SOUTHWELL AT WAR
1914 - 1919

Edited and Researched by:

Michael Austin

Michael J. Kirton

Lance Wright

Southwell and District Local History Society

2014

ABOUT THE EDITORS/RESEARCHERS

The Revd Canon Michael Austin, BD, MA, PhD served in several parishes in Birmingham and Derby before teaching theology at Bishop Lonsdale College, Derby (now incorporated into the University of Derby), and training clergy. A fellow of the Royal Historical Society, he has been a residentiary canon of both Derby and Southwell cathedrals and has published widely in church history, theology and aesthetics. Before retirement he was the Archbishops' Adviser for Bishops' Ministry.

Michael Kirton, ACIB, BA (Hons), MA (Hist) is a retired Bank Manager and is the Chairman of Southwell and District Local History Society.

Lance Wright is a retired teacher who has been undertaking historical research for many years in all aspects of local history. He is currently the Vice-Chairman of Southwell and District Local History Society.

COPYRIGHT NOTICE

© Michael Austin, Michael J. Kirton, Lance Wright and Southwell and District Local History Society.

All rights reserved. No part of this publication may be reproduced, stored or introduced into a retrieval system or transmitted in any form, by any means (electronic, mechanical, photocopy, recording or otherwise) without permission from the publishers.

Whilst every care has been taken to ensure the accuracy of the information contained in this publication, Southwell and District Local History Society cannot accept any responsibility for any error or omission.

ISBN: 978-0-9520503-8-4

Printed by: 4word Ltd, Bristol, 2014

To the men of Southwell who served their country in the First World War

and

to those who were left behind to support and, in many cases, to mourn them.

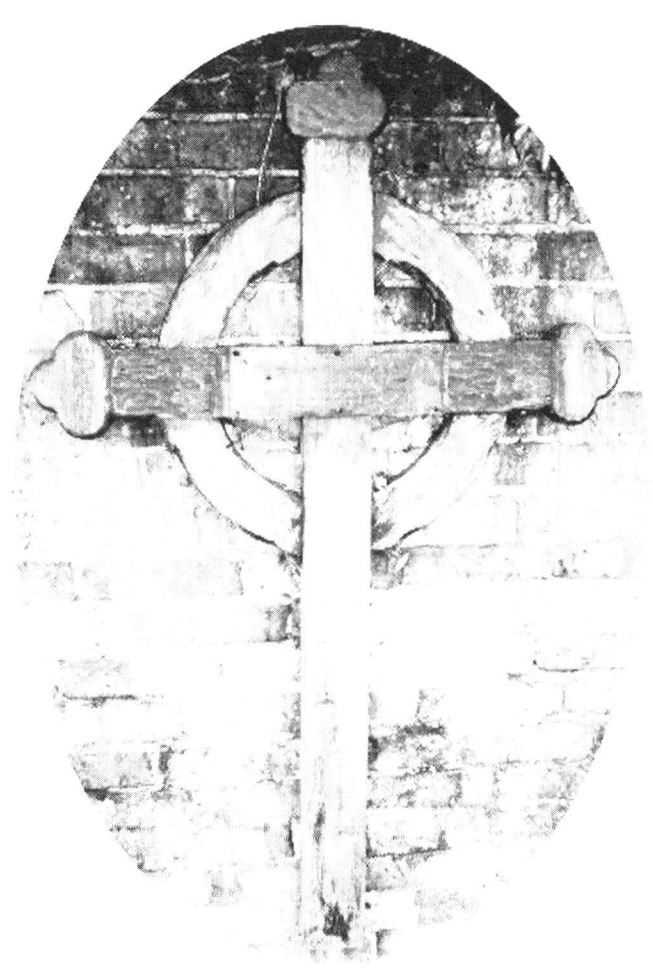

Memorial to Major John Pickard Becher, D.S.O. who led 'H' Active Service Company, 1/8th Battalion, Sherwood Foresters to war in 1914. He died of wounds on 1st January 1916.

The Memorial is on the wall surrounding Vicars' Court, Southwell.

*Badly shelled area near Chateau Wood, October 1917.
(Private Collection, c/o Southwell Minster)*

CONTENTS

Illustrations		vii
Preface		xi
Chapter 1	1.1 Roll Call, Southwell By Lance Wright and Mike Kirton	1
	1.2 Roll Call, surrounding villages By Lance Wright	75
Chapter 2	Southwell at War - The War Diary By Michael Austin and Mike Kirton	83
Chapter 3	3.1 Southwell Territorials go to War By Mike Kirton	201
	3.2 The War Diary of the 1/8th Battalion Sherwood Foresters By Mike Kirton	206
Chapter 4	Because it was expected of them - individual accounts of service men By Mike Kirton	247
Chapter 5	The Home Front	
	5.1 Women in the War and the Post-War Legacy By Mike Kirton	281
	5.2 Caring for the Wounded - Burgage Manor and Brackenhurst Hall By Mike Kirton	287
	5.3 Wartime School By Lance Wright	291
	5.4 The Minster Grammar School By Paul Birks	296
Chapter 6	Coming Home By Mike Kirton	309
Bibliography		315
Index		317

Ned Foster, The Forge, King Street, Southwell.
(Peter Cant)

ILLUSTRATIONS

Memorial to Major John Pickard Becher	iii
Near Chateau Wood, October 1917	iv
Ned Foster, The Forge, King Street, Southwell	vi
Southwell Branch of the British Red Cross	x
'Pals' from a painting by George Soper	xv
Field Marshall Viscount Allenby	3
Howard Barrett	5
William F. Bowes - Wedding	7
George W. Brown	8
Travel Pass - Bernard Bush	9
Fred Cooke	12
Arthur Cooling	12
Oscar Cottam	14
Dr T. S. Elliot	19
W. G. Elliot	19
Harold R. Ewers	19
Harry Foster	21
Edwin Gilbert	22
Frank Grimshaw	24
Alfred Hacking	24
Christopher Hall	25
Everard F. Handford	26
Henry B. S. Handford	26
Richard Harvey	27
Arthur Hazelwood	28
Arthur E. Horsley	30
Joseph Jones	33
Thomas W. Jubb	34
Albert J. Kendall	34
Herbert Kirk	35
Robert C. Lee at Machine Gun Corps Training Camp	37
Robert C. Lee in action	37
Alfred George Merryweather	41
Cyril R. Overton	44
George Peacock	47
Norman Powley	48
George Richardson	50
Cyril Rose	52
Richard Sharman	56
Arthur C. Sheppard	56
Albert V. Soar	58
Samuel Spall	58

Archibald G. Stanley	59
Charles Stimson	60
Alexander Straw	60
Harold Tyne	65
Ernest and Julia Ulyatt	65
William Ulyatt and family	66
John G. Waller	67
Frank Wilcox	69
Harry Wilkins	70
Bernard Willoughby	70
Arthur H. Wilson	71
Augustus Wyles	73
Soldier's Prayer Card	74
Advertisement - Holes Milk Stout	85
Recruitment Event 1915	86
Employees of E. Carey & Sons Ltd in 'H' Company	88
Troops gathered in Newark Market Place - August 1914	91
Recruitment Poster - Newark	92
Recruitment Poster - General	93
Concert Programme 1914	95
Officers of 8th Battalion, Sherwood Foresters 1914	97
J. H. Kirkby delivery cart	111
Southwell St. Mary's Football Team	115
War Loan Poster	144
Funeral of Driver J. W. Hindson 1918	175
'C' Company, 4th Battalion Nottinghamshire Volunteers	191
'H' Company at Summer Camp	203
'H' Company marching down Station Road, Southwell	204
'H' Company - Southwell Railway Station	205
Sherwood Foresters' Cap Badge	205
Mules at Southwell Railway Station	207
Map of Sanctuary Wood	210
Map of Hohenzollern Redoubt	213
Christmas Card December 1916 (2 images)	223
Map of Lens area	226
Christmas Card December 1917	230
Requival Bridge 1918	239
Map of Ramicourt	240
Prisches Church	244
Cartignes Church	244
Boulogne-sur-Helpe - old railway station house	245
General Allenby approaching Jerusalem on horseback	248
General Allenby walking into Jerusalem	248
John Pickard Becher	249
'H' Company Football team 1913	250
Abbeville Military Cemetery	251

Loos Memorial	251
Vincent Brown	253
Albert Edward Hopewell	255
John Henry Hopewell	256
William Hopewell	258
Conspicuous Gallantry Medal	258
Croix de Guerre	258
Albert Humberstone	259
Samuel Humberstone	259
Scroll - Death of Samuel Humberstone	260
Arthur Humberstone	261
Letter of sympathy from Revd W. J. Connybeare	261
Frank Paling	262
Albert Paling	263
Grave Marker - Albert Paling	263
Chris Rippin	264
Walter Frederick Saddington	266
'H' Company Orders (2 images)	267
John Sharman and Mary Walters	270
John Sharman	270
Samuel and Hannah Spall	272
Samuel Spall in later life	273
South Notts Hussars - officers	274
Philip A. Warwick	278
Regimental Christmas Card	280
Chilwell Munitions Factory	282
A nurse working on the front line	283
W.A.A.C.s baking bread in France	286
Hospital Group in Southwell	286
Burgage Manor - Patients and medical staff 1915	288
Another Air Raid - cartoon	289
Hospital fête	290
Church of England Infants School 1915	295
Science Laboratory, Minster Grammar School	296
Minster Grammar School, school photograph	299
Old Southwellians' Memorial	300
Samuel Humberstone's Remembrance Cross	303
Menin Gate, school visit	304
Wreath laying at Tyne Cot	304
School visit to Tyne Cot	305
Lochnagar Crater	307
Victory Parade 1919	311
Colour Party at the Minster 1919	312
Military Band at the Minster 1919	312
Dedication of the War Memorial	313
The Bishop of Southwell at the War Memorial	314

*Southwell Branch of the British Red Cross Society during the First World War.
Photograph by Howard Barrett.
(Peter Cant)*

PREFACE

On Remembrance Day each year the nation remembers its fallen from two world wars and other conflicts. With the centenary of the commencement of the First World War fast approaching, our thoughts focus on those who perished in that appalling war. Vast numbers of young men were plucked from the comfort of their families and friends and dropped into the trenches in a foreign field; many of them had previously travelled little further than to the nearest town or city. The purpose of this book is not just to honour those who were killed, but all those who fought and those left behind to worry about and support them in any way they could. Every community was affected and in the case of Southwell, with a population of about 3,200 people, around 650 men, many of them teenagers, served in the war at one time or another, some did not return until well into 1919. Those who survived were often scarred physically and mentally for life. They didn't want to talk about the nightmare of war, something that has become obvious as we have talked to their children and grandchildren. There were few families who were not affected in one way or another. The three of us involved in researching and editing this book have interesting and varied stories from our family histories.

Michael Austin's uncle, Frank Ridgwell, volunteered in 1915 and joined the Royal Fusiliers. He was sent to the Western Front and on one occasion kept a sick friend alive by rubbing dubbin on his chest. Later, whilst suffering from trench fever, he was posted to a shell-hole in No-Man's Land to observe enemy movements. In a dazed state he was alleged by a young officer to have fallen asleep and was court-martialled in the field. With no one to defend him he was sentenced to death. He was reprieved, given a suspended sentence of five years' penal servitude and immediately sent back to the trenches as his platoon was short of men. He volunteered for hazardous duty to obtain remission of part of his sentence, narrowly escaping death on one 'walk back over the top between machine-gun fire' to escort a rations and ammunition party. One bullet passed through his pay book (and a photograph of one of his sisters) in one tunic pocket and a second pierced his cigarette case in another. He was recommended for an award for bravery in the field. Although he never received any award above a Certificate of Honour, his prison sentence was quashed. Frank Ridgwell was taken prisoner on 25th March 1918 and was badly treated in captivity, spreading dubbin on crusts and eating horse flesh to keep alive. By October he had escaped and was living rough in civilian clothing, and helped by Belgians he made his way to the coast. Frank was arrested and interrogated by British military police, the pay book and certificate of honour saved him. He was put into khaki and shipped home. He left the Royal Fusiliers as he joined the regiment, as a private. This story illustrates the rough justice that many suffered in the army, although he survived others were put in front of a firing squad.

From time to time life on the 'Home Front' could be equally as hazardous as on the Western Front. Lance Wright's grandmother, Hannah Whitting-Shaw, was a housekeeper on Derby Road in Nottingham. In 1918, aged 38, she had volunteered to work in the National Shell Filling Factory, Chilwell. This was essential and hazardous war work and, apart from the obvious danger of working with high explosives, the skin of many of the workers turned yellow – they were known as 'Chilwell Canaries' or 'Canary Girls'. On 1st July 1918 Hannah woke up with influenza symptoms and was too unwell to go to work. Luck was on her side that morning as the factory suffered a massive explosion. It caused the deaths of 134 workers, only 32 were positively identified, and 250 were injured. There was national concern over the tragedy and the Minister for Munitions, Winston Churchill, sent the following message:

> Please accept my sincere sympathy with you all in the misfortune that has overtaken your fine Factory and in the loss of valuable lives, those who have perished have died at their stations in the field of duty and those who have lost their dear ones should fortify themselves with this thought, the courage and spirit shown by all concerned both men and women commands our admiration, and the decision to which you have all come to carry on without a break is worthy of the spirit which animates soldiers in the field. I trust the injured are receiving every care.

This was a tragedy felt by many and put a whole new understanding to the term 'Total War', which was, in fact, what the country was waging.

Few of us have been able to claim 'I was there when…' a significant historical event occurred. On 28th June 1914 my wife's paternal grandfather, Max Fredrik Minding, who worked for Electrolux, had travelled from Sweden and found himself in Sarajevo on the fateful day that Archduke Franz Ferdinand of Austria was assassinated by a Bosnian Serb. Along with many other visiting foreign nationals Max Minding was arrested by the police. Whilst he was not implicated in the plot, it must have become a memorable day of his life to have been there at one of the most significant events in modern history. It is interesting to note that in the 1930s he was still working for Electrolux, but in their Berlin office, and again witnessed the build-up to the next major conflict, although he did not live to experience that war.

These are just three individual stories that illustrate the horrors of the trenches, the commitment on the Home Front and the international nature of the war.

The purpose of this book is not to provide an account of the causes of the war – that could occupy a book in itself – but it would be wrong not to try to emphasise the enormity of the conflict. Later in this introduction we have included a comprehensive timeline of the war, aimed at covering the various campaigns that the men from Nottinghamshire are likely to have been involved in. The summary of the number of combatants from across the world and the vast number of casualties that resulted emphasise how devastating it was.

Southwell's commitment to the war was probably no greater than any other community, but it was still significant in relation to the size of the town. We have all heard of the various 'Pals' battalions' up and down the country and Southwell had its own company of 'Pals'. They were members of 'H' Active Service Company, 8th Battalion, Sherwood Foresters, numbering around 115 who, at the outbreak of war in August 1914, joined up with territorial companies from across Nottinghamshire to form the 1/8th Battalion, Sherwood Foresters (known as the 'Mad Eighth'). They were part of the first territorial division to go into the trenches, and many of the members of the battalion stayed in the front line for the duration of the war.

Captain W. C. C. Weetman of the 1/8th Battalion maintained the official war diary and in Chapter 3 we have summarised it in an effort to portray what the group of 'Pals' endured in the war. It should not in any way take away anything from the other 500 or so men who served in many different regiments, who would have had similar, and perhaps more horrific, experiences. Throughout the war the *Newark Advertiser* kept the people of Southwell informed of news from the front, although as the war progressed censorship prevented some of the news from being reported.

A major section of this book, Chapter 2, is dedicated to extracts from the *Newark Advertiser*, relevant to Southwell, from mid-1914 to late 1919. The various articles not only bring news from the front, but describe life on the 'Home Front'. The Home Front was vital to the war effort, not only in filling in for the absent men, but also in raising funds and looking after the many injured who came to Southwell for treatment and recuperation at Burgage Manor, Brackenhurst Hall and the fever hospital on Galley Hill. Many references are made to the weekly egg collections that were donated to the hospitals for the wounded soldiers. There are also reports of concerts for the troops that were billeted in and around Southwell and for their injured colleagues. This chapter paints a vivid picture of life in wartime Southwell and of the changing social attitudes.

Southwell sent some very brave men to the front and of these many were heroes. It would be a challenge to write about them all, as most were too modest to tell their stories when they returned. One such man who stands out for his bravery is William Hopewell who was awarded the Conspicuous Gallantry Medal for his contribution to the Zeebrugge Raid in 1918, and a summary of his exploits is recorded in Appendix 1. The much respected Major John Pickard Becher, D.S.O., who led 'H' Company to war, died on 1st January 1916 of wounds he received in October 1915 in the same battle in which his brothers-in-law, Henry and Everard Handford, were killed. These tragedies frequently hit local families, many of whom would have been dreading such news from the front. The war did not discriminate between officers and men, for too many there was no escaping the ultimate sacrifice of the First World War.

It is difficult to imagine the appalling conditions and horrors that our ancestors experienced in the trenches. None of the letters from the front, nor newspaper reports, painted a full picture of the sheer noise and terror of battle. However, one man, with his most descriptive language, attempts to convey this to his readers. In 1928 the poet Edmund Blunden published his own account of his experiences as a 20-year-old junior officer, serving on the Western Front in many of the places and actions that would have been familiar to the men of Southwell. In one passage he graphically describes his experience of an attack:

> A runner came round distributing our watches, which had been synchronized at Bilge Street. At 3.50, if I am right, shortly after Vidler had passed me growling epigrams at some recent shell-burst which had covered him with mud, the British guns spoke; a flooded Amazon of steel roaring, immensely fast, over our heads, and the machine-gun bullets made a pattern of sharper purpose and maniac language against that diluvian rush. Flaring lights, small ones, great ones, flew up and went spinning sideways in the cloud of night; one's eyes seemed not quick enough; one heard nothing from one's shouting neighbour, and only by the quality of the noise and flame did I know that the German shells crashing among the tree-stumps were big ones and practically on top of us. We rose, scrambled ahead, found No Man's Land a comparatively good surface, were amazed at the puny tags and rags of once multiplicative German wire, and blundered over the once feared trench behind them without seeing that it was a trench. Good men as they were, my party were half-stunned by the unearthliness of our own barrage, and when two were wounded it was left to me to bandage them in my ineffective way. (I have been reminded that two of our party were killed, but at the time the fact was lost in the insane realities all round.)...[1]

There is little wonder that the full horrors of the war were not passed on to soldiers' loved ones, as it would have made them more fearful for their sons and husbands. When they came home all they wanted to do was to blot out the memories, which, no doubt, were resurrected in nightmares.

Much has been written about the First World War and so often the emphasis has been on those who perished, with little about honouring all those who served and, just as important, those who were left behind to worry about them. The idea for this book came from our co-editor Michael Austin who felt that we should honour *all* those who served. Michael is an experienced author and a few years ago edited a book, *'Almost Like a Dream' - A Parish at War 1914-1919.*[2] This is

---

[1] Blunden, Edmund, *Undertones of War*, (London: Penguin, 2010), pp. 154-5 (First published 1928).

[2] Austin, Michael, *'Almost Like a Dream'*, (Whitchurch: Merton Priory, 1999).

an account of letters written to the vicar of St Michael's Church in Derby telling him of their experiences at the front. At the same time as completing his current book, *'Like a Swift Hurricane': People, Clergy and Class in a Midlands Diocese, 1914 - 1919,* Michael set about researching the reports from the *Newark Advertiser* that make up Chapter 2 of this book. We soon realised that to identify as many men as possible who served in the war we would need an experienced researcher, and our good friend Lance Wright eagerly volunteered for the task. Whilst the *Newark Advertiser* published an initial list, Lance soon nearly trebled this number to the 650 names we have listed in Chapter 1, with a further 550 from the surrounding villages (Caunton, Farnsfield, Morton, Fiskerton, etc.). He extracted names from voters' and absent voters' lists, school records, military records, and some more obscure archived records. This was only the start of the task as we decided to flesh out the names with biographical details, which we believe will prove a valuable asset to family researchers. We do, of course, apologise for any names we may have missed or any incorrect details.

Our work in tracing names has been supplemented by descendents of those who served, who, in many cases, have been able to supply family photographs and some reminiscences. However, it soon became obvious that most of the these brave servicemen did not want to talk about their experiences. There are a number of people we would like to thank for their assistance and support.

We are indebted to Joanna Parlby, Managing Director of the Advertiser Group and the editor of the *Newark Advertiser,* Chris Prime, for readily agreeing to our accessing the 1914-1919 copies of the newspaper, held in the archives of Newark Library. Tim Warner of the library service and the staff of Newark Library have been most helpful. Two local men, Peter Cant and David Hutchinson, have been most generous in allowing us access to their collections of local photographs, newspaper clippings, letters, etc., and we owe them our grateful thanks for their support. In addition, Geoffrey Bond, Roger Merryweather and Andrew Gregory have allowed us to use photographs and other interesting material, and we thank them. Some years ago local historian Doreen Stevenson had the foresight to interview a number of local people, from all walks of life, and record their memories, she has generously allowed us to use relevant transcripts of these interviews, for which we offer our thanks. The Dean and Chapter, Southwell Minster, are to be thanked for allowing us to publish images from the Loughton Collection of photographs, and Charlie Leggett is to be thanked for allowing us to use several images, including the one used on the front cover of this book. Derek Whitton, his mother Brenda and uncle Edward Kendall kindly supplied us with details of the Kendall family who served and we thank them for their interest in this project. The Sharman family historian, Robin Sharman, together with Olive Kitts and Bill Kemp spent several hours helping us with details of the Sharman men who served in the war and we are most grateful to them. Similarly, Tony Hopewell and Beatrice Thornton kindly provided us with details of the Hopewell brothers who served. In addition Peter Kendall, author of *The Zeebrugge Raid 1918, The Finest Feat of Arms* granted us permission to use extracts from his book about the exploits of William Hopewell in that daring raid. We would like to thank Julia Overton and her mother for providing us with the service records of Julia's grandfather, Cyril Overton, who served with Captain Handford. Some of the artefacts they have donated will be used in a forthcoming exhibition in Southwell Minster. Grateful thanks go to the following who have provided photographs and memories of family members who served in the war: Hayley Ayris, Ray Bush, Bridget Clarke, Frank and Suzanne Cooling, Colin Gabitas, Jean Hallam, Nancy Harrison, Heather Lee, Heather Price, Ruth Robinson, Chris Seglin, Carole Spall, Ann Warner, and Trevor Wilds. Thanks also to Margaret Peet who donated a postcard, which provided a further lead to a serviceman, and to Carol Bristow who put us in touch with further sources. Paul Birks of the Minster School History Department spent some considerable time researching the school records and providing us with an interesting chapter about life at the Minster Grammar School during the war period. Every year in February he and colleagues take a party of pupils to the Western Front where they visit important sites and memorials in the depth of winter, giving them an idea of what conditions may have been like in those long winter months. Christine Raithby kindly provided some background information on E. Carey & Sons, for which we are grateful. Many thanks go to the members of the Minster First World War Commemoration Committee for their ongoing support, including Robin Turner (Chairman), Andy Gregory, Charlie Leggett, Roger Merryweather, Judith Swann, and Tim Richmond. As with all local history projects, the staff of the Nottinghamshire Archives have earned our thanks. Many apologies to anyone we may have missed.

Of course, none of this project would have been possible without the support of the editors' wives, Ann Austin, Christine Wright and Anna Kirton. They have all played their part, and I am particularly grateful to Anna for the many hours she has spent in reading and giving constructive criticism of this book.

Mike Kirton
Managing Editor

Chairman, Southwell and District Local History Society
Southwell 2014.

'PALS'
From the painting by Geo. Soper.
(Roger Merryweather)

First World War Timeline

A timeline of the First World War giving campaigns in which servicemen from Nottinghamshire are likely to have been involved.

The causes of the First World War have their origin in complex interrelated political and economic factors, which cannot be covered here, not even briefly. They can be traced at least as far back as the 1870s and the development of war plans in the abstract by the Prussian military elite. This process gained momentum as the years passed and finally found expression in the so-called 'Schlieffen Plan', named after its principal architect. The historian John Keegan writes that 'the effect exerted by paper plans on the unfolding of events must never be exaggerated. Plans do not determine outcomes. The happenings set in motion by a particular scheme of action will rarely be those narrowly intended.' Yet once the decision to go to war had been taken this plan dictated where the war would begin and where its main focus would lie. Events then followed with astonishing rapidity.

1914

June	28	Archduke Franz Ferdinand assassinated in Sarajevo.
July	6	German government supports Austro-Hungarian reprisals against Serbia which in turn appeals to Russia.
	28	Austria-Hungary declares war on Serbia.
Aug	1	Germany declares war on Russia.
	3	Germany declares war on France.
	4	German troops invade Belgium. Great Britain declares war on Germany.
	5	Austria-Hungary declares war on Russia.
	10	France declares war on Austria-Hungary.
	12	Britain declares war on Austria-Hungary. Battle of Haelen, Belgium. First Austria-Hungary invasion of Serbia (to 25 August).
	14	France begins to invade Lorraine.
	15	Russia begins its invasion of East Prussia.
	16	Liège falls.
	18	Russian invasion of Austria-Hungary Galacia begins.
	20	Battles of the Frontiers in France and Belgium (to 24 August).
	21	Serbia wins battle of the Jadar River.
	23	Japan declares war on Germany. The British Expeditionary Force, Britain's profession-al army, in action at Mons, Belgium. In *The Times* of 30 August, its correspondent, Arthur Moore, told of the 'terrible defeat' of the BEF, and of the soldiers of 'the broken bits of many regiments . . . battered with marching' in its long retreat.
Sept	2	French government leaves Paris.
	3-4	German forces cross the River Marne and occupy Rheims.
	6-12	First Battle of the Marne.
	14	Allied forces recapture Rheims.
	15-18	Battle of the Aisne.
	26-28	Battle of the River Nieman.
Oct	1-4	First Battle of Arras.
	12	German forces take Ghent and Lille.

Oct	15 -	21 November. First Battle of Ypres, during which and its immediate aftermath 24,000 British and 50,000 German servicemen died, with negligible gains for the British. The professional BEF was effectively destroyed.

The [German] 'Western Front' now relatively static. 'From the air it had a drably uniform appearance, a belt of disturbed earth, ravaged vegetation and devastated buildings some four miles across. Later, as the power of artillery increased and local infantry fighting conferred advantage to one side or the other, the zone of destruction would widen. What would scarcely change for the next twenty-seven months was the length of the front or the geographical trace which it followed.'
(John Keegan *The First World War* [1998], p. 198)

Nov	5	Britain and France declare war on Turkey.
	29 -	13 December. Renewed German offensive at Ypres.
Dec		Stagnation on the Western Front. Large British garrison in Egypt, now a Protectorate. By the end of this month the BEF, originally of 100,000 men, had suffered 90 per cent casualties, of which 30,000 had been killed.

1915

Jan		German forces ordered to fortify their front line, the Western Front.
	8 -	5 February. Fighting in the area of La Bassée and around Soissons
Feb		Fronts in Palestine and Gallipoli established.
March	10	7th and 8th divisions of the BEF and the Meerut and Lahore divisions of the Indian Army commence the Battle of Neuve Chapelle (to 13 March).
April	22 -	24 May. German offensive leading to the Second Battle of Ypres. German forces first use poison gas successfully on the Western Front.
	24	Battle of St Julien.
	25	Anglo-French forces land at Helles and Anzac Cove, Gallipoli, in the Dardenelles.
May	6	German Supreme Army Command orders the Western Front to be further reinforced with a second line of trenches.
	9 -	19 June. Allied offensive, Artois, Western Front. Battle of Aubers Ridge.
	12	Windhoek, South-West Africa, taken by General Louis Botha.
June	8	Allied forces take Neuville.
	15	Battle of Givenchy.
July	9	German forces in South-West Africa surrender to General Botha.
Aug	6	New Allied landings at Sulva Bay, Gallipoli.
	8	Hostilities begin against German East Africa with shelling from the sea at Dar-es-Salaam. Allied casualties in East Africa were to be 1 battle casualty to 35 lost to illness and disease.
Sept	25 -	6 November. Allied forces launch Champagne and Artois-Loos offensives.
	25 -	8 October. Battle of Loos.
Oct	5	Allied troops land in Salonika.
Nov	22	Battle of Ctesiphon, Mesopotamia. Western Front remains relatively static through the winter months.
Dec	19	Sir John French replaced by Sir Douglas Haig as C-in-C, BEF. Allied forces evacuate Sulva and Anzac Cove, Gallipoli.

1916

Jan	8	Allied evacuation of Helles, Gallipoli, begins.

About 480,000 Allied troops had taken part in the Gallipoli campaign, including substantial New Zealand and Australian forces, French, Senegalese and Indian units. Total British and imperial casualties were 205,000, including 43,000 dead, 90,000 evacuated sick, and more than 33,600 ANZAC losses (one third killed). Turkish casualties were estimated at 250,000, with some 65,000 killed. This was the Turkish Army's most spectacular success, and the failure of the Allied campaign is generally

		regarded as 'an example of British strategic "drift" and tactical ineptitude' (Stephen Pope and Elizabeth-Anne Wheal, *The Macmillan Dictionary of The First World War* [1995], p. 184).
Feb	9	Military Services Act comes into force in Great Britain. This Act laid down that all single men between the ages of 18 and 41 were liable for conscription for military service, unless they were widowed with children or were ministers of religion.
	21	German Verdun offensive begins (to 18 December).
	29	First trial of a new weapon, the tank, in Britain.
March		French forces hold Verdun.
	8	Battle of Dujaila, Mesoptamia.
April	9	German offensive at Verdun renewed.
	24 -	1 May. Easter Rising, Dublin.
	30	Kut-el-Amara falls to Turkish forces.
May	29	German forces take Mort Homme Hill, Verdun.
	31 -	2 June. Battle of Jutland, North Sea.
June	5	Lord Kitchener killed when his transport, HMS *Hampshire*, was sunk by a mine off the Orkneys.
	13	Wilhelmsthal, German East Africa, captured by General Smuts.
July	1 -	18 November. The Somme offensive begins with 27 Allied divisions, seven-eighths of them British, advancing across No-Man's-Land against well-defended positions. On that one day British forces suffered 58,000 casualties of which 21,000 were killed. The losses were greater than on any other single day in the history of the British Army.
Aug		Western Front: stalemate.
	20	Allied offensive in Mesopotamia begins.
Sept	3	British forces occupy Dar-es-Salaam, East Africa.
	13	Allied Monastir offensive from Salonika begins (to 15 December).
	15	British forces first use tanks on the Western Front, at Fler-Courcelette, the Somme.
Oct	1-20	Renewed British offensive on the Somme, at Ancre Heights and Transloy Ridges.
	24	French counter-offensive takes Fort Douaumont, Verdun.
Nov	2	French recapture Fort Vaux, Verdun.
	13-18	Last Allied offensive in the Battle of the Somme begins.
	19	Allied forces take Monastir, Serbia (Salonika).
Dec	13 -	27 February. British offensive, Kut, Mesopotamia.
	21	British forces occupy El Arish, Palestine.
	29	Murder of Rasputin in Petrograd.
1917		
Jan		Western Front: stalemate.
Feb	21 -	31 March. German tactical withdrawal to the Hindenburg line between Arras and Soissons: Operation Alberich. Turkish forces retreat in Mesopotamia.
March		British setbacks in Palestine. Allied Lake Prespa offensive from Salonika.
	17-18	Allied forces take Bapaume and Péronne, Western Front.
April	9 -	17 May. Allied Nivelle offensive begins. British forces attack at Arras.
	16-20	Second Battle of the Aisne.
	18-19	British repulsed by Turkish and German forces in the Second Battle of Gaza.
May	3- 5	British forces attack the Hindenburg Line at Arras.
June	7-14	Battle of Messines, Flanders.
July	17	King George V changes his family name from Saxe-Coburg-Gotha to Windsor.
	31 -	6 November. The Third Battle of Ypres (known as Passchendaele).
Aug	20 -	15 December. French offensive regains territory in the Second Battle of Verdun. Third Battle of Ypres continues.
Sept	20	Second phase of the British offensive near Ypres begins.

	21	British capture Ramadi, Mesopotamia.
Oct	12	British assault at Passchendaele, Ypres.
	15	German forces renew offensive in East Africa.
	23	French force Germans back at Oise-Aisne canal.
Nov	6	British and Canadian forces take Passchendaele Ridge.
	7	British forces take Gaza.
	20	British massed tank assault at Cambrai, France (to 30 November).
	30 -	7 December. German counter offensive at Cambrai.
Dec	1	German forces cleared from German East Africa.

1918

Jan	21	German high command orders preparation for the 'Kaiserschlacht' ('Emperor battle'), the last great German offensive on the Western Front.
Feb	10	Trotsky declares Russia's abstention from the war.
	21	British take Jericho, Palestine.
	25	Food rationing in London.
March	21	German 'Kaiserschlacht' offensive begins, the Second Battle of the Somme, with an assault south of Arras (to 5 April) which surprised the Allies by its direction, speed and scale.
April	1	RAF formed to replace the Royal Flying Corps.
	9-29	German Lys offensive opens on the Western Front.
	12	German forces take Armentières.
	23	Zeebrugge Raid.
	24	British victory at Villers Bretonneux.
	30 -	4 May. British forces attack in Transjordan.
May	27 -	6 June. Third phase of German offensive on the Western Front, beginning on the Aisne.
	28	First American Expeditionary Force (AEF) assault on the Western Front at Cantigny.
	29	German forces take Soissons and Rheims.
June	3-12	German Aisne offensive halted at Château-Thierry and Belleau Wood.
	9-13	German offensive near Compiègne; Battle of the Matz, France.
July	15 -	3 August. Second Battle of the Marne.
	18	Allied counter-offensive begins.
	20	German retreat on the Marne.
	22	Allied forces cross the Marne.
Aug	8-15	Allied Amiens offensive forcing the collapse of the Second German Army.
	21-29	Allied Albert offensive.
	26-29	Allied Scarpe offensive.
	30-31	Police strike in London.
Sept	2	British forces breach the first Hindenburg Line positions.
	15	Allied breakthrough in Bulgaria.
	22	Turkish resistance in Palestine collapses.
	27 -	1 October. Allied forces assault on Canal du Nord, Hindenburg Line.
Oct	1	British and Arab forces occupy Damascus.
	5	German positions on the Hindenburg Line cleared by Allied forces.
	8	British forces begin assault on Cambrai and Le Câteau.
	14-20	Allied Courtrai offensive.
	17-24	British Selle offensive.
	30	Allies sign armistice with Turkey.
Nov	2-11	British Sambre offensive.
	8	British take Maubeuge.
	11	Allies sign armistice with Germany.

Nov	21	German High Seas Fleet surrenders at Rosyth.
	25	Last German forces in East Africa surrender.
	26	Last German soldiers leave Belgium.
Dec	6	British forces occupy Cologne.
	13	Armistice extended by one month.
1919		
Jan	12	Paris Peace Conference opens.
June	21	German High Seas Fleet scuttles at Scapa Flow.
	28	Treaty of Versailles signed.
Oct	12	Allied withdrawal from northern Russia completed.

An estimate of the total military casualties as a percentage of those mobilised[1]:

Country	Men Mobilised	Killed	Wounded	POWs + missing	Total casualties	Casualties as % of men mobilised
Russia	12m	1.7m	4.9m	2.5m	9.15m	76.3
France	8.4m	1.3m	4.2m	537,000	6.1m	73.3
GB + Empire	8.9m	908,000	2m	191,000	3.1m	35.8
Italy	5.5m	650,000	947,000	600,000	2.1m	39
USA	4.3m	126,000	234,000	4,500	350,000	8
Japan	800,000	300	900	3	1210	0.2
Romania	750,000	335,000	120,000	80,000	535,000	71
Serbia	700,000	45,000	133,000	153,000	331,000	47
Belgium	267,000	13,800	45,000	34,500	93,000	35
Greece	230,000	5,000	21,000	1,000	27,000	12
Portugal	100,000	7,222	13,700	12,000	33,000	33
Total Allies	**42m**	**5m**	**13m**	**4m**	**22m**	**52%**
Germany	11m	1.7m	4.2m	1.1m	7.1m	65
Austria	7.8m	1.2m	3.6m	2.2m	7m	90
Turkey	2.8m	325,000	400,000	250,000	975,000	34
Bulgaria	1.2m	87,000	152,000	27,000	266,000	22
Total	**22.8m**	**3.3m**	**8.3m**	**3.6m**	**15m**	**67%**
Grand Total	**65m**	**8.5m**	**21m**	**7.7m**	**37m**	**57%**

[1] See www.historylearning.co.uk (Does not include civilian dead.).

CHAPTER 1

1.1 Roll Call of Servicemen

The simple truth of 1914-1918 trench warfare is that the massing of a large number of soldiers unprotected by anything but cloth uniforms, however they were trained, however equipped, against large masses of other soldiers protected by earthworks and barbed wire and provided with rapid-fire weapons, was bound to result in very heavy casualties among the attackers…The first day of the battle of the Somme, 1 July 1916, was to be an awful demonstration of that truth…
(John Keegan, *The First World War* (1998), 315 ff.)

When we commenced this project in 2012 we aimed to provide as many details as possible of the men who served in the First World War and to include details of their post-war lives. Unfortunately, the sheer weight of numbers has forced us to restrict our research mainly to pre-war and wartime records, although family archives in some cases have added to the detail. However, we believe that the information provided will be of help to those researching their family histories and of interest to others. The sources we have used have been quite varied and our colleague, Lance Wright, has been particularly resourceful in unearthing some official records, which have greatly expanded our ability to identify individuals, particularly those with relatively common or similar names.

Good use has been made of the census returns, up to and including 1911, although at times searching for individuals has proved somewhat frustrating due to poor transcription and the apparent ability of some to have avoided the census altogether. The medal cards of the majority of servicemen are still available, but disappointingly many of the detailed full military records failed to survive the blitz during the Second World War. Of these many show evidence of fire and water damage; where they are available the detail is often very comprehensive. The *Newark Advertiser* has been an excellent resource for us, as illustrated in Chapter 2. Additionally, school admissions records proved to be invaluable in identifying individuals and a useful guide to pointing us in the right direction as far as the census returns are concerned. The voters' lists for the war period helped us to identify those men on active service. Finally, there has been some excellent input from children, grandchildren and other descendants of the servicemen.

Whilst every effort has been made to list siblings of the men, there may be missing names, particularly if they were not living at home when the census was taken. Please also note that some of the birth dates may be one year either way, depending on their birthdays in relation to the date of the census.

The men listed in this section either lived or worked in Southwell or had a direct link with the town. Those from the surrounding villages have been listed separately at the end of the chapter. Members of 'H' Active Service Company, 1/8th Battalion Sherwood Foresters who left Southwell in August 1914 are marked * after their surname. The majority of these men had been members of the Territorials pre-war. Service in France would often include Belgium.

This chapter also serves as an index for the Southwell men.

Abbreviations:

Bn.	Battalion	Minster	Minster School
Br.	Brother(s)	Natl.	Southwell National School
British	British Medal	*N/A*	Newark Advertiser
CWGC	Commonwealth War Graves Commission	No.	Service Number
Demob.	Demobilization	Occup	Occupation pre war
DoW	Died of Wounds	POW	Prisoner of War
F.	Father	Regt.	Regiment
Fam.	Family details	S.	Sister(s)
Fr.	France, including Belgium	S/F	Sherwood Foresters, Notts and Derbys Regiment
K-in-A	Killed in action	Theatre	Theatre of War
M.	Mother	Victory	Victory Medal
m.	Married	War Dead	*Italics*

Adams, Herbert. Born: Billinghay, Lincs, 1893; Lived: Southwell; Fam: F. Albert E Adams (Milking foreman and farm bailiff), M. Mary E. (Newton, m.1891), Br. John Edward (1900), Harold Newton (1905), Walter (1911-d. 1911), S. Alice Rachel (1895), Gertrude Mary (1896), Freda Elizabeth (1902), Eleanor Maude (1903), Agnes (1906); Occup: with J. H. Kirkby grocers; Service: Army Service Corps; Theatre/Medals: no details; See *N/A* 9/6/15.

Adlington, Walter James. Born: Ripley, 1879; Lived: Brackenhurst Farm, Southwell, later Westgate, Southwell; Fam: F. Henry (Pork butcher), M. Sarah (Bower), Br. Herbert (1878), S. Sarah Ann (1874), Florence (1890), married Ada Ellen (1901), children: George (1903), William Edward (1905), Walter James (1908), Sydney (1910), Albert (1913), Frank (1915) and Herbert (1917), S. Mary (1907); Occup: Farmer; Service: No. R214602, A.S.C. Remounts; Theatre: not known; Medals not recorded; See *N/A* 11/8/15.

Ainger, George. Born: Long Eaton, 1893; Lived Springfield Cottage, Nottingham Road, Southwell; Fam: F. Josia Ainger (Farmer), M. Eliza Ann (Wright), Br. Harry (1888), married Elsie J Roy 1920, children: Muriel J. (1922), Enid M. (1925); Occup: Gardener; Service: No. 11936, 2nd Bn. S/F, Sgt.; Theatre: Fr. Sept. 1914; Medals: Victory, British, 1914-15 Star; See *N/A* 5/12/17.

Allcroft, Walter. Born: Oswestry, 1887; Lived: Maythorne; Fam: F. Frank Allcroft (Silk trade), M. Fanny (Johnson), married Lucy K. D. Schumach, children: Dorothy (1916), three children died; Occup: Traveller – oil trade; Service: records not available.

Allen, Leonard. Born: Southwell, died 1918; Lived: Nottingham; Fam: No details; Occup: Not known; Service: No. 266946, 2/7th S/F; Theatre: Fr., K-in-A 21/3/18, during the German offensive known as Operation Michael. The battalion was in trenches in the Ecoust, Noreuil area when the Germans attacked and they were surrounded and running short of ammunition. His body was not found and he is commemorated on the Arras Memorial; Medals: Victory, British.

Allenby, Edmund Henry Hynman. Born: Brackenhurst Hall, Southwell, 1861-1936; Lived: Onslow Square, London (1911); Fam: F. Hynman Allenby (Norfolk land owner), M. Catherine Anne Allenby (née Cane), Br. Fred Claude (1865), Alfred (1870), S. Catherine M. (1860), Grace (1863), Helen H. (1867), married Adelaide Mabel (Chapman in 1896), children: Michael (1898) - K-in-A 1917; School: Haileybury and Imperial Service College, Hertford and Sandhurst; Occup: Professional soldier; Service: 1882, Lt. 6th (Inniskillin) Dragoons - see Chapter 4 for full career details; Theatre: Fr. 1914, Egypt and Palestine; See p. 211-2.

General Allenby

Alton, George Hugh. Born: Nottingham, 1887; Lived: Victoria Terrace, Southwell; Fam: Son of Jessie Alton; School: Infants & Natl. 1894-1900; Occup: Clerk at nurseries; Service: Attested 12/8/14, mobilized May 1917, No. 86083, 3rd Bn. S/F & No. 104025, 5th Cyclist Bn. East Yorks. Regt. & 29th Bn. Durham Light Infantry, also attached 524th Emp. Coy, Labour Corps, L/Cpl., demob. 19/2/19; Theatre: Fr., wounded 27/3/16 in arm; Medals: Victory, British.

Alvey, George. Born: Nottingham, 1889-1917; Lived: Southwell; Fam: F. Joseph, M. Elizabeth (Hook), Br. Albert Edward and Richard (both in Canada), Henry (1893), Francis Joseph, S. Annie (1882); Occup: Goods checker; Service: Attested Newark 31/8/14, No. 12389, Leicester Regt.; Theatre: Fr. July 1915, served at Kemmel in Belgium, the Somme, Bullecourt, Ypres, DoW 12/11/17, buried West Vlaanderen, grave III G19; Medals: Victory, British, 1914-15 Star; See *N/A* 29/5/18.

Anthony*, A. L/Cpl. No further details.

Arnold, Arthur Leslie. Born: Southwell, 1899-1918; Lived: Burgage, Southwell; Fam: F. George Arnold (lace curtain maker –E Carey & Sons), M. Rose (Randall), Br. George Irving (1910), Arthur Leslie (1899), S. Edith Emily (1902), Catherine Anne (1903); School: Wesleyan 1902-09, Minster 1909; Occup: with John Jardine, Nottingham; Service: Enlisted Nottingham, March 1915, re-enlisted 1917, No. 4666, 2/7th Bn. S/F, & No. 137583, Machine Gun Corps; Theatre: Fr. 1916, suffered trench feet and sent home when it was realised he was underage, returned France in 1918, DoW 20/7/18, buried Pas de Calais, grave VF 11; Medals: Victory, British; See *N/A* 31/7/18, this report gives a full account of Arthur Arnold signing up and serving whilst under age. Also pp. 272, 301.

Arnold, John Edwin. Born: Southwell, 1897; Lived: Burgage, Southwell; Fam: Br. of Arthur Leslie Arnold – see above; School: Wesleyan 1901-09, Minster, 1909-1913; Occup: Chemists' errand boy; Service: No. 124267, 3/A.M. 1st T. Wireless School, R.A.F.; Theatre: no record; Medals: no record.

Astill, Percy. Born: Southwell, 1898-1916; Lived: 5 Bruce Grove, Nottingham; Fam: F. Robert William Astill (Railway foreman), M. Arabella Sarah (Hayes), Br. William (1892), Cyril (1895), Bernard (1900); Occup: Ganger at Nottingham colliery; Service: Enlisted 24/8/14, No. 4896, 11th Bn. S/F; Theatre: Fr. May 1916, wounded at the Somme 1916. Whilst based in trenches at Le Sars, he was wounded when out on patrol on 28/9/16, DoW 3/10/16, buried Dernancourt Communal Cemetery; Medals: Victory, British.

Baguley, Kenneth. Born: Keele, Staffs, 1894; Lived: Kirklington Road, Southwell; Fam: F. Joseph Wright Baguley (Hotel coachman), M. Emma J. (Newell m. 1891), Br. Arthur Wilson (1892); School: Natl. Farnsfield, Natl. 1906-10; Occup: Clerk – J.H. Kirkby; Service: No. S4/059665, CQMS; Theatre: no record; Medals: Victory, British, Meritorious Service Medal; See *N/A* 9/6/15.

Baker, Alfred. Born: 1895; Lived: Oxton Hall with employer; Occup: Footman; Service: No. 6780, 9th Bn. East Surrey Regt.; Theatre: Fr., POW at Munster, captured Vermelles, 1915; Medals: Victory, British.

Ball, Albert. Lived: Southwell; Fam: Br. Fred, Herbert; Service: Labour Corps; No further details; See *N/A* 22/11/16, 12/2/19.

Ball, Cecil George. Born: Bilsthorpe, 1894; Lived: The Parks, Southwell; Fam: F. William Ball (Farmer), M. Susan (Pepper), Br. Leonard William (1889), Bernard Henry (1902), Frank (1903), S. Alice (1906); School: Minster 1907-10; Occup: Bank Clerk, National Westminster Bank; Service: Enlisted 1915, No. DM2/162969, 693rd MT Co., Army Service Corps, A/Sgt.; Theatre: India; Medals: British, G.S.M., India Gen. Service; See p. 306.

Ball, Fred. Died 1919; Lived: Southwell; Fam: Br. Albert – see above; Occup: Lace maker – E Carey & Sons; Service: Labour Corps; Theatre: Fr. 1916, died Calais 1919 – Influenza; See *N/A* 12/2/19.

Ball, Herbert. Fam: Br. Albert Ball – see above; Service: No. 2598, Royal Fusiliers, No. 611871, Labour Corps, Cpl.; Theatre: Fr. Sept. 1915; Medals: Victory, British, 1914-15 Star; See *N/A* 12/2/19.

Ball, Leonard W G. Born: 1889, Bilsthorpe; Lived: Nottingham; Fam: Br. Of C. G. Ball - see above; School: Minster; Occup: Corporation Clerk, Nottingham; Service: No. 056517, A.S.C. No. 4711, Royal Fusiliers; Theatre: No record; Medals: Victory, British; See p. 306.

Ball, Wilfred George. Lived: Adams Row, Southwell; Service: No. 167116, 355 Works Co.; Theatre: no details; Medals: no details.

Ballard, Frank Edgar. Born: Leicester, 1881; Lived: Church Street, Southwell; Fam: S. Kate Elizabeth (1892), married Louisa Johnson 1903, children: Beatrice May (1905), Constance M. (1911), Philip A. (1915), Geoffrey (1922); Occup: Painter's warehouseman; Service: No. 286213, 524 Employment Corps; Theatre: no record; Medals: no record.

Barker, John. Born: Bleasby, 1876-1918; Lived: Halam; Fam: Married Mabel Lamb, 1904; School: Natl.; Occup: Grocer – J.J. Bates; Service: Enlisted 9/8/16, No. 30551, Yorks and Lancashire Regt., No. 18009, Labour Corps; Theatre: Fr. 1917, K-in-A 10/3/18, buried Barlin Communal Cemetery Extension; Medals: Victory, British; See *N/A* 10/4/18.

Barlow, Alfred Henry. Born: Southwell, 1891; Lived: Westgate, Southwell; Fam: Br. of Thomas – see below, married Annie Ward, 1910, children: Thomas (1912), Mabel (1913), George E. (1916); Occup: Threader – E Carey & Sons; Service: Nos. 27230 & 52221, S/F & Lincolnshire Regt., Sgt.; Theatre: Fr.; Medals: Victory, British. See *N/A* 20/6/17.

Barlow, Ernest. Born: Southwell, 1895; Lived: Mansfield; Fam: F. Henry John Barlow (Farmer at Whitwell), M. Frances Louise Moss), Br. Cecil Pursey (1891), Ernest (1895), Kenneth (1898), S. Gladys Sarah (1892), Muriel (1893); Occup: Apprentice engineer; Service: No. 15951, 2nd Bn. Grenadier Guards; Theatre: Fr. August 1914; Medals: Victory, British, 1914-15 Star; See *N/A* 25/11/14.

Barlow*, Thomas F. Born: Southwell, 1893-1916; Lived: Westgate, Southwell; Fam: F. Alfred P. Barlow (Carrier), M. Sonata Charlotte (Schumach m. 1885); Br. Alfred (1892); S. Sonata

(1887), Ada (1889). School: Natl. 1899-1906; Occup: Threader, E Carey & Sons; Service: Nos. 877 & 305025, 1/8th Bn. S/F; Theatre: Fr. March 1915, returned to Belton Park (probably machine gun training), returned to Fr. March 1916, K-in-A 1/7/16, first day of the battle of the Somme near Gommecourt, commemorated on Thiepval Memorial; Medals: Victory, British, 1914-15 Star; See *N/A* 20/6/17, 8/8/17, also see 8th Bn. War Diary for further details of the attack during which he was killed. Also, p. 220.

Barrett, Arthur George. Born: Southwell, 1885; Lived: Camberwell, London; Fam: Brother of Howard Barrett – see below, married Nancy (Pugh in 1910), children: Arthur George (1910), Jessie N. (1915), Walter (1916), Margaret (1919), Lucas (1921); School: Easthorpe, Wesleyan 1893-?; Occup: Press photographer; Service: R.A.F.; Theatre/Medals: no record; See *N/A* 28/10/14, 7/8/18; Arthur Barrett was a highly regarded press photographer and a F.R.P.S.

Howard Barrett (Bridget Clarke)

Barrett, Howard. Born: London, Islington, 1875; Lived: King Street, Southwell; Fam: F. Walter Barrett (Lithographic Artist), M. Jessie (Taylor in 1868), Br. Walter Lucas (1868), Ernest Guy (1870), George Arthur (1884), Helen Kathleen (1872), S. Alice Maude and twin Violet Grace Winifred (1877), Jessie (1882); married Emma Elizabeth (Bee in 1902), children: Rowland Walter (1902-02), Harry (1904), Charles Howard (1906), Frank (1908), Fred (1910), Muriel (1913), Sybil (1917-18); Occup: Professional Photographer; Service: Prewar, No. 711 8th Bn., S/F T.A., drummer, wartime No. 148147, A/Cpl. 2nd Am. R.A.F.; Theatre: no record; Medals: Territorial Force Efficiency Medal, wartime – no record; See *N/A* 14/2/14, 3/6/14, 12/8/14, 28/10/14, 14/4/15, 7/8/18.

Barrow, Leonard Norman. Born: Southwell, 1861; Lived: The Hall, Normanton; Fam: married Mary (Mason) 1891, children: Nancy Mary (1893), Marjorie Grantham (1895), Hilda (1898), Sybil Grantham (1901), Leonard Valentine (1902), Vera Mary (1909); Occup: Private means; Service: R.A.M.C., Major; Theatre: not known; Medals: not known.

Bates, Frederick Machin. Born: Southwell, 1891-1918; Lived: Church Street, Southwell; Fam: F. John Joseph Bates (Grocer), M. Louisa (Machin m. 1890), Br. John Harold (1900), S. Madeline (1898); School: Mrs Macdonald's, Minster 1901-09, Arnold House School, Blackpool; Occup: Grocer; Service: No. 26874, 6th Bn. Northumberland Fusiliers and No. 72711, 9th Bn. Royal Fusiliers; Theatre: Fr. On 24th March 1918 the 9th Royal Fusiliers, part of the 9th Division, took up position north of Albert, aware that the German offensive Operation Michael had forced the British 3rd and 5th Armies back a considerable distance. The Germans made two attempts to cross the river during the night of 26/27th March and were held back. He was K-in-A 27/3/18 during this battle, commemorated Pozières Memorial, panels 19-21; Medals: Victory, British; See p. 301.

Bates, Walter Wood. Born: 1871; Fam: F. Thomas Bates (Grocer), M. Mary (Oldham), Br. John James (1863), Charles Arthur (1867), S. Mary Catherine (1869), Fanny (1872), Annie Elizabeth (1875), Married Ada Harriet (Girkin in 1898), children: Walter William (1901), John Oldham (1903), Ada Mary (1905); School: Minster; Occup: with J.J. Bates; Service: Nos. 1055 & 281956, South Notts Hussars; Theatre: Egypt; Medals: Victory, British; See *N/A* 9/6/15 & pp. 279, 306.

Baxter*, Samuel Ernest. Born: Sneinton, Nottingham, 1882; Lived: Westgate, Southwell; Fam: M. Ethel (Litchfield); S. Daisy (1892), married Kate Robinson, 1911, children: Ernest (1913), Francis W. (1918); Occup: Lace Maker, Carey & Sons; Service: No. 305121, 1/8th Bn. S/F, Sgt., also No. 235575, Sgt. Lincolnshire Regt., No. 4960109, C.Q.M.S., S/F; Theatre: Fr. March 1915; Medals: Victory, British, 1914-15 Star; Demob Nov. 1919.

Becher*, John Pickard. Born: Southwell, 1880-1916; Lived: The Elms, Southwell; Fam: F. John Henry Becher (Barrister), M. Alice Mary (née Pickard), Br. Lancelot (1883), S. Alice Joyce (1890), married Gertrude Veronica Gale (stepdaughter of Dr. Handford) 1911, children: John (1912), Mary (1913); School: Malvern Links and abroad; Occup: Solicitor, Larken & Co. Newark, Clerk to the Magistrates; Service: Enlisted as Territorial 1906 and commanded 'H' Company, Lt. 1907, Capt., Major Feb. 1915, 1/8th Bn. S/F; Theatre: Fr. Feb. 1915, wounded at Hohenzollern 15/10/15, DoW 1/1/16, buried Abbeville; Medals: Victory, British, 1914-15 Star, D.S.O.; See *N/A* 14/2/14, 15/7/14, 29/7/14, 5/8/14, 9/9/14, 23/9/14, 27/1/15, 24/3/15, 28/4/15, 5/5/15, 2/6/15, 8/9/15, 15/9/15, 22/9/15, 29/9/15, 6/10/15, 20/10/15, 17/11/15, 1/12/15, 12/1/16, 15/3/16, 18/4/17, 24/10/17, 14/11/17, see pp. xiii, 202, 207-12, 214-5, 249-51, 272.

Becher, Lancelot Edward. Born Southwell, 1883-1960; Lived: Army Quarters; Fam: Br. of John Pickard Becher – see above, married Margaret Lucy Lyttleton 1914; Service: Royal Fusiliers, Lt., H.Q. Staff, 16th Div. Royal Engineers, Lt. Col. at end of war; Theatre: Fr. December 1915; Medals: Victory, British, 1914-15 Star, D.S.O.; See *N/A* 5/8/14, p. 259.

Bell, Albert. Born: Southwell, 1889; Lived: Burgage Lane, Southwell; Fam: F. William Bell (Bricklayer's labourer), M. Emma, Br. Fred (1887), Albert (1889), Horace William (1894), Herbert (1899), Walter (1902), Arthur (1905), Edward (1907), S. Elsie (1896); School: Natl. Infants, Wesleyan 1894-1903; Occup: Gardener's labourer; Service: No. 33504, Northamptonshire Regt., L/Cpl., No. 83464, labour Corps, L/Cpl.; Theatre: France; Medals: Victory, British.

Bell, Fred. Born: Southwell, 1887-1919; Lived: Southwell; Fam: Br. of Albert Bell – see above; School: Wesleyan 1895-1901; Occup: Labourer – E Carey & Sons; Service: Called up 17/10/16, No. 5448, 2/4th Royal Scots, No. 404047, Labour Corps, although not fully fit and with poor eyesight he was drafted to France; Theatre: Fr. July 1917 and served with the 5/6th Bn. Royal Scots; Medals: Victory, British; Died of Influenza Rouen 22/1/19 whilst awaiting demobilization.

Bell, Herbert. Born: Southwell, 1900; Lived: Norwood Fields, Southwell; Fam: Brother of Albert Bell – see above; School: Infants and Natl. 1906-?; Service: No record, however listed as a veteran in 1928.

Bell, Horace. Born: Southwell, 1894; Lived: Southwell; Fam: Br. of Albert Bell – see above; School: Wesleyan & Natl. 1903-08; Occup: Gardener; Service: Enlisted 19/1/15, No. 3484, 8th S/F, discharged 28/4/16 – burns to fingers; Theatre: Home; Medals; no record.

Bell, William. Born: Mansfield, 1897; Lived: Saracen's Head, Southwell; Fam: F. William Bell, M. Emma, Br. Lawrence (1902), S. Martha (1898), Ethel (1900), Emma (1905), Rhoda (1910); School: Worksop, Natl. 1908-10; Service: no record, however listed as a veteran in 1928.

Bennett, Herbert. No personal details available; Occup: Butcher's assistant to William Brown, Southwell; Was deferred at a Tribunal on 1/4/16 until 1/6/16; Service: no records found.

Berrisford*, Alfred B. Born: Southwell, 1894; Lived: 6 Chatham Street; Fam: F. William James Berrisford (Fitter, E. Carey & Sons), M. Mary (Rowland m. 1883), Br. Herbert (1886), William James (1893), S. Annie (1889), Mary (1896), married Naomi Kirk 1918; School: Trinity and Methodist 1898-1907; Occup: House Painter; Service: No. 1235, 1/8th Bn. S/F (wounded 1915) and No. 164847 Labour Corps, demob. March 1919; Theatre: Fr. March 1915; Medals: Victory, British 1914-15 Star; See *N/A* 19/5/15.

Berrisford, William James. Born: Southwell, 1892; Lived: 6 Chatham Street, Southwell; Fam: Br. of Alfred B. Berrisford – see above, married Harriet Fisher 1915; School: Wesleyan 1898-1905; Occup: Lace maker – E Carey & Sons; Service: 2/8th S/F, No. 38532 158th

Protection Company, Royal Defence Corps, demob. 7/3/19; Theatre: no record; Medals: no record; See *N/A* 14/4/15, 9/6/15.

Bett, Joseph Henry. Born: Kirkby-in-Ashfield, 1882; Lived: Kirklington; Fam: F. William Bett (Farmer), M. Rebecca (Hand), Br. Percy (1881), John George (1888), S. Ellen Julia (1885), Elsie Jane (1891); School: Kirklington, Natl. 1895-?, Minster; Occup: Farm worker; Service: Nos. 1095 & 280237, South Notts Hussars; Theatre: Egypt April 1915; Medals: Victory, British, 1914-15 Star; See pp. 279, 306.

Bett, Percy William. Born: Woodborough, 1881; Lived: Burgage, Southwell; Fam: Br. of Joseph Henry Bett – see above; Occup: Farm worker; Service: No. SE/15538, Royal Army Veterinary Corps, No. 155387, Royal Field Artillery; Theatre: not recorded; Medals: Victory, British.

Bevell, William. Lived: Bradfield Cottages, Easthorpe, Southwell; Fam: married Frances Jebb 1927, child: William (1930); Service: Enlisted 25/1/15, No. 362343, Royal Engineers, L/Cpl., demob. 1/5/19; Theatre: not recorded; Medals: not recorded.

Birch*, Joseph E. No family details; Service: No. 1530 & 305166 1/8th Bn. S/F, demob. December 1918; Medals: Victory, British, 1914-15 Star.

Blanchard, W. No further details.

Blood*, J. No further details.

Blood*, W. E. No further details.

William F. Bowes
Minster Wedding 1917
(Jean Hallam)

Bond, Frederick. Lived: Easthorpe; Service: No. 235800, RAF.

Bowes, William Fieldstone. Born: Long Bennington, 1889-1991; Lived: Easthorpe, Southwell; Fam: F. Thomas Waugh Bowes (Tailor), M. Ann (Metcalfe m. 1878), Br. Aaron W (1885), S. Violet M. (1882), married Elsie Maud Dodsworth 1917, children: Barbara A. (1920), Basil C. T. (1922), Jean M. (1924), Derek M. (1932); Occup: Grocer's assistant with J.J. Bates; Service: Attested Newark 22/5/15, No. 26251, 16th Bn. S/F, Chatsworth Rifles, L/Cpl.; Theatre: Fr., wounded by shrapnel; Medals: Victory, British; Post-war worked for Knight Dickens, Newark.

Bowler, Bertie Herbert. Born: Southwell, 1891; Lived: King Street, Southwell; Fam: F. William Bowler, M. Eliza Collyer, Br. Joseph William (1882), Samuel (1885), S. Sarah Ann (1875), Georgina (1876), Eliza (1880) Emily (1886), Elsie (1889); School: Infants & Natl. 1897-1900; Occup: Professional soldier; Service: Nos. 3073, 4768, 267844, 1/6th Devonshire Light, C. Sgt.; Theatre: Egypt; Medals: Victory, British, 1914-15 Star.

Bowler, Stanley William. Born: Bawtry, 1888; Lived: Landseer Road, Southwell; Fam: F. Charles S. Bowler, M. Betsy Ann (Miles m. 1878), S. Beatrice E. (1879), Daisy E. (1891), Margaret Marion (1894); School: Private & Natl. 1901-02; Occup: Shop assistant; Service: No. 67635, Durham Light Infantry, No. 22483, Labour Corps, No. 59030, Northumberland Fusiliers; Theatre: not recorded; Medals: Victory, British.

Brailsford, Charles Frederick. Born: Lincoln, 1886; Lived: Private Road, King Street, Southwell; Fam: married Edith Ann Cooke 1884, children: Edward B. Metham (1907), Charles (1910); Occup: Farm labourer; Service: No. 63861, Royal Field Artillery, driver; Theatre: Fr. Sept. 1915; Medals: Victory, British, 1914-15 Star.

Brailsford, John Bellamy. Born: Edwinstowe, 1878; Lived: Adams Row, Kirklington Road, Southwell; Fam: married Lizzie Troops 1879, children: Harold (1903), Cecil (1904), Lois (1906), Leslie (1908), Ernest (1910), Ethel (1913), John (1915); Occup: Groom at hotel; Service: No.

R/4/063697, Army Service Corps Remounts, demob. 19/5/19; Theatre: Fr. April 1915; Medals: Victory, British, 1914-15 Star.

Brown, Charles. Born: Mansfield, 1871; Lived: 6, Victoria Terrace, Southwell; Fam: married Mary Ann, children: John H. (1889), Vincent A. (1890), Francis C. (1892); Occup: Painter; Service: Served 21 years with Volunteers and Territorials, retired in 1912 as Sgt., re-joined 1915, No. 5744, 165th Royal Defence Corps; Theatre: Home and Russia in 1919; Medals: Victory, British; See *N/A* 14/4/15, 19/9/17, 30/4/19, & p. 252.

Brown, Charles Henry. Lived: Westgate, Southwell; Service: No. 1017, South Notts Hussars, No. 259115, Agricultural Labour Corps, demob. 19/4/19; Theatre: Balkans April 1915; Medals: Victory, British, 1914-15 Star; See p. 279.

Brown, Duncan Carmichael. Lived: New Street, Southwell; Service: No. 117367, Machine Gun Corps; Theatre: not recorded; Medals: Victory, British.

Brown*, George William. Born: Hockerton, 1885; Lived: Brinkley, Southwell; Fam: F. John George Brown (Farmer at Brinkley), M. Mary Elizabeth, S. Louisa Maude (1891), Kathleen Edna (1893); School: Bleasby and Natl. 1893-99; Occup: Farming; Service: Enlisted in 1908, No. 717, promoted L/Cpl. Dec 1914, 1/8th Bn. S/F, wounded, September, 1915, demob. 31/3/16 – Termination of period of engagement; Theatre Fr. March 1915; Medals: Victory, British, 1914-15 Star;

*George W. Brown
(Newark Advertiser)*

Brown, John H. Born: Thurgarton, 1888-1919; Lived: Maythorne; Fam: Son of Charles Brown – see above, married Ada, children: two daughters; School: Wesleyan 1891-1900, Natl. 1900-01; Occup: Van man Kirkby's, previously prof. soldier with Royal Scots Fusiliers; Service: Enlisted Jan 1915, 1st Bn. S/F, Cpl.; Theatre: Fr. April 1915, wounded 3/7/17 at Westhoek, Belgium and discharged 1918; Medals: not recorded, but assume Victory, British, 1914-15 Star. Died 25/4/19, buried in the Minster Yard; See *N/A* 9/6/15, 5/9/17, 19/9/17, 30/4/19, & pp. 252-3.

Brown, Richard H. Born: Bleasby, 1888; Lived: Brinkley; Fam: F. George Brown (Farmer), M. Mary E, Br. George M. (1885), S. Mary (1882), Edith (1887); School: Easthorpe, Wesleyan 1897-1902; Occup: Farm worker; Service: No. 66432, Machine Gun Corps; Theatre: not recorded; Medals: Victory, British.

Brown, Thomas. Born: Ayrshire, 1885; Lived: Kirklington Road, Southwell; Fam: F. Alexander Brown (Twist hand – E Carey & Sons), M. Ellen, S. Marion Peggy, (1909); Occup: Twist hand – E Carey & Sons; Service: No. 437, S/F; Theatre: Fr. Feb. 1915; Medals: Victory, British.

Brown, Vincent Arthur Alphonso. Born: Nottingham, 1889-1916; Lived 6, Victoria Terrace, Southwell; Fam: Son of Charles Brown – see above, married Mary E. Haywood (1913); School: Wesleyan 1892-1900, Natl. 1901-02; Service: Enlisted 1907, No. 10651, 2nd Bn. S/F; Theatre: Fr. Sept 1914, K-in-A 13/9/16, buried Guillemont Cemetery; Medals: Victory, British, 1914-15 Star; See *N/A* 23/12/14, 11/10/16, 8/8/17, 19/9/17, 30/4/19 & pp. 252-3.

Buckels, Fred George. Born: Farnsfield, 1895; Lived: Farnsfield; Fam: F. William Buckels (Painter), M. Emma (Thomas m. 1876), Br. William (1887), Thomas (1876), Harry (1890), Alec (1893), S. Mary (1877), Ellen (1878), Jane (1880), Lucy (1881), Nellie (1884), Sallie (1897), Kathleen (1898); Occup: House painter; Service: Enlisted 26/4/15, No. 4369, 2nd Bn. Life Guards, Cpl. of Horse, Demob. 5/2/19; Theatre: Fr., wounded 1918; Medals: Victory, British; See *N/A* 9/10/18.

Buckels, Thomas. Born: Farnsfield, 1876; Lived: Westgate, Southwell; Fam: Br. of Fred Buckels – see above, married Ethel (Shooter in 1902), children: Eric (1903), Jack Robert (1905), Edith Mary (1907); Occup: House painter; Service: Previously served in Boer War, re-enlisted 7/6/16, No. SR 9370, Royal Garrison Artillery, demob. 21.5.17 to reserve; Medals: not recorded; See *N/A* 7/11/17, 9/10/18.

Burn, Charles. Born: North Cave, East Yorks, 1886-1915; Lived Park Street, Southwell; Fam: F. John Burn (Labourer), M. Elizabeth, Br. John (1874), Tom (1880), Harry (1890), Arthur (1895), Albert (1898), S. Isabella (1892); Occup: Domestic Groom for F. Hill, previously professional soldier; Service: One of the first men to volunteer. Previously attested at York in 1903 and transferred to the Reserve in 1906, No. 7316, 3rd Bn. Duke of Wellington's, West Riding; Theatre: Fr. 1914. Seriously wounded by shrapnel in early fighting and brought back to Glasgow, DoW and chronic dysentery 11/3/15, buried Glasgow Western Necropolis; Medals: Victory, British, 1914-15 Star; See *N/A* 31/3/15.

Burton, William. Born: Bulwell, 1882; Lived New Street, Southwell; Fam: married Florence (Egleshaw m. 1878), children: Florence May (1902), George William (1905), Ida Ellen (1907); Occup: Lace Maker – E Carey & Sons; Service: No. 286689, Royal Garrison Artillery, Gnr.; Theatre: not recorded; Medals: Victory, British.

Bush, Bernard. Born: Newark, 1896; Lived: Morton cum Fiskerton; Fam: In foster care, John K Ratcliffe (Farmer) and Emma Ratcliffe; Occup: Farm worker; Service: No. 54768, 7th Royal Berkshire, No. 24761, North Staffordshire Regt., Machine Gun Coy; Theatre: Mesopotamia, Basra; Medals: Victory, British; Post-war became manager of Southwell Sewerage Works.

Bush, Reginald F. H. Born: Nottingham, 1900; Lived: Gedling Road, Carlton; Fam: F. Frederick C Bush (Buyer Raleigh Cycles), M. Sarah E. Bush, S. Irene (1903); School: Minster 1910-16; Service: O.T.C. Nottingham University, Sandhurst 1918; Theatre/Medals: No record.

Butler, Alfred George. Born: Southwell, 1882; Lived Victoria Terrace, Southwell; Fam: F. William Wilson Butler (Blacksmith), M. Martha (Johnson m. 1865), Br.

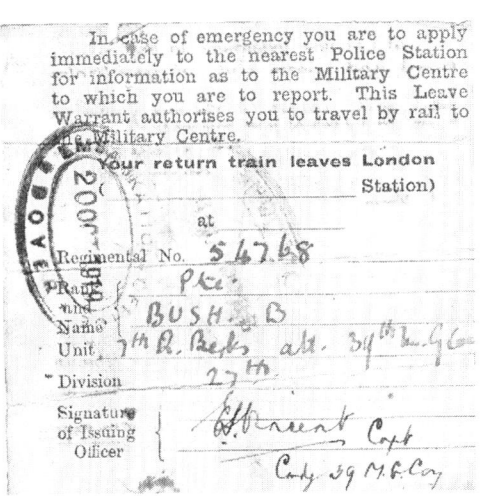

Travel Pass 1919 for Bernard Bush (Ray Bush)

William E. (1866), John L. (1869), Arthur A. (1875), Charles (1872), Charles F. (1880), Bertie R. (1883), S. Ada C. E. (1874); Occup: Grocer's Assistant, Kirkby's; Service: No. 82094, Lincolnshire Regt., No. 16292 Labour Corps; Medals: Victory, British.

Butler, Clifford William. Born: Southwell, 1897; Lived Norwood Villas, Southwell; Fam: Br. of Alfred George Butler – see above; School: Infants and Natl. 1904-11; Occup: Clerk, Kirkby's; Service: No. 21109, 13th and 10th Bn. S/F, No. 6195, Leicestershire Regt.; Theatre: Fr. 1915, wounded July 1916; Medals: Victory, British; See *N/A* 1/1/15, 20/1/15, 9/6/15, 12/7/16.

Cant, William. Born: Eagle, Lincs, 1878; Lived: King Street, Southwell; Married Gertrude (Peacock in 1904), children: James William (1905), Gertrude Olive (1906), Harold S. (1914),

Joyce M. (1916), Kenneth H. (1921); Occup: Baker, J.H. Kirkby; Service: 4th Bn. Notts Volunteers, Sherwood Foresters; Theatre: Home; Medals: no record.

Carey, William. Lived: Burgage, Southwell; Service: No. P7174, Military Police, No. 9 Area, Oswestry; Theatre: no record; Medals: no record.

Carvell, Frederick. Lived: Easthorpe, Southwell; Service: No. 5748, Royal Defence Corps; Theatre: no record; Medals: no record.

Cave*, Charles G. Born: Mortlake, Surrey, 1886; Lived: Westgate, Southwell; Fam: Married Hetty Cave in 1907, children: Constance (1910); Occup: Lace machine fitter, Carey & Sons; Service: No. 1427 & 305123, 1/8th Bn. S/F, demob. 2/3/15; Theatre Fr. March 1915; Medals: Victory, British, 1914-15 Star; See *N/A* 28/4/15, 22/9/15.

Chambers, Arthur Harold. Born: Nottingham, 1892; Lived: Westgate, Southwell; Fam: F. Arthur Chambers (Lay Clerk), M. Elizabeth (Woolley m. 1888), Br. Joseph Arthur (1891), Hubert Woolley (1898), George Edward (1906), Donald Woolley (1910), Hector Woolley (1910), S. Verity Emma (1900), Hilda Mary (1902); School: Natl., Minster 1902-09; Occup: Pupil teacher; Service: No. 21271, 5th Bn. S/F, 2nd Lt.; Theatre: Gallipoli & Fr. August 1915; Medals: Victory, British, 1914-15 Star; See *N/A* 6/1/15, 29/9/15, 10/11/15, 29/5/18 & p. 306.

Chambers, Hubert Woolley. Born: Nottingham, 1898; Lived: Westgate, Southwell; Fam: Br. of Arthur Harold Chambers – see above; School: Natl. & Minster 1906-12; Service: No. 480121 & T/3177, Royal Engineers; Theatre: not recorded; Medals: Victory, British; See p. 306.

Chapman, Charles William. Born: North Luffenham, Rutland, 1891; Lived: Winkburn; Fam: F. James Chapman (Gamekeeper), M. Emma, Br. Joseph (1894), Frederick (1897), married Sarah Elizabeth (Sturgess, m. 1915); School: Winkburn and Wesleyan 1900-05; Occup: Groom with Mr Small, Southwell; Service: Enlisted October 1914, Nos. 2847, 305793, 8th Bn. S/F, demob. Feb. 1919; Theatre: Fr., June 1915; Medals: Victory, British, 1914-15 Star; See *N/A* 4/11/14.

Chapman, Thomas Henry. Born/Fam: no details, died 1916; Lived: Southwell; Service: No. 3493, 2/8th Bn. S/F, L/Cpl.; Theatre: Ireland, died of wounds 27/4/16, buried Kilmainham Cemetery, Dublin

Charity, William. Born: Croxton Kervial, Leics, 1882; Lived: Private Road, Southwell; Fam: F. John Walton Charity (Woodman), M. Mary (Pike m. 1874), Br. Herbert (1875), Louie (1890), S. Emma (1879), Edith (1884), Mary (1886), married Mary Hannah Maria (Padgett m. 1900), children: Mary Ann Sissy (1902), Lucy Emma (1904), Louise Hannah Martin (1905), John William (1907); Occup: Lace hand – E Carey & Sons; Service: No. 85749, Royal Field Artillery, No. SE 35386, Army Veterinary Corps; Theatre: Fr. July 1915; Medals: Victory, British, 1914-15 Star.

Clarke, Cyril Thomas. Born: Skegby, 1893; Lived: The Police Station, Burgage, Southwell; Fam: F. George Clarke (Police Inspector), M. Sarah Ellen (Smith m. 1890), Br. Cyril Thomas (1894), Wilfred John (1896), S. Gertrude Janet (1885), Winifred Maria (1895), Nellie Davis (1900), married Constance Olive Mary (Clarke) of Sheffield 1918; School: Kirkby, Natl. 1903, Minster 1903-09; Occup: Asst. teacher; Service: No. 1490, 1st Bn. Brecknockshire Territorials, South Wales Borderers, Machine Gun Corps, 2/Lt, 62nd Squadron R.A.F., Lt; Theatre: Fr. July 1915; Medals: Victory, British, 1914-15 Star; See p. 306.

Clarke, T. No records

Clarke, Wilfred John. Born: Selston, 1896; Lived: The Police Station, Burgage, Southwell; Fam: Br. of Cyril Thomas Clarke – see above; School: Infants and Natl. 1903-08, Minster 1908-11; Occup: Gentleman's servant; Service: Enlisted 1914, No. 38356, Royal Field Artillery, Gunner; Theatre: Fr. July 1915; Medals: Victory, British, 1914-15 Star; See p. 306.

Clay*, Joseph H. Born: Arnold, 1895; Lived: Westgate, Southwell; Fam: F. William Clay (Cottons Patents Hand), M. Eliza, Br. William (1888), John (1891), S. Mary (1889); Occup: Clerk; Service: 1/8th Bn. S/F; Service: Fr. March 1915, reported in June 1915 he had been wounded in action; Medals: Victory, British, 1914-15 Star.

Clay*, William Henry. Born: Nottingham, 1890; Lived: Crowhill barracks; Fam: F. Joseph Clay (Plumber), M. Alice (Heaps m. 1889), married Elizabeth Richardson 1912, children: Joseph (1912-78), William Henry (1919-87), Arthur (1926-2006); Service: Professional soldier in 1911 – Crown Barracks, Crowhill R.S.O., 2nd Bn. S/F - No. 833 Cpl. 1/8th Bn. S/F (wounded), demob. 5/9/15; Theatre: Fr. Feb. 1915; Medals: Victory, British, 1914-15 Star.

Clulow, Henry Francis. Born: Bakewell, Derbyshire, 1874; Lived: Westgate, Southwell; Occup: Watch and Clock Repairer; Fam: married Kate, children: Annie (1902), Ernest (1906), Service: No. 266756; Medals: No details.

Cobb, George. Born: Southwell, 1899; Lived: Easthorpe, Southwell; Fam: F. George Cobb (Twist hand – E. Carey & Sons), M. Annie (Shephard m. 1898), Br. John William (1898); School: Easthorpe, Natl. 1906-12; Service: no details.

Cobb, John William. Born: Southwell, 1898; Lived: Easthorpe, Southwell; Fam: Br. of George Cobb – see above; School: Easthorpe, Natl. 1906-11; Service: Nos. 2961 & 268064, S/F, No. 457246, Royal Engineers, Sapper; Theatre: No record; Medals: Victory, British.

Cobb, John William. Born: Southwell, 1892; Lived: Spring Terrace, Southwell; Fam: F. John W. Cobb (Farm Labourer), M. Mary Elizabeth (Chambers), Br. William (1897), S. Annie (1893), Mary (1900), married Mary Annis Constance (Bancroft in June 1926), children: Douglas A (1926); School: Caunton, Natl. 1898-1905; Occup: Gardener; Service: Enlisted Nov. 1914, No. 20085, S/F, L/Sgt.; Theatre: Fr. July 1915-17, wounded and discharged Oct. 1917; Medals: Victory, British, 1914-15 Star.

Cobb, William. Born: Southwell, 1897; Lived, Westgate, Southwell; Fam: Br. of John W. – see above; Occup: Farm labourer with Leonard Hutchinson, Cork Hill Farm; Service: no records.

Coddington, George Ernest. Born: Balderton, 1883; Lived: King Street, Southwell; Fam: F. Thomas Coddington, M. Emma (Cutts m. 1867), Br. William Henry (1876), Thomas (1879), Frederick (1881); Occup: Hairdresser; Service: Enlisted June 1917, No. TRS/43721, Training Reserve and No. 88608, S/F, discharged sick 18/6/17; Theatre/Medals: no record.

Collinson, George William. Born: Swinderby, 1888; Lived: Crew Lane, Southwell; Fam: F. Thomas Collinson, M. Ettie Eliza (Brown m. 1886), Br. Herbert (1889), Thomas (1893), Walter (1900); Occup: Nurseryman; Service: No. 342464, Royal Engineers; Theatre: no details; Medals: no details.

Collinson, Herbert. Born: Swinderby, 1889-1918; Lived: Normanton; Fam: Br. of George William Collinson – see above, married Ellen (Ulyatt), child Gladys Mary (1907); School: Natl. ?-1902; Occup: Caudwell's Flour Mill; Service: No. 22008, 2nd Bn. S/F, Sgt.; Theatre: Fr. March 1916, fought with the battalion at Lens and later at the Battle of Cambrai. On 10/3/18 the battalion took over the line at Lagnicourt, where he was wounded, DoW 15/3/18, buried Achiet-Le-Grand, Communal Cemetery; Medals: Victory, British; *N/A 27/3/18.*

Collinson, William. No family details found; Occup: Lace maker - E. Carey & Sons; Service: applied to Tribunal 19/12/17 and refused, but no military records found.

Collis, Alfred. Born: no census details; Lived: Ormonde House, Easthorpe; Service: Nos. 480096, T/1988, Royal Engineers, Cpl.; Theatre: no details; Medals: Victory, British.

Cook, Charles. Born: Southwell, 1876; Lived: Westhorpe, Southwell; Fam: F. William Cook, M. Hannah (Richardson), Br. James (1874), Charles (1876), S. Annie (1877); Occup: Lace hand

*Fred Cooke - Front Centre
(Peter Cant)*

– E Carey & Sons; Service: No. T/405119, Army Service Corps; Theatre: no details; Medals: Victory, British.

Cooke, Fred. Born: Basford, (1879); Lived: Spring Terrace, Easthorpe; Fam: married Louise Annie Revill in 1898, children: Fred (1901), Annie (1900); Occup: Bricklayer; Service: No. M/348846, Army Service Corps, 4th Bn. Notts Volunteers, Sher wood Foresters; Theatre: no record; Medals: Victory, British.

Cooksley*, G. A. B. No details.

Cooling*, Arthur. Born: Southwell, 1891; Lived: Westgate, Southwell; Fam: F. Reuben Cooling (Gardener), M. Mary Ann (White m. 1888), Br. Frank (1898), S. Mabel (1893), Kate (1899), Hilda (1907), Winnie (1909); School: Trinity, Natl. 1898-?; Occup: Labourer and porter, E Carey & Sons; Service: No. 58991, 1/8th Bn. S/F., demob. 10/5/18; Theatre: Fr. March 1915, slightly injured July 1915; Medals: Victory, British, 1914-15 Star; See *N/A* 7/7/15.

*Arthur Cooling
(Frank & Suzanne Cooling)*

Cooling, Frank William. Born: Southwell, 1898-1917; Lived: Westgate, Southwell; Fam: Br. of Arthur Cooling – see above; Occup: Asst. miller, Caudwell's; Service: Called up February, 1917, No. 67395, 8th Labour Bn. Durham Light Infantry; Theatre: Fr. 1917, died of cerebral-spinal meningitis, 30/3/17, buried, Haute-Avegnes British Cemetery Pas de Calais; Medals: Victory, British; See *N/A* 18/4/17, 8/8/17.

Cooling, William. Born: Southwell, 1896-1917; Lived: New Houghton, Derbyshire; Fam: F. Edwin Cooling, M. Ellen (Scraton m. 1889), Br. Harold (1894), S. Mabel (1891), Lillian (1892), Elsie (1898), Ada (1900); Service: Volunteered at the outbreak of war, No. 16066, 2/7th S/F; Theatre: Fr. August 1915. The battalion was holding trenches in northern France where he was wounded - DoW 5/7/17, buried Metz en Couture Communal Cemetery; Medals: Victory, British, 1914-15 Star.

Cooper, Cecil E. Born: Normanton, 1888; Lived: Normanton; Fam: F. Edward Cooper (Farm foreman), M. Ada (Clarke m. 1885), Br. Leonard (1889), Elizabeth (1886), Eva (1887), Gladys (1892), Doris (1895); Service: No. M347543, Army Service Corps; Theatre: No record; Medals: British.

Cope, Thomas. Born: Newark, 1881; Lived: Church Street, Southwell; Fam: F. George Cope, M. Annie, Br. John (1887), S. Mary Ann (1882), Lydia Ellen (1890), Fanny (1891), May (1900), married Mary (Hampson in 1908), children: Douglas (1910), Mary (1912), Ronald (1921); Occup: Ironmonger's manager; Service: Enlisted 9/12/15, No. 151987, Royal Garrison Artillery, discharged 25/1/19; Theatre: Fr. wounded in right arm; Medals: Victory, British.

Coppock, George Ernest. Born: Southwell, 1898; Lived: Victoria Terrace, Kirklington Road, Southwell; Fam: F. Richard Coppock (Twisthand), M. Mary Jane (Tirrill m. 1883), Br. Richard W (1889), Leonard Raworth (1894), S. Harriet Elizabeth (1894), Agnes Emma (1902); School: Infants & Natl. 1905-10, Minster 1910-13 (Choral Scholarship); Occup: Chorister; Service: No. M/354043, 7th Aux. Army Service Corps; Theatre: no record; Medals: Victory, British.

Copson, Samuel. Born: Southwell, 1886-1917; Lived: Westgate, Southwell; Fam: F. Samuel (Basket maker), M. Annie (Lawson m. 1873), (Charwoman), Br. George (1882), Richard (1887), S. Jane (1879), Emma (1884), Mary (1890), Annie (1889); School: Trinity, Natl. 1893-95; Occup: Professional Soldier; Service: No. 8856, Royal Scots Fusiliers; Theatre: Fr. August 1914. Involved in the fighting at Mons, Le Cateau, and the Ypres Salient. The battalion took part in the Battle of Arras and he was K-in-A 3/5/17 in heavy shelling and gas attack, commemorated Arras Memorial; Medals: Victory, British, 1914-15 Star with Clasp and silver rosette and ribbon.

Corby, Will. Born/Fam: no details; Occup: with J.J. Bates; Service: No. 55278, Derbyshire Regt.; Theatre: no record; Medals: Victory, British; See *N/A* 9/6/15.

Cottam, Arthur. Born: Southwell, 1898; Lived: Easthorpe, Southwell; Fam: F. Henry Edwin Cottam (Carting contractor), M. Frances Annie (Drabble), Br. George Andrew (1894), Weightman (1897), Edwin Selby (1901), Harry (1906), Wilfred (1909), S. Winifred Annie (1893), Gladys (1909); School: Easthorpe, Natl. 1905-?; Service: Enlisted Aug. 1916, No. 329383, Agricultural Labour Corps, demob. 30/7/19; Theatre: most likely served in U.K.; Medals: no record.

Cottam, George Andrew. Born: Southwell, 1894; Lived: Easthorpe, Southwell; Fam: Br. of Arthur Cottam – see above; School: Easthorpe, Wesleyan 1901-08, Minster 1908-09; Occup: Butcher's apprentice; Service: Enlisted Jan 1914, No. 949, South Notts Hussars, discharged – ill health 17/3/15; Theatre: Egypt; Medals: no record; See pp. 279, 306.

Cottam, Harold Thomas. Born: 1891-1984; Lived: Church Street, Southwell; Fam: F. William Cottam (Builder), M. Jane, Br. Oscar (1895), Kenneth (1897), Angus Ivan (1907), Raymond (1909); School: Wesleyan 1898-1904, Minster, Marconi College, London; Occup: Merchant Navy; Service: Royal Navy Volunteer Reserve; Theatre: At sea; Medals: no record; Harold Cottam was the radio operator on the Carpathia and took the distress signal from the Titanic in April 1912.

Cottam, Kenneth Ellwood. Born: Southwell, 1897; Lived: Church Street, Southwell; Fam: Br. of Harold Thomas Cottam – see above; School: Wesleyan, 1901-09, Minster 1909-14; Occup: Clerk, Smith's Bank, Nottingham; Service: No. G21642, Sussex Regt.; Theatre: no record; Medals: Victory, British.

Cottam, Oscar William. Born: Southwell, 1894; Fam: Br. of Harold Thomas Cottam – see above; School: Easthorpe, Natl. 1900-08, Minster 1908-09; Occup: Builder with father; Service: Enlisted 1915, No. M2104940, Army Service Corps, demob. 26/3/19; Theatre: Fr. Sept. 1915; Medals: Victory, British, 1914-15 Star.

Oscar Cotton - Loughton Collection (By kind permission of the Dean and Chapter.)

Cox, Joseph. Lived: Nottingham Road, Southwell; Service: No. 203495, 4th Bn. South Staffordshire Regt.; Theatre: no record; Medals: Victory, British.

Cox, R. No records, but a brief mention in *N/A* 22/11/16.

Coy, George Islip. Born: Newark, 1896-1915; Lived: Bulcote; Fam: F. Thomas Islip (Horseman), M. Annie (Hazzard m. 1892), Br. Charles (1893), Thomas (1898), John (1899), Frederick (1900-01), Samuel (1902), Harold (1903-03), S. Mary Annie (1897-97); Service: Enlisted 12/10/14, 1/8th S/F; Theatre: Fr., June, 1915, K-in-A 30/7/15, commemorated Menin Gate, panel 39 & 41; Medals: Victory, British, 1914-15 Star.

Craggs, Percy H. Born: Southwell, 1892; Lived: New Street, Southwell; Fam: F. John Craggs (Sgt. Major – 4th Notts), M. Mary, Br. John (1883), Ernest (1887), S. May (1889); School: Wesleyan 1895-1904, Natl. 1904-05; Occup: Clerk; Service: Enlisted 3/10/07, No. 27293, Royal Garrison Artillery, demob. 2/10/19; Theatre; Fr. 1914, wounded in action with 20% disability, pension 8s 8p from 2/10/19; Medals: Victory, British, 1914 Star with Clasp and Roses.

Croom, Harry (Henry). Born: Southwell, 1894-1915; Lived: Beeston, Nottingham; Fam: F. Thomas Croom (Foundry labourer), M. Catherine (Curzon m. 1880), Br. Alfred (1885), Robert (1888), Leonard (1898), S. Emily, Kate (1892), Daisy (1896), Florrie (1904); Occup: Gas stoker and professional soldier from April 1914; Service: No. 13882 1st Bn. S/F, 4th Bn. & 1st Bn.; Theatre: Fr. December 1914. Wounded 5/5/15, DoW 20/5/15, buried Le Trepot Military Cemetery; Medals: Victory, British, 1914-15 Star.

Cropper, Edward William. Born: Upton, 1887; Lived: Easthorpe, Southwell; Fam: F. Joseph Cropper (dec'd – miller), M. Emma (m. 1886), Br. George (1883), Frederick (1890), Leonard (1892), William Edward (1887), Frederick (1890), Charles Leonard (1891), S. Edith (1885); Occup: Miller and baker; Service: No. 32648, Yorkshire & Lancashire Regt.; Theatre: no record; Medals: Victory, British.

Cross, George. Born: Southwell, (1889); Lived: Maythorne; Fam: F. Arthur Edwin Cross (Water bailiff), M. Alice Maud (Rex m. 1887); Br. Kenneth William (1894), S. Ada (1888); School: Wesleyan 1897-1903; Occup: Silk worker; Service: Enlisted September 1914, Nos. 2342 & 305511, 8th Bn. S/F, A/Sgt., demob. 10/3/19; Theatre: Fr. March 1915; Medals: Victory, British, 1914-15 Star.

Crouch, Fred. Born: Chard, Somerset, 1879; Lived: Easthorpe, Southwell; Fam: married to Kate Edith (Dennis m. 1901), children: Clara (1902), Arthur (1903); Occup: Coachman; Service: No. 113740, 204 S Bty. Royal Garrison Artillery; Theatre: not recorded; Medals: Victory, British.

Crow*, Henry Stevenson. Born: Cumberworth, Lincs, 1887; Lived: Concert Hall Yard, Southwell; Fam: Grandfather William Crow, married Sarah Ann (Henton m. 1910); Occup: Railway drag man; Service: No. 765 & 71053, 1/8th Bn. S/F, demob. 4/3/18; Theatre: Fr. Sept 1916, wounded in action; Medals: Victory, British.

Crowder, Charles Frederick Junior. Born: Southwell, 1898; Lived: 10, New Street, Southwell; Fam: F. Charles Crowder (Farm worker), M. Elizabeth (Morton m. 1884), S. Jane Hannah (1895), Alice (1898); School: Natl. 1905-12; Service: Enlisted July 1915, No. 55580, 24th Bn. Manchester Regt., demob. March 1919; Theatre: Fr. Nov. 1915, Italy Sept. 1917; Medals: Victory, British.

Crowson, Percy. Lived: 7 Victoria Terrace, Kirklington Road, Southwell; Service: No. 64962, Royal Field Artillery, 18th Brigade; Theatre: Fr. Nov. 1915; Medals: Victory, British, 1914-15 Star.

Curzon, John Henry. Born: Southwell, 1885-1918; Lived: Westgate, Southwell; Fam: F. Walter Curzon (Gardener), M. Mary Elizabeth (Smith m. 1875), S. Mary E (1877), married Daisy Barker 1909 , children: John Ernest (1910), Hilda (1917), Joseph J. (1918); School: Wesleyan 1888-89; Occup: Twist hand – E. Carey & Sons; Service: Nos. 2582 & 305657, 10th Bn. S/F, A/Cpl.; Theatre: Fr. March 1915, injured July 1915 following a mine explosion and sent to Woolwich Hospital to recover, returned to France and later gassed. In the line during the German offensive, Operation Michael, and K-in-A 23/3/18, commemorated Arras Memorial; Medals: Victory, British, 1914-15 Star; See *N/A* 7/7/15.

Daniels, Edward. Service: No. 45410, S/F; Theatre: Fr. 1915; Medals: Victory, British; See *N/A* 28/4/15, 25/8/15.

Davis, Harry Reginald. Born: 1894-1916; Lived: Lenton, Nottingham; Fam: F. Joseph Hill Davis (Secretary, Bailey & Co, Tanners), M. Mary Maria, Br. Fred James (1891), S. Gladys E (1893); School: Nottingham High School, Minster 1909; Occup: Bank Clerk; Service: Former Public Schools Bn., No. Z/1415, Hawke Bn., R.N.V.R., Reserve Bn. 4/5/15-1/7/15, re-joined 31/7/16 after illness; Theatre: Fr. 1916, K-in-A 13/11/16, buried in shell holes near German lines, commemorated Thiepval Memorial; Medals: not recorded.

Davis, William Edwin. Born: Southwell, 1897; Lived Easthorpe, Southwell; Fam: F. Harry Dunston Davis (Twist hand – E. Carey & Sons), M. Faith, Br. Ernest Richard (1908), Harry (1909), S. Mary Lilian (1892), Faith Ellen (1903), Mabel (1906); School: Wesleyan 1905-11; Service: Nos. 480488, (T) 3163, Royal Engineers; Theatre: not recorded; Medals: Victory, British.
Davison, George Robert. Born: Silvertown, Middlesex, died 1916; Service: Attested 1916 at Derby, No. 70437, 2nd Bn. S/F; Theatre: Fr. 1916. Was involved with the heavy fighting at Quadrilateral, near Ginchy, during the Battle of the Somme. In the trenches north of Les Boefs and K-in-A 13/10/16, commemorated Thiepval Memorial; Medals: Victory, British; See *N/A* 8/8/17.
Daws, John William. Born: Long Bennington, 1893; Lived: Kirklington; Fam: F. William Daws, M. Emma (Pounder m. 1889); Br. James Henry (1902), S. Ellen (1895), Mary (1897), Lizzie (1905), Alice (1909), married Mary (Taylor in 1922), children: Beatrice (1922), John William (1926), Reginald (1928); Occup: Waggoner; Service: Attested Newark Jan 1915, No. 3752, S/F, sent to work on J. Scott's farm at Kirklington, No. 24104, S/F, L/Cpl., demob. 22/2/19; Medals: Victory, British.
Deeley, Sidney Thomas. Born: Carlton, Newark, 1892-1914; Lived: King Street, Southwell; Fam: F. Henry Deeley (Miller's labourer), M. Abina Zingon Driphosa (Townsend), Br. Sidney, (1892), William A (1896), S. Ellen Prudence (1894), Edith Mary (1896), Lilian Agnes (1901); School: Trinity, Natl. 1900-1904, Wesleyan 1904-5; Occup: Professional Soldier; Service: No. 14657, 1st Bn. Grenadier Guards; Theatre: Fr. Sept. 1914. Was involved in the B.E.F. Retreat, moved to Flanders in late 1914 and was wounded whilst fighting near Ypres, DoW 12/11/14, buried Railway Chateau, West Vlaanders, Belgium; Medals: Victory, British, 1914 Star; See *N/A* 25/11/14, 28/4/15, 12/1/16. First Southwell death.
Deeley, William. Born: Southwell, 1896; Lived: King Street, Southwell; Fam: Br. of Sidney Thomas Deeley – see above; School: Trinity, Natl. 1904-05, Wesleyan 1905-09; Occup: Errand boy; Service: Nos. GS/20013, D/16174, Dragoon Guards, Cpl.; Theatre: Fr. 1915; Medals: Victory, British, 1914-15 Star and clasp.
Dennison*, J. No further details.
Deverill, Arthur Frederick. Born: Battersea, 1891; Lived: Halloughton with Mrs Mayfield; Fam: F. George Deverill (Solicitor's clerk), M. Ethel May, Br. George William (1885), S. Elsie (1890), married Ethel May (Poole in 1917); School: Thurgarton, Natl. 1904-06; Occup: Apprentice Electrical engineer; Service: Enlisted 19/9/14, Royal Flying Corps, Sgt. Major, in 1917 was a flying instructor; Theatre: Fr. and home; Medals: 1914-15 Star, no record of others.
Dixon, Alfred. Born: Farnsfield, 1880; Lived: Mountney's Cottage, Easthorpe, Southwell; Fam: married Elle, children: Elsie May (1905), Annie May (1911); Occup: General labourer; Service: No. 182653, Labour Corps; Theatre: no record; Medals: no record.
Dixon, Frederick Arthur. Born: Newark, 1887; Lived: Southwell; Fam: married to Gertrude Annie; Occup: Butcher's Assistant in Southwell; Service: Attested June 1916, No. 25919, 9th Bn. King's Own Royal Lancashire Regt.; Theatre: Salonika, died of pneumonia and malaria 3/1/19, buried Kirechkoi-Hortakoi Cemetery, Greece; Medals: Victory, British.
Dixon, John. Lived: Burgage Lane, Southwell; No other records.
Dixon, Walter Bradley. Born: Newark, 1884; Lived: Brookland Villas, Kirklington Road, Southwell; Fam: F. John Dixon (Inn Keeper, Black Bull), M. Annie, S. Phyllis A. (1890); School: Infants & Natl: 1892-?; Occup: Rural postman; Service: No. 2634, Lincolnshire Regt., No. 29549, Labour Corps, No. 388069, 8th Bn. London Regt.; Theatre: not recorded; Medals: Victory, British.

Dodd, John James. Born: Southwell, 1878; Lived: 'The Grapes', Westgate, Southwell; Fam: F. John H. Dodd (Publican), M. Martha Cousin (Wood, m. 26/3/74), S. Mary (1876), married Florence Ann (Outlaw in Sept. 1910), children: James W. (1913), Florence M. (1917), Thomas D. (1919); Occup: Publican and painter; Service: Applied to Tribunal 10/6/16 and deferred until 1/9/17, joined 4th Hussars, Cpl.; Theatre/Medals: No records; See p. 306.

Dodson, Dudley Paulson. Born: Lenton, Nottingham, 1898; Lived: School House, Upton; Fam: F. Thomas W Dodson (Schoolmaster), M. Mary A. (Schoolmistress), Br. Roland (1895), S. May (1895); Occup: Ironmonger; Service: No. C1159, 16th Bn. King's Royal Rifles, Cpl., demob. March 1919; Theatre: Fr. 1915, wounded 1916, P.O.W.; Medals: Victory, British, 1914-15 Star; Post-war joined Manchester Police as Pc.; See p. 269.

Dodsworth, Albert William. Born: Worksop, 1899; Lived: Easthorpe; Fam: F. Charles Dodsworth (Groom), M. Mary, Br. George Carlos (1888), S. Elsie Maud (1889), Mabel Annie (1896), Hilda Mary (1906), married Phyllis (Moore in 1921), children: Geoffrey (1921), Phyllis (1924), Daphne (1929), Gillian (1933), Robin (1934); Occup: Grocer's assistant; Service: Attested March 1917, No. TR/5/100867, discharged with illness after 9 months.

Donson, George. Born: Southwell, 1881-1917; Lived: Westhorpe, Southwell; Fam: married Mary A Kirk; Occup: Lace maker – E. Carey & Sons; Service: Enlisted November 1915, No. 19859, 36th Bn. Northumberland Fusiliers; Theatre; not recorded, died of influenza 8/1/17, buried Colchester Cemetery; Medals: no record.

Donson*, John. Born: Nottingham, 1873; Lived: Westhorpe, Southwell; Fam: F. George Donson (Nurseryman), M. Emma, S. Mary Ann (1882), married Jane in 1902, children: Harry (1902), Jack (1906), Wilfred (1909), Richard (1910); Occup: Lace maker, E. Carey & Sons; Service: Territorial 1893, No. 705, L/Cpl. 1/8th Bn. S/F from 1/4/04, 1/4/16 to No. 42626, Cpl. Royal Defence Corps, unpaid L/Sgt. 10/6/16, reverted to Cpl. 10/11/16, demob. 29/1/19; Service: It appears that in view of his age he did not serve outside the UK; Medals: Victory, British.

Donson, William. Born: Southwell, 1872-1916; Lived: Frome, Somerset; Fam: married May Elizabeth, children: William (1898), Cyril (1900), Ethel (1902), Bertha (1903), Louisa (1905), Annie (1907), John (1908), Thornley George (1910); Occup: Superintendent Refuge Assurance Co.; Service; No. SS/21101, 28th Labour Company, Army Service Corps; Theatre: Balkans Nov. 1915, DoW 26/10/16, buried Pieta Military Cemetery, Malta; Medals: Victory, British, 1914-15 Star.

Dovey*, Hubert. Born: Calverton, 1895; Lived: Calverton; Fam: F. Frank Dovey (Framework knitter), M. Elizabeth, Br. John (1897), Herbert (1901), Harry (1910), S. Ida (1903); Occup: Framework knitter; Service: No. 1582, 1/8th Bn. S/F, No. 157128, Machine Gun Corps; Theatre: No record; Medals: Victory, British.

Dovey*, Percy. Born: Calverton, 1897; Lived: Calverton; Fam: F. Frederick (Framework knitter), M. Harriet, Br. Horace (1899), Albert (1900), George (1902), William (1904), Arthur (1910); Occup: Factory hand – hosiery; Service: Nos. 1583, 330529, 1/8th Bn. S/F; Theatre: Fr. June 1915, Demob. 28/4/17; Medals: Victory, British, 1914-15 Star.

Doughty, Ernest Richard. Born: Southwell, 1898; Lived: Westgate, Southwell; Fam: F. Richard Doughty (Warehouseman), M. Annie Elizabeth, Br. Leonard (1907), John Phillip (1909), S. Edith Rose (1900), Minnie (1903); School: Trinity, Natl. 1906-11; Service: Enlisted late 1916, No. 203130, S/F, No. 60834, Leicestershire Regt.; Theatre: no record; Medals: Victory, British; See *N/A* 22/11/16.

Douthwaite, Robert Christopher Morris. Born: Derby, 1897-1919; Lived: College Street, Nottingham; Fam: F. Robert Edward Douthwaite (Timber Merchant), M. Beatrice Maud

(Haslop), Br. Philip Charlton (1900), S. Ursula Margaret Morris (1900), Millicent Morris (1903); School: Nottingham High School, Minster 1911-13; Occup: Insurance Clerk; Service: Royal Field Artillery, attached to Yorks and Lancashire Regt. Lt.; Theatre: Balkans, died of illness at Fiume 19/6/19, buried Kuzala Cemetery, Rijeka, Croatia; Medals: Victory, British.

Downham, Albert Arthur. Born: Camberwell, London, 1876; Lived: Pollards Lane, Southwell; Fam: married Elizabeth Stevens 10/2/12, children: Martha (1918); Occup: Professional soldier; Service: Enlisted 1894, No. 4010, Yorkshire and Lancashire Regt., Sgt. Major, retired 1918; Theatre: Home, although had previous service in South Africa and India; Medals: Victory, British.

Drabble*, Arthur E. Born: Winkburn, 1898; Lived: Easthorpe, Southwell; Fam: F. W. A. Drabble (Bricklayer), M. Alice, Br. William H. (1895), S. Phyllis (1906); School: Easthorpe and Wesleyan 1901-?; Occup: Grocer's assistant; Service: No. 1553, 1/8th Bn. S/F, demob. 7/3/18; Theatre: Fr. March 1915; Wounded 1915 and May 1916; Medals: Victory, British 1914-15 Star; See *N/A* 24/10/17.

Drabble, William H.* Born: Winkburn, 1895 - 1917; Lived: Easthorpe, Southwell; Fam: Brother of Arthur E – see above; School: Easthorpe and Wesleyan 1901-?; Occup: Grocer's apprentice – J.J. Bates; Service: No. 1433 & 305127, 1/8th Bn. S/F, promoted to Sgt.; Theatre: Fr. March 1915. Wounded at Hohenzollern Redoubt in October 1915, declined a commission. Shelled near Hill 70 where he was K-in-A 4/10/17, buried Philosophe, Mazingarbe; Medals: Victory, British, 1914-15 Star; See *N/A* 9/6/15, 24/10/17 & p. 230.

Ducker*, Ernest Arthur. Born: Rugby, Warwicks., 1897–1976; Lived: Brinkley Cottage, Southwell; Fam: F. Frederick William Ducker (Nurseryman), M. Charlotte Elisabeth, Br. Frederick Henry (1895), Richard Walter (1903), S. Alice Mary (1907), married Gladys E. Pead (1922), children: Ralph, Eva Mary; School: Burton Joyce & Natl. 1904-10; Occup: Nurseryman, Merryweather's, and lace maker E. Carey & Sons; Service: No. 74, 1/8th Bn. S/F & No. 18357 Army Cycling Corps; Theatre: Fr. February 1915, wounded in action, then transferred to Cycling Corps; Medals: Victory, British, 1914-15 Star; post-war worked for Feckinghams (nurseries), then Ransom and Marles, Newark laundry and Staythorpe Power Station. During WW2 he worked on munitions in Grantham.

Ducker*, Frederick Henry. Born: Rugby, Warwicks., 1895; Lived: Brinkley Cottage, Southwell; Fam: brother of Ernest Arthur Ducker – see above; School: Burton Joyce and Natl. 1904-08; Service: Nos. 1554 & 305178, 1/8th Bn. S/F; Theatre: Fr. February 1914; Medals: Victory, British, 1914-15 Star.

Dyer, Charles Alfred. Born: No family records; Lived: Alma Cottages, Westgate, Southwell; Service: Nos. 424018, 200214, 7250352, Royal Army Medical Corps, Cpl.; Theatre: Iraq; Medals: Victory, British, General Service Clasp Iraq.

Easter, Jonas C. Born: Kings Lynn, 1887; Lived: Southwell; Fam: F. William Easter, M. Susanna, Br. Alexander (1884); Service: Applied to Tribunal 3/3/16 - refused - no military records found.

Eaton, Ezekiel.* Born: Ilkeston, 1893 – 1915; Lived: Concert Hall Yard, Southwell; Fam: F. Ezekiel Eaton (Twist hand – E. Carey & Sons), M. Clara, Br. Edmond (1882), James Henry (1891), S. Rose (1896); School: Infants and Natl. 1900-07; Occup: Lace hand – E. Carey & Sons; Service: No. 1058, 1/8th Bn. S/F; Theatre: Fr. March 1915, DoW 17/5/15, buried Minster churchyard; Medals: Victory, British, 1914-15 Star; See *N/A* 26/5/15, 12/1/16.

Eaton*, James Henry. Born: Ilkeston, 1891; Lived: Concert Hall Yard, Southwell; Fam: Brother of Ezekiel Eaton – see above; Occup: Lace threader – E. Carey & Sons; Service: Nos. 1536 & 305169, 1/8th Bn. S/F, No. 733563 London Regt., 24th Bn. Signaller; Theatre: Fr. 1915; Medals: Victory, British, 1914-15 Star.

Egleshaw, John George. Born: Bulwell, Nottingham, 1883-1917; Lived: Southwell; Fam: F. James Egleshaw, M. Ellen (Truswell), married Ellen m. Sept. 1908), children: Florence (1909), Kenneth Maxfield (1911), Mary E. (1914), Grace E. (1917); Occup: Professional Golfer, Southwell Golf Club, previously with E. Carey & Sons; Service: Enlisted 1917, F/30578, Royal Naval Air Service, Aircraftman 2nd Class, died in an accident 14/8/17; See *N/A* 22/8/17.

Elliot, Thomas Stokoe, Dr. Born: Southwell, 1873; Lived: Colston Bassett, Bingham; Fam: F. Dr. George Elliott, The Old Rectory, Southwell, Br. Gilbert Henry (1867), William (1875), married Annie, children: Thomas Kendall (1907); Occup: General Practitioner; Service: Royal Army Medical Corps; Theatre: not recorded; Medals: not recorded; See *N/A* 4/11/14.

Elliot, William G. Born: Farnsfield; Fam: Br. of Thomas Stokoe Elliott – see above; Service: R.A.F.; Theatre: no record; Medals: no record.

Ellis, Robert. Born: Southwell, 1872; Lived: King Street, Southwell; Fam: married Charlotte, children: Audrey Elizabeth (1905), Margaret Edna (1909); Occup: Plumber; Service: Enlisted 28/6/15, No. 306354, S/F; Theatre: no record; Medals: no record.

Elsip, A. No records.

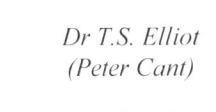

Elvidge, C. Born/Fam: no record; Occup: with J.J. Bates; Service: Army Service Corps Remounts; Theatre/Medals: no record; See *N/A* 9/6/15.

Ewers, Harold Richmond. Born: Burton-on-Trent, 1898-1918; Lived Burgage Villa, Southwell; Fam: F. Frank Ewers (Brewery Manager), M. Mary Emily (Collins); Br. Leslie Frank (1896); School: Minster 1909-14; Occup: Bank Clerk; Service: Enlisted 7/2/16, No. 29699, 2/7th Bn. Royal Warwickshire Regt.; Theatre Fr. July 1916, gassed 10/8/18, K-in-A 24/10/18, buried Cannone Farm British Cemetery, Sommaing, France Nord; Medals: Victory, British; See *N/A* 13/11/18, & p. 301.

Ewers, Leslie Frank. Born: Burton-on-Trent, 1896 1925; Fam: Br. of Harold Richmond Ewers – see above; School: Minster 1908-11; Occup: Civil Servant; Service: Border Regt. & Machine Gun Corps, Lt. & 71 Punjabi Indian Army, Captain; Theatre: India and Mesopotamia; Medals: Victory, British; See *N/A* 13/11/18, & p. 306; Died in 1925 in British Columbia,

Farr*, William. Born: Retford, 1894; Lived: Farnsfield; Fam: F. William (police pensioner), M. Louisa, Br. Charles Ernest (1896), John Lewis (1906), S. Gladys Mary (1898), Edith Emily (1900), Dorothy Helen (1905); Occup: Cowman; Service: Nos. 1771 & 305248, 1/8th Bn. S/F, demob. 19/9/18; Theatre: Fr. March 1915; Medals: Victory, British, 1914-15 Star.

Dr T.S. Elliot (Peter Cant)

W.G. Elliot (Peter Cant)

Harold R. Ewers (David Hutchinson)

Faulkener, P. No records; See *N/A* 4/11/14.

Fensome, Joseph. Born: Barnstable, 1885; Lived: Cricket Field Cottage, Southwell; Occup: Motor Car driver, Brackenhurst; Service: No. M1/09010, Army Service Corps; Theatre: Fr. Nov. 1914; Medals: Victory, British, 1914-15 Star.

Firth, Arthur Ernest. Born: Horncastle, 1877; Lived: Church Street, Southwell; Fam: married Mary Jane, children: Ernest William (1897), George (1898), Harry (1904); Service: no records.

Firth, George. Born: Horncastle, 1898; Lived: Church Street, Southwell; Fam: F. Arthur Ernest Firth – see above; School: Natl. 1902-11; Occup: Grocer's errand boy; Service: No. 126832, Machine Gun Corps; Theatre: no record; Medals: Victory.

Fisher*, William. Born: Nottingham, 1869 (?); Lived: Farnsfield; Fam: No details; Occup: Joiner; Service: No. 10571, 1/8th Bn. S/F & No. 31096, Yorkshire Light Infantry; Theatre; Fr. November 1914; Medals: Victory, British, 1914-15 Star.

Flowers, Benjamin. Born: Sutton Bridge, Lincs., 1876; Lived: Victoria Terrace, Southwell; Fam: F. George (Farm labourer), M. Harriet Emma (Hitch), Br. Edward (1880), Mahala Anderson (1881), George (1883), S. Jessie (1878), Lucy Anderson (1886), married Sarah Elizabeth (Harvey in 1899), children: Arthur (1911), Cyril (1915); Occup: Grocery deliverer, J.H. Kirkby; Service: applied to Tribunal 3/6/16 and deferred until 1/10/16 - no military records.

Fogg*, John T. Born: Farnsfield, 1893 - 1916; Lived: Quaker Lane, Farnsfield; Fam: F. Joseph Fogg – widower (Besom maker), Br. Henry (1877), married Elizabeth Macdonald 1915; Occup: Besom maker and general labourer; Service: Joined T.A. 1912, No. 1371, 1/8th Bn. S/F; Theatre: Fr. March 1915, wounded June 1915, re-joined unit Oct. 1915, gassed Oct. 1915, K-in-A 20/6/16 – CWGC no record of his grave; Medals: Victory, British, 1914-15 Star. Widow received a pension of 15/- p.w.; See p. 220.

Foster, Alfred. Born: Southwell, 1896; Lived: Back Lane, Southwell; Fam: F. James Foster (Lace maker – E. Carey & Sons), M. Lucy, Br. Arthur (1895), Joseph (1910), S. Edith (1900), Eleanor (1902); Service: no records.

Foster, Arthur. Born: Southwell, 1894; Lived: Back Lane, Southwell; Fam: Brother of Alfred Foster – see above; School: Infants and Natl. 1900-05; Service: No record, but listed as a veteran in 1928.

Foster, Charles Ernest. Born: Woodborough, 1887; Lived: Easthorpe, Southwell; Fam: Brother of John Leonard Foster - see below, married Martha Elizabeth (Richardson in 1907); Occup: Market gardener's assistant; Service: Applied to Tribunal 18/11/16 - exempt until 1/5/17 - no military records found.

Foster, Edward. Born: Southwell, 1876; Lived: Spring Terrace, Easthorpe, Southwell; Fam: married Sarah Jane, children: George (1906); Occup: Harness maker; Service: No. T8/5446, Army Service Corps, Saddler, S/Sgt.; Theatre: no record; Medals: Victory, British.

Foster, Ernest Burgess. Born: Southwell, 1891; Lived: Westhorpe, Southwell; Fam: F. John Foster (Blacksmith), M. Mary Elizabeth, Br. Edwin Robert (1889); Service: No. 466414, Royal Engineers, Sgt.; Theatre: no record; Medals: no record.

Foster, Frank. Born: Brinkley, 1896-1915; Lived: Mortonfields, Fiskerton; Fam: F. George Foster (Market gardener), M. Hannah, Br. George M. (1891), William (1892), May (1899); School: Morton, Natl. 1909-10; Occup: Market gardener; Service: No. 817, South Notts Hussars; Theatre: Egypt, K-in-A, Gallipoli 22/8/15, commemorated Helles Memorial; Medals: Victory, British, 1914-15 Star; See p. 279.

Foster, George Henry. Born: Southwell, 1894; Lived: White Lion Inn, Easthorpe, Southwell; Fam: George William Foster – see below; School: Easthorpe, Natl. 1901-08; Occup: Plumber; Service: No. 73102, Royal Field Artillery, Bombardier; Theatre: Egypt July 1915; Medals: Victory, British, 1914-15 Star.

Foster, George William. Born: Southwell, 1871-1918; Lived: White Lion Inn, Easthorpe, Southwell; Fam: married Euphemia Mary, children: Caroline (1891), George Henry (1894), Samuel Bernard (1897), William Hector (1901), Doris Elizabeth (1901); Occup: Landlord of White Lion & Curtain reader – E. Carey & Sons; Service: No. 905, Rifle Brigade, A/Sgt., No. 205928, attached Northumberland Fusiliers, Sgt.; Theatre: India, Palestine and Mesopotamia; Medals: Victory, British; Died of influenza at Cherbourg, en route for leave 24/10/18, buried, Tourlaville Communal Cemetery, Manche, France; See *N/A* 14/4/15, 6/11/18.

Foster*, Harry. Born: Upton 1895; Lived: Upton; Fam: F. Robert Samuel – widower (Miller and baker), Br. Herbert (1885), William (1898), married Mildred Devenport 1929; School: Upton and Minster School 1907-09; Service: 1/8th Bn. S/F & No. 11875 R.A.O.C. L/Cpl., Demob. 1919; Theatre; Fr.; Medals: Victory, British.

Foster, Henry. Born: Southwell, 1894; Lived: Easthorpe; Fam: F. William – no other record; School: Easthorpe and Natl. 1901-08; Service: no records, however listed as a veteran in 1928; See p. 306.

Foster, John Leonard. Born: Woodborough, 1891; Lived: Woodborough House, Church Street, Southwell; Fam: F. Thomas Foster (Market gardener), M. Mary, Br. Charles Ernest (1883), Tom Bernard (1898), S. Ethel (1895); School: Wesleyan 1895-1904; Occup: Asst. market gardener; Service: No. 335367, Royal Scots, L/Cpl.; Theatre: Fr. Feb. 1917, wounded Dec. 1917; Medals: Victory, British, Military Medal; See *N/A* 27/11/18.

Foster, Samuel Bernard. Born: Southwell, 1897; Lived: White Lion Inn, Southwell; Fam: F. George William Foster – see above; School: Easthorpe, Natl. 1904-08; Occup: Solicitor's Clerk; Service: Enlisted 5/9/16, No. 60788, S/F, No. 358044, Royal Engineers, L/Cpl. (Dec. 1917), demob. 25/11/19; Theatre: Fr. Nov. 1916; Medals: Victory, British.

Harry Foster (Peter Cant)

Foster, Tom Bernard. Born: Woodborough, 1897; Lived, Woodborough House, Church Street, Southwell; Fam: Br. of John Leonard Foster – see above; School: Wesleyan 1902-11; Occup: Asst. market gardener; Service: No. 330834, 5/6th Bn. Royal Scots; Theatre: Fr.; Medals: Victory, British; See *N/A* 9/6/15, 27/11/18.

Foster, William Edward. Born: Upton, 1898. Lived: Upton; Fam: Br. of Harry Foster – see above; School: Upton and Minster 1912-13; Occup: Grocer – J.J. Bates; Service: M/24273, Royal Navy, HMS Queen; Theatre/Medals: no record; See p. 306.

Fox, Charles Robinson. Born: Rolleston, 1884; Lived: Southwell; Fam: F. George R. Fox (Miller and farmer), M. Charlotte; Br. Harold (1886), George H (1895), Percy (1897), Cyril (1898), Sydney (1903), S. Millicent (1889), Elsey (1893); School: Rolleston, Natl. 1896-99; Occup: Miller, Caudwell's; Service: No. 305806, 1st Bn. S/F; Theatre: no record; Medals: Victory, British; See *N/A* 4/11/14.

Fox, George H. Born: Rolleston, 1895; Lived: Westgate, Southwell; Fam: Br. of Charles R Fox – see above; School: Rolleston, Natl. 1907-08; Service: No. 21597, 2nd Bn. Yorkshire and Lancashire, No. 229198, Labour Corps, 729 4th; Theatre: no record; Medals: Victory, British.

Frow, David. Born: Fullerby, Lincs., 1882-1917; Lived: Wong View, Westgate; Fam: F. John Frow (Farmer), M. Mary Ann (Thompson m. 1868), Br. George William & Henry (1869), Herbert John (1873), Hewson Edwin (1876), William Thomas (1879), David (1882), S. Alice Ann (1870), Fanny Emma (1877), married Emma Jane (Smith in 1914); Occup: Motor driver; Service: attested 10/12/15, mobilised March 1917, No. M/316774, Army Service Corps (MT Section); Theatre: Home; Medals: no record; Died 7/5/17, suffering acute mania and exhaustion, buried Holy Trinity Church, Southwell; His wife received a pension of 15/- p.w.
Fry, Worthy Edward. Born: Malmsbury, Wilts, 1879-1956; Lived: Brackenhurst, Southwell; Fam: married Hilda, children: Hilda (1907), Kathleen (1908); Service: Private, no further details.

Garratt, Arthur. Born: Halloughton, 1892-1918; Lived: Norwood Fields, Southwell; Fam: F. William (Horseman), M. Emma (Armstrong), Br. William (1888), Fred (1900), S. Maizie (1889), Annie (1898), Dora (1902), Mary Milbourn (1903); School: Infants & Natl. 1900-06; Occup: Miner at Rufford; Service: Enlisted Oct. 1914, No. 18654, 13th Bn. S/F & No. 43103, 2nd Bn. South Staffs; Theatre: Balkans 1/10/15, Egypt, Fr., Wounded in the German offensive, Operation Michael, DoW 27/3/18, buried Caberet Rouge British Cemetery, Souchez; Medals: Victory, British, 1914-15 Star.
George, Hubert Trehearn. Born: Southwell, 1898-1918; Lived: Park Street, Southwell; Fam: F. Walter George (former headmaster, Wesleyan School), M. Harriett; School: Wesleyan 1903-09, Minster 1909-13; Service: No. 11642, Royal Fusiliers, No. 104281, Machine Gun Corps, L/Cpl.; Theatre: Fr., K-in-A 19/6/18, buried Valenciennes Communal Cemetery; Medals: no record, but assume Victory, British; See *N/A* 24/4/18, & pp. 301, 306.
Gibson*, George. Born: Southwell, 1895 - 1936; Lived: Westgate, Southwell: Fam: F. William Gibson (Traction engine driver), M. Sally, Br. Henry (1897), Joseph (1906), William (1908), married Emma Blasdale 1927; School: Natl. infants & Natl. 1901-08; Occup: Grocer's assistant; Service: Enlisted T.A. 1912, No. 1364, 1/8th Bn. S/F, No. 165456 Labour Corps & Royal defence Corps; Theatre: Fr. March 1915; Medals: Victory, British, 1914-15 Star; Post-war was the Manager of the Co-op in Farnsfield and in Bilsthorpe. He died in 1936, believed to be as a result of rheumatic fever contracted in the trenches.
Gibson, Henry. Born: Southwell, 1896; Lived: Westgate, Southwell; Fam: Br. of George Gibson – see above; Occup: Grocer's assistant; Service: No. 249585, Royal Engineers, No. 75716, Royal Garrison Artillery; Theatre: no record, Medals: Victory, British; Post-war became a Police Constable.
Gibson, W. No records, but mentioned in Parish Magazine, July 1918.
Gilbert, Edwin. Born: Southwell, 1885-1916; Lived: New Street, Southwell; Fam: Br. of Harold Gilbert – see below; School: Infants, Natl. 1894-99; Occup: Lace maker – E. Carey & Sons; No. 2061, 8th Bn. S/F; Theatre: Fr., K-in-A 25/3/16 whilst the battalion was in trenches near Vimy Ridge, buried Le Treport Military Cemetery; Medals: Victory, British; See *N/A* 11/9/18.
Gilbert, Ernest John (Jack). Born: Southwell, 1888-1918; Lived: New Street, Southwell; Fam: Br. of Harold Gilbert – see below; School: Infant, Natl. 1895-01; Occup: Professional Soldier; Service: No. 6844, King's Royal Rifle Corps; Theatre: Fr. August 1914, wounded September 1918, having survived 4 years in France, DoW 4/11/18, buried St Sever Cemetery Extension, Rouen; Medals: Victory, British, 1914-15 Star; See *N/A* 11/9/18.

Edwin Gilbert (Peter Cant)

Gilbert*, Harold F. Born: Southwell, 1894; Lived: New Street, Southwell; Fam: F. William Gilbert –widower (Joiner), M. Edith (Davenport m. 1874), Br. William Henry (1877), Thomas (1879), Herbert Henry (1881), Robert S. (1884), Edwin (1886), William (1877), Robert James (1884), Ernest John (1888), S. Edith (1880), Charlotte Nora (1887); School: Natl.; Occup: Lace machine fitter – E. Carey & Sons. Service: No. 1052, 1/8th Bn. S/F, No. 104360, Mach. Gun Corps. Demob. 21/1/16; Theatre: Fr. Feb. 1915. Medals: Victory, British, 1914-15 Star; See *N/A* 11/9/18.

Gilbert, Leonard. Born: Farnsfield, 1889; Lived: Farnsfield; Fam: F. Benjamin Gilbert (Clothier), M. Marion, Br. Wilfred (1887); School: Minster, University College, Nottingham; Occup: Teacher; Service: 13th Bn. S/F, 2nd Lt., 15th Bn. Enniskillen Fusiliers, Lt. Colonel, promoted 1917; Theatre: Cape Helles & India; Medals: Victory, British, 1914-15 Star, Mentioned in Despatches; See *N/A* 23/9/14, 30/5/17, & p. 306.

Gilbert, Robert James. Born: Upton, 1884; Lived: Easthorpe, Southwell; Fam: Brother of Harold F. Gilbert – see above, married Edith (Watson in 1911), children: Edith (1912), Charles (1914), Helena (1917); School: Infants & Natl. 1894-97; Occup: Plumber; Service: Enlisted 21/6/15, No. 306320, S/F, No. 733570, 24th Bn. London Regt.; Theatre: no record; Medals Victory, British.

Gilbert, Robert S. Born: Upton, 1884; Lived: Easthorpe, Southwell; Fam: Br of Harold F Gilbert – see above; School: Caunton, Natl. 1898-99; Occup: Plumber; Service: No. 306320, S/F, No. 733570, 24th Bn. London Regt.; Theatre: Fr., wounded September 1918; Medals: Victory, British; See *N/A* 11/9/18.

Gilbert, William H. Born: Caunton, 1877; Lived: Sutton-in-Ashfield; Fam: Br. of Harold F. Gilbert – see above; Occup: Joiner; Service: No. 41366, Royal Engineers, Sapper; Theatre: Egypt; Medals: Victory, British, 1914-15 Star.

Glazebrook*, Ernest J. Born: Lowdham, 1896; Lived: Lowdham; Fam: F. George Glazebrook (Tailor), M. Sarah Anne, Br. Albert George (1903), Harold (1910), S. Grace (1906); Occup: Nurseryman/gardener; Service: No. 1422, 1/8th Bn. S/F, No. 98550, Mach. Gun Corps, A/Cpl.; Theatre: Fr. March 1915; Medals: Victory, British, 1914-15 Star.

Godber, Joseph. Born: Halam, 1881; Lived: King Street Southwell; Fam: F. Joseph Godber (retired farmer), M. Margaret, married Florence Margaret, children: John (1908); School: Miss Croft's Halam, Wesleyan 1892-93, Minster; Occup: Veterinary Surgeon; Service: Army Veterinary Corps, Captain; Theatre: Fr., Egypt; Medals: Victory, British, 1914-15 Star; See *N/A* 22/9/15, & p. 306.

Goodwin, Albert Gordon. Lived: Westgate, Southwell; Service: No. 63446, South Lancashire Regt.

Goulder, Alfred. Born: Radford, Nottingham, 1893-1915; Lived: Radford, Nottingham; Fam: F. Edwin Goulder, M. Elizabeth, Br. Edwin (1896), Ernest (1904), S. Nellie (1891), Beatie (1899); Occup: Solo Tenor, Southwell Minster; Service: No. 13478, 12th Bn. Northumberland Fusiliers, L/Cpl.; Theatre: Fr., K-in-A 25/9/15 whilst fighting in the Battle of Loos near Hill 70, memorial: Loos Memorial, Pas de Calais; Medals: Victory, British, 1914-15 Star.

Gray, G. W. No records.

Green, John. Born: Podhole, Lincs, 1889; Lived: Rose Cottage, Southwell; Fam: M. M. Green (Bourne Workhouse); Occup: Baker; Service: Attested 1915, No. S4/146942, Army Service Corps, demobbed 3/5/19; Theatre: Fr. 1916; Medals: Victory, British.

Greenfield, Joseph. Born: Ruddington, 1884; Lived: Burgage Lane, Southwell; Fam: M. Hannah Greenfield (Laundress), S. Hannah (1870), Elizabeth (1872), Eliza (1874), Temperence

(1877), Lily (1888); Occup: Twist hand – E. Carey & Sons; Service: Enlisted Sept. 1914, No. 2616, 2/8th Bn. S/F, discharged 7/12/15; Theatre: no record; Medals: no record.

Gregory, George. Born: 1901, Bulcote; Br. Of W. G. Gregory - see below; School: Miss Mason's, Natl., Minster 1909-14; Service: R.N.R.; Theatre/Medals: No records; See p. 306.

Gregory*, William Godfrey. Born: Bulcote, 1897; Lived: Westhorpe House, Southwell; Fam: F. William Gregory (Private means), M. Minnie Jane, Br. George (1902), Allen Augustus (1904); School: Miss Mason's, Natl. 1907-09, Minster, 1909-13, Nottingham University Service: Nos. 1814 & 305261, 1/8th Bn. S/F, Demob. 21/3/19; Theatre: Fr. March 1915; Medals: Victory, British, 1914-15 Star; See pp. 270, 306.

Grimshaw, Frank. Born: Nottingham, 1891; Lived: Leaworthy Cottages, Westgate, Southwell; Fam: F. Thomas Grimshaw (Picture framer), M. Ellen, Br. Lewis (1877), Alfred (1887), S. Ethel (1889), Evelyn (1894); Service: No. 6648, 18th Hussars, 40422, Yorkshire Regt., 30481, Royal Warwickshire Regt., W.O. II; Theatre: not recorded, Medals: Victory, British.

Frank Grimshaw (Newark Advertiser)

Hacking, Alfred. Born: Derby, 1885; Lived: Hill House, Southwell; Fam: F. Ven. Egbert Hacking (archdeacon of Newark); M. Margaret, Br. Egbert Melville (1882), S. Edith (1881, Alice (1884), Margaret (1887), Ann (1890); School: Marlborough; Occup: Solicitor, Chamberlain and Hacking, London; Service: 1/8th Bn. S/F, Lt. Col; Theatre: Fr. March 1915, wounded 4/10/18; Medals: Victory, British, 1914-15 Star, D.S.O., M.C., twice Mentioned in Despatches; See *N/A* 2/6/15, 1/9/15, 5/1/16, 19/1/16, 23/10/18.

Hacking, Egbert Melville (Rev). Born: Manchester, 1882; Lived, Hill House, Southwell; Fam: Br. of Alfred Hacking – see above; School: Aldenham and Cambridge University; Occup: Master and Chaplain at Aldenham School; Service: 1/8th Bn. S/F, Lt., Rifle Brigade, Capt.; Theatre: Fr. Feb. 1915, wounded September 1915; Medals: Victory, British, 1914-15 Star; Served as a combatant; See *N/A* 15/9/15, 19/1/16, 23/10/18.

Hackney, George Alfred. Born: Branston, Lincs, 1896; Lived: Adams Row, Kirklington Road, Southwell; Fam: F. George Hackney (Foreman plate layer), M. Mary, Br. John Robert (1888), Walter (1901); Occup: Gardener; Service: Enlisted 16/3/16, No. 5557, Lincolnshire Regt., No. 27000, 10th Bn. Royal Warwickshire Regt., demob 5/9/19; Theatre: Fr. 1916, wounded in chest 1917; Medals: Victory, British.

Alfred Hacking (Newark Advertiser)

Hailey, William Albert. Born: Southwell, 1882-1918; Lived: The Lodge, Hill House, Southwell; Fam: F. James Hailey, M. Ann, Br. Andrew (1889), S. Florence (1877), Elizabeth (1884); Occup: Chauffeur and motor mechanic; Service: Attested Dec. 1915, mobilized 16/2/17, No. M296463, Royal Army Service Corps, M. T. Section; Theatre: South Africa. Soon after arriving in South Africa was hospitalized with dysentery and transferred to Dar es Salaam, then on to Nairobi suffering malaria and then contracted measles and smallpox, died of illness 26/1/18, buried Nairobi South Cemetery; Medals: Victory, British; See *N/A* 29/5/18.

Hall, Arthur (Archie). Born: Southwell; 1888; Lived: Westhorpe, Southwell; Fam: F. James Hall (Nurseryman's labourer), M. Emma; School: Trinity, Natl. 1895-1901; Occup: Grocer's Assistant – J. H. Kirkby; Service: No. 28061, North Staffordshire Regt., L/Cpl.; Theatre: Fr.; Medals: Victory, British, Military Medal.

Hall, Christopher. Born: Southwell, 1883- 1917; Lived: Returned from Canada to fight; Fam: F. George (Nurseryman), M. Mary, Br. Arthur (1869), John James (1876), Herbert (1878), George (1881), S. Eliza (1868), Sarah Jane (1873), Minnie (1879); Service: Enlisted 1915, No. 21920, S/F, No. 19499, 2nd Bn. Northamptonshire Regt.; Theatre: Fr. July 1915. Wounded as the Germans were retreating to their new defences, the Hindenburg Line, DoW 5/3/17, buried Bray Military Cemetery; Medals: Victory, British, 1914-15 Star; See *N/A* 21/3/17, 8/8/17.

Christopher Hall (Newark Advertiser)

Hall*, George. Born: Southwell, 1881; Lived: Westhorpe, Southwell; Fam: Brother of Christopher Hall – see above; School: Natl. 1890-94; Occup: Labourer, Merryweather's; Service: No. 1426, 1/8th Bn. S/F, Sgt.; Theatre: Assume Fr. March 1915, believed to have lost a hand in the war; Medals: Victory, British, 1914-15 Star.

Hall*, Edwin Clarence. Born: Newark, 1892; Lived: Hall Cottage, Westhorpe, Southwell; Fam: F. Edwin Hall (Nurseryman), M. Fanny (Coulson); School: Newark Wesleyan, Natl. until 1906; Occup: Gardener's labourer; Service: 1/8th Bn. S/F, no other details; Theatre: Fr.; Medals, no record.

Hall, Fred. Born: Southwell, 1888; Lived: The Post Office, Westhorpe, Southwell; Fam: F. Charles Hall (Lace maker – E. Carey & Sons), M. Harriet, Br. Harry (1897), S. Alice (1886), Frances (1902); School: Trinity, Natl. 1896-1901; Occup: Grocer's Assistant; Service: no records.

Hall*, George Walter. Born: Southwell, 1890; Lived: Westhorpe, Southwell; Fam: F. John Hall (Lace Maker – E. Carey & Sons), M. Sarah (Jepson), Br. Percy (1893), John Wallace (1889), Allick (1907), Adrian (1910), S. Susie (1892), Doris May (1898), Sarah Elizabeth (1900), Barton (1903), Kate (1905); School: Trinity, Natl. left 1903; Occup: Hotel porter; Service: Enlisted 1912, No. 305122, 1/8th Bn. S/F, demob. 15/1/19; Theatre: France ?, but no details; Medals: No details.

Hall, Harry. Born: Southwell, 1897; Lived: Sunnyside, Westgate, Southwell; Fam: Br. of Fred Hall – see above; School: Trinity, Natl. 1905-10; Occup: Butcher's errand boy; Service: Nos. 2401 & 200502, S/F, Sgt., demob. 20/2/19; Theatre: Fr. February 1915; Medals: Victory, British, 1914-15 Star.

Hall, Horace. Born: Southwell, 1896; Lived: Westgate, Southwell; Fam: F. Thomas Hall (Lace maker – E. Carey & Sons), M. Mary, Br. Rowland (1900), S. Florence (1899), Hilda (1902), Annie (1906), Ida (1909); School: Trinity, Natl. 1904-10; Occup: Baker and confectioner; Service: no records, but mentioned as on leave in the Parish Magazine, July 1918.

Hall, Percy. Born: Southwell, 1893-1915; Lived: Westhorpe, Southwell; Fam: F. John Hall (Lace maker – E. Carey & Sons), M. Sarah (Jepson), Br. John Wallace (1889), George Walker (1890), Alick Stuart (1907), Adrian (1909), Sidney (1912), S. Susie (1892), Violet Lilian (1896), Doris May (1898), Sarah Elizabeth (1900), Barton (1903), Kate (1905); School: Trinity, Natl. 1900-07; Occup: Nurseryman's labourer; Service: No. 6678, Lancers of the Line, No. 10552, 1st Bn. Royal Munster Fusiliers; Theatre: Balkans. The battalion landed at 'V' Beach at Cape Helles on July 22nd 1915. Following being relieved by the Worcestershire Regiment they moved on 20th

August to Sulva Bay. From there they moved to Chocolate Hill and took part in the unsuccessful attack on Hill 112. There were around 300 casualties including Percy Hill whose body was never found. K-in-A 21/8/15, commemorated Helles Memorial; Medals: Victory, British, 1914-15 Star; See *N/A* 5/8/17.

Hallam, Marshall. Born: Chesterfield, 1881; Lived: Lord Nelson Inn, Southwell; Fam. M. Mary Hallam (Publican, Lord Nelson), S. Beatrice (1885); Occup: Clerk E. Carey & Sons; Service: No. 45941, S/F, No. 656074, Labour Corps; Medals: Victory, British.

Hancock, James William. Born: 1891; Lived: King Street, Southwell; Fam: F. James Hancock; School: New Milns, Scotland, Natl. 1899-?; Service: No. 45747, S/F; Theatre: no record; Medals: Victory, British.

Hancock*, James William. Born: Sneinton, 1881; Lived: New Street, Southwell; Fam: Married Gertrude Maltby (1882), children: Katherine (1902), Elsie (1905), Marjory (1909); Occup: Curtain maker/lace hand – E. Carey & Sons; Service: Enlisted T.A. 1899, No. 206, 1/8th Bn. S/F, North Midlands Div. Cycling Corps from 1916, No. 640592, Royal Field Artillery, Cpl., demob. 31/3/20; Theatre: Fr. Feb 1915; Medals: Victory, British, 1914-15 Star.

Everard F. Handford

Hancock, Robert. Born: Nottingham, 1889; Lived: Bradfield Cottage, Easthorpe; Fam: M. Annie Hancock, Br. Frederick (1904), S. Elsie Sarah (1894), Ellen (1899), Bertha (1897); Occup: General labourer; Service: No. 91450, S/F; Theatre: no record; Medals: Victory, British.

Handford, Everard Francis Sale. Born: Nottingham, 1895-1915; Lived: Elmfield House, The Burgage, Southwell; Fam: Br. of Henry Basil Handford – see below; School: Rugby, Cambridge University; Occup: Professional Soldier; Service: 2/8th Bn. S/F, Lt.; Theatre: Fr. July 1915, K-in-A 15/10/15, Hohenzollern, commemorated Loos Memorial; Medals: Victory, British, 1914-15 Star; See *N/A* 20/10/15, 12/1/16, 22/5/18, & pp. xiii, 210, 214-5, 249-50, 272.

Handford*, Henry Basil Strutt. Born: Nottingham, 1894-1915; Lived: Elmfield House, The Burgage, Southwell; Fam. F. Dr. Henry Handford (Senior Consulting Physician, Nottingham General Hospital), M. the Hon. Mary Emily (Strutt), Br. Everard Francis Sale (1895), S. (step) Sybil Augusta Gale (1875), Hilda Gale (1878), Veronica Gale (1884); School: Rugby and Cambridge University; Occup: Trainee lawyer; Service: 1/8th Bn. S/F, Captain; Theatre: Fr. Feb 1915, K-in-A 15/10/15, Hohenzollern, commemorated Loos Memorial; Medals: Victory, British, 1914-15 Star; See *N/A* 29/7/14, 1/9/15, 22/9/15, 20/10/15, 12/1/16, 22/5/18, & xiii, 202, 211, 214-5, 249-50.

Handley, Fred Coulam. Born: Killingholme, Lincs, 1887-1918; Lived: Private Road, Southwell; Fam: F. Joseph Handley (Farm labourer), M. Amelia, Br. Albert Ernest (1889), Joseph Conlan (1891), Wilfred (1897), S. Isabella (1900), married Florence; Occup: Farm labourer; Service: No. 22619, 1/5th Bn. S/F, Sgt.; Theatre: Fr. Aug 1915. Fought through the Somme and the Third Battle of Ypres. Won the M.M. during the German offensive, Operation Georgette, as they attempted to reach the Channel ports. Died of influenza 16/10/18, buried Tourgeville

Henry B. S. Handford (Julia Overton)

Military Cemetery; Medals: Victory, British, 1914-15 Star, Military Medal (awarded 'for his gallantry and devotion to duty at Kemmel during the German offensive when they attacked between April 12-17, 1918').

Hardstaff, Richard Edwin. Born: Mansfield, 1891; Lived: Thorney Abbey Farm, Oxton Road, Southwell; Fam: F. George Hardstaff (Farmer), M. Ann Hardstaff, S. Charlotte Mary (1880), Martha Ann (1882), Alice Miriam (1894); Occup: Farmer; Service: No. SE 19578, Royal Veterinary Corps; Theatre: no record; Medals: Victory, British.

Hargreave, Frederick Parker. Born, Glasgow, 1897-1917; Lived: 35 Percival Road, Sherwood, Nottingham; Fam: F. Charles Hargreave (Shopkeeper), M. Annie; School: Mrs Falconer's, Nottingham, Minster 1905-12; Occup: Accountant; Service: Kings Own Yorkshire Light Infantry, Capt; Theatre: Fr., K-in-A 20/11/17, commemorated Cambrai Memorial, Northern France; Medals: Victory, British.

Harrison*, Cyril Sydney. Born: Newark, 1896 - 1915; Lived: Easthorpe, Southwell; Fam; F. Thomas Harrison (Overseer roads, Borough Council), M. Emma, B. Percy (1893), S. May (1878), Laura (1876), Lily (1888), Olive (1889), Nellie (1894), Kathleen (1898); Occup: Clerk for civil engineer, Newark; Service: No. 2956, 1/8th Bn. S/F; Theatre: Fr. August 1915, K-in-A 14/10/15, commemorated Loos Memorial; Medals: Victory, British, 1914-15 Star; See p. 215.

Harrison, Coulson Taylor. Born: Southwell, 1879-1957; Lived: 75 Church Street, Southwell; Fam: M. Elizabeth Ann Harrison, married Carrie R. Templeman in 1919, children: Nancy Harrison (1920); School: Wesleyan 1892, London Orpham Working School; Occup: Midland Railway Clerk; Service: No. 17743, Coldstream Guards, Sgt., Nos. 308963 & WR/ 277733, Royal Engineers, Sgt.; Theatre: Fr.; Medals: Victory, British.

Harrison, Ernest. Born: Southwell, 1895; Lived: Easthorpe, Southwell; Fam: F. Thomas Harrison (Lace hand – E Carey & Sons), M. Annie (Williamson m. 1886), Br. James (1888), Thomas (1892), Harold (1893), William (1897), Herbert (1902), S. Emily (1891), May Elizabeth (1899), Florence (1900), 3 died in infancy; School: Easthorpe, Natl. 1903-04; Occup: Errand boy; Service: Nos. 17772 & 122293, 1/8th Bn. S/F,Theatre: Fr. 1915, wounded ; Medals: Victory, British, 1914-15 Star; See *N/A* 7/7/15.

Harrison, Harold. Born Southwell, 1893; Lived, Easthorpe, Southwell; Fam: Br. of Ernest Harrison – see above; School: Easthorpe, Natl. 1901-05; Occup: Threader – E Carey & Sons; Service: no record; Medals: No record.

Harrison, Herbert. No records.

Harrison, James. Born: 1888; Lived: Westgate, Southwell; Fam: F. Thomas Harrison – no other details; School: Wesleyan, Natl. 1896-1902; Service: No. 1762, 14th Bn. Kings Hussars, No. L9444, 21st Bn. Lancers, L9444, Corps of Hussars; Theatre: Fr. 1915; Medals: Victory, British, 1914-15 Star.

Harrison, William. Born: Southwell, 1897; Lived: Norwood Fields, Southwell; Fam: Br. of Ernest Harrison see above; School: Wesleyan 1905-07, Natl. 1907-10; Occup: Blacksmith; Service: Attested 2/7/15, No. 4165, Royal Warwicks Regt.; Theatre: Fr., gassed July 1917, and discharged August 1917; Medals: Victory, British.

Richard Harvey (David Hutchinson)

Harvey, John Robert. Lived: Easthorpe, Southwell; Service: No records.

Harvey*, Richard. Born: Southwell, 1895; Lived: Kirklington Road, Southwell; Fam: F. John Harvey (Nurseryman), M. Rebecca; School: Averham, Natl. left 1910; Occup: Junior law clerk; Service: No. 1240, 1/8th Bn. S/F, wounded 1915, demob. 19/3/19; Theatre: Fr. March 1915; Medals: Victory, British, 1914-15 Star.

Harvey*, Richard. Born: Southwell, 1893; Lived: Easthorpe, Southwell; Fam: F. John (Baker and confectioner), M. Elizabeth, Br. William (1898), S. Fanny (1900); School: Natl, infants and seniors, left 1907; Service: No. 305284, 1/8th Bn. S/F, Sgt.; Theatre: Fr. March 1915; Medals: Victory, British 1914-15 Star, Military Medal; See *N/A* 7/7/15, 11/12/18.

Harvey, William. Born: Southwell, 1897; Lived: Easthorpe, Southwell; Fam: F. John Harvey (Baker and confectioner), M. Elizabeth; School: Natl. Infants and seniors 1905-11; Service: Royal Marines; Theatre: Dardanelles, could be other theatres; Medals: no records; See *N/A* 13/10/15.

Haywood, Samuel. Born: Southwell, 1883; Fam: M. Charlotte Miller, S. Jenny (1888); Occup: Farm yardman; Service: No record; Medals: No record.

Haywood*, William Henry. Born: Calverton, 1893; Lived: The Flour Mill, Southwell; Fam: Henry Haywood (Carter at Flour Mill), M. Annie Elizabeth, B. Arthur (1893), Charles Frederick (1904), James (1907), S. Alice (1900); School: Wesleyan and Natl.; Occup: Threader – E. Carey & Sons; Service: No. 1238, 1/8th Bn. S/F, No. 179591, Mach. Gun Corps; Theatre: Fr. Feb. 1915; Medals: Victory, British, 1914-15 Star.

Arthur Hazelwood (David Hutchinson)

Hazelwood, Arthur (Pat). Born: Southwell, 1895- 1915; Lived: Private Road, Southwell; Fam: M. Martha Hazelwood (Laundress), S. Ethel (1892), Kathleen (1893), Alice (1899); School: Infants, Natl. 1902-09; Occup: Miller at Caudwell's; Service: Enlisted Oct. 1914, No. 2870, 2/8th S/F; Theatre: Fr. June 1915. Involved in the Hohenzollern Redoubt attack during the Battle of Loos. K-in-A 14/10/15, commemorated Loos Memorial; Medals: Victory, British, 1914-15 Star; See *N/A* 4/11/14, 2/2/16, 14/6/16.

Hearson, George Henry. Born: 1892; Lived: Bradfield's Cottages, Easthorpe, Southwell; Fam: F. John Hearson (Farm labourer); School: Wesleyan 1895-?; Occup: Grocer's boy; Service: No. 45594, Lincolnshire Regt., No. 29631, Labour Corps; Theatre: No record; Medals: Victory, British.

Hedderly, Henry. Born: Mansfield, 1895; Lived: West Lodge, Westgate, Southwell; Fam: F. Henry Slight Hedderly (Bank Manager), M. Eliza, Br. John William (1888), S. Sybil Mary (1884), Hilda Ruth (1886); Occup: Bank clerk; Service: No. 341083, 14th Bn. Northumberland Fusiliers; Theatre: No record; Medals: Victory, British.

Hedderly, John William Slight. Born: Southwell, 1888-1954; Lived: West Lodge, Westgate, Southwell; Fam: Br. of Henry Hedderly – see above; Occup: Engineer's apprentice; Service: No. 1767, Lincolnshire Yeomanry, No. M2/2046647, Army Service Corps; Theatre: Egypt, Oct. 1915; Medals: Victory, British, 1914-15 Star.

Hempshall, Charles. Born: Long Bennington, 1893; Lived: Westgate, Southwell; Fam: F. John Hempshall (Gardener's labourer), M. Mary Ann, S. Florrie (1903), Edith Connie (1907); School: Trinity, Wesleyan 1901-06; Occup: Gardener's labourer; Service: No. 67430, Lincolnshire Regt., No. 24805, Labour Corps; Theatre: No record; Medals: Victory, British.

Hempshall, G. B. No record, but see *N/A* 22/11/16.

Hempshall, T. No record, but see *N/A* 14/2/17.

Henderson, J. W. Born: No family records found; Occup: Horseman with J.H. Kirkby; Service: Applied to Tribunal 3/6/16 - exempt until 1/10/16 - no military records found.

Henton*, James John. Born: Southwell, 1884; Lived: Concert Hall Yard, Southwell; Fam: F. Henry Henton (Agricultural labourer), M. Jane, S. Eliza (1881); School: Wesleyan, 1888-1897; Occup: Lace threader – E. Carey & Sons; Service: Nos. 1434 & 305128, 1/8th Bn. S/F; Theatre: Fr.; Medals: Victory, British, 1914-15 Star; See *N/A* 7/7/15.

Herbert, Edward. Born: Durham, 1885; Lived: Landseer Road, Southwell; Fam: F. Thomas Herbert (Retired prison warden), M. Elizabeth, Br. George (1862), Harry (1879), Arthur (1883); Occup: Lay Clerk, Southwell Minster; Service: No. 113579, Royal Garrison Artillery; Theatre: No record; Medals: Victory, British.

Hewston, George (Thomas). Born: Southwell, 1882; Lived: George & Dragon Inn, Church Street, Southwell; Fam: F. George Hewston, married Minnie, children: Ernest (1903), Gladys (1907); Occup: Lace maker – E. Carey & Sons; Service: No. 137042, Royal Garrison Artillery; Theatre: No record; Medals: Victory, British.

Hewston*, John J. Born: Southwell, 1875; Lived: Back Lane, Southwell; Fam: F. John Hewston (Brewer's labourer), M. Mary, Br. William (1873), Thomas George (1881), S. Sarah (1873), married Mary; Service: 1/8th Bn. S/F and No. 272722, Royal Field Artillery, Gunner; Theatre: Not recorded; Medals: Victory, British.

Hewston, Thomas George. Born; Southwell, 1881; Lived: Southwell; Fam: Br. of John J Hewston – see above, married Minnie (Hall m. 1904), children: Ernest (1902), George Lawrence (1904), Gladys (1906); Occup: Twist hand operator- E. Carey & Sons; Service: 2/12/15, 460 Siege Battery, Royal Garrison Artillery; Theatre: Fr.; Medals: Victory, British.

Hewston, William. Born: 1873; Lived: Burgage Lane, Southwell; Fam: Brother of John J Hewston – see above; Occup: Lace maker – E. Carey & Sons; Service: Attested 8/4/15, No. 3683, S/F & No. 5774, Royal Defence Corps; No further records; See *N/A* 14/4/15.

Hill, George. Born: Normanton-on-Trent, 1885; Lived: Alma Cottages, Westgate, Southwell; Fam: F. William Hill (Farm worker), M. Anne, Br. Frank (1888), married Kate, children: Dorothy Annie (1910); Occup: Baker, Co-op; Service: No. 122517, Machine Gun Corps; Theatre: no record; Medals: Victory, British.

Hind*, William. Born: Wellow, 1880; Lived: Wellow Lodge; Fam: Not known; Occup: Woodman; Service: No. 17978, 1/8th Bn. S/F, Cpl., demob. 29/10/1; Theatre: Fr.; Medals: Victory, British, 1914-15 Star.

Hindson, John William. Born: Spilsby, Lincs., 1876-1918; Lived: The Ropewalk, Southwell; Fam: F. William Hindson, M. Hannah, Br. George (1889), Arthur (1891), S. Mary E. (1879), Annie (1884), Ada (1887), married Elizabeth Barlow (1900), children: Annie Elizabeth (1901), Gladys Mary (1902), Hilda (1910), Ellen (1912); Occup: Horseman, J. H. Kirkby; Service: Enlisted 1918, No. 252051, Royal Field Artillery 5th Reserve Brigade, Driver, died following an accident 14/5/18, buried Minster Yard – no further military records; See *N/A* 22/5/18.

Hives, Edwin Smith. Lived: Landseer Road, Southwell; No family or occupation information; Service: No. T4/251979, Army Service Corps, W.O. Class 2; Theatre: No record; Medals: Victory, British.

Hodges, Charles William George. Lived: Queen Street, Southwell; No family or occupation details; Service: No. 6914, Machine Gun Corps; Medals: No record.

Holland, Sydney Samuel. Born: Southwell, 1898; Lived: King Street, Southwell; Fam: F. John George Holland (Hairdresser), M. Alice, Br. John George (1905), S. Elsie Mary (1902); School: Infants, Natl. 1905-13; Occup: Hairdresser's assistant; Service: Enlisted 1916, mobilised 7/3/17, No. 341226, 36th Bn. Northumberland Fusiliers, No. 62416, Yorkshire & Lancashire Regt., Cpl.; Theatre: Fr. July 1918-Jan 1919; Medals: Victory, British.

Holmes, Robert John William. Born: Epperstone, 1890; Lived: Victoria Terrace, Kirklington Road, Southwell; Fam: F. Edwin Holmes (Cottager), M. Margaret Condie, Br. William (1897), S. Sarah Ann (1893), Minnie Gray (1895), Mary Ellen (1901), Margaret Condie (1904); School:

Epperstone Church, Natl. 1897-1904; Occup: Grocery shop assistant; Service: No. 26565, R.A.F.; Theatre/Medals: No records.

Holmes, William. Born: Epperstone, 1897; Lived: Station Road, Southwell; Fam: Br. of Robert J. W. Holmes – see above; School: Natl. 1901-11; Occup: Draper's errand boy; Service: No. M2/201412, Army Service Corps; Theatre: No record; Medals: Victory, British.

Hopewell*, Albert Edward. Born: Kimberly, 1888-1915; Lived: Chatham Street, Southwell; Fam: F. Henry Hopewell (Lace curtain corrector – E. Carey & Sons), M. Alice, Br. John Henry (1891-1915), William (1894-1973), Gordon (1898), S. Alice (1896-1991), Evelyn (1900-25), Elsie May (1905-78), Ada (1903), Millicent (1891-93), Ethel Ada (1907-07); Occup: Lace maker – E. Carey & Sons; Service: No. 2059, 1/8th Bn. S/F; Theatre: Fr. and Belgium Feb. 1915, K-in-A 15/4/15 at Kemmel, Belgium, buried Kemmel Chateau Military Cemetery – the first Southwell territorial to be killed; Medals: Victory, British, 1914-15 Star; See *N/A* 21/4/15, 28/4/15, 12/6/16. See pp. 254-5.

Hopewell, Gordon. Born: Bulwell, Nottingham, 1898; Lived: 8 Chatham Street, Southwell; Fam: Br. of Albert Edward Hopewell – see above; School: Bulwell National, Natl. 1906-?; Service: No. 133559, Machine Gun Corps; Theatre: Fr., P.O.W.; Medals: Victory, British; See pp. 254, 256.

Hopewell*, John Henry. Born: Kimberley, 1891-1915; Lived: 8 Chatham Street, Southwell; Fam: Brother of Albert Edward – see above; Occup: Threader –E. Carey & Sons; Service: Enlisted December 1907, No. 741, 1/8th Bn. S/F; Theatre: Fr. March 1915, K-in-A 30/7/15; Medals: Victory, British, 1914-15 Star; See *N/A* 21/4/15, 11/8/15, 12/1/16, & pp. 209, 211, 254-6.

Hopewell, Robert Arthur. Born: Kimberley, Nottingham, 1886; Lived: Burgage, Southwell; Family: Brother of Albert Edward Hopewell – see above, married Ethel, children: Iris and Ethel; Occup: Lace maker – E. Carey & Sons; Service: Enlisted 27/5/13, No. 1783, 8th Bn. S/F, discharged as medically unfit 6/8/14, however, family records suggest that he re-joined and was badly injured in a shell blast later in the war, no further records were identified; See pp. 254, 256.

Hopewell, William Albert. Born: Kimberley, Nottingham, 1894; Lived: 8 Chatham Street, Southwell; Fam: Br. of Albert Edward Hopewell – see above; School: Bulwell, County Road, Natl. 1906-07; Occup: Threader – E. Carey & Sons; Service: Enlisted, 7/1/13, No. PLY/15995, Royal Marines; Theatre: Served on various ships, took part in the heroic raid on Zeebrugge, discharged 7/7/22; Medals: 1914-15 Star, Victory, British, Conspicuous Gallantry Medal, Croix de Guerre and Palm, Territorial Efficiency; See *N/A* 8/5/18, 31/7/18, & pp. Xiii, 254, 256-8.

Hopkinson, Arthur. Born: Southwell, 1890; Lived: Westgate, Southwell; Fam: F. Charles Hopkinson, M. Sarah H. (Silk thrower), Br. George (1884), S. Ellen (1874), Sarah (1873), Gertrude (1887), married Mabel (Cooling m. 1913), children: Charles (1914); School: Wesleyan 1894-1904; Occup: Carter; Service: Enlisted 1914, Nos. 2962, 305858, 8th Bn. S/F, demob. 14/2/19, pension 5/6d p.w.; Theatre: Fr.; Medals: Victory, British, 1914-15 Star.

Hopkinson, George. Born: Southwell, 1884; Lived: Maythorne, Southwell; Fam: Br. Arthur Hopkinson – see above; School: Wesleyan, Natl. 1893-95; Occup: Twist hand – E. Carey & Sons; Service: No. 2963, S/F, No. 27548, Royal Warwickshire Regt.; Theatre: Fr. taken P.O.W. 1917 at Arras; Medals: Victory, British; See *N/A* 4/7/17, 12/9/17, & p. 269.

Hopkinson, Leonard. Born: Southwell, 1884; Lived: Alma Cottages, Westgate, Southwell; Fam: F. John Hopkinson (Over locker, Silk Mill), M. Lucy (Silk winder), S. Mabel (1884), Edith (1888), married Alice, children: Marian Emmelda (1911); School: Wesleyan 1889-?; Service: No. 23235, S/F; Theatre: No record; Medals: Victory, British.

Horsley, Arthur Edward. Born: Southwell, 1887-1918; Lived: Ormonde House, Easthorpe, Southwell; Fam: F. Robert Horsley (Private means, retired hotel keeper), M. Eliza Ostler, Br. Ormonde (1886), S. Hilda Mary (1890); School: Natl. 1894-1902, Minster; Occup: Former professional soldier, Apprentice grocer, J.J. Bates; Service: Professional soldier enlisted 1908, was in the Reserve by 1914 and was recalled to the colours, No. L/708, 12th Lancers; Theatre: Fr. August 1914. Saw service with the B.E.F. at Mons and during the great retreat to the Marne. Survived the war until he was wounded in the thigh and was K-in-A 9/10/18, buried Ramicourt British Cemetery; Medals: Victory, British, 1914-15 Star; See *N/A* 12/1/15, 3/3/15, 9/6/15, & p. 301.

Arthur E. Horsley (David Hutchinson)

Horsley, Ormonde Robert D. Born: Southwell, 1886; Lived: Ormonde House, Easthorpe, Southwell; Fam: Br. Albert Edward Horsley – see above; School: Natl. 1894-1901; Occup: Railway clerk; Service: No. S4/090173, Army Service Corps, S/Sgt., demob 25/8/19; Theatre: Fr. September 1914; Medals: Victory, British, 1914-15 Star; See *N/A* 21/4/15.

Hoskyns, Edwyn Clement (Rev.). Born: Notting Hill, London, 1884-1937; Fam: F. Edwyn Hoskyns (Bishop of Southwell), M. Mary, S. Phyllis (1887), Evelyn (1889); Occup: Clerk in Holy Orders, ordained 1908, served as a curate in Sunderland; Service: Chaplain in British Army; Theatre: Egypt and France; Medals: Mentioned in Despatches, Military Cross – London Gazette, 23/7/18: *For conspicuous gallantry and devotion to duty. Under heavy shell fire he personally placed wounded in a safe place, and was solely responsible for preventing them falling into the hands of the enemy. He remained with them until all had been evacuated, being slightly wounded himself. Next day he showed conspicuous courage in tending the wounded in an exposed position under heavy shell and machine-gun fire for nine hours without a break;* See *N/A* 18/5/18.

Hubbard, George William. Born: Edingley, 1886-1915; Lived: Edingley; Fam: F. Robert Hubbard, M. Lydia Jane, Br. Edward James (1886), Oliver (1892), S. Eliza Ellen; Occup: Professional soldier; Service: Enlisted 18/2/09, No. 11108, 1st Bn. S/F, L/Sgt.; Theatre: Fr. November, 1914. His battalion took part in the Battle of Neuve Chapelle and K-in-A 11/3/15, memorial Le Touquet; Medals: Victory, British, 1914-15 Star.

Humberstone, Albert. Born: Nottingham, 1887; Lived: Westgate, Southwell; Fam: Br. of Arthur Humberstone – see below, married Mabel Sharpe, November 1915; School: Infants and Natl. 1894-99; Occup: Professional soldier, saw service in India; Service: 1911 Census in South Africa, No. 9634, 1st Bn., Royal Scots Fusiliers, Sgt. Instructor; Theatre: Fr. August 1914; Medals: Victory, British, 1914-15 Star, D.C.M., Mentioned in Despatches 1915; See *N/A* 3/3/15, 11/8/15, 10/11/15, 4/7/17.

Humberstone*, Arthur. Born: Southwell, 1891-1917; Lived: Easthorpe, Southwell; Fam: William Humberstone (Lace maker – E. Carey & Sons), M. Annie Selina, Br. Albert (1887), William (1894); School: Easthorpe, Natl. 1900-1903; Occup: Curtain threader – E. Carey & Sons; Service: Enlisted March 1912, Nos. 1432 & 305126, 1/8th Bn. S/F, Cpl.; Theatre Fr. March 1915, wounded July 1915, K-in-A 23/6/17 near Lens, buried Noeux-Les-Mines, Communal Cemetery; Medals: Victory, British, 1914-15 Star; See *N/A* 11/8/15, 20/6/17, 4/7/17, 8/8/17, & pp. 227, 259-61.

Humberstone*, Samuel. Born: Southwell, 1889-1915; Lived: Westgate, Southwell; Fam: See Arthur Humberstone, married Lilla, children: Albert (1912), John William (1914); School: Natl. Infant and Seniors 1895-96; Occup: Lace maker – E. Carey & Sons; Service: Enlisted T.A 11/3/12, No. 1424, 1/8th Bn. S/F, Cpl.; Theatre: Fr. Feb. 1915, K-in-A 31/7/15, commemorated

Menin Gate; Medals: Victory, British, 1914-15 Star; See *N/A* 23/6/15, 7/7/15, 11/8/15, 18/8/15, 12/1/16, 20/6/17 & pp. 209, 211, 259, 261, 303.

Humberstone, William. Born: Southwell, 1894; Lived: Easthorpe, Southwell; Fam: Br. of Arthur Humberstone – see above; School: Easthorpe, Natl;. 1902-08; Occup: Curtain spooler – E. Carey & Sons; Service: No. 2126, S/F; Theatre: Fr. March 1915; Medals: Victory, British, 1914-15 Star.

Hunt, John Milward. Born: Southwell, 1896; Lived: Radley House, Southwell; Fam: F. William Hunt (Cottager), M. Annie Elizabeth, Br. William (1890), Edward (1901), S. May (1894); No further details.

Hutchinson, Arthur. Born: Newark, 1884-1917; Lived: Westhorpe, Southwell; Fam: Married Annie Smith 22/5/10 in Grimsby, children: Frank William (1912), Marjorie (1914); Occup: Baker; Service: Enlisted 10/10/15, mobilized 8/10/16, Nos. 5492, 201938, 2/4th Royal Scots; Theatre: Fr. 1917, missing presumed dead 22/8/17, commemorated Tyne Cot; Medals: Victory, British.

Hutchinson, Arthur. Born: Collingham, 1900; Lived: Farnsfield; Fam: F. Joseph Hutchinson (Farmer), M. Annie E., Br. Reginald (1902), Joseph (1910), S. Dora; School: Farnsfield Wesleyan, Minster 1911-15; Occup: Colliery Clerk; Service: No records.

Hutchinson, Fred Stanley. Born: Bradmore, Notts, 1891; Lived: Westwood Farm, Normanton; Fam: F. William Hutchinson (Farmer), M. Alice Mary (Grundy), Br. Harold (1883), Cyril (1885), Albert V (1888), Frank (1890), S. May (1902); Occup: Farming with father; Service: No. 201361, Royal Scots Fusiliers; Theatre: Fr.; Medals: Victory, British.

Hyde, Bernard. Born: Derby, 1889; Lived: Clinton House, Southwell; Fam: F. Gilbert Hyde (Coal Merchant), M. Mary; School: Leicester Mantle, Natl. 1903-04; Occup: Elementary school teacher; Service: 13th Bn. West Yorkshire Rgt., 2nd Lt.; Theatre: Fr.; Medals: No record; See *N/A* 7/7/15 & p. 306.

Jackson, Alfred. Born: No details; Lived: Nottingham Road, Southwell; Service: No. 11/1126, 11th East Yorkshire Regt.; Theatre: Egypt, Dec 1915; Medals: Victory, British, 1914-15 Star.

Jackson, Horace. Born: Southwell, 1888; Lived: Westgate; Fam: F. Thomas (Baker & Confectioner), M. Edith Eliza (Simpson), Br. William H. (1880), married Edith 1908, children: Edith (1908), Horace (1913); School: Wesleyan, Natl. 1897-1902; Occup: Twisthand – E Carey & Sons; Service: No. 2615, 8th Bn. S/F, discharged May 1916, following scalp wounds; Theatre: Fr. 1915; Medals: Victory, British, 1914-15 Star.

Jackson, William H. Born: Southwell, 1880; Lived: Southwell; Fam: Brother of Horace Jackson - see above; Occup: Lace maker - E. Carey & Sons; Service: Applied to Tribunal 3/6/16 - exempt until 1/10/16 - no military records.

Jacques, Arthur. Lived: Easthorpe, Southwell; Fam: Married Fanny Kate Goode, 1893; Service: No. 203780, South Staffordshire Regt., No. 140020, Machine Gun Corps; Medals: Victory, British.

Jacques, J. No family records: Occup: Lace maker - E. Carey & Sons; Service: Applied to Tribunal 3/6/16 - exempt until 1/10/16 - No military records.

Jebb, Arthur. Born: Southwell, 1861; Lived: Southwell; Fam: married Catherine Baker, children: Arthur (1897), Mary (1900), Percy (1902); Occup: Market gardener; Service: No. 200692, North Staffordshire Regt.; Theatre: No record; Medals: Victory, British.

Jebb, Arthur Jnr. Born: Southwell, 1897; Lived: Southwell; Son of Arthur – see above; School: Trinity, Natl. 1907-12; Occup: Grocer's boy, J. H. Kirkby; Service: No. 606688, S/F; Theatre: Fr. wounded 1917; Medals: Victory, British; See *N/A* 14/3/17.

Jebbett, Frank Arnold. Born: West Bridgford, 1894 - 1917; Lived: 26, Hampden Street, Beeston; Fam: F. Edwin (Lace manufacturer), M. Annie; School: Southwell Minster; Occup: left for Canada 1904 – farmer in Venn, Saskatchewan; Service: No. 875007, 8th Bn. Canadian Imperial Force, 1916; Theatre: Fr., K-in-A, Arleux en Gabelle, 28/4/17, memorial Vimy Ridge.

Jephson, William Edward. Born: Nottingham (?), 1898; Lived: West House, Southwell; Fam: M. Ada Jephson of Meadows, Nottingham; Service: Enlisted 14/6/17, No. 204563, 5th Reserve Bn. S/F, demob. 8/2/19; Theatre: Fr., wounded right hand and left knee; Medals: Victory, British; Pension 7/6d per week for one year.

Jepson, Fred. Born: Southwell, 1883; Lived: Westgate, Southwell; Fam: F. George Jepson (Painter's labourer), M. Eliza (Rogers m. 1868), S. Emma (1876), Eliza (1878), Martha (1880); Occup: Nurseryman/gardener; Service: Attested 27/11/15, No. 49072, Leicestershire Regt., No. 24428, Coldstream Guards; Theatre: Fr., wounded 4/11/18, demobbed 26/3/19; Medals: Victory, British.

Jepson, George. Born: Southwell, 1892; Lived: Trinity Place, Westgate, Southwell; Fam: Br. of John Thomas Jepson – see below; School: Trinity, Natl. 1897-1904; Occup: Confectioner's apprentice, Kirkby's; Service: No. 15321, 4th & 9th Bn. S/F; Theatre: Gallipoli & Fr. 28/8/15; Medals: Victory, British, 1914-15 Star, Military Medal; See *N/A* 20/1/15, 9/6/15, 18/7/17.

Jepson, Herbert. Born: Southwell, 1884; No further records.

Jepson, James Edward. Born: Southwell, 1896; Lived: Trinity Place, Westgate, Southwell; Fam: Br. of John Thomas Jepson – see below; School: Trinity, Natl. 1904-10; Occup: Iron monger's delivery boy; Service: Enlisted 1915, No. 5602, Army Cycling Corps, Cpl., demob. 14/2/19; Theatre: Fr. September 1915; Medals: Victory, British, 1914-15 Star.

Jepson*, John Thomas. Born: Southwell, 1894-17; Lived: Trinity Place, Westgate, Southwell; Fam: F. George Jepson (Groom & gardener), M. Mary Ann (Peacock, m. 1890), Br. George (1892), James Edward (1897), Sidney (1907), S. Florence (1899), Annie (1902); School: Trinity & Natl. 1901-07; Occup: Grocer's apprentice; Service: No. 1363, 1/8th Bn. S/F & No. 305107, S/F Cpl. 2nd Bn.; Theatre: Fr. March 1915, wounded at Kemmel March 1915, K-in-A 20/11/17, commemorated at Cambrai Memorial, Louverval; Medals: Victory, British, 1914-15 Star; See *N/A* 7/7/15, 28/11/17, 5/12/17, 29/5/18.

Jepson, Reginald. Service: 2/5th Bn. S/F, Capt.; Theatre: Fr. 1917; Medals: Victory, British.

Johnson*, William H. Born: 1886; Fam: no details; Service: No. 722, S/F. L/Sgt. His service number suggests that he was an early member of 1/8th Bn.; Medals: Victory, British, 1914-15 Star.

Jones, Jesse James. Born: Grandon Underwood, Birmingham, 1889; Lived: Woodborough House, Easthorpe; Fam: Thomas Jones, M. Rachel (Hunt), Br. Albert Ernest (1892), married Ethel E. Foster, 1920, children: James; Service: Attested 22/11/15, Nos. 242256, 53968, Northumberland Fusiliers, No. 245245, Durham Light Infantry, L/Cpl., demob. 16/5/19; Theatre: Fr. June 1917; Medals: Victory, British; By 1928 was living in the Market Place, Southwell.

Jones, Joseph. Born: South Normanton, Derbyshire, 1891-1917; Lived: Southwell; Fam: F. John Jones, M. Martha (both of Gornal, Staffs), Br. Eli (1895), Harold (1902), Enoch (1905), S. Emma (1889),

Joseph Jones (Colin Gabitas)

Sarah (1898), Eliza (1904) – and 4 died in infancy; Service: No. T4/091776, 2nd Mobile Veterinary Section, A.S.C., Driver; Theatre: Fr. Sept. 1915, DoW 30/4/17 at Rouen, buried St. Sever, Cemetery Extension; Medals: Victory, British, 1914-15 Star; See *N/A* 8/8/17.

Jordon*, Charles. Born: Lowdham, 1895; Lived: Lowdham; Fam: F. Frederick Herbert Jordon (House painter), Br. Alfred (1888), Josiah (1897), Arthur Seymour (1901), S. Stella (1899), Mavis (1904); Occup: Paper maker; Service: No. 1056, 1/8th Bn. S/F, demob. 19/11/15; Theatre: Fr. March 1915; Medals: Victory, British, 1914-15 Star.

Jordon, Frank. Born: Melbourne, Leics, 1899; Lived: Halam, Southwell; Fam: F. Joseph Jordon (Gardener), M. Mary (Earp), Br. Clarence (1890), Arthur (1895), Joseph (1896), John Eric (1897), Philip (1903), S. Mabel & Nelly (1892), Bertha Winifred (1894), married Molly 1925, children: Aubrey (1926), James (1930); Service: No. 53165, 2/5th Lincolnshire Regt., No. 46387, Gloucestershire Regt., No. 32190, Duke of Cornwall's Light Infantry; Theatre: No record; Medals: Victory, British.

Jordon, John Eric. Born: Melbourne, Leics, 1893; Lived: Halam, Southwell; Fam: Br. of Frank Jordon – see above; Service: No. 99682, 83rd Royal Garrison Artillery; Theatre: No record; Medals: Victory, British.

Jubb*, Thomas William. Born: Gonalston, 1893-1915; Lived: Main Street, Lowdham; Fam: F. Charles Jubb (Nurseryman), M. Elizabeth Ann, married Georgiana Kemp (1902); Occup: Groom/gardener; Service: Enlisted in T.A. 1912, No. 142, 1/8th Bn. S/F; Theatre: Fr. March 1915, K-in-A 30/7/15, commemorated on Menin Gate; Medals: Victory, British, 1914-15 Star; See *N/A* 11/8/15.

Thomas W. Jubb (Newark Advertiser)

Kay*, J W. No records.

Keetley, William Ewart. Born: Southwell, 1883-1927; Lived: Westgate, Southwell: Fam: F. William Keetley (Whitesmith & gas fitter), M. Ellen (Holmes), Br. Arthur Henry (1889), S. Annie Elizabeth (1879), Mary (1886); Occup: Twist hand operator- E. Carey & Sons; Service: No. 267482, 7th Reserve Bn. S/F. Sgt., No. 204314, 1st Norfolk Regt., Sgt.; Theatre: Not recorded; Medals: Victory, British; Died in 1927 of wounds he received in the war. His son died in Battle of Britain 1940.

Kemp, Edward James. Born: West Malling, Kent, 1880 - 1918; Lived: Brackenhurst Cottages, Southwell; Fam: Married Georgiana in 1902, children: Dorothy Violet (1903), Raymond (1904); Occup: Butler to Sir William Hicking for 12 years; Service: No. 109333, 59th Brigade and then 44th Brigade, Royal Garrison Artillery, Gunner; Theatre: Fr. August 1916. K-in-A 21/3/18 as the Germans launched operation Michael, buried Beuvry Communal Extension Cemetery, Pas de Calais; Medals: Victory, British; See N/A 3/4/18, 29/5/18.

Kendall, Albert Joseph. Born: Woodborough, 1894-1972; Lived: Westhorpe, Southwell; Fam: Br. of Percy Kendall – see below, married Louisa Sturgess, children: Margaret, Brenda, Albert Edward; School: Trinity & Natl; Occup: Butcher (Harvey of Southwell); Service: Enlisted 6/1/14, No. 480, Army Cycling Corps, No. 104226, Machine Gun Corps,

Albert J. Kendall (Kendall Family)

No. S/42084, Royal Army Service Corps, L/Cpl.; Theatre: Fr. June 1915; Medals: Victory, British, 1914-15 Star; Post War: Worked at Ransome & Marles, Army Reservist 17/21st Lancers, called up in August 1939, Sgt. in Royal Army Service Corps. One of the few to serve in both World Wars. Lived at 37 King Street, Southwell.

Kendall*, Percy. Born: Woodborough, 1894-1957; Lived: Westhorpe, Southwell, post-war lived: in Leicester; Fam: F. John Kendall (Market gardener), M. Frances Jane (Bacon, m. 1893), Br. Albert (1894), Wilfred Lancelot (1898), Lawrence Victor (1900), John Reginald (1919), S. Ida Gertrude (1904), married Mabel Rickett of Kirklington; School: Trinity & Natl. 1902-08; Occup: House painter; Service: No. 1241, 1/8th Bn. S/F, No. 25236, Durham Light Infantry; Theatre: Fr. June 1915, wounded 1915; Medals: Victory, British, 1914-15 Star.

Kendall. Wilfred Lancelot. Born: Southwell, 1898-1991; Lived: Westhorpe, Southwell; Fam: Br. of Percy Kendall – see above, married Dorothy Sarah Morgan – no children; School: Trinity, Natl. 1906-10; Occup: Grocer's assistant; Service: Enlisted June 1915, 11th North Staffordshire Regt., No. 86025, Machine Gun Corps, Cpl. (had reached Lance Sgt. Jan 1918), demob. 1919 – pension 5/6d p.w.; Theatre: Fr., gassed 1918, wounded; Medals: Victory, British; Post War: Kept the Workman's Rest, Southwell and worked on the Co-op mobile shop.

Kettle, W. Believed to be Police Constable Kettle who volunteered in August 1914 – see *N/A* 12/8/14.

Key, Albert. Born: Nottingham, 1870; Lived: 4, Victoria Terrace, Kirklington Road; Fam: Widower (m. Ellen Reddish, 1893 - died 1905), children: John William (1893), Fannie (1900); Occup: Mechanic – E. Carey & Sons; Service: No. 5784, 7th Co. 19th Bn. Royal Defence Corps; Theatre: not recorded; Medals: Not recorded; See *N/A* 14/4/15.

Key*, John William. Born: Nottingham, 1893; Fam: F. Albert Key – see above; School: Natl. 1899-1906; Occup: Threader – E. Carey & Sons; Service: Territorial 1/8th S/F, time expired and in 1917 became No. 228024A, mechanic 3rd R.A.F; Theatre: Fr. March 1915; Medals: No record; See *N/A* 1/8/17.

Kind*, H. No records.

King, Arthur. Born: Newark, 1893; Lived: Devon Street, Southwell; Fam: No record; Service: No. 309044, HMS Pembroke; See *N/A* 16/1/18.

Kirby, Harry. Born: Radford, Nottingham, 1870; Lived: Spring Terrace, Southwell; Fam: married Emma (Bamford m. 1890), children: Florence (1892), Leonard (1893), Henry (1898), Ethel (1900); Occup: Foreman – E. Carey & Sons; Service: No. 25168, 8th Bn. S/F; Theatre: No record; Medals: Victory, British.

Kirby, William. Born: Southwell, 1892; Lived: Westgate and later Upton; Fam: F. Arthur William Kirby (Greengrocer), M. Ruth (Pitchford, m. 1889); Br. Leonard (1890), Edward Christopher (1903), John George (1909), S. Louie D. (1897), Elsie May (1898), Dorothy (1904), Violet (1905), Olive (1907), Constance (1910); School: Easthorpe and Wesleyan 1896-1904; Service/Medals: No records.

Kirk*, George Edward. Born: Southwell, 1882; Lived: New Street, Southwell; Fam: Married Sarah (Blackshaw, m. 1908), children: Jessie (1909); School: Wesleyan until 1895; Occup: Twist hand – E. Carey & Sons; Service: Nos. 1430 & 305124, 1/8th Bn. S/F, demob. 8/3/19; Theatre: Fr. March 1915; Medals: Victory, British, 1914-15 Star.

Herbert Kirk (Newark Advertiser)

Kirk, George William. Born: Southwell, 1878; Lived: Burgage Lane, Southwell; Fam: Married Alice, children: Ethel (1899), Edith Lois

(1909); Occup: Nursery clerk; Service: Enlisted April 1915, No. 267489, 7th S/F, C.S.M.- no further details; See *N/A* 14/4/15.

Kirk, Henry Francis. Fam: No details; Service: No. 65669, 62nd Labour Corps; Medals: No details.

Kirk, Herbert. Born: Southwell, 1890-1916; Lived: Burgage Lane, Southwell; Fam: F. George Kirk, M. Sarah Jane (Hurt), Br. John James (1879), Harry (1880), Albert Edward (1887), S. Mary Lois (1882), Isabella (1885); School: Wesleyan 1893-1904; Occup: Lace maker – E. Carey & Sons, a talented footballer who played for Southwell City and as a professional for Mansfield Mechanics; Service: Enlisted June 1915, No. 70114, 1/8th S/F & 16th Bn. S/F (Chatsworth Rifles); Theatre: Fr. July, 1916. Involved in efforts to take Schwaben Redoubt, K-in-A 6/10/16, buried twelve months later at Mill Road Cemetery, Thiepval, Somme, France; Medals: Victory, British; See *N/A* 14/11/17, 29/5/18.

Kirk, John James. Born: Southwell, 1879; Lived: King Street, Southwell; Fam: Br. of Herbert Kirk – see above, married Eliza (Wyatt m. 1902), children: Lilly (1903), Charlotte (1905), Bella (1906), Lizzy (1907); Occup: Card puncher – E. Carey & Sons; Service: No. 12360, Military Police, L/Cpl.; Theatre: No record; Medals: No record; Post war lived on Station Road, Southwell.

Kirkby, James Henry, Jun. Born: Southwell, 1897; Lived: Queen Street, Southwell; Fam: F. James Henry Kirkby (Baker, grocer and general merchant), M. Hannah (Pettener), Br. John Nevil (1898), George Sydney (1899), S. Margaret Annie (1896); School: Mrs Macdonald's, Minster 1907-13, Private School, Blackpool; Service: Yorkshire & Lancashire Regt., 2nd Lt.; Theatre: Fr. August, 1916, lost a leg in 1917; Medals: Victory, British; See *N/A* 9/6/15, 4/8/15, 9/5/17, 23/5/17, 20/6/17, & p. 306.

Kirkby, John Nevil. Born: Southwell, 1898-1916; Lived: Queen Street, Southwell; Fam: Br. of James Henry Kirkby – see above; School: Mrs Macdonald's, Minster 1907-13, Private School, Blackpool; Service: O.T.C. Nottingham University College, 1914, 1915 enlisted Yorkshire & Lancashire Regt., 2nd Lt.; Theatre: France, June 1916. K-in-A 25/9/16 at Ginchy, whilst leading his platoon in the attack on Morval. His grave was lost and his death is commemorated on Thiepval Memorial, Somme, France; Medals: Victory, British; See *N/A* 9/6/15, 16/6/15, 7/7/15, 14/6/16, 7/10/16, 11/10/16, 8/8/17, & p. 301.

Knight, J. S. No family details; Service: 8th Bn. S/F; See *N/A* 21/7/15.

Labbett, **John William Hooper.** Born: Belize, British Honduras, 1894-1917; Lived: Southwell; Fam: F. Frederick Henry Labbett (Methodist Minister), M. Ines Bertha, Br. Sydney Bevan (1899), S. Bertha Evelyn Lily (1897); Service: Enlisted October 1914, No. 614, 10th Bn. Lincolnshire Regt., gazetted in 9th Bn. 2nd Lt.; Theatre: Mesopotamia, K-in-A 25/1/17 during advance on Kut, under the command of General Maude. Commemorated Basra Memorial, Iraq; Medals: Victory, British; See *N/A* 31/3/15, 7/2/17.

Labbett, Sydney Bevan. Born: Llanelli, 1899; Lived: Southwell; Fam: Br. of John William Hooper Labbett – see above; Service: No. J/42748, Royal Navy – no further details.

Landsell, Reginald George. Lived: Westgate, Southwell; no further details.

Lane*, John Kirkland. Born: Over Whiteacre, Nr. Tamworth, 1887; Lived: Trinity Villa (lodger) and later Church Street, Southwell; Fam: F. Rev. John George Lane, M. Mary Elizabeth (Kirkland), S. Alice (1882), Gladys (1885); Occup: Solicitor; Service: 1/8th Bn. S/F, Captain, Northumberland Fusiliers, Major; Theatre: Fr. Feb. 1915, wounded May 1915, but returned to front line later; Medals: Victory, British, 1914-15 Star; Post-war, Solicitor Kirkland and Lane; See *N/A* 2/12/14, 2/6/15, 18/8/15, & pp. 202, 207, 209, 222, 224, 228.

Larrington*, Lawrence. Born: Southwell, 1896; Lived: Lower Kirklington Road, Southwell; Fam: F. Arthur Morris Larrington (Foreman – E. Carey & Sons), M. Mary Ann (Boot, m. 1887), Br. Arthur (1888), Walter (1904), S. Minnie (1890), Louisa (1893), Gertrude (1895); School: Methodist 1900-08, Minster; Occup: Lace maker- E. Carey & Sons; Service: No. 1552, 1/8th Bn. S/F, demob. 1/9/16; Theatre: Fr. March 1915; Medals; Victory, British, 1914-15 Star; See p.306.
Law, C. F. No information. See *N/A* 22/11/16.
Lee, Fred. Born: Southwell, 1889; Lived: Market Place, Southwell, but moved to Australia in 1912; Fam: Robert Lee (Joiner and contractor), M. Millicent (Smedley), Br. Robert (1884), William Owen (1888), S. Kate (1878), Emma (1882), Millicent (1886), Annie (1886); School: Infants and Natl. 1896-1903; Service: Australian Light Horse & Artillery, Gunner; Theatre: Egypt and Fr., lost right arm in France, 1915; Medals: No record; See *N/A* 31/10/17.
Lee, Robert. Born: Newark, 1884; Lived: Market Place, Southwell; Fam: Brother of Fred Lee – see above, married Gertrude Janet Clarke, children: Gertrude M (1914); Occup: Joiner; Service: No. F/43734, R.A.F.; Medals: No record.
Lee, Ronald Leslie. Born: Southwell, 1895-1986; Lived: Spring Terrace, Easthorpe, Southwell;

Ronald L. Lee, front row second left, and below in action (Heather Price)

Fam: F. William Lee (Lace maker – E. Carey & Sons), M. Elizabeth, Br. William (1903), S. Hilda (1893), Elsie (1894), Constance (1897), Nora (1900), Olive (1901); School: Easthorpe, Natl. 1902-09; Occup: Gardener; Service: Enlisted August 1914, No. 12746 Lincolnshire Regt., Nos. 46620 & 7809079, 55th Machine Gun Corps, L/Cpl., demob. June 1919; Theatre: Fr. July 1915, and Gallipoli – wounded at Gallipoli; Medals: Victory, British, 1914-15 Star; Post War: Re-enlisted and served in India until June 1922. After service had a market garden in Southwell and the family ran a garage business. Home Guard in WW2.

Lee, Thomas Arnold, Revd. Born: Leicester, 1890; Lived: Southwell; Fam: F. Thomas C. Lee (Shoe & hosiery factor, Leicester), M. Mary (Romanis, m. 1872), Br. William (1879), S. Emma (1880), Margaret (1882), Helen (1883), Catherine (1885); School: Magdalen College School, Oxford, B.A. Hatfield, Univ. of Durham, 1912; Occup: Deacon 1913, priest 1914, curate Southwell Minster 1913-15; Service: October 1915 Army Chaplain; Theatre: Fr. October 1915; Medals: Victory, British, 1914-15 Star; Post war lived 6 Springfield Road, Leicester (1922); See *N/A* 26/5/15, 23/1/18.

Lee, William Owen. Born: Southwell, 1888; Lived: Market Place, Southwell; Fam: Brother of Fred Lee – see above; School: Wesleyan 1895-1902; Occup: Solicitor's clerk; Service: Enlisted November 1915, No. S4/215654, 3rd Res. A.T. Depot, Army Service Corps, demob. September 1919; Theatre: U.K.; Medals: No record.

Leek, John

Leonard, Harold Templeman. Born: Lincolnshire, 1899; Lived: Southwell; Fam: F. Thomas J. Leonard (Schoolteacher), M. Jane (Robinson), Br. Robinson (1882), Ebenezer (1886), John Windsor (1883), S. Mary (1878), Louisa Jane (1880), married Annie Elcome 1925; School: Farnsfield, Minster 1910-16; Occup: Student teacher; Service: No. 31173, East Lancashire Regt.; Theatre: Fr. 1917, P.O.W. 1918; Medals: Victory, British; See *N/A* 2/10/18, & p. 306.

Lester, George Frederick. Born: Kelvedon, 1898-1917; Lived: Hockerton; Fam: F. Henry Lester (Farm labourer), M. Ellen Elizabeth (Chetwynd), S. Mabel (1906), Hilda Isabella (1909), Clara (1910); School: Wesleyan 1907-1909, Natl.1909-10; Occup: Farm labourer; Service: No. 18606, 2/8th Bn. S/F; Theatre: Balkans December 1915, Fr., K-in-A near Arras 7/4/17, buried Vadencourt British Cemetery, Maissemy, France; Medals: Victory, British, 1914-15 Star.

Lewin, Frank. Born: Cotgrave, 1880; Lived: Halam, Southwell; Fam: F. James (Farmer), Br. Frederick James (1877), S. Alice Mary (1871); Occup: Farmworker; Service: M2/178112, Army Service Corps; Theatre: No record; Medals: Victory, British.

Lewin, Walter George. Born, Southwell, 1898; Lived: Norwood Fields, Southwell; Fam: F. Horace, M. Sarah (Hollingsworth), Br. William (1900), Harry (1901), Albert (1906), Fred (1907), S. Mary (1908), Rose (1910), married Bertha (Tyne) 1920; School: Cropwell, Wesleyan 1909-10; Service: 3rd Leicestershire Regt.; Theatre: No record; Medals: Victory, British.

Littlewood, Joseph. Born: Farnsfield, 1890; Lived: Southwell; Fam: F. Joseph (Boot repairer), M. Mary Ann (Green), S. Eva Jane (1885), Hannah (1886), Phoebe (1896), married Edith Redfern 1920, children: twins Gladys and Harry (1922); Occup: Railway porter's clerk; Service: Enlisted 1915, No. 267590, S/F, No. 362948, Royal Engineers, CC Sound Ranging Section; Theatre: Fr. May 1917, Medals: Victory, British.

Llewellyn, Charles. Born/Fam: No details; Service: No. 68870, Royal Horse Artillery, Ammunition Company, 3rd Cavalry Division, Staff Sgt.; Theatre: Fr.; Medals: Victory, British, 1914-15 Star.

Lomas, G. No family details; Occup: Clerk at E. Carey & Sons; Service: Applied to Tribunal 3/6/16 - exempt until 1/10/16.

Long, P. F. No family details; Occup: Clerk at E. Carey & Sons; Service: Applied to Tribunal 3/6/16 - exempt until 1/10/16.

Longmore, Oscar Frederic. Born: Southwell, 1884; Lived: Queen Street, Southwell; Fam: F. Edwin Longmore (Sub Postmaster, Southwell), M. Elizabeth (Bushell), Br. Robert Frederic (1889), married Constance Lee 1919, children: Desmond (1925); School: Minster; Occup: Clerk at flour mill; Service: Attested 1914, joined January 1915, No. 17572, 2nd Bn. S/F, L/Cpl., demob 15/4/19; Theatre: Fr. 1915, wounded September 1916 and returned home, posted again to France

January 1917, P.O.W. at Bullecourt 21/3/18, released 23/12/18; Medals: Victory, British, 1914-15 Star; See *N/A* 27/9/16, 12/9/17, 29/5/18, 15/1/19, & pp. 269, 306.

Longmore, Robert Frederic. Born: Southwell, 1889; Lived: Queen Street, Southwell; Fam: Br. of Oscar Frederic Longmore – see above, married Maude Marion (Parlette m. 1913), children: Edwin F. (1920); School: Infants & Natl. 1895-98; Occup: Clerk at flour mill; Service: No. 45785, Labour Corps, 505th Agricultural Co. – no further details of service.

Maidens, Reginald C. Born: Newark, 1898; Lived: Station Road, Southwell; Fam: F. Thomas Maidens (Stationmaster), M. Sarah Jane (Burton), Br. Cyril Francis (1896); School: Minster 1910-13; Occup: Clerk – Architect's office; Service: No record; See *N/A* 22/11/16.

Maltby, Charles Robert Crighton. Born: Nottingham, 1890-1916; Lived: Church Street, Southwell; Fam: F. Charles Langley Maltby (Bank Manager), M. Isaline Philippa (Bramwell), Br. Patrick Brough (1893); School: Magdalen College School, Worcester College, Oxford; Occup: Actor and assistant manager the Repertory Theatre, Liverpool – stage name Robert Crighton; Service: Rifle Brigade, Lt.; Theatre: Fr. July 1915, DoW 27/8/16, buried Dive Copse, Sailly-le-Sec, Somme, France; Medals: Victory, British, 1914-15 Star; See *N/A* 3/2/15, 8/8/17.

Maltby, Patrick Brough. Born: Nottingham, 1893; Lived: Church Street, Southwell; Fam: Br. of Charles Malby – see above; Service: Royal Navy Voluntary Reserve.

Marriott, Frederick Charles. Born: Southwell, 1885; Lived: 6 Victoria Terrace, Southwell; Fam: F. Samuel (Postman), M. Thirza (Wilson), Br. William (1875), Samuel (1879), Sydney Arthur (1889), S. Emma (1863), Mary (1864), Ellen (1870), Annie (1872), Ada (1882), Thirza (1887); School: Wesleyan 1892-?; Occup: Grocer's errand boy; Service: Enlisted 30/1/06, No. 6845, King's Royal Rifles, No. 21204, 3rd Bn. Oxford & Bucks; Theatre: Fr. 1914, severely wounded 8/5/15 at Ypres, discharged 20/7/16; Medals: Victory, British, 1914-15 Star; Received a pension of 8/3d + 1/6d per week; See *N/A* 11/11/14, 10/2/15, 25/8/15.

Marriott*, Thomas. Born: Wellingore, Lincolnshire, 1891- 1917; Fam: F. William Marriott (Farm foreman), M. Sarah Ann, Br. Allen (1878), Edward (1894), S. Annie (1880), married Louisa (Roome); Occup: Waggoner; Service: No. 4818, 1/8th S/F and 6th Bn. Oxfordshire and Buckinghamshires; Theatre: Fr., died 20/9/17, commemorated Tyne Cot Memorial; Medals: Victory, British.

Marrison, Oscar Jnr. Born: Southwell, 1895; Lived: Westgate, Southwell; Fam: F. Oscar (Wheelwright), M. Faith (Scraton), Br. Leslie (1900), Cecil Baden (1901), Gerald (1903), S. Elsie (1892), Phyllis (1893), Olive (1894), Gladys (1897), Maude (1898-99), married Ruth Boyall 1928, children: Nancy (1930); School: Trinity, Natl. 1904-10; Service: No. 477168, 649th West Riding Field Co., Royal Engineers; Theatre/Medals: No records.

Marrison, Oscar Snr. Born: Ranskill, Notts, 1865; Lived: Westgate, Southwell; Fam: Father of Oscar - see above; Service: No. 317259, Tank Corps; Theatre/Medals: No records.

Marsh*, George Herbert. Born: Bleasby, 1894-1929; Lived: Bleasby; Fam: F. Joseph Marsh (Wheelwright and joiner), M. Emily (Coleman, m. 1881), Br. Frank (1884), Alfred Joseph (1887), Charles (1890), George Herbert (1894), Joseph Edward (1896), Frederick (1899), S. Daisy (1883), Olive (1889); Occup: Apprentice wheelwright and joiner; Service: 1/8th Bn. S/F – no further details.

Marsh, George Robert. Born: Nottingham, 1884; Lived: Westgate, Southwell; Fam: F. George, M. Emma (Greensmith), Br. (half) Albert Greensmith, S. Nora (1888); Service: Attested 14/11/14, No. M/2/034629, Army Service Corps, 55th Auxiliary Co. M.T., demob. 4/4/19;

Theatre: Fr. February 1915-June 1915, home till 1917. Fr. April 1917; Medals: Victory, British, 1914-15 Star;

Marshall, Arthur. Born: Norwell, 1887; Lived: Southwell; Fam: F. Tilley Marshall (Blacksmith), M. Marie (Hollingsworth), Br. William (1881), George (1892), S. Annie Elizabeth (1879), Sarah (1883), Florence (1884), Emily (1896); Occup: Labourer – railway; Service: No. 1623, South Notts Hussars, No. 170027, M.G.C.; Theatre: Egypt; Medals: Victory, British; See p.279.

Marshall, Frank Reginald. Born: Newark, 1888; Lived: Brinkley, Southwell; Fam: F. John Clark Marshall (Boot maker), M. Elizabeth (Maltby, m. 1875), Br. John Sydney (1880), Charles Hedley (1885), Alfred (1888), Cecil S. (1892), S. Edna Mary (1878); Occup: Waggoner – farm; Service: No. G/52341, Middlesex Regt., 13th Bn. C Company; Theatre: Fr.; Medals: Victory, British.

Marson, Robert William. Born: Ashwell, Rutland, 1897; Lived: Prebend Yard, Southwell; Fam: F. Robert Marson (Carter), M. Mary (North), S. Emma (1887), Rose (1892), Eliza Edith (1895), Mary Ann (1899); Service: Attested 5/11/14, 8th Bn. S/F, No. 305857, 4th Co. Army Service Corps, demob 23/5/19; Theatre: Fr. March 1915; Medals: Victory, British, 1914-15 Star.

Martin, Leonard Lionel B. Born: Bromley, Kent, 1893; Lived: Southwell; Fam: married Mabel (Smith m. 1922); Occup: Baker with J. H. Kirkby; Service: Enlisted October, 1915, No. S4/143584, Army Service Corps; Theatre: Balkans, November 1915; Medals: Victory, British, 1914-15 Star; See *N/A* 20/10/15, 1/8/17.

Mashford, Thomas James. Born: Holbeach, 1889; Lived: Church Street, Southwell; Fam: F. William Edward Mashford (Grocer), M. Anne (Thwaite), Br. John Frederick (1893), Alfred Ernest (1895), S. Ada (1897); School: Natl. left 1903; Occup: Grocer's assistant; Service: No. 161894, Royal Garrison Artillery, Sgt.; Theatre/Medals: No records.

Maslen, Frank. Born: Cudworth, Yorks, 1873; Lived: 4 Station Road, Southwell; Fam: F. Charles (Railway porter), M. Hannah (Helman, m. 1869), Br. George Frederick (1874), Frank (1880), Edward Charles (1883), married Nellie (Andrews); Occup: Motor driver; Service: Enlisted 17/2/15, No. 049320, Army Service Corps; Theatre: No record; Medals: Victory, British, 1914-15 Star, G.C. Badge 11/2/1917.

McGowan, Charles William. Born: Newark, 1867; Lived: Spring Terrace, Southwell; Fam: married Ruth Mabel Virgo, children: William H. (1888), Harry (1893), Frank (1900), Bernard (1904), Elsie (1896), Lilly (1903), Constance (1909); Occup: Lace maker – E. Carey & Sons; Service: no record, but recorded as a veteran in 1928.

McGowan*, Harry. Born: Radford, Nottingham, 1893-1947; Lived: Spring Terrace, Southwell; Fam: F. Charles William McGowan – see above; School: Old Radford, Nottingham & Natl. 1903-05; Service: Nos. 1237 & 331309, 1/8th Bn. S/F, demob. To reserves 10/3/19; Theatre: Fr. March 1915, wounded Oct. 1916 & Nov. 1919; Medals: Victory, British, 1914-15 Star; Post-war: Lived in Easthorpe and re-joined 1/8th Bn. July 1920.

McGowan, William Harold. Born: Nottingham, 1888; Lived: Pollards Lane, Southwell; Fam: Brother of Harry McGowan – see above; School: Nottingham, Old Radford, Natl. 1903-05; Service: No. 34325, 2/9th & 20th Manchester Regiment, transferred to 8th Bn. S/F in 1920; Theatre: No record; Medals: Victory, British.

McMillan, B. No records.

Meads*, George William. Born: Calverton, 1896; Lived: St. Wifred's Cottage, Mansfield Lane, Calverton; Fam: F. William Meads (Farm labourer), M. Annie (Withers, m. 1895), Br. John Frank (1900); Occup: Hosiery machine minder; Service: No. 305186, 1/8th Bn. S/F; Theatre: No record; Medals: Victory, British.

Meads*, Harold. Born: Calverton, 1894; Lived: Burner Pool, Calverton; Fam: F. Matthew Meads (Hosiery hand), M. Ellen (Cooper, m. 1891), Br. Wilfred Bernard (1892), Lewis Edward (1904), S. Olive Elizabeth (1900); Occup: Gardener; Service: No. 1586, 1/8th Bn. S/F, No. 235427, Leicestershire Regt., Cpl., demob. 12/2/19; Theatre: Fr. March 1915; Medals: Victory, British, 1914-15 Star.

Meads*, Matthew. Born: Calverton, 1868; Lived: Burner Pool, Calverton; Fam: Father of Harold Meads, above; Occup: Hosiery hand; Service: Enlisted as volunteer in 1885, No. 702, 1/8th Bn. S/F, Cpl. 1899, Sgt. 1903, C. Sgt. 1911; Theatre: too old for France and served in U.K. until discharged in April 1916; Medals: Volunteer Long Service medal.

Meads*, Maurice. Born: Calverton, 1882; Lived: Windle Square, Calverton; Fam: married Martha Ann (Blood, m. 1906), children: Leslie (1908), Lloyd Maurice (1910), Alice (1914), Mavis (1923); Occup: Frame hand, hosiery; Enlisted 1912, Service Nos. 1543, 330567, 1/8th Bn. S/F, No. 860015, London Regiment and Rifle Brigade, demob. 1919; Theatre: Fr. July 1918; Medals: Victory, British.

Meads*, Wilfred Bernard. Born: Calverton, 1893; Son of Matthew Meads – see above; Occup: Hosiery hand; Service: Enlisted T.A. 1913, No. 1587, 1/8th Bn. S/F, L/Cpl., No. 396330, Army Service Corps, No. 35542, Leicestershire Regt., No. T/42387 R.A.S.C.; Theatre: Fr. March 1915 –home June 1915-Dec 1916; Medals: Victory, British, 1914-15 Star.

Merrin, Alfred. Born: Southwell, 1897-1917; Lived: Westhorpe, Southwell; Fam: F. Henry (Basket maker), M. Mary (Richmond), Br. Walter (1891), Thomas (1895), S. Ada Elizabeth (1889), Annie Amelia (1893); School: Trinity, Natl. 2010-15; Occup: Farm labourer; Service: Enlisted 1916, No. S/9891, 8th Bn. Seaforth Highlanders; Theatre: Fr. 1916, DoW at Rouen 6/2/17, buried St. Sever Cemetery Extension, Rouen; Medals: Victory, British; See *N/A* 8/8/17.

Merrin, Arthur. Born: Southwell, 1890; Lived: Church Street, Southwell; Fam: F. William Merrin (Agricultural labourer), M. Ann Elizabeth (Blatherwick), Br. John H. (1888), Lawrence Frederick (1900), S. Ada Elizabeth (1889), Georgiana (1893), Charlotte Ann (1895), Lucy (1896), Gladys (1898); School: Trinity, Natl. 1898-1905; Occup: Waggoner, Brackenhurst farm; Service: Attested 12/11/14, No. 305963, 2/8th Bn. S/F, 1916 Sgt., 9th Bn. S/F, demob. 4/3/19; Medals: Victory, British.

Merrin, Ernest. Born: Southwell, 1896; Lived: Oxton Road, Southwell; Fam: F. George Merrin (Farm labourer), M. Anna, Br. George (1901), S. Hilda (1897), Winifred (1906); School: Holy Trinity, Natl. 1905-10; Occup: Labourer – H. Merryweather; Service: Enlisted 18/11/13, No. 1878, 8th Bn. S/F, discharged 6/8/13 as medically unfit.

Merrin, Horace. Born: Southwell, 1899-1918; Lived: Westhorpe, Southwell; Fam: F. Charles Merrin (Hay trusser), M. Minnie (Booth), Br. Joseph Henry (1900), Harry Albert (1902), Charles T. (1915), S. Edith Hester (1905), Jane (1898), Hilda (1913); School: Wesleyan, Natl. 1907-13; Occup: Farm labourer; Service: No. 82578, 'A' Co. 20th Bn. Durham Light Infantry; Theatre: Fr. March 1918, K-in-A 4/9/18 as the Germans pulled back from the Ypres Salient, commemorated Tyne Cot Memorial, Belgium; Medals: Victory, British.

Merrin, Walter. Born: Southwell, 1891 - 1917; Lived: 2, Suez Street, New Basford, Nottingham; Fam: Br. of Alfred Merrin – see above, married; School: Trinity, Natl. 1899-1905; Occup: Stoker at

Alfred George Merryweather (Roger Merryweather)

Henry Ashwell Hosiery; Service: Attested December 1915, No. 30742, Leicestershire Regt., No. 31800 6th Bn. Yorkshire & Lancashire Regt., 10th Bn. Leicestershire Regt.; Theatre: Fr. September 1916, wounded 14/10/16, K-in-A 18/6/17, buried Wulverghem-Lindenhoek Road Military Cemetery, West Vlaanderen, Belgium; Medals: Victory, British.

Merryweather, Alfred George. Born: Southwell, 1878; Lived: Brinkley Castle then Brinkley House, Southwell; Fam: F. Henry Merryweather (Nurseryman), M. Emily Staniland, Br. Henry (1866), John Edward (1869), Ernest (1873), S. Elizabeth (1876), married Annie Clarissa (Fletcher, m 1902), children: Henry (1905), John (1908); Occup: Nurseryman, and orderly Burgage Manor Hospital; Service: Enlisted 1916, No. 113315, Royal Garrison Artillery, Cpl.; Theatre: Fr./Belgium January 1917, suffered gunshot wounds 5/10/17 and lost an eye in the Ypres sector, also served on Gibraltar, hospitalized with jaundice; Medals: Victory, British; See *N/A* 14/2/14, 10/10/17, p. 280.

Miller, Harry. Lived: White Swan Inn, King Street, Southwell; Occup: Employed by A E Hall, Cranfield House, Southwell; Service: No. M/2 054560, 7th Co. M.T. Army Service Corps; Theatre: Fr. July 1915; Medals: Victory, British, 1914-15 Star.

Mills, Reginald Eggleston. Born: 1899; Lived: King Street, Southwell; Fam: married Kathleen (Beckett m. 1926), children: Kathleen (1928); School: Newark Grammar, Minster 1910-14; Occup: Followed his father as a postmaster; Service: 'A' Co. Depot, S/F.; Theatre/Medals: No records.

Mills, Sidney Charles. Born: Southwell, 1898; Lived: King Street, Southwell; Fam: F. Charles Mills (Groom & footman, Westhorpe Hall), M. Elizabeth (Hollis); Br. Harry Hollis (1883), S. Kate Mary (1881), Kate Elizabeth (1890), Ethel (1896); School: Natl. 1906-11, Minster 1911-14, choral scholar; Occup: Footman, Westhorpe Hall; Service: No. T/384569, 143rd Co. Army Service Corps, Driver; Theatre: No record; Medals: Victory, British.

Milner*, Frederick T. Born: Sheffield, 1893; Lived: Railway Inn Lowdham; Fam: Details not known; Occup: Domestic servant at the Railway Inn; Service: No. 1588, 1/8th Bn. S/F, No. 403065, R.A.F; Theatre: Fr. June 1915; Medals: Victory, British, 1914-15 Star.

Minns, Percy. Born: Southwell, 1887; Lived: 1911 was serving in the Royal Navy, previously The Workhouse; Fam: Grandmother Susannah Hill of Lowdham; School: Natl, 1895-1900; Occupation: Gardener; Service: No. 220581, HMS Mantua, an armed merchant cruiser: 1915-16, Northern Patrols 1917-19, Sierra Leone and Cape of Good Hope convoys; Post-war lived Massey's Yard.

Moore, Richard. Born: Southwell, 1883; Lived: Back Lane & Burgage Lane, Southwell; Fam: F. George Moore (Shoemaker), M. Mary (Adamson), Br. Charley (1872), William (1877), S. Mary (1854), Harriet (1859), Jane (1863), Hannah (1865), Kate (1869); Occup: Farm labourer; Service: No. 4456, 3/8th Bn. S/F, No. 279903, Army Service Corps, demob. 23/5/19; Theatre: Fr. June 1916, shell shock and injuries July 1917, spending 52 days in hospital in Whitchurch; Medals: Victory, British.

Morley, Samuel.* Born: Calverton, 1894 - 1917; Lived: Burrows Yard, Calverton; Fam: F. Nathan Morley (Farm worker), M. Hannah (Watson, m. 1885), Br. Fred (1897), Joe (1903), S. Ada (1886), Ethel (1890); Occup: Farm labourer; Service: Nos. 1589, 305188, 1/8th Bn. S/F; Theatre: Fr. K-in-A 30/5/17, buried at Loos British Cemetery; Medals: Victory, British .

Morley-Richardson, Harry. Born: 1881; Lived: Easthorpe, Southwell; Fam: Married Ethel P. Smith Dec 1913, children: Marjorie (1914), Albert E. (1915), Dulcie N. (1919); Service: No. M/16905, Royal Navy, served on HMS Venerable.

Mosedale, Clement. Born: Southwell, 1887-1917; Lived: 3 Bishop Street, Mansfield; Fam: F. George Frederick Mosedale (Baker & Grocer), M. Emma (Randall), Br. George Richard (1884), Rupert (1889), S. Doris R. (1899), married Ethel Stevens 1909, children: Norman G. (1914); School: Wesleyan. 1890-97; Occup: Grocer's clerk; Service: Called up 1916, No. 61942, King's Own Yorkshire Light Infantry, G. 22846, 7th Bn., A Co., Royal West Surrey (Queen's); Theatre: Fr., taken P.O.W. at Wytschaete having been wounded, DoW 17/8/17 at Gullenghen Military Hospital, buried Harlebeke New British Cemetery, Belgium; Medals: Victory, British.

Mosedale, Rupert. Born: Southwell, 1889; Lived: Kirklington Road, Southwell; Fam: Br. of Clement Mosedale – see above, married Florence Smith 1919, children: Geoffrey C. (1923); School: Wesleyan 1892-1899; Occup: Baker's assistant; Service: No. 1259, South Notts Hussars, No. 82000, 3rd Reserve Cavalry Hussars, L/Cpl., medically discharged 8/8/17 following malaria; Theatre: Egypt 1915; Medals: Victory, British, 1914-15 Star; See *N/A* 23/9/14, & p. 279.

Moseley, John. Born: Southwell, 1896-1918; Lived: Beeston, in 1901 was living at Southwell Workhouse; Fam: Son of Eliza Moseley (Cook and domestic servant at Workhouse, spinster), S. Mary (1890); Service: No. 27676, 15th Bn. 1st S/F; Theatre: Fr. K-in-A 25/3/18, buried Beacon Cemetery, Sailly-Laurette, France; Medals: Victory, British.

Murden*, George Ernest. Born: Southwell, 1892; Lived: Kirklington Road, Southwell; Fam: F. William Murden (Lace maker – E. Carey & Sons), M. Ellen, Br. William Thomas (1891), George Ernest (1892), John Henry 1894-94), Frederick (1895), Harold (1900), Edward (1904), S. Mary Elizabeth (1890), Nellie (1893), Alice (1896), Annie (1898), Lucie Florence (1903), Doris (1907-08), May (1909), married Ethel M. (Seraton in 1920); School: Easthorpe & Natl. 1898-99; Occup: Threader – E. Carey & Sons; Service: No. 743, 1/8th Bn. S/F, low service number suggests that he enlisted some time prior to 1914, Nos. 640850 & 4961203, Royal Field Artillery, demob. 31/3/16; Theatre: Fr. Feb. 1915; Medals: Victory, British, 1914-15 Star.

Murden, Harold. Born: Southwell, 1899; Lived: Kirklington Road, Southwell; Fam: Br. of George Ernest Murden – see above; School: Wesleyan, Natl. left 1912; Service: No. 6107, North Staffordshire Regt., No. 2361, Guards Machine Gun Regt.; Theatre: No record; Medals: Victory, British.

Murden* William Thomas. Born: Southwell, 1891; Lived: Kirklington Road, Southwell; Fam: brother of George Ernest Murden – see above, married Mary L Sturgess 1917, children: Irene M (1922), Barbara (1923), Angus B. (1926); School: Easthorpe & Natl. 1898-99; Occup: Warper – E. Carey & Sons and later Grocer's assistant; Service: No. 742, 1/8th Bn. S/F, low service number suggests that he enlisted some time prior to 1914, Sgt., No. 78898, Durham Light Infantry, Sgt., No. S/49983, Cameroons, Sgt., demob 8/4/16; Theatre: Fr. Feb. 1915; Medals: Victory, British, 1914-15 Star; See *N/A* 19/8/14, 11/11/14, 10/2/15, 9/6/15, 16/6/15, 15/9/15, 29/9/15.

Murray, Royal. Born: Manchester, 1883-1917; Lived: Spring Terrace, Southwell; Fam: adopted son of Joseph (Railway porter) and Annie Lineker; School: Natl. 1892-1896; Occup: Brass bobbin winder – E. Carey & Sons: Service: Previous with 'H' Company, then National Reserve in early 1914, Nos. 2338, 20034, 242626, 1/6th S/F; Theatre: Fr. March 1915, April 1917 severely wounded and later K-in-A 4/11/17, buried Philosophe British Cemetery, Mazingarbe, Pas de Calais; Medals: Victory, British, 1914-15 Star; See *N/A*, 14/11/17, 29/5/18.

Murrell, William Henry. Born: Ruskington, Lincs, 1884; Lived: Easthorpe, Southwell; Fam: F. Thomas, M. Sarah Ann, Br. David Charles (1891), George Thomas (1896), S. Rebecca (1890), Susanna (1893), Mary E. (1898), Florence (1900), married Edith Ann Brown 1910, children: George W. (1911), Edith M. (1916); Occup: Grocer's carter; Service: No. 106470, 48th Machine Gun Corps; Medals: Victory, British.

Musgrove*, George. Born: Southwell, 1896; Lived: Easthorpe, Southwell; Fam: F. Henry Musgrove (deceased 1896), M. Mary Ann (Blanchard - Charlady), Br. Tom (1892), S. Lizzie (1890); School: Natl. Infants and Natl. 1902-05, Minster – choral scholar; Occup: Solicitor's clerk, Kirkland & Lane; Service: Enlisted 1912, No. 1428, 1/8th Bn. S/F, L/Cpl.; Theatre: U.K, did not go to France due to a knee problem; Medals: Not recorded; See p. 306.

Musgrove*, Tom. Born: Lowdham, 1892-1916; Lived: Easthorpe, Southwell; Fam: Brother of George Musgrove – see above; School: Easthorpe & Natl. 1900-02; Occup: Grocer's assistant, J. H. Kirkby; Service: Enlisted March 1912, No. 1437, 1/8th Bn. S/F; Theatre: Fr. March 1915 – Sept. 1915, discharged 15/5/16 as medically unfit and died 10/7/16, a full military funeral was held at Southwell Minster; Medals: Victory, British, 1914-15 Star; See *N/A* 20/1/15, 9/6/15, 12/7/16, & p. 301.

Musson, George Henry. Born: Southwell, 1879; Lived: Bulwell, Nottingham; Fam: F. Henry Musson, M. Elizabeth (Grey), Br. Harry (1862), William Augustus (1866), Walter (1867), Charles (1874), John (1876), S. Arabella (1859), Elizabeth (1869), married Harriet Ann Roe, children: Edith (1922); Occup: Shunter; Service: 1895 joined Yorkshire & Lancashire Regt., dismissed as he lied about his age, 1916, No. 55617, 4th Bn. West Yorkshire Regt., No. 51248, East Yorkshire Regt., ES/58808, Army Service Corps; Theatre: No record; Medals: Victory, British.

Musson, Walter. Born: Southwell, 1867; Lived: Westhorpe; Fam. Married to Eliza; Service: Formerly No. 9253 Grenadier Guards, joined 1884 and re-joined as No. 20473, S/F, Sgt.; Theatre/Medals: No records.

Musson, William Thomas. No family information; Lived: Victoria Terrace, Kirklington Road, Southwell; Service: No. 22987, Labour Corps; Theatre/Medals: No record.

Naylor, James H. No family information; Service: No. 32905, Leicestershire Regt., No. 138931, Machine Gun Corps; Theatre: No record; Medals: Victory, British; See *N/A* 9/6/15.

Newboult, Frank Oswald. Born: Tuxford, 1879; Lived: King Street, Southwell; Fam: F. Fred, M. Sarah Jane (Stokes), married Betsy (Turgoose, m. 1903), children: Maud Marion (1905), Enid (1907), Frank (1910); Occup: Ironmonger; Service: No records; See *N/A* 14/4/15.

Oliver*, Samuel. Born: Radcliffe-on-Trent, 1891-1915; Lived: Southwell; Fam: F. Albert Oliver, M. Alice, Br. William (1902), S. Annie (1898), May (1900), Norah (1908), Vera (1914); Occup: Carter with J. H. Kirkby; Service: No. 2750, 1/8th Bn. S/F; Theatre: Fr. March 1915. The 8th Battalion were fighting at Sanctuary Wood and fought off a determined effort by the Germans to take their trenches, and Sam Oliver was K-in-A 30/7/15, several other Southwell men died in the same action. Commemorated on Menin Gate; Medals: Victory, British, 1914-15 Star; See *N/A* 28/10/14, 20/1/15, 9/6/15, 11/8/15, 18/8/15, 15/9/15, 22/9/15, 12/1/16, & pp. 211, 259.

Osborne*, John Neville. Born: Bulwell, 1896; Lived: Westgate, Southwell; Fam: F. John Osborne (Lace maker – E. Carey & Sons), M. Sarah Elizabeth Persall m. 1895); School: Trinity & Natl. 1903-10; Occup: Office boy, wines and spirits; Service: Nos. 1431 & 305125, 1/8th Bn. S/F, Cpl.; Theatre: Fr. March 1915; Medals: Victory, British, 1914-15 Star.

Otter, Joseph. Born: 1882; Fam: F. William, M. Ellen (Rastrick, m. 1878), Br. William (1887), S. Sarah (1878), Louisa (1881), married Elizabeth (Padley in 1902), children: Fred (1902), Joseph (1903), Leslie (1903), Eileen H. (1912); Occup: With J. H. Kirkby, originally professional soldier with Royal Marines; Service: Royal Marines Artillery & No. 12188, 8th Bn. Lincolnshire Regiment;

Theatre: Fr. September 1915, wounded 1916, demob. 6/2/19; Medals: Victory, British, 1914-15 Star; See *N/A* 9/6/15, 20/1/15.
Overton, Cyril Richard. Born: Newark, 1894; Fam: F. Isaac, M. Sarah (Stevenson m. 1886), Br. Isaac (1888), S. Florence Louisa (1890), married Edith E. (Darnell m. 1924), children: Geoffrey W (1925) John M. (1927), Malcolm A. (1934); Occup: Clerk; Service: Enlisted 12/5/13, Nos. 1742 & 305239, 1/8th S/F, L/Cpl., Signaller, demob. 1/4/19; Theatre: Fr. March 1915; Medals: Victory, British, 1914-15 Star.

Cyril R. Overton (Julia Overton)

Pacey, Arthur. Born: Thurgarton, 1893; Lived: Church Street, Southwell; Fam: F. Charles Pacey (Gardener), M. Clara Ann (Darmens), Br. Charles (1892), John (1897), Joseph Richard (1899), Samuel (1901), Henry (1903), Ernest (1905), Norman George (1907), Walter (1909), Robert (1910), S. Alice (1894), Sarah Ann (1895), Lois (1900); Occup: Gardener; Service: No. 24235, 1st Bn. East Lancashire Regt., A/Cpl., (wounded); Theatre: Fr.; Medals: Victory, British; See *N/A* 19/8/14, 25/8/15, 25/11/16, 10/4/19.
Pacey, Charles. Born: Barningham, Suffolk, 1892; Lived: Church Street, Southwell; Fam: Br. of Arthur Pacey – see above, married Nellie W Adams 1915, children; Margaret (1916); Occup: Gardener; Service: No. 470171, West Yorkshire Regt.; Theatre/Medals: No records.
Pacey, John. Born: Thurgarton 1898; Lived: Church Street, Southwell; Fam: Br. of Arthur Pacey – see above, married Gladys M. Revill 1923, children: John R. (1927); School: Natl. 1907-11; Occup: Gardener; Service: No. 3154, 1/8th Bn. S/F; Theatre: Fr. June 1915; Medals: Victory, British, 1914-15 Star; *N/A* 9/6/15.
Pacey, Joseph Richard. Born: Thurgarton, 1899; Lived: Church Street, Southwell; Fam: Br. of Arthur Pacey – see above; School: Natl. 1911-12; Service: No. 93221, Durham Light Infantry: Theatre: No record; Medals: Victory, British.
Pacey, William. Born: Thurgarton, 1896; Lived: Church Street, Southwell; Fam: Br. of Arthur Pacey – see above, married Lily S. Holden 1925, children: Jean (1928); School: Natl. 1907-10; Occup: Grocer's van boy, Kirkbys; Service: Nos. 5806, 201970, 2nd 4th Bn. Leicestershire Regt.; Theatre: Fr., wounded; Medals: Victory, British; See *N/A* 20/1/15, 10/4/18.
Padgett, George. Born: Hyson Green Nottingham, 1885; Lived: Market Place, Southwell; Fam: F. George Padgett (Letterpress printer), M. Eliza Ann (Spencer, m. 1880), S. Mary E. (1882), married Hilda M. (Wagstaff, m. 1923); Occup: Stationer's assistant; Service: No. 47334, 27th Bn. Durham Light Infantry; Theatre: No record; Medals: Victory, British.
Page*, Thomas. Born: Cossall, 1893; Lived: Sunnyside, Westgate, Southwell; Fam: F. Harry Page (Lace hand – E. Carey & Sons), M. Emma (Horridge), S. Sarah Ann (1896), married Mabel A. Jackson 1925; School: Trinity & Natl. 1900-06; Occup: Lace hand – E. Carey & Sons; Service: Enlisted T.A. 1912, No. 1436, 1/8th Bn. S/F, No. 567250, Labour Corps, demob. 5/3/19; Theatre: Fr. Feb 2015; Medals: Victory, British, 1914-15 Star.
Paling*, Albert Ernest. Born: Normanton, 1896-1916; Lived: 17 Station Road, Southwell; Fam: F. John Paling (Boarding House proprietor), M. Annie (Gibson, m. 1890), Br. George (1891), Frank (1893); School: Trinity & Natl. 1903-10; Occup: Miller at Caudwell's; Service: Enlisted Oct. 1914, No. 2872, 1/8th Bn. S/F, Cpl.; Theatre: Fr. June 1915, Sept. 1915 suffered a gunshot wound to his neck, Oct 1915 he was gassed and away from his unit for a period. He was wounded

at Bellacourt, near Arras on 13/7/16 – DoW 14/7/16. Buried Walincourt Halte British Cemetery, Grave I H 11; Medals: Victory, British, 1914-15 Star; See *N/A* 26/7/16, & pp. 221, 262-3.

Paling*, Frank. Born: Normanton, 1893-1915; Lived: 17 Station Road, Southwell; Fam: brother of A. E. Paling – see above; School: Wesleyan & Natl. 1905-1907; Occup: Gardener and nurseryman; Service: Enlisted 8/9/14, No. 2344, 1/8th Bn. S/F; Theatre: Fr. Feb/Mar 1915. K-in-A Kemmel 12/6/15, buried Kemmel Chateau Military Cemetery, Grave D. 62; Medals: Victory, British, 1914-15 Star; See *N/A* 23/6/15, 18/8/15, & pp. 259, 262-3.

Paling, Robert. Born: Beeston, 1881; Lived: Southwell; Fam: F. Robert Paling (Railway foreman), M. Rebecca (Allen), Br. William (1866), John (1867), George (1870), Arthur (1875), Frank (1883), S. Susan (1878), married Eleanor Ann Ebelwhite 1902, children: Frederick Arthur (1910), John E. (1913); Occup: Lace maker; Service: No. 44963, Royal Army Medical Corps; Theatre: Fr. April 1915; Medals: Victory, British, 1914-15 Star.

Paling, Samuel. Born: Lowdham, 1891; Lived: Southwell; Fam: F. Samuel Paling, M. Sarah Ann (Knowles), S. Mary E (1872), Florence (1874), married Ida E. (Rowett m. 1917), children: Margaret (1923), Barbara (1925); Occup: Tailor; Service: No record.

Parker, Harry. Born: Southwell, 1898; Lived: Kirklington Road, Southwell; Fam: F. James Parker (Labourer), M. Mary Jane (Howard), Br. James (1900), S. Emma (1895), Clara (1897); School: Wesleyan from 1901; Service: No. 476618, 448th Field Co., Royal Engineers, Driver; Theatre: No record; Medals: Victory, British; See *N/A* 19/8/14.

Parker, John William (Willie). Born: No family details; Lived: Landseer Road, Southwell; Service: No. S4/059999, Royal Army Service Corps, Sgt.; Theatre: Fr. May 1915; Medals: Victory, British, 1914-15 Star; See *N/A* 1/9/15.

Parker, Richard Jnr. Born: Southwell, 1886; Lived: Westhorpe, Southwell; Fam: F. Richard Parker (Farm labourer), M. Elizabeth (Marriott), Br. Thomas (1877), William (1879), Arthur (1881), Frederick (1883), S. Kate Eliza (1887); School: Natl. 1894-99; Occup: Postman; Service: No. 3148, R.A.F., Sgt.

Parkes* (Parks), Arthur. Born: Lowdham, 1890; Lived: Main Street, Lowdham; Fam: F. Reuben (Rubin) Parkes (Railway platelayer), M. Ann (Reason, m. 1869), Br. Samuel (1869), Henry (1873), Walter (1875),William (1879), S. Ellen (1876), Emma (1885), Sarah (1887); Occup: Farm labourer; Service: Enlisted T.A. 1912, No. 1375, 1/8th Bn. S/F, discharged 21/3/16; Theatre: Stayed in U.K.; Medals: No record.

Parkin, George. Born: Doncaster, 1885; Lived: King Street, Southwell; Fam: F. William Henry (Farmer), M. Mary Ann (Kent, m. 1882), Br. Frederick John (1887), James (1889), Ernest (1894), S. Alice (1883), Mary (1891), married Sabina Mashford 1909, children: Reginald (1910), Lucy (1912), Frederick, Jim & Mabel; Occup: Foreman horseman; Service: Enlisted 1917, No. 143214, Royal Garrison Artillery, Gnr., demob. 25/1/19; Theatre: Fr. wounded and hospitalized Oct/Nov 1918; Medals: Victory, British.

Parlby, George. Born: Southwell, 1883 - 1915; Lived: Asfordby; Fam: F. George, M. Mary (Brown), Br. John James (1875), William Leslie (1909), Sidney (1913), S. Lois Ann (1889), Gwendoline (1908), Frances Mary (1915); Occup: Gardener at nursery; Service: No. 2394 Leicester Yeomanry, Household Cavalry; Theatre: Fr. February 1915, died at home of illness 14/12/15, buried Asfordby Church Yard; Medals: Victory, British, 1914-15 Star.

Parr, George Leonard. Born: Farnsfield, 1901-1916; Lived: Broomfields, Farnsfield; Fam: F. John Parr (Farmer), M. Edna, Br. John Richard (1897), S. Kathleen (1899); School: Farnsfield Wesleyan Elementary, Minster 1913-16; Occup: Royal Navy; Service: Royal Navy, Boy 2nd Class,

No. J/61127, H.M.S. Powerful, died of disease at Devonport, buried Ford Park Cemetery, Plymouth.

Partington, John (Jack) Lennox. Born: Southwell, 1899; Lived: Kirklington Road, Southwell; Fam: Thomas David Partington (Lace manager – E. Carey & Sons), M. Sarah (Paulson), Br. Robert Walker (1901), married Clara M Gilman 1925; School: Natl. 1907-14, Minster; Occup: Clerk – E. Carey & Sons; Service: No. 30907, 4th Bn. East Lancs, No. 76834, King's Own Yorkshire Light Infantry; Theatre: Fr., P.O.W. 1917; Medals: Victory, British; See *N/A* 15/1/19 & pp. 269, 306.

Pashley, Thomas Alfred. No family details; Occup: Slaughter man with W.J. Adlington; Service: Applied to Tribunal 1/4/16 - exempt until 1/10/16 - no military records.

Peacock, Charles. Born: Southwell, 1888; Lived: Westhorpe, Southwell; Fam: F. James Martin Peacock, M. Charlotte B.(Blackwell), Br. Thomas (1870), William (1886), George (1889), John Cosby (1890), George (1894), S. Sarah (1878), Alice (1879), Alice Belinda (1892), Susan (1895); School: Wesleyan 1896; Occup: Domestic groom; Service: London Yeomanry; Theatre: No record; Medals: Victory, British; See *N/A* 14/6/16.

Peacock, George. Born: Southwell, 1889-1916; Lived: Kirklington Road, Southwell; Fam: Br. of Charles Peacock – see above; School: Grimsby Board, Wesleyan 1897-1902; Occup: Robinson's flour mill, Rotherham, previously at Caudwell's Mill; Service: No. 4720, 2nd Bn. Yorkshire and Lancashire Regiment; Theatre: Fr. March 1916, K-in-A 21/4/16, buried Essex Farm Cemetery; Medals: Victory, British, 1914-15 Star; See *N/A* 14/6/16, 7/3/17.

Peacock, John Crosby. Born: Southwell, 1890; Lived: Landseer Road, Southwell; Fam: Br. of Charles Peacock – see above, married Annie; School: Wesleyan, 1897-?; Occup: Threader, E. Carey & Sons; Service: Enlisted 23/9/14, No. 280376, 8th Hussars, S. Notts Hussars, Cpl.; Theatre: Egypt; Medals: Victory, British, 1914-15 Star; See *N/A* 14/6/16, p. 279.

Peacocke, Joseph Evelyn. Born: Upton, 1873-1952; Lived: Clyde House, Southwell; Fam: F. William James Peacock; Occup: Clergyman, C of E; Service: Attested 8/7/15, No. 60998, R.A.M.C., discharged as medically unfit a week later.

Pearsall, Walter. Born: Southwell, 1877; Lived: Kirklington Road, Southwell; Fam: F. John Pearsall (Shoemaker), M. Ann (Beardow, m. 1859), Br. John James (1861), Benjamin (1863), Joseph (1863), Arthur Edwin (1865), Herbert (1867), George Henry (1870-72), Jonathan (1871), S. Mary Ann (1873), married Agnes Davies (Sandever, m. 1908), children: Walter Arthur (1910), Frederick H. (1913); Occup: Clerk – E. Carey & Sons; Service: No. 295697, R.A.F.; Theatre/Medals: No records..

George Peacock (Newark Advertiser)

Peet, Alexander. Born: Southwell, 1890; Lived: Kirklington Road, Southwell; Fam: F. William Peet (Baker & confectioner), M. Emma (Hallam), Br. John William (1874), Frederick Frank (1879), Archibald (1884), Edward B. (1888), S. Sarah Ellen (1876), Ada Cuckson (1881), Gertrude Jesse (1893); School: Wesleyan 1893-?; Occup: Carter with J.H. Kirkby; Service: Attested October 1914, No. 2749, 8th Bn. S/F, No. 82557, Machine Gun Corps, demob. 5/7/18; Theatre: Fr. March 1915, wounded in right arm June 1915, and left arm amputated, April 1917, pension 16/6p p.w.; Medals: Victory, British, 1914-15 Star; See *N/A* 28/10/14, 20/1/15, 9/6/15, 16/6/15, 30/6/15, 22/9/15, 18/4/17, 9/5/17, 26/9/17, 18/4/17, 9/5/17, 26/9/17, 21/11/17.

Peet, Harold Randall. Born: Grantham, 1890; Lived: Private Road, Southwell; Fam: F. John Peet (Saddler & gardener), M. Annie (Randall), married Ethel Mary Hazelwood 1913, children: Kathleen (1917); School: Wesleyan 1899, Natl. 1902-04; Occup: Soldier; Service: No. 599, South

Notts Hussars until 1916, then No. 193780, B Section, 8th Mobile A.A. Bty., Royal Garrison Artillery; Theatre: No record; Medals: Victory, British; See p. 279.

Perkins, Francis. Born:1888-1917; Lived: Old Kent Row, Southwell, later in Hyson Green, Nottingham; Fam: F. Charles Perkins (Lace maker- E Carey & Sons), M. Adelaide Peach (Hickling, m. 1880), Br. Alonzo (1884), Herbert (1884), Horace (1892), Eric (1895), Sydney (1900), S. Ophelia (1898), married Nellie (Squires, m. 1910), children: Francis Alonzo (1911); School: Radford, Natl. 1896-1901; Occup: Lace curtain maker in Nottingham; Service: No. 13190, 17th Bn. S/F; Theatre: Balkans, Fr. His battalion took part in the Battle of Menin Road Ridge, part of the Third Battle of Ypres, it was whilst they were digging in at Bulger Wood that he was K-in-A 20/9/17, commemorated Tyne Cot, Memorial; Medals: Victory, British, 1914-15 Star.

Perkins*, Horace Graham. Born: Stapleford, 1892; Lived: Adams Yard, Westgate, Southwell; Fam: Br. of Francis Perkins – see above, married Rosetta Turner 1916, children: Sarah (1917), Rosetta (1920), Rita (1930); School: Trinity & Natl. 1900-02; Occup: Threader – E. Carey & Sons; Service: No. 882, 1/8th Bn. S/F, No. 477538, Labour Corps; Theatre: Fr. discharged 7/4/16 following wounding; Medals: Victory, British, 1914-15 Star; See *N/A* 20/6/15.

Pickersgill, Frederick George. Born: Worksop, 1880; Lived: New Street, Southwell; Fam: Married Beatrice Sanderson 1911, children: Renie (1912), Denis (1913), Kathleen (1915), Mary (1924); Occup: Coachman; Service: Attested 11/2/15, No. 88202, 69th Brigade, Royal Field Artillery, QMS, demob. 8/4/19; Theatre: Egypt, Mesopotamia; Medals: Victory, British, 1914-15 Star.

Pitchford, George. Born: Southwell, 1893; Lived: Private Road, Southwell; Fam: F. James Pitchford (Roadman), M. Clara (Dowsell), Br. William (1892), S. Florence May (1903), Annie (1907), married Lilian Wilson 1916, children: Lilian M. (1917), George (1920), Dulcie (1923), Clara (1925), Sheila (1927); School: Wesleyan 1898-1906; Occup: Roadman; Service: Attested June 1917, No. 52993, Army Service Corps, No. M2/183579 & No. 50611, 3rd Bn. Northants Regt., demob. 17/1/19; Theatre: Eastern; Medals: Victory, British.

Pitchford, James. Born: Southwell, 1867; Lived: Southwell; Fam: Father of George and William – see above and below, married Clara (Dowswell in 1890); Occup: Roadman; Service: Attested 25/11/14, No. 20088, 2/8th Bn. S/F, discharged as medically unfit 3/5/16; Theatre/Medals: No record.

Pitchford, William. Born: Southwell, 1891; Lived: Back Lane, Southwell; Fam: Br. of George Pitchford – see above; School: Old Basford, Wesleyan 1898-1904; Occup: Tailor & with Merryweather & Son; Service: 1907, 4th Notts Volunteers; 1908, No. 772, 1/8th S/F, discharged as unfit 28/9/14.

Plowman, Samuel. Born Stapleford, Nottingham, 1884; Lived: Spring Cottages, Easthorpe, Southwell; Fam: married to Mabel; Occup: Offal warehouseman; Service: Possibly, No. T4 058092, Army Service Corps & 48387, Hampshire Regt.; Service: Egypt, May 1915; Medals: Victory, British, 15 Star.

Plummer, Edward. Born: Southwell, 1881; Lived: Oxton Road, Southwell; Fam: Br. Richard (1874); Occup: Labourer; Service: Attested 1902, No. 8873, Northumberland Fusiliers, transferred to reserve 1906, mobilized 5/8/14, but discharged 15/8/14 as medically unfit.

Poole*, J. Pte. S/F, no further details.

Powley*, Norman William. Born: Southwell, 1894; Lived: Brinkley; Fam: F. John Powley (Farmer), M. Agnes; School: Natl. 1899 - ?; Occup: Farm

Norman Powley in later life. (Ann Hurt)

worker; Service: No. 1242, 1/8th Bn. S/F, wounded (lost a hand) and discharged 6/9/16; Theatre: Fr. March 1915; Medals: Victory, British, 1914-15 Star.

Pratt, Charles. Born/Family: No details; Service: No. 162374, Royal Garrison Artillery; Medals: Victory, British.

Pritchett, Charles Gill. Born: Southwell, 1882; Lived: New Street, Southwell; Fam: F. William Pritchett (Farmer), M. Emma (Gill), Br. Frank (1884), Thomas (1889), S. Alice (1881), Annie Maria (1893), married Eleanor Goodson 1912, children: Edith J. (1912); Occup: Baker; Service: Enlisted 8/4/15, No. S/408162, Royal Army Service Corps, demob. 30/1/19; Theatre: No record; Medals: Victory, British.

Pugh, Thomas. Born: 1899, Southwell; Lived: Kirklington Road, Southwell; Fam: F. Edward John Pugh (Engine driver – flour mill), M. Matilda, Br. Edward J. (1893), Herbert (1908), S. Norah Alice (1898), Eliza (1904), Harriet (1895); School: Infants & Natl. 1906-11; Service: No record; See Parish Magazine July 1918.

Pulford, Reginald B. Born: Loughborough, 1893; Lived: Pollards Lane, Southwell; Fam: F. Stephen Pulford (Farmer), M. Clara (Daykin), married May Wagstaff 1923, children: Stephen (1924) – teacher at Minster School, Elizabeth C (1926); Service: RAF, attached to 316th Siege Bn. Royal Garrison Artillery; Theatre/Medals: No records.

Randall (or Randell), Frank Conway. Born: Tipton-on-the-Hill, Leics, died 1917; No family details; Lived: Southwell; Occup: Baker with J.H. Kirkby; Service: No. S4/143586, Army Service Corps; Theatre: Salonika, India, Egypt and Mesopotamia, suffered from fever in October/November 1916, died of heat exhaustion 16/7/17, buried, Basra War Cemetery; Medals: Victory, British; See *N/A* 20/10/15, 1/11/16, 1/8/17, 8/8/17, 12/9/17.

Raworth, George H. Born: Southwell, 1891; Lived: Westhorpe, Southwell; Fam: Br. Leonard Raworth – see below; School: Bleasby, Natl. 1903-05; Service: No. 55150, Worcester Regt., No. 40034, South Staffordshire Regt.; Theatre: No record; Medals: Victory, British.

Raworth*, Leonard. Born: Southwell, 1893-1918; Lived Kirklington Road, Southwell; Fam: F. Nathan Raworth (Labourer), M. Sarah, Br. William (1885), George H. (1891), S. Mary (1871), Georgina (1879), Edith (1891); School: Wesleyan 1896-?; Occup: Carter – J. H. Kirkby; Service: Enlisted 1911, Nos. 243 & 1243, 1/8th Bn. S/F, discharged 7/6/16; Theatre: Fr. March 1915; Medals: Victory, British, 1914-15 Star. Discharged as medically unfit and died 10/8/18, buried Minster Church Yard with full military honours; See *N/A* 14/8/18.

Raworth, William. Born: Southwell, 1885; Lived: Bradfields Cottages, Easthorpe, Southwell; Fam: Br. of Leonard Raworth – see above; School: Wesleyan 1891-1896; Occup: Grocer's errand boy; Service: No. 67003, Durham Light Infantry, No. 22549, Labour Corps; Theatre: No record; Medals: Victory, British.

Raynor, Frank. Born: Southwell, 1893-1915; Lived: King Street, Southwell; Fam: Br. of George Henry Raynor – see below; School: Wesleyan, Natl. 1903-05; Occup: Gardener, Merryweather's, Silk Hand, Maythorne; Service: Enlisted 1911, No. 11852, 1st Bn. S/F, served in India pre-war; Theatre: Fr. Nov. 1914. His battalion was involved in the Battle of Neuve Chapelle where there were heavy casualties and he was K-in-A 12/3/15, memorial Le Touquet; Medals: Victory, British, 1914-15 Star; See *N/A* 5/5/15, 15/9/15.

Raynor*, George Henry. Born: Southwell, 1892; Lived: Easthorpe, Southwell; Fam: F. Arthur Raynor (Lace maker – E. Carey & Sons), M. Sarah (Henton, m. 1889), Br. James William (1891), Frank (1894), John (1902), S. Eliza (1895), Fanny (1899), married Mary Ellen Shaw 27/4/14, children: Eva Ellen (1917), Nellie (1919); School: Wesleyan 1896-1905; Occup: Lace threader –

E. Carey & Sons; Service: No. 1019, 1/8th Bn. S/F, signed on again in T.A. 11/6/20; Theatre: Fr. March 1915; Medals: Victory, British, 1914-15 Star.

Reddish, William George. Born: Nottingham, 1884; Lived: Westgate, Southwell; Fam: M. Edith Ellen (Hall); Service: Attested 26/9/14, No. 2572, 8th Bn. S/F, No. 83714, 229th Machine Gun Corps; Theatre: Fr. March 1915, Egypt, suffered two knee injuries and malaria, resulting in pension of 5/6d p.w. increased to 8/1 p.w.; Medals: Victory, British, 1914-15 Star.

Redmile, John William. Born: Bulwell, Nottingham, 1898; Lived: Back Lane, Southwell; Fam: F. William Redmile (Twisthand – E. Carey & Sons), M. Sarah Ann, Br. George Herbert (1899), S. Mary Ellen (1894), Ada (1895), Annie (1897); Occup: Gardener, Merryweather's; Service: Enlisted Nov. 1916, No. 161216, Royal Army Medical Corps 8th Coy, No. 42001, 5th Reserve, Durham Light Infantry, demob. January 1920; Theatre: Salonika, April 1917, suffered severe malaria; Medals: Victory, British.

Reeves, Frederick James. Born: Upton, 1889: Lived: King Street, Southwell; Fam: Brother of George William Reeves - see below; School: Natl. 1897-1902; Occup: Assistant butcher; Service: No. BZ5719, RNVR, President Div. III; Theatre/Medals: No record.

Reeves, George William. Born: Upton, 1894; Lived: King Street, Southwell; Fam: F. Obediah Reeves (Butcher), M. Anne, Br. Robert Sydney (1898), Frederick (1889), John (1892), George (1894), Walter (1900), S. Lillie (1887), Winnie (1893), Olive (1897), Ethel (1908); School: Upton, Natl. 1909-10; Occup: Grocer's Assistant; Service: No. 7625, 5th Dragoon Guards, Cpl.; Theatre: Fr.; Medals: Victory, British, 1914-15 Star.

Reeves, Robert Sydney. Born: Upton, 1898; Lived: King Street, Southwell; Fam: Brother of George William Reeves - see above; School: Upton, Natl. 1909-12; Service: No. 480296, Royal Field Artillery; Theatre: Fr.; Medals: Victory, British.

Renshaw, Frank. Born: Salterford House, Calverton, 1888; Fam: F. Thomas Renshaw (Gamekeeper), M. Hannah (Kitchen), Br. John Joseph (1877), George Jarvis (1878), Tom (1882), S. Lilly (1880), Minnie S. Annie (1887), Charlotte (1893), Olive Annie (1910); Service: No. 020895, Army Ordnance Corps; Theatre/Medals: No records.

Revill, Frank. Born: Southwell, 1880; Lived: Easthorpe, Southwell; Fam: Br. of Richard Revill – see below, married: Kate (Cottam m. 1901, children: George R. (1911); Occup: Lace maker – E. Carey & Sons; Service: Attested August 1914, No. 2069, 8th Bn. S/F, No. 79643, wounded 1915, Royal Defence Corps; Theatre: Fr. Feb 1915; Medals: Victory, British, 1914-15 Star; See *N/A 8/9/17*.

Revill*, Richard Junior. Born: Southwell, 1886 - 1942; Lived: Spring Terrace, Southwell; Fam: F. Richard Revill (Labourer), M. May (Stanfield, m. 1880), Br. Frank (1880), John (1881), Tim (1891), S. Louie (1879), Winnie (1894), Gladys (1896), married Jessie Louisa A. (Rudge, m. 1917), children: Robert (1921), Vera ((1923), James R. (1930), Ronald (1932), Alan A. (1934); School: Infants and Natl. 1893-1897; Occup: Warper – E Carey & Sons; Service: Enlisted T.A. 1908, No. 730, 1/8th Bn. S/F, L/Cpl., No. 82569, Machine Gun Corps, Cpl.; Theatre: Fr. March 1915, wounded 10/8/15 and returned to U.K., discharged 31/3/16; Medals: Victory, British, 1914-15 Star; See *N/A 8/9/17*.

Revill, Timothy. Born: Halam, 1892; Lived: Easthorpe, Southwell; Fam: Br. of Richard Revill – see above; School: Easthorpe, Natl. 1909-15; Occup: Domestic gardener; Service: No. 201914, Royal Scots; Theatre: Fr., wounded April 1918; Medals: Victory, British; See *N/A 24/4/18*.

Richardson, George. Born: Halam, 1888-1916; Lived: Easthorpe, Southwell; Fam: Br. of William J. Richardson – see below; School: Trinity, Natl. 1897-1901; Occup: Gardener Merryweather's, Coal merchant's labourer, Midland Railway Co; Service: Enlisted 1914, No. 63348, 117th

Ammunition Column, Royal Field Artillery; Theatre: Fr. Sept. 1915, and Salonika, died 21/10/16 in Malta from malaria and dysentery; Medals: Victory, British, 1914-15 Star; See *N/A* 8/8/17.

Richardson*, William John. Born: Halam, 1883; Lived Carlton, Worksop; Fam: F. Samuel Richardson (Agricultural labourer), M. Mary (Dixon, m. 1882 - Charlady), Br. John (1885), George (1888), S. Sarah (1888); Occup: Gardener, formerly at Norwood Park; Service: No. 2031, 1/8th Bn. S/F, No. 32546, Oxford & Bucks Light Infantry, demob. 13/3/19; Theatre: Fr. March 1915; Medals: Victory, British, 1914-15 Star.

Rick, George Arthur. Born: Rolleston, 1883; Lived: King Street, Southwell; Fam: F. George Rick, M. Anne (Bramley, m. 1882), married Minnie (Hale, m. 1908), children: Constance (1909), Florence (1910), George (1911); Occup: Engine driver, flour mill; Service: No. 25966, 9th Bn. King's Own Royal Regt.; Theatre: No record; Medals: Victory, British.

George Richardson (David Hutchinson)

Rickett*, John Robert. Born: Southwell, 1879 - 1941; Lived: King Street, Southwell; Fam: F. John Rickett (dec'd), M. Mary Ellen (Horsley, m. first 1878, married second George Childs 1886, died 1900), S. Mabel Elizabeth (1883), Florence Annie (1888), George Cyril (1891), Bertie Harry (1894), married Susan (Leeson, m. 1900), children; Annie (1900), Ellen (1902), Francis (1906), Florence (1908); Occup: Lace maker – E. Carey & Sons; Service: Enlisted T.A. 1908, previously Volunteers, No. 753, 1/8th Bn. S/F, demob. 31/3/16; Theatre: No foreign service.

Ridgard*, William Henry. Born: Woodborough, 1871-1915; Lived: Main Street, Woodborough; Fam: F. William Henry (hairdresser), M. Elizabeth (Shipley), Br. James (1874), Richard (1880), Claude Harold (1891), S. Elizabeth Ann (1872), Gertrude (1875), Emily Martin (1886), Beatrice Lilian (1889), married Lilly (Stevenson, m. 1890), children: they had 5 children, 4 died in infancy; Occup: Hairdresser; Service: No. 755, S/W, L/Cpl. – long serving in T.A.; Theatre: Fr. March 1915, K-in-A 8/5/15, buried Loker Churchyard, West-Vlaanderen, Belgium, grave 11 B 4; Medals: Victory, British, 1914-15 Star.

Ridge, A. Born: Southwell; Lived: Back Lane, Southwell; Fam: Believed to be brother of Ernest and Harold Ridge – see below; Service: 3/8th S/F; See *N/A* 9/6/15.

Ridge, Ernest. Born: Southwell, 1895; Lived: Back Lane, Southwell; Fam: F. James M Ridge (Carter), M. Harriett Ann (Wombwell), Br. Harold (1897), James (1901), Albert (1905), Wilfred Eric (1909), S. Olive (1894), Hilda (1899), Frances Ann (1909); School: Wesleyan 1898-?; Occup: Boot repairer; Service: Nos. 2127, 305399, S/F, L/Cpl., demob. Feb 1919; Theatre: Fr. March 1915; Medals: Victory, British, 1914-15 Star.

Ridge, Harold. Born: Southwell, 1897; Lived: Back Lane Southwell; Fam: Br. of Ernest Ridge – see above; School: Wesleyan, 1900-?; Occup: Telegraph boy; Service: Enlisted 1/6/15, No. 4054, 2/8th S/F; Theatre: Ireland, wounded May 1915, lost foot June 1916, discharged 7/10/16; Medals: Victory, British; See *N/A* 10/5/16, 6/6/17.

Ridge, James Edward. Born: Southwell, 1900; Lived: Back Lane, Southwell; Fam: Br. of Ernest, Harold and James – see above; School: Wesleyan, 1909-13; Service: Attested 21/4/18, No. 110320, 5th Bn. Durham Light Infantry, demob. 24/1/19; Theatre/Medals: No records.

Rippin, Archibald. Born: Hawton, Newark, 1894; Lived: Cross Keys, Upton. Fam: Brother of John Christopher Rippin – see below; Occup: Grocer's assistant; Service: Attested 25/1/15, No. 85132, Royal Field Artillery, Driver; Theatre: Fr. 8/6/15; Medals: Victory, British, 1914-15 Star.

Rippin, John Christopher (Chris). Born: Kelham, 1898-1993; Lived: Cross Keys, Upton; Fam: F. Joseph Rippin (Publican and pig breeder), M. Ann (Mann, m. 1876), Br. Archibald (1894),

Arthur (1900), Marmaduke (1902), Raymond (1904), Joseph (1911), S. Blanche (1889), Olive (1991), Gertrude (1891), Dorothy (1893), May (1895), Kathleen (1899), – they had 16 children, 5 of whom had died by 1911; School: Upton, Wesleyan 1908-11; Occup: Grocer's assistant - J.J. Bates; Service: Attested 28/10/16, No. 31716, South Staffordshire Regiment; Theatre: Fr.; Medals: Victory, British; See pp. 264-5.

Robinson, Frank. Born: Southwell, 1895; Lived: Queen Street, Southwell; Fam: F. Frederick Robinson (Hairdresser), M. Edith (Stanley, m. 1892), Br. Walter (1896); School: Miss Mason's, Natl. 1907-10; Occup: Apprentice hairdresser; Service: No. 70161, 16th Bn. S/F, Cpl.; Theatre: Fr. wounded near Thiepval 1916; Medals: Victory, British; See *N/A* 4/10/16, 24/10/17.

Robinson, George William. Born: Southwell, 1884; Fam: No record; Service: No. 11692, 2nd Bn. S/F, A/Sgt.; Theatre: Fr. September 1914, P.O.W. at Mons; Medals: Victory, British, 1914-15 Star.; See p. 269.

Robinson, Walter. Born: Southwell, 1897-1917; Lived: Queen Street, Southwell; Fam: Br. of Frank Robinson – see above; School: Miss Mason's, Natl. 1907-10; Occup: Apprentice hairdresser; Service: Called up January 1916, No. 306547, 2/8th Bn. S/F, L/Cpl.; Theatre: Ireland, April 1916, Fr. February 1917, K-in-A 26/9/17, buried New Irish Farm Cemetery; Medals: Victory, British; See *N/A* 24/10/17.

Robotham, James. Lived: Pollards Lane, Southwell; Service: No. 239649, Durham Light Infantry; Medals: No record.

Roe, Richard Chapman. Born: Worksop, 1894; Lived: Westgate, Southwell; Fam: F. John Roe (Oil merchant & general dealer), M. Lois (Brailsford), Br. John (1901), William Edgar (1907), Eric (1909), Herbert (1911), S. Doris (1899), married Emma Jane Cox, 1916, children: Marjorie (1919); School: Wesleyan, 1897-?; Occup: Assisted in family business; Service: Enlisted June 1916, called up August 1917, Royal Army medical Corps, No. 2R/5/126737, 7th Tank Regt., discharged 26/6/18 on health grounds; Theatre: No record; Medals: Victory, British.

Rogers, William John. Born: Bolsover, 1900; Lived: Upton; Fam: F. William John Rogers (Farm labourer), M. Annie (Elston, m. 1898), Br. Bailey (1903), S. Annie (1905), Mary (1910); Theatre/Medals: No records.

Rose, Cyril Purnell. Born: Stafford, 1895-1915; Lived: Easthorpe, Southwell (1910); Fam: F. William Rose (Schoolmaster), M. Brittania (Bethel), Br. Frederick William (1890), S. Elsie Brittania (1889), Hilda Tryphenia (1893), Marjorie Victoria May (1897); School: Grasmore, Chester; Natl. 1904-07, Minster 1908-1910 (Choral scholar); Occup: Clerk, Ironworks, motor engineer; Service: King's Royal Rifles; Minster School records state K-in-A 29/3/15.

Rose, William. Born: Southwell, 1883; Lived: Westgate, Southwell; Fam: F. Mark Rose (Joiner), M. Eliza (Goodrum, m. 1878); Occup: Twist hand – E. Carey & Sons; Service: No. 133341 A/M 3rd/34th Royal Artillery, R.A.F.; Theatre/Medals: No records.

Rumford, Edwin Cecil. Born: Southwell, 1891; Lived: King Street, Southwell; Fam: Br. of Herbert William Rumford – see below, married Jane T. (Edward, m. 1916); School: Infants & Natl. 1897-1902,

Cyril Rose
(Newark Advertiser)

Minster; Service R.A.F., Lt.; Theatre: Fr.; Medals: include St George's Medal 2nd Class, awarded by Czar of Russia; See *N/A* 8/9/15 & pp 307.

Rumford*, Herbert William. Born: Southwell, 1889; Lived: King Street, Southwell; Fam: F. William Rumford (Grocer and confectioner), M. Frances Ann R. (Tuck, m. 1887), Br. Edwin Cecil (1891), married Violet (Scarborough, m. 1914), children: Frances M.; School: Infants and Natl. 1895-1900; Occup: Assisting in family business; Service: No. 875, 1/8th Bn. S/F, Sgt. – long serving in T.A., No. 240699, R.A.F.; Theatre: Believed to be France; Medals: Not recorded as he transferred to R.A.F., assume Victory, British, 1914-15 Star, also Territorial Force War Medal.

Rumley, Arthur. Born: Ollerton 1891-1916; Lived: Lockwell Farm, Bilsthorpe, previously Union Workhouse, Upton with his siblings; Fam: F. William Rumley, M. Annie, Br. John William (1880), Thomas (1886), Arthur (1888) S. Agnes (1880), Jane (1887); School: Dame School, Natl. 1897-1900; Occup: Waggoner; Service: Attested September 1914, No. 12085, 2nd Bn. Leicestershire Regt., Theatre: Mesopotamia February 1916, wounded March 1916, DoW 7/4/16, buried Amara War Cemetery; Medals: Victory, British; See *N/A* 14/6/16.

Russell, Sidney. Born: Cardiff, 1899; Lived: Westgate, Southwell; Fam: Living with guardian, William Taylor (Lace maker – E. Carey & Sons); Service: No records; See Parish Magazine July 1918.

Saddington*, Walter Frederick. Born: Oakham, Rutland, 1866; Lived: Westgate, Southwell; Fam: married to Helena in 1895, children: Frederick (1905), Eveline (1907); School: Minster 1910-14; Occup: Professional soldier; Service: Enlisted in 1883, Derbyshire Regt., Sgt., served in India, East Indies and Aden, discharged 1912, re-enlisted No. 26571, 1/8th Bn. S/W. C. Sgt., demob. 1919; Theatre: Fr. March 1916 – March 1917; Medals: Victory, British, India Medals (2) from previous service; See pp. 266-7.

Salt, Arthur Herbert Lloyd. Born: Southwell, 1898; Lived: Station Road, Southwell; Fam: F. Arthur Salt (Schoolteacher), M. Emilie Charlotte (Niblett), S. Emily Gertrude (1881), Edith Winifred (1885), Ethel Constance (1889-93); School: Natl. 1905-10, Minster 1910-16; Occup: Clerk Smith's Bank; Service: No. 340937, 37th Bn. Northumberland Fusiliers, L/Cpl.; Theatre/Medals: No record; See *N/A* 22/11/16 & p. 307.

Sargeant, Edward. Born: Newmarket, 1889-1916; Lived: Westgate, Southwell; Fam: F. Thomas Sargeant, S. Fanny (1893), Nester (1895), married Ethel Smith August 1914, children: Florence Ethel (1915); Occup: Baker; Service: Previously A.S.C., attested April 1916, No. 24602, 3rd Bn. later 8th Bn. North Staffordshire Regt., L/Cpl.; Theatre: Fr., involved in an attack on German trenches south of Gradcourt, there was hand-to-hand fighting, the men were cut off and he was K-in-A 19/11/16. Memorial Stump Road Cemetery; Medals: Victory, British.

Savage, George Anthony. Lived: Halam Road, Southwell; Service: No. 276590, R.A.F.

Sayers, Alfred. Born: Easton, Suffolk, 1896; Lived: Norwood Fields, Southwell; Fam: Married Annie Elizabeth (Eaton), children: Joseph Alfred (1906), Walter Robert (1909), Florence Ann (1908); Occup: Horseman/Waggoner J. H. Kirkby, previously miller; Service: Southwell Tribunal, exempt until October 1916, No. M/323565, Army Service Corps; Theatre: Fr. June 1918; Medals: Victory, British.

Scarborough, Edward. Born: Southwell, 1893; Lived: Shoulder of Mutton, Westgate, Southwell; Fam: F. Frederick Scarborough (Licensed Victualer), M. Eliza Anne, S. Violet (1991); School: Holy Trinity, Natl. 1900-07; Occup: Solicitor's Clerk, J.K. Lane; Service: 4th Bn. Notts Volunteers; Theatre: Home; Medals: No record.

Schumach, Frederick Cornelius Henry. Born: Southwell, 1891; Lived: Church Street, Southwell; Fam: F. Henry John Schumach (Taxidermist), M. Lucy Kate (Doncaster); Br. Henry John (1886-7), George John D. (1893), Lucy Kate D. (1885), Mary Winifred (1889-96), married

Nora Marsh 1915, children: Henry J. G. (1920); School: Infant & Natl. 1897-99; Occup: Taxidermist, Lay Clerk at Minster; Service: No. DM2/169380, 738th MG Co., Army Service Corps; Theatre: Fr. 1916, wounded and suffered meningitis; Medals: Victory, British; See *N/A* 31/5/16, 14/6/16, 19/7/16, 2/1/18.

Schumach, George John Darcy. Born: Southwell, 1892-1973; Lived: Church Street, Southwell; Fam: Br. of Frederick Schumach – see above. Married Jessie Young 1928, children: David 1934; School: Infant & Natl. 1898-1900, Minster 1900-11 – choral scholarship, Nottingham University; Occup: Trainee teacher; Service: 2/8th Bn. S/F, Q. Sgt. Maj., London Regt., Lt.; Theatre: Fr. February 1917, wounded twice, latterly November, 1917; Medals: Victory, British; See *N/A* 27/1/15, 31/5/16, 2/1/18, see pp. 302, 307.

Scott, John William. Born: Southwell, 1886; Lived: Southwell; Fam: F. James Scott, M. Fanny (Lacey m. 1885), Br. Donald (1889), Walter (1904), Harold (1908), S. Eliza Ann (1885), Janet Jessie (1888), Margaret (1891), Ann (1894), Katie (1897), Alice (1906) – there were 13 siblings in total, of which 3 died, married Mary Lettice (Gilbert m. 1911), children: Florence Hester (1913), John William (1914), Gilbert H. (1917), Dorothea M. (1919), Margaret (1923); Occup: Wagoner; Service: Attested 26/1/15, No. 6046, Royal Engineers; Theatre: Dardanelles & Fr.; Medals: Victory, British.

Scott, Sydney James. Born: Appleby, Westmorland, 1882; Lived: Station Road, Southwell; Fam: Married Maude Cicely Witherbed 1910; Occup: Buyer – Caudwell & Sons; Service: Conditional exemption until Jan 1916, No. A/358107, Army Service Corps, Cpl..; Theatre: Fr.; Medals: Victory, British; See *N/A* 31/10/17.

Scraton, Arthur. Born: Southwell, 1893; Lived: Back Lane, Westhorpe, Southwell; Fam: F. William (Builder's labourer), M. Charlotte (Laughton), 13 children, 4 died; Br. William (1882), Henry (1885), Frederick (1886), Thomas (1899), Frank (1890), Ernest Walter (1902), S. Ada (1895) and a further child; School: Trinity, Wesleyan 1903-07; Occup: Farm labourer; Service: T.A. 8th Bn. S/F, but unfit, later re-joined, No. 476624 Royal Engineers; Theatre: No record; Medals: Victory, British.

Scraton, Frank. Born: Southwell 1890; Lived: Back Lane, Westhorpe, Southwell; Fam: Br. of Arthur Scraton – see above, married Georgina (Stanley m. 1918); School: Trinity, Wesleyan until 1902; Occup: Farm labourer; Service: No. 11786, 2nd Bn. S/F, C.S.M., Theatre: Fr. September 1914, P.O.W.; Medals: Victory, British, 1914-15 Star; See *N/A* 10/10/17, 15/1/19, & P. 269.

Scraton, Robert. Born: Southwell, 1894-1918; Lived: Holy Trinity Cottage, Westhorpe, Southwell; Fam: F. Frederick Scraton (Domestic gardener), M. Ellen (Brown, m. 1893), Br. Marshall (1903), S. Elizabeth (1896), Annie (1897), Laura (1898), Clara (1899), Sarah Ellen (1901), Kate (1905); School: Trinity, Natl. 1902-08; Occup: Telegraph messenger & auxiliary postman; Service: No. 34295, S/F & No. 128677, 47th Bn. Machine Gun Corps, L/Cpl.; Theatre: Ireland, Fr. December 1916, K-in-A 3/6/18, buried Franvillers Communal Cemetery Extension; Medals: Victory, British; See *N/A* 26/6/18.

Scraton, Thomas. Born: Southwell, 1899; Lived: Back Lane, Westhorpe, Southwell; Fam: Br. of Arthur Scraton – see above; School: Trinity, Wesleyan 1907-14; Occup: Farm labourer; Service: Enlisted 23/2/17, Nos. 78925, 65942, Durham Light Infantry, P.O.W.; Theatre: Fr. March 1918; Medals: Victory, British; See pp. 268-9.

Selby, James Henry. Born: Southwell, 1899; Lived: Kirklington Road, Southwell; Fam: F. Henry Selby (Warehouseman), M. Emma (Gascoine), Br. Joseph (1896), S. Olive (1895), Emma (1896), Joseph (1896) – all siblings dead by 1911, married Mary Flaherty, children: Patrick (1923), Emma (1924), Kevin (1930); School: Infants & Natl. 1905-11; Service: No. 480515(T)3049, 62nd Division

Royal Engineers; Theatre: No record; Medals: Victory, British; Post war lived in Private Road, Southwell.

Selwyn, Edward Gordon (Revd.). Born: Liverpool, 1886; Lived: Bishop's Manor, Southwell, prior to schooling; Fam: F. Edward Selwyn (Clerk in Holy Orders), M. Lucy Ada (Arnold), married Phyllis Eleanor Hoskyns (Bishop's daughter), children: Christopher A. (1915), Edward C. J. (1925); School: Eton; Occup: Lecturer at Cambridge University; Service: Royal Artillery, Chaplains Division; Theatre: No record; Medals: Victory, British.

Sensecall, Charlie. Born: Southwell, 1878; Lived: Westhorpe, Southwell; Fam: F. James Sensecall (Farm labourer), M. Agnes (Shevings, m. 1861), Br. William (1862), Henry (1863), George (1866), John (1867), James (1869), Frank (1871), Edwin (1873), S. Agnes (1865), Bertha (1875); Occup: Postman; Service: No. 41560, Yorkshire & Lancashire Regt., No. 39564, S/F, No. 23461, South Staffordshire Regt., No. 55796, Durham Light Infantry, No. 17859, Labour Corps, No. 132599, Royal Army Medical Corps, No. WR/ 344732, Royal Engineers; Theatre: no record; Medals: Victory, British.

Seward, Harry. Born: Bridgwater, 1883 - 1916; Lived: Southwell; Fam: F. George Seward (Gardener), M. Elizabeth, Br. George William (1879), James Leonard (1881), Harry (1882), Charlie (1885) S. Ada Elizabeth (1889), Lily (1894), Daisy (1898); Occup: Grocer; Service: No. 806, Rhodesia Regiment; Theatre: Africa, March 1915, K-in-A Kenya 11/3/16, buried Taveta Military Cemetery, Grave No. IXA6; Medals: Victory, British, 1914-15 Star; Does not feature amongst Southwell War dead on Minster memorial.

Sharley, Arthur. Born: Heanor, 1887; Lived: Station Road, Southwell; Fam: F. Frank (Groom), M. Sarah, Br. William (1886), Walter (1889), Ephraim (1906), Ernest (1908), S. Betsy (1884), Alice (1892), Evelyn (1897), Gladys (1901) – there were 16 children, of which 10 survived; Occup: Coal miner; Service: Attested 29/11/15, No. 129439, Royal Garrison Artillery, 91st Brigade, invalided home after illness Jan. 1917; Theatre: No record; Medals: Victory, British.

Sharman, Charles. Born: Counthorpe, Lincs, 1888; Lived: Halam, Nr. Southwell; Fam: Br. of John Sharman – see below, married Hannah (Holmes m. 1909), children: Emma (1909), John Henry (1912), Barbara (1916); Occup: Market gardener; Service: Called up 1916, S/F, No. 65937, Machine Gun Corps, demob. 1919 to Army Reserve; Theatre: Fr.; Medals: Victory, British.

Sharman, Henry. Born: Counthorpe, Lincs, 1893; Lived: The Holme, Westhorpe, Southwell; Fam: Brother of John Sharman – see below, married Frances Cooling 1914; children: Ernest (1913), Frances (1915); School: Woodborough, Natl. 1904-05; Occup: Flour miller; Service: Enlisted 1917, No. M351256, 52nd M.T. Company, Royal Army Service Corps; Theatre: U.K.; Medals: No record.

Sharman, Herbert. Born: Appleby, Lincs, 1879; Lived: Burgage, Southwell; Fam: Married to Annie, children: Mary; Occup: Delivery man, J.H. Kirkby; Service: Applied to Tribunal 3/6/16, exempt until 1/10/16 - no military records.

Sharman*, John (Jack). Born: Counthorpe, Lincs., 1895-1915; Lived: The Holme, Westhorpe; Fam: F. Thomas Sharman (Traction engine driver), M. Hannah, Br. Thomas (1885), Charles (1888), William (1891), Henry (1893), Michael (1896), Richard (1897), James (1900), George (1908), S. Elizabeth (1883), Anne (1886), Jane (1890), Ruth (1903), May (1906); School: Woodborough, Natl. 1904-07; Occup: Gentleman's servant; Service: Enlisted 3/11/11, No. 1245, 1/8th Bn. S/F, Cpl.; Theatre: Fr. March 1915, K-in-A 14/10/15 at Hohenzollern Redoubt, commemorated Loos, Pas de Calais; Medals: Victory, British, 1914-15 Star, D.C.M., St George's Order (Russian award); See *N/A* 23/6/15, 7/7/15, 15/9/15, 20/10/15, 12/1/16, & pp. 215, 270-1.

Sharman, Richard. Born: Counthorpe, Lincs, 1896; Lived: The Holme, Westhorpe; Fam: Br. of John Sharman – see above, married Hannah Mary Pitts in 1921, children: Edward (1921), Robert (1922), Mary (1925), Betty (1929); School: Woodborough, Natl. 1904-09; Occup: Nurseryman, with Merryweather's, and Grummitt of North Fen; Service: Enlisted 14/4/14, No. 11379, Leicestershire Regt., 3rd Bn., Cpl. (1917), demob. 19/2/19 to Army Reserve; Theatre: Fr. 1915 with 3rd Bn., Basra 1915, India 1916, Egypt 1916, wounded March 1916 and suffered malaria, hospital treatment in Basra, Bombay and Alexandria, Palestine in 1917/18; Medals: Victory, British, 1914-15 Star; Post War lived in Bourne Lincs., and was a rose grower and agricultural contractor, also dealt in army surplus vehicles.

Sharman, William. Born: Counthorpe, Lincs, 1891; Lived: Westgate, Southwell; Fam: Br. of John Sharman - see above; Occup: Head roller man, Caudwell's flour mill; Service: Applied to Tribunal 3/6/16, exempt until 1/10/16 - no military records.

Sharpe, Oliver. Born: Leicester, 1868-1918; Lived: Westgate, Southwell; Fam: Wife Elizabeth Harriet, children: Oliver (1903), Walter (1906), Horace (1908), Ernest (1910), Mabel (1891), Gertrude (1895), Ethel (1897), Minnie (1899); Occup: Boot maker; Service: No. 09187, Army Ordnance Corps, died 15/1/18, buried Leeds, Harehills Cemetery; Theatre: Assume UK; Medals: No record.

Richard Sharman (Robin Sharman)

Shaw, Thomas. Born: Bulwell, Nottingham, 1890; Lived: Vine Cottages, Southwell; Fam: F. Thomas Shaw (Twisthand – E. Carey & Sons), M. Maria, S. Nancy (1893), Florence (1897); School: Bulwell Natl, Natl. 1898-1903; Occup: Twisthand – E. Carey & Sons; Service: No. 295709, R.A.F. – no further details.

Shelbourne, William H. Born: Welby, Lincolnshire, 1893; Lived: Southwell; Fam: F. John W. Shelbourne (Pyclet salesman), M. Mary Eliza (Barker, m. 1872), Br. Herbert (1896), H… A (1901), J… (1907) (initials only on Census form), S. Ethel (1895), Florence (1899); Occup: Baker, J. H. Kirkby; Service: No. S1435889, Army Service Corps; Theatre: No record; Medals: Victory, British; See *N/A* 20/10/15, 1/8/17.

Sheppard*, Arthur Cyril. Born: Mansfield Woodhouse, 1889 - 1915; Lived: Waterloo House, Southwell; Fam: F. Arthur Sheppard (Jobbing gardener), M. Fanny, Br. William (1881), Charles (1885), John (1894), S. Lilly, (1883), Hetter (1887), Fanny May (1892), Helling (1897); School: Wesleyan 1895-97, Natl. 1897-1902; Occup: Lace hand – E. Carey & Sons; Service: Enlisted 1908, No. 752, 1/8th Bn. S/F, Sgt.; Service: Fr. March 1915. Awarded the D.C.M. – see *Newark Advertiser*. In November 1915 the battalion was in the Richebourg sector when part of the trench parapet collapsed and he was killed by machine gun fire - K-in-A 22/11/15, buried St. Vaast Post Military Cemetery, Richebourg-L'avoue; Medals: Victory, British, 1914-15 Star, D.C.M. (leading a bombing party under heavy fire); See *N/A* 22/9/15, 1/12/15, 12/1/16, & p. 215.

Arthur C. Sheppard (David Hutchinson)

Sheppard*, J. T. No biographical record; Service: 1/8th Bn. S/F; Theatre/Medals: No records..

Sheppard, John Winfield. Born: Radcliffe-on-Trent, 1894; Lived: Waterloo House, King Street, Southwell; Fam: Br. of Arthur Cyril Sheppard – see above; School: Wesleyan, Natl. 1903-05; Service: No. 40380, Royal Army Medical Corps; Theatre: Fr. January 1915; Medals: Victory, British, 1914-15 Star; See *N/A* 22/9/15.

Sheppard, William A. Born: Mansfield Woodhouse, 1881; Lived: Burton-on-Trent; Fam: Br. of Arthur C. Sheppard – see above; Occup: Estate labourer; Service: No. 2972 Staffordshire

Yeomanry, No. 300306, Corps of Hussars, Cpl., demob. 24/3/19; Theatre: Egypt, November 1915; Medals: Victory, British, 1914-15 Star; See *N/A* 22/9/15.

Shepperson, William Henry. Born: Bingham, 1899; Lived: Ropewalk, Southwell; Fam: F. Henry (Market gardener), M. Julia (Rolfe), Br. James (1902), S Lilian (1891), married Alice V. Clyne, children: Arnold H (1925), Julia V. (1931); Service: Enlisted 23/2/17, No. 71066, Durham Light Infantry; Theatre: Fr. March 1918, P.O.W.; Medals: Victory, British; See p. 269.

Sheward, William Henry. Born: Southwell, 1897-1916; Lived: Meadows, Nottingham; Fam: F. William Henry Sheward (Railway guard), M. Anna (Meadon), Br. Walter (1898), Arthur Redvers (1900), Francis Hector (1903), S. Edith Alice (1905); Service: No. 63364, 'A' Battery, 110th Brigade, Royal Field Artillery; Theatre: Fr. September 1915, K-in-A 29/7/16, buried Becourt Military Cemetery; Medals: Victory, British, 1914-15 Star.

Sides, Archibold Wilfred. Born: Oxford, 1880; Lived: King Street, Southwell; Fam: Married Kate Saxe (Holness m.1906), children: John Wilfred (1909), Stella K. (1910), Eric F. (1912); Occup: Grocery manager; Service: No. A/386616, E.F.C., Army Service Corps; Theatre: no record; Medals: Victory, British.

Simpkins, Arthur Thomas. Born: Braybrooke, 1881; Lived: Norwood Fields; Fam: F. George Simpkins (Farm labourer), M. Mary A, Br. Charles A (1882), George Edward (1885), Walter J. (1887), S. Ada E. (1880), Annie (1889), Ethel (1890), married Mary J. Bacon 1901, child: George A. (1911); Occup: Chauffeur; Service: No. M-281103, Royal Army Service Corps, A/Cpl.; Theatre: No record; Medals: Victory, British.

Simpkins, Charles Alfred. Born: Braybrooke, Northants, 1882; Lived: Westhorpe, Southwell; Fam: Brother of Arthur Thomas Simpkins –see above, Married Jane Osborne 1908, children: George A. (1913), Edith A. (1916); Occup: Carrier; Service: No. 5787, 717th Labour Corps; Theatre/Medals: No information.

Smith, Albert R. Born: Grantham, 1881; Lived: Maythorne, Southwell; Fam: F. William Smith (Shoemaker), M. Elizabeth Mary (Widdowson), Br. George W. (1882), Charles Ernest (1885), Herbert H. (1887), Walter Henry (1892), Joseph Ernest (1893), Thomas Harold (1904), Leonard (1908), S. Mabel E. (1884), Charlotte Annie (1895), Dorothy Blanchard (1900); Service: No. 431528, 3rd Bn. S/F, L/Cpl.; Theatre/Medals: No records.

Smith, Arthur. Born: Southwell, 1877-1917; Lived: Norwood Lodge, Southwell; Fam: F. William, M. Elizabeth, Br. George (1866), Edmond (1872), Thomas (1881), S. Mary Jane (1868), Annie (1870), Ellen (1875), Bessie (1879), married Florence Bingham 1912, children: Arthur William (1913); Occup: Former professional soldier gardener for J. R. Starkey M. P.; Service: Enlisted 1st Bn. S/F August 1896 – served Boer War winning D.C.M. in 1900 for his actions at the Battle of Diamond Hill for re-supplying ammunition whilst under heavy fire. Also served in China and India, discharged in 1908. Re-joined S/F at outbreak of war. No. 5157, 17th Bn. S/F, Sgt.; Theatre: Dardanelles – took part in Sulva Bay landings, and evacuated with the army to Egypt. Sent to France July 1916. Fought on the Somme and at Ypres, K-in-A 4/8/17; Medals: D.C.M., Queen's South Africa medal with clasps, King's South Africa Medal from previous service, Victory, British, 1914-15 Star; See *N/A* 17/1/17, 29/5/18.

Smith, Charles, Ernest. Born: Grantham, 1885; Lived: Maythorne, Southwell; Fam: Br. of Albert R. Smith – see above; Service: No. 5759, S/F, Cpl.; Theatre: Fr. 27/12/14; Medals: Victory, British, 1914-15 Star.

Smith, George. Born: Halam, 1882; Lived: Halam, Southwell; Fam: F. John Smith (Labourer), M. Elizabeth Jane (Allen), S. Sarah (1868), Mary (1874), Emma (1877), Jane (1879); School: Halam, Natl. 1892-94; Service: No identifiable record.

Smith, John Ernest. Born: Southwell, 1893-1918; Lived: Westgate, Southwell; Fam: F. William Smith (Shoemaker), M. Elizabeth, Br. George (1882), Charles (1885), Herbert (1887), Walter (1891), Arthur (1898), S. Mabel (1884), Dorothy (1900); School: Trinity, Natl. 1901-06; Occup: Butcher's assistant; Service: Enlisted 1914, No. 305794, 1/8th Bn. S/F; Theatre: Fr. June 1915, K-in-A 3/10/18 near Ramicourt having assisted in the breaking of the Fansomme Line (21 men killed and 89 wounded in this action), buried Joncourt East British Cemetery; Medals: Victory, British, 1914-15 Star.

Smith, John Henry. Born: Southwell, 1871; Lived: Burgage Lane, Southwell; Fam: F. John (Labourer), M. Mary (May), Br. Walter (1878); Occup: Labourer; Service: No. 38519, 67th Protection Company, Royal Defence Corps; Theatre/Medals: No records; See *N/A* 14/4/15.

Smith, John William. Born: Radford, Nottingham, 1900; Lived: Oxton, Southwell; Fam: F. James Arthur (Farmer and woodman), M. Lucy Ellen (Beardsley), Br. Arthur Edward (1902), S. Evaline (1896), Clara (1904); School: Oxton, Minster 1912-17; Occup: Student teacher at Calverton; Service: No record.

Smith*, N. Born/Fam: No details; Service: No. 1366, 1/8th Bn. S/F, wounded; Theatre: Fr. Feb. 1915; Medals: Victory, British, 1914-15 Star.

Smith, Samuel Vernon. Born: Ilkeston, 1894; Lived: Westgate, Southwell; Fam: F. George Smith (Gardener), M. Ellen, S. Florence (1894), married Mary J. Mallinder 1915; School: Trinity, Natl. 1902-05, Minster, 1911-17, Choral scholar; Occup: Clerk in wholesale silver merchants and later E. Carey & Sons; Service: No. 2128, S/F, No. 487933, 4th Railway Telegraph, Signal Bn. Royal Engineers, No. 305400 S/F; Theatre: Fr. 26/2/15; Medals: Victory, British, 1914-15 Star; See p. 307.

Smith, Thomas Marriott. Born: Nottingham, 1883; Lived: Westgate, Southwell; Fam: F. Thomas M. Smith, M. Elizabeth, S. Elizabeth A (1887); Service: No. 476440, 62nd Division, Royal Engineers, L/Cpl.; Theatre/Medals: No record.

***Soar*, Albert Victor.** Born: Nottingham, 1897-1915; Lived: Victoria Cottages, Lowdham; Fam: F. Marcus Thomas Soar (Secretary of Builders' merchants), M. Charlotte L. (Newman, m. 1887), Br. Marcus (1892), S. Gertrude Jenny (1899), 4 siblings died before the 1911 Census; Occup: Paper maker; Service: Enlisted T.A. 1912, No. 1374, 1/8th Bn. S/F; Theatre: Fr. March 1915, K-in-A 8/5/15, buried Kemmel Chateau Military Cemetery; Medals: Victory, British, 1914-15 Star.

Albert V. Soar (Newark Advertiser)

Soar, Marcus Thomas. Born: Nottingham, 1892; Lived: Lowdham; Fam: Br. of Albert Victor Soar – see above; Occup: Professional soldier; Service: Enlisted 1909, No. 838, North-Midlands Cycling Division, discharged 18/10/15 due to sickness; Theatre: Belgium 1915; Medals: No record; See *N/A* 19/5/15.

Spall, Samuel. Born: Southwell, 1897; Lived: Concert Hall Yard, Southwell; Fam: F. Samuel Spall (Bricklayer), M. Eliza (Walker), Br. Bertie (1899), Walter (1901), S. Doris (1902), Florence Gertrude (1904), married Hannah Bertha (Cooper m. 1918), children: Philip (1919), Ronald (1923), Yvonne (1927), Ian Gwynvor (1930); School: Infants & Natl. 1905-10; Occup: Butcher's errand boy with S. Swift pork butcher; Service: Enlisted 22/10/14 (lied about his age to join), Nos. 2849 & 307680, 1/8th

Samuel Spall the Boy Soldier (Carole Spall)

Bn. S/F, in Jan. 1918 to 5th Reserve Bn. S/F, demob. 18/3/19; Theatre: Fr. June 1915, wounded March 1917 at Gommecourt; Medals: Victory, British, 1914-15 Star; See *N/A* 4/11/14 and full story pp. 272-3..

Spencer*, Arthur. Born: Woodborough, 1892-1915; Lived: Woodborough; Fam: F. Richard Spencer (Framework knitter), M. Elizabeth, Br. James (1878), George (1890), Arthur (1893), S. Lucy (1881), Elizabeth (1885), Alice, (1887), Louise (1898); Occup: Framework knitter; Service: Joined T.A. pre war, No. 758, 1/8th Bn. S/F, L/Cpl.; Theatre: Fr. March 1915, K-in-A 14/10/15, memorial at Loos; Medals: Victory, British, 1914-15 Star; See p. 215.

Spencer, John William. Lived: Chatham Street, Southwell; Fam: Married to Nellie; Service: No. 127532, 42nd Bn. Machine Gun Corps; Theatre: No record; Medals: Victory, British.

Spendlove, Frank. Born: Oxton, 1897; Lived: Southwell; Fam: F. James Frederick (Farmer), M. Annie Elizabeth (Fulbrook), S. Dorothy (1891), Florence (1904); Service: Attested 10/12/15, No. 203480, 1/5th S/F; Theatre: Fr., K-in-A 1/7/17, commemorated Arras Memorial Bay 7; Medals: Victory, British.

St. Clair, Ernest Vaughan. Service: No. 331375, A/C2, R.A.F.; No records.

Stafford, George. Born: Southwell, 1877; Lived: Back Lane, Burgage, Southwell; Fam: lived with aunt Ann Kemp – no further family details; Occup: Twisthand – E Carey & Sons; Service: Previously served, joining S/F in 1894, serving in Malta, Cyprus and South Africa. Re-joined 18/9/14, No. 7391, S/F, No. GS/101895, Royal Fusiliers, No. 405086, Labour Corps; Theatre: Fr. 2/5/15; Medals: Victory, British, 1914-15 Star.

Stanley, Archibald George. Born: Southwell, 1898 - 1918; Lived: Queen Street, Southwell; Fam: F. Herbert Stanley (House painter), M. Mary Annie (Milner); School: Miss Mason's Prep, Minster 1909-11; Occup: Painter and decorator; Service: Attested 6/6/16, mobilized October 1917, No. 79595, 'W' Company, 2/6th Bn. Durham Light Infantry; Theatre: Fr. May 1918, K-in-A 28/10/18, buried Esquelmes Churchyard; Medals: Victory, British; See *N/A* 13/11/18, & pp. 301, 307.

Archibald G. Stanley (David Hutchinson)

Stephenson, Baden. Born: Southwell, 1900; Lived: Easthorpe, Southwell; Fam: Br. of Thomas Stephenson – see below; School: Infants & Natl. 1909-13; Service: No. 484432, Royal Engineers, Bugler; Theatre/Medals: No records; See *N/A* 8/9/15.

Stephenson, Fred. Born: Southwell, 1887; Lived: Easthorpe, Southwell; Fam: Br. of Thomas Stephenson – see below; School: Infants & Natl. 1895-98; Occup: Professional Soldier; Service: Cameron Highlanders, L/Cpl.; Theatre: Fr. December 1914; Medals: Victory, British, 1914-15 Star; See *N/A* 8/9/15,

Stephenson, George. Born: Southwell, 1892; Lived: Easthorpe, Southwell; Fam: Br. of Thomas Stephenson – see below; School: Infants, Wesleyan & Natl. 1903-08; Occup: Professional Soldier; Service: No. 8881, Cameron Highlanders; Theatre: Fr. December 1914; Medals: Victory, British, 1914-15 Star; See *N/A* 8/9/15.

Stephenson, J. Born/Family: No information; Lived: Southwell; Occup: With J.J. Bates; Service: 8th Sherwood Foresters; Theatre: Assume Fr.; Medals: No record; See *N/A* 9/6/15.

Stephenson, Leonard. Born: Southwell, 1894; Lived: Easthorpe, Southwell; Fam: Br. of Thomas Stephenson – see below; School: Wesleyan, Natl. 1906-08; Occup: Grocer's errand boy, J.J. Bates; Service: 8th Bn. S/F & No. 13733, 1st Bn. North Derbyshire Regt., No. 142849, Machine Gun Corps; Fr. August 1915; Medals: Victory, British, 1914-15 Star; See *N/A* 9/6/15, 8/9/15.

Stephenson*, Thomas. Born: Nottingham, 1884 - 1916; Lived: Easthorpe, Southwell; Fam: F. Thomas Stephenson (Lace maker – E. Carey & Sons), M. Emma (Briley, m. 1885), Br. Fred (1887), George (1893), Leonard (1894), William (1896), Arthur (1897), Baden (1900), John (1902), Hector (1909), S. Selina (1889), Louisa (1891), Alice May (1910), married Louise, children: Roland (1908), Alfred Frederick (1909); School: Infants & Natl. 1897; Occup: Lace maker – E. Carey & Sons; Service: Member of T.A. for 14 years, No. 70767, 1/8th Bn. S/F; Theatre: Fr. March 1915, K-in-A 26/10/16 whilst in trenches near Le Transloy and the men were under continuous pressure from shelling and raiding enemy trenches. Commemorated Thiepval Memorial; Medals: Victory, British, 1914-15 Star; See *N/A 8/9/15, 8/8/17*.

Stephenson, William. Born: Southwell, 1896; Lived: Easthorpe, Southwell; Fam: Br. of Thomas Stephenson – see above; School: Wesleyan, Natl. 1906-10; Service: No. 48100, 3rd Bn. S/F, Cpl., No. 17222, Labour Corps, Cpl.; Theatre: no record; Medals: Victory, British; See *N/A 8/9/15*.

Stimson*, Charles. Born: Upton, 1896 - 1915; Lived: Carr Holt Farm, Lowdham; Fam: F. William Stimson (Roadman, County Council), M. Sarah (Roberts), Br. George (1882), John (1885), Frank (1892), William (1894), Ernest (1899), S. Nellie (1886), Mabel (1887), Sarah Ann (1888), Mary Elizabeth (1890), (13 children, 2 died in infancy); Occup: Farm labourer; Service: Previously T.A., re-joined 1914, No. 2903, 1/8th Bn. S/F; Theatre: Fr. June 1915, K-in-A 14/10/15, commemorated Loos Memorial; Medals: Victory, British, 1914-15 Star; See p. 215.

Straw, Alexander. Born: Farnsfield, 1898 - 1918; Lived: Farnsfield; Fam: F. Alexander Straw (Corn dealer and Grocer), M. Lilian Mary, Br. Walter (1895); School: Minster Boarder, 1912-14; Occup: Solicitor's clerk; Service: Officer training, Nottingham, 1st Bn. S/F, Lt., Theatre: Fr., wounded at Messines 1917, DoW 3/6/18, buried Sissonne Military Cemetery; Medals: Victory, British; See p. 269.

Charles Stimson (Newark Advertiser)

Straw, Frederick Walter. Born: Farnsfield, 1898 - 1916; Lived: Farnsfield; Fam: Walter Straw (Earthenware maker), M. Annie Elizabeth (Larder, m. 1891), S. Olga Mary (1895); School: Minster 1911-1914; Service: Enlisted 1915, Yorkshire & Lancashire Regt., Lt.; Theatre: Fr. attached to 14th Bn., K-in-A 7/11/16, commemorated Thiepval Memorial, Somme; Medals: Victory, British; See p. 307.

Straw*, Walter William. Born: Farnsfield, 1895; Lived: Farnsfield; Fam: Br. of Alexander Straw – see above; Occup: Grocer's shop assistant; Service: T.A. No. 2339 S/F, No. 305509, S/F, No. 239513 Gloucestershire Regt., demob. 31/3/19; Theatre: Fr. March 1915; Medals: Victory, British, 1914-15 Star; See *N/A 22/5/18*.

Alexander Straw (David Hutchinson)

Stubbs, James Sidney. Born: Halam, 1889-1918; Lived: Southwell; Fam: F. Aram Stubbs (Farmer), M. Sarah Elizabeth (Wignall), Br. William Sampson (1881), Robert Adam (1883), S. Gladys Victoria (1888), married Alice Margaret Jordon; Occup: With Southwell Gas Company, previously farm worker; Service: Called up July 1917, No. 123238, 42nd Bn. Machine Gun Corps; Theatre: Fr. January 1918, K-in-A 21/10/18 during the German offensive, Operation Michael, buried St. Aubert Cemetery; Medals: Victory, British; See *N/A 6/11/18*.

Sturgess, George Henry. Born/Fam: No information; Service: No. 6896, Lancers, L/Sgt.; Theatre: Fr. August 1914, Medals: Victory, British, 1914-15 Star.

Suggitt, George. Born: Barton le Street, Yorks, 1875; Lived: 10, Station Road, Southwell; Fam: married Lauretta Peel Kerr, 1907, children: John Craven (1908), Mary Ellen (1910), George David (1917); Occup: Domestic gardener; Service: Attested 30/8/16, Nos. 88359 & 136389, 19th Company, Royal Army Medical Corps; Theatre/Medals: No record.

Summers, Hugh Francis. Born: Southwell, 1881; Lived: Southwell; Fam: F. Charles Summers, M. Ellen (Allwood), S. Harriett (1867), Jane (1869), Ann (1870), Mary (1877); Occup: Tobacconist Market Place, Southwell; Service: Attested 31/8/16, No. 12848, No. 2 Yorkshire Army Pay Corps, & No. 48695, King's Own Yorkshire Light Infantry; Theatre/Medals: No records.

Suter, John William. Born: Southwell: 1886; Lived: King Street, Southwell; Fam: F. William Suter, M. Anniss (Hayes), Br. Walter (1889), Fred (1904), S. Elsie Sarah, in 1911 was living with his Aunt Mary Suter; School: Infants and Natl. 1894-98; Occup: Postman; Service: No. 30129, Yorkshire & Lancashire Regt., No. 18184, 31st Labour Corps; Theatre: No record; Medals: Victory, British.

Suter, Walter. Born: Southwell, 1889 - 1918; Lived Spring Terrace, Southwell (1911); Fam: Br. of John William Suter – see above, married Annie C. Shilcock 1914, children: Florence (1915); School: Natl. 1895-98, Wesleyan 1898-1903; Occup: Grocer's assistant; Service: No. 63205, Durham Light Infantry, Sergeant; Theatre/Medals: No record; Died 12/12/18, buried Minster Church Yard.

Swallow, Eustace Claude. Born: North Muskham, 1879; Lived: Norwood Cottages, Southwell; Fam: F. William Crampton Swallow, M. Fanny (Banks), Br. Samuel (1878), married Aida Wall 1911, children: Eustace Stanley (1912); Occup: Horseman at Starkey's; Service: Attested 28/1/15, No. 84990, Royal Field Artillery, Driver; Theatre: Fr. June 1915; Medals: Victory, British, 1914-15 Star.

Swift, John Crispin. Born, Southwell, 1894; Lived: King Street, Southwell; Fam: F. George Swift (Labourer); School: Easthorpe, Wesleyan 1898-1909; Service: Nos. 3115 & 265915, Royal Warwickshire Regt.; Theatre: No record; Medals: Victory, British.

Swift*, John George. Born: Southwell, 1895; Lived: Maythorne; Fam: F. George Swift (Labourer), M. Nelly, married Sarah E. Radford 1926; School: Wesleyan 1898-?; Occup: Lace maker – E. Carey & Sons; Service: Nos. 1359 & 305105, 1/8th Bn. S/F; Theatre: Fr. March 1915; Medals: Victory, British, 1914-15 Star.

Swift, William R. Born: Southwell, 1877; Lived: King Street, Southwell; Fam: F. Frank Samuel Swift (Pork butcher), M. Mary (Whitworth m. 1875), married Miriam Clara (Rhodes in 1906), children: Constance (1907), William (1910), John & Molly (1918); Occup: Pork Butcher; Service: 1915 8th S/F and R.D. Corps, but discharged as unfit; Theatre/Medals: No record; See *N/A* 24/4/15.

Taylor, George Charles. Born: Nottingham, 1895-1918; Lived: Nottingham; Fam: F Charles Taylor (Veterinary Surgeon), M. Georgina; School: St Annes on Sea and Minster 1906-11, Royal College of Vets; Occup: Veterinary Surgeon; Service: Army Veterinary Corps, attached to 26th Army Brigade, Royal Artillery, Captain; Theatre: Fr., K-in-A 6/9/18, buried Sun Quarry Cemetery, Cherisy, Pas de Calais; Medals: Victory, British

Taylor, William. Born: Southwell, 1887; Lived: Westgate, Southwell; Fam: Married Edith Hopkinson, child: Kenneth Victor (1910); School: Wesleyan and Natl. 1896-97; Occup: Lace maker – E. Carey & Sons; Service; No records, but noted in 1928 as a veteran.

Teather*, George. Born: Woodborough, 1886; Lived: Main Street, Woodborough; Fam: M. Mary Ann Spencer (Framework knitter); Occup: Framework knitter; Service: Joined T.A. 1910, No. 1057, 1/8th Bn. S/F; Theatre: Fr. March 1915; Medals: Victory, British, 1914-15 Star.

Templeman*, George (Jim) H. Born: Southwell, 1894; Lived: Easthorpe, Southwell; Fam: M. Mary Ann Templeman, Br. John Thomas (1888), S. Ruth (1886), Agnes (1893), married Ellen Skinner of Croydon; School: Easthorpe & Natl. 1901-08; Occup: Grocer's clerk – Kirkby's; Service: No. 1435, 1/8th Bn. S/F, Sgt., No. 95/129407, Royal Fusiliers, Sgt., demob. 1919; Theatre: Fr. March 1915, transferred to the Russian Front after 4 years; Medals: Victory, British, 1914-15 Star, D.C.M.; Learnt Russian and post-war returned to Kirkby's before moving to London to work in the Russian Record Office; See *N/A* 20/1/15, 9/6/15, 22/9/15, 5/1/16, 15/11/16, 22/10/19.

Templeman*, John Thomas. Born: Norwell, 1888; Lived: Easthorpe, Southwell; Fam: Brother of George H. Templeman – see above, married Jessie May Boyd of Little Sailing, Essex; School: Trinity, Natl. 1894-1898; Occup: Twist hand threader – E. Carey & Sons; Service: Nos. 1508, 305158, 4960752, 1/8th Bn. S/F, Sgt., demob. 19/3/19; Theatre: Fr. March 1915; Medals: Victory, British, 1914-15 Star, M.M.; See *N/A* 15/11/16, 17/1/17, 22/10/19, & pp. 209, 218, 227.

Templeman, Thomas. Born: 1885; Lived: Westhorpe, Southwell; Fam: F. Thomas Templeman; School: Trinity, Natl. 1894-98; Service: No record.

Terry, George Thomas. Born: Watford, 1882; Lived: Compton House, Southwell; Fam: F. Joseph Terry, M. Annie (Atkins), Br. Joseph John (1876), Leonard James (1884), S. Alice Ruth (1879), Annie Elizabeth (1886); Occup: Groom to Capt. Hume, previously professional soldier; Service: Attested 1901, No. 6816, Derbyshire Regt. Served: Malta 1901-02, S. Africa 1902, China 1902-04. Demob. 1904. Re-engaged 10/10/14, No. 33841, Royal Munster Fusiliers; Theatre: Fr. November 1914, severely injured 3/3/15 and returned home; Medals: Queen's South Africa, Cape Colony Clasp, Transvaal, Victory, British.

Terry, Thomas Bernard. Born: Daybrook, 1895-1916; Lived: Burnell Arms, Winkburn; Fam: F. Henry Terry (Drayman), M. Jane (Wealthall, m. 1886), S. Ann (1897); Occup: Farm worker; Service: Enlisted 1915, No. 3492, 1/8th S/F; Theatre: Fr. June 1915, wounded October, 1915, but was able to re-join his unit. Was at wounded again at Vimy Ridge and DoW 20/4/16, buried Aubigny Communal Cemetery; Medals: Victory, British, 1914-15 Star.

Thompson, Alfred. Born: Southwell, 1890; Lived: Westhorpe, Southwell; Fam: F. William Thompson (retired), M. Eliza (Jeal), (father married twice), Br. William (1871), George (1874), Henry (1876), Frank (1879), S. Mary Jane (1873); School: Wesleyan 1897-1902, Natl. 1902-04; Occup: Gardener; Service: Attested September 1914, No. 238106, 8th Bn. S/F, transferred to 1st Bn. No. 2337, York and Lancaster Regt., A/Cpl., demob. 13/3/19; Theatre: Fr. and Italy (1917); Medals: Victory, British, 1914-15 Star; See *N/A* 11/11/14, 26/5/15.

Thompson, Frank. Born: Southwell, 1879 - 1918; Lived: Birrell Road, Sherwood Rise, Nottingham; Fam: Br. of Alfred Thompson – see above, married Elizabeth Ada 1905, children: Phyllis (1906), Sydney (1907); Occup: Seed man's assistant; Service: No. M/344372, Army Service Corps; Theatre: Middle East, died in an accident 14/7/18, buried Jerusalem Cemetery, Israel; Medals: Victory, British.

Thompson, Henry. Born: Southwell, 1876; Lived: Westgate, Southwell; Fam: Br. of Alfred Thompson – see above, married Jane 1914, children: George (1915), Mary (1916), Henry (1920); Service: No. 152783, Royal Field Artillery, Gnr.; Theatre: No record; Medals: Victory, British.

Thomson, David. Born: 1888 - 1919; Fam: Wife M L Thomson of Church Street, Southwell - no further information; Service: 9th Bn. Rifle Brigade, 2nd Lt.; Theatre: No record but died 1/5/19, buried Minster Yard; Medals: No record.

Thorpe*, Charles. Born: Woodhouse, Yorkshire, 1890 - 1915; Lived: Farnsfield and Papplewick; Fam: S. Gladys M. Thorpe of Goole, married Betsy; Occup: Houseman on farm in Papplewick;

Service: enlisted 1913, No. 1770, 1/8th Bn. S/F; Theatre: Fr. March 1915, K-in-A 30/7/15, commemorated Menin Gate; Medals: Victory, British, 1914-15 Star; See p. 211.

Thraves, Horace. Born: Caythorpe, 1887; Lived: Lowdham; Fam: F. Richard Thraves (Bricklayer), M. Ellen (Allwood), Br. Richard (1890), Frank (1892), S. Louise (1884), Minnie (1886), married Alice Spencer 1911, children: Richard (1912), Queenie M. (1914), Masie (1920), Peggy (1922); Occup: Flour carter; Service: Nos. 914 & 206959, Rifle Brigade, A/Sgt.; Theatre: No record; Medals: Victory, British; See *N/A* 14/4/15.

Tilson, Thomas. Born: Stronground, Hunts, 1896 - 1916; Lived: Southwell; Fam: F. William Tilson (Brickyard labourer), M. Fanny, Br. Arthur (1891), George (1899), S. Fanny (1904); Occup: Bishop Hoskyn's Footman; Service: Enlisted January 1915, No. 17009, 6th Bn. Northamptonshire Regt.; Theatre: Fr. July 1915, K-in-A 2/7/16, buried Dantzig Alley, British Cemetery, Mametz; Medals: Victory, British, 1914-15 Star.

Tinley, Edward. Born: Southwell, 1882; Lived: Radley Farm, Oxton Road, Southwell; Fam: F. George Glasier Tinley (Farmer), M. Mary Ann (Simpson), Br. Charles Glasier (1882), Frank Percival (1884), S. Gertrude Mary (1875), Catherine (1876), Florence Annie (1877), Mary Jane (1880); Occup: Farm worker; Service: Attested Boscombe 23/2/15, No. T3 02097, Army Service Corps, No. 48820, East Surrey; Theatre: No record; Medals: Victory, British, 1914-15 Star; Post war lived at Park farm, Crink Lane, Southwell.

Toder, Harold Cyril. Born: Newark, 1894; Lived: Southwell; Fam: F. John William Toder (Chimney sweep), M. Mabel (Widdowson m. 1892), Br. Percy (1897), Clarence (1900), Bernard (1901), Charles (1902), Rowland (1904), Albert (1910), S. Doris Irene (1896), Gladys Mabel (1899), Constance (1906), married Mary W. (Furniss in 1921), children: Winifred (1923), Joyce (1927); Occup: Chauffeur to Dr. George Polson of Southwell; Service: No. M2/104941, Motor Transport A.S.C.; Theatre/Medals: No records; See *N/A* 9/6/15.

Toder, Percy Walter. Born: Southwell, 1896 - 1918; Lived: King Street, Southwell; Family: F. John W Toder (Labourer), M. Mabel, Br. Harold (1894), Clarence (1900), S. Doris (1896), Gladys (1899); School: Natl. 1905-07, Wesleyan 1907-10; Occup: with J. J. Bates; Service: Enlisted October, 1914, Nos. 3143, 20025 & 242617, 2/5th Bn. S/F; Theatre: Fr. June 1915, wounded at St. Eloi, P.O.W. March 1918 at Bullecourt, released November 1918 and died of influenza, 10/12/18; Medals: Victory, British, 1914-15 Star; See *N/A* 9/6/15, 11/12/18, & p. 269.

Tongue, Ernest. Born: Southwell, 1899; Br. of J. W. Tongue - see below. School: Minster 1908-14; Occup: Clerk, Wine and Spirits Merchant, Newark; Service: Sherwood Foresters; Theatre/Medals: No records; See pp. 270, 307.

Tongue, Frederick Charles. Born: Southwell, 1897; Br. of John William Tongue – see below; School: Infants & Natl. 1903-09, Minster 1909-12; Service: Nos. 4032 & 306272, 3/8th S/F; Theatre: Fr. Oct 1915; Medals: Victory, British, 1914-15 Star; See *N/A* 9/6/15, p. 209.

Tongue, George Arthur. Born: Lowdham, 1891; Lived: Barleythorpe, Oakham; Fam: Br. of John William Tongue – see below, married Lillian Nellie Easton; School: Infants & Natl. 1895-1903; Occup: Footman to Earl Lonsdale, Oakham; Service: Attested September 1914 in Dublin, No. 16722, 11th Bn. S/F, Cpl. reduced to Pte following disciplinary hearing; Theatre: Fr. August 1915; Medals: Victory, British, 1914-15 Star; See *N/A* 5/5/15.

Tongue*, John William. Born: Southwell, 1894; Lived: Elm Bank Villas, The Burgage, Southwell; Fam: F. George Tongue (Bricklayer), M. Elizabeth (Harmston m. 1885), Br. Frederick Charles (1897), Ernest (1900), George Arthur (1891), Ernest (1899), S. Ada (1885), Bertha (1892), Lillian Beatrice (1887), Nellie (1895); School: Infants & Natl. 1899 - ?; Occup: Lace spooler –

E. Carey & Sons; Service: No. 876, 1/8th Bn. S/F, No. DM 207122, Army Service Corps, demob 16/3/16; Theatre: Fr. March 1915; Medals: Victory, British, 1914-15 Star.

Townsend*, Alfred. Born: Sneinton, Nottingham, 1882; Lived: Private Road, Southwell; Fam: F. Walter Townsend (Lace maker – E.Carey & Sons), M. Mary (Sensecall, m. 1881), Br. William Henry (1882), Walter (1883), Robert (1892), S. Elizabeth (1888), Priscilla (1889), Fanny (1904), Alice (1905); Occup: Twist hand – E. Carey & Sons; Service: Enlisted 1903, Nos. 734, 307647, 1/8th Bn. S/F, Cpl., re-joined 1920, No. 4960751; Medals: Victory, British, 1914-15 Star.

Townsend, Robert. Born: Southwell, 1892-1915; Lived: Easthorpe, Southwell; Fam: Br. of Alfred Townsend – see above; School: Easthorpe, Natl. 1899-1904; Occup: Miller; Service: No. 11739, 8th Bn. Lincolnshire Regt., Cpl.; Theatre: Fr. September 1915. Took part in the Battle of Loos in October 1915, K-in-A 25/11/15 when the trench he was in was subject to a heavy artillery barrage, buried Chapelle d'Armentiers; Medals: Victory, British, 1914-15 Star.

Townsend, Walter. Born: Sneinton, Nottingham, 1883 - 1916; Lived: Hull; Fam: Br. of Alfred Townsend – see above, married Lottie Townsend; School: Dane School, Nottingham, Natl. 1892-1897; Occup: Baker – J H Kirkby; Service: Enlisted September 1914, No. 11/948, East Yorkshire Regt., Sgt.; Theatre: Egypt, 1915, Fr. 1916. Suffered shell shock 8/4/16 and returned to duty a week later. Taken ill 17/6/16 died of uraemic convulsions, buried Beauval Communal Cemetery – wife received a pension of 16/3d per week; See *N/A* 12/7/16.

Townsend, William Henry. Born Sneinton, Nottingham, 1882; Lived: Chatham Street, Southwell; Fam: Br. of Alfred Townsend – see above, married Mary Jane, children: George (1906), Grace Mary (1909), Hilda (1911); Occup: Lace maker E. Carey & Sons; Service: Enlisted 6/12/15, No. 38736, Lincolnshire Regt., demob. 25/7/18; Theatre:No record;Lived: Medals: Victory, British.

Truswell, Henry. Born: Southwell, 1869; Lived: Flour Mill, Southwell; Fam: F. James Truswell, M. Ann; Service: Attested 25/11/14, No. 20087, 2/8th Bn. S/F, discharged with ill health 25/7/16; Theatre/Medals: No records.

Tuckwood, Walter. Born: Nottingham, 1888; Lived: Westgate, Southwell; Fam: F. Charles Tuckwood, M. Eliza Ann (Brooksby), Br. Edwin (1890), Charles (1892), Claud (1896), S. Katherine (1884), Edith (1886), Rosa (1899), married Alice (Murden in 1916); Occup: Baker; Service: Attested 21/7/15, No. S4/125394, Army Service Corps, discharged as unfit 13/10/16; Theatre: Home; Medals: No record.

Turner, George. No family records; Lived: Southwell; Service: Nos. 2081 & 860605, Royal Field Artillery; Theatre: no record; Medals: British.

Twells*, Edward. Born: Halam, 1866; Lived Burgage Lane, Southwell; Fam: Wife Susannah (Hewston), children: William (1894), John (1902), Lizzie (1897), Mary (1904); Occup: Bricklayer; Service: National Reserve, No. 3191 and King's Own Yorkshire Light Infantry, No. 267672, 1/8th Bn. S/F, & 7th Bn., attached to 29th Pioneer Bn. & Protection Co. Royal Defence Corps, demob. 18/2/19; Theatre: Served in UK; Medals: Victory, British.

Twells, Herbert. Born: Southwell, 1892-1917; Lived: Kirklington Road, Southwell; Fam: F. Robert Twells (Bricklayer's labourer), M. Ellen (Clarke, 1888), Br. Robert (1901), S. Evelina (1890), Emma (1895), Florence (1897), Nellie (1909); School: Wesleyan 1895-1903, Natl. 1903-04; Occup: Corn warehouseman; Service: Enlisted Southwell in Army Veterinary Corps, transferred to No. 149670, Royal Garrison Artillery, Gnr; Theatre: Egypt, Salonika with R.A.V.C., Fr. with R.G.A., K-in-A 21/10/17 at 3rd Battle of Ypres, buried Ypres Reservoir Cemetery; Medals: Victory, British; See *N/A* 29/5/18.

Twells*, William. B. Southwell, 1894; Lived: Burgage Lane, Southwell; Fam: Son of Edward Twells – above; School: Wesleyan 1897 - ?; Occup: Threader – E. Carey & Sons; Service: Enlisted

1910, Nos. 1017, 1/8th Bn. S/F, No. 26772, 7th Bn. S/F; Theatre: Fr. March 1915, wounded, demob Feb. 1919; Medals: Victory, British, 1914-15 Star.

Twidale, Leslie Francis. Born: Southwell, 1899 - 1918; Lived: Home Farm, Westhorpe, Southwell; Fam: F. George Twidale (Farmer), M. Emma Jane (Herrod), Br. George (1879), Herbert (1881), Henry (1883), Matthew Herrod (1885), Sleightholm (1886), David (1896), S. Margaret (1875), Ethel Annie (1888), Kate Mabel (1890), Annie Maria (1891), Fanny Edith (1893), Hannah Herrod (1894), 17 children, 2 died by 1911; School: Trinity, Natl. 1907-12; Occup: Chemist's apprentice in Newark; Service: Called up 1917, No. 94159, West Yorkshire Regiment, No. 44647, 2/5th Bn. Lincolnshire Regt.; Theatre: Fr. wounded and captured 14/4/18, DoW in German hospital, following the amputation of the lower right thigh and contracting septic poisoning, 10/5/18. Buried Cologne Southern Cemetery and memorial on family grave at Holy Trinity, Southwell; Medals: Victory, British; See p. 269.

Harold Tyne
(Newark Advertiser)

Tyne, Harold. Born: Southwell, 1895 - 1918; Lived: Kirklington Road, Southwell; Fam: F. Charles Tyne (General labourer), M. Elizabeth (Gray), Br. Walter Ernest (1892), Charles Thomas (1893), S. Lilian (1888), Bertha (1898), Minnie (1900), Ada (Nellie (1903); School: Wesleyan 1898-1903, Natl. 1903-08; Occup: Grocery warehouseman; Service: Enlisted September 1914, No. 305752, 1/8th S/F, L/Cpl.; Theatre: Fr. May 1915. Won D.C.M. at Sanctuary Wood 30/7/15. K-in-A 22/3/18 whilst defending trenches and a tunnel near Cambrin; Medals: Victory, British, 1914-15 Star, D.C.M; See *N/A* 20/1/15, 12/5/15, 9/6/15, 8/9/15, 15/9/15, 22/9/15, 20/10/15, 14/2/17, 18/4/17, 4/7/17, 29/5/18, 29/10/18.

Ulyatt, Ernest. Born: Southwell, 1892; Lived: Mill House, Station Road, Southwell; Fam: F. Henry Ulyatt, M. Mary (Berridge), Br. William (1885), John Henry (1893), S. Nelly (1898), married Julia; School: Trinity, Natl. 1900-05; Occup: Gardener; Service: No. 118351, Royal Army Medical Corps; Theatre: No record; Medals: No record.

Ulyatt, George Henry. Born: Southwell, 1882; Lived: 7, Carholme Road, Lincoln; Fam: M. Eliza Ulyatt, married Rose, children: George Henry (1902), Leonard William (1904); Occup: Cab driver; Service: Enlisted 9/9/14, No. 15848, S/F, discharged as unfit 5/12/14.

Ulyatt, John Henry. Born: Southwell, 1888; Lived: Burgage Lane, Southwell; Fam: F. George Ulyatt, M. Eliza (Bacon, m. 1872), Br. Matthew (1877), William H (1884), S. Eliza (1875); School: Natl. 1893-1900; Occup: Carter – County Council; Service: No. 40218, 18th Bn. S/F, No. 170588, Labour Corps; Theatre: No record; Medals: No record.

Ernest & Julia Ulyatt
(Heather Price)

Ulyatt, Percy Webberley. Born: Southwell, 1894 - 1917; Lived: Westgate, Southwell; Fam: F. John Ulyatt, M. Sarah Ann (Marshall) (Dressmaker), S. Florence; School: Trinity, Natl. 1903-07;

Occup: Grocer's assistant; Service: Called up 1916, No. 26570, 1st Bn. S/F; Theatre: Fr. 1916, K-in-A 31/7/17, 3rd Battle of Ypres, during heavy fighting. Buried Hooge Crater, Cemetery; Medals: Victory, British.

Ulyatt, Robert. Born: Little Carlton, 1896; Lived: Normanton, Southwell; Fam: F. W. H. Ulyatt (Farmer), M. Annie (Smith), Br. Samuel (1898), William (1908), S. Rebekah (1905), May (1910); Occup: Colliery horse keeper; Service: No. 85620, Royal Field Artillery, Gunner; Theatre: Fr. Sept. 1915, Salonika; Medals: Victory, British, 1914-15 Star; See *N/A* 8/8/17.

Ulyatt, Samuel. Born: Little Carlton, 1898-1917; Lived: Normanton, Southwell; Fam: Br. of Robert Ulyatt – see above; School: Selston, Natl. 1909; Occup: Colliery horse keeper; Service: No. 27091, S/F; Theatre: Fr. 1917, DoW 7/7/17, buried Lussenthoek Military Cemetery; Medals: British, Victory; See *N/A* 8/8/17.

Ulyatt, William. Born: Southwell, 1884; Lived: Kirklington Road, Southwell; Fam: Br. of John Henry Ulyatt – see above; School: Wesleyan 1891-1896; Occup: Carter – County Council; Service: No record.

Ulyatt, William. Born: Southwell, 1885; Lived: Westgate, Southwell; Fam: F. Henry Ulyatt (Farm foreman), married Annie (Skillington m. 1906), children: Willie (1907), Herbert (1909), Mary (1915); Service: No. 67397, Durham Light Infantry, No. 23246, Labour Corps, demob. August 1919; Theatre: Fr.; Medals: Victory, British.

William Ulyatt and family (Heather Price)

Underwood, Christopher Green. Born: Ollerton, 1899; Lived: Westhorpe Cottage, Westgate, Southwell; Fam: F. George T. Underwood, M. Ann (Wells), Br. Frank (1901), Harold (1903), Ernest (1905), S. Elsie (1898), Annie May (1910), married Florence A. Suckling 1919, children: Eric N. (1920), George W. (1921); Service: No. 59344, West Yorkshire Regt.; Theatre: No record; Medals: Victory, British.

Underwood, George Thomas. Born: Marton, Lincs., 1872; Lived: Westhorpe Cottage, Westgate, Southwell; Fam: father of Christopher Green Underwood – see above; Occup: Forester; Service: No. 476265, Royal Engineers, Sapper; Theatre: Egypt 30/3/15; Medals: Victory, British, 1914-15 Star.

Underwood, H. T. No family details; Occup: Lace maker - E. Carey & Sons; Service: Applied to Tribunal 3/6/16 - exempt until 1/10/16 - no military records found.

Vernon*, W. T. No details.

Vickers, Ernest Charles. Born, Southwell, 1894 - 1917; Lived: Westgate, Southwell; Fam: F. Wistow Vickers (President, Southwell Traders' Association), M. Rachel (Scarliff, m. 1894), S. Dorothy (1897); School: Mrs MacDonald's Prep, Minster 1906-10; Occup: Bank clerk, Smith's Bank and Nottingham & Nottinghamshire Bank, Worksop.; Service: Volunteered Nov. 1915, No.

PS/9350, Royal Fusiliers, Pte., Essex Regt., Lt.; Theatre: Fr. Dec. 1916, K-in-A 26/1/17, commemorated at Thiepval Memorial; Medals: Victory, British; See *N/A* 4/4/17, 28/4/17, 30/5/17, 8/8/17, & pp. 301-2.

Vickers, Archibald Frank. Born: Brant Broughton, 1899; Lived: The Holme, Westhorpe, Southwell; Fam: F. William Vickers (Groom/Gardener), M. Sarah Ann, Br. William Henry (1893), Arthur Ernest (1904), S. Edith Ann (1884), Gertrude Alice (1891), Florence Sarah (1896), m. Florence G. Spall 1927; Service: Served in the Army in Palestine; Medals: No record.

Wagstaff, George. Born: Farnsfield, 1898; Lived: Station Villas, Southwell; Fam: Br. of William Henry Wagstaff – see below; Occup: Farm worker; Service; Enlisted, 1915, No. 19635, S/F, L/Cpl.; Theatre; Fr. 1917, wounded 1917 & 1918; Medals: Victory, British, 1914-15 Star; See *N/A* 15/5/18.

Wagstaff, William Henry. Born: Farnsfield, 1896; Lived: Station Villas, Southwell, later Normanton; Fam: F. William Cook Wagstaff (Farmer), M. Sarah Elizabeth (Pinder), Br. John (1891), George (1898), Frank (1906), S. May (1892), Margaret (1893); Occup : Farm worker; Service: No. 165010, South Notts Hussars, Machine Gun Corps, Sgt., No. 280044, 1/1st South Notts Hussars, Sgt., No. 539170, Royal Artillery, Sgt., No. 53251, Notts Yeomanry, Sgt.; Theatre: Egypt and Fr.; Medals: Victory, British, 1914-15 Star; See *N/A* 8/5/18, & pp. 279, 307.

Walker, Hugh William. Born: Southwell, 1891; Lived: Westgate, Southwell; Fam: F. William Abraham Walker (Medical Doctor), M. Fanny Sarah (Hill), Br. Joseph (1894), Reginald (1896), S. Florence (1894), Fanny (1911- died in infancy); School: Minster 1903-09, Arnold House, Blackpool; Occup: Bank Clerk; Service: No. 568473 & T1619, Signal Co., Royal Engineers, Cpl.; Theatre: No record; Medals: Victory, British.

Walker, Joseph. Born: Southwell, 1894; Lived: Westgate, Southwell; Fam: Br. of Hugh William Walker – See above, married Cecily E. Carey 1926, children: Martin (1926), Patrick (1929), Cornelius (1931), Dennis (1932), Margaret (1934) – lived in Stepney; School: Minster 1911-16, Arnold House, Blackpool; Occup: With cycle works, Nottingham; Service: Attested Royal Engineers, No. 612150, Royal Horse Artillery; Theatre: Egypt 25/4/15, Palestine 23/3/17-16/4/19, suffered malaria and received a pension; Medals: Victory, British, 1914-15 Star; See p. 307.

Walker, Reginald. Born: Southwell, 1896; Lived: Westgate, Southwell; Fam: Br. of Hugh William Walker – see above, married Olive G. Lee 1929, children: David G. (1934), Reginald A. (1937); School: Minster 1909-15, Arnold House, Blackpool; Occup: Bank clerk; Service: Enlisted 1915, 3/8th S/F and No. 487218, 3rd Special Co. Royal Engineers, No. 280792, South Notts Hussars, No. 76877, Derbyshire Yeomanry; Theatre: No record; Medals: Victory, British; See *N/A* 9/6/15 & p. 279.

Waller, John Gamble. Born: Longsite, Lancs., 1888 - 1916; Lived: Brinkley, Southwell; Fam: F. Herbert Gamble Waller (Teacher), M. Marion (Barlow, m. 1878), Br. Edgar (1883), Arthur Frederick (1892), Sidney Horace (1894), S. Flora Emma (1881), Eva E. (1882), Lilly Beatrice (1886); Occup: Elementary teacher; Service: Volunteered 1914, No. 1519, 1/5th The Queen's, Royal Surrey Regt., Sgt.; Theatre: India November 1915, appointed Sergeant-Instructor at Martiniere College, Mesopotamia, K-in-A 11/9/16, buried Basra War Cemetery; Medals: Victory, British, 1914-15 Star. The Colonel of his regiment wrote: 'Doubtless by this time you have heard the sad news of the death of your son in action. Last Monday we had to attack an Arab village and destroy it. Your son was

John G. Waller (Newark Advertiser)

in the thick of the fighting and early on in the action he was struck by a bullet and killed instantly. His death is a great loss to us as he was one of our best sergeants, and a type of man we can ill afford to lose. I trust that the thought that he gave his life for his country may be of some consolation to you in your loss. On behalf of the battalion I desire to offer you our sincerest sympathy.'

Wallis, John Grise. Born: Burton-on-Trent, 1886; Lived: Landseer Road, Southwell, later Westgate; Fam: F. George Wallis (Railway shunter), M. Emma (Grice, m. 1885), Br. Henry (1891), George (1892), William (1901), S. Mary E (1889), Daisy (1895), Mabel (1896), Emma (1889); Occup: Baker & confectioner's assistant; Service: No. S4/20611, 351st Company, Army Service Corps, Service/Medals: no record.

Ward, George. Born: Southwell, 1891; Lived: Burgage Lane, Southwell; Fam: Br. of Robert Ward – see below; School: Wesleyan, 1893-99, Natl. 1899-1901; Occup: Threader – Lace factory Ilkeston; Service: No identifiable records, however, a report in the *N/A* 17/2/15 states that he had been wounded.

Ward, Harry. Born: Southwell, 1898; Lived: Burgage Lane, Southwell; Fam: Br. of Robert Ward – see below; School: Infant & Natl: 1905-1910; Occup: Spooling hand – E. Carey & Sons; Service: No. 306453, S/F; Theatre/Medals: No records.

Ward, Herbert Johnson. Born: Long Eaton, 1887; Lived: Boarder Minster School (1911), then Beeston; Fam: F. Herbert J. Ward (Butcher), M. Kate (Jackson), Br. Norman (1904), S. Marjorie (1888), School: Beeston & Minster 1910-12; Occup: Draper's apprentice; Service: No. 1673, 14th Brigade, Royal Field Artillery, Cpl.; Theatre: No record; Medals: Victory, British.

Ward, Percy. Born: Kneesall, 1878 - 1916; Lived: Southwell; Fam: F. William Ward, M. Mary; Service: No. DM2/270256, Motor Transport Works, Army Service Corps, Grove Park; Theatre: Home, died 23/12/16 at Bromley, Kent after a short illness; Medals: No record.

Ward*, Robert. Born: Southwell, 1897; Lived: Burgage Lane, Southwell; Fam: F. William Ward (Bricklayer), M. Mary (Heuston, m. 1883), Br. William (1887), Harry (1898), S. Annie (1885), Lilly (1892); School: Wesleyan & Natl. 1905-10; Service: No. 2378, 1/8th Bn. S/F, demob 30/4/16; Theatre: Fr. Feb. 1915; Medals: Victory, British, 1914-15 Star.

Ward*, William. Born: Southwell, 1887-1917; Lived: Bradfield Cottages, Easthorpe; Fam: Brother of Robert Ward – see above, married Annie Pitchford 23/11/12; Occup: Lace hand – E. Carey & Sons; Service: Enlisted 1913, No. 1774, 1/8th Bn. S/F, No. 11134, Military Foot Police, demob. 18/7/19; Theatre: UK; Medals: Victory, British; See *N/A* 8/8/17, & p. 226.

Warren, Frank. Born: Farnsfield, 1881; Lived Farnsfield and then Southwell; Fam: F. Henry Ward, M. Annie (Smalley), Br. Henry (1875), George (1890), S. Ann (1872), Kate (1880), Annie Ellen (1884), Alice Maud (1886), Dora (1888), Althea (1891); married Lilian Asher, children: Lilian (1914), Frank (1916), Arthur (1920), George Henry (1923); Occup: Bricklayer's labourer; Service: Attested 7/4/08, No. 738, S/F Reserve Regt., 158823, Machine Gun Corps, discharged 6/4/16; Theatre: No record; Medals: Victory & British.

Warriner, Cedric. No records

Warriner, Harry. No records.

Warwick, Hugh Branston. Born: Southwell, 1879 - 1958; Lived: c/o Army & Navy Club; Fam: F. Richard H. Warwick (Director, Warwick & Richardson Brewery, Newark), M. Florence Mary (Branston, m. 1877), Br. Philip Huskinson (1880), S. Mary K (1888), married Frances Laura Pratt in 1908, Christine Stops in 1922, Mary E Millidge in 1954; Occup: Professional Soldier; Service: R.A.O.C. rose from Major to Lt. Colonel, Northumberland Fusiliers; Theatre: Fr. 1915; Medals: Victory, British, 1914-15 Star, D.S.O.

Warwick, John Cedric Geoffrey. Born: Upton, 1894 - 1918; Lived: Upton Hall, Southwell; Fam: F. John Francis Warwick (Director, Warwick & Richardson Brewery, Newark), M. Eliza Gertrude (Branston, m. 1881), Br. Guy Ranson (1884), Kenneth Gilbert (1897), Douglas Vivian (1890), S. Phyllis Dulce (1887), Violet Marjorie (1893); School: Harrow and Royal Agricultural College, Cirencester; Service: South Notts Hussars; Theatre: Egypt, April 1915. Killed at sea whilst in transit from Egypt to France, 27/5/18 – ship torpedoed, commemorated on the Chatby Memorial, Egypt; Medals: Victory, British, 1914-15 Star; See pp. 274, 277-9.

Warwick, Norman R. C. Born, Southwell, 1892 - 1962; Fam: Half-brother of Hugh and Philip Warwick, (mother Joyce Ransom); Service: East African Mounted Rifles, Captain; Theatre: East Africa 1914; Medals: Victory, British, 1914-15 Star; Knighted post war; See p. 274.

Warwick, Philip Huskinson. Born: Southwell, 1880 - 1954; Lived: Normanton Prebend; Fam: Br. of Hugh Branston Warwick – above; School: Parkestone, Poole, University of Oxford; Occup: Director, Warwick & Richardson Brewery; Service: South Notts Hussars, Lt. Colonel; Theatre: Egypt, April 1915, Fr. 1918; Medals: Victory, British, 1914-15 Star, D.S.O.; See pp. 277-9.

Warren* Frank. Born: Farnsfield, 1882; Lived Farnsfield; Fam: F. Henry Warren (Farm worker), M. Ann (Smalley, m. 1871), one of 6 surviving children of 12; Occup: Bricklayer's labourer; Service: North Notts 4th Volunteers, enlisted 1908 with T.A., No. 738, 1/8th Bn. S/F, No. 158823, Machine Gun Corps, demob. 6/4/16; Theatre: No record; Medals: Victory, British.

Watchorn, William. Lived: Kirklington Road, Southwell; Service: No. 111257, Royal Field Artillery, Gnr; Theatre/Medals: No records.

Watson, John. Born: Southwell, 1889 - 1916; Lived, Sheppards Row, Southwell, then 21, Cedar Street, Mansfield; Fam: M. Sarah Ann Watson (Charwoman), Br. Herbert (1882); Occup: Barrington's Tin Works, Mansfield; Service: Enlisted June 1915, No. 27203, 17th Bn. S/F, L/Cpl.; Theatre: Fr. 1915, K-in-A 5/9/16 as part of the ongoing Battle of the Somme near Beaumont Hamel. There were 454 casualties that day, including John Watson who had been shot in the knee. Buried Dullens Communal Cemetery Extension, No. 1; Medals: Victory, British (possibly 1914-15 Star – record unavailable); See *N/A* 11/8/15, 12/1/16, 8/8/17, & pp. 211, 259.

Webb, Henry George. Born: Essex, 1886; Lived: Oxton Hall, Nr. Southwell; Fam: Married Lily (Belwood in 1914); Occup: Chauffeur; Service: Attested 16/8/15, No. M2/117255, Army Service Corps, demob. 29/4/19; Theatre: Fr. Sept. 1915; Medals: Victory, British, 1914-15 Star.

Weeks, Harry Sidney. Born: Family details not found; Lived: Westgate, Southwell; Service: No. 204647, 660th M.T. Co. Army Service Corps, Cpl., No. 2918, Royal Engineers, Cpl.; Theatre: Salonika, contracted malaria; Medals: Victory, British.

Wells, George. No records.

Whitworth, Arthur. Born: Kneesall, 1898 - 1917; Lived: Kneesall; Fam: F. George Whitworth, M. Kate (Wilkinson, m. 1891), S. Daisy (1894), Florence (1896); Service: Called up 1916, No. 31578, 7th Bn. Leicestershire Regt.; Theatre: Fr., K-in-A 8/11/17, commemorated Tyne Cot Memorial; Medals: Victory, British; See *N/A* 29/5/18.

Wilcox, Bernard Oliver. Born: Kimberley, 1892; Lived: Waterloo Yard, Southwell; Fam: F. Henry Oliver Wilcox (Lace machinist), M. Annie Maria (Attenborough), Br. Francis Henry (1892), John Robert (1895), S. Phoebe Annie (1897), married Lizzie Redgate 1930; School: Natl. 1898-1905; Occup: Clerk, Midland Railway Electrical Department;

*Frank Wilcox
(Newark Advertiser)*

Service: Attested 10/12/15, Nos. 189182 & 257778, 5th TN Stores, Royal Engineers; Theatre: No record; Medals: Victory, British, First Good Conduct Medal.

Wilcox, Francis Henry. Born: Kimberly, 1892; Lived: Southwell; Fam: Br. of Bernard Oliver Wilcox – see above, married Constance Harrison, children: Sybil (1921); School: National 1898-1901; Service: No. 286782, 2nd Bedfordshire Regt., Cpl.; Theatre: India; Medals: No record; *See N/A* 9/5/17.

Wilcox Frank.* Born: North Muskham, 1891 - 1915; Lived: Hill House Stables, Burgage, Southwell; Fam: F. George Wilcox (Coachman), M. Mary Ann (Spencer, m. 1886), Br. Raymond (1907), John (1908), S. Christine, (1903), Kathleen Emily (1910); Occup: Lace hand – E. Carey & Sons; Service: Enlisted 1907, No. 767, 1/8th Bn. S/F L/Cpl.; Theatre: Fr. March 1915. Wounded May 1915, returned to the front June 1915 and caught up in a mine explosion, K-in-A 15/6/15, buried Kemmel Chateau Cemetery 15/6/15; Medals: Victory, British, 1914-15 Star; See *N/A* 20/1/15, 28/4/15, 23/6/15, 7/7/15, 21/7/15, 11/8/15, 18/8/15, 17/11/15, 12/1/16, & p. 259.

Wilcox, John Robert Attenborough. Born: Kimberley,1895; Lived: Waterloo Cottage, King Street, Southwell; Fam: Brother of Bernard Wilcox – see above; Occup: Clerk at nursery; Service: No. 2343, 1/8th Bn. S/F, discharged 28/4/16; Theatre: Fr. March 1915; Medals: Victory, British, 1914-15 Star.

Wilkins, Harry. Born: Southwell, 1889 - 1915; Lived: 41, King Street, Southwell; Fam: F. Frank Wilkins (Cowman and dairyman), M. Elizabeth (Henton, m. 1882), Br. Arthur (1887); School: Infants & Natl. 1895-1903; Occup: Professional soldier; Service: No. 10534, 1st Bn. S/F; Theatre: Fr. November 1914, K-in-A 11/3/15 during the Battle of Neuve Chapelle, commemorated Le Touret Memorial; Medals: Victory, British, 1914-15 Star; See *N/A* 14/10/14, 24/3/15, 28/4/15, 5/5/15, 12/1/16.

Wilkinson, William Jefferson. Born: South Collingham, 1883 - 1917; Lived: Kirklington Road, Southwell; Fam: F. Joseph Wilkinson, M. Annie (Anderson, m. 1886), married Annie, children 3; Service: Called up 1916, No. 122701, Royal Garrison Artillery; Theatre: Fr. 1917, K-in-A 5/7/17, buried Dickebusch New Military Cemetery; Medals: Victory, British; Pre war William Wilkinson had returned from Canada and set up a poultry farm at Edingley, Notts., which he had to sell when he was called up for military service. Following his death his Battery Major wrote: 'It is with the deepest regret that I have to inform you that your husband was killed on the afternoon of 5th July. He was in company with others, resting in a dugout, when about 2.30 the enemy commenced shelling the battery position. The men all cleared out for safety and your husband had got well clear of the shelling when a piece of shell struck him on the head, killing him instantly. We found him lying on the road face downwards and after removing him from further harm, we buried him reverently in the evening, together with four others of his companions who had similarly suffered. He was a hard and willing worker, and of a cheerful nature and I feel his loss very keenly. Although poor comfort, you have the entire sympathy of his Battery in this your sad and irrevocable loss.'

Harry Wilkins (Newark Advertiser)

Wilks, Norman. No details.

Williams, Archibald C. R. Born: Newport Monmouthshire, 1900 - 1916; Lived: 1911 Minster School Boarder; Fam: F. David Williams (Clerk in Holy Orders), M Sarah Ann (Nippers, m. 1878), Br. David (1880), Frederick G. (1882), Joseph (1887), Samuel (1894), Archibald (1899), S. Janet (1885), Sarah Ann (1889), Jesida (1892); School: Home educated, then Minster 1911-1914; Occupation: Royal Navy; Service: HMS Conway & HMS King George V, K-in-A 12/11/16.

Willoughby, Archibald Macdonald. Born: Southwell, 1886-1943; Lived: Church Street, Southwell; Fam: Br. of Bernard Digby Willoughby – see below; Occup: Naval Officer; Service: Lt-Commander Royal Navy, no further details.

Willoughby, Bernard Digby. Born: Southwell, 1896-1997; Lived: Church Street, Southwell; Fam: F. Dr J. F. D. Willoughby, M. Mary Elizabeth (Randolph, m. 1881), Br. Ronald (1885), Archibald Macdonald (1886), S. Katherine (1882), married Ruth Barber 1944; Service: Army Service Corps, 2nd Lt., R.F.C, Lt., 1/21st Punjabi, Captain; Theatre: India; Medals: Victory, British, 1914-15 Star; Post war took Holy Orders.

Willoughby, Ronald James Edward. Born: Ilkeston, 1885; Lived: Church Street, Southwell; Fam: Br. of Bernard Willoughby – see above, married Constance Louisa (Sherbrooke); Occup: Royal Navy; Service: Listed in HMS Dido in 1914 as Lt. Commander; Theatre/Medals: No records.

Bernard Willoughby (RFC Records)

Wilson, Albert Henry. Born: Nottingham, 1881 - 1917; Lived: Kirklington Road, Southwell; Fam: F. James Wilson, married Nellie, children: Leonard Eric (1904), Phyllis (1908); Occup: Letter press compositor, also served at Burgage Manor Hospital, Minster bell ringer; Service: Called up 1916, No. 53483, S/F, No. 242102, 1/5th Bn. Border Regt.; Theatre: Fr. October 1916, K-in-A 25/4/17 at Arras, commemorated Arras Memorial; Medals: Victory, British; See *N/A* 16/5/17, 23/5/17, 8/8/17. The following letter was received by Mrs Wilson:

'Dear Mrs Wilson – You will no doubt have received by now official news regarding the death of your husband Pte. A. H. Wilson, but I feel it my painful duty to give you as full as possible details. He started with me in the attack on the 25th inst. And came through successfully out of the charge, and it was whilst holding the trench that a shell came close by and he was killed instantaneously. We carried the body back well to the rear, and gave him a decent burial and a cross has been erected above his grave. Speaking on behalf of the N.C.O.s and men of the Company, I must say he was a great favourite and ever ready to lend a hand to anyone. He always did his work uncomplainingly, and was a great help to me, and his platoon sergeant. I will now draw to a close by tendering my deepest sympathy to you and your family.'

Albert H. Wilson (David Hutchinson)

Wilson*, Herbert John. Born: Radford, Nottingham, 1887; Lived: King Street, Southwell; Fam: F. Albert Edward Wilson (Lace maker E. Carey & Sons), M. Harriett (Gee, m. 1882); School: Radford Buildings, Natl. 1897-1901; Occup: Cycle maker, Raleigh; Service: Nos. 746, 305019, 1/8th Bn. S/F, Col. Sgt., Wounded, demob. 15/3/19; Theatre: Fr. March 1915; Medals: Victory, British, 1914-15 Star.

Wilson, Randall Richard. Born: Southwell, 1900; Lived: Easthorpe, Southwell; Fam: F. John Henry Wilson (Labourer), M. Elizabeth, Br. Cecil Henry (1903), S. Laura (1895); School: Natl. 1908-13; Service: No record; See Parish Magazine July 1918.

Wilson*, William. Born: Southwell, 1893; Lived: King Street, Southwell; Fam: F. Edward Wilson, M. Mary Ann (Jerves, m. 1886), S. Elizabeth (1889); School: Wesleyan 1896-?; Service: No. 1016, 1/8th Bn. S/F, No. 30929, Yorkshire and Lancashire Regt., No. 18481, Labour Corps; Theatre: Fr. Feb. 1915; Medals: Victory, British, 1914-15 Star.

Wombwell, Walter. Born: Thurgarton, 1881 - 1918; Lived: Westgate, Southwell; Fam: F. Christopher Wombwell (Farm labourer), M. Elizabeth, married Ethel, children: Noel Walter (1909); School: Natl. Infants, Wesleyan 1892-94; Occup: Basket maker; Service: Attested 2/7/17, West Yorkshire Regt., No. 79035, 9th Platoon, 7th Bn. Durham Light Infantry; Theatre: Fr. January 1918, K-in-A 23/3/18 on the third day of the German offensive, Operation Michael, buried Assevillers New British Cemetery; Medals: Victory, British; His widow received a pension of 20/5d per week.

Wombwell, William. Born: Thurgarton, 1888; Lived: Westgate, Southwell; Fam: Brother of Walter Wombwell – see above; School: Trinity, Wesleyan, 1897-1902; Occup: Gardener's assistant; Service: Attested June 1915, No. 27196, S/F, transferred to Royal Army Ordnance Corps, L/Cpl.; Theatre: Siberia, Vladivostok 23/11/18 – 6/12/19, demobilized 3/3/20; Medals: Victory, British.

Wood, Arthur. Born: Newark, 1884; Lived: King Street, later Pollards Lane, Southwell; Fam: F. Earnest Wood, married Mary, children: Joyce M. (1915); School: Wesleyan, 1889-99; Occup: Grocer's traveller; Service: No. 49665, 3rd North Staffordshire Regt.; Theatre/Medals: No records.

Wood, Arthur. No biographical details; Service: No. R/5641, AB, Royal Naval Voluntary Reserve, 2nd Reserve B. Royal Navy.

Wood, Walter. Born: Upton, 1886; Lived: Upton; Fam: Married Mary Emma in 1907, children: Ethel Mary (1907), Olive (1914); Occup: Twist hand - E. Carey & Sons; Service: Attested 6/12/15, No. 032171, Royal Army Ordnance Corps; Theatre/Medals: No records.

Woodruff, Leonard Arthur. Born: Basford, 1888; Fam: F. Edward Woodruff (Textile traveller), M. Ellen (Marriott), Br. Horace Edward (1873), Robert Haydon (1881), S. Jessie (1876), Annie (1878), married Eliza Wallace, children: Olive K. (1915), Dorothy M. (1920); Occup: Groom; Service: No. 22834, Royal Army Veterinary Corps; Theatre: No record, Medals: Victory, British.

Woodward, Cecil G. Born: Tring, Herts, 1898; Lived: Maythorne, Southwell; Fam: F. George Woodward (Estate Carpenter, Starkey's), M. Emily (Edmonds), Br. Leonard (1910), S. Primrose (1906), Marjorie (1908), m. Clara Keetley, children: Cecil G. (1928), Florence (1928), George J. (1932); School: Wesleyan, Natl. 1906-8, Minster 1908-12; Occup: Carpenter at Starkey's; Service: Enlisted 1914, No. 5/7666, A.O.C; Theatre/Medals: No records; See p. 307.

Woodward, George William. No details; Service: 1/1st South Notts Hussars; See p. 279

Worman, Arthur Lawrence. Born: West Bridgford, 1894 – 1916; Lived: Nottingham; Fam: F. Walter (Clerk Advertising Dept.), M. Maria, Br. Walter Cecil (1879), Harry Dean (1887), S. Mabel (1883), Hilda (1884), Constance (1890); School: Mrs Hatfield's, Minster 1903-08; Occup: Apprentice lace maker; Service No. 12693, 8th Bn. Leicestershire Regt., L/Cpl.; Theatre: Fr. July 1915, wounded 15/1/16, died 18/1/16 at Rouen, buried St Sever Cemetery, Rouen; Medals: Victory, British, 1914-15 Star.

Wright, Alfred Godfrey. Born: Swineshead, 1874; Lived: The Burgage, Southwell; Fam: Married Dora Wood 1899, children: May (1899), Kathleen (1901), Dora (1903); Occup: Twisthand – E. Carey & Sons; Service: Nos. 20627 & 203474, S/F; Theatre: No record; Medals: Victory & British; See *N/A* 14/4/15.

Wright, Gervase. Born: No record; Lived: Morton Manor, Rolleston; Fam: No record; School: Minster; Service: S/F. Captain; Medals: Victory, British; See p. 307.

Wright*, Harry Gordon. Born: Calverton, 1897 - 1917; Lived: Foxwood Terrace, Calverton; Fam: F. John Livington Wright (Framework knitter), M. Rebecca (Beardall), Br. Joseph (1893), James (1900), S. Florence (1894), Nellie (1898); Service: No. 307044, 1/8th Bn. S/F, Cpl.; Theatre:

Fr. March 1915, K-in-A 30/1/17, commemorated Loos Memorial; Medals: Victory, British, 1914-15 Star; See p. 229.

Wright*, Henry Gordon. Born: Nottingham, 1887 - 1915; Lived: Trinity Villas, Southwell; Fam: F. Thomas Wright (Architect), M. Mary, Br. Thomas (1879), Edward (1882), William (1885), S. Caroline (1876), Evelyn (1881), Octavia (1889), Kathleen (1891); Occup: Bank clerk; Service: 1/8th Bn. S/F, Captain; Theatre: Fr. March 1915, K-in-A 6/6/15, buried Kemmel Chateau Military Cemetery; Medals: Victory, British, 1914-15 Star; See pp. 207, 229.

Wright, John Robert. Born: Newark, 1890; Lived: Farnsfield; Fam: F. Robert Wright (Foreman maltster), M. Sarah, Br. Richard Harold (1895), Clive (1899), Clement &Joseph (1905), S. Hetty (1901), married Ethel Wilson 1916, children: John Robert (1916), Olive G. (1919), May (1921), Victor W. (1921), William E. (1922), Constance (1927); Occup: Maltster; Service: Nos. 48206, S/F, 17286, 28th Labour Corps; Theatre: No record; Medals: Victory, British.

Wright*, John T. Born: No record found; Lived: Park Street, Southwell; Fam: No details of parents, although *N/A* reports a brother, George; Service: 1/8th Bn. S/F, No. 144488, Machine Gun Corps; Theatre: Fr. 1915, wounded twice; Medals: Victory, British, 1914-15 Star, Military Medal won in France 1917; See *N/A* 10/10/17.

Wyer, Cecil. Born: Southwell, 1887; Lived: King Street, Southwell; Fam: F. William Edward Wyer (Shoemaker), M. Elizabeth (Clifton), S. Elsie Mary (1896), Esmey Ethel (1898), married Ada E. Gilliver, children: Hazel M (1925); School: Natl. 1902-05, Minster 1905-14 – choral scholar and pupil organist; Service: No. 306706, 2/5th S/F; Theatre: No record; Medals: Victory, British.

Wyles, Augustus. Born: Southwell, 1870-1917; Lived: The Hop Yard, Southwell; Fam: M. Anna M. Wyles, Br. Arthur (1863), John (1865), S. Eliza (1858), Mercy (1868); Occup: Labourer and former soldier; Service: Served with 4th Notts Volunteer Bn. in the Boer War, No. 3419, Nottinghamshire & Derbys., No. 204220, 21st Bn. Rifle Brigade, 802nd Area Company, Labour Corps; Theatre: Egypt and Salonika died of pneumonia 19/10/17, buried Alexandria (Hadra) Memorial Cemetery; Medals: Queen's Medal and four clasps from Boer War, Victory, British; See *N/A* 7/11/17, 29/5/18

Wyles, Wallace. Born: Southwell, 1887; Lived: Maythorne, Southwell; Fam: F. Arthur Wyles (Labourer), M. Fanny, Br. Arthur (1888); School: Wesleyan, Natl. 1895-?; Occup: Twisthand – E. Carey & Sons; Service: Attested 28/9/14, Nos. 602 & 612250, 19th Brigade, Royal Horse Artillery; Theatre: Egypt, April 1915; Medals: Victory, British 1914-15 Star.

Augustus Wyles
(Newark Advertiser)

The men of Southwell's commitment to the First World War was probably no greater than any other community in Britain and the Empire, but the price they paid was high with 16% dying as a result of the war, and many wounded, both physically and emotionally. Across the Empire 8.9 million men were mobilized and the death rate was 10%, with a further 2 million wounded. The deaths amongst young officers was higher than for other ranks and in just one action, Hohenzollern, October 1915, two young local officers died – the Handford brothers - and a few weeks later their brother-in-law, Major John Becher, D.S.O., died of wounds he received in the same action. In the introduction to *Up The Line To Death*[1] Brian Gardner states: 'The life expectancy

---
[1] Brian Gardner, ed., *Up The Line To Death, An Anthology* (York: Methuen, 2007), p. xxiii.

of a young officer was about nine months – or one summer's push.' This one sentence speaks volumes about the harsh reality of the First World War.

The anthology contains a poem written by the war poet Richard Aldington (1892-1962), who was an officer in the Royal Sussex Regiment and was wounded in 1917 whilst serving on the Western front, which graphically describes the experience of life at the front.

Bombardment

Four days the earth was rent and torn
By bursting steel,
The houses fell about us;
Three nights we dared not sleep,
Sweating, and listening for the imminent crash
Which meant our death.

The fourth night every man,
Nerve-tortured, racked to exhaustion,
Slept muttering and twitching,
Whilst the shells crashed overhead.

The fifth day there came a hush;
We left our holes
And looked above the wreckage of the earth
To where the white clouds moved in silent lines
Across the untroubled blue.

Richard Aldington

SLIP THIS INSIDE YOUR CAP.

A SOLDIER'S PRAYER.

Almighty and most Merciful Father,
Forgive me my sins:
Grant me Thy peace
Give me Thy power:
Bless me and mine in life and death
for Jesus Christ's sake. Amen.

Cyril Overton's Prayer Card
(Julia Overton)

1.2 Roll Call - The Surrounding Villages

The following lists are a roll call of the men and women from villages surrounding Southwell who served in the First World War. Those in bold lost their lives. A few of the men may also appear in the Southwell list because they are known to have a connection with the town. The total number listed is 574, there are likely to have been more.

AVERHAM

Ansell, William Edward
Dickinson, Frederick Johnson
Finn, James William
Gent, John Henry
Hunt, Harry Lawford
Ingamells, Reuben

Ingamells, Charles Frederick
Johnson, Charles Thomas
Lee, Robert
Smith, George William
Watts, Harry
Williamson, John

BLEASBY

Andrew, George William
Barker, John
Baydon, W.
Brothwell, J.
Brown, William Arthur
Cox, Charles Enos
Cox Harry
Crowther, T.
Dewhurst, George Herbert
Elmer, Charles William
Faulkner, John Jessop
Fields, Ernest
Gill, Leonard Edward
Hind, William Vincent
Holmes, C.
Holmes, George
Holmes, Samuel
Hyde, B.
James, H.
James Jack Leslie F.
James, William Henry
Kelham, Cecil Herbert Langdale
Kelham, Philip Varasour Langdale
Kemp, Albert
Lidgett, George D.
Limb, Walter Edward
Marsh, Charles
Marsh, Frederick
Marsh, Joseph Edwin
Marshall, L.R.

Mason, A.
Mason, W.O.
Mason, W.W.
Mills, Herbert
Musgrave, G.
Naylor, H.V.
Nuthall, J.W.
Oliver, Harold
Oliver, Owen
Oliver, Sidney
Palmby, Henry
Panton, J.W.
Picksley, F.
Rayworth, H.
Rosen, Henry Samuel
Sharp, J.
Sheppard, Thomas Henry
Smith, J
Sneath, Thomas
Spike, Charles
Spike, Henry Cope
Stonehouse
Storer, Leonard
Sullivan, M.
Truman, Harold Edmund
Weston, John Geoffrey
White, Sampson Ernest
Wilson, George Albert
Wilkinson, Harry

CAUNTON

Antcliffe, Alexander
Antcliffe, Charles Edward
Baines, John Thomas
Barker, George William
Bartle, Albert
Bartle, Sidney
Bartle, Walter
Bickerton, Charles
Bland, William Percy
Boddy, Wilfred
Brown, John George
Burrows, Ernest
Butterfield, David
Carrott, Fred
Chappell, Ernest Henry
Drabble, Henry Mann
Drabble, William
Elvidge, Albert
Elvidge, George
Elvidge, Heber
Fincham, Cyril
Fincham, Horace
Fincham, Thorald
Frecknall, Thomas
Gibson, Sydney
Gilbert, Edwin
Gilbert, Frederick
Godson, Edward
Graves, Arthur
Hage, Arthur

Hickman, Walter
Hole, Hugh F.S
Hole, John
Hopkinson, Richard
Jaques, Frank
Lacy, Henry Percy
Lord, Frank
Lord, George Henry
Lord, Joseph J.
Moody, George Samuel
Ogden, Frank
Pearce, John
Pinder, Charles
Pinder, George
Pinder, George Alfred
Poole, Charles
Poole, Walter
Potterton, John Frederick
Reynolds, Albert George
Reynolds, Sydney
Rushby, Herbert
Saxby, William
Schwabe, Alexander George Thackeray
Sharp, Herbert Francis William
Smith, George William
Turner, G.
Wells, Ernest
Wells, George Henry
Wombwell, Francis Arthur

EDINGLEY

Barratt, Edrick Richard
Breedon, Ephraim
Butcher, Arthur
Cope, John
Dance, Edward
Dance, William
Heighton, John
Hubbard, John
Hurst, John William
Judge, John Frederick

Parlett, Henry
Pearson, William
Robinson, William James
Skelcher, Bertram
Smith, George
White, Frederick
White, Sydney
Whitehead, James Alfred
Whitworth, Ernest William

FARNSFIELD

Alsop, William James
Baguley, William
Barlow, Samuel
Bartlett, Alfred
Bartlett, Robert Ernest
Bartle, G.
Barton, R.F.
Beighton, Graham
Bennett, George
Bowler, Eustace John Harold
Bowman, F.
Bowmer, Fred
Broadhurst, William
Buckles, Alec
Buckles, Harry
Buckles, William
Bullock, Frank jun.
Burton, Bruce
Castle, Harold William
Challand, Arthur Douglas
Challand, Walter
Chantry, Joseph
Christian, Bert
Coldham, Frederick
Coleman, H.
Compton, Frederick Henry
Cooledge, William
Copeland, Walter
Crofts, Shirley
Davis, Arthur
Davis, Thomas Percy
Dean, Arthur Edward
Easter, Jonas Collett
Emmons, William
Farr, C.G.
Farrow, George
Felton, Sidney
Fogg, John
Fogg, William
Fortis, William
Gilbert, Leonard
Godden, Albert Edward
Goulding, Joseph
Goulding, N.C.

Graves, George
Gray, Norman Benjamin
Gray, Oliver Marshall
Haigh, Frederick
Haynes, Richard William
Hogg, John Henry
Isgar, Percy William
Jackson, Charles Albert
Kew, John Robert
Knowles, George
Marriott, Alfred
Marriott, J.
Marshall, Herbert
Marshall, James
Miller, Edward Alexander
Millington John Duffin
Milner, J.
Moakes, George
Musson, George Henry Tipping
Musson, Leonard
Musson, William
Musson, William John
Nairn, Robert William
Odlin, Ernest
Osborne, Arthur
Palmer, Harry
Parker, Walter
Parr, H. George Leonard
Parr, John Richard
Phillips, Arthur
Phillips, Herbert
Potton, John Walter
Powell, Charles William
Radford, George jun.
Ramsden, Elsworth
Randall, Albert
Robinson, Frank
Rosling, George
Ross, George
Ross, William
Skelton, Ben
Smith, George William Harcourt Avondale
Smith, Henry Ivor
Smith, Richard

Farnsfield continued

Spittlehouse, A.J.
Spittlehouse, Harold
Stafford, George Arthur
Stanley, Philip
Stanley, W.
Stocks, Fred
Straw, Alexander
Straw, Frederick William
Straw, Walter William
Swift, Thomas
Talbot, Frank
Talbot, Guy
Thorpe, Charles

Wagstaff, John James
Warren, Frank
White, T.E.
Whitten, William
Whitworth, Leonard
Wilson, John Naylor Hodgson
Wilson, Laurence Naylor Hodgson
Wilson, Wm. Hodgson Sugden
Withers, Frank
Woodward, Harry
Woodward, Percy
Wright, Harold
Wright, Henry D.
Wright, Thomas

FISKERTON cum MORTON

Akrill, George
Antcliffe, Elijah
Antcliffe, Walter
Brown, Cephus John
Brown, Charles Stafford
Bryan, George
Bryan, Herbert
Carpendale, Harold Bert
Cox, Samuel
Crowder, Arthur Foster
Crowder, George
Crowder, Thomas
Cullen, Charles Frederick
Cullen, Harold
Dabell, Walter
Elliott, Thomas Wilfred
Elliott, William Ernest
Foster, Frank
Foster, George Cornelius
Foster, William
Fox, William jun.
Gilliatt, Christopher J.
Gilliatt, Cyril
Hammersley, Frederick Charles
Hancock, George Thomas
Hardy, Frederick

Jarvis Charles
Lawson, Arthur
Lees, Frank
Longdon, Reginald William
Marsh, George
Midgley, Richard Marriott
Midgley, Robert Howsin
Parker, John
Pickup, Gilbert Charles
Sawyer, Fred
Shrewsbury, George Edward
Smith, Leonard
Templeman, George
Townrow, Sydney
Usher, William Lawson
Voce, Charles William
Voce, George Walter
Voce, Thomas Dennis
Wagstaff, Bernard Eric.
Waller, Arthur Frederick
Waller, Sidney Horace
Widdowson, Frank Christian
Widdowson, Norman Stuart
Willows, Charles
Wing, Henry
Wright, Gervase

GONALSTON

Arliss, Thomas Ward
Butterfield, Percival John
Buxton, Christopher
Francklin, Philip
Francklin, William Robert
Jubb, Thomas William

Kemm, Frederick Gilman
Lindsey, Horace
Midgley, Richard Marriott
Pearson, Oliver
Sheppard, Wilfred
Vann, Arthur

HALAM

Barlow, Walter
Bust, Eric
Cragg, Percy
Cragg, Thomas Cyril
Hallam, William Smith
Hayes, Charles Henry
Haywood, Arthur
Haywood, William
Hill, John Percy
Hurt, John
Hurt, Seth
Lawson, George
May, Harry

Ricketts, Arthur
Ricketts, David
Rogers, William
Sharman, Charles
Smith, Arthur
Tinley, Charles
Tinley, Edward John
Ware, Henry
Weightman, Fred
Whysall, German
Whysall, John
Wilkinson, John James

HALLOUGHTON

Osborne, Thomas William
Wales, William Henry Brett
Wilson, William Henry

HOCKERTON

Naile, Henry
Smith, Philip St George Duncan

KIRKLINGTON

Baxter, John William
Daws, John William
Drabble, William
Fox, Edwin
Fox, Ernest
Gilbertson, Ernest
Handley, Frederick Coulam
Hayes, Henry
Hayes, James Christopher

Martin, Reginald Hall
Midgley, Arthur William
Pattle, Jonas
Pattle, William
Rickett, Harry
Smith, James
Stubbins, Thomas
Whitworth, Ernest William
Wright, George

Henrey, George William
Knight, Cyril
Knight, Horace
Rickett, Albert Edward

MAPLEBECK

Whitworth, Reuben Percy
Williams, Arthur Ernest
Wright, Harold Thomas

OXTON

Abbott, William Harris
Adkin, Stanley
Argyle, George
Argyle, Samuel
Argyle, Walter
Barnby, Harrison
Bell, Albert William
Bell, Alfred
Berridge, James
Bramble, Arthur
Bramble, Frank
Carter, Charles Richard
Catlin, Ernest
Dickman, William
Evans, Vincent
Evans, William
Fox, George Henry
Freestone, Arthur
Green, Charles
Halford, Henry
Hart, Frank
Hart, Joseph William
Hart S. H.
Hindson, Arthur
Hindson, Robert
Holdershaw, Frank
Jackson, Edwin

Martin, George
Reader, Thomas
Reavill, John William
Reeve, Henry
Richards Arthur
Sherbrooke, Henry Graham
Sherbrooke, Robert Lowe
Spendlove, Frank
Statham, George
Stevens, Herbert
Strutt, Arthur
Strutt, Bertie
Strutt, Frederick.
Strutt, George Frederick
Taylor, Sydney
Templeman, Thomas
Turner, William
Upton, George
Upton, George Frederick
Upton, Herbert
Wain, William
Wells, John Robert
Whitelock, Edward
Whitelock, James
Whitelock, Matthew
Whitelock, Victor

ROLLESTON

Bemrose, Charles William
Bryan, Charles Henry
Bryan, George Ernest
Bush, Henry Christopher
Cox, Samuel
Dickinson, Sam
Facer, Archibald
Facer, Herbert Edward
Fox, Charles Robinson
Fox, George Henry
Fox, Percy William
Hollingsworth, Percy William
Hyde, Herbert Edmund

Hyde, J. W.
Long, George
Pepper, Cecil
Pepper, Francis Walter
Pepper, Samuel
Rick, Robert Broadberry
Rick, Thomas Samuel
Sharpe, Harry
Smith, George
Stanfield, John William Wellings
Swann, Thomas Humphrey
Thurston, Thomas Charles
Waller, John Gamble

STAYTHORPE

Herrod, William
Ingamells, Charles Frederick

Thompson, George Driver
Thompson, Henry Edward

THURGARTON

Ainger, Harry
Baylay, Charles
Bentley, John William
Bird, Henry
Booker, Edward William
Featherstone, Arthur
Featherstone, Harry
Fisher, Alfred
Fisher, George
Fisher, Harry
Fletcher, Leonard
Francis, Sydney James
Heather, Robert
Jackson
Kaye, Isabel
Kaye, Walter Rockley
Lovett, Aaron
Marson, Arthur James
Marson, Robert
Massey, Matthew

Paling, Thomas
Pearson, William
Richardson, Frank William
Sharpe, George
Smith, George
Statham, Joseph Palesthorpe
Taylor, Edgar
Taylor, George Edward
Taylor, Harry
Thornton, Noel William
Thornton, Richard
Tyler, Arthur David
Tyler, William
Tyler, William James
Upton, Thomas Francis Joseph
Usborne, Thomas Richard Guy
Warrener, John Vincent
Warrener, William Henry
Wise, George
Wombwell, Walter

UPTON

Abbott, Robert Ward
Abbott, William Harris
Arnold, Joseph
Beale, Clarence
Bently, Lionel Charles
Brooks, Charles
Brooks, James Edward
Brooks, Robert Harold
Brown, Harry
Chambers, Joseph Arthur
Clements, Sydney William
Cortby, George
Cox, Philip
Cropper, George
Daniels, Edward
Dodson, Dudley Paulson
Foster, Charles
Foster, Harry
Hague, William Webster
Hemstock, Herbert
Hemstock, Percy
Hilton, Shepherd Alfred Sydney
Hilton, Shepherd Basil Algernon
Hunt, Arthur Godfrey
Keyworth, Edward Thomas
Kirby, Leonard
Kirby, William
Lester, Frank
Lowe, Alfred Henry
Martin, Cyril Victor
Martin, Edwin
Parker, Ernest
Porter, William Ernest
Proctor, Albert
Proctor, Thomas

Rawson, Arthur
Reeves, Frederick James
Reeves, George William
Reeves, Robert Sydney
Richardson, Edmund
Rippin, Archibald
Rippin, John Christopher
Rockley, Arthur
Sheppard, George William
Sheppard, Harry
Sheppard, Herbert
Simpson, Albert
Simpson, Ernest
Smith, Frederick
Smith, William Henry
Smithson, Harry
Stimson, Charles
Stimson, Ernest
Stimson, Frederick
Stimson, George
Stimson, William
Story, William
Sumner, John Wesson
Suter, Cyril Barton
Todd, Tom
Walker, Percival Thomas
Walster, William James
Warwick, Douglas Vivian
Warwick, John Cedric Geoffrey
Watt, Thomas
Wells, William Henry
Wilkinson, William Jefferson
Wood, Walter Oliver
Wynne, Abraham S.B.
Wynne, William Henry

CHAPTER 2

SOUTHWELL AT WAR

1914 - 1919

The Newark Advertiser
AND SOUTH NOTTS GAZETTE

The Southwell War Diary

This is an edited version, with notes, of the 'Southwell News' column from the Newark Advertiser from January 1914 to November 1919. Additional information has been incorporated from reports of meetings of the Southwell parish council, Southwell rural district council, the Southwell Board of Guardians, the Southwell tribunal, the 'Fallen Heroes' notices, and articles, letters and editorial comments that appeared elsewhere in the paper. The Advertiser was published weekly on Wednesday with its 'Southwell News' column being supplied by 'a local correspondent'. The principal local regiment was variously referred to in this newspaper as the Notts and Derby Regiment (its official title) or the Sherwood Foresters (its popular title). The Territorial battalions of the regiment were the 5th, 6th, 7th and 8th. The 7th battalion was popularly known as the 'Robin Hoods' and the gallantry of the 8th Battalion, to which H company (the Southwell company) belonged, caused them to be known by some in the regiment in 1915 as the 'Mad 8th.'

We have here an almost week-by-week account of how a small but by no means untypical community lived out its life in the months before the war, how it responded to a conflict that was to bring so much sorrow to many of its families, and what the effect of the war was on its social life and institutions. By mid-1917 it was claimed that over 500 young men from Southwell had been mobilised, though this number may include men from the villages nearest to the town.[1] Well over a fifth of them were to be killed in action, and at least as many more were wounded or suffered in other ways. Hardly a family in the town was untouched by the war. All the families with young men serving in the armed forces would have daily feared the letter or telegram telling them of the death or injury of a husband, son or brother. In the first months of the war, before censorship was imposed with increasing severity, letters from men at the front told their families at home, often in vivid detail, of the actions in which they had fought.

    As a community Southwell coped with the regulations under the Defence of the Realm Act: lighting restrictions were imposed, licensing hours reduced, and food and fuel rationed. The Southwell tribunal, established here as elsewhere under the Military Service Acts of 1916, heard hundreds of appeals against conscription from Southwell and a wide area around. The parish council, the rural district council and the Board of Guardians dealt as best they could with the restrictions imposed by war. Two auxiliary military hospitals, one in Burgage Manor and one in

---

[1] The final total from Southwell was at least 650.

Brackenhurst Hall, took numbers of wounded men, as did the fever hospital on Galley Lane, and were actively supported by the people of Southwell, who provided weekly entertainments, certainly in Burgage Manor and Brackenhurst. From early 1915 the national egg collection scheme, designed to provide fresh eggs for the wounded, was supported in Southwell and the villages, and weekly reports of the number of eggs collected were published. Servicemen training in a camp in Norwood Park were befriended, and school premises and private social clubs were opened to them. In the earliest days of the war no less than 25 refugees from the atrocities following the German invasion of Belgium were welcomed into the town by the town council and by individuals.

Some individuals and businesses profited from the war. That was inevitable. Others were forced to restrict their opening hours. There is evidence that by late 1917 food and fuel price increases were imposed despite price controls designed to protect the poor, and the working people of Southwell established a Workers' Defence League to 'bring the workers' complaints in a regular manner to the proper authorities'. At this sign that workers were beginning to organise, in May 1918 the chairman of Southwell Traders' Association, representing local employers, 'hoped to see the Traders' Association and Labour so organised as to work amicably for mutual benefit'.

Comrades' associations for ex-servicemen were actively supported, not least because some discharged and disabled servicemen were being ignored or treated unfairly.

Through these reports we can share something, far removed as we are in time and circumstance, of the fears and hopes of Southwell servicemen and of their families in what several servicemen called 'the dear old town' during a war which, though it did not initiate radical change in the ways in which men and women regarded themselves, each other and their communities, certainly accelerated it, often, for some, with unwelcome and disturbing consequences that are still resisted, but for others were to bring greater freedom and opportunity.

Southwell before the war

In early 1914 Southwell was still firmly rooted in Victoria's England. Veterans of the Crimean War and the Indian Mutiny were still alive. The *Newark Advertiser* shows its middle-class inhabitants were enjoying a vigorous social life with golf and rifle club competitions, cattle fairs, horticultural shows, billiards and tennis tournaments, pigeon races, debating society, 'amateur theatricals', Red Cross Society meetings and demonstrations, dances, balls, and annual dinners. The town's working class had more limited opportunities, but the 'Pleasure Fair' and 'Mr Ginnett's circus' and the town's ale-houses would have catered for its needs and relied on its support, and the Warwick penny bank offered some security for what savings they could accumulate. The workhouse was governed by Guardians sharing many of the assumptions about poverty, and what was still called 'feeble-mindedness', prevalent fifty and more years earlier, and who were governed by the Poor Law rules governing 'settlement' in the Union. The town's employers, particularly in agriculture and horticulture, treated their workers with the distant patronage, which had marked the relationship between capital and labour for generations.

By the close of 1919 one can still hear strong echoes of that England, but the impact of the war had been profound. Many of the town's young men had been killed. Those that returned – many of them shell-shocked and wounded – wanted, demanded, the new world they had been told they were fighting for and believed that they deserved. Social class divisions persisted of course, officers and men had died together but they were still divided by class, but the war had destroyed forelock-touching deference for ever. Capital and labour were better organised. Above all, virtually all men over 21 (but not, until 1928, all women) had the vote [see the next chapter]. By 1919 Southwell was a more democratic, but still socially divided, place.

7 January 1914

A report that Mr. W. N. Hicking, high sheriff of Nottinghamshire, of Brackenhurst Hall and Burgage Manor, had donated new uniforms to surviving members of the Nottingham and Nottinghamshire Crimean and Indian Mutiny Veterans' Association. This took place in a ceremony in the Mikado Café in Nottingham, after which the veterans were taken to a show in a picture palace. Mr Hicking provided new top coats, uniforms, peaked hats, gloves, and socks, to replace the existing 'neat, blue serge uniforms' worn by the veterans. The Association saw to it that these men 'never want, provides them with medical attendance, and finally buries them with military honours.' To Mr Hicking's gift the Mayor of Nottingham added 'half a pound of tobacco', apparently to each man. Of the original veterans, 121 had died since the formation of the association in 1899. At the Mikado Café 23 veterans attended, though 'some . . . were too feeble to turn out in such severe weather'.

'THANKS   On Christmas Eve the workmen and tenants of Mr. Wm. Cottam were each presented with a barrow-load of logs. On New Year's Eve the workmen were entertained to dinner, and for this seasonable generosity all who participated wish to heartily thank Mr. Cottam.'

'WARWICK PENNY BANK   This useful institution was re-opened on Saturday and the Trustees have adopted a regulation that any depositor giving notice of withdrawal must take out the whole of his or her deposits, and will not be entitled to receive a fresh card during the current year.'

- HOLE'S -

MILK STOUT.

PRICES—Half-pints, per dozen, 2/-.

Pints,   „   3/6.

UNDER LETTERS PATENT 13535—1908, 1369—1909.

'CHRISTMAS TREE AT THE WORKHOUSE'   On Monday week the children in the Workhouse, Southwell, were entertained by a Christmas tree, the gifts being subscribed for by the Guardians, and the tree supplied by Mr. Webb. Mr. and Mrs. Lewin came and assisted and helped to amuse the children. Afterwards games of all kinds were indulged in and the children had a most enjoyable time. The Master and Matron worked very hard in their efforts to afford the children all the enjoyment possible out of the event. On Tuesday a concert was given by Mr. Foster, a member of the Board, and a number of friends from the Baptist Chapel. The first part of the programme was entirely vocal, the second portion being devoted to a humorous sketch, entitled "Wanted a Wife". At the conclusion each woman was presented with an orange and each man with an ounce of tobacco.'

14 February 1914

A report of the ninth annual dinner of Southwell Rifle Club held at the Hotel lists among those present most of the influential men in the town. Among the many listed by name were: Dr. Walker, Dr. Willoughby, C. L. Maltby, R. A. Millington, J. H. Kirkby, E. A. Merryweather (captain of the club), A. T. and N.A. Metcalfe, C. G. Caudwell, Harold Browne, A. G. Merryweather, G. W. Kirk (hon. secretary), H. Barrett, A. Woodruffe, J. P. Becher and 27 others. Apologies were received from Archdeacon Hacking, Dr Handford, Dr Polson, J. E. Merryweather, A Salt, and several clergy together with some fourteen others. [From these men were drawn many who served, or were to serve, on the town and rural district councils, the Board of Guardians, the petty sessions bench, the Southwell Traders' Association committee, and committees for good causes. They and their wives were also key figures in the social life of the middle class in the town.]

A recruitment event sometime in 1915
(Photographed by Howard Barrett)

21 February 1914

'QUADRILLE CLASS' This is a notice of the annual Shrove Tuesday Dance to be held in the Assembly Room on 24 February. Mr F. A. Marshall's band had been engaged, 'and lovers of the light fantastic know what this means'. An extension until 2 a.m. had been granted. 'An early application for tickets is requested, as the supply will be strictly limited.'

At their recent meeting the Southwell Board of Guardians discussed the case of a 'feeble-minded' girl from Grantham 'whose "settlement" is on the Southwell Union', though it noted that from 1 April responsibility for placing such cases would devolve to the county council.

28 February 1914

A notice that the Southwell Debating Society was to hold a special meeting at Rumford's room on the following Thursday evening 'when the subject will be as follows: "That the practice of

Vivisection has resulted in the highest benefits to humanity'. The case for the motion was to be made by R. A. Millington and the case against by J. E. Ellis. Harold Browne would be in the chair. 'As this meeting is open to non-members, including ladies, it is fully expected that there will be a large assembly.' A subsequent report, on 4 March, noted that the motion was carried by a majority of 13 votes. Several local medical practitioners had spoken in support.

22 April 1914

TERRITORIALS   Lieutenant McMillan was in charge of a number of men of the South Notts. Hussars Maxim Gun Section at Brackenhurst last week. They spent a busy time in tactical drill and firing under war conditions. Brackenhurst is an ideal spot for training with hills and valleys, and plenty of farms in the neighbourhood for giving shelter to scouts when on the march.

27 May 1914

A notice that a 'Pleasure Fair' had been held in 'Mr Jackson's field, near the Gas Works'. This was an attempt to revive the traditional Southwell Fair. There were 'motor cars, cakewalk, bread-making competitions, steam roundabouts, coconut shies', while 'the usual side shows did a good trade on Friday and Saturday nights, although the weather was not all that could be desired'.

3 June 1914

A notice of the forthcoming visit of 'Mr Ginnett's circus', including the final circus appearance of Mona Conner, 'the finest bareback rider in the country' according to Mr Ginnett.

24 June 1914

An article headed 'Southwell the Birthplace of the Poor Law. Sir George Nicholls the Author' begins by saying that 'the following interesting historical summary has come into our hands by the courtesy of the Clerk to the Southwell Board of Guardians (Mr. Ellis). It was written for Mr. Eustace Barlow, late Chairman of the Southwell Board, by a well-known and highly-placed Inspector of the Local Government Board.' What follows is a very one-sided (and in part erroneous) account of the establishment of the Poor Law regime in Southwell in the 1820s, the success of which led to the provisions of the infamous Poor Law Amendment Act of 1832. George Nicholls is given all the credit for this reform and the crucial initiative of John Thomas Becher is not mentioned at all. This reflects the bitter dispute between Nicholls and Becher about who was responsible for 'the Poor Law Reform in England'.

15 July 1914

'CHURCH PARADE   On Sunday last the streets were lined with spectators to see the Church Parade of the local Territorial Force, who formed up at the new drill hall under the command of Captain Becher, and accompanied by Southwell Brass Band, marched by the way of Easthorpe to the Minster. The local branch of the National Reserve, in strong force, formed the rear guard, and the members of the British Red Cross Society with Miss E. M. Small, commandant of the women's detachment, and Mr A. E. Merryweather, in charge of the men's detachment, were assembled in the Market-place, and fell in with the procession to church. The local members of the Church Lads' Brigade, under the command of Capt. Brown, also took part. The sermon was preached by the rector, the Venerable Archdeacon Wild, who delivered a stirring discourse from the text, "There is another King." After the service the procession was reformed in Westgate, and with the strains of music, marched to Burgage Green, where they were addressed by Capt. Becher, who urged the members of the Territorial Force to join the National Reserve when they had completed their term with the Territorials.'

29 July 1914

'TERRITORIALS   On Sunday last the Southwell detachment of the Notts and Derbys paraded at the Drill Hall, where they were formed into line under the command of Captain Becher and Lt. Handford. They were marched to the station and entrained for the camp at Hunmanby, near Filey, Yorkshire, for a fortnight's training under canvas. There were 76 rank and file, including the new drill instructor Sergeant Walker. The men were supplied with refreshments for the long railway journey, and were given an enthusiastic send-off by hundreds of friends and relatives who went to the station to see them start.'

Employees of E Carey & Sons Ltd, members of 'H' Company, Sherwood Foresters, 1913 (Andy Gregory)

Southwell during the war

5 August 1914 (the day war was declared)

The following quote preceded a full report on the outbreak of the war:

> The earth is full of anger,
>   The seas are dark with wrath;
> The Nations in their harness
>   Go up against our path;
> Ere yet we loose the legions –
>   Ere yet we draw the blade,
> Jehovah of the Thunders,
>   Lord God of Battles, aid.
>
>   - Kipling

Reports of a lawn tennis tournament, amateur theatricals, a Church Lads' Brigade camp at Southport, and the wedding of Lancelot Edward Becher of the Royal Engineers and second son of the late John Henry Becher, to Margaret Lucy Lyttleton, only daughter of the bishop of Southampton. [Note: Lancelot Edward Becher, younger brother of John Pickard Becher, ended the war as a lieutenant colonel serving with the headquarters staff of 16th division, Royal Engineers. He had been awarded the DSO, been mentioned in dispatches, and been granted the three campaign medals. He had been sent to Western Europe on 18 December 1915.]

12 August 1914

'SOUTHWELL WAR NEWS   H Company of the 8th Battalion Sherwood Foresters returned from camp on Monday, and during the week members from Oxton, Bleasby, Farnsfield, Epperstone, and other villages have been billeted in various hotels and other places.

   The first man to rejoin the colours from Southwell was P.c. Kettle, who is a Reservist. At Southwell Police Court on Friday, Mr Wright of Fiskerton, who presided, said, "Before we begin business I should like to say a few words with regard to P.c. Kettle, who had to answer the call to arms. I have always found he has done his duty as an officer in the police force, and no doubt he will do the same in the Army. He has gone to uphold the flag of Old England and we wish him success and a safe return." Inspector Clarke expressed his thanks to Mr Wright for his kind remarks.'

   H Company contains no fewer than 36 employees of Messrs Carey and Sons, lace factory, Southwell, and the manager, Mr T. D. Partington, himself an ex-sergeant in the Company, has received the following telegram:- "I am proud to think we have so many men ready to respond to the call of duty in national defence. Please assure them of my good wishes and hopes for their safe return. – Durose, chairman."

                            HORSES

Demands for horses have been made on Mr W. N. Hicking J.P., Brackenhurst, Mr J. J. Bates, Mr J. H. Kirkby, and the Co-operative Stores. The two principal firms in the town – Mr J. H. Kirkby and Mr J. J. Bates – have notices affixed to the front of their establishments stating that only normal quantities will be sold to ordinary customers.

RED CROSS SOCIETY

The Southwell detachment of the Red Cross have received orders to mobilise, but the instruction was also officially conveyed that there was no necessity to leave situations and places of business until a further order was issued. Arrangements have been made for 60 beds in the town, in which the sick and wounded can be accommodated, and these beds must be ready at a moment's notice. Mr W. N. Hicking, with his accustomed generosity, has placed the commodious and new empty Burgage Manor at the service of the Society, and has promised to find a number of beds; while a portion of the Bishop's Manor and the Grammar School will also be utilised if necessary. There was a meeting of the detachment in the Trebeck Hall on Friday to consider the making of various articles for the comfort of the fighting men. [Note: William Hicking, chairman of the Nottingham and Notts Banking Company, was made a baronet in 1917. He owned Brackenhurst Hall and Burgage Manor, both of which became Red Cross auxiliary military hospitals.]

MEMORABLE SERVICE IN THE MINSTER

On Thursday evening a memorable and historic service was held in Southwell Minster. H Company and the National Reserve marched to the Minster, and a large number of residents of the town accompanied them. The Bishop of Southwell and Archdeacon of Nottingham intoned prayers which were for the restoration of peace and the good and security of the country, and the Bishop of Southwell (Dr Hoskyns) gave an eloquent and inspiring address. He asked them to be loyal and to serve their officers well and truly. His lordship left the pulpit and, walking down the nave, presented each Territorial with a small but handsomely bound prayer-book. And before dispersing the National Anthem was most enthusiastically sung.

H COMPANY DEPARTS

'H Company left Southwell shortly after eight o'clock on Friday morning. As they marched to the station, many inhabitants, old and young, went with them, and they were given a rousing send-off as they entrained for Newark. Mr Howard Barrett, the up-to-date photographer, took several pictures of them. Previously he promised to give a portrait to each individual member of the Company, and nearly 40 availed themselves of the offer.'

[Note: In 1912 Howard Barrett described himself in *Kelly's Directory* as a 'photographer, thrice patronised by his late Majesty King Edward VII; horses, cattle and premises photographed by appointment; distance no object; residence, King Street; studio, Station Road'.]

A full report and photograph recorded the
HISTORIC SCENE IN THE MARKET PLACE
as the official ceremony was held to send off the men of the 8th Battalion Sherwood Foresters, as Newark Market Place was on Monday morning filled with a dense throng of townspeople who had come to give a good send-off to the Sherwood Foresters, who were 'going out to save'…

Newark Advertiser

19 August 1914

Complete list in this edition of Southwell men in H Company and other companies of the Sherwood Foresters, the Sherwood Rangers Yeomanry and other units.

2 September 1914
NATIONAL RESERVE

Report of a parade of a 'large number' of local members of the National Reserve. Under the command of Capt. J. R. Starkey they went on a six mile march. 'The men looked very fit. A short time drilling has worked wonders in their appearance, and if wanted at any time for active service will no doubt be able to render good work.' The reservists were ordered to parade on Thursday 27 August at 7 p.m. and Sunday 30th August at 10.15 am, with shooting practice on the Westgate range every weekday after 6 pm.

NEW DRILL HALL

A long report of a 'very influential and enthusiastic' meeting in the new drill hall when 'Capt. H. P. G. Branston, appointed by the War Office to be in charge of this district, explained a scheme under which all able-bodied persons between the ages of 16 and 50 may learn to use the rifle'. Mr J. R. Starkey made a 'spirited appeal to the inhabitants of Southwell and district to do what they could at this critical moment to make themselves useful. If ever the time came that they were called upon to defend their native town, it was essential that they knew how to handle a rifle.' A committee was elected to carry forward the scheme, with T. D. Partington and J. Ellis as joint secretaries.

THE PRICE OF BREAD

A letter to Mr Arthur Woodruffe of Southwell [Note: he was warehouse foreman at J. H. Kirkby, grocers, general stores and bakers in Southwell] 'writing in a Nottingham contemporary', in response to a letter there from 'Consumer'. 'Consumer' had complained about the differences of the price of bread charged by bakers. Woodruffe defends the practice based on the economics of scale. He offers detailed statistics, and argues that the trade is just about paying its way with flour costing over 30s a sack, and a 4lb loaf selling for 6d.

9 September 1914

'WELL DONE, SOUTHWELL' Report noting that so many local players 'having gone away with the Territorials and others joining their regiments', it was thought possible that none of the town's sports clubs would operate that season.

'TERRITORIALS "H" Company require 36 recruits to complete their establishment for general service at home and abroad . . . . Capt. J. P. Becher has been in Southwell this week and gives a very favourable account of the general progress of the Southwell men.'

To the Men of Newark.

Join your local Territorial Regiments.
400 to 500 MEN WANTED for
Sherwood Rangers.
Apply MR G FOSTER, STODMAN STREET.

1,000 MEN WANTED for New Battalion
Sherwood Foresters.
Home Defence or Foreign Service.
Apply Drill Hall, Newark; or
Lieut. Barrow, The Barracks,
Hawton Road, Newark.

23 September 1914

The number of Southwell men now enrolled in the National Reserve [is] now 95, and 11 have joined the Regulars and Territorials.

'HORSES FOR THE WAR. Officers from the Remount department of the War Office . . . have taken some more horses, including two from Mr J. Bates and two from Mr J. H. Kirkby to make good the losses caused by the serious fighting during the last few weeks.'

Report that 'Several local men recently joined the South Notts Hussars, including Mr Lynn, the Rural District Council's sanitary inspector, Mr Mosedale, son of Mr F. Mosedale, baker, and Mr W. W. Bates, brother of Mr J. J. Bates, who lately resided at Collingham.'

AN APPEAL FOR THE 8™ BATTALION – The following letter has been sent for publication:-
    Depot, 8th Sherwood Foresters,
    Drill Hall, Newark,
    17th September, 1914.

My Dear Sir, - The North-Midland Division of which the 8th Battalion Sherwood Foresters forms part, has the honour of being selected for service abroad.

    In order that the regiment may be thoroughly equipped, it is desirable that it should be in possession of certain articles beyond those mentioned in the War Office schedule. Among these are travelling field cookers, which are most essential for the comfort and efficiency of the men. The City of Nottingham and the Duke of Portland, the Hon. Colonel of the Regiment, have presented one to the 7th Battalion (Robin Hoods). The cost is approximately £160.

    Is it too much to ask the county to do likewise for its Battalion?

    An early reply is essential, as it is expected that the Regiment will leave England at the end of the month. Subscriptions will be gladly received by Mrs. Foljambe, Osberton, Worksop. – Yours truly
    G. S. FOLJAMBE. Lt.. Col.,
Commanding Depot, 8th Sherwood Foresters.

[NOTE: The outcome of this appeal was not recorded, but it was to be a further six months before the Battalion left for France.]

'HOSPITAL FOR BELGIAN REFUGEES   A movement is afoot in the town to give relief to some of the large number of destitute people from Belgium . . . . Mr J. J. Bates will be glad to receive the names of any persons who can give assistance in this noble cause, either food, lodging, or clothes.'

TERRITORIALS   Report of H Company of the 8th Sherwood Foresters in training in Harpenden. Capt. Becher was 'very proud' of his men, who had been on route marches of 30-40 miles a day.

'LETTER FROM THE FRONT   Gymnastic Instructor Sturgess, of the Royal North Lancashire Regiment, writing to his parents in Southwell, says,: "At last I am able to write to you. We have had a rough time of it since we left England. On the 16th we got it hot. There were 50 killed and wounded. I was one of them, and got a bullet through my knee. I am going on well, and shall be about in a few weeks. There is only one lieutenant and about 150 men left in my regiment now. We had nothing but rain for a week, night and day, and only the clothes we stood up in. Had to throw everything else away, but we got

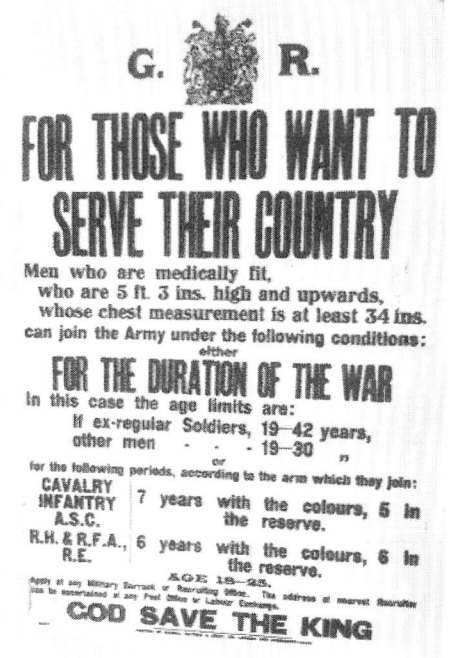

Early Recruitment Poster
(Mike Kirton)

plenty to eat, which is a blessing. Last Monday we gave the Germans "sock." Had to walk over them to get to the others.'

Report that Leonard Gilbert, youngest son of Mr B. Gilbert of Farnsfield, had been gazetted second lieutenant in the 13th Sherwood Foresters. An old Southwell grammar school boy he had graduated from University College, Nottingham and had taught at Andover Grammar School and the Duke of Northumberland's Grammar School, in Alnwick.

14 October 1914

'HOME FROM INDIA   Private Harry Wilkins, son of Mr F. Wilkins, King Street, has paid a flying visit to his native town this last week, just to see his parents and friends for a few days previous to going to France. He is a member of the Telegraph Section of the 1st Battalion Notts and Derby, and has been stationed in India since 1909. The following is an account of his interesting and eventful journey home, which his many friends in Southwell will be pleased to read: – "We received orders for Europe on the 1st September, and embarked next day on the S. S. 'Thongwa', along with seven more ships, loaded with Indian troops, and escorted by the cruiser "Dartmouth." Stayed in Aden for a few hours, and were joined by the armed cruiser "Norfolk", and the "Dartmouth" returned to Bombay. Pleasant voyage through the Red Sea and Suez Canal. Stayed at Port Said for coaling and were joined the following day at Alexandria by 19 ships, loaded with Indian troops, as well as two fresh cruisers, making a total of about 28 ships. Just before arriving at Malta we were passed by about 14 boats, which we supposed were taking some of the Territorials to India. Two days after passing Malta we left the remainder of the convoy; they to proceed to Marseilles and we to England. After staying at Gilbraltar about 14 hours we were joined by a man-o-war which stayed with us until arrival at Plymouth. We had a full regiment on board, and in addition to the crew there were about 1,100 of us. It was rather rough in the Bay. My impression of the Russians is that they are just proving themselves to be entitled to the name of 'The Russian Bear,' and although rather slow he is terribly sure. We arrived in Plymouth on 1st October." '

28 October 1914

'RECRUITING   The Minster town is doing its share in supplying recruits for Lord Kitchener's Army. Another party left this week for their respective units, including three more from Mr J. H. Kirkby's establishment – Messrs S. Oliver, H. Tyne and Alec Peet – and their employer has promised to keep their situations open for them until their return from military service.'

'COMFORTS FOR THE "SHERWOODS"   A notice of a smoking concert to be held on 29 October at the Admiral Rodney Hotel. Tickets are 6d each and all proceeds 'will be handed over to the local committee to provide comforts for the Sherwood Foresters'.

'HOSPITALITY FOR THE BELIGIANS   A party of Belgians, named Degroote, from Ostend, left their country last week with many other families, numbering about 1,300. After a very stormy voyage of two days in a fleet of 40 fishing boats and other small vessels, they arrived at Lowestoft, but as all the east coast is now a prohibited area the people were compelled to carry on. The Degroote family were commended by some friends in Southwell, who met them at the station on their arrival in the town on Tuesday evening, and escorted them to a house prepared by willing hands, where everything was done to make them comfortable. Mr Degroote is a marine engineer, and his two sons, who are with him, are telegraph operators. He is also accompanied by his wife and daughter and wife's sister.'

'A SOUTHWELL INVENTION AERIAL PHOTOGRAPHY Mr Howard Barrett is showing some remarkable landscape photos of Southwell and district taken with a camera recently patented by his brother, Mr A. G. Barrett. The invention is an automatic photographic kite trolley, attached to a line, the distance of travel being controlled by a block running along a screw thread. When the kite has reached the required altitude the aluminium camera attached takes a photograph of the landscape below. When taken at a height of 450 feet it gives a view of several miles, showing houses and fields and a wonderful panoramic picture of the country. It was originally intended for obtaining topographical surveys of the Sudan and other tropical countries, where aeroplanes and balloons would be useless owing to the intense heat. The War Office are now negotiating with Mr Barrett and making experiments with a view to purchase. The whole structure is light and very portable and the operator has complete control over the kite. The action of the slide in the camera closes the wings and it at once descends, bring the apparatus gently to earth.'

[Note: A regulation prohibiting the flying of kites was issued later under the Defence of the Realm Act. It may well have resulted from the success of this experiment, demonstrating that enemy agents could also use this method for surveillance.]

4 November 1914

A report that seven men from Southwell enlisted the previous Saturday. 'Mr Caudwell, the miller, supplied three: C. Fox, A. Paling, and A. Hazlewood, the others being S. Spall, P. Faulkener, C. Chapman and J. Smith.

'REAL PATRIOTISM: OUR MEN AT THE FRONT' A report that Dr T. S Elliot 'has been asked by the War Office to undertake special duties in connection with the Expeditionary Force in France. Mr Godber, the local veterinary surgeon, has been at the firing line since the outbreak of the war, tending to sick and wounded horses.'

'BELGIAN REFUGEES' A report of a town meeting in Trebeck Hall chaired by the rector, Archdeacon Wild. It was decided to take a house in the town 'for the purpose of entertaining Belgian refugees, the cost of same to be met by subscription . . . . In

Grand Concert
(SALLE MAUPERTIUS)

On Tuesday, October 27th, 1914.

Chairman — 2nd-Corpl. Vickery, R.E.
Vice Chairman — Corpl. Begley, R.E.

PROGRAMME.

1. Pianoforte Solo — Sapr. Brand.
2. Song — "Fall in and follow me" — Sapr. Bryan.
3. Vocal Duo — "Sweet 72" — Saprs. Pope & Fellows.
4. Song — "Naughty Boy" — Sapr. Hall.
5. Farce — "PHŒBE'S VISITORS"
   Scene—Drawing Room.
   Phœbe (Charwoman) — Sapr. Allday.
   Ike (Jew) — Sapr. Hollis.
   Buckskin (Cowboy) — Sapr. Chapman.
6. Songs at the Piano — Pte. Wallis, R.A.M.C.
7. Song — "The White Man" — Sap. Pope.
8. Song — Selected — Corpl. Glazier.
9. Comedy Quartette — The Four Would-be's.
10. Song — Selected — Corpl. Smith, C.L.I.
11. Song — "Be a Man" — Corpl. Maitland.
12. Duet — "The Battle Eve" — Saprs. Pope & Fellows.
13. Song — "The Ragtime Curate" — Sapr. Bryan.
14. Song — "What a norful thing is work" — Sapr. Hollis.
15. Song — Selected — Sapr. Hedges.
16. Humourous Sketch — "THE EGYPTIAN MUMMY"
    Scene—The Professor's Studio.
    The Mad Professor — Lce.-Corpl. Hall.
    The Mummy — Sapr. Pope.
    Mary — Sapr. Fellows.
    Burglars — Saprs. Havies & Parkes.

"GOD SAVE THE KING"

(David Hutchinson)

addition to the above . . . Mr and Mrs W. N. Hickling are taking a house, and having a family under their care.' An appeal was made for money, food and furniture.

A report of a smoking concert at the Admiral Rodney 'to provide comforts for the local men of the Sherwood Foresters in training at Harpenden'.

'BURGAGE MANOR HOSPITAL AT SOUTHWELL' A report that the War Office was to utilise Burgage Manor and the Trent Bridge pavilion as auxiliary hospitals. Patients would initially be transferred from Lincoln, Leicester, and probably Leeds.

11 November 1914 A complete roll of honour of the men from Southwell who had enlisted or been mobilised.

25 November 1914

A report of the death in action of Pte. Sidney Deeley of the Grenadier Guards, the first soldier from Southwell to be killed in the war. His parents lived in King Street. They had received a letter from their son the previous week saying that he was 'all right and in the thick of the fighting. On Thursday the War Office notified his friends that he had died from wounds received in action at Ypres, and conveyed the sympathy of Lord Kitchener in the loss they had sustained'.

'A LETTER FROM THE TRENCHES Private E. Barlow, of the Grenadier Guards, writing to his sister last week, says: "We are getting it rough. Every day and every night we have been in the trenches for twelve days. We do not get a chance to sleep, as the Germans are only 200 yards from us, and we can see them running about. We have lost a lot of men this last week or two, but we have put a good lot of Germans out of mess this week. The fighting has been terrific. I have not been able to leave the trenches to have a wash for twelve days, and have only had one clean shirt while I have been out. They have only hit me once, and that was in the leg, but not very bad. It will soon be Christmas now, but there will not be many of us left, and fewer Germans if we go on at the same rate as the last week or two." '

2 December 1914

A report that Lieutenant J. K. Lane, of Southwell, in the 8th Sherwood Foresters, had been promoted Captain.

9 December 1914

A report of a 'meat tea' to be held on 15 December for wives and mothers of the men on the Southwell roll of honour.

16 December 1914

Photograph of the officers in the 8th Battalion, Sherwood Foresters - see following page.

OFFICERS OF THE 8th BATTALION SHERWOOD FORESTERS

23 December 1914

'DECORATED BY THE KING' A report of the personal decoration by the king of the D.S.M. to Pte. Thomas Tinker of the 2nd battalion, the Lancashire Fusiliers. He was the grandson of the late Mrs Tinker of Park Street, Southwell. In a letter to his parents a few days previously he told that, 'The Prince of Wales gave me the bar, and the King pinned the medal on me.' Thomas Tinker had joined the Lancashire Fusiliers 12 years before the outbreak of war (at which time he was a reservist) and had seen service in Egypt and India.   When war was declared he was an attendant at Prestwick Asylum.

'RECRUITING MEETING' A long report of a 'well attended and enthusiastic' recruiting meeting at the Assembly Hall chaired by the rector of Southwell, Archdeacon Wild, with most of Southwell's notables on the platform.

'A SOUTHWELL SOLDIER   HIS ADVENTURES WITH THE SHERWOODS The following extracts are from a letter to his parents in Southwell, written by Private V. A. A. Brown, a signaller in the Sherwood Foresters, and published in the *Nottingham Guardian*:– "On the 19th September we took over some trenches for a few hours. Here was where we got our first man wounded (by shrapnel). Early on the 20th September (Sunday) we relieved the Queen's Regiment, two companies in the firing line, and two in support. Here is where the fun started.

About two in the afternoon we were all sitting about the dugouts. We saw a lot of our men coming over the sky-line on our right. We did not know who they were at first, but did so soon afterwards. All glasses were focused on them. We didn't know until we saw one up a telegraph pole cutting a wire. They were coming over the sky-line in hundreds. Down comes the general.

Our commanding officer says, "They have taken our trenches", "No," says the general. "They have, sir," says our commanding officer. The general had another look. "Yes," he says.

THE WORST PART OF THE LINE

Then the orders came – A and C Companies in the firing line, B and C in support. We had got the worst part of the line to attack, too, but off they went. As soon as they came over the crest of a little rise our fellows met a murderous fire. The Germans had got several machine guns hidden in a haystack and they caught us in the flank. We had to go over a little rise down a hollow and the enemy was on the other ridge, and they were still running over the other ridge. They were in and out of our trenches in a little over half an hour.

The West Yorkshires were coming over in solid masses, but our fellows went up that hill like a lot of madmen. The Germans never stayed to face the bayonets but we lost a lot that day, about 250 killed and wounded. One of our sections got caught by a machine gun just as they came out of a wood. They all lay dead nearly in a straight line with the officers in the centre.

We saved the situation, but at what cost? As soon as the West Yorks saw us coming they turned and joined up, what was left of them. Of course, they were retiring, also the Durhams on our left. I can honestly say if it had not been for the Sherwoods the situation would have been lost there, and I expect the battle of the Aisne would have been lost to, as for several days that part of the line was the key to the situation.

One of our officers, Mr Barnard, was leading his men, swinging his walking stick in one hand and his revolver in the other. He got wounded once but still went on, and got killed before he got to the trench. I think the bravest man was Captain Popham. He was wounded five or six times, nearly all in the head. Although his face was streaming with blood he kept on shouting, "Come on lads, get at the devils." One man wanted to bind him up but he said, "Get on, lad, with the others." He is Irish, so you can understand.

On the 19th October, at night, we took over some trenches at Ennetieres and that night passed off all right. About seven next morning they started shelling, and one burst just outside the house we were in and shifted all breakfast pots off the table. We shifted out there quick and went on several more miles before the day was over.

Well, about four in the afternoon – the shelling was on all day – the Buffs [Note: Royal East Kent Regiment] on our right retired, and we didn't know that we had lost a lot during the day, though we had a lot more to go through before the day was over. The C.O. sent down to the general to say they were closing on our trenches. The general says you must not retire on any account, so the general sent to the trenches that message. But we got an order to retire, what was left, of course, and you ought to have seen the thin khaki line nipping down the road. We went into action 973 strong that day, and at roll call next day we mustered 243 all told. Just fancy, we had lost 730 in one engagement but I believe 500 or more were prisoners. There were some bad cases among the wounded, too.

Well, we nipped down the road, and it was swept by shell fire and two machine guns all the way until we got over a rise and got against some sand pits.

I will tell you what the Germans had done. There was a big fort, called Fort Aiglais; it was one of the outlying forts of Lille, and the Germans knew if they could get a house down there they could sweep the road we had to retire down. So we shelled this house until they knocked the corner off and then their maxims swept straight down this road. A lot of our chaps had been captured by this time. Some of them got away from the Germans though. We retired down the road under fire, and when we got over this little rise we thought we should be safe, but the Germans had got round on our right and the sandpits came under fire from the right. Bullets were whistling around us. The general says: "Collect all the men you can and line that ridge on the left." There was a windmill there. And it was about 8 by this time and fairly dark. We lined the ridge by the windmill and all the C.O. could muster first was 83 of us. I got sent out on lookout to a burning house about 20 yards to the right of this windmill. The Germans charged our chaps so they had to retire, and we got the order and got left there. We got to know later that a whole Brigade of Germans charged our 83 men. We heard the Germans yelling "Hoch! Hoch!" [Note: 'High']. Then we thought it about time to move, so we moved. We could not go through the village, us three, as the Germans were in possession of it, so we went across country and found the battalion next morning three or four miles away. We got there just as they were having breakfast, so I was all right. It was about the worst night I have had, and the tightest corner I have been in. I thought my time had come that night, especially when the Germans got up to the windmill. We crawled away very quietly, I can tell you.'

30 December 1914

A report that a party of four Belgian refugees had been located in the King Street house as guests of the town, making eight in the care of the local committee, and 26 in the town altogether.

A report that Dr Willoughby was to give a course of lectures on first aid for the Red Cross, and was recruiting young men to the Red Cross 'who are unable to join the army'.

6 January 1915

A report that Clifford Butler, a clerk in J. H. Kirkby's office, son of W. Butler, Clerk to Southwell Parish Council had joined the Sherwood Foresters. A. Chambers, a master at Southwell National School, son of Mr Chambers, a Lay Clerk at the Minster, 'had gone into Lord Kitchener's Army.'

20 January 1915

A report that the first of a series of first aid lectures to local members of the Red Cross had been delivered by Dr Willoughby, a local GP, on 'First Aid to the Wounded.' The lecture was attended by 27 people.

'MR J. H. KIRKBY'S ROLL OF HONOUR'   A report that Joseph Otter, one of Kirkby's employees, had joined the Royal Marines, making 12 that had volunteered for HM forces from the firm. They were Messrs Wilcox, Smith, Otter, Drabble, Butler, Oliver, Peet, Tyne, Jepson, Pacey, Musgrave and Templeman. [no initials in this report]

A report that the parish of Halam had received two Belgian ladies, who were guests of the parish and residing at Maythorne.

27 January 1915

A report that Capt. J. P. Becher had given his sister Joyce away in marriage to Charles T. A Pollock. The officiant, at Holy Trinity, Brompton, was the bishop of Norwich [Bertram Pollock], uncle of the bridegroom.

'FLYING VISIT FROM THE TRENCHES. Private Arthur Horsley, of the 12th Lancers, got permission on Sunday morning last to come home for a few days furlough. Leaving France he crossed the Channel, and getting a fast train, arrived in Southwell the same evening. He has been through numerous engagements, and in the thick of the fight on several occasions, but got through safely.'

'MILITARY   We are still sending men for the army. Several more have gone during the past few days, and the Cathedral city has not lost its enthusiasm yet. Many of our men have been promoted, some very rapidly, notably G. Schumach, who we hear has been made sergeant. We congratulate him in his success, as he has only been in the Army a few weeks, which plainly shows that men of the right stamp are quickly picked out for promotion.'

3 February 1915

'ENTERPRISING TRADESMAN   Mr J. H. Kirkby of the supply stores, has just been successful in getting the contract to supply the Army Camp at Clipstone with bread; the quantity to be supplied daily is five thousand loaves. His model bakery is equipped with all the latest machinery for dealing with a large output, and the fact that the firm is able to deal with such a big contract, is evidence that the tradesmen of the Minster town are up to date in their business methods.'

'MORE MEN FOR THE ARMY   Several men left the town this week for the Army. Mr Cyril Maidens, son of Mr T. Maidens, has joined the Army Service Corps (Mechanical Transport Section)' having learned his trade at the noted garage of Messrs Simpkins and Co. of this town. Mr K. Baguley, clerk in Mr J. H. Kirkby's office, has gone to Aldershot as a clerk in one of the Army offices. Mr Claude Swallow, farm foreman to Mr J. R. Starkey, has, we understand, gone to Glasgow. Other men have gone to their respective units.'
[Note: In the 1911 census return Eustace Claude Swallow was 32 years of age; Kenneth Baguley was 16 years old in 1911; The *Newark Advertiser* regularly carried advertisements for Kirkby's; 'the cash supply stores'. It sold everything from bread, 'Prime Yorkshire Ham', Stilton cheese, bottled beer, stout and 'Devonshire Cyder', to 'Clover and Mangel seeds. 'Special quotations and Samples on application'; George Edwin Simpkins was an automobile engineer, with premises in King Street.]

'COMMISSION Mr. C.R.C. Maltby has been granted a commission as temporary 2nd Lieutenant in the Rifle Brigade. Mr. Maltby, who is the son of Mr. & Mrs. C.L. Maltby, Southwell, has been serving for the past five months in the 3rd Battalion University and Public School Corps at Epsom.'

WEDDING AT SOUTHWELL A full report of the wedding of Miss Hilda Margaret Starkey, daughter of Mr. J.R. Starkey, M.P., to Lieutenant Parker. Miss Starkey had been nursing the wounded at Nottingham General Hospital.

10 February 1915

A report that a roll of honour had been set up in the Minster to record the names of the men from the Minster parish who had enlisted, and which 'will be added to from time to time' so that 'a true record may be handed down to future generations of those who have done their duty to King and country in the hour of direct need'.

17 February 1915

A report that Frank Maslem, the bishop of Southwell's chauffeur, had left Southwell that week for London, en route to France, 'where he has volunteered to drive wounded soldiers from the firing line to hospitals at the Base'.

'LOCAL MAN SHOT IN THE NECK   Private G. Ward, of the 1st Sherwood Foresters, writing to his relatives in Southwell, says: "I was going into the trenches one night when it was dark. I was carrying two rifles, and my chum had got a bag of cokes, and when about 100 yards from the trench I got a bullet in my neck. And it came out again at the left eye. I laid there about an hour before I was found, then, two of the Lancashires picked me up and carried me down to the dressing station, where I was attended to, and then sent straight away to the No. 13 General Hospital at Boulogne, where I am writing this, I am getting on fine, and hope to be in England soon. They look after me well in the hospital, and the doctors and sisters are very good. Hope I shall have luck to get to Nottingham". Pte. Ward has now arrived in Southwell, and is getting on well, and hopes to get back to France in a short time.'

24 February 1915

'LETTER FROM A PRISONER OF WAR   Sergeant W. Robinson, of the 2nd Sherwood Foresters, who was captured by the Germans on October 20th, writes to his parents in Southwell, from Hamelyn Weser, Hanover, under date Jan. 20th, and which arrived in Southwell on February 23rd, says: "I am quite well, and have received all the parcels and boxes you have sent me. We were not allowed to smoke until Christmas Day, then we had a regular "beano." Don't forget to send me some more cigarettes, they will come through all right. There are eight of us for the parcels when they arrive, and we always share up. E. Castle is with us. We are only allowed to write one postcard a month."'

3 March 1915

A report that L/Cpl. Albert Humberstone, 1st battalion, Royal Scots Fusiliers, had been mentioned in dispatches for 'gallant and distinguished service in the field.'

C.L.B. MEMBERS IN THE ARMY. There are about 60 members of the above now serving in the Army and Navy, several of whom have been in the thick of the fighting, A. Horsley of the 12th Lancers, who helped to cover the retreat of the infantry from Mons has been in two cavalry charges.

COOKING LECTURE AT TREBECK HALL – A report that Miss Florence Petty, known all over the county as the 'Pudding Lady' gave an exhibition of how to cook a variety of dishes.

10 March 1915

A report of an 'inspiring lecture' delivered in Trebeck Hall on 2 March by Fr David Jenks, director of the Society of the Sacred Mission, the Anglican religious order based at Kelham in Nottinghamshire, 'on points likely to lead to controversy at the conclusion of the war'. He argued that Europe 'would be the centre of great anxiety when the map is being re-painted. What would become of Turkey and Austria? Another great political problem would be the treatment of India and her soldiers, who were now fighting side by side with ours. In one day the Irish question, the Welsh Church Bill and the Women's Franchise agitation were dropped. The masses of the people had been noble and heroic and followed the call of the country in a manner unsurpassed in the history of the world. The wives and mothers, sisters and sweethearts were the bravest of the king's soldiers. Women who could give up all they loved best in the world to lay down their lives on the battlefield were going to rule the country. We were fighting for honour and principles of truth and justice; for the safety and integrity of small nations: and they must not forget that religion would play a large part in the settlement after the war.' [Note: With two exceptions this was a remarkably prescient analysis. Religion did not play a large part in the post-war settlement, and it could not be said that after the war women ruled the country, as they did not secure adult suffrage on equality with men until 1928 and, despite legislation, did not secure equal pay in many fields of employment.]

A report of the annual meeting of local members of the National Deposit Friendly Society. The meeting noted that there were 143 male and 29 female members of the Deposit section. Of the male members, 27 were in HM forces.

24 March 1915

Report that Capt. J. P. Becher has been gazetted major in the 7th Notts and Derbys [though this is a newspaper error and should read 8th Battalion.] Becher, with Robert James Wordsworth of the 8th battalion, was promoted major on 18 March 1915 and gazetted on 12 March 1915. John Pickard Becher led H Company (the Southwell Company) of the Territorials 8th Battalion Notts and Derbys when it was mobilised in August and was to die of wounds sustained on 14 October 1915 during the assault on Hohenzollern Redoubt during the Battle of Loos. He had been a partner in Larken and Huskinson, solicitors, of Newark.

Pte. Harry Wilkins, son of Mrs F. Wilkins of King Street, killed 'in the terrific fighting that took place at Neuve Chapelle last week'.

'The Headquarters' staff of the Signalling Section of the Derbyshire Yeomanry and South Notts Hussars have arrived in the town for training purposes, the high hills around the Minster being ideal for signal operations, and the men have been at work every day. They are billeted at the Saracen's Head and the Crown Hotel. Capt Jardine being in command.'

31 March 1915

COMMISSION – A report that J.W.H. Labbett, the son of Rev. F.H. Labbett, circuit minister of the Wesleyan Society, has been granted a commission as 2nd Lieutenant 9th [later 10th Bn.] Battalion Lincolnshire Regiment.

ROLL OF HONOUR – It was also reported that Private Charlie Burn, who was in the employment of Mr F. Hill, Park-street, had died following serious wounds received in early fighting in France. He died in hospital in Glasgow. He had been a member of the West Riding Regiment, The Duke of Wellington's.

7 April 1915

80 members of the Southwell Company [St Mary's Company] of the Church Lads' Brigade serving with the forces, 'and the fact that so many of them wear stripes points to the value of their early training'.

14 April 1915

'Last week Mr G. W. Kirk enlisted at Newark in the 2nd 8th Sherwood Foresters, and was made a sergeant the next day and has been sent to Luton. Mr Kirk has done good work in Southwell, and will be much missed. As Quartermaster of the local branch of the Red Cross Society he has been the means of bringing the members up to a very high standard of drill, and he was also secretary of the Rifle Club at the same time, where his ability showed itself in the increased membership and high marksmanship of it members.'

'NATIONAL RESERVES   The War Office recently sent notices to the local members of the above asking them if they were prepared to sign on for either active service or home defence. A good number signed on for foreign service and several for home defence. Quite a small minority found it inconvenient to leave their business at the present time; one in particular is enlarging a local bakery to supply the camp at Clipstone; another is in bed ill; another has just returned from hospital in the Midlands. Dr Willoughby conducted an examination in the New Drill Hall on Thursday last and those who passed the test were sworn in by Mr J. R. Starkey M.P. and expect to leave Southwell in a few days for their respective depots. The following are the names of those who passed the examination: Howard Barrett, W. Beresford, C. Brown, F. Cavill [Carvell], G. W. Foster, J. Hall, W. Heuston, A. Key, F. O. Newbolt, C. G. Pritchett, H. H. Smith, J. H. Smith, A. Wright, and H. Thraves. The following were passed from the Farnsfield branch: A. Cope, J. Goulding, J. Milner, J. Sullivan, W. B. Whitten, W. Wiseman, J. R. Wright.'

[Note: Dr Willoughby was James Frederick Digby Willoughby, a medical practitioner, who in 1911 lived in Church Street in Southwell. His two sons both served in the war – see Roll Call]

21 April 1915

'FIRST SOUTHWELL TERRITORIAL KILLED' This is the caption beneath a photograph of Pte. Albert Hopewell. He was the brother of John Henry Hopewell who was to be killed in action in August 1915. The two brothers had worked at Carey's lace factory in Southwell.

PREPARATION FOR WOUNDED SOLDIERS The commandant of the local branch of the Red Cross Society received notice yesterday morning to prepare the hospital [Burgage Manor] to receive fifteen wounded soldiers who will arrive in Southwell this (Wednesday) afternoon.

ROLL OF HONOUR Mr W. R. Swift, of King Street, left the town on Monday to join the National Reservists at Worksop…Mr Ormonde Horsley has also joined the Army Service Corps.

NATIONAL PATRIOTIC ORGANISATION A lantern lecture, under the auspices of the above, will be given on Monday April 26th, in the Assembly Rooms. The Association is giving these lectures to show the reason we are at war, and also to counteract the mischievous efforts of those who are trying to bring about a premature peace. All are cordially invited to attend.

NATIONAL EGG COLLECTION FOR WOUNDED An egg depot in connection with the National Egg Collection for the wounded has been started at Southwell, the organiser being Miss Ida K. Fairweather, of Clinton Cottage, Southwell. The first consignment numbers 321 eggs was sent off on Thursday, and the promoters desire through the 'Advertiser' to thank very heartily all who have contributed to the success of this first effort. Especial thanks are due to the Southwell Guides, who collected 160, the Wesleyan Day School scholars, who collected 84, and the National scholars who collected 27… [Note: this was a response to the national campaign to collect eggs for the wounded. Several posters were produced in 1915 to advertise the national egg collection. The most striking shows a large white hen wearing a broad olive green sash bearing the insignia of a crown, similar to the arm bands issued to men recruited under the so-called Derby or Group scheme. The poster says: 'Enlisted for Duration of the War. Help the National Egg Collection for the Wounded.' It was designed by R. G. Praill and published by Avenue Press, London WC.]

28 April 1915

Report of an 'entertainment' in Trebeck Hall for soldiers staying in the town (these were the signallers referred to on 24 March) Miss Elliot and Mr R. W. Kiddle arranged this. 'The programme consisted of songs and solos from the lay clerks, violin solos by Mr Liddle and other items. Refreshments were handed round during the interval.' Capt Jardine proposed a vote of thanks to 'the artistes.' [Note: this was an example of what Herbert Wild, the archdeacon of Nottingham and rector of St Mary's, Southwell, was to call the 'rational' entertainment that was the only kind that should be offered to soldiers!]

By this date three Southwell men had been killed in action: Ptes. Sidney Deeley, Harry Wilkins and Albert Hopewell. A memorial service was held for them in the Minster earlier in the month.

'Considerable excitement was caused in the town on Wednesday last [21 April] when 14 wounded soldiers arrived from Lincoln and were located in the Manor House, which has been prepared as a temporary equipment hospital for some time. The men were met at Fiskerton Station by the men's detachment of the local Red Cross Society under Commandant A. E. Merryweather, and conveyed to Southwell in motor cars, where they were placed under the care of the women's detachment of the same Society. None of the cases is serious, and all were able to walk.'

'SOUTHWELL TERRITORIAL WOUNDED, AN EXPLOSIVE BULLET   L/Cpl. Wilcox, of the 1st 8th Sherwood Foresters, who is wounded and now in a London Hospital, was the first Southwell Territorial to be wounded in France.. Writing to his mother and father, at Southwell, he says: "Just a line to let you know I am now in a hospital in London. I think you have had a card, so you know which. I came across on Friday. I was wounded on Tuesday morning. The bullet went through my left arm, but I am going on nicely. I was taken from the trench at night to hospital and then next day was conveyed to Baileul, and from there to Boulogne. I am going on all right up to now. We used to take duty in the trenches for four days at a time, and it was our lot to go in again on Sunday night. Major Becher and Lieut Hollins were very good, and the former said he would write to Mrs Becher so that she could come and see you. Remember me to all. I expect to have a furlough when I am right."'

In a further letter he writes: 'I am pleased in one way to be here, for I am certain some of them have got to be killed before so long. It is awful – like hell. The day I was wounded they took me in a dugout, and I had to lay from 5 in the morning till 8.30 at night, and then Ted Daniels and Chas Cave brought me out, under fire all the time. Bullets were flying on all sides but thank God I got there with a bit of luck. Major Becher said he would come if I wished him to, but what good was it risking his life like that. The bullet went in the back of my arm at the top, and came out the other side. It was an explosive bullet.'

5 May 1915

'SOUTHWELL SOLDIER MISSING   Mr A. Rayner, who is employed at the lace factory, on Friday received a communication that his son, Pte. F. Rayner, was reported missing since March 12th. Pte. Rayner was in the 1st Sherwoods, and he had been stationed in India prior to the outbreak of the war, and went to France with the original British Expeditionary Force.'   [Note: he may have gone missing during the Battle of Neuve Chapelle, which began on 10 March and during which Harry Wilkins was killed.]

'ROLL OF HONOUR   Mr H. Pointon has joined the National Reserve (Active Service Branch), and gone to Worksop for duty. He was previously in the Sherwood Foresters but discharged owing to a kneecap giving way, due to an accident several years ago. G. A. Tongue, son of Mr and Mrs Tongue, Burgage, has been promoted to Lance-Corporal.'

'MAJOR BECHER'S THANKS   Mr E. Herbert, Hon. Secretary of the concert arranged by the lay clerks for providing comforts for local soldiers at the front, which realised £3, has received the following letter from Major J. P. Becher on receipt of some of the articles purchased:- "The sweets you so kindly sent out arrived safely during our last turn in the trenches, and have been distributed. I can assure you that they like all sweet things out here, and these are much appreciated. Will you please convey the thanks of myself and the Company to all the lay clerks? I have heard nothing of cigarettes yet, but no doubt they will turn up in due course. Today is the first nice Sunday we have had for a month, as during the last three we have either been going into or actually in the trenches. I am sure Southwell ought to be proud of its men. They have all done splendidly, and I should not be surprised if you do not get some wounded back before long, as I think they are sure to be sent back to England. – Yours faithfully, J. P. Becher, Major.'

'FOOD FOR THE TROOPS   An officer of the Commissariat Department at York had just recently paid a visit of inspection to the bake house of Mr J. H. Kirkby, and expressed himself highly pleased with the manner in which the bread is turned out, and the cleanliness of the bake house and machinery. Troops are expected at Clipstone Camp in a few days, and bread for them will be baked in six large ovens, and delivered in a large motor van, specially built for the purpose by Messrs Thornycroft, the well-known motor engineers, and will carry 50 cwt of bread and make two or three journeys to the camp each day; 4,000 men are expected in camp now, and the number will gradually increase up to 40,000 or 50,000 as the huts and other accommodation is complete'.

'WOUNDED SOLDIERS   The people of Southwell are doing everything possible to relieve the monotony of the wounded soldiers who are recuperating at the Burgage Manor lent by Mr W. N. Hicking. On Wednesday the Rev. T. A. Lea and Mrs C. L. Maltby kindly took the black and white minstrels to the hospital, and a capital programme was gone through, the appreciation of which was adequately voiced by Dr. Willoughby J.P.; while on Thursday they were entertained at tea at Westhorpe Hall by the Rev. H. K. and Mrs Warrand. They inspected the beautiful grounds, played bowls and billiards, and spent a most enjoyable time.'

'ENTERTAINMENT FOR SOLDIERS   Report of another entertainment at Trebeck Hall for soldiers stationed in the town. This is a lengthy report which noted that the soldiers 'were delighted with the singing' of Mr Schmach who provided 'the comic element'.

12 May 1915

'NATIONAL EGG COLLECTION'   This was a regular weekly report at this time. It was a typical week, with 842 eggs collected 'and 196 were delivered to the Burgage Manor Auxiliary Hospital'.

Report that a party of Royal Engineers had camped in Norwood Park, the forerunners of some 500 who would come for training, and were engaged in building bridges over the Greet and the Trent (obviously for training purposes).

'LOCAL SOLDIERS GASSED   Private Harold Tyne of the 8th Battalion, Sherwood Foresters, writing to friends in the town, says, "I am sitting in the trenches to write this letter, and shells are flying about. We leave one company in the village behind, and their duty is to carry rations to us. Every time we go in one or two get picked off by snipers. A few days since, as soon as we get inside, the enemy begin to shell, and they blew the trench all up just at the side of us. The sandbags flew up into the air as the shells exploded, and when they dropped a lot of men were buried underneath, thus killing and wounding several of them. But the Germans are not satisfied with a fair fight. They were firing at us the other day, and when they were finished there was not one of us that could see at all; they had been firing shells charged with a horrible kind of gas." '

19 May 1915

Report noting that Pte. Alfred Beresford had been wounded in the arm and was in hospital in Aylesbury.

Headline: 'Carey's Men in the Army' This reported that 60 were now serving representing 82 per cent of those eligible to enlist: out of those left, 11 were married men with families. [Sixteen men from Carey's died in the war and are commemorated on a war memorial at the entrance to their former premises.]

BURGAGE MANOR HOSPITAL   This report noted that six more wounded men had arrived the previous Saturday. 'The last contingent are more serious cases, some of them suffering severe bullet wounds.' Concerts and 'other entertainments' are given by 'local talent, and everything is done to make their lot as pleasing as possible'.

NATIONAL EGG COLLECTION   A report that the total eggs collected for the week amounted to 938, of which 280 were sent to Burgage Manor.

LETTER FROM BELGIUM   One of the local territorials writing from the trenches in Belgium last week, says: - 'We had a very exciting week, the Germans have been shelling us continually all the week. One of the shells dropped on the parapet where I was on sentry duty, but did not harm me at all. Last Sunday, May 9th, we saw a very exciting incident, about 5.50 pm a large German aeroplane came over our lines. He had not been there long before one of our own machines saw him, and made a dash for the enemy. They started firing at each other, dodging and flying, and firing for the mastery, when all of a sudden, when the excitement was most intense the German came crashing head first from a height of 900 feet or more. You can guess that there would not be much left of him when he reached earth. On Monday they tried to blow up the trenches, but they had not sapped far enough, and blew up more of theirs than ours, but they are dead shots, and if one puts his thumb above the trench they can hit it.' [At this time the 1/8th Battalion were dug in in the Ypres Salient, and experiencing heavy fighting.]

26 May 1915

Report of the funeral of Pte. Ezekiel Eaton, 1/8 Sherwood Foresters in the Minster on 19 May. The son of Mrs and Mrs E. Eaton of King Street, Southwell. He had been in the 'local company' of the 8th Battalion for five years, and was wounded in the trenches with a 'bullet penetrating his thigh where it remained for three days before being extracted'. He had worked at Carey's lace factory, and had attended the National Day School in Southwell. He was 'an ardent member of Southwell City F. C. for which he occupied the position of goalkeeper'. The report continues: 'Practically the whole of the townsfolk of Southwell turned out and lined the route to pay their last tribute to a fallen hero who had made the great sacrifice.' There is a detailed list of family members and others in the cortege, but included in them were the Southwell Company of the CLB, and 'a detachment of wounded soldiers being cared for at Burgage Manor' and 'the families of Belgian refugees now located in the town'.

2 June 1915

'SOUTHWELL EGG COLLECTION   Dear Sir, We very greatly regret having to record a decrease in our total for the egg collection this week. We think the chief cause has been because the school children have had this week holidaying, and their weekly contributions have not been organised in the usual splendid way. We should like to take this opportunity of publicly thanking the teachers for their willing co-operation in this work so far, and should like to suggest that when the next holidays come along some arrangements might be made for collecting the eggs as usual. We know that eggs are getting rather more scarce, but unfortunately wounded men are not, and we urgently ask that both contributors and collectors will do their utmost to keep the supply regular of this most important item in a sick man's diet. It seems the least we can do when these men are suffering so much for us. The National Egg Collection Committee are now publishing a little magazine each week, entitled "Eggs Wanted," and in it they give most interesting accounts of the work that is being done all over the country by all sorts and conditions of people. The total number of eggs received for the week ending May 22nd at the Central Depot was 367,663, and that was a decrease on previous weeks. But if one begins to add up what two eggs per day per man will come to, after reading the daily casualty lists, it is quite easy to realise that even all those are not enough.

Very many thanks indeed for all that you have done for our collection by publishing the reports each week, and if you can still further help the cause by publishing the above we shall be very greatly obliged.

The total this week is 756. Sent to Burgage Manor Hospital, 364. The chief returns are as follows:– Southwell Girl Guides, 144; Farnsfield Boy Scouts, 139; Eakring Boy Scouts, 100; Fiskerton village, 96; Morton village, 40; Halam Boy Scouts, 51; Rolleston village, 40; Southwell National School, 25; Kirklington village, 24; Bilsthorpe village, 22; small amounts, 49; total, 756.

May we suggest that school children should write their name and address on their eggs in pencil then it will not rub off when boiled, and perhaps some wounded Tommy might write his thanks to them. Many such letters are published in "Eggs Wanted." Yours sincerely, Ida K. Fairbrother, Clinton Cottage, Southwell, May 27th 1915.'

'THE TREBECK HALL   It has been decided to open the above Hall as a soldiers' club, where they can go and write letters or play games, several of which are permitted; also for a small charge they can buy refreshments; tea, coffee, cocoa etc, being provided. A special feature of the rules is that they can take a lady friend with them. Many soldiers are in Southwell at the present time and the Hall is much used and appreciated by them,'

'CAPTAIN J. K. LANE WOUNDED   News was received in Southwell on Friday that Captain J. K. Lane had been wounded, but had a wonderful escape from death. Previous to the war Captain Lane, a partner in the firm of Southwell solicitors, Messrs Kirkland and Lane, held a commission in the Southwell Company of the 8th Sherwood Foresters, his senior officer being Captain (now Major) J. P. Becher. The intimation that he was wounded was conveyed in a letter to Mrs Kirkland at Southwell from the Chaplain, (Rev. [J.] P. Hales) as follows: "Dear Mrs Kirkland, –Just a line if I can catch the early post to relieve your anxiety if you hear that Jack Lane is wounded. He is all right; I mean there's no danger. A most miraculous escape. The bullet went through both breast pockets and through his right arm. He is smoking a pipe and very cheery when I left him a few minutes ago. They have come for the letters. Jack is a fine soldier and man." Capt. J. K. Lane was very popular with the men, and, in fact, with anyone with whom he came into contact, and we all congratulate him on his miraculous escape, and wish him a speedy recovery.'

'LETTER FROM A SOUTHWELL TERRITORIAL   LOCAL BUGLERS LEAD IN THE BRAVE CANADIAN SURVIVORS   A Southwell Territorial, writing to his friends this week, gives an interesting account of life in the battle line. He says:– "I have been out all night mending the telephone wires. We have miles and miles of it out, and the shells play havoc with it. I was at headquarters last week – it's a pretty village, a lovely chateau, with a large moat all around. I had a swim in it, but cannot again, as the water may be wanted for drinking. The trees were all in full bloom, flowers galore, and a nightingale singing in the village every night. We never see any birds near the trenches, but one day I was in a fortified farmhouse and a cock pheasant walked past. Of course, we dare not show a hand, or we should have drawn shells. I have been in some houses where the walls were covered with blood-stains, ladies underclothes in the bedrooms soaked in blood (enough to make one sick), gas meters opened and robbed, safes broken open, things wantonly destroyed, furniture and all pictures smashed, all bottles and barrels in the cellar empty (worse luck), and all ornaments broken. We had a taste of the gas last week, but it did not affect us much, as we only got the tail end. They have just brought a man in here with a bullet through one thigh, and it has stopped in the other. Expect you have heard about our little losses by now. Southwell was well in it, right in the worst fighting. Major Becher was grand. I was close by him all the time. I believe our lot would have gone straight for the Germans if they would have let us. Young Mr Hacking [Lt. Alfred Hacking, one of the sons of the archdeacon of Newark, Egbert Hacking] was "copping it" with his platoon also, but my word he did shine. He's a fine soldier and quite fearless, and his chaps can't do enough for him; but all the officers did wonders that night. We are well off for officers. Our Colonel, Colonel Fowler, is a proper one, you know, one of the scrapping sort, and you can bet your boots we shall give nothing while he is there. We used to talk about the Terriers and wonder if they would be any good in war, but it's come now, and you can take my tip that our regiment will go all the way, and we are right in the thick of it now. The other night the remnants of the Canadians were relieved, and we all turned out in the middle of the night to cheer them, as well as sending our bugle band to lead them a mile or two. Poor devils, although few, they went through well. They had no end of German helmets and other souvenirs, but they were so tired they soon had to throw them all away. They were singing, "It's a long, long way to Vancouver." As they marched past us they shouted, "We've not done with 'em yet boys." They are a hetty [manly] lot, all big, strong, fellows. Well, you know, it's a bit rotten, after seeing a sight like that, to pick up a "Mirror" next morning, dated two days previously, and see a picture of 2,000 men on strike outside Woolwich Arsenal striking for two pounds a week. I wonder what would have happened if the Canadians had downed tools. There would have been no Sherwoods left, and precious little of the Belgian army. But war's a great leveller and all who come back will have learned a lot. I for one shall not be sorry to see the enemy on the run and home in view. But, never fear, they will get it in the neck soon.'

[Note: The passage about the Canadians was quoted by Edwyn Hoskyns, the bishop of Southwell, in his letter in the Southwell Diocesan Magazine (no. 327, June 1915, 71-2). Evidently taken from this edition of the Newark Advertiser, Hoskyns says that the letter was written by a private in the Sherwood Foresters.]

9 June 1915

'SANDBAGS FOR THE TROOPS   All those willing to help make sandbags to send to the front for our soldiers should apply to Mrs Godber, Moor Lane, on Tuesday or Friday mornings between the hours of 10 and 12, when they will be supplied with materials and instructions.'

'MILITARY HOSPITAL   Burgage Manor, which has been converted into a military hospital continues to do excellent work. A number left on Tuesday week, and there were fresh arrivals on Wednesday. Some of the cases are very serious, while others have been more in the nature of recuperation from wounds and shock. An appeal is earnestly made for the supply of blankets, sheets, counterpanes, and rugs for beds, bath and face towels, dressing gowns and cigarettes, which seem inevitable and in great demand for the wounded Tommy.'

'THE "ADVERTISER" IN THE TRENCHES   Pte. Harold Tyne, of the 8th Sherwood Foresters, and formerly an employee of Mr J. H. Kirkby, who, with three other former employees, is in the same trenches, writes as follows to Mr. A. Woodruffe:– "Thank you very much for the 'Advertiser' which you send us every week. The last three we received just when going into the trenches, and we can assure you it is a treat to read about the news of our native town. If we buy an English paper out here it is either the 'Mirror' or something like that, and they cost us two pence.. We came out of the trenches in the middle of the week, after having a quiet time for us. We got the tail end of a peculiar sort of gas that affected our eyes for a long time. Our officer said they were high explosive shells charged with gas, but we are all right up to now." '

[Note: In 1911 Arthur Woodruffe was 40 years old and living with his family at Thorne Cottage in Southwell. He was employed as a warehouse foreman.]

ENLISTMENT During the past week or so Mr. Oscar Cottam, son of Wm Cottam, builder, and Mr Cyril Toder, chauffeur to Dr Polson, J.P., have joined the Motor Transport Corps, while Mr Reggie Walker, third son of Dr Walker, Fred Tongue, Burgage, and Mr A. Ridge, Back Lane, have been enlisted in 3/8th Sherwood Foresters.

'CATERING FOR THE SOLDIERS   This was a further report on the use of Trebeck Hall as a soldiers' club. It provided writing paper, pen and ink, billiards, bagatelle. There is 'a piano for the musically inclined, of which there are many in the army . . . . About 200 men were already members of the club. The charge for membership is a nominal 6d for three months. The Wesleyan School is used on similar lines. The Westhorpe Institute is thrown open to the soldiers, and the Minster Institute provides one of the finest billiard tables in the town, which, with the baths belonging to the same committee, are much appreciated.'

EGG COLLECTION   Last week 1001 eggs were collected, of which 364 were sent to Burgage Manor.

NEWARK GROCERS   A list of men from various grocers and provision merchants who were serving was published. The Southwell list was as follows:

J. H. KIRKBY'S STAFF

William Murden	8th Battalion Sherwood Foresters
Thomas Musgrove	8th Battalion Sherwood Foresters
Geo H. Templeman	8th Battalion Sherwood Foresters
Arthur Drabble	8th Battalion Sherwood Foresters
Samuel Oliver	8th Battalion Sherwood Foresters
Alex Peet	8th Battalion Sherwood Foresters
Harold Tyne	8th Battalion Sherwood Foresters
John Pacey	8th Battalion Sherwood Foresters
Kenneth Baguley	Army Service Corps
Herbert Adams	Army Service Corps
Clifford Butler	13th Battalion Sherwood Foresters
J. H. Kirkby Jnr.	Officer Training Corps
J. N. Kirkby	Officer Training Corps
Joseph Otter	Royal Marine Artillery
Harry Brown	3rd Battalion Sherwood Foresters
Frank Wilcox	5th Devonshires
George Jepson	4th Sherwood Foresters

Messrs J H Kirkby making deliveries
(Private Collection)

JOHN J. BATES STAFF
W. W. Bates	South Notts Hussars
A. Horsley	12th Lancers
W. Foster	Royal Navy
W. Drabble	2/8th Sherwood Foresters
L. Stephenson	8th Sherwood Foresters
J. Stephenson	8th Sherwood Foresters
W. Corby	Derbyshire Regiment
C. Elvidge	Remount Dept.
P. Toder	2/8th Sherwood Foresters

16 June 1915

Report of the death in action of Captain Henry Gordon Wright, 'well known and highly respected in Southwell' and a member of the Southwell Company of the 8th Sherwood Foresters, and had been a member of the Southwell Rifle Club, 'one of their finest shots.' He was on the staff of the Southwell branch of the Nottingham and Nottinghamshire Bank. Captain Wright was shot in the head by a German sniper 'on Sunday week'. Aged 30, he was engaged to be married to Miss Gwen Pratt of Bleasby. [See report below, 14 July, and was due to marry the previous month 'but the young officer was unable to obtain leave'.]

SOUTHWELL SOLDIER WOUNDED A report that Alexander Peet, 8th Sherwood Foresters, of Kirklington Road, formerly employed by Mr J. H. Kirkby, was engaged digging trenches last Thursday, when he was wounded by a bullet passing clean through the muscle of his right arm. After being attended to at the dressing station he was removed to the base.

23 June 1915

Photograph of Pte. Frank Paling of Southwell, killed in action.

Report of Cpl. F. H. Wilcox of Southwell Company, 8th Sherwood Forester, killed in action 'last week'. He had been employed by Carey and Co, lace makers of Southwell, and was 'very popular in his regiment and highly esteemed in the town'. He was a member of the local branch of the Church of England Men's Society, and was the first man in the branch 'to lay down his life in the great war for justice and freedom'.

NEWS FROM THE FRONT A Southwell soldier, writing on Thursday last to Mr A Woodruffe, describes the severe fighting that took place on June 15th, when there were several casualties among the local men. The lieutenant mentioned may be Lt. Hollins of Mansfield, whilst Cpl. Wilcox of Southwell was also killed about that time [see below]. The writer says: 'We were coming out of the trenches on Tuesday night, June 15th, after having had a very hot time. The enemy shelled us every night and day, and I can tell you it was not very pleasant. Well, everything went on all right so far as the shelling was concerned, until Tuesday night, when we were to leave the trenches. It would be about 9.30, and we had just been 'stood-to' for about a quarter of an hour when the enemy blew up one of our trenches, and then started shelling and trench mortaring us. They also turned the machine guns on us, and then opened rapid rifle fire. The trench which they blew up was the one where the brave Southwell lads were in, and when it went up in the air the Germans started off and charged the trench. But our brave boys stuck to them. Several other trenches went through it as well, but I think this particular trench got the worst. We got several wounded, and a corporal and lieutenant killed, but nothing to compare with what the Germans got. Dead bodies of the enemy were lying in all directions, and the trench where our Company was in was just like a slaughterhouse. One of the Southwell lads distinguished himself in the fight, but we have not heard how he will be rewarded for doing so well.'[Several Southwell men distinguished themselves, particularly John Sharman and Sam Humberstone – see report 7th July 1915.]

30 June 1915

Full report of the 'Military Sports' organised by Southwell Golf Club for the men of the West Riding and Northumbrian Engineers training in the vicinity.

WOUNDED SOLDIER Private Alexander Peet, of the 8th Bn. Sherwood Foresters, who was wounded last week at the front, has arrived at a private hospital in Manchester, and is going on very favourably. He was shot through the thick muscle of his right arm.

7 July 1915

Report that J. N. Kirkby, son of Mrs and Mrs J. H. Kirkby [Southwell bakers, etc.], had been gazetted 2nd Lt in the Yorks and Lancashire regiment, and Bernard Hyde of Clinton House, a temporary 2nd Lt in the 13th West Yorkshires. Also that QMS Howarth of the 3/1 West Riding Company, RE, and QMS Hutson of the 2/2 West Riding company, RE, both of Southwell, had been given commissions. 'The promotions from the ranks have given much satisfaction in the town.'

Letter from Pte. J. J. Henton of the Southwell Company (H coy) of 1/8th Sherwood Foresters who worked formerly at Carey's in Southwell. Writing to his wife 'and evidently speaking of the incidents of June 16th, which were referred to in last week's *Advertiser* says:– "The Germans attacked us the last time we were in the trenches. They thought they would break through us because we were only Terriers, but we stuck to them like glue. We had a few casualties, but the Germans lost heavily. You will be surprised to hear that poor old Jerry got wounded, but I think he will get over it. Sam Humberstone and Jack Sharman have been spoken of very highly. They ought to get a medal, for they have earned one, but I was sorry I was not at it at the time. We had to go before the Brigadier for the second time for doing such good work; they are always praising the 8th Battalion, and the Robin Hoods call us 'the Mad 8th'. I was in a support trench this last time. We could not fire at all, but the Germans were shelling us every day, and we had to shift out of the trench to get out of the road of them." Private Henton wishes to thank local friends for a parcel of chocolate'.

[Note: The edition of the *Newark Advertiser* for 30 June carried a report of an action 'somewhere in Belgium' by the 8th Battalion, Sherwood Foresters: 'It appears, according to the official dispatches, that the Germans, on Tuesday, 15th June, mined the lines held by the Battalion, but fortunately the loss of life only occurred in one trench. A terrible bombardment followed the mining, in which heavy artillery, "Jack Johnsons" [German high explosive shells], machine guns, mortars, and rifles belched out shot and shell for over one hour. The Newark lads, however, held on, and inflicted heavy losses on the enemy who were hopelessly defeated in their endeavour to break the Battalion's lines. Lt. Dobson and Lt. Hollins (of Mansfield), two officers of the 8th Battalion, and several men were killed and wounded, but up to now it is ascertained that the Newark Company only lost two men, and, strange to say, both were named Richardson, whilst the Southwell Company lost Corporal Wilcox in this encounter.' The report continues by quoting a letter from Lieutenant Colonel Fowler, C.O. of the 8th Battalion saying that 'the Battalion did splendidly, and worthily upheld the name it has made for itself.' Seventy-six men of the 1/8th Battalion were killed and wounded in this encounter, 23 from Mansfield and Forest Town, and seven from Sutton. Among the wounded Pte. J. H. Curzon of C Company, from Southwell, was wounded in the left arm, Pte. J. T. Jepson, from Southwell and in B Company, suffered a fractured arm, Pte. R. Harvey from Easthorpe, B. Company, had a grazed back, Pte. A. Cooling, from Southwell, B Company, a sprained shoulder, Pte. E.. Harrison, from Southwell, B Company, an injured forearm, Pte. A. McGowan, from Southwell, B Company, a cut hand, and Pte. J. Sharman, from Westhorpe, B Company, a wounded thigh.]

EGG COLLECTION   This week's total was reported at 767, with 392 eggs going to Burgage Manor Hospital.

14 July 1915

Report of an entertainment for soldiers at Norwood Park camp organised by Mr A. N. Metcalf. It was attended by a large number of soldiers and a party of wounded men from Burgage Manor Hospital. Also present were Mons and Mdlle de Groot, two of the Southwell Belgian refugees. The entertainment included a contribution from Miss Gwen Pratt [see 16 June above] 'who showed talented skill in her recitation'.

LETTER RE EGG COLLECTIONS Ida K. Fairweather – letter: 'Once more I greatly regret having to report a decrease in our egg collection. We have only received 773 this week for this depot…Surely we of Southwell district will not fail to do our best…'

21 July 1915

Cpl Frank Wilcox of 5th Devonshires was married to Miss Connie Harrison, daughter of Mrs Harrison of Queen Street. Frank Wilcox, formerly an employee of J. H. Kirkby, enlisted at the outbreak of the war. 'He has got a few days furlough previous to going to the front.'

Report of the meeting of the Southwell RDC about the national appeal to assist Belgian refugees. One member pointed out that some Belgian refugees were demanding 5 shillings before they would agree to work for an employer in this country.

4 August 1915

Harry Kirkby, eldest son of Mr and Mrs J. H. Kirkby, commissioned as 2nd Lt in the Lancashire Fusiliers.

Full report of a dance held for soldiers in Trebeck Hall.

Southwell St. Mary's Football Team in 1913
Back Row L-R: A. Moore, R. Revill*, S. Humberstone**, G. Donson**, J. Dixon*, W. Johnson*,
D.F. Longmore, E. Bancroft (Trainer)
Middle Row L-R: J. Watson**, E. Gilbert**, A. Henton, R. Scott, G.D. Mosedale (Capt), G. Cross*
Front Row L-R: W. Tinley (Chairman, A. Humberstone**, T. Shaw*, H. Kirk**, E. Scarborough*,
A. Townsend*, F. Scarborough (Treasurer)
(Collection - Peter Cant)

**Died in the war *Served in the war

'DR HANDFORD'S APPOINTMENT Dr Handford of Southwell, and Medical Officer for the county, has been called up for military duties at the Cannock Chase Camp. He was for many years in the Army Medical Corps, and has two sons in the army at the present time.'

11 August 1915

Report of the death of Pte. John Watson of Southwell, aged 23, 1/8th Sherwood Foresters. He had been employed for a time at the Southwell Co-operative Stores and was born in Skellwyth Bridge, Westmoreland. He was shot in the knee and died in hospital. For two and a half years he was goalkeeper for Southwell Thursday FC in the Notts Mid-Week league.

Report of the death in action of Cpl. Sam Humberstone, with photograph. His wife lived in Westhorpe and his mother in Burgage Lane. The report noted that 'kind friends, as tactfully as possible, broke the sad intelligence to the bereaved. Cpl. Humberstone leaves, in addition to the widow, two little sons, the elder of whom is not yet three years old. He would have been 26 on the 18th of this month, and only quite recently he wrote a most cheery letter to his wife, explaining that he had every prospect of coming home from the trenches on furlough, and hoped to be with her to celebrate her birthday. Later a letter was received from another relative, who is also fighting, explaining that poor Sam was instantly killed, and he did not suffer, but died like a hero. He was an employee at Messrs Carey and Sons' lace factory, where he was employed up to going to camp shortly before the outbreak of hostilities. He was an enthusiastic footballer, and had played regularly for Southwell City. Another son of Mrs Humberstone, Pte. Arthur Humberstone, has been wounded. Lance-Sgt. Albert Humberstone, the elder brother, who was home a few weeks ago and is in the 1st Battalion Royal Scots Fusiliers, has been awarded the D.C.M. The youngest boy of the family is also in the 8th Sherwood Foresters.

Report of the death in action of Pte. J. H. Hopewell, with photograph: 'Mr and Mrs Hopewell of 8, Chatham Street, lost their second son, Pte. A. E. Hopewell, last April when he was killed in action, and now they have received the sad intelligence that their third boy, Pte. John Henry Hopewell, has also made the supreme sacrifice. He was 25 years of age on the very day that he was shot. A native of Kimberley, he went to school at Bulwell, afterwards removing with his parents to Southwell, where he entered Messrs Carey and Son's lace factory, and was also a member of the Boys' Brigade, being in the bugle band. Some seven years ago he joined the bugle band of the 8th Sherwood Foresters. A letter to his parents states that "he always did his duty without grumbling, and consequently was appreciated by his officers." Much sympathy is felt with the parents at their double loss. A fourth son, William, is with the Royal Marines on board H.M.S Exmouth which is "somewhere" in the Mediterranean. Mr and Mrs Hopewell have been greatly touched by the many messages of kindly feelings of which they have been the recipients.'

Report of the death in action of Sam Oliver. Pte. Sam Oliver served with the Sherwood Foresters and was killed on 30 July 1915. He is commemorated on the Ypres (Menin Gate) Memorial.
Report of the death of Pte. T. W. Jubb, only son of Mr and Mrs Jubb of Lowdham. Pte. Jubb had served in 'B' Company of the 1/8th Sherwood Foresters with his Southwell colleagues who he had trained with. He was shot whilst at his post in a trench.

Report of an open recruiting meeting in Southwell which attracted a 'large crowd'. It was addressed by, among others, Sgt. Brundell, 'one of the wounded soldiers at the local Red Cross hospital' in Burgage Manor. He appealed for more men to join the army, saying: "The English soldier is more than a match for the Germans, but one Englishman could not beat half a dozen Germans" and "Although Southwell had done magnificently in sending men to the war, yet he still saw strong, healthy, young fellows walking about the streets who ought to be doing their bit in the trenches." The report continued: 'Mr Adlington, a local builder, said that he would join and do his bit, and, amid much enthusiasm, another man said that he had tried twice, but would have another go.'

Report of a well attended service in the Minster on the first anniversary of the declaration of the war. The bishop of Southwell, Edwyn Hoskyns, in his address said that 'they must be aware they were engaged in a most righteous cause, realising that life would be worth nothing in this world if brute force and militarism conquered, for then Christ would be banished from their homes.'

18 August 1915

NATIONAL RESERVE   The members of the National Reserve now attached to the 8th Battalion Sherwood Foresters . . . have all been passed for Imperial Service. The medical inspection, which was conducted by Army doctors from Thoresby Camp, was a very severe one, and speaks well for the men, most of whom are over 40 years of age.

MEMORIAL SERVICE   The Venerable the Archdeacon of Nottingham conducted a memorial service in the Minster on Thursday night. The nave was full of relatives and friends of the brave men in whose memory the service was held. The address was given by the Rector. Deputations were present from the firms where the men worked previous to the war. The dead heroes are Cpl. S. Humberstone, Cpl. F. Wilcox, Pte. F. Paling, Pte. S. Oliver, and Pte. J. Watson. Mr Wyer played the Dead March in "Saul", and the whole congregation sang the National Anthem. In a conspicuous position in the central aisle was the Union Jack draped in black and crowned with a magnificent laurel wreath sent by Messrs H. Merryweather and Sons. Capt. J. K. Lane was present at the service, and members of the Girl Guides were in uniform.

The following letter, whilst sent by a Newark member of the Sherwood Foresters, has been reproduced as it illustrates the horror of the battlefield that the 1/8th Battalion Sherwood Foresters suffered in the trenches:

WITH THE SHERWOOD FORESTERS IN ACTION   'Dear Dad, Once more I am able to write to you, and I am a very lucky chap to be able to do so, but, thank goodness, I came through it all right with nothing worse than a bruised back and a shaking. But I am about all right again now. It was an awful day and a battle that will never be forgotten, and all who came through are worth all the praise that the people of England can give them. I will try and give you an idea of what it was like. First of all I will tell you the position. The Germans are in possession of a ridge, with our lines at the bottom and a village at the back, and that enables them to do as they like with the chaps in our trenches. So we had to shift them out of it. Several attacks have been made, but all have been failures. So the Sherwoods and Durhams were put to it, and we made the attack at daybreak on August 9th. Six hundred big guns were to play on the trenches first, besides a battery of the famous French 75 guns which came up for the occasion, and they were to fire 800 shells in eight minutes. I know it seems unbelievable, but that is the [undecipherable] we got, and goodness knows how many guns the Germans used. It is absolutely impossible to describe the scene of the bombardment. All I can say it was one continuous bursting of all kinds of shells. They even sent great trees up into the air. We started in a wood, but I can tell you there is very little of the wood left now; it has been blown to pieces. The Germans started to use liquid fire on us, but we did not give them a chance to use much. We went over the top and got at them. And what a fight. I will never forget it as long as I live. The men were falling like rabbits, but we kept on, and when we got to the Germans' trench it was full of dead and dying, and the dying and captured were crying for mercy, but none was shown to them. They said, 'Me no fight English, but Kaiser make us. We want peace.' When we took the second line we captured about 127 men, but the third line was different. The Germans did not stop to wait for us there; they dropped everything and ran for it. So you see, we made a complete victory of it. When we got possession of their trenches we had an awful time of it. They bombarded us with their siege guns, and they had got the range to perfection. Every shell came into the trench and nearly every man in 'B' Company was killed, and I must say we paid a heavy price for what we did. A shell burst in front of me, and I was completely buried, but I worked myself out all right, and all that happened to me was I got my back bruised with the falling earth. I was the last man in the trench who was not wounded, one of my own regiment and one of the D. L. I. [Durham Light Infantry], and I got them into shelter all right, and after a while we crawled out on our stomachs. That was around eight o'clock at night, and we had been fighting hard since 2 o'clock in the morning, and when we got into safety I was completely done up; but the wounded men, I am pleased to say are safe in hospital. When the Queen's Westminster Rifles relieved us it was a very small battalion of Sherwood Foresters that formed up and answered the roll-call, but, I am pleased to see that the British are still holding the line we fought for. Well, dad, I must close now. Please send me the paper as soon as you can, as I want to see what they say about it. Give my love to all, and tell them I am all right. Good-bye for the present. – Your son, Frank.' [This letter describes one of the incidents whilst the 1/8th Battalion were in trenches near Sanctuary Wood, in the Salient.] - See Chapter 3.

25 August 1915

ROLL OF HONOUR The roll of honour in the Minster, containing the names of local men serving in His Majesty's forces, had been altered and brought up to date. The list now comprising 23 officers, 242 men, 1 chaplain, 10 killed, 16 wounded, 2 sick, 1 wounded twice, 1 missing, 1 prisoner of war, 1 mentioned in dispatches for gallant and distinguished service in the field.

THE SOLDIERS' CLUB, held in the Trebeck Hall, is proving very popular with the men now training in the district. It is open every night for writing purposes, and refreshments are served at a moderate charge. Concerts and dances are run by a committee of ladies. Last Thursday the orchestra for the dance was provided by Mr Litchfield, and about a 100 men were present with their lady friends.

HEROES AT HOME Several of the local heroes are home from the trenches this week, having been granted a few days leave after a very severe time in the fighting line. Major J. P. Becher, who has done magnificent work in the furious fighting of the last month, is again home for a flying visit. Pte. J. Sharman, who was recommended for the D.C.M. on account of great bravery, is also at home looking fit and well. Pte. E. Daniels arrived on Saturday and Pte. F. Marriott is again home to recuperate after his second wound. He was in the great retirement from Mons, where his regiment was severely cut up, he received a bullet wound in the thigh, and after getting over that he again went into the firing line, where he was wounded a second time.

1 September 1915

Report of a dance attended by 100 soldiers of the West Riding engineers 'and lady friends' in Trebeck Hall.

PROMOTIONS Two local officers have been promoted this week, both being on active service at the front. Lt. Henry B.S. Handford, son of Dr and Mrs Handford of Southwell, has been gazetted temporary Captain in the Sherwood Foresters, and Second-Lieutenant Alfred Hacking, son of the Archdeacon of Newark and Mrs Hacking of Southwell, has been gazetted temporary lieutenant in the same regiment.

8 September 1915

Report that Flight-Sgt E. C. Rumford, son of Mr W. Rumford of King Street had been mentioned in dispatches and awarded the St George's Medal, 2nd class, by the Czar of Russia. [Note: Herbert William Rumford was a 'refreshment contractor and confectioner' of King Street, see entries for 21 November and 19 December 1917.]

'SIX SONS IN THE ARMY   With the enlistment of their son Baden in the Engineers last week Mr and Mrs Stephenson of Easthorpe, Southwell, now have six sons serving with the colours, and hold the record for Southwell. The following is the list:– Thomas, 8th Sherwood Foresters; Fred, Cameron Highlanders; Leonard, 1st Sherwood Foresters; George, Cameron Highlanders; William, 3rd Sherwood Foresters; Baden, Royal Engineers. Mr Stephenson, who is a lace maker, employed at Messrs Carey and Sons Ltd, Southwell, has 19 years service to his credit in the old 4th Notts VB [Volunteer Battalion], and is now a member of the National Reserve, 3rd Class.'

HELD A TRENCH ALONE   Many messages have been received that Private J. Sharman, of Southwell, has distinguished himself with the 8th Battalion Sherwood Foresters, but up to the present no particulars of the actual circumstances have been sent. The splendid performance of the Southwell lad, whose portrait is given in this issue, is described in the following words from his commanding officer:-
> 'At Kemmel, on June 15th, for holding trench 'J3 left' by himself after it had been blown by a German mine. He repelled the enemy's attack, killing one man and putting the remainder to flight.'

Pte. Sharman, who is only 20 years of age, is the son of Mr T. Sharman, Westhorpe, and was employed before the war by Mr H. E. Steel, Westhorpe. When war broke out he left Newark Market-place with the remainder of the Battalion. A week ago he returned home for several days' leave, looking very fit and well. He would not speak of the war or his own gallantry in the field, and has since returned to the front.

THE 8TH SHERWOODS (NEWARK BATTALION - A FINE REPUTATION – SIR J. FRENCH'S CONGRATULATIONS   A full report appeared in the newspaper regarding the congratulations that had been read to the troops on behalf of Sir John French. He congratulated the 8th Battalion, along with members of the Robin Hoods for their excellent fighting at the front.

PROMOTIONS AND DISTINCTIONS L/Cpl. Harold Tyne, of the 8th Sherwoods, writing to his parents on Saturday last and received by them on Monday night, says: 'I am pleased to tell you that Major J.P. Becher has won the D.S.O., and Arthur Shepherd and myself have been awarded the D.C.M.. ...'

NATIONAL EGG COLLECTION   The total this week had amounted to 810 eggs for the wounded.

SOUTHWELL PASSENGER ON THE HESPERIAN   Miss Nellie Fisher, of Southwell, granddaughter of Mr John Fisher, Westhorpe, was a passenger on the Allan liner R.M.S. Hesperian, and was on her way to Canada to be married. She left Southwell on Friday morning to join the ship at Liverpool, travelling second class in the vessel. Her friends were much alarmed when the news came through that the liner had been torpedoed, but a wire was received on Monday morning saying 'Safe, and landed at Queenstown. Writing particulars.'

[Note: The liner *Hesperian* was the first passenger ship to be attacked after all passenger vessels had been armed for their own defence after the sinking of the steamer *Arabic*. The *Hesperian* was sunk on 4 September 1915 by the *U-20* commanded by Capt. Schwieger. He had earlier torpedoed and sunk the *Lusitania* in an action regarded at the time as a monstrous disregard for the safety of civilians. The *Hesperian* was carrying the body of a one of the *Lusitania*'s passengers that had been recovered from the sea. Nellie Fisher was saved, but 32 passengers were drowned. The week prior to the sinking, Count Bernstorff, the Imperial German Ambassador to the United States, had assured Washington that 'passenger liners will not be sunk without warning' following the Lusitania sinking. When word reached Germany of Walter Schwieger's actions he was ordered to Berlin to justify his actions and apologize officially. Schwieger was killed later in the war whilst in command of SM U-88.]

MORE SHERWOODS WOUNDED   News has reached Mr and Mrs J Brown, Brinkley, Southwell, that their eldest son, Pte. George Brown, 8th Sherwood Foresters, has been in hospital some time suffering from rupture, in the severe fighting recently when the Germans blew up their trenches. Pte. Brown was engaged in throwing up the bags of sand protecting the trench, when he overstrained himself in the effort to rebuild the parapet. He was sent down to the base, and thence to England. Pte. Richard Revill, son of Mr and Mrs Revill, Easthorpe, has had a marvellous escape from death, a bullet from a German rifle hit him in the right arm, passed clean through the muscle, and through his tunic, in the pocket of which was a bundle of letters and a Bible. The bullet ploughed its way through the letters and stopped near the outer cover of the Bible, thus no doubt saving his life. He is at present home on sick furlough. His brother Frank also of the 8th Sherwoods has been wounded with shrapnel in the ankle, and is in hospital in the south of England.

15 September 1915

'DOES SOUTHWELL COMPANY HOLD THE RECORD? Sgt. W. Murden, 8th Sherwood Foresters, in an interesting letter to Mr Woodruffe, says:– "We have been through a most trying time a few weeks since. We went into the trenches to relieve the 7th Battalion. All went well for a time until just before daybreak when the Germans made their attack preceded by liquid fire. It is hard to make anyone understand what the latter was like. It was a flame that seemed to belch forth from a cylinder, burning everything that it came into contact with. It only burns for about five minutes, then gives off a dense smoke, under cover of which they make their attack. That is as well as I can describe it, and when they had allowed time for [the] device [to work] they came on, fully equipped, but they never succeeded; our men stuck to them like leeches, especially the bomb throwers, some of whom, I am sorry to say, we lost, including Sam Oliver, from our firm. He was in my platoon. He died gallantly fighting to the last, and never changed in his manner at all – as cool as if he was driving his horses in Southwell. We kept on at this for several days; then they gave up, and never attempted to come again. We are hardly doing anything with the infantry now. We can always say that Southwell has done its share in this war, and done it voluntarily and thoroughly. A volunteer is worth three pressed men. It is wonderful to see our men out here. They are always the same. I have close on fifty men under me, and it's no trouble to look after them. I am now going to tell you some news that has come to our Battalion, and our Company in particular, concerning the engagement just referred to, Sgt. Arthur Shepherd and L/Cpl. Tyne were complemented by the General, and to crown the event it has just come to us that Major Becher has had the D.S.O. conferred upon him, and Segt. Shepherd and L/Cpl. Tyne (who belongs to the old firm) the D.C.M. That is making a D.S.O., two D.C.M.s and one St George's Order (Pte. J. Sharman) all given to men in our Southwell Company. You will forgive me saying we are proud of ourselves, but I am sure Southwell will be proud of its men. There are other things I should like to tell you, but they would not pass that gentleman, the censor. It is a good idea having him or we might send something that would not be to the advantage of our Army.'

[Note: William Thomas Murden was aged 20 in 1911 and employed as a warper in Carey's lace factory. When he enlisted he was working at Kirkby's, the grocers, bakers and general stores in Southwell, with Sam Oliver, a carter, and Arthur Woodruffe, warehouse foreman.]

ARCHDEACON OF NEWARK'S SON WOUNDED   Amongst the wounded in the casualty list issued on Monday appears the name of Second Lieutenant E.M. Hacking, of the 8th Sherwood Foresters, and son of the Venerable Archdeacon Hacking of Newark. The gallant officer obtained his commission in the County Battalion shortly after the outbreak of war, and was at Luton. He went to the front in February last.

ANOTHER SOUTHWELLIAN KILLED   News has been received of the death of another Southwellian belonging to the 8th Sherwood Foresters – Private Frank Raynor, second son of Mr Arthur Raynor of Carey's lace factory. On March 12th he was reported as missing, and nothing more was heard by his father until Saturday morning week, when a communication was received from the Records Office, Lichfield, informing him that his boy was killed in action on the date it was reported he was missing, enclosed with an expression of sympathy of the King and Queen, signed by Lord Kitchener. Private Raynor, who was 22 years of age, was a native of Southwell, and attended the Wesleyan Day School, and on leaving there he went to work at Messrs Merryweathers Ltd., and from whence he entered the silk mill at Maythorne. He enlisted in the army some four years ago, and was drafted to India, being in the section which went out with Capt. Hume, and remained there until the outbreak of the war, when he proceeded with the regiment to the front, where he has now laid down his life.

[Note: Censorship was applied with increasing severity as the months passed. By at least the autumn of 1916 it was possible for many front-line soldiers to send home only a Field Service post card printed with the following phrases for deletion as applicable:

I am quite well. I have been admitted into hospital sick/wounded/ and am going on well/and hope to be discharged soon. I have received your letter/telegram/parcel dated . . . . Letter follows at first opportunity. I have received no letter from you lately/ for a long time. A signature 'only' could be added with the date. Postage had to be prepaid by the soldier.]

22 September 1915

'CAPTAIN J. GODBER ON LEAVE   The many friends of Capt. J. Godber MRCVS are pleased to see him home for a short time from his arduous duties in France. He is looking well like all the men who are home on leave. Capt. Godber gave up a lucrative practice in Southwell a year ago to take up veterinary work for the Army. His term of service is up, but he is taking on again for another term. Mrs Godber has, in the absence of her husband, being doing splendid work making sandbags for the troops.'

[Note. In 1912 Joseph Godber was 'a veterinary surgeon and veterinary inspector under the Diseases of Animals Acts for the Southwell district', with premises in King Street.]

'CAPT. HANDFORD WOUNDED   In the list of casualties under date Sept. 11 appears the name of Capt. H. B. S. Handford, wounded. The gallant officer, who is a son of Dr. and the Hon. Mrs Handford, Elmfield, Southwell, was in charge of a number of men digging trenches, when a stray bullet hit him in the hand. The wound is not serious. One of the men had a narrow escape, the bullet grazing his neck and causing a slight flesh wound before hitting Capt. Handford, who is a popular and capable officer in the 8th Sherwood Foresters.'

'MISS FISHER SAILS FOR CANADA   Writing to her friends in Southwell, Miss Nellie Fisher says she is having another try for Canada. "At the time of the attack on the Hesperian", she says, "I was feeling a little seasick, and had just gone to lay down in my cabin, when all of a sudden there was an awful thud, and passengers rushed for their lifebelts. The ship began to quiver and shake, and the feeling that came over one was something awful; but after a time I was lowered with a rope round my waist, to a boat that was in the water. After about two hours we were rowed across in the boats to a destroyer. There they took us on board, made us some tea, and revived us. We were then taken on to Queenstown, then to Dublin and by another boat to Holyhead, thence by train to Liverpool. I lost everything except money, which I had on me. I shall get across all right this time." '

Report of the award of the DSO to Major J. P. Becher (with photograph). This noted the personal congratulations of Sir John French, c-in-c BEF, to the 8th Sherwood Foresters for 'their magnificent behaviour in the fighting around Ypres' when Becher was in temporary command of the battalion.

'D.C.M. AWARDS FOR SOUTHWELL TERRITORIALS (with photographs)
Two other, members of the same battalion, and both Southwell lads – Sergeant Arthur Sheppard and Lance-Corporal Harold Tyne – have been award the Distinguished Conduct Medal for conspicuous gallantry at Ypres on July 30th. Lance-Sergeant Sheppard led a bombing party on his own initiative under a heavy bomb and rifle fire against the attacking enemy. Having thrown all his grenades, he went back and brought up a fresh supply, and later, having lost five men, he brought up reinforcements.

Private Tyne, at the same time and place, picked up several unexploded German grenades when his own failed to explode, and threw them, killing several of the enemy. Later he held his trench with great coolness and bravery under a heavy bomb and machine gun fire until reinforced, performing a similar action the following day.

[Note: The Distinguished Conduct Medal was second only to the Victoria Cross in awards for gallantry made to soldiers below the rank of officer. It was awarded for gallantry in the field in the face of the enemy. It was equivalent to the Distinguished Service Order awarded to officers. It was won by at least one other serviceman from Southwell, Sgt. G. H. Templeman (see entry for 22 October 1919).]

'HEROES AT HOME   Lance-Corporal Harold Tyne, who has won the D.C.M, is now at his home on a short furlough. Leaving the trenches in Flanders on Wednesday at 4 pm, he arrived at Boulogne about 9 pm, and reached Southampton at 10 o'clock on Thursday morning. He looks fit and well. He enlisted in the Army in October last year, three of Mr J. H. Kirkby's employees who enlisted at the same time being Harold Tyne, Alex Peet, and Sam Oliver. The last-named was killed on July 30th at the time that Tyne won his D.C.M., and Peet was wounded at Kemmel on June 9th. The Germans made a determined attack on the trench (says Tyne in an interview) that was occupied by him and eight companions, and after being bombarded for some time the trench was raked with a machine gun. In a short time all eight men were killed, all shot through the head, and only Tyne was left. He threw bomb after bomb at the advancing enemy, and after his supply was finished he picked up the Germans' unexploded bombs and threw them back at them, getting a good height with their bombs, which then exploded. In this way, running from one end of the trench to the other, and hampered with the dead bodies of his comrades, he managed to hold his trench and kept the enemy at bay until reinforcements came to his aid.

Private Peet is also home on sick furlough. The two men, who live next door to each other when at home, had a dramatic meeting in Southwell Station on Friday morning, not having seen each other since Peet was wounded in the arm while digging trenches on the above date. The bullet, which he carries in his pocket as a memento, entered his left arm at the biceps muscle. Just touching the bone, it stopped under the skin on the other side of the arm. He was sent down to Boulogne, where the bullet was extracted, and thence to Stockport, where he has since been under treatment.

Mr and Mrs Sheppard have three sons and a son-in-law serving their King and country. The eldest, Trooper W. A. Sheppard, who is married, with two children, is in the South Notts Hussars; the second son is Sgt. Arthur Sheppard, who has won the D.C.M; while the third son, Pte. J. W. Sheppard, is in the R.A.M.C. and has been wounded. The son-in-law is Pte. C. G. Cave, who is in the 8th Sherwood Foresters, and has been in hospital in France some time suffering from [trench] fever. All Mr and Mrs Sheppard's sons had a splendid training in the Church Lads' Brigade in their younger days, and they have also been prominently identified with football in Southwell.'

'A TERRIBLE SCENE Lying wounded in a hospital at Chislehurst, L/Cpl. J. Mosley, of the 2nd Notts. and Derby Regiment, has written an interesting letter to a friend describing the successful charge of his regiment at Hooge. "We were in the hottest fighting area – Ypres," he says, "and had been in the trenches many days, when we came out for two days' rest. Then came the order to prepare for a tough job, at least that's what the general told us, and he said we should do it. We did it, too, in good old English style. We started on the march for Hooge, being shelled on the way, and losing a few wounded and one killed, our good old commanding officer, Leveson-Gower, being one of the wounded. I myself was following the battalion up with five men, and had the misfortune to have two of the men slightly wounded. We were lucky not to be blown to atoms, but got to the trenches about midnight."

"The position looked awful, I shall never forget the terrible sight. The bombardment was awful. I have never known it so bad. We made the charge about three in the morning, and I can tell you we let them have some steel. Our fellows fought like lions, and made a terrible mess of them. There were about 20 of us in one trench, when all of a sudden I got buried, and when I managed to free myself it was to find only three of us left, all the other poor fellows had disappeared. I saved two that had got buried, one just in time, with shells and bombs dropping almost on top of us…"

"I have nearly been blown up time after time. Only those at the front know the horror of day and night. It's awful to see your chums falling at your side, some blown to atoms and others with heads off. I have seen civilians killed, and thousands of poor women and children terror-stricken. We have put them in the trenches for safety.'"

29 September 1915

Report of a meeting of the parish council. It congratulated J. P. Becher and other men from the town had gained awards for gallantry. It was noted that 'upwards of 200 "old boys" from Southwell National Schools' were serving with the forces.

'LIFE IN GALLIPOLI – SHERWOOD CORPORAL PREFERS SOUTHWELL Corporal A.H. Chambers, of Southwell, who is now with the 9th Battalion Sherwood Foresters in the Gallipoli Peninsula, speaking of an attack made on August 21st writes: "It was awful to see the dead and wounded lying about in front of the trenches. Our doctor was a hero, going out under the hottest fire to the wounded, always hopeful and cheerful, never resting and always regardless of self. Lt. Carr, of the R.A.M.C., deserves the V.C. if anyone does. Our battalion is holding a line on the slope of a high ridge, the soil on which is only two inches deep, and underneath is solid rock. To entrench this is an arduous task, six inches per night being rapid progress. Of course, the front is sand-bagged, but snipers pick out all the low parts. We have suffered very heavily in our division. Numbers of men are down with dysentery, and I have had slight attacks. It is a very lowering disease. The smells and flies are responsible."

Writing on Sept. 4th, Corporal Chambers says: "We vary our grub as much as possible. Our dishes include rice pudding sweetened with jam, prunes and raisins (once a week), fried potatoes and onions cooked in bacon fat (every two days), stew, and porridge made from biscuits. We see bread occasionally. I expected to be home by Christmas, but may not be now, as this looks like being a terribly hard job. No navy in the world but ours could have effected this landing."

On Sept. 10th Corporal Chambers writes that the weather is now becoming cooler, and the tropical khaki cloth clothing is much too thin. The country consists of ridges of parallel hills from 150 to 300 feet high. "I never realised what a lovely spot Southwell was until I saw Gallipoli." He adds, "However, we shall soon polish them off."'

Collection organised locally for Belgian refugees.

6th October 1915

COUNTY MAGISTRATES' MESSAGE   On Wednesday the magistrates at the Newark County Police Court passed a resolution of congratulation to Major Becher, Clerk to the Court, on his being made a Companion of the Distinguished Service Order. They also expressed their admiration for the excellent work of the 8th Sherwood Foresters at the front…

RED CROSS HOSPITAL   The Red Cross Voluntary Equipment Hospital has been cleared for a short time to undergo repairs and necessary cleaning, and has now been opened again to receive 25 wounded soldiers from Nottingham. The cases were not serious, most of them being convalescent, and wearing the special hospital dress. They attended the Sunday morning service at the Minster.

13 October 1915

Pte. W. Harvey, serving with the Royal Marines, home on leave from the Dardanelles having contracted dysentery. [Note: The Dardanelles operation in February and March 1915 was an attempt by British and French warships to force a passage through the Dardanelles Straits, held by Turkey. The straits were the key link to the Black Sea ports of Russia and the Mediterranean and provided a direct route to the centre of Ottoman Turkey. This operation culminated in the ill-fated Gallipoli front, the Allied invasion of western Turkey form April 1915 to January 1916.]

'A VOYAGE TO EGYPT   Cpl. Frank Wilcox of the 5th Devons, formerly an employee of Mr J. H. Kirkby, and whose parents reside in King Street, writes from Polygon Camp, Abhassia, Egypt, to Mr Woodruffe, an interesting account of his voyage to Egypt. "Just a few lines", he says, "hoping to find you well, as it leaves me in the pink, although I must admit it's awfully hot. We only drill first thing in the morning and last thing at night. We are on the edge of a big desert, so you can bet it's lively; but you know I shall stick to it and see the thing through. These people here are terrors for charging. I went into a barber's shop yesterday and paid three piastres for a shave – that's 7½d in our money; so I shall shave myself in the future." Cpl. Wilcox pays a warm tribute to the White Star liner which took them over and also refers to the cheers of the people as the great liner put to sea. They reached the Bay of Biscay, and he was pleased to say he was a proper old sailor. He put that down to the ship being such a monster. She didn't rock a bit. There was such a demand for photos of the ship that he could not get one to send home. They touched at Malta, and later reached Alexandria. "I have been to Cairo once," he says, "I must admit it's a fine place, but give me dear old England, and not so much of the black people. But we shall stick it and see it through. It's all for the good of King and country. I hope they will make a few of the slackers join up before it's all over. From what I hear we shall be top-note at the Dardanelles. I am busy washing my clothes today, but don't need to dry them; the sun does that, and irons them too." Cpl. Wilcox concludes by sending kind regards to his fellow-employees with Mr J. H. Kirkby.'

20 October 1915

Report that L/Cpl Tyne D.C.M. wounded though not seriously. Ptes. Drabble and Kendall, both local Territorials, also wounded.

Report that three more employees of J. H. Kirkby have enlisted showing that the firm 'has done exceedingly well in this respect'. They were L. L. B. Martin, F. C. Randell, and W. H. Shelbourne. They joined the Army Service Corps.

'SOLDIER'S LETTER   Recently Mr Sharman, of the Home, Westhorpe, Southwell received a most interesting letter from his son Richard, who is in the 2nd Battalion of the Leicestershire Regiment, "Somewhere in France." The latter is the brother of Pte. J. Sharman, 8th Sherwood Foresters, who has been awarded the D.C.M. Pte. R Sharman was over at Southwell about a month ago, and has been on active service since then. He writes as follows: – "Dear Dad, – Just a few lines to let you know that I got through the attack safely. It was hell with the cover off. You couldn't realise the things that took place. There we had gas bombs, artillery, maxims, and rifle fire against us, the only wonder being that any are left at all. We attacked early in the morning, and captured three lines of trenches, but had not enough men to hold them. There had been a lot of rain, and the trenches are about a foot deep in soft sludge. It looks like treacle. We came through two miles to get out, up to our thighs in places, so you know what we look like. If ever I hear anyone give the Germans any praise I should feel fit to shoot them, for they even shot our wounded as they were crawling in. We were praised by the General for our work. I've lost all my pals, but there will be a reckoning yet. I can't write to all, so give my respects to the lot. We are not in billets, and I am in a cart shed."'

Report, with photographs, that Capt. Henry Basil Strutt Handford, aged 21, and 2nd Lt. Everard Francis Sale Handford, aged 20, Henry's only brother, have both been killed on the same day, 14 October. They were the sons of Dr and the Hon. Mrs Handford. This was the same day and in the same action that Major J. P. Becher, their brother-in-law, was seriously wounded, subsequently to die of his wounds. They were killed during the assault on the Hohenzollern Redoubt during the Battle of Loos. Speaking in Nottingham in October 1919, John Percy Hales D.S.O., rector of Cotgrave and chaplain of the 8th battalion throughout the war, said that he was speaking on the anniversary 'of one of the worst nights of my life – The Hohenzollern Redoubt'.

27 October 1915

'THE TERRIBLE NIGHT OF SEPT. 24TH   A graphic description of the Sherwood Foresters in the battle of Hooge on Sept. 24th is given in a letter from one of the men, who says:-
   "Fifteen of us were detailed off for a fatigue of carrying bombs and grenades to a disused trench about three-quarters of a mile behind the firing line. We finished this about midnight, and were then unexpectedly commandeered to stay there and carry the bombs up, as they were wanted. At 3.45 a.m. all our batteries started shelling like one, and I never heard any German shells for the noise that ours made passing over-head. At 4.30 a.m. we went to the officers' dug-out, as it was time for us to take up our first box of grenades, but found the dug-out blown in and portions of human anatomy on the opposite parapet.

Myself and another fellow started out with the first box of grenades. We were just on the point of starting when a mine went up and the trench bottom heaved up and sank again and the parapets rocked.

As we got nearer the firing line and to one of the high roads the state of the trench got worse and worse and the shell fire heavier. Finally a bit of shrapnel hit the box we were carrying and ricocheted off, so we got out of the trench and ran along the top in the direction we thought our destination lay.

When I got back I got into the dug-out with four others; it was so small we couldn't lie down, so we sat up with our backs against the wall and dozed. Suddenly I heard myself groaning, and the dug-out was filled with acrid smoke, and the roof and sandbags were dropping on me. The man on my right swore violently, and hurled himself out of the dug-out. After a struggle I freed myself and got out, too. He had gone, but the man inside who could speak begged me to help him out, and I had to stop. The first man was nearly gone with concussion, and couldn't speak. He sank in the bottom of the trench when I pulled him out. The next chap had been hit between the shoulder-blades by the shell and was obviously dead, so I left him. The third man was imprisoned by a beam, so I left him to be liberated by some from another dug-out who had just come up. I was unhurt, and so was the first man to get out, but it was a marvellous escape. What had happened was that a whizz-bang had come through the back of the dug-out.

All this time we had had no food, and we were all of us feeling absolutely famished. I expect rations had been arranged for us, but as our officer had been killed we didn't know the arrangements. To add to our discomfort it had been raining and the trench was ankle-deep in water. During the day another officer came to take charge, and he let us go back to our company for tea. We were under cover and though they were shelling us, it wasn't nearly as heavy as that we had been through. I had my equipment and rifle smashed by a shell outside the dug-out.

It was hard to have to go back to the bombs, but this time we were provided with food. The night seemed interminable and we shivered with cold. The water was over the boot-tops, and we couldn't lie down. This was the third night we had been without rest; the first we were trench digging; the second bomb guarding and carrying, and the third ditto.

I am utterly disgusted with the slackers" he concludes, "and I am also convinced that we shall need all our men if we are to win soon and avoid a protracted struggle. No one suggests that life out here is all roses, but a little hardship is a small matter ranged against the horrors of a war on our own soil."'

The losses suffered by the 8th Battalion are graphically recorded in the following extract from the newspaper, the 8th Battalion War Diary gives a detailed description of the battle (Chapter 3).

'8TH BATTALION SHERWOOD FORESTERS – IN BRILLIANT BAYONET CHARGE – TRENCHES IN REDOUBT CAPTURED AND HELD – COMMANDER AND OTHER OFFICERS KILLED
By piecing together news which is slowly filtering through to Newark from the front it is evident that our local territorials – the officers and men of the 8th Sherwood Foresters – have covered themselves with glory in the field of battle, but at a terrible cost.

The information already to hand is that the Commanding Officer, Colonel Fowler, has been killed; the second in command, Major J.P. Becher, D.S.O., of Southwell, has been severely wounded, Captain H.B.S. Handford and Second-Lieutenant C.F.S. Handford, of Southwell, and brothers-in-law of Major J.P. Becher, were killed on the same day; Lt. Vann has been wounded;

Lt. W.M. Hemmingway is missing, and Lt. Strachen killed; and the casualties to the rank and file number hundreds.'

3 November 1915

8TH SHERWOOD'S GALLANTRY – LETTER FROM MAJOR BECHER, D.S.O.
The Newark County magistrates the other day passed a resolution congratulating Major Becher and the men of the 8th Battalion Sherwood Foresters on the excellent work they were doing at the front, and at the last sitting of the Court on Wednesday, at which Colonel E.H. Nicholson presided, with Mr S. MacRae and Mr G.B. Naylor, a letter acknowledging the receipt of resolution was read from Major Becher, D.S.O. as follows:-

'I have just received a copy of the resolution passed by the magistrates, which I really appreciate. I like the wording of the resolution immensely, as it recognises what I have always felt pleased and proud of, viz. that the distinction conferred upon me is a recognition of the good work done by the men of the battalion. At present, it is rather difficult to write letters as one cannot give any information which might furnish a clue to our doings and whereabouts, so you must excuse such a short one.'

Colonel Nicholson said that since the letter was written Major Becher had been dangerously wounded, while gallantly leading his men against the Germans on the Hohenzollern Redoubt. Their heartfelt sympathy would go out to him in the terrible suffering he must have undergone during the 48 hours' exposure before he was found, and their earnest hope for his speedy and complete recovery.

Major Becher, D.S.O., is clerk to the Newark Magistrates.

The seventh son of Mr Thomas Stephenson of Easthorpe has enlisted: Thomas, Fred, Leonard, George, William, Baden, and now Arthur, who enlisted in the Royal Engineers.

10 November 1915

Letter to the *Advertiser* from Field Marshall Lord Grenfell proposing to recruit a second (reserve) CLB battalion of the 16th KRRC.

MILITARY WEDDING   On Saturday last the Minster was the scene of a pretty but quiet wedding, the contracting parties being Sergeant Albert Humberstone, of the 1st Battalion Royal Scots Fusiliers, and Miss Mabel Sharpe, of West Bridgford, Nottingham, formerly of Westgate, Southwell. The bride was given away by Mr F.G. Hewston (brother-in-law of the bride-groom). The bridesmaid was Miss Ethel Sharpe, sister of the bride. The officiating clergyman was the Rev. J.R. Thomas, senior curate.

'THIS VILE CLIMATE' – SOUTHWELL MAN'S EXPERIENCES IN GALLIPOLI
"I have never been in better health than I am at present," writes Pte. A.H. Chambers from the Gallipoli Peninsula to his parents in Southwell, "but a man needs a constitution of iron to stand this vile climate. Conditions here have not been heavenly. After about six hours' rain a heavy snowstorm came on and did its best to cheer us up for a whole day and night. On its cessation a hard frost set in, and this, together with the cold winds and water, makes the conditions terrible. Our battalion got off lightly, only 97 men suffering from exposure and frostbite. The other

battalions suffered more heavily. The weather has now become much milder, but it may break up at any time. From letters received I gather that many of my long-lost letters have at last reached their destination. One written during the first week of September arrived in Southwell on November 6th, so you see the authorities have at last commenced to bustle."

In another letter Pte. Chambers writes: "You would have smiled to see us fishing valises, rifles, etc., out of the flooded dug-outs with the aid of a pick. The trenches are neck-deep in water in parts, and several communication trenches are impassable.

We are now in the grip of winter, and a cold winter it is. On the night before last it started to rain, and rained for six hours without a stop. Naturally we retired to our dug-outs, but although we had dug a trench at the bottom, the dug-out soon began to fill with water. I started baling out with a mug and canteen, but the water gained on me so rapidly that very soon our blankets were under water, and we were over the boot tops in it. The rain seemed to descend in sheets – never have I seen such a terrific downpour.

After a time the storm abated a little, and we soon had the water under control again. When the rain ceased we cleared the dug-out of mud and water by digging down about a foot until we came to dry earth. Since our blankets are wet through we sat in one corner of the dug-out and tried to sleep until the morning, which was again stormy.

Dozens of fellows had their dug-outs flooded right over to a depth of six feet. Down the footpaths there were rushing torrents, strong enough to carry a man off his feet.'"

CONCERT – On Wednesday night a miscellaneous programme of music was given to the wounded soldiers at the Red Cross Hospital by Mr F. Litchfield's band, and songs were given by some of the soldiers. At the close the soldiers passed a vote of thanks to Mr Hempshall, the cornet player of the band, for the pleasure he had given them, and wished him every success in the Army, which he joined on Nov. 6th.

17 November 1915

Full report of an "Entertainment for Soldiers" for wounded soldiers in Burgage Manor.

Report of the annual meeting of Southwell Church of England Men's Society, under the chairmanship of Dr J. D. F. Willoughby. The branch membership numbered 46 of which 11 were serving in the army. One member, Cpl. F. Wilcox, had been killed, and another, Major J. P. Becher, had been severely wounded.

'LOCAL HERO AT THE DARDANELLES   Pte. G. Twells, of the 9th Sherwood Foresters, who, when the war broke out, was employed at the local post office as rural postman for Oxton, is now at Bagthorpe Military Hospital [note: on what is now the City Hospital site] slowly recovering from wounds received in the hard fighting at the Gallipoli Peninsular. Seen by our local correspondent at the above hospital on Saturday, he has a stirring story to tell. Private Twells was called to the colours on August 5th, 1914, and went to Derby. As he was used to horses, Major Sadler picked him out as his servant, and in a few days they went to Plymouth en route to France, but the Major was kept back, and promoted to Colonel, in charge of the 9th Sherwood Foresters at Belton Park [note: near Grantham], where they stopped for some months. As Twells was used to teaching officers to ride, he was put in charge of this branch: he also holds a certificate as a first class farrier. While at Belton, he was offered the position of staff transport sergeant, but preferred to keep his position as officer's servant. Colonel Sadler soon afterwards volunteered for the front with the 9th Sherwoods, and went out to the Dardanelles. Of the terrible time they had in landing he will not easily forget. He had no sooner got on the land than his helmet was riddled with shrapnel, set on fire, and burned to cinders, but there was no time to wait for another. They went up the almost perpendicular sides of the cliff till they got to the top. On the fifth day of continuous fighting the Colonel asked for volunteers to go forward in the night and cut down two trees near the enemy's trenches, which were in the way and must be cleared at any cost. Private Twells volunteered for the job and crept out, saw in one hand and rifle in the other. Although under heavy fire for over an hour he succeeded in bringing down the trees, and got safely back to our lines, which were found untenable, and the troops had to go back to the boats. On the 6th of August the 9th Sherwoods made another landing on the peninsular, where the adjutant was wounded. Continuous fighting took place day and night until the 21st August, when a big attack was made on Hill 70. The Sherwoods made a dash across the ground, making straight for the Turks' trenches. Colonel Bosanquet was in the front leading his men, and suddenly the Turks began their cry, "Allah!"

"Allah!" sounded from one part of the ground on to another part, until the air was rent with the noise. Colonel Bosanquet called out to his men, "Look out! The devils are going to charge" and at the same moment about a dozen big fellows, shouting "Allah! Allah!" with all their might, rushed at the Colonel, but he shot three or four with his revolver, but was being overpowered when Pte. Twells ran to his assistance. He bowled five or six over with his bayonet: then in the melee other men of both sides rushed up, and Twells received a bullet through his groin and fell to the ground. Immediately shrapnel burst in the midst of the struggling mass of men, killing and wounding all the struggling soldiers. Twells remembers Colonel Bosanquet patting him on the shoulder and saying, thank you my man, you will be rewarded for this, before swooned away, and coming to himself sometime after he found dead and dying men, some on the top of him, some around, friends and foes mixed up together: in a few minutes he liberated himself from the heap and crept as best he could to his own lines. Beside the bullet wound he got a piece of iron from the shrapnel shell in his leg, which fractured the ankle, from which he is slowly recovering. While crawling along he passed Lord Henry Bentinck [note: MP for Nottingham South, 1910-1929] who lay on the ground severely wounded, but he told Private Twells to make his way to the lines. The Turks, says Twells, are big lusty fellows, fine shots, but clean fighters. The officers, always with flashes in their eyes to see the men don't fire on a hospital ship or Red Cross wagon. It is wonderful to see them at their prayers every morning at sunrise, they are seen at their devotions and very little firing goes on at this time. The country, says Twells, swarms with snipers, many of whom are women dressed in soldier's uniforms, often taken from the dead.' [Note: see entry under 8 December 1915.]

1 December 1915

Sgt. Arthur Sheppard D.C.M. killed when 'part of the parapet near Sgt. Sheppard, having been blown down by shellfire, the Germans trained a machine gun on the breach and Sgt. Sheppard was killed.' He had recently been awarded the D.C.M. for 'leading a bombing party on his own initiative under a heavy bomb and rifle fire against an attacking enemy. Having used all his grenades he went and got a fresh supply, and having lost five men, he brought up reinforcements.' Arthur Sheppard had been employed at Carey's.
Report that Major J. P. Becher is gravely ill.

8 December 1915

'WELL DONE CAREY'S   Very few firms in the country have sent more men pro rata to the Army in this critical time in the nation's history than Messrs Carey and Sons the well known lace-makers of the Minster town. In addition to those serving in the Army, the whole of the men who are left, and are of military age, have been enrolled in their respective groups under Lord Derby's scheme.'

[Note: The Derby or Group scheme was an attempt to increase voluntary recruitment without recourse to compulsory conscription. Men who attested under the scheme were assigned to the group based on year of birth. New recruits were issued with a card, given one day's pay at infantry rates (2s 9d), and sent home to resume their employment until their respective Groups were called up. They wore a grey armband with a red crown as a sign that they had volunteered. The scheme was devised by Edward Stanley, 17th Lord Derby, who was appointed Director-General of Recruiting in October 1915. The scheme did not succeed in recruiting sufficient men to replace those lost, and it was abandoned in December 1915. Compulsory conscription was introduced in the Military Service Act of January 1916.]

'SOUTHWELL SOLDIER AT SULVA BAY - STIRRING DEEDS OF THE 9TH SHERWOODS' [Note: this is a slightly different account given by the same soldier to another journalist of the story published on 24 November, with some additional details. 'Pte. George Twelves' here is the Pte. G. Twells in the earlier account.]

'Stirring details of a hand-to-hand encounter which Colonel Bosanquet, the gallant commander of the 9th Battalion Sherwood Foresters, had with a number of Turkish soldiers, were supplied to a Press representative by Private George Twelves, of the 9th Sherwood Foresters, and formerly a postman at Southwell, who is now a patient in the Bagthorpe Military Hospital. Twelves arrived at the institution recently, after serving with his regiment at the Dardanelles. A native of Lenton and a reservist, he was acting as a postman for the Southwell district when the war broke out, his duty being to cycle to and deliver letters in Oxton. He answered the call to the colours, and rejoined his old regiment, the 2nd Battalion Sherwood Foresters.

FACING DESPERATE ODDS

When the Battalion went to the Dardanelles Twelves was among those who were landed at Achi Baba [note: the height commanding the Gallipoli peninsular and the principal defensive position of the Turkish army in 1915] under heavy fire, the enemy overcoming the difficulty of observation at night by lighting fires on the hills which rendered the gallant attackers visible. Many men fell to rise no more, and others were grievously wounded, but the main body landed in spite of the desperate odds they had to face. For a week or two the battalion remained on that part of the peninsula, and about five days after reaching the trenches volunteers were asked for to undertake the hazardous task of cutting down two trees growing near the British firing line and used by the Turks as aids to accurate marksmanship. A comrade and he at once stepped out, but by the time he had crept to the first of the trees he found himself alone, and he still wondered how he managed to escape the enemy's crack shots. He did so, however, and with a collapsible saw began to cut into the trunk of the tree, which at length lay on the ground. Another twenty yards he had to go before he could accomplish the destruction of the other tree, and while he was at work on it Captain Randle, of whose bravery he spoke with admiration, went to him. The trees having been removed, officer and man returned to cover, neither being as much as scratched. Capt. Randle, it will be remembered, was one of the gallant officers to fall not long afterwards, his loss being keenly regretted by the men who worked under his direction.'

22 December 1915

Report of the contribution being made by Carey's employees to the war effort (see under 8 December 1915). On the outbreak of war Carey's employed 159 men. By 22 December 1915, 63 were serving in the Army; 16 had enrolled in their age-groups under Lord Derby's scheme; 24 had attempted to enlist but had been declared medically unfit; 40 were over military age; 6 were under military age; 8 had left the firm; two had died. Total 159.

5 January 1916

MENTIONED IN DESPATCHES – A report that Lieutenant Hacking and Corporal Templeman had been Mentioned in Despatches.

12 January 1916

A report of the recent Southwell Petty Sessions. W. Wright, presiding, paid tribute to the Southwell war dead: Maj. J. P. Becher D.S.O., Capt. Handford, Lt Handford, Sgt. Sheppard D.C.M., Cpl Sharman, Cpl. Wilcox, Ptes. Burn, Deeley, Eaton, A. Hopewell, J. H. Hopewell, Humberstone, Oliver, Payling, Raynor, Watson, and Wilkins. A vote of sympathy for the relatives was passed and the court rose 'in appreciation of the resolution.'

'SOUTHWELL MAN IN EGYPT   Corporal Frank Wilcox (formerly an employee of Mr J. H. Kirkby), and now of the 8th Devonshire Regiment, sends an interesting letter to our local correspondent, in which he says that they are encamped in the finest city in the world, Cairo. He thinks it contains the most wonderful and beautiful building that it is possible to build. "During the short stay we have had here, I have had a good run round; been to the Pyramids, and to Alexandria, which is a fine place. We camped near the Pyramids for a long time. Now we are "somewhere". We have a large hospital here with wounded Indian soldiers. Sorry shall not be able to help you at Christmas time, but we shall keep smiling all the same. We are glad to hear of the number of men joining up. If the Turks get here we shall give them a warm time. I have done one year now, and am pleased to think I am getting quite an old soldier. This writing paper and envelopes are sent to us by the children of Australia."'

19 January 1916

LT. A. HACKING   Lt. A. Hacking, who has been awarded the Military Cross, is a son of the Ven. J.G. Hacking, Archdeacon of Newark, who resides at Hill House, Southwell. Educated at Marlborough College, Lt. Hacking is a member of the firm of solicitors and Parliamentary agents,

Messrs Chamberlain and Hacking, of Parliament-street, London. At Marlborough he was a distinguished cricketer, and was a member of the Marlborough Blue Cricket XI, after leaving school. He obtained a commission in the 8th Sherwood Foresters in October, 1914, and at the front was appointed bombing officer to the Sherwood Foresters' Brigade. On one occasion he was called before the whole Brigade and complimented on his gallantry.

The Archdeacon of Newark has another son at the front, Lt. Egbert Melville Hacking, who was educated at Aldenham School and Cambridge University. He is a prominent Association footballer, and has played for his college. Although ordained he is a combatant officer, and prior to the war was a master at Aldenham School.

2 February 1916

'THE STRICKEN BRAVE' A report that Arthur Hazlewood of 2/8th Sherwood Foresters 'better known as "Pat" ', son of Mrs Hazlewood, laundress at Southwell Workhouse, had been killed. He had been born in Southwell and had attended the National School. On leaving school he went into the reading room at the lace factory before working for Mr Caudwell at the flour mill. He enlisted on 9 October 1914. 'Pte. Hazlewood was of a most amiable disposition, and a footballer of some considerable merit, playing for Southwell Town.'

8 March 1916

'DRINK FOR WOUNDED SOLDIERS   SOUTHWELL WOMAN FINED   Mrs Maria Clay, of Kirklington-road, Southwell, appeared at the local Petty Sessions on Friday, summoned under the Defence of the Realm Act for procuring and giving ale to two soldiers undergoing hospital treatment, viz: Walter Maltby, Royal West Kent Regiment; and Walter Tovey, Army Service Corps.

Asked whether she pleaded guilty or not guilty defendant said she gave them a quart. P.c. Pass said he saw the wounded soldiers go into defendant's house at 11.15 a.m. on February 18th. At 11.40 defendant's daughter went out with a basket and returned with two bottles. Witness went into the house and saw the two wounded soldiers sitting with two pint bottles of beer on the table. The men told the officer they were just going to enjoy themselves. When told she would be reported, defendant said the men were going away on the morrow, and invited the policeman to sit down and have a glass with them.

This defendant denied. She said she was very sorry if she had done anything wrong.

Miss Small (Matron) said considering the number of men who had gone through the hospital, they had not much trouble with the men on account of drinking.

In fining defendant 20s., the chairman (Mr W. Wright) who was accompanied by Mr L. Brodhurst and Mr F. Hill, said it was a serious offence, and defendant was liable of a fine of £100 or six months' hard labour. Any future case would be severely dealt with.'

[Note: Under the Defence of the Realm (Consolidation) Act, 1914, the 'Competent Military Authority', in this case Major J. A. Reeks commanding 45 Regimental District and based in Derby, could issue an order prohibiting the sale of intoxicating liquor within his area to any one resident in the scheduled area after 9 p.m., and all members of the armed forces except within specified hours – in this case 12 noon and 1 p.m. and 6 p.m. and 9 p.m. A 'Closing Order' to this effect was issued by Major Reeks and published in the *Newark Advertiser* on 6 January 1915.]

15 March 1916

'LETTER FROM EGYPT   A Southwell non-commissioned officer, writing from Pharaoh's country says: – "We are somewhere in the land of Egypt. Our camp is pitched on a pretty spot, right away from all human habitation, but as the tribes around us are somewhat hostile we don't go out of camp, except when on duty. But we are enjoying ourselves and having a good time. I was sorry to hear the sad news you told me in your letter, which reached me on Feb. 5th that Major Becher had passed away. He will be a great loss to Southwell and district. I never shall forget the happy times we spent in camp with Southwell H Company. Major Becher used to sit among his Company at night like a private soldier, and spin a few yarns in his turn. Those were happy times, now, alas! Never to return. I think I am right in saying that his place will never be filled in H Company again. On our arrival at this place we had a miserable time – no water, and, worst of all, no tobacco, in fact, we are, as the old song goes, "ten miles from nowhere", but we are making the best of it. It's all for the good of the dear old country. All we do at nights is sit in our tents and spin a few yarns, and then have a sing-song. But we shall be on the move shortly, perhaps to a more lively spot.'

22 March 1916

'FOOD FOR PRISONERS OF WAR   A Southwell lady who sends a parcel of bread every week to prisoners of war in Germany, has received a letter from one of them in which he says that they have to rely to a great extent upon what is sent out to them by good friends in England, and although the bread is three weeks on the way yet it arrives there in good condition, and it is a great treat to them to eat a good bit of English bread.'

A report of a meeting of the Southwell tribunal which heard appeals against conscription. The area covered by the tribunal included Southwell and villages in a wide area around the town. Early appeals were frequently from farmers applying for exemption for their sons. In one case one son was a cowman and another a horseman and their father appealed on the ground that he could not maintain his farm without the help of both. This report noted that 'It seemed to be the policy of the Tribunal that under such circumstances one of the sons ought to be serving.' The chairman of the tribunal, J. W. A Bonner JP referred to 'the splendid record of the Society of the Sacred Mission [at Kelham] and said he considered Father Jenks had behaved very well'. This referred to the fact that clergy were exempt from conscription, as were Roman Catholic seminarians. Anglican theological students were not exempt unless they were within a year of ordination. It seems that Fr. David Jenks, director of SSM, did not try to protect members of his order from conscription.

[Note: Reports of meetings of the Southwell Tribunal now appeared regularly in the *Newark Advertiser.* The Military Service Act of 27 January 1916 introduced conscription for the first time in the war, and, together with the Defence of the Realm Act of 8 August 1914, was the most important legislation enabling the UK to marshal its resources on a war footing. Under this first Military Service Act every British man who, on 15 August 1915, was between the ages of 19 and 41, and, on 2 November 1915, was unmarried or a widower without dependent children, was deemed to have enlisted for general service with the armed forces or in the reserve, and therefore could be mobilised at any time. The Act came into force on 2 March 1916, and after that date all men that fell within its provisions became subject to the Army Act 1881. Appeals could be made against conscription on various grounds and a system of local, central and appeal tribunals was established to hear appeals. These tribunals contained between 5 and 25 members, usually under the presidency of a magistrate, or could work through a committee appointed by the full tribunal. Decisions of the Southwell tribunal could be appealed, and were heard by an appeals tribunal meeting in Nottingham.]

29 March 1916

'WE ARE SEVEN' A report of a meeting of the Southwell Tribunal notes that three brothers, George Twidale (37), H. Twidale (34) and Matthew H. Twidale (30) had applied for exemption from conscription. 'The two latter brothers are in partnership in a farm at Westhorpe, which belongs to their mother, their father being dead. George Twidale has a business in the cattle and milk trade on his own account; – It transpired that of the [seven] brothers none is serving. Two brothers are married. They are engaged as follows:– A chemist in Newark, a chemist in Mansfield, a chemist's apprentice at Newark; the three applicants; and another aged 18, not subject to the Military Service Act. George Twidale and H. Twidale were put to May 1st, and the application of Matthew Twidale was refused.'

6 April 1916

Thomas Smith of Waterloo Yard, was fined 5 shillings for allowing 'an external light attached to Messrs Caudwell's Mill' to be illuminated contrary to the Lighting Regulations. These regulations, issued under the Defence of the Realm Act of 8 August 1914 (known popularly as 'DORA'), were intended to protect against attack by Zeppelins. The regulations also applied to bonfires burning at night.

12 April 1916

A report of a concert for wounded soldiers on 5 April. Concerts or 'entertainments' for these men were staged several times each month. This was another of the popular concerts which do so much to relieve the monotony of the life of the wounded soldier at 'the Red Cross Hospital' at Burgage Manor. Mr Alfred Merryweather (the hospital commandant) was 'the principal vocalist' and 'Mr Litchfield's band . . . gave several compositions by high-class authors, and 'the wounded themselves contributed songs, recitations and trombone solos'.

A lantern lecture on the 5th and 6th June by Mr H. Summers was based on actual photographs 'showing the conditions of modern warfare and the result of the invasion of Belgium and France'. Patriotic music was played throughout, including the national anthems of the allies played 'as the different flags were thrown upon the screen'.

A letter to the editor of the *Newark Advertiser* headed 'SOUTHWELL EGG COLLECTION':

'Dear Sir, – This week we complete a full year of work for the National Egg Collection, and we think that all who have in any way helped, will be glad to have our first report. Although everyone has worked so cheerfully and well, we shall be only too thankful if we do not have to publish a second. Where so many people have helped both in giving eggs and money, it is impossible to thank them individually; but we should just like them to see some of the letters that children in the neighbourhood have received from wounded soldiers, and they would feel well repaid for their sacrifice. It is impossible to speak too highly of the way that some of our collectors have worked. They have tramped many weary miles in dusty heat and blinding snowstorms, carrying heavy baskets and collecting odd eggs from scattered farms, but they have never flagged in their zeal, and have always turned up smiling with their spoil every week. As for the children – well, they have worked like little Britons, and we do not like to think what we would have done without Mr Merrryweather's dray, which calls every week and delivers our cases both to the hospital and the station. The total number of eggs which this depot has received is 28,958. Of these, 11,322 have been sent to Burgage Manor, so that we may feel we have saved our local hospital at least £50 during the year. We have received in cash £9. 11s. 8½d, nearly the whole of which has been collected in odd pence. As all the work is voluntary, and the London cases go carriage forward, and return carriage paid, and nothing has been deducted for postage, we have had no expenses; so that all money handed in has gone direct to the London Central Office. We were hoping to give the total amount collected by all the individual sub-depots, but only the following have handed in reports on their year's work: Kirklington, 618 and 6d cash; Rolleston, 1,437; Upton, 764; Halam Scouts, 1,711 and 16s. 5½d. cash; Averham, 913; Wesleyan Day School, 635; Eakring Guides and Scouts, 818 (for four months); Morton, 2,922; National School, 1,725 and £1 15s. 10d. We have only a limited number of collectors' badges sent down, so decided that anyone who collected 60 eggs or 5s in cash should be entitled to wear one. This has promoted healthy competition and already about 30 children in the district have them. We still have a few waiting to be won! Nearly a million eggs a week are now required by the War Office for our men. Need we say more? If anyone in the district within a radius of 5 miles, can promise one or two eggs a week, we shall be glad to put them in touch with the nearest collector, who will call every week. Once more thanking you for your great help in publishing our weekly reports, I remain, yours faithfully,

Ida K. Fairweather
Depot Controller
Clinton Cottage, Southwell
April 6th, 1916.

19 April 1916

A report of gifts received for Southwell Auxiliary Military Hospital from Mrs Webb and Miss Wright, Fiskerton, apples, oranges, cigarettes, tobacco, cakes, tinned fruits and flowers; Mrs Litherland, Westhorpe, eggs, flowers, apples and cigarettes; Mrs Ibbotson, Hockerton, apples.

'SOUTHWELLIAN FINED' Mr F. A. Robinson, of Hardwick House, Queen street, was fined 5s at Southwell petty sessions for allowing a bonfire to stay alight contrary to the Lighting Regulations.

26 April 1916

It was reported to a meeting of Southwell Rural District Council that only two conscientious objectors had appeared before the Southwell tribunal. The chairman remarked that 'in some places there was a large number, but people seem to be made of better stuff in this district from some of the others (Hear, hear).' It was also reported that the last meeting of the Southwell tribunal heard 75 cases, 'and not one conscientious objector among them.'

[Note: To declare oneself a conscientious objector was a courageous act. Broadly, conscientious objectors fell into two groups, those who refused combat roles on religious or moral grounds, but were prepared to serve at the front in non-combat roles such as stretcher bearers, ambulance drivers, medical orderlies, cooks and labourers, and 'absolute conscientious objectors' who refused any involvement at all in national or imperial conflicts. Under the early Military Service Acts of 1916 conscientious objection was a ground of appeal against conscription. Absolute conscientious objectors were usually not recognised by any of the belligerent nations, and were generally imprisoned if they persistently refused a non-combat role. Conscientious objectors were frequently insulted and ostracised in their local communities, particularly in this country.

The despising, and the defence, of conscientious objectors continued well after the Armistice. This was illustrated in a bitter correspondence in the *Advertiser* in August and September 1919 between 'Ex-serviceman', who claimed that Newark Labour Party, local trade unions, and the Newark branch of the Federation of Discharged and Demobilised Sailors and Soldiers encouraged conscientious objection, and E. A Pettit, secretary of the Newark branch of the Federation, together with Walter Everton and Walter H. Neale. So abusive did the letters from 'Ex-Serviceman' become that the editor had to stop the correspondence. He had, he said, been tolerant of 'Ex-Serviceman' but 'there are limits'.]

3 May 1916

A hundred people were present at 'a very successful dance' at Trebeck Hall on 26 April to raise funds for 'comforts for soldiers'. The regimental march of the Notts and Derbys regiment, 'The New May Moon', was played twice, once in each half.

10 May 1916

'CASUALTIES Many Southwell men have been in Ireland during the disturbances, and although several had narrow escapes, only two were wounded, viz., Harold Ridge who was wounded in both legs, and Cecil Wyer, who was shot in the right arm. The casualty lists this week from the Expeditionary Force also contain the names of Private P. W. Toder, wounded, and Private P. Kendal, wounded.' [Note: This is a reference to the famous Easter Rising, beginning on Easter Monday, 24 April 1916 and lasting until 30 April. This was organised by the military council of the Irish Republican Brotherhood. Its immediate cause was the Military Service Act of January 1916 which threatened conscription of Irishmen into the British army, but its principal aim was to end British rule in Ireland. It was the first major disturbance in Ireland since the United Irish Rising of 1798. Among the troops sent to put down the insurrection were 2/8th Sherwood Foresters. A long report in the *Newark Advertiser* for this date details the part taken by 2/8th battalion during fighting which claimed the lives of 64 rebels and 134 troops and policemen.]

A report of another concert for the wounded at the Burgage Manor hospital. Mr Litchfield's band performed, with songs from Miss Gwen Pratt of Bleasby and from Cpl. Hayden and Ptes. Simpkins, Edwards and Dyer. The chairman was 'the popular commandant, Mr A. Merryweather'.

17 May 1916

A report, with the full programme, of an 'entertainment' for the soldiers in Burgage Manor hospital at the Wesleyan day school in Southwell.

24 May 1916

The Duke and Duchess of Portland inspect the Burgage Manor hospital. The Wounded soldiers were paraded and addressed by the duchess who wished them well.

31 May 1916

A report of the celebration of Empire Day on 24 May by the children of Southwell National Schools. This day was first celebrated on 24 May, Queen Victoria's birthday, in 1902, the year after her death. At the height of the war it was kept with patriotic fervour. This year, in the morning the children were taught about the significance of the Empire 'its extent, influence and importance; Queen Victoria, and the King, etc.', they were shown the Union Jack and instructed as to its 'construction, uses, and meaning'. In the afternoon the boys marched to 'the Recreation Ground Hollow . . . there forming a living G. and M., and singing the National Anthem. The girls had a very pretty and effective Empire tableau in the school playground, some of the characters represented being Britannia, Ireland, Scotland, Wales, India, and the Colonies. The whole proceedings were interspersed with the singing of national and patriotic songs and recitations, and with country dances, the daisy, the Empire flower, being much in evidence in buttonholes or as coronets and garlands.' A number of parents and friends supported the proceedings, and the children sent £1. 3s. 3d. to the Overseas Club for Soldiers' and Sailors' Comforts.

'PTE. F. C. SCHUMACH   Quite a gloom was cast over the minster town on Friday last when it became known that Pte. F. C. Schumach was lying in a Rouen hospital in a very critical condition, suffering from spinal meningitis. Well known and very highly respected in his native city. He was ever ready with his trained and pleasing voice to help forward any good work, and was frequently heard on the local concert platform. He joined the Mechanical Transport Corps only a few weeks since, and has been training at Rouen, France. His only brother, Sgt. Geo. Schumach, has been in the Army sometime and made rapid promotion. Much sympathy is extended to his wife and mother, and it is hoped a speedy recovery will take place. Pte. Schumach was lay clerk at the Minster, and carried on the business of taxidermist before joining the army.'

7 June 1916

'RED CROSS HOSPITAL   Miss E. M. Small, the commandant, has received a most excellent report from the military authorities in regard to the working of the hospital.'

A last weekly meeting of the Southwell Tribunal heard as one of its cases an application by Carey's for exemption from conscription for 17 of its employees. Representing the company, Mr T. D. Partington said that when war broke out 46 of its employees 'were embodied with the local territorials'. From a normal staff of 147, the company was now employing only 67. The cases of all 17 were put back to 1 October, with power to appeal again. J. H. Kirkby appealed on behalf of nine employees. Eight were put back to 1 October and one to 1 July.

14 June 1916

Pte. Fred Schumach reported to be recovering in a Rouen hospital.

A concert in support of Southwell auxiliary hospital at Bishop's Manor on 23 May raised £54 12s 6d. [Note: In purchasing power in 2011, according to a conservative calculation based on the retail price index, this was worth £2,880.] The hospital also recently received seeds and a sack of potatoes from Mr Hickling; the Southwell Children's Guild sent £1 8s.; Mrs Conybeare, wife of the rector of Southwell, contributed spinach and lettuce; Miss Freer, rhubarb and lettuce; Mrs Ibbotson of Hockerton, a regular supporter, sent £2 14s. 2d. the proceeds of an 'entertainment and dance' that she had organised; and Mrs Moore and the National Egg Collection supplied eggs.

'PRIVATE GEORGE PEACOCK KILLED   Southwell mourns the loss of yet another of her gallant sons, the news being just received that Private George Peacock, of the Trench Mortar Battery, York and Lancaster Regiment was killed in action on Good Friday at the age of 27 years. The brave hero was the son of Mr James Peacock, Westhorpe, Southwell, and after leaving school worked for several years at Mr J. H. Kirkby's Stores, afterwards going to Mr E. Caudwell's flour mills, and finally to Messrs Robinson and Son's roller flour mills at Rotherham, from which he enlisted in the Yorks and Lancasters. After getting into khaki he was transferred to Durham. And it was a curious coincidence that the first time he turned out on parade it was to find that the officer in charge of his Company was Lt. Neville Kirkby, of Southwell, son of one of the deceased's former employers. One of Private Peacock's mates, who saw him killed, writes an account of how it happened. He says: "Our Battery went up to the trenches to reinforce another battery. George and four of his pals were in one bay, and me and my pals were in another, next to him, when a big shell came over from the enemy. It just missed my head and dropped right into the next bay, where George and his pals were working their mortar. The trench and all the lot went up in the air, and when we found his body we hardly knew it was him: he had been killed instantly. And he never knew what hit him, so you have the consolation that he died a painless death. And now he is buried with his pals in a nice little spot, far from the monsters of the Huns. We have got a little cross made of wood, with his and his mate's names painted on it, and while I am spared you may be sure that it will be well looked after and cared for. You have the consolation of knowing that he died for King and country, and he met a hero's death. His life is not only mourned for at home, but by scores of pals out here in the trenches." Two of the deceased's brothers are also serving in the Army – Charles in the London Yeomanry, and Crosby in the South Notts Hussars: the latter is now in Salonika.' [Note: George Peacock died on 21 April 1916. He is buried in the Essex Farm cemetery on the Ypres Salient where he was killed. Second Lieutenant John Nevil Kirkby, Yorks and Lancasters, aged 19, was killed in action on 25 September 1916. He is commemorated on the Thiepval Memorial.]

A memorial service in the Minster was held on 7 June for Arthur Hazlewood, Edwin Gilbert, George Peacock, Arthur Rumley; all who had died in the Battle of Jutland; and for Lord Kitchener.

21 June 1916

'BIPLANE VISITS KIRKLINGTON HALL   A monster biplane of the latest Army type sailed over the Minster town on Sunday and planed slowly to earth in a large field near Kirklington Hall, where the officer in charge was paying a visit. He was accompanied by a Sergeant of the Royal Flying Corps. Hundreds of people visited the machine during the day, and it started away again at 5.30 in the evening, its destination being a large flying depot in the Midlands.'

The recent meeting of the Southwell Tribunal heard the case of George Baines, a tailor of Southwell and a conscientious objector. 'It appeared that the man had applied to a Lincoln firm for employment in the aeroplane construction department, but they refused to set him on until he produced a certificate of exemption. The Clerk had been in communication with the military authorities, and it was decided that he write to the firm, saying that the military authorities in Derby were willing to allow the man to undertake the work, as it was a work of national importance.' [Note: In 1911, George Baines was 18. He was a tailor and was living with his mother, Sarah Jane Pyzer, his brother John Thomas Baines (21) and three step-sisters, Sarah Ann (7), Lydia (6), and Theodosia (4) at or near 4, Westgate, which in 1901 had been occupied by her husband William G. Pyzer[2]. In that year he was a widower aged 46 and a tailor living at this address which may have been the shop mentioned in the entry for 2 August 1916. George Baines was 23 when he declared himself a conscientious objector. See entry for 26 April.]

12 July 1916

'MEN WHO HAVE SUFFERED   The firm of J. H. Kirkby has sent a large proportion of its employees to fight for King and country, and this week has been recorded the fact that more of the employees have been killed or wounded. Sgt. Walter Townsend, who died in France from shell shock, was before the war employed in the bake house. After the war broke out he joined up with the Hull Commercials, and after severe fighting in France, showing conspicuous bravery on several occasions, was buried in a hole made by a big shell from the enemy, and died from the shock. Private Clifford Butler, the only child of Mr W. Butler, clerk to the Parish Council, who before the war was in Mr Kirkby's office, writes to his parents to say that in the great advance he had been wounded. A bullet went in his left ear, passing through his head downwards, and came out on the right side of the neck. Although only 19 years of age, he joined the Army in December 1914, and with the 10th Sherwoods has seen much fighting in France. He pluckily says in his letter that he is in hospital at Rouen, but hopes to be up again shortly. Private Thomas Musgrave, who before the war was a grocer in the retail department, has been ill at home as a result of exposure in the trenches, and has succumbed.'
[Note: The 10th battalion of the East Yorkshire Regiment was known as the 'Hull Commercials'. The 'great advance' may be a reference to the Battle of the Somme which began on 1 July 1916.]

19 July 1916

Pte. F. Schumach out of hospital in Rouen and now in England.

---

[2] In 1912, William Guest Pyzer was a tailor with a business in Westgate.

26 July 1916

Private Albert (Bab) Paling died of wounds in France. 'He had been in the trenches a few days when his brother was killed by his side, and now his turn has come to take the great sacrifice.'

2 August 1916

A War Savings Campaign, part of a national campaign, launched by the parish council at a meeting addressed by Capt. J. R. Starkey MP and W. J. Conybeare, the rector of Southwell. 'After the meeting opportunity was given for the public to purchase war vouchers and pay in contributions of 6d and upwards. Many people responded. A shop in Westgate, formerly occupied by Mr Pyzer, has been taken for the purposes of receiving contributions every Friday night.'

30 August 1916

The Minster Institute, closed during the summer, reopened for the benefit of wounded soldiers 'as most members are now fighting in the Army, and the income is not sufficient to pay expenses'. Capt J. R. Starkey M.P. had offered to pay the expenses of all wounded soldiers using the Institute.

It was reported that in July 1916 the Southwell Tribunal had dealt with 194 appeals against conscription. [Note: The geographical area covered by the Tribunal was wide, from Lowdham to Sutton on Trent and an equal distance north and south.]

13 September 1916

'NURSING ASSOCIATION   Since the war began the wives and families of soldiers have been nursed on special terms. The report for the year ending August 31st shows that the number of cases nursed is 200; of these 180 are new cases, 171 of these are Southwell patients, 9 Halam, 6 Hockerton, 5 Edingley, 4 Upton, 3 Kirklington and 2 Halloughton. Fifty-nine maternity cases have been attended; the number of visits paid is 6,599.'

20 September 1916

A flower day in support of the Nursing Association raised £21 13s. 2d., with 'the young ladies of the town busy all day . . .'.

27 September 1916

A report that Pte. Oscar Longmore had been wounded. He was the eldest son of Mr E. Longmore (a lay clerk at the Minster) and Mrs Longmore and served with 2/8th Sherwood Foresters. He was shot in the leg, 'but not seriously', and was recovering in hospital.

4 October 1916

A report that Cpl. Frank Robinson had been wounded. He was the son of Mr and Mrs F. Robinson of Queen Street and served with the Sherwood Foresters. He had been wounded in an action in

France, 'a large piece of shrapnel having penetrated the right arm, while in the trenches preparing for the charge at Thiepval. His Sergeant-Major, writing to the parents, said Robinson was a good reliable soldier, always at the post of duty. He was very sorry to lose him, but hoped for a speedy recovery'.

11 October 1916

This edition carried photographs of 2nd Lt. (John) Nevil Kirkby and Pte. Vincent Brown, both of Southwell and recently killed in action. Vincent Brown died on 16 September 1916 and Nevil Kirkby on 25 September. [See 14 June 1916 above for Nevil Kirkby. Vincent Brown, who served with the Sherwood Foresters, is buried in Ecoivres military cemetery, Mont-St Eloi, Pas de Calais.]

1 November 1916

A report that Pte. Con Randall, formerly a baker with J. H. Kirkby and serving with the Army Service Corps, 'lies in a very weak condition at a convalescent home in Egypt from a severe attack of fever which he caught when engaged in his army duties somewhere in the Mediterranean. He was a prominent member of the local Baptist Church'.

8 November 1916

Another concert by Mr Litchfield's band for the soldiers in Burgage Manor. Good wishes were extended to Mr Hempshall, who played the cornet in the band, who joined the army on 6 November.

15 November 1916

'MILITARY MEDAL   In the list of men who have gained the Military Medal, issued this week by the War Office, appears the name of Corporal J. T. Templeman, of the Notts and Derbys. This gallant soldier is a native of Southwell, a prominent footballer, and formerly an employee of Messrs Carey and Sons. He was with his regiment in camp when the war broke out, and has been at the front since the dark days at the commencement of the great conflict. He has been in the thick of the fighting on many occasions, and was previously mentioned in dispatches for doing some fine work on the battlefield. His brother Jim has also been in the same regiment since the local men first went out.'

'SUNDAY POSTAL DELIVERY   An important meeting of the Traders' Association was held at the Admiral Rodney Hotel on the 16th inst. There were present: Mr W. Vickers (chairman), Messrs J. H. Kirkby, J. J. Bates, N. A. Metcalfe, G. E. Mills, W. Leek, S. J. Scott, T. D. Partington, S. Booth, A. Salt, F. Tinley, G. L. Knowles, T. Maidens, F. Ewers (hon. Sec.), &. – A letter was read from the Rector of Southwell (The Venerable W. J. Conybeare), enclosing a resolution from a meeting over which he had presided just recently, setting forth the desirability of doing away with the delivery of letters on Sunday in Southwell, providing it does not effect the postmen's wages; and asking that the matter should be brought before the meeting. A lengthy discussion took place on the subject and ultimately the following resolution was passed:– That this meeting at the present time entirely disapproves of any alteration whatever in the Sunday postal facilities, not only on account of business, but also from the fact that so many people have sons and daughters engaged in warfare and from whom they are at all times anxious to obtain news and information.'

[Note: Although the strict sabbatarianism of the Lord's Day Observance Society was generally avoided by the mainstream churches, Sunday observance had been strongly advocated by them for very many years. This had been resisted by business interests, not only on account of trade, but the wartime separation of families bolstered the opposition of tradesmen to the cancellation of Sunday postal deliveries.]

22 November 1916

The following men from Southwell had recently enlisted: G. Donson, C. F. Law, A. Ball, A. L. Smith, R. C. Maidens, G. B. Hempshall, A. H. Salt, E. R. Doughty, and R Cox.

29 November 1916

A flower day in Southwell for the fund which sent parcels of comforts to soldiers raised £58. [Note: £58 in 1916 was worth over £3,000 in 2011, as measured by the retail price index.]

6 December 1916

A report, with a full programme, of a 'social and dance' for 'Soldiers' Presents' organised by the Girls' Friendly Society.

SOCIAL AND DANCE FOR SOLDIERS' PRESENTS The Trebeck Hall was filled with young people on Thursday night, when the members of the Girls' Friendly Society gave a social evening and dance to help the fund now being raised to send a present to every soldier and sailor gone from Southwell.

20 December 1916

A most enjoyable concert was given to the wounded soldiers at Burgage Manor Hospital on Saturday night.

EGG COLLECTION   Total for the week ending 13th December was 201, with 123 bought with cash in hand…

3 January 1917

THANKS   Pte. F.M. Bates, 2nd -6th   Northumberland Fusiliers, writes: - 'May I, through the *Advertiser* thank the Southwell Traders' Association and those who kindly contributed towards the soldiers' parcels? The men appreciated the contents very much, and on behalf of those stationed at Cleveland, Somerset, I am sending this word of thanks.'

17 January 1917

'THANKS FOR PARCELS   Miss Cullen, the mistress of the infant department of the Wesleyan Day School, who organised a concert to provide funds to send the old scholars in the Navy and Army a box of good things for Christmas, has received a number of letters from men in all parts of the Continent and the home country, thanking her for the interest she was taking in them, and making touching reference to their days of childhood in the old school, thoughts of which often came to them in the darkness of the night, when shells from the enemy were falling fast and furious, comrades killed by their side, and not knowing when their turn would come, but thankful that they were enabled to do their bit for King and country.'

AWARD AND PRESENTATION   Cpl. T. Templeman, who was awarded the Military Medal some time ago, was formerly an employee of Messrs Carey and Sons, lace manufacturers. As a recognition of his bravery, his colleagues opened a fund and sent him a wristlet watch. Mr W. Taylor has now received a letter, in which Cpl. Templeman says: "I received the beautiful wrist watch a few days ago, and beg to offer my most sincere thanks, through you, to my fellow workers for their kindness in presenting to me such a handsome gift, which I feel to be altogether undeserved. While there are such warm hearts at home, one can't fail to do one's duty out here, and, in conclusion, I must urge you all to cheer up and not listen to peace talk, as I feel sure we can make a much better finish a little later on in the year."

'DEATH OF PTE. G. DONSON   The many friends of Private George Donson will be sorry to hear that he has died from pneumonia at the Hamilton-road Military Hospital, Colchester, and was buried on Friday last at Colchester. Pte. Donson was well known in the Minster town, where for several years he was a noted football player. He was formerly employed by the Prudential Assurance Company, and latterly worked at Carey and Sons' lace factory. He joined the Army on November 18th last year, and although he had not been well for several years, it was hoped that the open-air life of the Army would do him good, but a short time ago he got influenza, which developed into pneumonia, which proved fatal. Much sympathy is felt for his wife and one child, as well as for his aged mother, who are left to mourn their loss.'

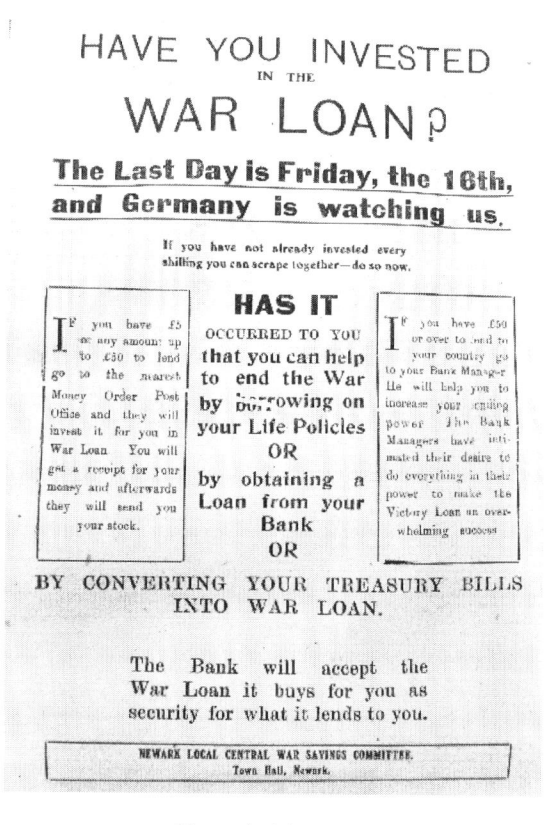

Newark Advertiser

HERO OF MANY BATTLES   The Minster town has sent many gallant lads into the army to fight for King and Country, but few of them have seen so much service as Corporal Arthur Smith, who has just been home for a flying visit from the trenches of France. Joining the 1st Battalion of the Sherwood Foresters many years ago, he was sent out to India with his regiment, and shortly afterwards the South African War broke out. They were embarked at a few hours' notice, and after a record voyage from India to the Cape they were rushed up the country, and were soon in the thick of the fight; and although our hero went through the Boer War from start to finish, and was in many tight corners, he came through without a wound. He was under General Smith-Doreen [Dorrien], and speaks in glowing terms of his abilities as a commander in the field. At the close of this war the Chinese Rebellion started, and leaving Africa for China, the 1st Sherwoods were soon in at the trouble. After serving his time in the army Smith came home to the reserve, and at the outbreak of the present war was free; but knowing that the country needed men he volunteered his services, was accepted, and again joined his old regiment. After a short period of training he went out to the Dardanelles, and thinks the finest feat in the world's history of wars was the marvellous evacuation of that large army of men who came away from Gallipoli unknown to the enemy; although for a long time the two armies had been fighting at close range. Our local man next went to Egypt where they had a 'brush' or two with the enemy in the desert; and shortly afterwards they were transferred to France where he has had many narrow escapes. His good luck never left him, and he has returned to the Front to put the finishing touches to the Great War.

31 January 1917

A recent meeting of the Southwell Board of Guardians was told by the Master of the Workhouse that 'a few tramps of military age who came to Southwell had been dealt with by the recruiting officer'.

7 February 1917

Typical of the many appeals against conscription heard by the Southwell Tribunal at its weekly meetings was that of G. Ullyatt, 37, of Southwell. He was married with three children and was employed by his father as 'a dairyman, milk deliverer, etc.'. His appeal was refused subject to a substitute being provided.

MINISTER'S DOUBLE BEREAVEMENT   Much sympathy is felt with the Rev. F.H.H. Labbett, Wesleyan Minister at Southwell, in the double loss he has sustained. On Thursday Mr Labbett received official confirmation that his eldest son, Lt. J.W. Hooper Labbett, had been killed on the Tigris, in Mesopotamia, while in the evening of that day Mrs Labbett had a seizure following an attack on Monday previous, and passed away without being informed of the death of her son. The funeral of Mrs Labbett took place on Monday.

14 February 1917

RED CROSS HOSPITAL CONCERT   The Southwell Orchestral Band paid a visit to the wounded soldiers' hospital on Wednesday night, and gave a musical programme which was much appreciated by the men. Mr T. D. Partington was in the chair, and Miss Edna Booth the principal soloist, her songs being received with loud applause.   Pte. T. Hempshall, the solo cornet player with the band, was home on furlough, and he received many congratulations on his return. Mr R. Rawson was at the piano.

CPL. TYNE, D.C.M., of the Sherwood Foresters, has sent home to Southwell a photographic group of his section in full war kit, including steel helmets. Those shown in the photograph are:– Front row: Privates J. Johnson, S. Coppin, J. Smedley, J. Brewitt, G. Morrell, C. W. Golland, H. Lewis, E. Buck. Second row: J. Hoe, A. Pinford, L/Cpl H. Barthorpe, Corpl. H. Scrimshaw, Lt. J. B. White, Cpl. H. Tyne, D.C.M., Lance-Cpl. G. Chester, Ptes. A. A. Huntbock, C. Ogden, Third row: Privates J. Schofield, A. Flowers, G. Storry, F. W. Watson, J. H. Boulton, J. A. Crag, Wilson, E. Dickinson.

'IN AID OF BLINDED SOLDIERS   The Holy Trinity Schoolroom was well filled on Thursday night last, when a concert was given on behalf of St. Dunstan's Homes for Blinded Soldiers. The programme submitted was of a miscellaneous character, and all the items were of exceptional merit. The singing of Miss Richards, Nottingham, and Cpl. Walter Lomax, R.E., Newark, and the violin solos of Mr. R. W. Liddle received rounds of applause. The programme was as follows: – "Christians Carol Sweetly", the Choir; song, Cpl. W. Lomax; song, "Rose Softly Blooming", Miss Richards; violin solo, "Romayne" (Beethoven, Op. 40), Mr R. W. Liddle; carol, "The First Nowell", the Choir; song, "My Dearest Heart", Miss Richards; violin solo, "Perpetuam Mobile" (F. Reis, Op. 34), Mr Liddle; song, Cpl. Lomax; carol, "The Manger Throne", the Choir.'

21 February 1917

'RED CROSS HOSPITAL EFFORT' Report of a concert by Southwell Amateur Dramatic Society, with the full programme.

28 February 1917

'THE PATRIOTIC SALE   The inhabitants of the Minster town are most enthusiastic in their endeavour to make the Newark and District Patriotic Sale a success, and the money given amounts to £90 from Southwell and the immediate neighbourhood, in addition to nearly 100 articles of various kinds for the sale. [Note: £90 in 1917 was worth £3,930 in 2010, measured against the retail price index.]

MUSIC FOR THE WOUNDED   Mr. Hugh Summers gave an interesting lecture on Tuesday last week to the wounded soldiers at Burgage Manor Hospital. On Wednesday night Mr. Litchfield's orchestral band gave several pleasing selections, and on Thursday Mr. N. A. Metcalfe gave a concert, when songs, recitations, and violin solos were given by Miss Wales, Miss Millington, Miss Dowse, Miss Jones, Mr. R. Ross, and Mr. E. Allcroft.'

7 March 1917

A report of the annual meeting of the Southwell branch of the National Deposit Friendly Society. Its annual report disclosed that 58 members of the branch were serving in the armed services, and that two had lost their lives, George Peacock and Edwin Gilbert.

14 March 1917

'PTE. A. JEBB WOUNDED   Mr. and Mrs. A. Jebb, of the Pollard-lane farm, Southwell, have been officially notified that their son, Arthur, was wounded in action last week. Pte. A. Jebb, of the Notts. and Derbys, was an employee of Mr. J. H. Kirkby, where he worked for several years. He joined up last year on attaining the age of 18.'

The weekly report of the local response to the national egg collection showed that for the week ending 8 March 1917, 437 eggs had been collected, and 78 bought 'with cash in hand'. Seventy-eight eggs had been sent to the Burgage Manor hospital.

'ARCHIE HALL WINS THE MILITARY MEDAL   Southwell men who have gone to the front to uphold the honour of the British flag now number about 500, and the latest to gain distinction is Pte. Archie [Arthur] Hall, of Westhorpe, who, previous to the war, was an employee of Mr. J. H. Kirkby. He was a well-known football player and sprinter, winning several times at the local flower show sports. Details are not yet to hand as to how he won the distinction, but in a letter to his father and mother, who reside in Westhorpe, he says: "You will be surprised to hear that I have won the Military Medal; so you see Southwell is keeping up its reputation in turning out useful boys. I will tell you all about it if I have the luck to get through this lot. I won my medal on my birthday, so shall easily remember the day." Pte. Hall joined up in 1915, and was attached to the Lewis Gun Section of the 1st Staffordshire Regiment, going out to France a few weeks back. During this time he has seen much fighting, and been in some tight corners, in which his Lewis gun has done useful work.'

A report of the recent meeting of the Southwell Board of Guardians noted that the Board considered reducing the rations of the inmates of the Workhouse. Members thought that 'it was inadvisable to make alterations, seeing that these were well below the requirements of the Food Controller'. However they thought that 8lbs of bread each week for each inmate was too much, and 'considered that this should be cut down to 4lbs, and substituted with oatmeal, cornflour and other things'. It was felt that the inmates would approve of this change because it would not reduce 'the amount of nourishment that they had received hitherto'. It was also suggested that the officers' rations should be reduced, 'but that each officer should receive 4s. per week in lieu of the reduced rations'. The report noted that 'after further discussion the subject was referred back to the House Committee'.

There was also a discussion of a letter from the Local Government Board about the enrolment of officials of local authorities in National Service. Mr Gregory, a member of the Board of Guardians said that 'he strenuously objected to Sanitary Inspectors going'. Mr Simpson said that, 'he was quite willing to enrol for National Service, but he could not altogether neglect his own business, and where would the country be if all commercial undertakings were abandoned. Yet there was this side to it: he might be able to spare a certain time each week to do something in what was termed the National Service, but could he be asked to surrender all, and leave his business at the mercy of someone else?' There were similar comments from other members. There is more than a hint here of the notion that 'surrendering all' could be left to the young men at the front, but that commercial interests should be left as unaffected as possible by the war.

[Note: The difficulty of importing food had, by this time, threatened an acute shortage of basic supplies. On 3 February 1917 the national press reported that Lord Devonport, the government's food controller, wanted to avoid compulsory food rationing but that this could only be achieved by economy and the avoidance of waste. Individuals were asked to consume no more than 4lbs of bread, 2lbs 8oz. of meat and 12 oz. of sugar each week, but were told that there was no shortage of eggs and fish. The appeal largely failed, and late in December 1917 food rationing was imposed on a regional and area basis, with the first rationing of civilians imposed in Pontypool on 17 December, soon to be followed by its imposition in Birmingham, with other areas of the country a little later.]

21 March 1917

A report that the names of men from the parish of Holy Trinity in Southwell who have enlisted in the armed services had been inserted on a roll of honour in the church.

'ANOTHER LOCAL MAN DIES OF WOUNDS   Mr and Mrs G. Hall, of Westhorpe, have received a telegram from the War Office conveying the intelligence that their son, Pte. Chris Hall, has died from wounds received in action, and the following letter has also come through:– 5th Casualty Clearing Station, B. E. F.   Dear Mr and Mrs Hall, – I regret very much to inform you that your son, 19499 Pte. C. Hall, 2nd Northamptons, died in this hospital of wounds, on March 7th. He was badly wounded in the shoulder and back, and did not live long after he was brought into hospital. I am glad to be able to say he did not suffer. He will be buried in the cemetery allocated to this hospital. With every sympathy, yours truly, K. C. Todd, sister-in-charge. March 7th – Pte. Hall was 33 years of age, and had been in the Army one year and nine months. He went out to Canada some years since, but came home and joined up with the Sherwood Foresters, being transferred to the Northamptons when he went to the front. He was home on furlough last October, and seemed to have a premonition that he should not get back again.'
[Note: Christopher Hall died on 5 March 1917 and is buried in Bray Military Cemetery, on the Somme.]

4 April 1917

A report that Lt. E. C. Vickers, only son of W. Vickers, president of Southwell Traders' Association, had been killed in action.[Note: 2nd Lt. Ernest Charles Vickers, serving with the Essex Regiment, died on 26 January 1917, he was 22 and is commemorated on the Thiepval Memorial.]

'NATIONAL SERVICE CAMPAIGN   In connection with the above a public meeting was held in the Assembly Hall on Friday night. There was a satisfactory attendance, considering that over 500 men have gone to join the Army and Navy. Mr J. R. Starkey, M.P., was chairman, and in the audience were Rev. K. Warrand, Rev. E. A. and Mrs Coghill, Mr and Mrs C. L. Maltby, Mr H. Lewin (Halam), Mr A. T. Metcalfe, Mr N. A. Metcalfe, Mr A. Salt (Chairman of Parish Council), Mr. J. H. Kirkby, Mr and Mrs Wagstaffe (Hockerton), Mr J. Tatham, Mr H. Heald, Mr G. Cholerton, Mr T. Maidens, Mr J. Ellis (clerk to Board of Guardians), Mr Harrison, and others . The Chairman gave a characteristic speech, and urged upon those present the necessity of supporting the movement in order to make it a success. Mr A. Wilson, of London, gave an interesting account of the working of the scheme, and alluding to the marvellous organising power of the Germans, said they had a method whereby every man in each district could be traced in a few minutes, with a record of his trade abilities, whether he was a good workman or a drunkard, and it was not to be supposed that our scheme would be perfect as that in a few months, but the idea was to get every man to enrol in order to make the national labour mobile or fluid in order to move it about from place to place where it was most needed. Archdeacon Conybeare also gave an interesting speech and hoped Mr Wilson would not go away with the idea that because the room was not crowded with men Southwell was not patriotic. Our men were where they ought to be – in the trenches and in training for the trenches; but still there was a great national need for more men in order to produce food and munitions. In regard to the former, 80 pounds out of every hundred of our food was imported, whereas the Germans produced 87 per cent of their food, and 95 per cent of their meat. Dr J. F. D. Willoughby proposed a vote of thanks to the speakers, and this was seconded by Mr A. Salt, and carried unanimously.'

18 April 1917

PRIVATE F.W. COOLING, SOUTHWELL The official intimation was received on Wednesday of the death in France from cerebro-spinal meningitis of Pte. Frank Cooling (19), Durham Light Infantry. He was the third son of Mr and Mrs R Cooling, of Westgate, Southwell. As a boy he attended the National School, but owing to eye trouble went to the Colville-street, (Nottingham) Blind School, where he remained for two years, but always had to wear glasses. Later he was employed by Messrs Merryweather and Sons, at The Nurseries, and afterwards was at Messrs F. Caudwell's flour mills until enlisting on Feb. 26th, 1917. It is only six weeks ago he left home to join the Army. Mrs Cooling has another son who has been out on active service, but is now at home. Much sympathy is felt with the bereaved family.

'SOUTHWELL (Alexander Peet) The sad intelligence reached Southwell on Monday that Pte. Alexander Peet, Kirklington-road, had been seriously wounded, and it had been necessary to amputate the left arm. Pte. Peet was before the war employed for many years by Mr J.H. Kirkby. He enlisted in the 8th Sherwood Foresters soon after the outbreak of war, with two other employees, Corporal Harold Tyne, who won the D.C.M., and Pte. Sam Oliver, who was killed at Kemmel in Belgium on June 9th, 1915, with shrapnel in his leg, in an attack led by Major J.P. Becher. On recovery he was attached to a Lewis gun section, and again went out early this year. Letters have been received from the Chaplain and Matron of the hospital, and the latter states: 'I am sorry to say your brother, 82557 Pte. A. Peet, M.G.S., has been admitted to this hospital, suffering the loss of his left arm. He is considered very seriously ill, but we hope to send you better news in a few days. He is having every care and attention, and being well looked after.'

'AN EXCELLENT REPORT Ida Fairweather, the honorary depot controller of the National Egg Collection submitted her second annual report in which she thanks the egg collectors for their ongoing efforts in all weathers. A total of 23,606 eggs had been given and every week eggs are sent to the V.A.D. Hospital at Burgage Manor. However, the number of eggs given locally had reduced as the London Central Committee wished that as many eggs as possible be sent to the Base Hospitals abroad. She comments: 'So we workers for the N.E.C. must adopt the Army watchword and – if necessary – "carry on" for another year.'

28 April 1917

A report of a concert for 'soldiers' comforts' by the Girls' Friendly Society in Holy Trinity schoolroom. It was a 'pleasing entertainment' with proceeds donated to soldiers' comforts and to support of GFS huts for munitions workers. [Note: Several Church of England organisations such as the Church Army and the GFS provided recreation facilities for men at the front and for munitions workers at home.]

A report that the Red Cross hospital at Burgage Manor had now been open for two years. Another concert had been held in support of the hospital (full programme noted) including songs from Miss D. Vickers [Dorothy Gertrude Vickers]. [Note: Her brother, 2nd Lt Ernest Charles Vickers was killed in action in January.]

2 May 1917

'CAPTAIN R.C.WATSON, SOUTHWELL Mr J.H. Watson the London director of Messrs Carey & Sons Ltd., lace manufacturers, Bulwell and Southwell, has received the sad news that his second son, Captain Robert Carey Watson, Middlesex Regiment, was killed in action on 16th April. Captain Watson was for a time identified with the factory in the Minster town, and was a prominent member of the Debating Society…'

9 May 1917

THE WOUNDED Lt. J.H. Kirkby is progressing satisfactorily, and Pte. A. Peet, who recently had an arm amputated, has been moved to England, and is now in a Red Cross Hospital at Manchester. Cpl. Frank Wilcox, of the Devons, is just recovering from a bad attack of malaria fever at Napier Barracks Hospital, Lahore, India.

'RATIONING OF TRAMPS   Rev. S. Bredison said reference had been made that morning at the House Committee about the Notts and Derbyshire Vagrancy Committee. Some casuals were getting 12½ lbs of bread per week, and the Master had been asked what could be done.

Mr Simpson inquired whether or not the Local Government Board had issued a rationing order? The Master said that the dietary for casuals had not been altered, and averaged something like 10½ lbs of bread per week, which was 6½ [lbs] above the Food Controller's order. The casuals received no meat; he had knocked them off potatoes and half-an-ounce of margarine, while he had decreased the allowance of bread from eight ounces to six, but they were entitled to a bread ticket to get their mid-day meal: but if there were no bread stations in the direction in which they were going they had to be given bread, which brought it up to 10½ lbs a week. He urged that this should be laid before the Notts and Derbyshire Vagrancy Committee, and mentioned that the casuals at Southwell averaged two per night. He advised that their casual wards should be closed altogether, because no men of 50 or 60 need be out of work; but he was of the opinion that in going about their greatest fear was lest they should find something to do.

The Chairman observed that they had knocked the dietary in the Workhouse down by 50 per cent.

The Clerk stated that he did not think they could close the casual wards.

The Master pointed out that if it were done it would make the casuals work, or drive them into workhouses. Some were halt and lame, but they could do light employment.

Mr Straw: Do you think any hardship would be caused if the wards were closed?

The Master replied in the negative.'

[Note: The report continued further, but this extract illustrates contemporary attitudes to what would now be regarded as the homeless unemployed during a critical period in the war and at a time of food shortages.]

'BRACKENHURST HALL AS A RED CROSS HOSPITAL   Mr & Mrs W. N. Hicking have most generously turned their beautiful house and garden into a Red Cross Hospital, with Mrs Hicking as Commandant… About 30 wounded men arrived last week, and more are expected in a few days.'

16 May 1917

A photograph of Pte. A. Wilson, of Southwell, killed in action. [This was 242102 Pte. Albert Henry Wilson, Border Regiment, who was killed, aged 36, on 25 April 1917 and is commemorated on the Arras Memorial. In 1911 Albert Henry Wilson, aged 29, was living in Southwell].

FUNERAL OF PTE. D. FROW   The sad news conveyed to Southwell in the early part of the week that Pte. David Frow, of the Machine Gun Corps, had died in a military hospital, and on Friday the remains were interred in the churchyard at Holy Trinity. The Vicar (Rev. E. A. Coghill) conducted the service. The deceased, who was a sides man at Holy Trinity, had been in the town about three years, and formerly lived at Wong View, Westgate. He joined the Army a short time since, and was attached to the Machine Gun Section, but being of a quiet and studious disposition, the noise of the guns brought on sleeplessness, and medical aid being of no avail, he gradually sank and passed away at the age of 35 years. Many friends and relatives attended the funeral to pay a last tribute of respect and regard, and there was a large number of wreaths and floral emblems.'

[Note: David Frow may have displayed the severe symptoms of what was then called shell-shock, so-called because it was thought to be caused by heavy enemy shelling over a prolonged period. It was also called neurasthenia, a term no longer used. We might now describe it as post-traumatic stress. Even if the condition was recognised, First World War medical treatments were crude. Officers were often sent home to recuperate, but other ranks were usually sent back to the front, often accused of being malingers. Some deserted, later to be shot after a field court martial. Other 'punishments' could be horrific, including being bound for hours a day to a gun carriage within range of enemy shelling. It has been estimated that 80,000 British servicemen, or 2 per cent of those that saw active service, suffered from the condition. If David Frow was suffering from shell-shock then he seems to have been treated well.]

23 May 1917

A report of a recent meeting of Southwell Parish Council at which sympathy was expressed to J. H. Kirkby whose son had recently been seriously wounded in France. Kirkby replied that he had recently received a letter from his son saying that he was going on well, and hoped soon to be home. [Note: Another son, John Nevil Kirkby, had been killed in action on 25 September 1916.] The Council voted £100 to support the Red Cross hospital. They also considered a proposal from the Local Government Board that a 'Rat and Sparrow Club' be formed and awards given 'for the destruction of rats, house sparrows etc' (evidently to help alleviate the food shortage). It was decided, after considerable discussion, to delay a decision until the next meeting.

A report that Pte. A. Wilson, a photograph of whom was published on 16 May 1917, had been a member of the Southwell Fire Brigade.

A reference is made in this edition of two Red Cross hospitals in Southwell 'doing splendid work for the wounded'. [Burgage Manor and Brackenhurst.]

30 May 1917

At the annual prize-giving at the Minster Grammar School, the headmaster made reference to old Southwellians who were serving in the armed forces, and named those who had died in action. The latter were 2nd Lts. N. Kirkby, Vickers and F. Shaw, and also (but no rank or initial given) Davis, Moore, Taylor, Worman, Rose, Williams and Parr. Mention was also made of Leonard Gilbert who had risen in rank from 2nd Lt. to Lt. Colonel during the war.

FIRE AT THE MILL   A report of a fire at Caudwell's flour mills. Prompt action by the mill manager and members of Southwell Fire Brigade saved the building from destruction. Damage was estimated at about £1,000.

6 June 1917

'ECHO OF THE IRISH REBELLION   The many friends of Harold Ridge will be sorry to hear that it has been found necessary to amputate his foot, and the operation was carried out at Nottingham Hospital on Sunday. Ridge was a soldier with the Sherwood Foresters. And being ordered out to Ireland to help quell the rebellion, was soon in the thick of the fray at Dublin, and received two wounds, one in the hip and an explosive bullet in the right foot. The latter was a serious wound, and although for a year the doctors have done their best, it was recently found necessary to take off the limb just below the knee. He is progressing favourably.'

20 June 1917

A report that Lt. J. H. Kirkby is progressing satisfactorily in a convalescent home for officers in Oxford.

A report that Capt. Douglas Watson, son of the London director of Carey and Sons had been awarded the MC 'for distinguished conduct in Palestine.'

'PTE. T. BARLOW, SOUTHWELL   A year ago Pte. Thomas F. Barlow, youngest son of Mr Alfred Barlow, Westgate, Southwell, was reported missing, but on Thursday the worst was confirmed, for the following communication was received from the Records Office at Lichfield:–

"It is my painful duty to inform you that no further news having been received respecting your son, the Army Council have been regretfully constrained to conclude that he is dead, and that his death took place on July 1st, 1916." Pte. Barlow was a native of Southwell, and as a boy attended the National School, after which he worked at the factory, and was in camp with the Territorials at the outbreak of war. He went to France at the beginning of 1915, and returned to his home in February of that year for a month's leave having signed on again, though his term of service had expired. Later he was stationed at Belton Park, and during his period there on several occasions he visited Southwell, going out again at the end of March 1916. About the middle of last July his father was officially notified that he was missing, and now his death is safely presumed. He was a footballer who played for the local teams, and was also fond of other forms of sport. His elder brother, Sgt. A. H. Barlow, is with the Sherwood Foresters at the present time in France.'

[Note: The death of 305065 Pte. T. F. Barlow, Sherwood Foresters, is recorded by the CWGC as 1 July 1916. He is commemorated on the Thiepval Memorial. The Thiepval Memorial to the Missing, Somme Battlefields, records the names of 72,204 identified officers and men of the UK and South African forces. 1 July 1916 was the first day of the battle of the Somme, when the British army lost 58,000 men, 20,000 of whom were killed on that day alone, a tragedy not surpassed in British military history. The Somme offensive lasted until 18 November 1916. This offensive resulted in 419,654 British dead and wounded, with a further 194,451 French casualties. German dead and wounded were estimated at 500,000. The Allies gained seven and a half miles. John Keegan noted that 'The Somme marked the end of an age of vital optimism in British life that has never been recovered' (*The First World War* [1998], 321).]

4 July 1917

'PTE. GEORGE HOPKINSON MISSING   The War Office has recently notified the friends of Pte. George Hopkinson that he has been missing since March last, and that as no further news has come to hand, it is feared that he has been killed or taken prisoner. Pte. Hopkinson resided at Maythorne, Southwell, and went out to France with the Sherwood Foresters, being wounded shortly afterwards. He was then transferred to the Warwickshire Regiment, and after returning to France saw much fighting with that celebrated regiment, which was in the advance on several occasions.' [See report 12th September, 1917.]

'VOLUNTEER COMPANY   In connection with the Notts. Volunteer Regiment a meeting will be held in Southwell on Monday night next, July 9th, at eight o'clock, to urge the necessity of forming a Company for the town and district. The chair will be occupied by Mr. Harold Browne, and an address is to be given by Colonel Sir Lancelot Rolleston, K.G.B., D.S.O., supported by the Lord Bishop of the Diocese, the Archdeacon of Nottingham (Ven. Conybeare), Colonel Frank Seely, Sir William N. Hicking, and others.'

'CPL. TYNE, D.C.M., ON FURLOUGH   The many friends of Cpl. Tyne, D.C.M., were pleased to hear that he had returned to his native town on Sunday night for a few days furlough, looking well and in the pink of condition. He has many tales to tell of Fritz and the hairbreadth escapes from the trenches of Fritz during the last year and a half. It was in September, 1915, that nearly all Southwell gathered together on the lawn of the Bishop's Manor, where his lordship presented H. Tyne and A. Shepherd with the D.C.M, and these two heroes returned to France on Sept. 21st.

Arthur Shepherd was killed shortly afterwards, but the good luck of Tyne still enabled him to pull through, and since then he has taken parties of our men over to the German trenches innumerable times and brought back numbers of prisoners. Yet he has always got back safe. On one occasion he was hit in the nose with a piece of shell, but the wound was only slight. He has brought back several mementoes of the fray, and thinks that time and patience will see us triumph over the enemy, who nevertheless still keeps a bold front and does not give in until there is no hope of escape.'

'PRESENTATION TO SOUTHWELL HERO   D.C.M. FOR A BRAVE DEED   There was a large gathering of people on the lawn of Burgage Manor Hospital, Southwell, on Monday afternoon, to do honour to one of the wounded soldiers in that institution, Corporal Albert Woodroffe, 12602, Royal Fusiliers, who was in action at Potaguee Wood, Belgium, on July 21st 1915, when one of his comrades was severely wounded, and under very heavy shell-fire, and with the ground raked with shot and shell, Cpl. Woodroffe bandaged up his comrade's wounds and brought him to the dressing-station. The presentation was made by Lt. Col. Battersby, Medical Officer for the City and County of Notts., who was supported on the platform by Archdeacon Conybeare, Mrs Hoskyns, Mrs J. R. Starkey, Miss E. Small (Commandant), Dr. J. F. D. Willoughby (Medical Officer), Messrs T. D. Partington, A. Salt, and H. Merryweather, J.P., and Lady Norton Hicking. . . ' A list follows of 36 Southwell notables who were in 'the large concourse of people'. At the end of the ceremony 'Miss Small, the Commandant, amid the continued cheering of the large gathering, and on behalf of the nurses and staff of the hospital, then presented Cpl. Woodroffe with a silver luminous watch, which had the following inscription engraved upon it: "Presented to Cpl. Albert Woodroffe, Royal Fusiliers, by the Staff of the Burgage Manor Auxiliary Hospital, Southwell. July 2nd, 1917."
[Note: Although the heading refers to a 'Southwell Hero' this seems to refer to Albert Woodroffe being a patient in Burgage Manor. He does not appear in the 1911 census return for Southwell. It seems that he was not a native of or normally resident in Southwell.]

'CPL. A. HUMBERSTONE, SOUTHWELL   Mrs Humberstone, Southwell, has received the sad news that her son, Cpl. Arthur Humberstone, 25, of the Sherwood Foresters, has been killed. A telegram was received in Southwell on Sunday, from the Records Office, stating that he was badly wounded, and a further one came on Wednesday, to say that he was dead. Cpl. Humberstone attended Southwell National School, under Mr A. Salt, and afterwards worked for Messrs Carey and Sons at the lace factory. He joined the Sherwood Foresters five years ago, and was with the regiment when they were embodied at the outbreak of war. He was wounded at Ypres in July 1915. He was a well-known footballer, playing for Southwell City, and was one of the team when they won the Newark Charity Cup, whilst he had also played for Southwell at cricket, in which sport he likewise showed much ability.

   The following letter was received from the Chaplain: – "Dear Mrs Humberstone, It is with deep regret that your son was brought into this hospital so badly wounded that he soon passed away, in spite of attempts to save his life. He was unconscious when he died, and it will comfort you to know that he suffered no pain. I saw him when he first came in, and he asked me to send you his love. Please accept my sincere sympathy in your great trouble. I shall bury him tomorrow at —, and will remember you in my prayers at the grave."

   Cpl. Humberstone was home on leave some 15 months ago, and was due for a month's leave, being time-expired last March. His brother, Cpl. Sam Humberstone, was killed in action in July,

1915, and he has two more brothers with the colours, Sgt.-Instructor Albert Humberstone, R.S.F, who has been awarded the D.C.M., and Pte. William Humberstone, who is still in the trenches with the Sherwood Foresters. This latter member of the family was able to see Arthur after he was wounded, and was allowed with three more chums to go to his funeral. Writing home, Pte. Will Humberstone states: – "I hardly know how to write this letter to tell you the news that poor Arthur has got severely wounded this morning with a trench mortar. I saw him when he was on the stretcher, but he hardly knew me. His wounds are in the neck and right side, and the doctor says they are very serious." In a later communication he states: – "I expect you have my letter telling you about Arthur being wounded. I am awfully sorry to tell you he died on Saturday, the 23rd, at 9 o'clock. I have got permission to leave the trenches to attend his funeral, and three chums are to go with me."'

[Note: 305126, Cpl. Arthur Humberstone, aged 26, Sherwood Foresters, died on 24 June 1917 and is buried in Noeux-Les-Mines Communal Cemetery, Pas de Calais.]

11 July 1917

A report that 2nd Lt. G. P. Gregg, 1/7 Battalion Cheshire Regiment, previously reported wounded and missing, has been killed in action. 'He was the younger son of Mr and Mrs Oliver Gregg, West Kirkby, Cheshire, and grandson of the late Mrs Henry Machin, Southwell, and well known in the neighbourhood.'

A report of concerts at Burgage Manor at one of which (by Mr Leek and his friends from Newark). Cpl. Albert Woodroffe D.C.M. thanked the staff for the present given him that afternoon which 'would be a constant reminder of the kindness he had received from them at Southwell'.

18 July 1917

'NOTTS. VOLUNTEER TRANSPORT On Sunday morning many of the residents went to the Market-place to watch the arrival of the Newark Motor Transport Section of the Nottinghamshire Volunteer Regiment, which lined up in the Market-place and Westgate. Temp. 2nd Lt. J. Mather was in command and after a short stay the cars went on to Newstead Abbey, where the drivers had refreshments and looked round the world-famous gardens. Inspector W. Clarke and P.c. Copeland were on duty in the Market-place to regulate the traffic while the Transport was in the Town.'

'CPL. G. JEPSON WINS THE MILITARY MEDAL Cpl. George Jepson is now home on a few days leave, and the inhabitants of the Minster town learn with pride that he has been awarded the Military Medal for good work done on several occasions, but chiefly on the 10th of June last. Jepson was an employee of Mr J. H. Kirkby's bake house, and, like many of his mates, joined the Sherwood Foresters soon after the outbreak of the war. When he had finished his training he went out to Gallipoli, and took part in the memorable landing at Sulva Bay. Here he was wounded, and when better went to France, where he was soon in the severe fighting on the Somme, and his regiment did some good work. He was next transferred to the Tunnelling Section of the R.E.s, and in the early part of June this year was engaged as a listener to his section while they were working their way under the enemy trenches at La Bassée, and finding that a section of the enemy was also at work near to, it was decided to make a raid on his trenches, and, if possible, blow his trenches up. So on June 10th a party of our men went over and drove them out of their front line. Our hero, with his officer and sergeant, then ran across No Man's Land with the necessary powder etc., and quickly finding the shaft, went down a distance, laid a mine, and exploded it in the workings, thus destroying the labour of many months. All the men returned safely, and were complemented by the C.O., and on June 15th Jepson was called out, told to get into a car, and taken to headquarters, where he was warmly congratulated by Sir Douglas Haig and awarded the Military Medal. The gallant Corporal is a native of Southwell, his father being for many years gardener to the late Mr John Kirkland, and is still with Mrs G. E. Kirkland, Church-street.'

1 August 1917

A report of a concert for the wounded soldiers at Burgage Manor hospital, including a note that Pte. White 'caused much amusement with his song "As we come up from Zummerzet"'. Gunner Hiskerton 'finely rendered "Ring Down the Curtain" and Pte. Henderson, A.S.C., 'gave a splendid exhibition of the "Highland Fling", his dancing being received with much applause'. Mr Litchfield's band was again in attendance. On this and other occasions the patients themselves provided much of the entertainment.

'PTE. F. C. RANDALL, SOUTHWELL   Another Southwell man has given his life in the Great War, the news reaching Southwell on Friday last that Pte. F. C. Randall (familiarly known as "Con" Randall), had died on July 14th, on a small island a few miles north-east of the Persian Gulf. Pte. Randall enlisted in the Army Service Corps on October 15th, 1915, with Ptes. L. L. B. Martin and W. H. Shelbourn, all of whom were engaged in the machine bakery of Mr J. H. Kirkby, the Supply Stores, Southwell. Randall went out to Mesopotamia, and the extreme heat of last summer laid him up for a time, but after recuperating in Alexandria he was sent to this small island, which has a population of about a thousand Arabs, he and a black boy being the cook for the garrison there. As a member of the local Baptist Church, he was a faithful and zealous worker in the Sunday School and Band of Hope, and also took a prominent part in other departments of church life. He is the first of their members to die in the Army, and a memorial service will be held. Much sympathy is felt for Miss Burge, Easthorpe, Southwell, to whom he was engaged to be married.'

'AIR-MECHANIC KEY   A Southwellian's record deserving a mention is that of Air-Mechanic [John William] Key, who formerly worked for Messrs Carey and Sons, at the lace factory, during which time he joined the Territorials. Being with them in camp when war broke out, he went to France with the 1st-8th Sherwood Foresters, and saw considerable service. He became time expired, and returned home, entering the works of Messrs A. Ransome and Co. Ltd., Newark, but later joined the Naval Section of the Air Service, having been attached to the local aerodrome for a considerable time. He is now in the vicinity on furlough. He is a boxer of considerable merit, and has taken part in the tournaments between R.N.A.S. and the R.E.s, and on the last of these, given in the Corn Exchange, he was one of the victors. A-M Key has established himself a warm favourite, and his many friends will be interested to know that in his newer capacity he is once more doing battle with the Huns. He leaves these parts shortly for that purpose, and all who know him will join in wishing him the best of luck.'

8 August 1917

'PTE. S. ULLYAT, SOUTHWELL
Another Southwell man has given his life in the Great War, the news reaching Southwell that Pte. Samuel Ullyat (19), of the Sherwood Foresters, second son of Mr and Mrs W. H. Ullyat of Normanton, Southwell, who was wounded on June 29th, died on July 7th at a Canadian Casualty Station in France. He was a native of Little Carlton, and while very young went with his parents to Selston, Notts. Deceased, who worked on a farm with his grandfather and father, enlisted in June, 1915. He was home on leave in December, 1916, and went to France in April this year. He has another brother, Pte. Robt. Ullyat, who enlisted in February, 1915, and is now with the R. F. A. [Royal Field Artillery] at Salonika.'

A report of the effort that Southwell Traders' Association had made to support a fund to send Christmas presents to serving military personnel from Southwell 'at home and abroad, including every name on the Roll of Honour'. Donations came to £42. 13s. flag day raised a further £29. 1s. 6d., making a total of £71. 14s. 6d. . Out of this, expenses were paid: 'Parcels: £52. 4s. 9d; artificial flowers for Flag Day, £1. 8s. postage on parcels, £12. 4s. 6d.; sundry expenses, 3s; balance in hands of treasurer, £5. 14s. 3d. Total £71. 14s. 6d. No fewer that 338 parcels were sent out to the men, also to 26 officers were sent one tin of 50 cigarettes each. The parcels contained dates, chocolates, cigarettes, Nestlé's milk, cocoa, tablets etc., and enclosed in each one was a greeting card, "From the Southwell Traders' Association and the old Home Town". That the parcels were appreciated by the recipients has been shown by the 111 letters of grateful acknowledgement received by the hon. secretary.' The report ended by recording that to the credit balance of £5. 14s. 3d had been added £8. 2s. 6d. sent in by the Holy Trinity branch of the Girls' Friendly Society, 'which amount will form the nucleus for any further effort that may be made for those for whom the fund was initiated'.

[Notes (a): £72 in 1917 would have been worth £3500 in purchasing power today.
(b) This report confirms the large number of Southwell men that were serving with the armed forces, noting that 364 parcels were sent to officers and men at Christmas 1916. Reports in the *Newark Advertiser* on 14 March and 4 April 1917 had spoken of about 500 men from Southwell serving with the armed forces.]

A report of a memorial service held on 2 August in the Minster for the war dead: Percy Hall, Charles Maltby, John Watson, Vincent Brown, Nevil Kirkby, John Waller, George Richardson, Harry Seward, Thomas Stephenson, George Davison, Ernest Vickers, William Labbett, Chris Hall, Frank Cooling, Joseph Jones, Albert Wilson, Alfred Merrin, Tom Barlow, Arthur Humberstone, Will J. Wilkinson, Conway Randle [*sic*, F. C. Randall], and Walter Merrin. The service was 'beautiful in its simplicity' with all the hymns sung unaccompanied. The report notes that as the rector, W. J. Conybeare, read out these names 'one caught a glimpse of the horrors of war and of the fine men, noble in character, who, alas! will never return to their homes and families; who died bravely facing the foe on the battlefield in Flanders or France and in the lonely islands of the Mediterranean Sea'.

15 August 1917

A report of the recent meeting of the Southwell Rural District Council that had received a letter from Lady W. N. Hicking, Brackenhurst. She had suggested that seats for the wounded should be provided between Brackenhurst and Southwell. The Clerk to the council said that it had no power to provide seats, but it could give permission for them to be placed by the roadside, so long as they did not obstruct the highway. Permission was given, 'and it was stated that there would be no difficulty about the provision of seats'.

'SOUTHWELL LAD IN GERMANY   The soldier whose portrait accompanies this notice is Sgt. G. W. Robinson of the 2nd Battalion, Sherwood Foresters, one of the so-called contemptible little Army who so heroically held up the massed troops of the Germans at Mons. The photo is unique, in that it was taken in Germany a few days ago, and just received in Southwell by the mother of Sgt. Robinson, who is Mrs R. Doughty, Kents-row, Westhorpe. Sgt. Robinson was, before joining the Army seven years since, an employee of Mr J. H. Kirkby, and, joining the Sherwood Foresters, did his training at Aldershot, Salisbury, and several other depots in this country. At the outbreak of the War he was one of the Expeditionary Force that, in August 1914, left these shores and landed in France to oppose the oncoming hordes of the Kaiser. After being in the thick of the fighting on many occasions the Sherwoods made their celebrated stand at Mons, and Sgt. Robinson was taken prisoner. He had sent many cards to his parents and friends in Newark and Southwell, and they will no doubt be pleased to see this photo of him.'

'GUNNER [W. J.] WILKINSON, SOUTHWELL   During the last week the sad news has been confirmed that Gunner William Jefferson Wilkinson was killed on July 5th while resting in a dug-out after being engaged in shelling the enemy position. Wm. Jefferson Wilkinson, eldest son of Mrs and the late Mr Wilkinson, of Rose Cottage, Southwell, was apprenticed to Mr Copestake, of Mansfield, where he remained for eight years, leaving there to go out to Canada in 1905, where he was a keen member of the Church, holding the office of sides man, and helping to build a Church College in Saskatchewan. He returned to England in 1914, and set up as a poultry farmer at Holly Cottage, Greaves-lane, Edingley, which he had to sell up to join the Army last year. He went to France in March this year, and was killed at the age of 35 years, leaving a widow and three children. Information was received on July 19th from the Dover Depot that he was killed, but no particulars were given.

The sad news was confirmed in letters received. Deceased's Major wrote:– "It is with the deepest regret that I have to inform you that your husband was killed on the afternoon of the 5th July. He was, in company with others, resting in a dug-out, when about 2.30 the enemy commenced shelling the battery position. The men all cleared out for safety, and your husband had got well clear when a piece of shell struck him in the head, killing him instantly. We found him lying on the road face downwards, and after removing him from further harm, we buried him reverently in the evening, together with four others of his companions who had similarly suffered. He was a hard and willing worker, and of a cheerful nature, and I feel his loss very deeply. Although poor comfort, you have the entire sympathy of the officers and men of the Battery in your sad and irrevocable loss." The Chaplain wrote:– "I have just obtained your address and am writing to express my deep sympathy with you in the loss of your husband, who was killed on the afternoon of July 5th. The battery was not in action, and the men were resting in their dug-outs when suddenly, between 2.30 and 3 o'clock, they were shelled. In trying to escape from the shelled area, your husband and three other companions were hit and killed instantaneously. I buried him the following day in the little British cemetery at Dicksbusch [sic]. I pray that He who came into the world to heal the broken-hearted, will comfort you in this terrible sorrow and give you the strength to bear up under so heavy a blow," '

[Note: 122701 Gunner William Jefferson Wilkinson, Royal Garrison Artillery, aged 35, was killed on 5 July 1917. He is buried in Dickebusch New Military Cemetery Extension, West-Vlaanderen, Belgium.]

22 August 1917

A report of the death of Air Mechanic John George Egleshaw, aged 34. He had been the Southwell Golf Club professional, and died as the result of an accident at a Royal Naval Air Service headquarters 'somewhere in England'. The report continues: 'It appears that he was at work on Monday when the propeller of a seaplane struck him on the head and back inflicting terrible injuries.' He died from shock 'on Tuesday week'. He was born in Bulwell and had come to live and work to Southwell 20 years previously. He was initially employed at Carey's, and in 1910 was appointed the professional at the golf club. He had joined the RNAS two months before his death. He was a member of the Cycle Company of the Notts Volunteers. He left a widow and four children, the youngest under six months old. The report continues with details of the inquest and of the funeral. The latter mentions that wounded soldiers from Brackenhurst and Burgage Manor hospitals were present.

[Note: The CWGC debt of honour register has F/30578 Aircraftsman 2nd Class John George Egleshaw, Royal Naval Air Service, aged 32, died 14 August 1917. He is buried in Southwell Minster churchyard, near the north side of the church.]

5 September 1917

CPL. HARRY BROWN. The many friends of Cpl. H. Brown of Maythorne will be interested to hear that he is now at Blackburn Hospital, recovering from the effects of wounds. Cpl. Brown was in severe fighting around Arras early in August, and was hit by shrapnel breaking his leg in two places. He had to lay in the open for one and a half days and a night before the Red Cross men could get to him. On arrival in this country his friends were asked to visit him owing to his precarious condition, but we are glad to state he is now progressing satisfactorily. [Note: A report on 19th September suggests that he was wounded at Westhoek, Belgium.]

12 September 1917

A report that Mrs S. Hopkinson, of Maythorne, having previously been told that her son, Pte. George Hopkinson, was dead, had now received the news that he was a prisoner of war. He was captured at Arras. He had attended the Wesleyan Day School in Southwell, and had then worked at Carey's. He was 'a footballer of considerable merit and had played for Southwell St Mary's as well as other local teams'.

A report of a memorial service for Frank Conway Randall in Southwell Baptist Church, noting that he served with the A.S.C. in Salonika, India, and Mesopotamia, and that he had died 'after illness, in hospitals, [and] after loneliness on the little island of Kharak in the Persian Gulf'.

19 September 1917

Reports of entertainments for wounded soldiers at Burgage Manor, and flag days for the Southwell nurses.

A report that Cpl. J. H. Brown had been wounded at Westhoek in Belgium on 31 July 'but is progressing favourably'.

'He was shot through the right leg which was broken in two places and was also badly fractured. He managed to crawl to a shell hole where he lay for two days and nights, until picked up by stretcher-bearers, and is now in Queen Mary's Military Hospital, Whalley, near Blackburn, Lancashire. Vincent Brown, his brother, made the supreme sacrifice, having been killed on the Somme, Sept. 16th, 1916, and had served nine years with the Sherwood Foresters.
   Cpl. J. H. Brown, who enlisted with the Royal Scots Fusiliers in 1907, was for some time stationed at Ayr, Scotland, and later in Dublin. In 1908 he proceeded with his regiment to India, and subsequently to Pretoria. Returning to Southwell he was for some-time in the employ of Mr Kirkby, and in January 1915, he joined the Sherwood Foresters and has seen two year's hard fighting. Pte. C. Brown, father of the above, served 21 years with the old Volunteer and Territorial Corps, six years as sergeant in the latter, retiring in 1912. He also joined up in 1915 in the Royal Defence Corps, and is at present engaged in guarding a prisoner of war detention camp near Sutton Bridge, Lincolnshire.' [See entry for 30 April 1919. John Harry Brown's father was Pte. Charles Brown.]

26 September 1917

'PTE. S. J. PLOWMAN   The many friends of Pte. S. J. Plowman will be pleased to hear that he is getting better from a bad attack of malaria. He has been in hospital at Salonika for 34 days, but returned to his duties on the 4th of this month. He says they have had no rain for 10 weeks, and the harvest is all in except maize. Fruit is very plentiful; a good supply of figs, melons and tomatoes can be bought from the natives for a few pence.'

'WOUNDED SHERWOOD HOME   Pte. Alex Peet has just arrived in his native town after serving in the Army since October 24th, 1914. He went out to France early in 1915, and on June 9th received a bullet in his right arm which fractured the bone. After recovery he joined the Machine Gun Corps, leaving England for France on Feb. 19th 1917. On April 9th, with many other local lads, he took part in the gallant charge upon Vimy Ridge, in the midst of shrapnel and machine gun fire from the German trenches. Peet was coolly working his Lewis gun when a large shrapnel shell burst and shattered his left arm. He was taken to the base, and from leaving France to arriving at a Manchester hospital it was only a matter of 24 hours. He is now awaiting his turn to go to Roehampton to be fitted with an artificial limb.'

[Note: Vimy Ridge was a tactically significant chalk ridge running about 12km northeast of Arras and overlooking the town. It was the focus of almost continues fighting from September 1914, when it was occupied by German forces, until the Allied offensive in late 1918 which moved the front line eastwards. German engineers constructed in the ridge a network of artillery-proof trenches, bunkers and other defensive positions which were added to passages that had existed since the Middle Ages.]

10 October 1917

'CPL. A. G. MERRYWEATHER WOUNDED   The news reached the Minster town this weekend that Cpl. Alfred Merryweather had been wounded with shrapnel in the forehead, and had gone to a hospital in France. Cpl. Merryweather, before joining the Army, did good work as an orderly at Burgage Manor Hospital. He joined the R.G.A. last year and went to France in January this year. He has been in the thick of the fighting on many occasions, and was wounded on October 3rd. Alfred Merryweather's home is at Brinkley, where his wife and family reside.'

'THE MILITARY MEDAL   Mr and Mrs Wright, of Park-street, Southwell, have been notified that their son, Pte. Tom Wright, of the Sherwood Foresters, has been awarded the Military Medal. He was in action with Sgt.-Major Scraton, of Westhorpe, and Pte. Wright secured the honour during dawn, when attacking a strong enemy position, which was taken with slight loss. During the engagement the officer of the platoon was taken ill and Pte. Wright coolly led men across No-Man's Land to the new position which was taken over. He then instructed the men to make secure. He joined Kitchener's Army, and went to France in 1915. He has been twice wounded, the last occasion being in the big push on July, 1916. He lay for some time in a dangerous condition in Glasgow. His brother, Pte. Geo. Wright, was for some time in hospital at Malta with malaria.'

[Note: The 'big push' refers to the Battle of the Somme which began on 1 July 1916. 'Kitchener's Army' was the New Army created independently of the Territorial Force late in 1914. Field Marshall Lord Kitchener, appointed War Minister by Asquith on 3 August 1914, was initially unsure of the efficiency of the Territorial battalions, and declined to use the Territorial Force as the basis of the vastly greater military force needed for what he foresaw would be a long war. The huge number of recruits that responded to his call for volunteers formed new battalions within existing regular army regiments. The new battalions were in action for the first time in the Artois-Loos offensive on the western front in September 1915.]

24 October 1917

'SGT. W. H. DRABBLE, SOUTHWELL The war has dealt cruelly with another Southwell lad. Mr and Mrs A. Drabble, Easthorpe, Southwell, have received the news that their eldest son, Sgt. W. H. Drabble, Sherwood Foresters, has given his life for his country. On Thursday afternoon they received letters from an officer and sergeant stating that he was killed in action on October 4th. It is understood that he was struck on the head with a shell, while taking his men into the trenches, death being instantaneous. His birthday would have been last Saturday week, when he would have been 23 years of age. As a boy he attended Southwell Wesleyan Day School, and afterwards he was apprenticed to the grocery business with Mr J. J. Bates, King Street, where he remained for about five years, and later he went to Worksop to take up a position in the same trade, where he stayed for nearly eight months, up to the time of the outbreak of war. He was in the Territorials, and was with them at Camp during the crisis of August, 1914, being one of the number present in Newark Market-place at the service prior to the march to Nottingham and Derby. He was wounded about the same time that Colonel Fowler was killed and Major J. P. Becher received injuries which proved to be fatal, after which he returned to England and was here until March, 1916. He went to France again and was home three months ago, when he was in the best of health and spirits. After a month's furlough, he returned to France. Sgt. Drabble was offered a commission in February last, but this he declined. He was a footballer, and played for Southwell Thursday, of which team he was captain. A brother of his, Pte. A. E. Drabble, who was with him in the 1st-8th Sherwood Foresters, was dangerously wounded two years since, and in an engagement last May he was shot through the leg, and is at present with the Colours.

Mr and Mrs Drabble and family desire to thank all friends for their kind expressions of sympathy.'

LANCE-CPL. W. ROBINSON, SOUTHWELL   Mr and Mrs F. Robinson, Queen-street, Southwell, received the sad news on Friday that their son, Lance-Corporal W. Robinson, a Lewis machine gunner, 2nd-8th Sherwood Foresters, has been killed in France. This gallant soldier joined the colours on January 24th, 1916. Very shortly afterwards the Irish rebellion broke out, and he, along with his comrades, went over and helped to quell the riots. Going out to France on February 17th this year, he has been through many engagements, and rendered signal service with his Lewis gun. Many are the regrets at his untimely end, at the age of 21. His older brother, Frank, is a corporal in the 16th Sherwoods, and is now in France. The following letter has been received by the parents, who wish to thank their friends for sympathy and kindness shown to them in the past few days of sorrow and anxiety:– "I am afraid that you have received the terrible blow in the death of your son out here. It was one unlucky shell which landed right in the middle of the position which A Company had consolidated, and caused five casualties. Although I was only about 100 yards away at the time, I did not know until afterwards that your son was one of them. I am sure, however, you will be glad to hear that he was asleep at the time, and probably never knew anything about it. He had done good work with his Lewis gun during the engagement, and the officers and N.C.O.s say he was simply splendid. I would have written to you before, but there has been a great rush of work this last week or two, and I have had little time. It has been a sad time for us out here, in the absence of so many of the old faces, but I sometimes think that the lot of the people left behind, who have to wait in continual anxiety for news of those who have left them, is harder still. You have my sympathy and all his friends in your great loss. Yours sincerely, Geo. Elliott."

31 October 1917

'4TH NOTTS. VOLUNTEER REGIMENT   The Southwell Company, now in course of formation, promises to be a success. A considerable number of very suitable recruits have come forward and the first parade will shortly be fixed. The Company has been fortunate enough to obtain permission from the Territorial Association for the use of the splendid Drill Hall. Intending recruits must send their names to Mr. G. H. Waller, Fiskerton-cum-Morton, and Mr Waller will be pleased to give any particulars required.'

PTE. F. LEE LOSES HIS RIGHT ARM   The news has just reached Southwell that Gunner Fred Lee has been wounded in battle, and the surgeons had to amputate his right arm in order to save his life. Many people will remember this gallant soldier going out to Australia about five years ago. The younger son of the late Mr Robert Lee, joiner and contractor, and brother of the present proprietor of the old-established business, he was doing well in the colony, but joined the Australian Light Horse at the outbreak of war. He saw service in Egypt and later transferred to the Australian Artillery, going to France, and being in action during the battle of the Somme with the Howitzer Brigade. Altogether he has been in numerous battles for over two years. We are pleased to hear he is progressing favourably, and hopes to be in his native town for his Christmas dinner.

PTE. SIDNEY J. SCOTT   Our local correspondent has received an interesting account of his travels and experience in France from Pte. S. J. Scott who was well known in Newark and district as cashier and traveller to Mr Caudwell, Greet Lily Flour Mills, Southwell. After referring to the recent orders from our Food Controller, he says: "I believe there are breadless and meatless days in France, but if so, the business is managed with so little ostentation that one never notices anything different. The French are so adaptable that meals seem as good and food as plentiful as ever. When our rations are short we buy French bread. This is made all one shape – long rolls about 2½ feet long and very palatable and tasty it is slightly brown in colour like our standard bread used to be. I should think it is made from flour milled to about 85 per cent. The only fault appears to be the amount of salt they put in. There is a large modern mill near to where I am stationed, a fine stone structure, I hope to have a trip around it before long. Since I landed in this part of the country I have only experienced one heavy rain and hot broiling sun for three months. We have the minimum of clothing and Indian helmets. Beef has to be practically killed and eaten the same day. Mutton we hardly ever see. Most of food, therefore, is of the tinned variety. I had no idea, before coming to the South of France, that so many articles of food were put into tins. We, however, get plenty of fruit, melons, peaches, grapes, tomatoes etc., about 4d per pound. Figs and lots of other fruits can be obtained at very cheap prices. Although I am a long way from the scene of hostilities, one has not to be long in this country before seeing the terrible effects of the war, also I find out what a great part our country is playing. I was posted to Boulogne from London, which is a busy but picturesque place. I was some time there learning the system of accounts and French money, all our transactions being in French currency and most of our business in the French language. My office was close to the station gates, and it was an inspiring sight to see our troops arriving from the trenches to go on leave. I could well have completed my soldiering there but early one morning had orders to pack kit, draw five days rations, and, along with five others, entrained at 11 a.m. to proceed to —. We got into the Paris express, and stayed one night in the "Queen of Cities", resuming the journey early next morning by a troop express, accompanied by French, French Colonial, Algerian, Arab, Indian, and various other soldiers. Ours was the only British party on board. This part of the journey was most impressive, the natural scenery unsurpassable. I shall never forget such an enjoyable period. Many lovely little woods and forests, pretty little villages dotted here and there in delightful situations. Fine towns, apparently up-to-date in all that constitutes a modern town: and, above all, a well-cultivated and productive countryside. Corn was cut and being led, and although the crops were rather thin, agriculture seemed well done, nothing neglected. But what struck me particularly was that the work was mostly done by oxen and women. There are very few men left in this country. Our train continually took up or put down soldiers just released from farm work, or those returning to the front after a period of such work. Later on we passed through a famous wine-growing district. It was an education to see hundreds of acres of grapes growing out in the open like potatoes in our country, loaded with fruit, and to note the names of the various places in passing, many of them names of well-known wines, and to see the hundreds of barrels stacked up and some barrels on trucks, like our oil tanks in England. It was worth going a long way to see. We arrived here after our long journey, and are camped outside the city. It is a picturesque place in the grounds of a French chateau, on the hillside amongst the trees and flowers, with gardens sloping down to the open sea, and from our dormitory in the morning we get an unparalleled view of the — Ocean. On one side of us is an Indian camp and hospital, below us live the Egyptians, who do all the labouring work, etc. From the nature of my address you will get an idea of what we are doing here. Cannot tell you in this letter. In the next will tell you something of life here. I am fit and well at present, although hours of duty are long. We have comfortable quarters, but are subject to strict discipline. This is necessary in such a cosmopolitan place, but we are doing our best to make the most of the work and situation.''

7 November 1917

'Mr Arthur Wyles, Maythorne, received an intimation from the War Office on Saturday last, that his brother Augustus Wyles, died at Alexandria on the 19th October, from pneumonia. "Gus" Wyles, as he was familiarly known by everyone in the Southwell district, was an old soldier, a member of the old Fourth Notts Volunteer Battalion, who, at the commencement of the Boer war, along with Mr T. Buckels of Westgate, volunteered for active service. They saw much fighting in that campaign, and at the close Wyles had a bad attack of fever, being treated at Netley Hospital for its after effects. He was a fine shot, a marksman, and rendered good service in South Africa, gaining the Queen's medal and four clasps. He again volunteered for active service at the beginning of the present war, and was attached to the 21st Midland Battalion of the Rifle Brigade and did duty at Cairo and other places in Egypt afterwards proceeding to Salonika, being finally transferred to the 802nd Area Company of the Labour Corps. He again went to Alexandria, where he died of pneumonia on the above date, at the age of 48 years.' [photo of Augustus Wyles in the edition for 14 November 1916].

'FOR THE MEN ON ACTIVE SERVICE   The members of the Southwell Traders' Association are making a special effort to send the men on active service a present from the home town this Christmastide. The subscriptions up to Monday amounted to £60 17s. 6d. The flag day on Saturday last produced (thanks to the splendid work of the ladies engaged) £21 9s. 7d. and last year's balance of £13 16s. 9d. makes a total of £96 3s. 4d. Several subscriptions promised are not yet paid in but Mr F. Ewers, the secretary, will be pleased to complete the accounts in order to make the necessary report to the authorities. It is proposed to send the officers a tin of the best cigarettes, and the N.C.O.s and men a postal order, also a greeting card and the best wishes from the old home town. Many of the men have expressed the desire for a P. O., as at the festive season they get boxes of food from friends and relatives; also a more liberal ration is served out to them by the Army authorities. It is hoped to still further increase the subscriptions in order to send the men a money order worthy of the great effort they are making to bring the war to a successful termination.'

'BURGAGE MANOR AUXILIARY MILITARY HOSPITAL   The soldiers at this hospital have for some time past been doing a lot of needlework and when Miss Pavey of Westhorpe Lodge discovered how interested they were and knowing how very heavily time hangs on the hands of our men in the hospitals, she kindly promised to teach them embroidery and offered prizes for the best regimental crests. More than half of the patients entered for the competition, and many more would have done so had it been possible to secure in time the crests drawn for embroidery and the materials. At the invitation of Miss Small, the commandant, and the wish of Miss Pavey, Mrs Battersby adjudicated upon the needlework, and found it no easy task. She expressed herself greatly surprised at the fine quality of the work, the beautiful stitches, and the great attention given to detail and colouring, and said she considered everyone far surpassed her expectations. The prizes presented by Miss Pavey, according to Mrs Battersby's judgment, were:– 1st (wrist watch), Pte. Cutler, Manchester Regt.; 2nd (safety razor) Gnr. Wilshaw, R.F.A.; 3rd (silver cigarette case), Pte. Kirk, Lincoln Regt.; 4th (letter cases), Pte. Beach, Warwick Regt., and Pte. Wilcox, Royal Sussex. Hon. mention; Spr. Wood, R.E. (work unfinished).

Colonel Battersby, in the name of the men, thanked Miss Pavey for her kindness and patience in teaching the needlework, and for the prizes, and said that he would be glad if other hospitals would follow the example of Burgage Manor and arrange needlework competitions for the coming winter. He also thanked Miss Small for the great interest she had shown.'

14 November 1917

'BRACKENHURST HOSPITAL   The Commandant of Brackenhurst Auxiliary Military Hospital wishes to thank Mr C. L. Maltby and friends for so kindly continuing to provide funds for purchasing tobacco and cigarettes for the wounded soldiers; also to gratefully acknowledge the following gifts to the hospital:– Mrs Bainbridge, venison; Mr Wm. Wright, Fiskerton Manor, apples; Mr W. Mountney, honey; Mrs Starkey, rabbits; Mr Kelham, Bleasby Hall, vegetables; Mrs C. L. Maltby, apples and pears; Mr Tatham, partridges; Rev. G. F. Wintour, fruit and vegetables from Upton Church harvest festival.'

ANOTHER NOTED FOOTBALLER KILLED   Many of the noted football players of the Minster town have done heroic service in the battlefield, and another has, alas!, laid down his life. Pte. Herbert Kirk, of Burgage-lane, Southwell, enlisted in the 8th Sherwood Foresters in June 1915, went to France in July 1916, and on October 6th of that year was reported wounded and missing. Nothing further was heard until last week, when the War Office notified his friends that he was killed in action on October 6th, 1916. Herbert Kirk was well known in Newark, since he played in the ranks of Southwell City football team many times against their clubs. He was the professional for Mansfield Mechanics, and also played for several Newark clubs, always being a big scorer. In one season he scored 51 goals for Southwell City, which great feat was acknowledged by that club in the presentation to him of a gold medal. He was a lace maker at Messrs Carey and Co.'s factory, where he will be much missed, his genial nature making him a great favourite with all his workmates. He was killed at the age of 27 years.

'PTE. ROYAL MURRAY KILLED IN ACTION   Mrs Lineker, of Spring-terrace, who adopted the above soldier when a boy, received the sad news last week that he had been killed in action. Pte. Royal Murray, 1/6th Sherwood Foresters, was for many years in the Territorials. Early in 1914 he left them and joined the National Reserve. When war broke out he joined his old Company, and went out to France with the late Major Becher in the spring of 1915. He was sent back to England completely worn out, and having scratched his leg with barbed wire in France, septic poisoning ensued which delayed his recovery. He again went out in December, 1916, and was attached to the 2/6th Sherwoods. In April this year he was seriously wounded near Lens. A shell burst near a big wall, part of which fell on him, and he lay for ten hours before being discovered.

He sustained a fractured collar bone, a fractured knee, and a severe cut under the left eye. After being in hospitals for some time he recovered and again went to France in September this year, this being his third and last time to go to the scene of war, being killed in action on the night of November 4th, at the age of 34. In civilian life Murray was employed by Carey and Sons. He was very intelligent, a great reader of classical books, and studied astrology. In one of his letters to a friend he regretted that he was unable to see the planet Mercury, as although it was placed well for observation where he was wounded but Fritz had upset his calculations. The following letter has been received by Mrs Lineker, who wishes to thank, through the "Advertiser", all friends for their kindness and sympathy in her great sorrow. Captain Maugham, writing to Mrs Lineker, says: – "It is with the deepest regret that I write to inform you that Pte. Murray 242626 was killed in action on the night of Nov. 4th. He died almost instantly after being hit. He is being buried in a British cemetery behind our own lines. Although he had not been with us long, he always did his job well and never complained. With every sincere sympathy, in which the whole Company joins me.''

21 November 1917

'COMRADES OF THE GREAT WAR   An interesting meeting in connection with the above was held in Mr Rumford's large room on Tuesday night last week. Mr T. D. Partington was in the chair, and many of the local men who have done their bit and been discharged were present to hear an address from Major Enderby, but that gentleman had to go to London on important business, and two ex-soldiers from Nottingham gave interesting speeches in explanation of the aims and objects of the movement. Sgt.-Major H. B. Burrows, ex-Sherwood Foresters, said they did not want the discharged soldier to be treated like he was after the Boer war, but to get all money due to him, to find employment for disabled men, to promote the welfare of the wives and children of men who had fallen. The association was absolutely non-political, and the men themselves would have a voice in the management of it. The smallest branch in the country would have all the privileges of the great cities, and it was hoped to embrace not only the N.C.O.s and men but the officer who had risen from the ranks and would return to his former occupation after the war. The subscription was 1s. per year. S.Q.M.S. R. H. Jay, ex-South Notts. Hussars, said they read in the papers, and Parliament had said, that the British Army saved England in the early stages of the war, and they were saving England today. When these brave men came home from the wars they would want a friend to help them to get their pensions and to obtain work. This was what this association existed for, and he hoped a branch would be formed in Southwell. Several questions were put to the speakers and answered, after which ex-Sgt. Spray proposed, and ex-Sgt. Newboult seconded that a branch be formed. This was put to the meeting and carried unanimously. Ex-Sgt. S. Wilson, Farnsfield, was elected secretary pro tem, and the following committee appointed: W. Tuckwood, F. Newboult, A. Peet, J. Spray, and W. Johnson. The chairman was thanked for his interest in the movement and in reply said he should always do what he could for the men who fought the battles in vindication of right against wrong, and wished the association every success in its efforts to benefit the discharged soldier.'

[Note: This is evidence that associations for ex-servicemen had been established before the end of the war, primarily from the experience of the poor treatment shown to returning Boer War military personnel. The Royal British Legion web site notes that it was formed on 15

May 1921 bringing together four national organisations of ex-Service men that had established themselves after the Great War of 1914-1918.]

BRACKENHURST AUXILIARY HOSPITAL   Following the example of other hospitals in the neighbourhood, a very successful competition was held last week among the patients for the best worked regimental badge. Many thanks are due to Mrs Warrand, Westhorpe Hall, who gave the prizes (six in number), and to Lady Savile, who very kindly came from Rufford to judge the work. Her task was not an easy one as some really wonderful specimens were produced. Mrs Wordsworth, who had shown great interest in the men and their work, was present at the competition.

WOUNDED SOLDIERS' CONCERT   A full report of a further concert for wounded servicemen appeared in the paper. Mr Litchfield's orchestral band played for the men.

28 November 1917

'DISABLED SOLDIERS   A flag day was held on Saturday last on behalf of the Nottingham and Notts. Home for Paralysed and Disabled Soldiers. Ladies sold a beautiful autumn leaf and were successful in obtaining the sum of £13 14s. 6d. and there is still one more box to come in.'

A report notes that the annual meeting of members of the Minster Institute 'decided to again allow the wounded soldiers in the town to use the billiard table and other rooms all day free of charge' and that 'about 50 of the members are now serving with the Forces'.

'LANCE-CPL. J. T. JEPSON REPORTED KILLED   Although not officially announced it is feared that Lance-Cpl. John T. Jepson has met his death in the battle area of France. Mr and Mrs Ainger, of Southwell, received a letter on Monday morning from their son at the front asking them to break the sad news to Mr and Mrs Jepson that their son, Tom, was killed on Nov. 20th and buried in a pretty cemetery near to the fighting line. L/Cpl. Jepson was in private life employed by the Southwell Co-operative Society, and joined the Sherwood Foresters. He was wounded at Kemmell [sic] in November 1915 and had been out again for seven months. He had two brothers serving, one of whom recently won the Military Medal. Killed at the age of 23, he will be much missed by a large circle of friends.   His father has been for many years in the employ of the late Mr Kirkland and now of Mrs Kirkland as gardener.'

[Note: Kemmel is a village about six miles south-west of Ypres.]

5 December 1917

'LOCAL CHAPLAIN LOSES ARM   One of the Minster clergy, the Rev. T. W. Windley, has received news that his son, the Rev. F. M. Windley [Francis Morse Windley], chaplain to the forces, was severely wounded in the advance towards Cambrai on Nov. 20th. He was going to a clearing station when a shell exploded over him. The shrapnel cut through the steel helmet he was wearing but, the force being reduced, it only inflicted a scalp wound which was not serious. His left arm, however, was badly shattered. He was conveyed to a base hospital, and there the arm was amputated. He is said to be going on well, and will probably be sent to England soon.

Mr Windley, who only went out earlier this year, previously held a curacy in a large parish near Middlesbrough.'

'LANCE-CORPORAL J. T. JEPSON   The sad news of the death in France of the above soldier is confirmed in a letter received by his parents on Monday. L/Cpl. Jepson was mobilised with the 1/8th Sherwood Foresters in August 1914, and went out with the local territorials in March 1915. He was badly wounded at Kemmel in June of that year, and was sent to Tunbridge Wells Hospital, thence to Ripon Convalescent Home. He was drafted to the 2/8th Sherwoods in March 1917, and killed at the age of 23 on Nov. 20th last. Mrs and Mrs Jepson wish to thank the many kind people who have written and personally conveyed messages of sympathy and condolence to them. The letter from his Platoon Sergeant says: "25th Nov. 1917. I am very sorry indeed to have to convey the very sad news of your son's death. He was a very good lad, and much esteemed by all his chums in the platoon. He died like a hero. I had just put him and another fellow on their post, when a shell dropped among us and killed him immediately and stunned his chum. His death was instantaneous: he never spoke after he was hit. His personal belongings were taken and handed over to Headquarters, and I suppose you will receive them in due course. We buried him and put a cross to mark his grave; it was the only thing we could do for him. I may tell you he was in the big push, and we had reached our objective when he was killed. I showed Sgt. Ainger his grave; he comes from the same place, so if he gets home he will be able to tell you all about it. All his comrades wish me to express their deepest sympathy in your great bereavement to which I add my own."'

SOUTHWELL VOLUNTEERS The enrolment of the Southwell Section of 'C' Company of the 4th Battalion has been performed in a brisk, business-like manner, and between 40 and 50 were enrolled last week. The parade on Saturday and Sunday will be under a special instruction sent from Clipstone Camp. The rifle range is being put in order so the musketry instruction and practice will be carried out.

12 December 1917

A report of Southwell Girls' Club giving 'a most successful entertainment' in support of the fund to send presents to local servicemen.

19 December 1917

'WORKERS' DEFENCE LEAGUE   A meeting of the working class in Southwell was held in Mr. W. Rumford's room on Saturday Dec. 15th, when a large number of both sexes attended to discuss the difficulties of the workers regarding the distribution and prices of food and fuel. Mr G. A. Arnold was voted to the chair, and briefly stated the objects of the meeting and asked those present to suggest some practical method of bringing the workers' complaints in a regular manner to the proper authorities. He quoted the speech of Lord Rhondda, reported in that day's papers, in which the Food Controller stated that he had made many regulations, which should help the poor, but these were not being enforced. Mr J. Osborne proposed that an organisation be formed in Southwell to look after the consumers' interests in these matters and this proposal was carried unanimously. Several titles were suggested, the one finding general favour being the Workers' Defence League. It was further agreed that the subscription be 1s. per annum, payable quarterly if desired in order that the poorest worker might come in. Mr G. A. Arnold was elected president; Mr J. Osborne, treasurer; and Mr J. E. Arnold, New-street, Southwell, secretary. A large and representative committee was elected, with power to add suitable persons. Some discussions took place regarding excess prices of controlled articles, and it was agreed that the committee should enquire into any definite complaints.'

A report of special services in the Minster the previous Sunday 'to commemorate the liberation of Jerusalem from the Turks who have held it for 1200 years.'

[Note: Jerusalem taken by General Sir Edmund Allenby (later Viscount Allenby of Megiddo). He commanded the BEF's cavalry division at Mons and Le Cateau, the first Aisne battle, and the first battle of Ypres. He then commanded an infantry corps in the second battle of Ypres and took over the Third Army on October 1915. He had a poor relationship with Lord Haig. That, and the failure of his cavalry to exploit inadequate German defences during the battle of Arras, led to some loss of reputation. He was transferred to command the Palestine front in October 1917. He was brilliantly successful, capturing Jerusalem in December 1917. Edmund Henry Hynman Allenby was born on 23 April 1861 at Brackenhurst Hall, the family home of his mother, Catherine Anne Allenby, *née* Cane, daughter of the Revd Thomas Coats Cane of Brackenhurst. Allenby Road is named after him.]

A report of a 'Volunteers' Smoker', a 'very pleasant evening' enjoyed by the Southwell Section of the 4th Notts. Volunteer Regiment and their friends who held a 'smoking concert' at the Admiral Rodney. 'Mr Carle's string band was in attendance and performed various selections in most excellent style, contributing in a large measure to the success of the evening's entertainment. Mr R. Ross rendered a couple of patriotic songs in grand style. Pte. Best, Lance-Cpl. Marshall, Sapper Frampton and Sapper Cummings contributed humorous songs and monologues which delighted the audience and fairly brought down the whole house, encores being the rule.' In a speech, Captain Ringrose noted that 'this old island was in about as tight a spot as it had ever been during the war' and said that the local section had instructors who 'were the pick of the experts' who would rapidly train the volunteers into 'an efficient, trained and fully-equipped body of men'.

'COMRADES OF THE GREAT WAR   A report of a meeting in connection with the Comrades of the Great War movement held in Southwell the previous Thursday. It was addressed by Major H. H. Endersby, the district organiser of The Comrades. He pointed out that The Comrades differed from the Soldiers' and Sailors' Federation only in this – that The Comrades included officers as well as men in its membership and the Federation did not, and the Federation strongly opposed the recruitment of discharged men. A point at issue was the working of the Review of Exceptions Act. Until it was repealed the hands of The Comrades were tied. Nevertheless, he said that 'if it could be proved that any discharged soldier had been unjustly or unfairly got at by the working of the Act; "The Comrades" would certainly take up the case and see it through. He personally considered it a shame that any discharged man should be called up again until all the young men who had rushed off to the protected trades, etc, to escape service had been combed out (Hear, hear). He said that he was sorry to say there were a few "artful dodgers" sheltering behind their silver badges – which only they knew how they had managed to get – but for the honour of the nation he trusted they were very few (Hear, hear). Personally he thought the Review of Exceptions Act was for the benefit of these cold-footed gentlemen.'

[Note: The Military Service (Review of Exemptions) Act 1917 was designed to meet the increasing need for soldiers by 'combing out' (the phrase used) men who had claimed exemption from military conscription because they were occupied in civilian occupations essential to the war effort. Evidently there had been cases where men discharged from military service had been recalled to service contrary to what Major Endersby said were 'black and white assurances . . . that no overseas discharged man should be called up again'. The Silver War Badge was issued on 12 September 1916 to men who had served in the armed forces subsequent to 4 August 1914 and who had been discharged or retired from the military forces as a result of sickness or injury caused by their war service.]

2 January 1918

'TWICE WOUNDED   The news has just come through that Lt. and Quartermaster G. J. D. Schumach has again been wounded. Son of the late Mr and Mrs Schumach, Southwell, he was educated at the Grammar School, and when war broke out joined up with the 8th Sherwood Foresters. His ability soon showed itself, and he made rapid progress, gaining the position of Quartermaster in April 1915. He has seen much fighting, and was wounded about two months ago. His brother Fred will be remembered as a lay clerk at the Minster and is also on active service.

'PRESENTATION OF THE MILITARY MEDAL   Private A. Hall, of Westhorpe, Southwell, was presented by General Maxwell, at Newcastle, on Friday week, with the Military Medal, which was given him for bravery in the field on February 10th this year. On that date the Germans made a raid on our trenches, and Hall, hearing a noise at the wire entanglements near to where he was on sentry in the darkness of the night, immediately got his Lewis gun into position and, guided entirely by sounds, commenced to fire. Many of the enemy were caught in the wire and killed, and an officer and nine men taken prisoners. The night before the raid Fritz called over from his trenches, only 40 yards away at this point, that he would come over and fetch the gun, which had been doing deadly work a few days before. Hall is now at home for a few days furlough. '

9 January 1918

A report that the Southwell company of the Volunteers under Sgt.-Major North, R. E. and Sgt. Haddon, R. E., 'are rapidly being trained' and that they were to hold a smoking concert with Sir William Hicking of Brackenhurst in the chair.

16 January 1918

A report that the butchers of Southwell are to close on Mondays and Tuesday until further notice, supplies 'having been cut down by 50 per cent'.

A report that as the billiard table in the Minster Institute was now used by wounded soldiers from the two hospitals in the town, 'it is absolutely necessary' to recover it at a cost of £12 (£460 in today's values). Donations were sought. The Minster Institute was reputed to have the finest billiard table in the area before the facility was made available to the local military.

'SEAMAN'S THANKS   A letter from P.O. [Petty Officer] A. King thanking the people of Southwell for 'Christmas comforts'. 'It is so good of you at home to think of us away; how that small gifts brought back memories of the happy days we spent in that old town of ours. But how many dear ones have left home and will never return. God bless and comfort all who are bereaved and who mourn the loss of their dear ones. Bereavement is never easy to bear. All our hearts go out in love and sympathy to all the poor mothers, wives and sweethearts who are mourning for their loved ones who have gone out to fight for the freedom of our country. We know how they feel as they think of their dear ones in a foreign land or amid the waves without the sight of a loved face or the touch of a mother's or a wife's or a sweetheart's hand to cheer their last moments. May the New Year 1918 bring to us victory and peace, and see us again in the dear old town.'

23 January 1918

'VISIT OF THE REV. T. A. LEE   The Rev. T. Arnold Lee, who left his curacy at Southwell Minster to go as a chaplain to the forces in France, has been on a weekend visit to his former parish, and preached to a large congregation on Sunday afternoon. In the course of an interesting discourse the rev. gentleman said, "It is now 2½ years since I stood in this pulpit. Mine has been a strange experience. Going first to a St John Hospital, I had three months among the wounded, then on to the Somme, where I saw all the fighting. One is filled with admiration at the spirit of the men; their cheerfulness is proverbial, their patience is marvellous. There is no better fighter in the world than the average Englishman. They are ready to go anywhere and do anything. The morale of the Army today is splendid. Those who are wounded and lying at the clearing stations are, in the majority of cases, really anxious to get back to the front. The work of the chaplain is a mixed one. We run concerts, sports, football matches, and work behind the counter at the canteen, and do anything to help the men. There is no cause for pessimism, but a lot for optimism. We work amongst men from all parts of the world, and they are generally glad to see the parson."'

6 March 1918

'A SOLDIER'S DEATH   Mr Henry Brown, Westhorpe, has received the sad news that a grandson, Pte. J. H. Brown of the Cheshire Regiment, who has frequently stayed in Southwell, has given his life in his country's cause. Deceased was the nephew of Mr and Mrs C. Brown, King Street, Southwell, and removed to Colne, Lancashire, some 30 years ago. Pte. Brown, who was 26 years of age, enlisted two years ago in the Motor Transport Corps and was later transferred to the infantry.'   He had been in France for 8 months and was married.

13 March 1918

'LOCAL PIGEONS DOING THEIR BIT   Mr Francis Stout, the secretary of the local flying club, is to be congratulated on the success of his pigeons at the front line. When the War Office asked for a supply of birds to carry messages at the front, Mr Stout sent 20 young birds, and he has been notified that the whole of these birds have rendered conspicuous service, and are worthy of special mention. Major Asman sends his best wishes and thanks for the patriotic assistance rendered, and the Major-General of the General Staff, says, "Reports from France indicate that many lives have been saved and the success of operations assisted in an ever increasing number of cases by the agency of these birds."'

A report of a well attended local meeting of discharged soldiers with a view to establishing a branch of the National Federation of Discharged and Disabled Sailors and Soldiers.

27 March 1918

A notice of the death of Sgt. Herbert Collinson, Normanton, Southwell. He was the second son of Mr and Mrs Thomas Collinson of Morton. He died of wounds on 15 March 1918. He had been employed for eight years at Caudwell's flour mills. His widow was the daughter of Mr and Mrs Ullyatt. 'He died two years to the day on which he went out to France.'

3 April 1918

'BOMBR. E. J. KEMP, SOUTHWELL   Mrs Kemp of Brackenhurst Cottages has received the news that her husband Bombardier E. J. Kemp of the 44th Brigade, R. G. A., aged 37, has been killed in France. No official confirmation has up to the present been received from the War Office, but Mrs Kemp has received letters from the Brigade-Major, the Brigade Chaplain, and the owner of the house in which Bombardier Kemp was billeted. From information contained in these letters it appears that a German shell fell on to the deceased whilst he lay asleep at 5.30 a.m. on the 21st March, killing him instantaneously. Before joining the Army Bombardier Kemp was butler to Sir William Hicking, Bart., of Brackenhurst Hall, with whom he had been for 12 years. He enlisted on July 11th, 1916, joining the 59th Brigade, R. G. A. He went to France in August of the same year, and had been on home leave twice. On returning to France from his second leave, just before last Xmas, he was transferred with his colonel to the 44th Brigade R. G. A. (a South African Brigade). And the Major says in his letter to Mrs Kemp:– "Kemp was very popular with officers and men, and we all recognised him as a fine fellow, a good soldier, and a brave man, and we are going to miss him tremendously." Bombardier Kemp was well known in Southwell and the vicinity, and much sympathy will be felt for Mrs Kemp and her son and daughter. Mrs Kemp wishes to thank all friends for their kind sympathy with her and her family.'

10 April 1918

'PTE. J. H. CURZON, SOUTHWELL   Mrs Curzon, of Westgate, Southwell, wife of Pte. John Henry (Jack) Curzon, Sherwood Foresters, received the sad news in a letter from a Chaplain on Sunday that her husband died on March 23rd, doing his duty for King and Country. Pte. Curzon was the only son of Mr Walter Curzon, gardener, and leaves a widow and three young children for whom much sympathy is felt. As a boy he attended the Southwell Wesleyan School, and later was employed at Messrs Carey and Son's lace factory. At one time he was in the old Volunteers and enlisted in the army as soon as war broke out. He was buried in one of the trenches, recovered, following which he was gassed, and came home about six weeks ago. Pte. Curzon was in the big offensive, and there met his death in the early stages. He was a well-known local footballer, occupying the position of centre-half or full-back for Southwell Town. He had the nickname of "Jolly" and took part in the Notts. League and the Newark and District League.'

'PTE. J. BARKER, HALAM, SOUTHWELL   A notice that Pte. John Barker, Labour Battalion, had died of wounds. 'It appears he was struck by a bomb which was believed to be a stray shot, for he was working at the time and was not supposed to be really in the danger zone nor the line of fire. He was severely injured in the lower part of the body and both legs and on being admitted into the hospital he died immediately afterwards. Pte. Barker, who was 42 years of age, was a native of Southwell, and his parents, now deceased, at one time occupied Rodney Farm, near Bleasby. He went to Southwell National School, and was afterwards with Mr. J. H. Whittingham, printer and stationer, later going to Mr Baldry, contractor. Subsequently he was with Mr Roe, of the Elms, and for the past 15 years he had been employed by Mr J. J. Bates, grocer and provision merchant, King Street, with whom he was up to the time of his enlistment on Aug. 9th, 1916. He was home last December and left on Boxing Day, shortly after which he went to France. Mrs Barker desires to thank all friends for their sympathy in her great bereavement.'

[Note: John Whittingham was a 'bookseller, stationer, printer, book-binder, newsagent' of King Street.]

24 April 1918

A notice that Hubert (Bert) George, son of a former head of the Southwell Wesleyan Days School, was missing. His company commander had written to say that he had been missing since 28 March 1918, 'although it is possible that he may have been attached to another unit temporarily'.

'LOCAL WOUNDED' A notice that Pte. F. M. Bates had been wounded on 27 March. He was the son of Mr and Mrs J. J. Bates (J. J. Bates was a grocer and provision merchant in Southwell). Tim Revill had been wounded and his parents had been allowed to visit him in France. Mr and Mrs Hopewell 'had seen their wounded son in Leicester'. He had been badly wounded in the foot. Mrs and Mrs F. Robinson, Queen Street, had visited their injured son. No first names were given for either.

8 May 1918

'ZEEBRUGGE HERO   Of the volunteers for the daring attack on Zeebrugge very few of the men belonged to Nottinghamshire. Southwell, however, sent one of these gallant boys — Pte. William Albert Hopewell of New Street, Southwell. This lad is now home on leave.'

[Note: The Zeebrugge Raid was mounted by British forces on the night of 22/23 April 1918. It was an attempt to block the exists to Zeebrugge and Ostend harbours by scuttling old cruisers loaded with concrete, thus denying their use to German light naval surface forces and submarines. The operation was conducted with great gallantry at a cost of 500 casualties, but, although it was hailed as a triumph, it was a virtual failure, resulting in only minor damage and disruption. See Chapter 4.]

15 May 1918

'DECORATION FOR BISHOP'S SON   The Rev. E. C. Hoskyns, chaplain to the forces, son of the Bishop of Southwell, has been awarded the Military Cross on the field for conspicuous bravery. Among other acts of gallantry, he successfully brought to safety 50 or more wounded men when there was a real danger of their being taken prisoners during the advance of the enemy. He had been on active service for nearly two years.'

'LANCE-CPL. G. WAGSTAFF WOUNDED   The news has just reached Southwell that Lance-Corporal G. Wagstaff, third son of Mrs Wagstaff, Station Villas, Southwell, and the late Mr William Wagstaff, of Farnsfield, has been badly wounded in the left shoulder. He enlisted in the Sherwoods at 17 years of age, and was wounded in February 1917, sent to France, and wounded again on April 18th last. His relatives have been granted permission to visit him at a Birmingham hospital, and have found him going on satisfactorily.'

A report of the annual general meeting of Southwell Traders' Association notes that the chairman, C. G. Caudwell, in his résumé of the work of the Association during the past year, 'hoped to see the local Traders' Association and Labour so organised as to work amicably for mutual benefit.'

22 May 1918   A report of the dedication, by the Bishop of Newcastle, of a window in the Minster in memory of the two sons of Dr. and the Hon. Mrs Handford, Capt. Henry Basil Strutt Handford, aged 21 and Lt. Everard Francis Sale Handford, aged 20, who were killed in action on the same day, 14 October 1915, during the Sherwood Foresters' assault on the Hohenzollern Redoubt during the Battle of Loos (see entry for 20 October 1915).

In a report of a recent meeting of Southwell Board of Guardians sympathy was expressed to one of its members, Mr A. Straw, who was in London visiting his eldest son in hospital where he was 'suffering from German gas'.

[Note: Alexander Straw was a prominent member of the Southwell Traders' Association. He was a corn miller, baker and grocer with his business in Farnsfield where, in 1918, he lived at The Grange and had two sons. The eldest, Nos. 2339 TF, 239153 and 305509 Pte. William Walter Straw, served with the Sherwood Foresters and the Gloucestershire Regiment, going to France on 2 March 1915. Before he enlisted he was a grocer's assistant in his father's business. The younger son, also Alexander, was born in Farnsfield. In 1911, aged 12, he was a boarder at Southwell Grammar School. He was commissioned 2nd Lt in the 13th Battalion, Notts and Derbys Regiment in 1915, having attended the Officers Training College in Nottingham from where he was posted to Lichfield (report in the *Advertiser* 18 August 1915). A lieutenant, aged 20, he died of wounds on 3 June 1918, and is buried in Sissonne British Cemetery, Aisne, France.]

DEATH AND FUNERAL OF DRIVER J. W. HINDSON   Southwell has lost many of its sons in this present war, but the death of Driver Will Hindson at Catterick Camp, Yorkshire, during the course of his training, is in some respects the most pathetic of all. Joining the Army in January this year, he was attached to A Battery, Reserve Brigade, R. F. A., Scoton Camp, Catterick, and although making several applications for furlough to see his wife and three daughters, was never able to get home, and unfortunately being thrown from a horse about three weeks since, was not admitted to hospital until a few days before he died, his wife being sent for last Monday week, and just got there in time to see him pass away. A wire was received from the camp last Thursday to say the body was on the way to Southwell. Arrangements were made for the funeral at one o'clock on Saturday, a firing party, bearer party, and buglers of the Royal Engineers at Newark were detailed to attend the funeral, and on Friday morning a wire was received saying the funeral must be postponed. The remains of Driver Hindson arrived at Fiskerton on Sunday morning, and was met by members of the Southwell Branch of the Discharged Soldiers, who conveyed the coffin, covered with the Union Jack, to his residence, Rope-walk, Southwell. He had been head horseman to Mr. J. H. Kirkby for seven years, and was highly esteemed by his employer and fellow-workmen, having charge at one time of nearly 40 horses. He died at the age of 41, and was buried in the Minster Churchyard on Monday afternoon. 'Vast crowds lined the route through the town, and many friends and relatives followed him to his last resting place.' These included 'the wives and mothers of those who had fallen in the war'. A report of the funeral follows, noting that 'the body was met at the west entrance by the Bishop of Southwell', the rector (who gave 'a very touching and inspiring address') and the assistant curate. This suggests that even at this stage of the war, the death of every serviceman was keenly felt in the town.

Military Funeral of Driver J.W. Hindson - A. J. Loughton Collection

29 May 1918

'NEWS OF "THE MISSING" The hearts of many have been gladdened this week by the news that Lance-Cpl. Oscar Longmore, son of Mr. and Mrs. E. Longmore, and Pte. P. W. Toder, son of Mr. and Mrs. Toder, King-street, are both well and are prisoners of war in Germany. The former writes a postcard saying that he was taken prisoner on May 21st, and cannot give a definite address; but Toder, in a long letter, says he hopes they have received his postcard (but this has not yet come to hand). "I am allowed to send (he writes) two letters and two postcards a month. My pal and I have received a parcel from the Red Cross Society. Send me plenty of fags, then I shall be quite contented. You can write me as many times as you like; they do not mind at this end, but if you send money send a 10s note, else I cannot change it. I shall only be allowed to write to you, so tell all my friends. I have seen the post-master's son, Oscar Longmore, and Arthur Chambers. I am quite happy and well. Don't worry." Mr. and Mrs. Toder and family wish to thank through the *Advertiser*, the many friends who have been so kind to them in their time of anxiety and distress.'

'MEMORIAL SERVICE AT THE MINSTER' A report of a service held as a 'memorial and thanksgiving' for the fallen. The 'relatives and friends of the noble men who have given their lives in a noble cause' were in the congregation. The names on the Minster Roll of Honour added since the last memorial service had been held were read: Arthur Smith, Walter Robinson, William Drabble, Herbert Twells, Herbert Kirk, Augustus Wyles, Royal Murray, Thomas Jepson, Arthur Whitworth, George Alvey, William Hailey, Herbert Collinson, Edward Kemp, Harold Tyne, John Curzon, John Moseley, and William Hindson. By this date the Roll of Honour contained 67 names.

A case before the previous sitting of Southwell Petty Sessions illustrated the complexity of the food control regulations and local confusion about how they should be interpreted and applied. J. J. Bates, the grocer, answered a summons at the instance of the Southwell Food Control Committee that he 'did unlawfully supply to the Hon. Mrs Handford, of Southwell, for consumption certain bacon not in accordance with the directions prescribed by the Food Controller'. Mr J. Ellis, the Food Controller's executive officer, produced a copy of the regulations which provided for 5 ozs. of bacon per coupon. 'Mary Ellen Knowles, cook to the Hon. Mrs Handford, said that on May 2nd she ordered 2 lbs. of sausages at Mr Bates's grocery shop, left six coupons, and asked that the balance for the coupons should be made up with bacon. Besides the sausages, 2½ lbs. of bacon were sent, and Mrs Handford thereupon returned 2lbs. of the bacon.'

Mr Bates represented himself and cross-examined Miss Knowles. She said that the bacon was supplied from his shop and from nowhere else. Mr Bates, in his own defence, pointed out that there were two kinds of sausages, for one of which double the amount of meat was allowed per coupon. 'It was this latter kind of sausage that Mrs Handford had.' 'Mr Metcalfe pointed out that after allowance for the sausages the coupons remaining were sufficient for 10 ounces, whereas he understood that the amount delivered was 40 ounces.' Mr Bates had to agree with this, but pleaded mitigation. He had read the regulations as saying that one coupon carried an entitlement to 10 ounces of bacon whereas he understood now that one card carrying two coupons qualified for 10 ounces, or five ounces per coupon. A newspaper (the *Newark Advertiser* no doubt) was then produced which ran a report that the Newark executive officer (Mr Ellis's counterpart) had stated that until further notice the value of one coupon would be 10 ounces of bacon. Mr Ellis thereupon told the bench that 'Newark has no jurisdiction in Southwell' whereupon Mr Bates said, not unreasonably, that he had assumed that 'the law for Newark would be the law for Southwell'. From the bench, Mr Merryweather asked, 'Do they vary?', to which Mr Ellis replied that, 'There is only one law throughout the country.' Mr Bates, to laughter in court, said that he could not make bricks without straw, and, extending the biblical analogy, said that, 'The Israelites passed through the Red Sea, but he had been entangled in a sea of red tape.'

For what the bench described as a technical offence, Bates was fined 30s. It was the first case of its kind to be heard by the Southwell magistrates.

26 June 1918

'PTE. ROBERT SCRATON, SOUTHWELL   'The sad news has reached Southwell that Pte. Robert Scraton, son of Mr and Mrs Scraton, Holy Trinity Cottage, Westhorpe, was instantaneously killed by a shell while working his machine gun on June 3rd last. Pte. Scraton was well known in his native town. He was connected with the Post Office from the age of 14, first as a telegraph messenger, and afterwards as auxiliary postman. He joined the Army on February 21st, 1916, and went out to the Irish Rebellion, where he was made Lance-Corporal. He went to France on December 25th, 1916, where he saw much action, and contracted trench fever in June 1917. When convalescent he was transferred to the Machine Gun Corps and went to France again on February 17th, 1918. Letters have been received showing that he was killed instantaneously by a shell while at his gun. His officer wrote: "He was a man I would always have trusted anywhere, and whatever the circumstances he would always be at his gun, ready. From the very first I marked him out as one of my best men. We all feel the loss very much, as in our days we do not meet so many of his sort, always cheery, bright, and willing."'

10 July 1918

The *Advertiser* carried an advertisement for Southwell Aeroplane Week which was to begin on the following Monday. Subscriptions were invited for National War Bonds and for Savings Certificates. If the town and district were to raise £15,000, 'the authorities will give to an Aeroplane the name of our town'. Yet it seems that the town already had an aircraft named after it, for 'Thanks to our civic pride we read in an official dispatch that the Aeroplane "Southwell" has carried the war into enemy territory and harried the lines of communication of the foe — perhaps that it has saved Southwell men from the deadly attack of the Hun, enabling them to return unharmed to their wives and children.'

24 July 1918

A report of the last meeting of Southwell Parish Council noted that the town and district had raised £15,000, or £5 per head of population, during Aeroplane Week. In 2010 this was equivalent to £570,000 and £190 respectively, according to the retail price index. The parish council had also noted the keen demand for council-owned allotments on land on Newark Road, and that more land for allotments was needed in Westgate and Westhorpe.

A further report of the 'great success' of Aeroplane Week noted that a meeting in support of the week had been held in the Assembly Room the previous Tuesday. It had been organised by the W.A.A.C. (Women's Auxiliary Army Corps) for the dual purpose of promoting the W.A.A.C. movement and to give information about investments to further the war. It was chaired by the archdeacon of Nottingham and rector of Southwell, W. J. Conybeare. A Mr Salt said that the W.A.A.C existed 'to get women workers'. This was 'personal service', whereas investment in government securities was 'the service of [our] money'. He argued that if money was not provided voluntarily by investing in government securities [war bonds and national savings certificates], the government would raise it through taxation. 'Therefore, which was better, to invest in Government securities, where the money remained their own at good interest, doing service to their country, or pay it in taxes, when it would no longer be their own?' The sum raised at this meeting alone was £2,664. 11s. 0d. 'including £2,000 from Sir William Hicking' (an investment equivalent to £75,000 in value in 2010). The following Thursday, 'a short dinner-time meeting' at Carey's lace factory raised a further £1,895.

[Note 1: These very large sums were investments that, as the meeting at Carey's was assured, were 'safe, profitable, placed in a good cause, and not locked up'. In fact the subsequent history of war bonds issued by the UK government in the First World War, suggests that, as the Labour Party MP Tom Johnson was to say of the 1917 War Loan: 'No foreign conqueror could have devised a more complete robbery and enslavement of the British Nation.' Successive governments were in effect largely to default on the loan. In March 2012, £1,939 million was still outstanding.

2. The Women's Army Auxiliary Corps (W. A. A. C.) was established in 1917 at the suggestion of Lt. Gen. Sir Henry Lawson. It consisted of volunteers. They were not accorded full military status even though they were subjected to enemy action throughout their service in France.]

31 July 1918

A report notes that the Bishop of Southwell's Sherwood Foresters Fund had made the following grants: £600 to the Sherwood Foresters Regiment Prisoner of War Fund; £600 to the Nottingham Comforts for Troops Fund; and £300 each to the Ilkeston Prisoner of War Fund and the Newark Prisoner of War Fund. [In today's values these grants amounted to over £68,000.]

'SAILOR DECORATED   Pte. W. Hopewell, R.M.L.I. [Royal Marines Light Infantry], son of Mrs Hopewell, 8, Chatham-street, Southwell, has been decorated for distinguished service in the recent Zeebrugge affair. The official description says: – "After the No. 1 and No 2. of his Lewis gun section had become casualties in the ship in which Pte. Hopewell was serving, he took the Lewis gun ashore and brought it into action. He continued to fire the gun through the action, and was almost the last man to retire, bringing the gun out of action with him, until it was rendered useless by a direct hit from a shell." '

'OPEN-AIR WAR AIMS MEETING'   This is a report of a meeting held in Southwell market place the previous Friday to promote 'National War Aims.' It was addressed by J. R. Starkey MP who 'gave an account of the negotiations that led up to the war, and stated in clear and unmistakable language what our war aims are and what we are fighting for. He was repeatedly cheered in the course of his speech.'

[Note: Early in 1918 a National War Aims Committee was established as the principal agency of domestic propaganda within the newly created Ministry of Information, headed by Lord Beaverbrook. In the fourth year of the war, and with, at this stage no early end of it in sight, it was evidently believed that war-weariness had to be combated.]

'PTE. A. L. ARNOLD, SOUTHWELL   Although only 19 years of age last April, Pte. A. L. Arnold, M.G.C. [Machine Gun Corps], son of Mr G. A. Arnold, of Southwell, served at the Front in 1916, and has a splendid record of service up to his death, which event was notified to his parents on Thursday last. Deceased as a boy attended the Wesleyan School at Southwell, and won a scholarship at the Minster Grammar School from whence he entered the employ of Messrs Jardine and Sons, Nottingham [probably John Jardine Ltd., bobbin and carriage maker]. In the fateful week of August 1914, when war broke out, he was at a Scouts' camp at Skegness, and wrote home saying he should join up at once, although only 15 years of age. Failing to get enlisted, he served as a Scout boy at the Territorial Headquarters, Nottingham, until he got a friendly sergeant to stretch his age and chest sufficiently to pass him into the 2nd-7th Sherwoods, in March, 1915, but it was February, 1916, before he landed in France. Owing to the weather, he was soon in hospital with trench-feet. His next birthday came when he was in hospital, and when he confessed to having arrived at 17 years, a kindly doctor chalked up "Blighty" on his bed-head, and to Blighty he came for convalescence. He was then persuaded by his parents to allow his birth certificate to be sent to the Army authorities, with the result that he was transferred to the Army Reserve. In October, 1917, he was recalled to active service. And after a period in the Training Reserve, was posted to Clipstone Camp for machine gun work, and early in May once more went to France, where he has met his death. In a recent letter to his brother, he wrote: "Paradoxical as it may seem, while you are a veritable slave in the Army, it is the most free and glorious life possible."

The first notification that parents received was a letter, dated July 19th, from the C.E. Chaplain, stating that their son was wounded on the previous Thursday. No bones were broken, but he was badly hit in the right leg and thigh, and had lost a lot of blood. The Chaplain wrote: "I was immensely struck by his example of steadfastness and thoughtfulness and his wonderful smile." His lieutenant also wrote, on July 21st, that he was a decent acquisition to the Company. He stated that although badly wounded Pte. Arnold was quite himself all the while he was being taken to the Casualty Clearing Station. The hope was expressed that he would have a speedy recovery, but unfortunately he succumbed to his wounds.

Mr and Mrs G. A. Arnold and family desire to thank all friends for their kind expressions of sympathy in their hour of trial. While it has been impossible to personally reply to all the kind letters received, they assure their friends that their kindly thoughts have greatly helped them in their great sorrow.'

7 August 1918

In a report of the death of Walter Barrett, mention is made of his two sons, Howard and Arthur, both of them photographers, who were with the RAF. (see entries for 12 August 1914, 28 October 1914 and 14 April 1915).

14 August 1918

A report suggesting that a coal rationing scheme is shortly to be introduced.

'OPEN-AIR MEETING' This is a report of a 'demonstration' of 'an enthusiastic character', in the Recreation Ground the previous Thursday, by members of the local branch of the Federation of Discharged Soldiers and Sailors. They had 'paraded the town with the Federation banner' and met to hear speeches from H. Seely-Whitby and a Mr Little from Nottingham.
, the chairman of the meeting, said that it had been 'my duty for some time – and not a pleasant duty – to help men into the Army. Southwell, I am pleased to say, did not want much helping.

The men are most patriotic, and respond loyally to the call of duty. The local tribunal has had a good deal of disagreeable work to do, but it has always been most fair and impartial. Now it will be my duty, and a pleasant duty, to help the men on their discharge from the Navy and Army. In previous wars the men who fought for us were, I am sorry to say, soon forgotten; but we are determined that we shall not forget the noble men who are fighting for us in this war. (Cheers). We shall not forget our duty to them, nor their wives and relatives. When they return we must see to it that we were in honour bound to go into it, and when the men return home, we must see to it that they are not forgotten.' Seely-Whitby, in a characteristic speech', said that 'after other wars the old soldiers had to be collected out of the workhouses, but after this war there would be a transformation scene. They were out to fight for the men who fought for us.'

[Note: These were fine and well-intentioned words, but post-war Britain did not turn out, as Lloyd George had famously promised, to be a land 'fit for heroes to live in' and that the Federation and its supporters hoped for. Initially the post-war programme of reconstruction created jobs, but the huge war debt, and the need for industry to re-tool, created deep economic uncertainty. Unemployment rose sharply and plans to rebuild had to be set aside during the economic slump of 1921. As well known as Lloyd George's hopeful slogan was the sight of unemployed ex-servicemen selling matches from the gutter to scrape a living. Virginia Nicholson quotes one young woman describing the all too common sight in 1920 of 'patient queues of hollow-eyed men outside factories hoping to be taken on . . . who by a nervous movement, a twitching muscle, or a too rigid tension, would betray the fact that they were all in some greater or less degree suffering from shell-shock.' (Virginia Nicholson, *Singled Out* (Penguin 2007), 241).]

An advertisement for a 'Patriotic Fete', to be held at Brackenhurst Hall on 22 August, from 3 to 9 p.m., in aid of the Southwell Red Cross hospitals, promised the following 'entertainments' in the grounds of the Hall: Half-hour Concerts [by the band of the 3rd Reserve, R. E., based in Newark], Silhouette Artist, Palmist, Hoop-La, Fish-Pond, Zoo, Hat-Trimming Competition, Strafing the Kaiser, Soldiers' Work Stall, and dancing on the lawn from 6 to 9 p.m. Tea and light refreshments would be available. The entrance fee was 1s. from 3-5 p.m., and 6d. thereafter, with children admitted half-price. [Note: It is difficult to know what 'Strafing the Kaiser' refers to: it was probably a game of some kind. A silent film *Pimple Strafing the Kaiser* was produced in 1916/7, but the British Board of Film Classification rejected it as unsuitable for screening.]

A report, with a photograph, of the funeral in the Minster of Leonard Raworth, 'formerly with the Southwell Territorials'. His funeral, with full military honours provided by Royal Engineers from Newark, was conducted by the bishop of Southwell and the Revd. J. R. Thomas. The report continues: 'The deceased went to France in February, 1915, and participated in the severe fighting at Kemmel, Hooge, Loos, and the attack on the Hohenzollern Redoubt. He gave many instances of his bravery, and on one occasion was congratulated by the General for voluntarily taking rations up to the line despite very heavy fire. Invalided home in 1916 for a severe operation, he had been more or less an invalid ever since. And passed away on Saturday.'
[Note: Nos. 243 and 1243 Pte Leonard Raworth went to France on 1 March 1915. Before enlisting he had been employed by the Co-operative Society in Southwell before he enlisted. He died on 10 August 1918, aged 25, is buried in the Minster churchyard, and is on the Commonwealth War Graves Commission Debt of Honour index.]

28 August 1918

'LOCAL LAD IN THE FLYING CORPS IN FRANCE   The following is culled from an interesting letter sent by a local flying boy to his parents in Southwell. He says:– "Our surroundings are very pleasant, but the weather very hot. We are down in the south of the country, at a French aerodrome camp, and have done some good work. One day our captain swept a German trench with his machine gun, and then gave the signal to our Scottish and Yorkshire boys to go over the top, and they were soon over and captured the trench. Again we were on the move, the captain and I flying north again. The morning was very dull and cloudy, although the clouds were high. After ascending 2,000 feet we were flying over beautiful country for 50 minutes, when a big black cloud loomed ahead. The machine started rising and falling like a cork on the water, and in two minutes we were surrounded by a thick white mist. It is a funny sensation when you cannot see the ground, and maps are no good at a time like that. The pilot just has to carry on with the aid of his compass. Then he put the nose down and came out of the cloud only 200 feet from the ground. Seeing an aerodrome on our left, we just managed to clear some trees and land. We resumed the flight after lunch, and landed at "the city", where we had to stay four days, and had a nice time. The large buildings, beautiful gardens, and avenues surprised me. On Friday we were all in the air again early and speeding on our way. The course took us quite near the firing line, and we could see the flashes from our guns, and the town being shelled was on fire. Sir D. Haig's army was on the advance, and we heard they did very well. We flew for four hours at an average speed of 70 miles an hour." '

11 September 1918

'PTE. R. S. GILBERT WOUNDED   Mrs. Gilbert, of Easthorpe, has received a letter from the Chaplain of a French Casualty Clearing Station, informing her that her husband has been wounded in the chest, and urging her to keep her spirits up, as he is going on as well as can be expected. On Friday morning she had a letter from the Private himself, informing her that he was wounded, but was going on all right. Prior to his enlistment three years ago he was with Messrs Berry Bros., coal merchants, and joined the Sherwood Foresters, but has since been attached to a London regiment. He went out to France a year ago last February, and was home on leave about eight weeks ago, when he was quite well, so it appears he had only just gone up to the line again when he was wounded. A brother, Pte. Edwin (Tich) Gilbert, Sherwood Foresters, was killed in action three years ago (23/3/16), and three other brothers are serving, one in England and two in France – viz., Pte. Harry Gilbert, M.G.C., Pte. Jack Gilbert, K.R.R., and Pte. William Gilbert, R.E.'

A report of the wedding in the Minster of Lieutenant Cyril Thomas Clarke, the eldest son of Inspector and Mrs Clarke, and Constance Olive Mary Clarke, daughter of Mrs and the late Mr John Clarke, of Sheffield. 'The bridegroom, who is well known and highly respected in Southwell and district, joined the Army at the outbreak of war. He served in France for many months, and having shown conspicuous ability as a machine-gunner, was sent back to England to take a commission and is now a machine-gun officer in the R.A.F.'

[Note: Lt. Cyril Thomas Clarke served with 62 Squadron RFC/RAF as squadron armaments officer.]

2 October 1918

A report that Pte. H. T. Leonard was missing in action. He had attended Southwell Wesleyan church 'for some years' and was a local preacher. He was educated at Farnsfield School and Southwell Grammar School, and had matriculated in London University. He served with the East Lancs. Regiment.

[Note: In 1911, Harold T. Leonard was 12 years old and was a boarder at Southwell Grammar School.]

9 October 1918

A report that Cpl. of Horse Fred Buckels, son of the late Mr W. Buckels of Farnsfield had been wounded and was in hospital in France. He served with the 2nd Battalion the Life Guards, having joined the army in 1915 at the age of 23. Cpl. Buckels was 6' 6" tall with 'a magnificent physique, and had been serving in France 'in the thick of the fighting'. He had been made an orderly to the king. Fred Buckels had four brothers who were serving, or had served, in the army, one of whom, Tom Buckels, had recently been discharged after many years including service in the Boer War.

23 October 1918

'LT. COL. A. HACKING WOUNDED'   A report that Alfred Hacking, a son of the archdeacon of Newark, Egbert Hacking, of Hill House, Southwell, was in hospital suffering from wounds to the right arm and right thigh sustained on 4 October.

Note: Alfred Hacking and his brother Capt. the Revd Egbert Melville Hacking (who served as a combatant and not as a chaplain), had together been gazetted second lieutenants on 3 October 1914 into the 1/8 Notts and Derbys. Both were wounded in action. Alfred Hacking went to France in March 1915. He served throughout the war, was mentioned in dispatches and won both the DSO and the MC.

6 November 1918

'SGT. G. W, FOSTER, SOUTHWELL Sgt. G. W. Foster, landlord of the White Lion, was in the National Reserve at the outbreak of war, and afterwards went with the London Rifle Brigade to India, where he passed an examination for the Sanitary Section, and, after volunteering for Mesopotamia, was attached to the Northumberland Fusiliers. He was out three years, during which time he saw service in India, was through Palestine, and for a year had been in Mesopotamia. He wrote home from Italy on the 7th, saying that he was leaving on the following day for England, as he had obtained a furlough, and hoped to arrive in Southwell within nine days for a month, but on Tuesday night a telegram came from the Records Office, York, stating that he was in a rest camp at Cherbourg dangerously ill with pneumonia. Another telegram on Friday conveyed the sad intelligence that he had died early on Thursday morning. He was 48 years of age, and leaves a widow, three sons and two daughters, two of the sons being in France, as well as a son-in-law. He was the eldest son of Mr. Wm. Foster, White Swan, King Street, and much sympathy is felt for his family.

[Note: No. 205928 Sgt. George William Foster died on 24 October 1918, aged 47, and is buried in Tourlaville Communal Cemetery, Manche, France.]

'WAR MEMORIAL   In this month's magazine the Rector (Ven. Archdeacon W. J. Conybeare) says: – "I venture to suggest that it is time we all began to think about what should be our local war memorial. Should it be a building which could be used for the good of the community, where lectures could be given, where books could be had, and where there would be room for quiet reading? It might prove best to enable our ancient Grammar School to be better equipped for the exceedingly important work it has to do. This would be of general use owing to the free places which are yearly offered to boys of Southwell and district. The school dates from Saxon times, and is nearly 900 years old. How grand it would be to give it new vigour as a memorial for our Southwell lads. I only throw out these ideas so as to set us thinking, and very likely some other idea may be suggested which would prove better."'

A report of the death in action of Pte. G. F. Rose. He had worked at Kirkby's, and went to France in 1916 with the Sherwood Foresters. He went 'over the top' on 14 October 1918, 'and afterwards his dead body was found, death having been instantaneous from a shell'. He was the son of Mr and Mrs T. Rose of 69, Wood Street, Mansfield.

[Note: There is not record of this Pte. G. F. Rose, Notts and Derbys Regiment, on the CWGC debt of honour index.]

A report of the death in action of Pte. James Stubbs, son of Mrs James Stubbs, of Shepherds Row, who had been killed 'in the recent fighting'. He also had been an employee of Kirkby's, and, later, of the Southwell Gas Company. 'He was very popular in the Minster town, and much sympathy is felt for his widow and little daughter.' [

Note: No. 123238 Pte. James Sidney Stubbs served with the Machine Gun Corps (Infantry). The CWGC gives his date of death as 21 October 1918. In 1911 he was 22 years of age and living in Southwell. He is buried in St Aubert British Cemetery, Nord, France.]

13 November 1918

'PTE. H. R. EWERS, SOUTHWELL A life of promise has been brought to an abrupt termination by the death of Harold R. Ewers, Royal Warwickshire Regiment, younger son of Mr and Mrs F. Ewers, of Burgage, Southwell. He was only 20 years of age, and the following letter has been received:– "Dear Mrs Ewers, It is with my deepest sympathy that I write to inform you of your son's death. He died almost instantly, a bullet going through his head. He was a good lad and showed great pluck. Pte. Ewers, your son, was in my Platoon, and was always willing and well liked. You can rest assured that he has been buried respectably. You may wonder who is writing. I am his Platoon Sergeant, and I am sure you will understand how I feel, so I will close with my deepest sympathy to all of you, Yours respectfully, Glaister Diggins." Harold Ewers was born at Burton-on-Trent. And was only five years of age when his parents came to Southwell, his father being the worthy manager of the local branch of Messrs Marston, Thompson Evershed and Co. He was educated at the Minster Grammar School, and while there was a member of the Cadet

Corps, being one of the team selected for shooting at Bisley, when he won the Donegal badge. He was appointed a clerk at the London, City and Midland Bank at Kettering on August 1st, 1914, and was subsequently transferred to Mansfield in a similar position in the same Company. He joined the Army on February 7th, 1915, and on arrival in France was posted to the Royal Warwickshire Regiment. He came home on leave in March 1918, while he was gassed on August 10th last, during the whole of which period he was a runner, and was in the fighting line again on October 8th, as a rifleman, being killed in action between the 20th and the 27th of that month. Much sympathy is felt for Mr. and Mrs. Ewers in their sad loss, especially considering that peace is approaching so rapidly, and they wish to thank all kind friends for the consideration shown to them in the death of their dear son, whose elder brother Lt. Leslie Ewers, is with the Border Regiment, on the Tigris, and of whom no news has been forthcoming for some weeks.'

[Note: No. 29699 Pte. Harold Richmond Ewers was killed on 24 October 1918, aged 20. He is buried in Cannone British Cemetery, Sommaing, Nord, France. Marston, Thompson and Evershed were brewers, with its Southwell premises in Westgate. Frank Ewers was its local agent and manager. He was also the secretary of the influential Southwell Traders' Association.]

'PTE. A. G. STANLEY, SOUTHWELL "He gave his life for his God and his fellow men", is the apt description of the death of Pte. Archibald George Stanley, Durham Light Infantry, in which he was a patrol scout, only son of Mr. and Mrs. Herbert Stanley, Queen-street, Southwell, to whom a chaplain has written stating that death was caused by a machine gun bullet on the night of October 28th. Deceased attended the Minster Grammar School, and afterwards entered his father's business as a painter and decorator, and for a year was the sole head of the firm owing to Mr. Stanley's illness. He enlisted on October 4th, 1917, and went into training at Catterick, being ultimately placed in the Durham Light Infantry, and was stationed at Westgate, Kent, previous to going to France.'

[Note. No. 79595 Pte. A. G. Stanley is buried in Esquelmes churchyard, Pecq, Hainaut, Belgium.]

20 November 1918

A report telling of the impact of the influenza epidemic on Southwell which was resulting in 'many deaths'. Several businesses had been 'finding it difficult to carry on'. All of the Minster choirboys had been affected and had been absent the previous Sunday, and two organists were 'severely ill.' On that Sunday, 'Miss Calvert came to the rescue and played the hymn tunes on the harmonium, while the Rector read the prayers. The afternoon musical service had to be abandoned.'

[Note: The 'Spanish' 'flu pandemic, 'La Grippe', in late 1918 and into 1919 was devastating, killing more people than was claimed by the Great War. It has been variously estimated that between 20 million and 40 million people were killed world-wide and that about one-fifth of the global population was affected.]

27 November 1918

A report of the award of the MM to Lance-Cpl. J. L. Foster, of Woodborough House, Southwell, the second son of Mr T. Foster. The medal was awarded 'for gallant service rendered to his country on October 1st and 2nd'. J. L. Foster went to France in February 1917, and had been wounded at Christmas 1917. He served with the Royal Scots, as did his brother Pte. T. B. Foster who was a battalion runner with the regiment in France.

The 'flu epidemic was still having a severe effect on the town.

4 December 1918

The Roll of Honour in the Minster now contained the names of 82 officers and men from the town who had been killed in the war. The report noted that this was from a population of 3,000, and 'shows how well the Minster town responded to the call of King and country, and given their lives for the cause of the great ideals which brought us into the conflict'.

The Residence was being used as a soup kitchen for the town's many 'flu victims.

11 December 1918

A report that the MM had been awarded to Cpl. Richard Harvey, eldest son of Mr and Mrs John Harvey of Easthorpe. He had served with 1/8th Sherwood Foresters since the outbreak of the war, before which he had been an employee at Carey's lace factory. The report continued: 'He had received a card from his Brigade-Major, of 46th Division congratulating him for his conspicuous bravery in the field.'

18 December 1918

'DIED ON THE WAY HOME   Very pathetic is the death of Pte. Percy Walter Toder, third son of Mr. and Mrs. J. Toder, of King-street, Southwell, who have received the following telegram: – "Rotterdam. Regret to announce the death of Pte. P. W. Toder. Died yesterday (Tuesday) from pneumonia. – Oldbert, British Red Cross, Rotterdam." Pte. Toder was employed by Mr. J. J. Bates when the war broke out, and joined the Army in November, 1914. He was in the 2/5th Notts and Derbys, and in all the battles fought by them in 1915 was always in the thick of the fighting. Wounded at St. Eloi, and later suffering from trench feet, our hero came home for a short time, then went back to France, and was captured by the Germans at Bullecourt on 21st March this year, being sent to a coal mine at Dulmen. He often complained of the hardships endured by the prisoners. He left Germany on Nov. 26th, and in the long march to Holland was the first man in the column, cheering the men on who were lagging behind, and calling out, "Come on lads; never mind being tired. We're going home now." Arriving in Holland, he was attacked with pneumonia, and died as above stated, at the early age of 22. In a letter to his aunt at Mansfield, Toder said the Germans were working them all to death. Mr. and Mrs. Toder and family wish to thank all the friends who have been kind to them in their time of great sorrow.'

[Note: No. 242617 Pte. Percy Walter Toder died on 10 December 1918. He is buried in Numegen (Rustoord) cemetery, Netherlands.]

1 January 1919

A long article in *The Newark Advertiser,* reviewing the past year, carried a paragraph on the effect of food rationing. It asked, 'What mark has the past year left on the social life of Great Britain?' The transformation since 1914 had been gradual, but 'in some respects the changes of the last nine months of the war were the most striking of all. It is hard now to realise that the food ration system dates from February. The Food Ministry had long prepared us for this radical interference with our habits, but Lord Rhondda, like Lord Devonport who preceded him, had naturally shrunk from so forbidding a task. On February 25th meat and sugar were rationed in London, and a fortnight later the schemes came into operation in the provinces. Butter, margarine, fats and jam have successively come within the scope of the arrangement, which must outlast the war for a considerable time.'

The article congratulated the government on carrying out this policy so successfully, though 'the Ministry has made some of the mistakes which are inseparable from bureaucracy. That it has made so few may well be the wonder of posterity' – a comment which Mr J. J. Bates, the Southwell grocer, may well have read somewhat ruefully! (See entry for 29 May 1918).

8 January 1919

How the men from Southwell who had died during the war should be commemorated was a question that exercised many. The rector, W. J. Conybeare, had argued that a memorial should take the form either of a library and reading room open to all or equipping the grammar school 'for the exceeding important work it has to do' (see entry for 6 November 1918). A recent meeting of Southwell Parish Council had considered the question. Arthur Salt, the chairman, said that 'several different things had been mentioned to him, such as a public hall with offices and rooms for the Council, a reading room and library, baths and washhouses, almshouses for the disabled in the war, a large public monument for those who had fallen in the war, and various other schemes.' Although 'nothing could be too good to commemorate the great sacrifice the men had made' the question was what was 'the most fitting thing within their grasp': in other words, though he did not say this so directly, what could the town afford to pay? Mr Merryweather proposed that a committee be formed to consider the question. Whatever form the memorial took, he said, it 'must be undenominational in character'. This was put to the meeting and carried.

15 January 1919

A report that Miss E. M. Small, commandant of Burgage Manor auxiliary hospital since August 1914, had been awarded an OBE.

[Note: the Order had been created by George V only a few months previously, on 4 June 1917.]
'C. L. B. AND PRISONERS OF WAR   A very pleasant gathering took place in the Trebeck Hall on Thursday, when the local troop of the Church Lads' Brigade held their annual social, presided over by the Rector (the Ven. Archdeacon Conybeare). The guests included the following

local men who have been prisoners of war in Germany and now returned home: – Sgt.-Major Scruton, Lance-Cpl. Oscar Longmore, Pte. W. Shepperson, Pte. Jack Partington, and Pte. Scraton. Several other local prisoners were prevented from attending by prior engagements. Others present were the wardens of the Minster, Mr. T. D. Partington, Lt. F. Murden, Sgt.-Instructor North, R. E., Mr J. Sturgess (bandmaster), Mrs Conybeare, Miss Leah Sturgess, and others. After tea the Rector said he had a very pleasant duty to perform. The Southwell Traders' Association had very kindly sent all the soldiers and sailors a present of money from the home town, and as it was difficult to locate the exact place of the prisoners of war, it was decided to keep theirs back until they arrived home, and it was his pleasing duty to now ask them to accept their present, and he, in the name of Southwell and especially the Church he represented, gave them a hearty welcome home. The men thanked the Rector for his kind remarks, and the remainder of the evening was spent in games, songs, etc. Mr Partington very generously presented the men with cigars, and Mr Henry Merryweather, Jun., brought a basket of fine apples.'

'PTE. J. W. TODER   Private J. W. (Jack) Toder, 2nd/5th Notts and Derbys, third son of Mr. and Mrs W. Toder, King-street, Southwell, has unfortunately died while on his way home from captivity. He had been a prisoner in Germany since March 21st. After great hardships he and others reached Sittard, Holland, in sore plight, their boots having been worn through, while their socks and clothing were in rags. Pte. Toder was attacked by influenza, which developed into pneumonia, and he passed away on December 10th. Born in Newark, he had lived in Southwell since seven years old. After leaving school he worked for Mr J. J. Bates, at the Central Stores, from whence he enlisted in October 1914, in the 8th Sherwood Foresters, and was transferred several times, finally into the 2nd-5th. He saw much fighting, and was wounded at St Eloi. On Thursday morning his parents received photographs of the grave at Sittard, together with the ribbons from the wreaths, which had been placed upon the coffin by some friends out there. Only 22 years of age, he was greatly liked because of his genial disposition. Mr and Mrs Toder wish to thank all friends for sympathy shown to them.'

[Note: This is another version of the notice of the death of Percy Walter Toder in the edition for 18 December 1918, with additional details. The name here is erroneously given as J. W. Toder.]

29 January 1919

'CAREY'S VICTORY BALL'   A report of a ball held in Trebeck Hall. Music for dancing was provided by the Southwell Orchestral Band under the direction of F. Litchfield. Mr N. [Neville] A. Metcalfe and Pte. Jack Partington were the MCs. Two hundred people attended.

5 February 1919

'AUXILIARY HOSPITALS CLOSING   This month will see the end of the splendid work accomplished by the two Red Cross Hospitals. Great credit is due to Lady Norton Hicking, and Miss E. M. Small, the Commandants, for the excellent work done in nursing the wounded soldiers back to health and strength. The staff of nurses and all engaged in the good work are worthy of the highest praise for the many hours they have given to the discharge of their self-imposed task; and also Sir William Hicking for so generously allowing the use of his two houses, Brackenhurst Hall and Burgage Manor.'

The local branch of the Discharged and Demobilised Sailors' and Soldiers' Federation held a dance in the Assembly Rooms the previous Thursday. Two hundred attended, 'including wounded soldiers from Burgage Manor and Brackenhurst Auxiliary Hospitals'. Mr Litchfield's band once again supplied the music.

'LAND WORKERS' RALLY   An interesting gathering was held in the Trebeck Hall on Friday week, when the village land workers of the Southwell Petty Sessional Division met to receive the armlets, certificates and stripes to which they were entitled for the work on the land during the war. The workers were composed of women and girls from 15 years of age and upwards, and accompanied by the registrar from each village. All of them had a splendid record of work accomplished on the land; several had worked continuously since the commencement of the war, and were worthy of even greater honours than were bestowed upon them. The presentation was made by Miss New, the county organising secretary of the Women's War Agricultural Committee. She was introduced to the audience by Mrs Conybeare (the president of the Southwell branch). Miss New gave a most interesting address on the valuable work being done by women in food production during the war, and the great need that still exists for them to do all in their power to help, both on account of the scarcity of labour and the great shortage of food supplies all over the world, due to the war and the poor harvests of recent years. She expressed great pleasure at the number of workers in the local branch and the excellent record of work done. "I have wondered," she said. "why so few of the regular Land Army girls were employed in the Southwell district. Now I know, because you have such a fine body of local women at work. Though you are not enrolled in the Land Army and cannot wear the uniform, you are none the less an integral part of the great Women's Land Army, and are also recognised by the Government as such." After the presentation tea was handed round by the registrar and Boy Scouts, who had kindly given their services for the afternoon; and the meeting concluded with an enjoyable entertainment, consisting of songs and sketches by Miss Pitchford, Southwell, Mrs. and Miss Bond, Eakring, and the Misses Wagstaffe. The audience of about a hundred women and girls showed their appreciation of each item by loud applause.'

12 February 1919

'ANOTHER LOCAL LAD DIES IN FRANCE   The parents of Private Fred Ball, of Norwood Fields, received the sad intimation last week that he was lying in the Canadian Hospital, Calais, dangerously ill with influenza, and next day came a wire to say that he was dead. Pte. Ball was in the Labour Corps, and had been in France over two years. Before joining the colours he was employed at the lace factory. And joined up in October 1916. At the time of his death he was waiting to be demobilised. The other brothers in the Army are: Albert, in the Labour Corps, and Herbert, in the Royal Fusiliers. The two latter are still in France. Much sympathy is felt for the family in the painful bereavement, as he was expected home in a few days.'

26 February 1919

A report that the local egg collection will cease at the end of March because the National Egg Collection was 'purely a war measure'. The last local collection would be on 19 March.

A Victory Ball had been held at the Saracen's Head the previous Friday evening. Dancing had commenced at 10.30 p.m. and continued until 2.30 a.m., with 'music supplied by local gentlemen with piano and violins'.

A report that the local 'Labourers' Union' had nominated a Mr Willoughby to serve on the Southwell Food Control Committee, but that a Mr Moore, nominated by the Co-operative Society, had been elected. It was noted that no retail traders now served on the committee. (See entry for 19 December 1917).

12 March 1919

Report of a public meeting that had been held by the Southwell branch of the National Federation of Discharged and Demobilised Sailors and Soldiers, presided over by Mr T. D. Partington. 'The audience included several recently demobilised servicemen.'

A meeting of Southwell Board of Guardians the previous Friday had been told by a Mr Richardson that he thought 'that the Old Age Pension was very inadequate for those old people unable to work and in view of the likelihood of a further increase in the price of coal'. In the light of this he gave notice that at the next meeting of the Board he would move that it approach the Government, calling attention to the inadequate allowance. Mr Marriott observed that the Board would 'have to raise the allowance to their own poor people'.

19 March 1919

'PARISH COUNCIL ELECTION   It is many years since so much excitement and interest was exhibited in the local parish council election. Some weeks since a meeting of the various workmen's organisations was held to consider a more democratic representation on the District and Parish Councils, the outcome being that the members are being nominated by the Southwell Co-op Society, the Workers' Defence League, the local Lace-Makers' Union, the Federation of Discharged and Demobilised Sailors and Soldiers, and the Women's Institute. About 13 of the present parish council are standing again, and several ladies and gentlemen of the town are coming forward as candidates, so that very keen competition is looked forward to.'

[Note 1. This is an example of the extent to which the First World War energised local working class organisation. One crucial effect of the war was that working men and women now expected some reward for their sacrifices. With so many of the young men of the town having enlisted, either as volunteers or as conscripts, and experiencing the need to accept responsibility and to show mutual loyalty and discipline under fire, it was inevitable that they would demand a voice in the democratic process, now open to all men over the age of 21 and women of 30 and over (providing that they held property) under the provisions of the Representation of the People Act 1918. This Act enfranchised more British citizens than all the previous Reform Acts put together, with the total electorate increasing from 7.5 million in 1910 to some 20 million. It was argued that only women aged 30 and over should be enfranchised because had women of 21 and over been granted the vote they would, owing to the carnage of the war, have outnumbered men. In this event the majority of voters would never have exercised the right to vote before, and it was feared that this might destabilise the political process. This argument was disputed, but women of 21 and over were not enfranchised until 1928.

Note 2. The Women's Institute was established in 1915 in part to promote to wartime food production but, at least as significantly, to provide women with a forum and experience practical democracy. This they did by voting for their officers by secret ballot. So it was that the WI put up a candidate at these local elections. However, every chairwomen of the national WI until 1961 was a titled Lady. For the result of the election see the entry for 9 April 1919.]

2 April 1919

A long letter from Ida K. Fairweather, of Clinton Cottage, Southwell, the local depot controller of the national egg collection since its inception, giving statistics both for the previous year and for the four years of the scheme's operation. As to the latter, the letter continued: 'Eggs given, 84,305 (estimated value £850), bought, 3,777, sent to London Central Depot, 59,293.' It seems that the balance had been given to the Burgage Manor auxiliary hospital. It had received regular supplies of locally collected eggs throughout the war. In the early months of the scheme in an average week 25 - 30 per cent of eggs collected were donated to this hospital.

In her letter Ida Fairweather paid warm tribute to the egg collectors, many of whom 'had worked for the whole of the four years, since April, 1915, and all of them have our very sincere thanks for the splendid way they have carried on, often under extremely trying weather conditions, but it was never neither too cold, hot or wet to bring along the eggs for our wounded men, and it has meant much personal sacrifice on the part of both collectors and contributors alike, to make up our splendid total.' Ida Fairwweather also thanked 'Messrs Merryweather and Sons for the help they have so willingly given in carting the full cases to the station and the hospital each week; while many thousands of eggs would never have reached the soldiers without the help of Messrs Kirkby's and Mosedales's bakers' and to 'Messrs Hall and Harvey who have delivered to us, free of charge, the country consignments'.

9 April 1919

'PARISH COUNCIL   For the Parish Council the candidates and number of votes cast were as follows:– Elected: J. Leek, 577; T. Foster, 528; N. A. Metcalfe, 436; L. N. Barrow, 392; J. H. Kirkby, 387; A. T. Metcalfe, 384; A. Salt, 382; J. J. Bates, 366; E. A. Merryweather, 352; C. L. Maltby, 333; H. Merryweather, 326; R. S. Stanley, 295; F. Ewers, 291; A. Woodruff, 274; A. M. Larrington, 240. Not elected: R. Sale, 236; Mrs Arnold, 214; F. Porter, 207; H. Stanley, 193; J. Moore, 175; F. Preston, 162; W. Beresford, 156; H. T. Jackson, 145; Mrs Grocock, 138; G. Greenfield, 138; Mrs Brown, 126; Mrs Butler, 108; and G. Bancroft, 97.

The former members of the Council who were candidates were re-elected, with the additions of Mr F. Ewers, secretary of the Traders' Association, and Mr A. M. Larrington, a member of the Democratic Union.'

[Note: Former members of the council who chose to stand again were re-elected. They very largely represented the town's traders, its principal employers, despite a substantial working class opposition, many of whom, both men and women, would have been exercising, for the first time, a newly-won right to vote and therefore to stand for election. The total votes for the candidates who were elected, 5563, was some 73 per cent greater than for those who were not elected. The only obvious representative of the working class on the new council was Arthur Morris Larrington, who secured the final place on the council. He was 53. In the 1911 census he gave his occupation as 'Foreman, Lace curtain trade'. Mrs Arnold may have been the wife of a 'local labour leader' (see entry for 30 July). J. Moore represented members of the Southwell Co-operative Society (see entry for 26 February 1919).]

16 April 1919

'VILLAGE WAR MEMORIALS'   A report quoting a letter to the *Nottingham Guardian* suggesting that a new general hospital be built 'as a town and county memorial to our fallen'.

23 April 1919

'C' Company, 4th Battalion Notts Volunteers, photographed during the war opposite the Drill Hall, Newark Road, Southwell. They later became 12th Volunteer Battalion, Sherwood Foresters
Private Collection, P. Cant.
   Back Row, left to right, No. 1 Fred Cook, No. 2 Bill Cant, No. 4 Arthur Chamberlain,
      No. 5 Ted Scarborough, No. 9 Mr Pickard, No. 11 Tom Shaw, No. 12 Jack Dolby.
   Front Row, left to right, No. 4 Mr Smith, Middle Sgt Instructor North of Farndon,
         No. 12 George Mosedale, No. 13 Sam Ulyatt.
               (Peter Cant)

At the recent meeting of Southwell Board of Guardians the question of the working hours of the Poor Law officers was raised. Mr Shipsides observed that 'as employers of labour [the Board] should try, by better methods to strikes, to give to the people they employed better conditions'.

[Note: Mr Shipsides, who served on the Southwell RDC also, was evidently one of the more liberal and socially sensitive of members of these influential local committees.]

For many months after the Armistice the *Newark Advertiser* ran a regular and comprehensive column under the headline 'Demobilisation Notes'. It covered all aspects of demobilisation including the pressing issues of civilian employment, unemployment benefits, housing, and the support of disabled men. In this edition it noted that by this date, nearly 600,000 servicemen still awaited demobilisation, of which 47,000 were officers and 550,000 were other ranks. Of this total one third had served with the Expeditionary Force in France, very many from the early days of the war.

30 April 1919

'DEATH OF AN EX-SOLDIER   Many local people will learn with regret of the death of ex-Private John Harry Brown of Maythorne, Southwell. Deceased joined the 1st Sherwood Foresters in January 1915 and went out to France in April the same year. He was in the severe fighting at Ypres, Cambrai, and several places on the Somme, being wounded in July 1917, his injuries being a bullet wound and fracture of the shin bone. He was in hospital many months, and underwent several operations. The effect of his hardships in the war told upon his constitution, but being discharged in 1918 he again took up his duties as van man with Mr Kirkby, delivering bread in Newark, where he was well-known. He was taken ill a few days ago and pneumonia attacking an enfeebled constitution he passed away on Friday night at the age of 31, leaving a wife and little daughter to mourn their great loss. His other brother, Vincent, was killed in 1916, and his father, one of the old Southwell Volunteers, is now fighting at Archangel.'   (See the entry for 19 September 1917.)

[Note: British troops were sent to Archangel and Murmansk in 1918 as part of an international force defending UK interests during the Russian Civil War, and providing support for the pro-monarchist White Russian forces opposing the Bolsheviks. With other Allies they formed the North Russian Expeditionary Force. The NREF, in which 13,000 British and Commonwealth personnel served, with more than 600 being killed and wounded, was finally withdrawn from Archangel in October 1919. The campaign was popularly known as 'Churchill's War', 'the Great Russian Gamble', and 'Whitehall's Folly'. See the entry for 22 October 1919.]

14 May 1919

The annual dinner of C Company (Southwell section) of the 12th Volunteer Battalion of the Sherwood Foresters was held on 8 May in the Crown Hotel. Lt. Page recalled the time when volunteers had 'a very important and necessary duty in mounting guard over the pontoon ground at Farndon, and the trio on duty on alternate Friday nights included a representative of that district, as well as another, and Newark. Two of them were the sole representatives of their district, and the result of a midnight discussion was a determination on the part of their good friend Cpl. Waller, to endeavour to raise a section at Southwell. As to the success of his efforts this section spoke for itself. Unfortunately, Cpl. Waller had not enjoyed the best of health, but he had been ably assisted by Cpl. Mills in the raising of the section, and by Sgt. North and Sgt. Slaney on the training. While they were proud of the Newark Company, he felt especially and particularly proud of the two country sections because he had had some hand in their raising and training. At the very enjoyable camps the Southwellians were always very happy soldiers. In shoots too they had made their mark, and he was sure that in the years to come they would look back with the greatest possible pleasure to the time they had spent in the Volunteers.'

21 May 1919

At the recent meeting of Southwell Rural District Council the clerk reported that the following war trophies had been offered to the RDC: a damaged German machine-gun, a German ammunition box and a German ammunition belt. A Mr Chadburn remarked that 'he was under the impression they would have a German field gun in addition to these. The chairman remarked that they would not need a very large site.' The clerk had written accepting the trophies 'and [had] asked the War Office to consign them to the Midland Station, Southwell'.

18 June 1919

A report of the recent meeting of the Southwell war memorial committee noted that it had been decided that a memorial hall, fully equipped, would cost £5,000, and it was agreed that 'the cost of either cottage homes or a memorial cross could be accommodated to the amount of subscriptions received'. Nevertheless an amendment was proposed by Mr W. H. Smith that 'a scheme for a Public Hall be carried out. Sir W. N. Hicking said he was really in favour of the last gentleman's remarks, and wished to ask the Rector if he knew whether they could raise £5,000. The Rector said he was afraid he could not tell. Upon being put to the vote there were 14 for the proposal and 9 against. Mr Kirkby said he did not think the majority wished to impose their idea upon the minority, and suggested that the nine be formed into a committee to try to raise the money. Sir W. Hicking said they were there to get up a memorial to those who had fallen and he would like to see something done so that everyone would take an interest in it and give their quota. Ven. Hacking [the Venerable E. Hacking, archdeacon of Newark] supported what Sir W. N. Hicking had said, but thought the cross should be in the churchyard. Mr. F. Robinson said the majority of those who had lost sons in the war were in favour of a cross. Mr Caudwell was in favour of a cross and moved the following proposition: "That a suitable cross be erected upon the Green (in addition to the tablet in the Minster) as a war memorial," Mr. F. Robinson seconded, and it was carried. After further discussion a committee was appointed to carry the scheme into effect.'

[Note: We can see from this and previous references in the *Advertiser* that several suggestions, other than a memorial cross, were made about how best to commemorate Southwell servicemen who had died in the war. All would have benefited the generations to come. Yet an appeal to Southwell's inhabitants did not raise enough to put any of these imaginative ideas into effect.]

On 1 June the government issued a new ultra-long dated security, the 4% Victory Bond. This loan was intended principally to help repay government debt arising from the war. Lloyd George told potential investors that they would get 'the premier security of the world'. It proved popular with individuals and local authorities. The Local Government Board sent a circular letter to all local authorities encouraging them to invest in the bond.

In its 18 June edition the *Advertiser* reported on the meeting of the Southwell Board of Guardians on the 13th under its chairman, H. Lewin of Halam. The letter from the LBG was discussed at this meeting. T. Foster, a Southwell member of the Board, opposed investment, and 'urged that the Board had already invested enough in War Loan', but G. Simpson, of Caythorpe, was more outspoken, saying that 'the more money they subscribed the more extravagant the Government became, and it was quite time they put a scotch on the wheel. As long as the Government got money they seemed to squander it in eery direction. Every day and in every department of State money was being squandered in a most scandalous way, and he, for one, would oppose any further investment of the funds of the Union at the present time.' The Board agreed not to invest and that the letter should 'lie on the table'.

[Note: In 1911, Herbert Lewin, 46, was a farmer living at Halam House Farm; Thomas Foster, 48, was a market Gardener, living in Easthorpe; and Gershom Simpson, aged 54, was a salt refiner living at 'Charnwood', Lowdham. Each employed members of their family in the family business, and each employed servants. They were typical of the men who served on the local Board of Guardians, Southwell Rural District Council, Southwell town council and committees of residents promoting good causes.]

A report of the recent meeting of the Southwell RDC in this edition noted the discussion about the high cost of building houses in the area. One member observed that 'owing to the high cost of building material and labour it was impossible to build a cottage in Southwell for less than £750'. [It is worth noting that £750 in 1919 was, according to a conservative estimate using the retail price index, worth about £26,900 in 2010]. Other costs being faced by the RDC were also increasing. The clerk told the council that a steam motor wagon would now cost £1,100, whereas a steam motor roller had cost £540 before the war. This discussion followed receipt of an application from the council's highways surveyors who had asked for an additional road roller, a water cart, a scarifier and a steam motor wagon. The clerk said that a one penny rate would raise £600, and a 3½d. rate would cover the cost of all the items the surveyors had asked for. Gershom Simpson, of Caythorpe, the member of the Board of Guardians who had objected so strongly to the Board investing in the Victory Loan, said 'they would all remember when the Council invested money in the War Loan it was distinctly understood at the time it was to have it until after the war and then expend it on material for the roads . . . The chairman [J. W. A. Bonner] observed that 'it was not a very good time for withdrawing money from the War Loan in view of the new [Victory] Loan.' The discussion continued, with Simpson asserting that the government had plenty of road rollers that it could sell cheaply to local authorities. The surveyors' application apparently held over, because, on the proposal by Alexander Straw, the RDC instructed its Clerk 'to make enquiries as to what Government stores and material were available and the price required'. An amendment that no further action be taken was defeated.

To give weight to the discussion by Southwell RDC of the cost of providing housing, a note in this edition of the *Advertiser* listed local properties sold at a sale recently held in the Admiral

Rodney: freehold farmhouse at Upton with over one acre of land, £1,300; Rose Cottage, Farnsfield, copyhold, £300 (producing an annual rental of £18); Compton House, Southwell, £650; a freehold house in Southwell, £270 (annual rental, £22); three cottages in Southwell, £480 (annual rental, £47 4s. 0d.).

25 June 1919

The decision of the Southwell Guardians not to subscribe to the Victory Bond, brought a sharp and lengthy rebuke from 'Sphinx', a columnist on the *Newark Advertiser*. This column had been running from before the outbreak of the war, carrying the editorial disclaimer: 'We do not necessarily identify ourselves with the views expressed in this column.' In this issue 'Sphinx' wrote:

'The Southwell Guardians decision not to entertain subscribing to the new Victory Loan does not cast a very creditable reflection. The whole country is agog with enthusiasm for the loan, but Southwell has treated it with hostile criticism, and has left a communication on the subject from the Local Government Board to lie ignominiously on the table. The Local Government Board carefully pointed out the great assistance rendered to Boards of Guardians in previous loans, and the present occasion was one in which local authorities could be of the utmost value. If they threw their whole weight into the campaign, the L. G. B. continued, they would contribute greatly towards ensuring success. But this appeal did not move the Southwell Board. They were undoubtedly imbued with the merciful fact that "the fighting had finished". Granted. The war to all intents and purposes is over. The guns have ceased their fire, the bloodshed has ended. The public have therefore to use a little imagination to understand why money is still required to bridge the gaping gulf between war and peace finance. But money is necessary, and as pointed out by the Chancellor of the Exchequer, it is immediately wanted to fund the existing short period floating debt, which will strengthen the national credit and thus help to re-establish industry, increase production, reduce unemployment, and lower the cost of living. These points, however, did not appeal to the gentlemen at Southwell. On the contrary, one of their number, a representative from Caythorpe, brings a serious indictment against the government: "The more money we subscribe," he says, "the more extravagant the Government becomes, and it is quite time we put a scotch on the wheel. When the Government gets more money they seem to squander it in every direction, Every day and in every department of the state, money is being squandered in a most scandalous way."'

For 'Sphinx' the Board's refusal was 'tantamount to hamstringing the State'. He did not deny that governments, and, he pointed out acidly, even Boards of Guardians, had mis-spent money and had displayed extravagance, ignorance or carelessness, but 'this is a Victory Loan' and unless the nation subscribes the government will be forced 'to resort to the compulsory levy to pay the debts, re-cast the finances, and re-establish credit and industry'. He added: 'The Southwell Guardians' minute book contains the record that the Board would not support the Loan. In other words, the Guardians refuse to assist the Government in its final effort to put the National house in order. It is not a minute to boast about!'

The Southwell Board of Guardians were by no means alone in refusing to subscribe. On 16 July the *Advertiser* carried a long letter, headed 'Victory Loan Campaign', from J. Payne, the honorary Nottinghamshire organiser for the government's war savings programmes. He said that in the previous two weeks he had been in touch with almost all war savings committees in the county, and 'in almost every instance I have found the secretaries fully alive to the enormous difficulties confronting them'. Foremost among these was the 'sheer ignorance as to the true purpose of this Victory Loan' and, indeed, hostility. But he personally had encountered an even more serious phenomenon. This was what he bluntly described as 'gross selfishness'. He wrote: 'I myself have lately met with instances where men have made much money during the war, while those at the Front have been risking life and limb, and have been making the supreme sacrifice, and I have been told by these men that the terms of the Loan are too disappointing to be entertained.' He continued, with increasing bitterness, 'they have not subscribed to that heart-rending human loan, for which the only dividends are constant heartache and privation, and for which the only Certificates of investment are the memorial Scrolls which are shortly to be issued to those bereaved of their loved ones.' The letter concluded: 'To refrain [from investing in the new bond] would be suicidal, as the welfare of everybody, worker and employer, is bound up in the success of the campaign.' The 1919 Victory Loan was not redeemed by the Treasury until 1954. In March 2012 nearly two billion pounds of earlier 1914-18 war loan remained unredeemed, and had been virtually defaulted.

2 July 1919

'PEACE CELEBRATIONS   The signing of the Peace terms was made known in Southwell about five p.m., when the streets began to fill with inhabitants and flags and banners were soon in evidence. Streamers were stretched across the roads, and the whole town gave itself over to quiet rejoicing. The bells of the Minster rang in the evening, and a dance was held in Mr Rumford's room.'

16 July 1919

A report notes that the Southwell Board of Guardians had met on 11 July. The Board had received a circular from the Local Government Board stating, so this report said, that 'in view of the general desire to celebrate peace they had issued an order enabling Boards of Guardians and other local authorities to make such modification with regard to the discipline as they thought advisable. The letter also stated that in order to celebrate peace they would authorise any reasonable expenditure.' The Board's discussion of the circular was predictable:

   'Mr Straw [Alexander Straw, Farnsfield] asked if the matter had been dealt with by the House Committee.
      The Chairman replied that the Committee recommended that similar fare as provided at Christmas be granted the inmates, and on behalf of the Committee he proposed that be passed.
      Mr Straw seconded, and inquired whether they would be supplied on Saturday and Sunday.
      The Chairman replied that they could have two days if they wished.
      The Clerk said he had received several letters from other Boards, asking them to grant 2s. 6d. per week additional out-relief in the case of adults, and 1s. and 6d. for children during peace festivities, and this was agreed to.'

30 July 1919

A report noted that a tablet had been erected in the grammar school recording the names of 23 Old Southwellians in the armed services who had been killed during the war.

'WORKPEOPLE ENTERTAINED   Under the auspices of the Southwell Lace Operatives' Society, a tea was given to Messrs Carey's employees on Saturday, and a very enjoyable time was spent. After tea, Mr Partington, manager, said he was pleased to see such an enjoyable party. The firm was anxious to raise the standard of their workpeople, and he was glad to see the baths that had recently been installed were so popular among the employees. Also, the interest that was shown by the facilities provided by the firm at the golf course and tennis court. The Rector said he was very pleased to receive the invitation to be present at that gathering, and to meet the workers. He hoped that now the war was over those social gatherings would become more frequent and social intercourse be renewed. Mr Arnold, local labour leader, expressed regret that both the Chairman and Secretary of the Society were both away on business in connection with the Society. He expressed pleasure in the efforts the firm (Messrs Careys) were making to make the condition of life and work more congenial.'
Sports were held on the golf course, and a long list of events and prize-winners follows which gives a number of names of employees.

27 August 1919

'EASTHORPE PEACE CELEBRATIONS   The inhabitants of Easthorpe, Southwell, celebrated the conclusion of hostilities in a fitting manner on Saturday. A meat tea was given to every grown-up person, in the New Drill Hall, and 400 sat down to a menu of ham, beef, sauces, pickles, cakes, pastry, bread and butter and tea, after which the tables were laid and 130 children partook of tea.' After tea, 'the scene changed and everyone gathered in Mr Cottam's field in Easthorpe for races, games, bowling competition, pea guessing, tug-of-war, fancy dress parade etc.' These also included slow cycle races for both ladies and gentlemen, egg and spoon races, sack races, veterans' races, and much else. A complete list of events and prize-winners follows.

24 September 1919

The report of a meeting of the Board of Guardians held in the Workhouse on 18 September included a note of its consideration of a letter received from the Ministry of Health about the employment of disabled soldiers by local authorities. The Ministry had asked the Board 'to undertake to employ at least 5 per cent disabled men on their staff'. A lengthy discussion followed. The report gives us a revealing glimpse of the attitudes and assumptions of, in the main, local employers as they exercised a modest responsibility in face of what had become an acute social problem, the unemployment of disabled servicemen.

'Mr Richardson asked if there were any of the staff now serving.
The Clerk replied in the negative, and after reading the form enclosed in the letter, remarked that they wished the Board to sign that undertaking.
The Chairman [J. W. A. Bonner] observed they could consider the recommendation if the occasion arose when they were effecting a change in the staff of the institution.

Mr Simpson remarked that it was just a question of giving disabled ex-service men preference when making fresh appointments. He thought they could easily sign that agreement.

Mr Francklin [Gonalstone, a county councillor] moved that the Board acknowledge receipt of that recommendation, and consider every case as it arose, giving preference to ex-servicemen whenever possible. He did not think they ought to sign that undertaking to employ a certain percentage.

The Chairman intimated that they only employed two males.

Mr Simpson pointed out that they could easily keep up to that percentage.

Mr Straw said they should all be in favour of doing so if it were possible. Mr Richardson seconded.

Mr Simpson urged that so far as they were concerned the percentage did not count at all. He moved an amendment that the Board give the undertaking as it stood at the present time.

Mr Chadburn said they must count the females on the staff.

Mr Simpson: It does not apply to females.

The Clerk said the percentage was to be taken on the whole of the establishment, including females and juveniles. Five per cent was the usual figure, or one in twenty.

The Chairman intimated that unless they gave the undertaking it was no use writing at all, because it did not affect them. They could not undertake to employ less than five per cent.

Mr Straw seconded the amendment, which on being put was carried by 9 votes to 8.'

The Southwell War Memorial Fund had reached £466 19s 0d. by this date.

'SOUTHWELL EVENING SCHOOLS' This is a lengthy report of a public meeting held in Trebeck Hall to consider establishing evening schools in the town the following winter. It was chaired by T. D. Partington. The meeting was called following the passing of an Education Act which made it compulsory for young men and women ('youths and girls') under 18 who had left school at 13 or 14 to attend evening classes. A local committee had been established 'consisting of a representative of every important business place in the town and a representative of each of the day schools', and it had arranged 'Monday night for English and geography; Tuesday night, arithmetic and book-keeping; and Wednesday night shorthand and dressmaking. An arrangement had been made with the Mothers' Union with regard to the latter, and a competent teacher would be appointed from the County Council for dressmaking. They had also appointed an extra night, Friday night, with the object of doing away with a lot of homework.' In short, this was an evening class programme modelled almost exactly on the elementary school pattern, and, it seems, held in the elementary schools.

Harold Brown, a county councillor, then spoke of the ideals of education, which was not, he said, 'merely the teaching of children, but the development both of the physical body and mind. Advanced education must not be looked on as a task . . . [for] education afforded much pleasure because it could bring so much happiness.' They were high-sounding words, but Mr R. Matthews, headmaster of Southwell Grammar School, brought to the meeting some reality. He had, he said, some experience of teaching evening classes, but his experience had not been a happy one:

'He did not think evening classes were a success for two reasons. First, they were carried out in places that were totally unfit. Growing youths and girls between 14 and 18 seemed very clumsy about the knees and shoulders when they had to sit at the desks made for children, and their hands seemed much too big. (Laughter). Another disadvantage was that no person coming to school in the evening could expect great vitality from the students when they had been at work all day.

Neither did the teacher feel like exerting himself much after teaching all day. Evening classes will eventually be linked up with the classes that are to come, and young persons will have opportunity for refreshment and rest, and better buildings will be provided. Anyway something will be done. He was inclined to think that if the programme were a little more varied it would be better.'

22 October 1919

'TOOK PART IN RUSSIAN EXPEDITION   Last week Sgt. G. H. Templeman, Easthorpe, who has been with the Russian Relief Force, has returned home. He has been awarded the Distinguished Conduct Medal for conspicuous gallantry. He served four years in France, and afterwards volunteered to go to Russia. His brother, Sgt. T. Templeman, the well-known footballer, also gained the Military Medal. The former was employed at Mr J. H. Kirkby's, and the latter is at Messrs Carey and Sons' lace factory. They were both born in Southwell and are to be heartily congratulated on the service they have rendered to King and country.'

[Note: G. H. Templeman served with the Royal Fusiliers (City of London Regiment).]

5 November 1919

A report of the latest meeting of Southwell RDC noted that a circular letter had been received from the League of Nations Union stating that the national campaign of the League had been inaugurated and asking that 11 November, the anniversary of the Armistice, be celebrated throughout England and be known as League of Nations Day. The circular appealed to the RDC to give the campaign 'its valuable support'. A typical discussion followed:

'The Chairman [J. W. A. Bonner] observed that they [the League of Nations Union] did not realise what a large area the Southwell district covered.
Mr. Simpson: It is rather premature; the League of Nations is not yet an accomplished fact.
Mr. T. Shipsides remarked that it never would be unless they did their best to make it so. He felt it would be a disgrace if they did not support a letter like that. They had spent their time and money for the last few years trying to beat Prussian Militarism. They had had flag days and everything else to raise money, and he could not express his feeling, but at the bottom of his heart he felt that they, as representatives of public bodies, should support that League of Nations. That would do more than warships and armies could do to provide them with a new and better England and a better world. He had great pleasure in moving that they did something to support the object for which the letter was written.
Mr. Simpson said that he did not think there would be any two opinions about the League of Nations being the finest thing ever proposed in the world, but at the present moment it was not an accomplished fact of any importance. If they could do anything to further the inauguration of the League of Nations, he thought they would do everything possible, he would personally, because he believed it was a movement they ought to strive for, but at the same time he did not see what they could do at the moment.
The Chairman remarked that it was a matter for the parish meetings to take up.
The Clerk agreed, and suggested that the Press convey the discussion to the public.

Mr. Newman asked what lines they wished the Council to take. Was it to have church services, a tea, or what? (Laughter).

And so the discussion continued, with the Clerk suggesting that he send the names of all chairmen of parish councils to the League of Nations' Union so that the Union could send circulars to them direct, 'or he could send a copy of their communication from his office'. Mr Shipsides pointed out that most of those present were chairmen of their parish councils. They should 'carry out what they had in their hearts' and call parish council meetings and 'tell the people exactly what it meant to foster that idea [of the League of Nations], not only for the country but for future generations. Such a course would be far better than spending their time and money preparing for war.' This was agreed.

[Note: The constitution of the League of Nations was established by the Paris Peace Conference in April 1919. The League consisted originally of 28 nations that had been at war with Germany, together with 14 states that had remained neutral. The United States, which had proposed the idea, refused to join. The League was governed by an Assembly, which consisted of representatives of all member states, but all important decisions had to be unanimous. The Council of the League consisted of the great powers. They had permanent seats but they could be outvoted by 12 other states elected to the council by rotation. The main purpose of the League was to prevent further war, and member states entered into a covenant not to resort to war until every other avenue for resolving international disputes had been explored, and then only after nine months. After initial successes the League failed in its primary function not least because if, in its view, the vital interest of a member nation was at stake it could, and did, withdraw from the non-aggression covenant.]

An altar had recently been dedicated for use in the Minster. Its panels had been made parts of British aircraft 'shattered in the air in France' and consisted of panels made 'from the broken propellers, the cross from cylinders, and vases from aluminium and plates from copper used in aeroplanes.' These were made by mechanics at RAF Norton camp [this was No. 2 Aeroplane Repair Depot, situated 5 miles south of Sheffield and in the diocese at that time] in memory of men from Norton who had lost their lives in action over France, and had originally been given to the Church Hut at Norton before the camp was closed in October 1919.

End of Reports

These reports drawn from the *Newark Advertiser* have provided a valuable and interesting insight into life in Southwell from early 1914 to late 1919. They have touched upon the part the town's women played in the war effort, particularly in charitable work, entertaining the troops and nursing the sick and wounded. However, this is not a full representation of the important part that women played in the war effort and the next chapter summarises the wider role of women in the First World War. In addition some changes on the 'home front' deserve a mention.

CHAPTER 3

3.1 SOUTHWELL TERRITORIALS GO TO WAR

'H' Active Service Company, 8th Battalion Sherwood Foresters

Southwell and district has had a long and distinguished association with the Sherwood Foresters, and this was never more evident than in the First World War. Much has been written about the 'Pals' Brigades' from various parts of the country, but how many have realised that Southwell had its own 'Pals' - 'H' Active Service Company, 1/8th Sherwood Foresters? On 20th January 1915 the *Newark Advertiser* published a list of 267 Southwell men who were on active service. Of these 115 were serving in 'H' Company under the command of Captain J. P. Becher, a local solicitor. The remainder were spread across various regiments of the British Army. In addition to these men there would have been a number serving in the Royal Navy and the Royal Flying Corps.

'H' Company joined with other territorial companies to form the 1/8th Battalion, Sherwood Foresters, the first territorial battalion to be on active service in the Great War. They were in and out of the front line for the duration and fought bravely throughout, earning the title 'The Mad 8th' from other battalions. As part of the 1/8th Battalion they were considered fit for front line duties. The following section is an edited version of the battalion's war diary, which illustrates their deep involvement in the conflict, but first a brief history of the 1/8th Battalion showing how 'H' Company became part of 'The Mad 8th'.

A Short History of 8th Battalion, Sherwood Foresters

Local Volunteer Corps were formed up and down the country in the late eighteenth century, in response to the invasion threat of the French Revolutionary and Napoleonic Wars. Newark was one of the first places to have such a Corps, formed in 1793.

Although these Volunteer Corps were disbanded after the wars, similar companies were again founded at various times of National Emergency. Seven such companies formed in Nottinghamshire in 1859/60 were the more direct forerunners of the 1/8th Battalion the Sherwood Foresters. The seven companies were:

>
> The 2nd or Retford Corps
> The 3rd or Newark Corps
> The 4th or Mansfield Corps
> The 5th or Thorneywood Chase Corps
> The 6th or Collingham Corps
> The 7th or Worksop Corps
> The 8th or Southwell Corps

In 1862 these were amalgamated to form the Administrative Battalion, The Notts Rifle Volunteers. This battalion became in 1880 the 2nd Notts Rifle Volunteer Battalion, and in 1887 the 4th Notts Volunteer Battalion. By 1908 the volunteer battalions were reorganized and the 4th Notts Volunteer Battalion became the 1/8th Battalion Nottinghamshire and Derbyshire Regiment (Sherwood Foresters), Territorial Force.

In 1914 came the test of war. On 4th August 1914 the battalion was recalled from Annual Camp and mobilized. At this time there were eight companies, 'A' to 'H' coming from Retford, Newark, Sutton-in-Ashfield, Mansfield, Carlton, Arnold, Worksop and Southwell respectively. In France and Flanders, during the following four years, the battalion - part of the 139th Brigade, 46th Division - had through its ranks 193 officers and 2,650 other ranks. Perhaps the best remembered engagements in which the battalion fought were Hooge (July 1915), Hohenzollern Redoubt (October 1915), Gommecourt (July 1916), and Bellenglise (St. Quentin Canal, September 1918). The battalion's part in the last battle is commemorated by the lifebelts, which form part of the decoration of the screen round St. George's Chapel, Newark Parish Church.

The battalion was re-formed in 1919 with only four companies. 'A' Company was recruited from Arnold and Carlton, 'B' Company from Newark and Southwell, 'C' Company from Mansfield and Sutton-in-Ashfield, and 'D' Company from Worksop and Retford; Battalion H.Q. still remaining in Newark.[1]

'H' Company

Official records of the men on active service in The World War are sparse as many were destroyed in air raids in the Second World War. Whilst, in general, medal cards have survived, individual service records are few and far between, but where they have survived they are very useful. However, we have been fortunate to find a list in the *Newark Advertiser* of the men who were on active service in early 1915. With the help of the 1901 and 1911 census returns we have been able to build up a picture of most of the men who made up Southwell (H) Active Service Company, 1/8th Sherwood Foresters.

The names of 115 men appear on the list and they were led by a local solicitor, Captain (later Major) John Pickard Becher, great-grandson of the poor law reformer Reverend J T Becher of Southwell. Two other officers in the company were also well known: Captain John Kirkland Lane, another local solicitor, and Lieutenant Henry Basil Strutt Handford a 20-year-old Cambridge law student, who was the Regimental Signalling Officer. The ages of the men of 'H' Company ranged from 17 to 48 (most of them were in their late teens and early twenties) and the men had a wide variety of occupations. There were lace makers, painters, shop workers, farm hands, gardeners, servants, framework knitters, bricklayers, a cigar maker, and a cycle parts maker. However, at least thirty-eight of the men were employed at the local lace factory, E. Carey & Sons Limited. Of these thirty-eight men, eight were to die in action. A further eight Carey employees, who served in various regiments, were also to die. Their sixteen names are remembered on a plaque outside the House of Correction, the site of the former lace factory. Most of 'H' Company lived in Southwell, with just a few from the surrounding villages. The company seemed to be quite healthy, unlike some of their city counterparts. A few medical records remain and the striking detail is that, by modern standards, the men were relatively short in stature. However, fit enough for the 1/8th Battalion, which were front-line troops.

'H' Company were typical of the many volunteers up and down the country who had played and worked together before they were thrown into the nightmare that was to be a war like nothing any of them could imagine. Much has been written about the battalions of 'Pals' – the Accrington Pals usually comes to mind - and we now realise that the 1/8th Battalion Sherwood Foresters was made up of groups of 'Pals' from around Nottinghamshire and Derbyshire.

As Europe lurched into war in the summer of 1914, many of these Territorials were at their two weeks' annual camp. For the 1/8th Battalion these had taken place at Scarborough, Thoresby,

---

[1] For a history of the Sherwood Foresters visit:
http://www.wfrmuseum.org.uk/wfr_history.htm#thesherwoodforesters

Aberystwyth and in 1914 at Hunmanby, on the edge of the Yorkshire Wolds – two weeks of fresh air, training and a break from work. The photograph below, from 1908, shows a group of Southwell lads enjoying a smoke near their tents.

'H' Company at summer camp 1908.
Back row, left to right; Herbert Rumford, Frank Wilcox, Ezekiel Eaton, unknown, G. Tomkins.
Front Row, left to right: Arthur Hopewell, possibly Albert Hopewell, Len Raworth, George Gibson.
(Peter Cant)

As they went off to Hunmanby in late July there was a diplomatic crisis looming, but some would not have given much regard to it as so often in the past crises had blown over. However, this time it was different, the battalion diarist noted:

> …the atmosphere was so charged with electricity that it was impossible to settle down to the normal routine of training, and there was little surprise when on August 3rd, Bank Holiday, Germany declared war on France, and when on the following day, August 4th, Great Britain herself, following upon the violation of the neutrality of Belgium, joined forces with Russia and France.[2]

As the news broke the Territorial Camps were immediately broken up, the men were sent home and told to be ready for any emergency. Later in the day a Royal Proclamation for the embodiment of the 1/8th Sherwood Foresters (Notts. and Derby Regiment) was issued and all companies

---

[2] Weetman, W.C.C., *The Sherwood Foresters in the Great War 1914-1919 - History of the 1/8th Battalion* (Nottingham: Thomas Forman & Son, 1920 - reprint by LLC/Qontro).

received a one word telegram – 'Mobilise'. During the next two days there was frantic activity as essential supplies were obtained, particularly underclothing and other necessaries for the men.

On Friday 7th August the battalion gathered in Newark and the photograph below shows 'H' Company marching down Station Road, Southwell, to the railway station to catch a train to Newark – they were now on active service. Perhaps they thought that it would all be over by Christmas, clearly it wasn't. There were to be very many casualties, which was to be a concern to many in the high command.

General Nevil Macready, Adjutant-General of the B.E.F. is recorded as having stated that the casualties in Territorial units were a cause of a greater feeling of loss than those in the Regular Army because of the closer sense of personal involvement among men from small, local communities.[3]

'H' Company, led by Captain J.P. Becher, in Station Road, Southwell, waiting to turn right into the railway station to catch the train to Newark-on-Trent, on the first leg of their long journey to the Western Front.
(Peter Cant)
Original photograph by Howard Barrett of Southwell.

---

[3] David Ascoli, *The Mons Star: The British Expeditionary Force 1914* (London: Harper, 1981), p. 64n.

*'H' Company departing Southwell railway station for Newark-on-Trent on Friday 7th August 1914
on the first leg of their journey to the Western Front.
(Loughton Collection - by kind permission of the Dean and Chapter, Southwell Minster.)*

*Sherwood Foresters'
Cap Badge*

(Julia Overton)

3.2 THE WAR DIARY OF THE 1/8TH BATTALION SHERWOOD FORESTERS
- *The Mad Eighth*

The following is an edited version of *The Sherwood Foresters in the Great War 1914-1919 – History of the 8th Battalion* by W. C. C. Weetman.

The various companies were billeted in schools in Newark, and 'H' Company were put in charge of guarding the bridge and other parts of the Great Northern Railway. According to the war diary little of interest happened, except that one too keen (or nervous) sentry fired some shots at a group of suspicious looking persons, who were innocent plate-layers returning home from work. Thankfully there were no casualties.

On Monday 10th August the battalion paraded on Newark Market Place and the Mayor and Corporation, accompanied by Canon Hindley, Vicar of Newark, wished them God speed. After a short service the battalion, minus 'H' Company who were left to guard the railway, marched off to Radcliffe-on-Trent and eventually to Derby, via Nottingham. Captain Becher's men followed later. As the battalion was short of military transport, locally sourced carts and vehicles were purchased. Floats and drays from Warwick and Richardson's, Hole's, Dicken's Minerals and Davy's Brewery were utilised for ammunition and general service wagons. The collection was completed with a furniture van full of blankets, two corporation water carts, and a bread cart with red crosses painted on each side. The whole collection apparently looked more like a circus than a military column as it departed from Newark.

This was the battalion's first test of endurance as they marched to Radcliffe-on-Trent and the following morning completed a further twenty-three miles to Derby. The men were then subjected to a number of route marches, on three very hot days spent in Derby, in an attempt to toughen them up. Whilst in Derby, those that had not already volunteered for service abroad were asked to do so.

Membership of the Territorials had been on an annually renewable basis and as they signed on they completed an agreement that they would serve 'in the Territorial Force, in any part of the United Kingdom for the defence of the same, provided my service should so long be required'. Their new agreements were to serve outside the U. K. on what was known as Imperial Service. During the temporary stay in Derby the unfit were weeded out and the rest were asked to volunteer. In the first instance the response was not very positive, but a second appeal resulted in over 800 volunteers. Members of the battalion who refused to volunteer were apparently paraded in front of the battalion C.O. and given a 'military' dressing down. It would seem that all of 'H' Company volunteered for service abroad.

Training in Hertfordshire and Essex

The whole division was sent to Hertfordshire for training and, after a delay, arrived near Luton in the early hours of 16th August. They had an uncomfortable few days and then moved on to Harpenden for three months' intensive training. Here conditions were much better and they enjoyed ample rations. In Harpenden they were joined by 5th, 6th and 7th Sherwood Foresters, which, with the 1/8th, formed the Notts and Derby Infantry Brigade, under the command of Brigadier General C.T. Shipley.

The battalion diarist looked back at their time at Harpenden with a certain amount of affection. The territorials were trained to be front-line infantry and their officers were even trained as swordsmen – a skill they would not need to use in the future. Trench digging was practised - little did they realise that they would be spending much of their time in France and Belgium in such dire conditions. A succession of senior military figures, including Lord Kitchener, inspected the battalion during this period of intensive training as they were converted into an effective fighting force.

Rumour was rife during this period, and as early as 1st September they thought they would be off to France within a month. By early November a farewell sermon was preached, but still they remained in the U.K. By mid-November they were on the move to Braintree and Bocking in Essex. Again the troops were happy with their accommodation, which included the Convent at Bocking, where they were well looked after. However, serious work commenced as they received orders to dig defensive lines of trenches for the protection of London. The terrain was difficult, there being much heavy clay, but was good training for when they eventually crossed the Channel. The trenches were completed by Christmas, but leave was cancelled due to a false alarm concerning a possible invasion following the bombardment of Scarborough on 22nd December. Despite the disappointment of leave being cancelled, the men were well entertained with football matches and dances in Braintree. By the end of December the battalion returned to the Luton area to carry out firing practice at the Wardown and Galley Hill Ranges and field firing in appalling weather at Dunstable. A week later they were back in Bocking. The remainder of their time in Essex was spent re-equipping both uniforms and transport, including mules (see below). When not training the men were kept busy searching for elusive spies and on road block duties. They also witnessed their first air raid.

In mid-February orders were received to move to France without too much further delay, and a few days later the Division was inspected by His Majesty the King at Hallingbury Place, near Bishop's Stortford. A certain amount of re-organization took place in the last few days before leaving for France, including the doubling up of the various companies as follows:

A Company - formerly E (Carlton) & F (Arnold) Companies
B Company - formerly B (Newark) & H (Southwell) Companies
C Company - formerly C (Sutton-in-Ashfield) & D (Mansfield) Companies
D Company - formerly A (Retford) & G (Worksop) Companies

The individual identity of 'H' Company had now been lost, but the leading officers of 'B' Company were certainly Southwell men: Captain J.P. Becher and Captain J. K. Lane. 'C' Company had a former Southwell territorial in charge, Captain H. G. Wright. The battalion, with Lt.- Colonel G. H. Fowler, in command was made up of 31 officers and 996 other ranks.

On 25th September they left Bocking for Southampton Docks. Whilst they were reasonably well trained in ordinary methods of fighting, they were not that well acquainted with the many practical points appertaining to trench warfare. This was to come 'in the hard school of bitter experience'. However, they were proud to be part of the first complete territorial division to embark for France.

Mules ready to be transported from Southwell railway station to the front.
(Peter Cant)

To France and the trenches

February 25th 1915 – June 20th 1915

In late February the battalion was transported to Southampton and was eventually crowded into a small Clyde pleasure steamer, the 'King Edward', except for 101 men under Captain Becher who were embarked on the 'Caledonian'. There were further delays, but they eventually arrived at Le Havre and had a less than comfortable train journey in cattle trucks, marked 'Hommes 40', 'Chevaux 8' and taken north via Rouen, Abbeville, Calais and St. Omer to Cassel. From Cassel station they were subjected to a seven-mile route march to the village of Oudezeele. Here they were accommodated in scattered farms, billeted in barns. Their first impressions of France were not that good, particularly as the route march, with many in new boots, had left them weary and sore. Captain Becher's company arrived a day later, having been kept for three days on the 'Caledonian'.

With the battalion now all together, further training took place in very cold weather. It must have been a daunting experience for these young men to be suddenly in a foreign war zone, most of them had probably travelled little further than to their annual summer camp. This is illustrated by the battalion diarist who notes their first encounter with French troops in the small village of Wormhoudt, where they marched through to a warm welcome from the locals, with the whole battalion whistling the 'Marseillaise'. It was in this area that they witnessed their first signs of warfare with shell-scarred buildings and a scattering of French and English graves. On 9th March the 1/8th Battalion marched with the Lincoln and Leicester Brigade and joined up with the remainder of their brigade.

The intention had been for the brigade to join in a major offensive at Neuve Chapelle. Whilst waiting to be sent to the trenches, they were in sight and sound of the ongoing battle, however, the British attack was not successful and they were stood down. A considerable number of men were taken ill as a result of the infamous French water as they waited at Neuf Berquin. The fit continued with trench warfare training – all this to prepare them for their first experience in the trenches.

The battalion was attached to the more experienced 10th Infantry Brigade and, whilst they had a relatively quiet time, they soon learned to keep their heads down. They witnessed their first casualty when C.S.M. Hopkinson of 'C' Company was wounded by a sniper, closely followed by two men from 'D' Company. The harsh realities of the war were being swiftly experienced. When they stood down from these trenches the battalion was complemented on their discipline and keenness and that 'they came in so much better than Regulars, and I was genuinely filled with admiration for them. They were a splendid body of men'.[1] They were now ready to take over their own section of the front line, the first Territorials to do so.

On 1st April 1915 the 8th Battalion received orders to move to Locre in Belgium. The diarist notes their disappointment at the reception they received from the Belgian civilians and there was evidence that they had been stealing British supplies – no doubt the Belgians were feeling the effects of the war. Following a Church parade on Easter Eve, taken by the Bishop of London, they moved into the front-line trenches at Kemmel on 4th April. The opposing front lines varied from 25 to 300 yards apart. Easter Day was quiet with 'C' Company experiencing a short truce with the Germans opposite, only to be spoilt by one of the Germans shouting unflattering remarks that quickly ended the truce.

---

[1] An officer of the 2nd Seaforths. Weetman, pp. 37-38.

The early days were relatively quiet, but with ongoing annoyance from German snipers, one of whom claimed his first fatal casualty, Private Hyde of 'A' Company. The battalion rotated 4 days on and 4 days off. Bathing at Locre had been difficult until they received three galvanised iron baths from Miss Gilstrap of Winthorpe, Newark. A similar consignment from Mrs Becher was lost in transit, no doubt a welcome gift to another unit. During this relatively quiet period the battalion spent much of their time improving their defences. However, by 22nd April life became more difficult when they were subjected to gas, which had been aimed at the Ypres Salient a few miles away, fortunately the results were not too serious, but the men had learnt to be wary.

Two days later life became more serious as Lt. Vann and his platoon from 'B' Company (Southwell and Newark men) suffered their first heavy bombardment. Severe damage was done, but any raid was prevented by a machine-gun team consisting of L/Cpl. Sharrock and Ptes Hopewell and Davis. Lt. Vann and his men were in severe difficulties and had to dig out wounded men, during this action Vann was blown several yards by a shell, which killed four men and buried another three. Major Becher came up with reinforcements from other members of 'B' Company to dig out and dress the wounded, with the enemy only 70 yards away. This action saw the death of fourteen men and a further fourteen men and two officers wounded. It was the battalion's first serious experience of trench warfare – there were many more to come. The first cases of shell shock were experienced, one of these being Lt. Vann, however, he quickly recovered and was leading daring night patrols in early May. Earlier in April Capt. Lane of Southwell had been put in command of 'D' Company, unfortunately he was badly wounded and hospitalized – he returned to the front line much later.

During June a number of men were transferred from the battalion to the Brigade Mining Section. Both offensive and defensive mining was very important. In mid-June the Germans exploded three mines and the bravery of 1/8th Battalion prevented a breakthrough, with 'B' Company men again being complimented for restoring order and repairing communications. These included Cpl. Humberstone, L/Cpl. Templeman and Pte. Tongue. This particular skirmish had caused further heavy casualties with eleven killed and twenty-nine wounded. Following this damaging action the battalion was removed from the Kemmel sector. The total casualties included four officers and forty-nine other ranks killed and one hundred and twenty wounded, with only twenty replacements. The diarist recorded: 'As a school of instruction our time at Kemmel undoubtedly provided a very valuable lesson not only to officers, NCOs and men of the battalion, but to officers of the Brigade and Divisional staffs, whose experience of the new form of warfare could hardly have been learnt under better conditions than those obtained during our first two months of trench warfare.'[2] This was just the start, the battalion now moved on to the Salient where they were to be subjected to more intensive fighting.

The Salient
June 20th 1915 - October 1st 1915

With the experience of fighting in the Kemmel sector under their belts the 1/8th Battalion marched towards the Salient, or 'Bloody Ypres' as it had been described by the Canadians. The battalion diarist described the three months that followed as almost the hardest months of the war.

They had left Locre on 20th June and marched with the rest of the brigade to the Ouderdom Huts, situated on the Reninghelst-Vlamertinghe Road. The huts were somewhat exposed to a long-range German gun, which ensured that care needed to be taken when moving around. There

---
[2] Weetman, pp. 33-46.

FIGHTING AT SANCTUARY WOOD - JULY-AUG 1915

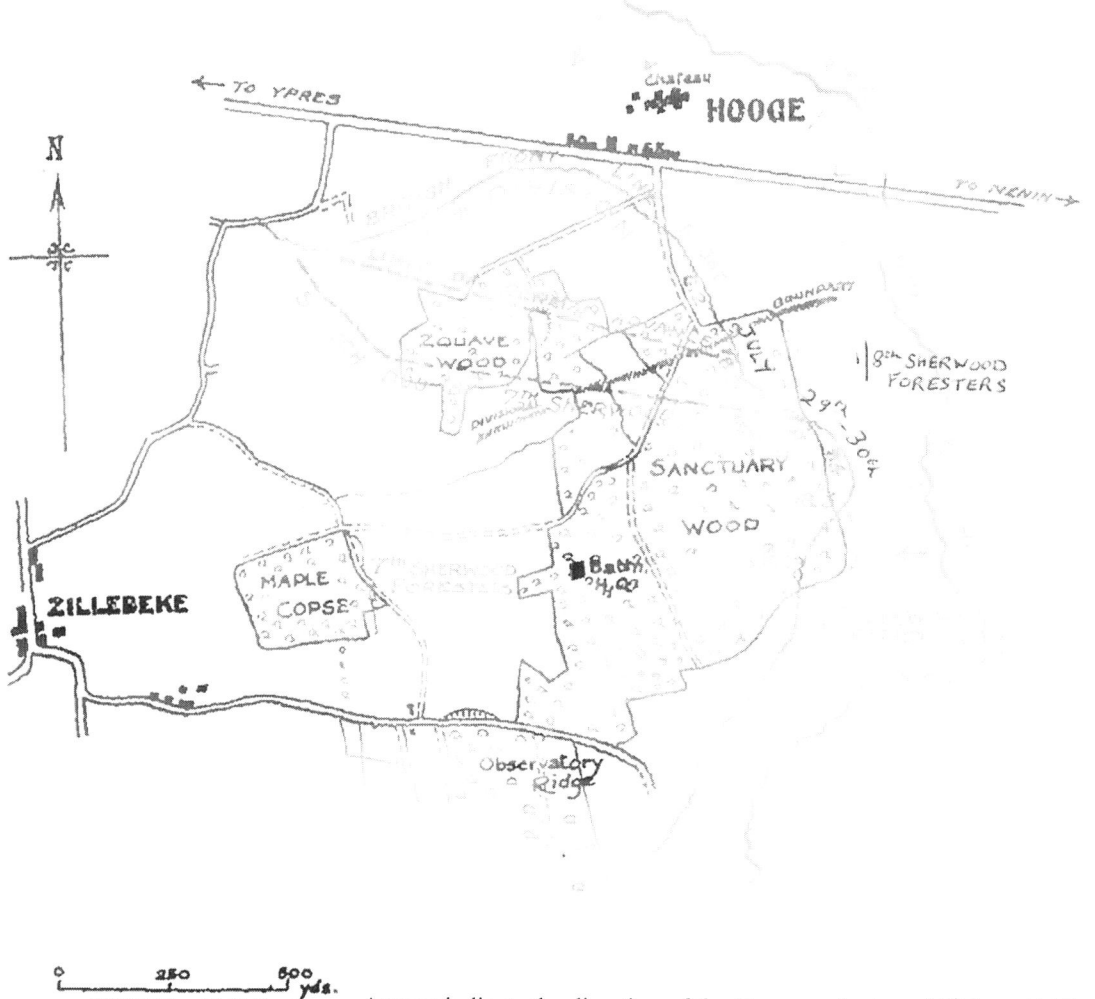

Arrows indicate the direction of the German attack on 30th June 1915

Map adapted from Weetman, p. 52.

were good sheltered trenches around the huts and the men escaped without casualty. Within three days they were on the move again to the front line at 'Sanctuary Wood', where they replaced the 5th East Yorkshires. According to the diarist 'things were anything but pleasant in the region of the woods, whose title was something of a misnomer.' Rations and stores, including water, had to be collected each night and due to the congestion this was a seven hour round trip.

The troops were kept busy maintaining their trenches, which were very uncomfortable when it rained. During their first stint in Sanctuary Wood they saw little in the way of action, except for 'A' Company (Arnold and Carlton men) that suffered around twenty casualties, including four fatalities. After seven days the battalion was relieved by the 5th Lincolns and rested at a camp near Poperinghe, where they spent twelve nights of what were described as the 'most enjoyable days we ever had in France'. The weather was noted as 'glorious'.

After their well-earned rest near Poperinghe the men were marched back to the front to relieve the North Staffords in the Hooge sector. Here they were exposed to extreme danger, as in some cases the trenches were only twenty-five yards apart and were protected by wire netting to try and prevent the enemy throwing hand grenades directly into them. Constant shelling caused increasing numbers of casualties, including eight fatalities, none of them Southwell men, between 11th and 23rd July. On completion of this difficult period they were relieved by the 7th Battalion and marched back to bivouacs near Ouderdom. This was a long trek and they did not arrive until 7.00 a.m. and were immediately shelled out of the camp as the Germans spotted four white tents that had been erected in sight of their artillery – a bad mistake by a well-meaning officer who was attempting to improve their comfort! A swift move was made to a secure camp near Busseboom, where they were left in peace to service their kit and catch up with their washing.

At this camp they were joined by 2nd Lt. Everard Handford (2/8th Battalion), brother of Capt. Henry Handford, both of Elmfield House, Southwell. In addition, due to the C.O., Col. Fowler, being on leave and his second in command being ill, Major Becher was now in temporary command of the battalion – a rapid rise in responsibility from his command of 'H' Company in pre war Southwell.

Following their short rest on 29th/30th July the battalion returned to Sanctuary Wood to take over from the 7th Battalion. The trench system ran partly on the outskirts of the wood and partly through the wood itself, which still had wild flowers and thick undergrowth. Within a few hours of their return they were subject to a huge bombardment, which was the prelude to an attack led by 'flammenwerfer'[3]. The troops were taken by surprise and the attack had some success with 'D' Company in danger of being cut off and attacked from the rear. A dangerous gap had appeared in the line, which was quickly filled by a platoon of 'B' Company (Southwell and Newark men). They were raked with machine-gun fire, resulting in many casualties. The day was saved by Sgt. Foster who managed to throw a well-aimed bomb at the machine-gun post, which also destroyed the 'flammenwerfer'. However, the attack continued and reinforcements from the Reserve Company were sent in by Major Becher, followed by the Brigade sending in the 7th Battalion to assist. As the battle progressed more reserves were called in to re-establish the situation. Some saw the incident as a massive blunder, but this did not detract from the bravery of the troops, most of whom were deprived of sleep and food, as well as artillery support. During this skirmish over the 30th/31st July the 1/8th Battalion suffered twenty-one killed and forty wounded. The dead in these early days included Privates J. Watson[4], C. Thorpe, S. Oliver and Cpl. S. Humberstone and on 1st August Private J. Hopewell, all from Southwell. As the attack continued the casualty list grew over a period of two weeks to ninety-four wounded (including four officers) and thirty-six other ranks killed. The battalion had to stay in the line until 17th August, when they were finally relieved by the 7th Battalion. A much depleted and tired force, now well tried and tested in battle, returned to Ouderdom for a well-earned rest. They were highly praised by General Allenby:

---

[3] The flammenwerfer was a flame thrower, and it was their first experience of this weapon that had been developed by the German army in the early days of the war.

[4] Private Watson was not with the original deployment from Southwell, but must have joined them shortly afterwards.

> I have read with great pleasure and pride the report of the General commanding your Division, telling of the arduous work which you recently did in the neighbourhood of Hooge. By your boldness, tenacity and gallantry, you did work of very great importance. Perhaps you do not know that not only did your action have an important bearing on that particular bit of line, but on the whole campaign, because of the political reason for holding the Salient. The town of Ypres is nothing to us, but if the Boche took it they would publish it to the world that they had captured the fortress of Ypres, which we have held since November, 1914.

Major John Becher was awarded the D.S.O. in recognition of his work whilst in command of the battalion, with other officers and men receiving suitable honours.[5] Regular reports were printed in the *Newark Advertiser* during this difficult period – see Chapter 2.

At the end of August the battalion returned to the line, strengthened by some replacements, but 41 of their original number returned home having completed their terms of enlistment. Their new trenches were at 'Middlesex Wood', which was astride the Ypres-Comines Canal, close to St. Eloi. According to the diarist the period was one of normal trench life, however, they suffered 11 fatalities up to the end of September. During this period new equipment appeared including sniper scopes, which were fitted with periscopes so that they could be fired without looking directly over the parapet. They also had 'fun' with Colonel Fowler's Elephant Gun that caused the enemy some annoyance. Their biggest risk came from Belgian guns that were covering this sector, but they were not as accurate as they should have been with rounds falling into friendly positions.

On 30th September, having suffered 61 fatalities in this period, the battalion was relieved by the 8th Lincolns and they marched back to their tents at Ouderhom. General Allenby paid them another visit, wishing them well on their next deployment. Little did they know that their next move would once again put them in the thick of the fighting.

Hohenzollern Redoubt

October 1st 1915 – October 17th 1915

With little time to rest the battalion packed up and moved to Béthune and within two days were in the nearby village of Mont-Bernenchon. It was a clean and attractive place, but their hopes of a few days' rest were short-lived as they were moved to Vermelles, where they were taken to trenches that had recently been occupied by the Germans. They were set to work to turn the defences round to face the enemy. The work was relatively safe being half a mile from the German line, however, on 5th October a stray shell struck them and three men died. That evening, in heavy rain and darkness, they were marched back to what were described as unpleasant billets in Mazingarbe. The diarist made it clear that they thought the last few days had been a 'purposeless expedition'.

The following day the battalion moved on to more salubrious facilities at Fouquières, near Béthune, where they learnt that the next task was to assist in the capture of the 'Hohenzollern Redoubt' and 'Fosse 8'.[6] The officers were briefed and informed that they would be supported by:

---

[5] Weetman, pp. 47-54.
[6] Fosse 8 was a colliery.

...the heaviest concentration of artillery yet known in the war – 400 guns of all calibres - that all contingencies had been provided for, and that in spite of the strength of the position we should probably encounter very little opposition before reaching our objective.[7]

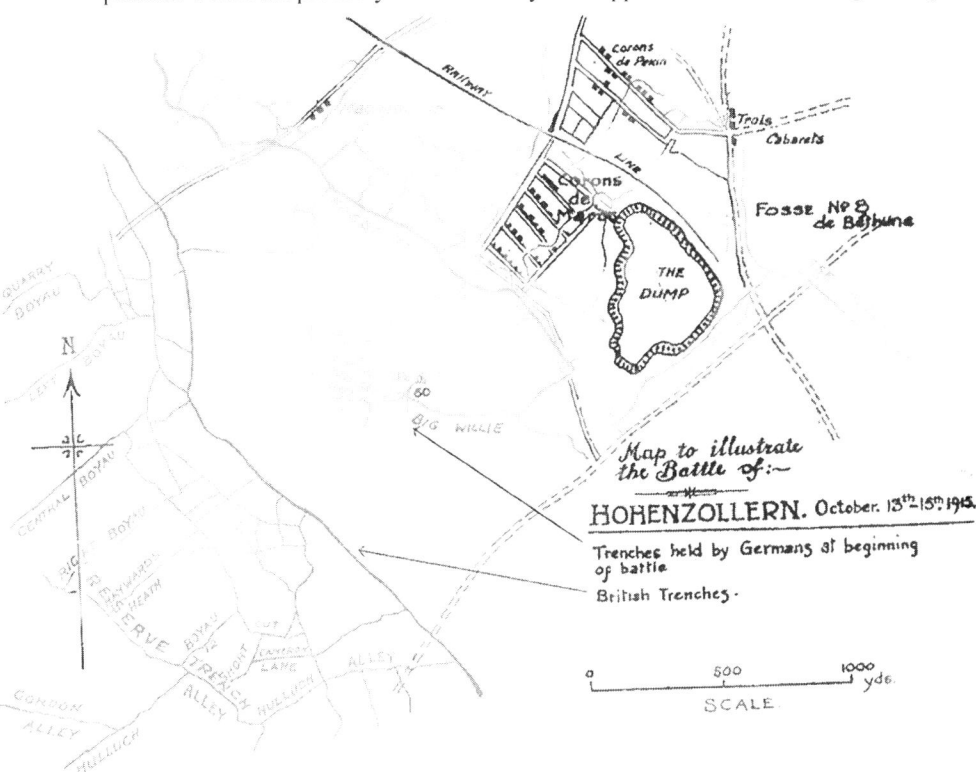

The Hohenzollern Redoubt (Weetman p. 94)

In spite of the last statement, the planning seemed somewhat complex from the details described in the battalion diary. The following few days at Fouquières passed very quickly as the maps and plans of the attack were studied and various bombing squads were trained. The men wrote 'last letters home'. However, the diarist noted that there was little or no excitement as they had already experienced a good deal of fighting. The first steel helmets had arrived and were distributed to the machine-gunners along with new box respirators instead of the previous smoke helmets.

With preparations made the battalion set off on October 12th for their battle. After a march through Vermelles, which was extremely busy with troops and transport, they arrived at their assembly position in 'Sussex Trench'. By 6.00 a.m. around 300 of the battalion were allocated to carrying rations, water, grenades, and rum to the front line. Apparently one ill-disciplined member of the team took full advantage of the rum and was found flat out in the bottom of a trench!

During the morning the artillery fire was kept to normal levels, but at noon the barrage commenced in earnest and they were able to observe the shells bursting over the German lines.

---
[7] Weetman, p. 56.

So much so that they thought there would be little resistance remaining – how wrong they were. As the smoke cleared they observed the Staffords going over the top, only to hear the 'tap-tap' of enemy machine guns. By 3.00 p.m. the 1/8th Battalion was ordered to move up the trench system, but progress was slow as the casualties poured back and carrying parties and reserves moved up. It soon became clear that all was not well and two of their own men, who had been allocated to bombing squads, were seriously wounded. As it became dark, there appeared to be an air of confusion. It was obvious that the bombardment had not been as effective as had been expected. The advance had been held up by well dug in machine guns and the attackers had been forced back.

So far the 1/8th Battalion had avoided the front-line fighting, but this was soon to change as Lt. Colonel Fowler gave orders that they be made ready for an attack on the right of the Redoubt. 'B' Company (Newark and Southwell) were excluded from this action and the remainder moved forward in the dark. In the early hours of 14th October they received orders to attack. Because of the darkness, it was necessary for Major Becher to be sent to the extreme right flank to show a light to guide in the advance. The troops found navigation very difficult and they finished up too far to the left. When this was realised 'A' Company, with Everard Handford in command, pushed on just as the Germans were becoming aware and increasing their rate of fire. In the process Lt. Handford was killed with a single bullet to the head, there were many wounded and the advance came to a halt. Meanwhile 'D' Company, led by Captain Vann, foiled a counter attack further to the right. Vann was wounded in the action and after having his forearm dressed he returned to the line, but was sent back by the C.O. They were now very close to the German lines and had to build up barricades for protection.

'C' Company, commanded by Captain Basil Handford, had been supplying the front with water and grenades across open ground. As light came at around 7.30 a.m. they were spotted and machine-gunned, resulting in the death of Basil Handford and several others. Meanwhile 'B' Company, commanded by Captain Turner, had remained in the old support line and had been ordered to dig a communication trench to link up the Redoubt with the old front line. They had worked throughout the night under heavy rifle fire and were congratulated on their achievement.

The diarist noted that October 14th 'seemed a never-ending day for those in the Redoubt'. The lines were too close for shelling, but the casualties mounted as grenades were constantly thrown. In the confusion of the battle promised relief did not materialise and they had to remain in the Redoubt in spite of relatively little sleep or food for 48 hours. They were finally relieved the following day and withdrawn to 'Railway Reserve Trench'.

Major Becher was missing and there was concern for him. The C.O., Lt. Colonel Fowler, in an effort to spot him, put his head above the parapet and was killed instantaneously by a sniper's bullet. Earlier he had been out during the night with Sgt. Stokes in an effort to find Major Becher. This was indeed a sad loss to the battalion as Lt. Colonel Fowler had been well liked.

Shortly afterwards news was received that Major John Becher had been found. He had been accompanied by his batman; they had been bombed by the Germans and both badly wounded. Although they had become separated, they had both crawled away, but John Becher had been forced to lie in an old trench until he was discovered by an officer of the Leicesters. He was finally rescued and under heavy fire was carried to safety across open ground. Sadly he did not recover from his injuries and died ten weeks later on 1st January 1916. The diarist paid great tribute to John Becher, stating that he often went out on night patrols into 'no man's land' and would never tell a man to do something that he wouldn't do himself. In the space of a few hours he had been struck down in the same battle as his two brothers-in-law, the Handfords. On 16th October a bedraggled and depleted battalion returned to Vaudricourt, arriving at 6.30 a.m. for a much needed sleep in billets, which were described as some of the poorest they had been assigned to. [For a further account see Chapter 4.]

The Hohenzollern Redoubt was described as a fruitless battle and was looked upon as a dismal failure. The 1/8th Battalion lost 7 officers and 35 other ranks killed or later dying of their wounds, in addition 14 were missing and subsequently found to have died. Of the deaths, 7 were Southwell men: the Handford brothers, John Becher (died of his wounds 10 weeks later), Cpl. John Sharman, L/Cpl. Arthur Spencer, Pte. Charles Stimson and Pte. Cyril Harrison. This tragic engagement illustrates the pain felt up and down the Empire when members of the 'Pals' battalions' were killed in their numbers in individual battles.

Whilst there were going to be further devastating losses, the Hohenzollern Redoubt must be recorded as the battalion's darkest period. In October 1919 John Percy Hales, D.S.O., rector of Cotgrave and chaplain to the 1/8th Battalion throughout the war, said on the anniversary of the battle that it was one 'of the worst nights of my life – The Hohenzollern Redoubt'[8].

Richebourg – Marseilles – Candas

October 18th 1915 – March 5th 1916

The much depleted battalion welcomed the arrival of 103 reinforcements, but was still somewhat short of officers. On 18th October they were paraded in front of Major General Stuart-Wortley, who thanked them for their work at Hohenzollern and spoke personally to those who had excelled themselves in the recent battle.

The following day they were not sorry to leave their uncomfortable billets and marched to Lapugnoy for a week in very comfortable quarters. Here several new junior officers joined them and the various companies were able to get themselves into shape. They were entertained by the 'Whizz-bangs' theatre group who put on a few good shows. The local wine took its toll on a number across all ranks. After their week's rest they moved back to Béthune.

At the end of the month the 46th Division was reviewed by the King and the Prince of Wales. Around 250 men represented the 1/8th Battalion in a ploughed field that had been subjected to heavy rain. The diarist noted that the King suffered a nasty accident and was driven away looking very ill, he did not elaborate on the nature of the accident.

The battalion received further reinforcements at Béthune and on 4th November they left for their next front-line assignment near Vieille Chapelle, relieving the 58th Rifles (Meerut Division) in trenches close to Neuve Chapelle. The land was very wet and they took over a badly maintained set of trenches, which were affected by standing water. The previous occupants had done little to make them comfortable. However, the line was very quiet and the opposing Germans were quite talkative. One shouted over, 'I don't want to fight, I've had enough of the war.' A few days later another enquired about which regiment they were and made remarks about cigarettes and plum puddings. Being relatively quiet there were few casualties, however, when they moved along this particular sector they were regularly swept by machine-gun fire and sadly Sgt. Arthur Sheppard of Southwell was killed on 22nd November. He had been awarded the D.C.M. for gallantry whilst they had been in the Hooge sector earlier in the summer.

The battalion only spent 16 days in the trenches in this sector, but they witnessed some cold, wet weather resorting to thigh length 'gumboots', and had to treat their legs and feet daily with

---

[8] See note following the *Newark Advertiser* report of 20th October, 1915.

whale oil in an effort to avoid 'trench feet'. The men were relieved every 24 hours to allow them to dry out and have a decent rest before returning to the line. Unfortunately, during these so called periods of rest they had to undertake much work on strengthening the trenches in their sector. On 2nd December they were relieved by the 7th Battalion, having lost 3 men killed and 15 wounded during this apparent quiet period.

Following their withdrawal from this sector the battalion returned to Vieille Chapelle and were instructed by Brigade H.Q. that they should be ready at short notice to move to an 'unknown destination'. Rumour was rife whilst they cleaned off the mud from the trenches and smartened themselves up once again. They soon found out that they were scheduled to go to Egypt.

Early December was spent on drill, briefings and re-equipping, in the process of which they had to part company with 'Big Ben' and 'Old Bob' and other heavy draught horses that had been with them since leaving Newark. They were replaced by mules, bearing names such as 'Harry Thaw' and 'Legs Eleven'. Once again the battalion was moved to new billets, this time at Wittes by the La Bassée Canal where they spent Christmas 1915. The troops all received gifts from home, including a parcel from the Nottingham Comforts Fund. However, Christmas was short-lived as on Boxing Day they were moved to fresh billets at Molinghem, which were full of vermin. Despite this they had a good time and enjoyed some football with the 11th Sherwood Foresters, and managed to win the brigade championship.

Between 7th and 9th January the battalion was moved by train to Marseilles where, according to the diarist, they spent their happiest fortnight in France. Whilst they had to undertake some training and preparation for their forthcoming voyage, their afternoons were free to enjoy the cafes and bars of Marseilles. Arrangements were well underway for their sea journey to Egypt, when on 24th January they were disappointed to hear a change of plan and that they would be returning to Northern France the next night to join the 3rd Army. The reason for this sudden change was not immediately clear, but it transpired that as Gallipoli had been evacuated much easier than anticipated there was no need for further troops to be sent to the region. The battalion marched to the railway station through crowds of cheering French people, which no doubt boosted their morale somewhat. These young men from Nottinghamshire were a long way from home, but must have appreciated the experience, not least of all a well-earned rest after the traumas of the front line.

After an uncomfortable journey the battalion arrived at Pont Remy on the morning of 28th January 1916 and stayed for 2 weeks prior to moving to Ribeaucourt. Here they parted company with the Machine Gun Section, consisting of an officer and 35 men, along with their equipment. As a replacement for the machine guns they received the new, much lighter Lewis Guns. There followed further training before being moved to Candas where they undertook work on the extension of the railway in preparation for a new offensive. Following their 3 months' diversion from the front, the battalion was now ready to play a further active part in the war – Vimy Ridge.

Vimy Ridge

March 6th 1916 – April 21st 1916

On hearing the news that the next move was to Vimy Ridge, the one word that went round the battalion was 'mines'. So much had been heard about mining warfare and their fears of the unpleasant nature of this form of warfare were soon to be realised, particularly during the latter part of their stay in this sector. The whole area proved to be a mass of mines.

The front line in 1915 had run through the east end of Lorette Ridge to Carency and then to La Targette, however, on September 25th 1915 the French had pushed the Germans back a mile virtually to the foot of Vimy Ridge. Running north to south was the Arras – Béthune road (the Route de Béthune), about a mile behind the front line and two miles in front of Mont St Eloy. The forward area was one of desolation, with trenches, wire, shell holes, mine craters, and shattered trees in what had been 'no man's land'.[9]

Vimy Ridge was held by the French when the 1/8th Battalion arrived and this was their first experience of taking over from them. They were very well received by the French, who, no doubt, were destined to support their hard-pressed colleagues at Verdun. The British officers were invited to drink a toast in sweet sparkling wine to 'confusion to the enemy'. In the midst of the meeting they were soon reminded, after their sojourn in Marseilles, that the war was still in progress as they were shelled by the opposing line.

On 6th March the battalion moved up towards the front and the following day they set about cleaning and repairing the trenches. Here they found huge dugouts and caverns in the chalk that had been fitted out with wire beds, having accommodation for two companies. The dugouts gave them good protection from incoming shells. After a week they were relieved by the 2nd Royal Irish Rifles and withdrew to rest billets, which were in a mess. As the diarist recorded, they could not give the previous occupants a 'billet clean' certificate with the piles of rubbish that had been left behind. Nor were there any baths so they had to improvise. However, they did recruit 'a fascinating crowd of French ladies' to assist with clothes washing.

During the periods of 'rest' the battalion was called upon to provide men to the Brigade Mining Section, which was giving assistance to the French miners. This involved an officer and twelve men, but on the credit side they received 140 reinforcements that were very welcome.

The front lines were often only 70 yards apart and in some cases bombing posts were only 10 – 15 yards apart and conversations could easily be overheard. Meanwhile mining was taking place and working parties were formed to take over craters quickly when a mine was blown, making sure the lip of the crater was occupied and linked up to their trenches before the enemy took advantage. During this period the diarist noted that there was little special activity by the Germans apart from regular shelling and trench mortars being fired, which from time to time created a need for serious repairs to their defences. Additionally, the Germans were sending over 'lachrymatory' gas shells, which had a sweet smell and did little harm except to make their eyes water.

Because of the closeness of the lines, it was necessary at night to erect 'white boards' so that their gunners could identify friendly trenches. These boards had a white backward facing face and were placed in such a position that the Germans could not see them. The main activity was to harass the Germans continuously with mortars and sniper fire. It seems that the battalion held

---

[9] The modern day visitor to Vimy Ridge can still see a large area covered in shell holes, but as the grass has grown and the trees have recovered one can only start to imagine the scene of desolation that greeted the troops.

its own with sniping, and were annoyed when their champion sniper Sgt.-Drummer Clewes, who had been responsible for killing over 100 Germans, was sent home as his contract had expired – he later received the D.C.M. (he must have been one of the longer serving territorials). Once again Col. Fowler's Elephant Gun was put to good use in blowing out several of the enemy's loophole plates. A rather bizarre piece of equipment had been left behind by the Germans in the form of a dummy tree, which consisted of a 20 feet high structure made of steel casing and covered in imitation bark with ledges inside, allowing someone to climb up and observe the enemy's positions. During this period new items to improve intelligence gathering were introduced, including the 'I-Tok', which was a device intended to pick up enemy telegraph and telephone messages. The efficiency of the device was doubted as most of the messages picked up were their own! A little later a 'Fullerphone' was provided which replaced the ordinary telephone and was supposed to be able to transmit messages in a secure way.

One benefit of following the French was that they had organized 'Trench Coffee Shops', which proved to be a great success in providing hot drinks when needed. On the other hand the diarist noted 'the casual sanitary arrangements of the French', which resulted in the presence of many rats in the sector, some of which were 'such colossal specimens as we found during our stay in the Vimy trenches'.

On April 12th the battalion moved back to the trenches for what proved to be an eventful tour. Following heavy rain and snow the trenches were in a deplorable state and they had to resort to gum boots again. In the first three days they were faced with heavy shelling and on 16th April the French had arranged to blow one of their mines, following which a raiding party was to rush forward and capture any remaining Germans in their forward trenches. However, all did not go to plan due to bad synchronization and the Germans being somehow aware of the plan, which took the raiding party by surprise and, faced with heavy resistance, they had to retire under fire. Fortunately another group managed to consolidate the trenches following the mine being blown.

In retaliation the Germans blew one of their mines the following night, which caused a lot of damage and heavy losses. There followed three very miserable nights as members of the battalion managed to occupy the lip of the crater. There was a lot of bravery shown in re-establishing their position and L/Cpl. J.T. Templeman of Southwell was commended for carrying out repairs to telephone wires 'with his usual skill and courage'.

A further mine was blown by the French on 19th April, which resulted in hostile shelling, and another mine was set off by the Germans on the following day. Much to their relief the battalion was relieved by the 10th Cheshires and had a very weary trudge along endless duck boards to Écoivres, were then taken by bus to Tincques and Bethencourt where they were billeted across the two villages. They arrived in a bedraggled state, having spent eight days in waterlogged trenches, just as the ladies of the villages were setting off to church in their Sunday best.

This short excursion to Vimy Ridge had cost the battalion 17 killed, 69 wounded and 5 missing. It is rather chilling to read these numbers that were recorded in a very matter-of-fact way, at the same time the diarist mentioned that the men expressed concern for their replacements, who were to suffer even greater losses as the Germans made a determined attack and recaptured their trenches.

The Battle of Gommecourt – The Somme Offensive

April 22nd 1916 – July 2nd 1916

Within a few days of arriving at Tincques the men had managed to clean off the mud and filth of the Vimy trenches and felt fit for their next assignment. On April 26th the battalion was inspected by General Shipley who commended them on their smart turnout.

The weather had improved and they were back in training. This time they were drilled in a new form of bayonet fighting and practised advancing under the shelter of a smokescreen. It is interesting to note that as the war progressed new forms of fighting were devised and implemented. This time it was to prepare them for the 'big push' that was to be the Somme Offensive. By April 29th the battalion was moved to Averdoignt, near St. Pol, and 60 members of 'B' Company and 100 of 'C' Company were sent to Third Army Headquarters for a short period of duty. They were subsequently praised for their smartness and good work. By early May they were on the move again, arriving at Bienvillers on 10th and were under the command of VII Corps.

At that time this part of the line was the quietest on the Western Front. So quiet that, even when holding the line, commanders slept in their pyjamas. The feeling was that the dugouts had been made for comfort and there were small garden plots scattered around without the risk of shelling and sniper fire. However, it transpired that the Germans at this point were short of ammunition, but when a German diary was recovered later it appeared that the Germans had been making a note of all movements and had gained a good idea as to the forthcoming attack.

The attack that the 46th Division was preparing was to be against the German trenches west of Gommecourt, immediately opposite the village of Foncquevillers. The idea was to cut off the German salient - the most westerly point that they had held as a permanent line. With this objective in mind a tremendous amount of preparation was taking place. Old trenches were improved and around a dozen of them had been given local names, such as Lincoln Lane, Nottingham Street, Rotten Row, Derby Dyke, etc. The trenches were dug out a further two feet and barbed wire was removed. In addition a tremendous amount of munitions and rations were put in place – all of this observed by the Germans who, according to the captured diaries, were impressed with the preparations.

During their stay at Bienvillers the 1/8th Battalion busied themselves with improving the defences of the village until they were sent to relieve the 5th North Staffords in Foncquevillers on 19th May. Two uneventful weeks later they were relieved by the 4th Leicesters and sent to Humbercamp, prior to receiving their final training for the forthcoming 'Big Push'. On 7th June they moved on to Le Souich, where the diarist noted that they spent one of the least enjoyable weeks out of the line in intensive training and work details in very wet weather. The training involved a four hour march to the training ground, two hours soaked to the skin in growing corn whilst they practised for the battle, and a further four hour return march. The feeling was that it had been totally overdone and the men became stale. In addition to all the practical training the officers were carefully briefed by means of a full-scale model of the German lines at Gommecourt.

Following this extensive, if not overdone, training the battalion marched back to Humbercamp where they were informed that the 1/8th Battalion would be held in reserve with the main assault being undertaken by the 5th and 7th Battalions. Once again the 1/8th were involved in numerous working parties in readiness for the attack. They moved to Foncquevillers on 18th June and were besieged with visitors, resulting in the rapid depletion of their victuals and drinks.

During this period there was a general feeling of confidence. However, on 23rd June the heavens opened and there was a violent thunderstorm, which virtually wrecked all the good work they had done, with the trenches filling up to a depth of two feet in mud and water and needing constant pumping out. There was now a great deal of work to be undertaken to make good the damage before the forthcoming offensive was due to start.

The diarist noted how difficult it was to move along the line with knee-deep mud and water. Whatever happened the movement of supplies had to proceed. In the midst of this 'B' Company came under attack from Adinfer wood and their casualties rose. In this period Pte. John Fogg of Southwell was killed along with several other men. Fortunately the battalion was relieved on 27th June and they moved back to Pommier. They had spent nine difficult days holding the line and the casualty list showed 16 men killed and 46 wounded. During their short stay at Pommier they were lucky to avoid further casualties when the local church was shelled as some of the officers were taking tea in an adjoining building; they escaped covered in dust and a little shaken.

The bad weather meant that the attack was postponed until 1st July and the night before the battalion took up their positions at Foncquevillers. They arrived at 10.00 p.m. and were issued with soup and rum, together with rations for the following day, iron rations and a bacon sandwich. They were loaded up with 200 rounds of small arms ammunition, four sandbags, two Mills grenades, two gas helmets, haversack, waterproof sheet, and a supply of wire cutters and gloves.

They reached their assembly point in the early hours and the first bombardment started at 6.25 a.m. The assaulting battalions moved off at 7.30 a.m., supported by a heavy bombardment. By 8.00 a.m. the 1/8th Battalion started moving forward, but were hampered by deep water and mud. The trenches were blocked by the dead and with the wounded trying to make their way back. As a result, little progress was made and it soon became clear that the attack on their front had not succeeded. The main reason given was that the bombardment had done little damage to the opposing defences and covering smoke had dispersed before the main assault had got across 'No Man's Land'. Those that did reach the German trenches met with heavy resistance and were soon overwhelmed. By late afternoon volunteers were called for to go out and ascertain the state of affairs ahead of them. Stretcher bearers and others worked for 36 hours under constant bombardment to bring in the wounded. The battalion was relieved by the 5th Lincolns on the morning of 2nd July.

Even as they withdrew four men were wounded as a shell from one of their own guns burst prematurely. Whilst the Somme offensive accounted for 50,000 casualties on the first day, the 1/8th Battalion escaped relatively lightly with 3 killed, 37 wounded and 3 missing, one of those was Pte. Thomas Barlow of Southwell who was later confirmed as killed in action.

Upon reflection the diarist noted:

> We cannot look back with anything but regret on the awful battle, when so many lives were sacrificed apparently to no purpose. July 1st is not our happiest of days – indeed on two successive occasions it was our most unfortunate day of the year.

He went on to mention that the enemy must have been aware of what was planned and made preparations accordingly. In addition he said,

> …barely a man had had a full night's sleep for a week prior to the attack, and there had scarcely been a day or night when rain had not fallen consistently and heavily, and working parties had not been soaked to the skin.

The diarist further noted that most officers in the attacking battalions had been killed or wounded along with a large proportion of the men. It would seem that at the time of writing, whilst there was an acknowledgement that many had died, the full extent of the casualties had not been calculated.

There was a message of thanks from the Corps Commander in appreciation of their effort, '… we had a share in the success of the great Somme attack, and that our own terrible losses were not entirely in vain'.

Bellacourt

July 2nd 1916 - October 29th 1916

The battalion moved to Bavincourt expecting to take a well earned rest following the traumas of the Somme offensive. However, after just two days orders were received to move again on July 7th to Bienvillers. Here they spent two unpleasant nights moving gas cylinders. The fear was that a bursting shell would rupture a cylinder and cause huge problems. To guard against this they wore smoke helmets at all times. Fortunately the gas was moved to the front without incident.

After this nerve-racking diversion on July 10th the battalion moved to Bellacourt, almost 5 miles south-west of Arras. This proved to be, on the whole, a very quiet sector. In the early part of their stay they welcomed a number of new officers and men and were quite well off for numbers. The various companies took up their positions on July 11th, relieving the Liverpool Scottish. The diarist recorded the commanders of the various companies:

    'A' Company - Captain Vann
    'B' Company - Captain Turner
    'C' Company - Captain Pigford
    'D' Company - Captain Hill

At this stage each company had two platoons in the front line and two in support, a system that worked very well. They held quite a long frontage of the line and were up to 200 yards away from the enemy. The sector was reckoned to be the quietest on the British Front, but not totally so during the three months that they were there. Even the weather was reasonable during this period after the mud of their last assignment.

Although the diarist had noted that this was a quiet sector during their first tour of the trenches, in the early hours 'B' Company were given an unexpected reminder of the war with a well aimed bombardment that killed four men and wounded nine. One of the fatalities was Corporal A.E. Paling of Southwell [see Chapter 4]. It was believed that the Germans had a visit from their 'travelling circus', a hit squad that was brought up from time to time to strafe a section of the line. Following this incident the line was quiet and the battalion settled into a 'humdrum' existence, being rotated in and out of the line every six days.

During their rest periods the troops were entertained by the 'Whizz-bangs' and played the usual football games. However, they were not without inspections by the new Divisional Commander, Major-General W. Thwaites, who had been nicknamed 'The Mushroom Picker' because of his surprise early morning visits. Whilst he was said to find this amusing, he was a stickler for smartness and insisted that salutes went without fault. The commander of 'B' Company, Captain Turner, received a polite rebuke for failing to keep his horse under control when it was 'spooked' by the men fixing bayonets. Whilst the line was generally quiet, a well planned raid took place headed by Captain Vann of 'A' Company consisting of 5 officers and 136 other ranks from his company. The objective was to secure a prisoner and, in the event, they killed 5 Germans and brought back 5 prisoners at a cost of 8 wounded. The raid was heralded a success and Captain Vann received a bar to his M.C. and subsequently the French Croix-de-Guerre.

By the time the battalion was relieved they had suffered a total of 7 killed and 37 wounded. On 29th October they moved on to a training area to prepare for their next assignment.

The Capture of Gommecourt

October 29th 1916 – March 17th 1917

Between 29th October and 3rd November the battalion marched 40 miles from Bailleulval to Maison Ponthieu, which was situated in the Third Army (St. Riquier) training area. Once again the billets were not up to standard and the men had to spend some time making improvements to ensure adequate bathing and cooking facilities. There was little opportunity for entertainment and if they wanted to shop it meant a journey to Auxi-le-Chateau.

During their stay of three weeks they undertook training with a view to them taking a further part in the Somme offensive, this included practice formations for open warfare. The military training was interspersed with football matches, aimed at keeping the men fit. Training for open warfare was essential, as for the most part they had been confined to trench fighting. Getting to and from the training grounds required a somewhat tedious six mile journey. Further changes of personnel took place, the most notable being the return of Southwell solicitor Major Lane, who 18 months previously had been wounded at Kemmel and had recuperated in England. Major Lane took over the command of 'A' Company.

Following this period of training the battalion returned to their old trenches at Foncquevillers. Initially on 22nd November they set off from Humbercourt, where they undertook further training in cold and wet conditions. There was more football and a cross-country run, with a further inspection by Major-General Thwaites on a cold and foggy day, which meant he was unable to spot some of the more unconventional manoeuvres. The following day they were issued with new, more effective gas masks, which stayed with them until the end of the war. By 6th December they were deemed ready for a return to the front line and were in rotation with the 7th Battalion. Unfortunately, they were again subjected to trenches that were deep in mud and water and 'gumboots thigh' were in great demand. The dugouts were also quite poor, making life in the trenches very uncomfortable. Whilst conditions were bad, the front was quiet, apart from occasional shelling, and they were only a short distance from the village where they could dry out and clean their kit. Christmas day 1916 was spent in the line, but was peaceful, although they did not enjoy their Christmas dinner until the New Year. The gifts from home were most welcome, including the card reproduced overleaf.

Although this period had been quiet, their last relief of the 7th Battalion on 16th February was a bit of a shock as they were subjected to a heavy bombardment of gas with between 500 and 600 shells, mostly filled with phosgene, coming over and, as a consequence, they suffered heavy casualties with 4 men killed and 24 wounded. During this stretch at the front they were helping to train men from three battalions of the London Regiment. The diarist noted their concern as 'they were almost like the proverbial sardines', and if the enemy had decided to shell them whilst they had been training these troops, the casualties would have been very high.

Post Card

For Correspondence | Address Only

SOUTHWELL MINSTER,
December, 1916.

Dear Friend,

This card takes to you, wheresoever you may be, my best Christmas and New Year wishes. It is a picture of the little War chapel we have fitted up in the Minster. The list of the names of all those who have left this parish to serve is, as you see, decorated with flags, and surmounted by the crucifix, to remind us how all human suffering is shared by Jesus Christ, and how He saved us by His own death from the eternal consequences of sin. On the table are some well-known pictures, and some flowers. The flowers are kept fresh by children, or by someone who has lost her husband, and being unable to put flowers on his grave far away, places them here instead in memory of him. Here prayer is said every day by children or by others for you. So you are not forgotten.

May Christmas bring us all some better hope of peace and goodwill, and help us to trust in Him Who came from heaven to earth so as to lead us from earth to heaven.

Your Minister in the Lord,
W. J. CONYBEARE.

Christmas Greetings, 1916 (Mike Kirton - courtesy of Margaret Peet)

Further personnel changes took place as Major Lane succeeded Major Ashwell as second in command and a number of officers were relieved, as they were deemed to be unfit. Casualties during their time in this sector amounted to 7 killed and 47 wounded, but they received 243 reinforcements, which included several men from the Sherwood Rangers Yeomanry. The battalion handed over their trenches on February 19th and marched back to St. Amand.

A period of refitting and reorganization followed after moving to Ivergny. The diary entries at this time provide an interesting insight into the way the army was reorganized with the benefit of experience to date. In the early days specialist bombing or 'Grenade Platoons' had been set up and these were now disbanded. In the future each platoon would have its own section of bombers along with other specialist sections:

- Riflemen
- Bombers
- Rifle Grenadiers
- Lewis Gunners

This restructuring was to last for the remainder of the war. The signallers were also divided into 'battalion' and 'company' signallers.

By late February 1917 the Germans were starting to retreat – the 'great Somme Retirement' - and the battalion moved to St. Amand, near Foncquevillers, where they relieved members of the 138th Brigade who were following the retreating Germans. On 3rd March they took over the old German trenches at Gommecourt from the 5th Leicesters. However, the Germans were still on the eastern outskirts of the village and the line was in a 'fluid' state. As the German retreat gained pace it was difficult to keep up, however, they did have time to burn their dugouts before vacating them, leaving just a few souvenirs, including a 'Boche bugle' that eventually found its way into the battalion museum. The British did not have it all their own way as the Germans mounted a counter-attack against 'C' Company on 4th March, resulting in 7 deaths and 17 wounded. Fighting continued backwards and forwards around Gommecourt as the Germans resisted and much gallantry was demonstrated during this period of 'moving' warfare. As the front moved, keeping up essential supplies proved to be a challenge. The roads were in a sorry state and every night they were 'thronged with horses and vehicles'. By mid-March the battalion was established in Gommecourt where they found the once prosperous village had been virtually destroyed. The German trenches had been very well constructed and in some of the deep dugouts they found long subterranean passages where looted tapestries and valuable furniture from the local chateau had been secreted by the Germans. They were shocked to come across bodies of British officers and men who had not been buried after the Somme offensive on 1st July, although there was a grave for one officer with a cross bearing an inscription in English: 'To the memory of a very gallant British Officer and Gentleman, killed 1st July 1916.'

Lens

March 17th 1917 – July 4th 1917

The battalion's departure from the Gommecourt line was something of a relief for them, but they were faced with a march to Contay where they arrived on 23rd March. It was not an easy journey as the roads were subject to shelling and, having been in constant use, were very muddy. At times vehicles were up to their axles in mud, all adding to the difficulty in moving around. However, they realized that footslogging was the easiest mode of transport. Those on bicycles proved to be a source of amusement as they tried to negotiate the mud. From Contay they went through Amiens and eventually reached Revelles where they awaited a train north. En route they met men of the 2/8th Sherwood Foresters, who had recently arrived in France, and enjoyed a bit of banter with them, one conversation was recorded: 'Who are you?' – '1/8th' was the reply', 'Who are you?'- '2/8th' – 'Right, you can tell your mother you've seen some real soldiers now!'.

Upon reaching Revelles there was a delay due to the number of divisions that required transport and the battalion enjoyed a short rest. Visits to Amiens, which had only been slightly damaged, were appreciated and they found the town full of life. On 24th March they entrained for the north and experienced a slow journey, arriving the following morning at Hazebrouck where they were told there would be a 15 minute stop. Some of the officers decided to chance their luck and raced to the buffet to order 'omelettes et café', the train moved off without warning and they were stranded until they had the good fortune to find a freight train that was heading their way and fortunately arrived at Bergette just as the rest of the battalion was detraining. Following a few hours march they arrived at Westrehem and comfortable billets.

The battalion was now part of the First Army commanded by General Horne and spent the first two weeks at their new location refitting and practising the new platoon formation for attack using a creeping barrage, a technique that had been developed as the war progressed. Again football played an important part in keeping the men fit and active. Recreation time was also spent visiting the Divisional Cinema and obtaining personal supplies from the village shop – Lane's Emporium. They also found that the locals were very welcoming and they lacked for little, although the weather was still cold and there were heavy snowfalls.

In mid-April the battalion once more moved towards the line and they stayed under canvas at Houchin, where they shared a camp with the 7th Battalion. Inevitably there were further personnel changes as officers were transferred in and out and others were sent home sick. By 18th April another move took them to Liévin, passing close to the front line where they were warned to be careful of roads being shelled and saw signs instructing them to wear 'small box respirator's – clearly there was a threat from gas. Liévin had only been evacuated by the Germans two days earlier as a result of the Canadians capturing Vimy Ridge. However, the enemy still held some strategic positions, including Fosse 3, Hill 65, and Hill 70 as illustrated on the map overleaf.

Liévin lay astride the Souchez River and was three miles west of Lens, which was still held by the Germans. It had been a thriving mining centre, but was now badly damaged by shelling. However, many of the cellars had been adapted as defensive positions, but all the defences were facing the wrong way. Some of the cellars had been furnished with tables, chairs, and beds.

Intelligence obtained from interrogating prisoners suggested that the Germans were ready to retreat from Lens and that little pressure would be required to push the enemy outposts out of Cité-de-Riaumont and Hill 65. Unfortunately, the information had been obtained when the Germans were in a panic, but they had since had time to re-establish themselves. This proved to be a costly error.

On 19th April the 1/8th Battalion took over a section of the line from the 7th Northamptons and were informed that they would be involved in capturing Hill 65. However, before that could be attempted the enemy needed clearing from the village of Riaumont. This was partially achieved the night after their deployment in conjunction with the 6th Battalion. There were no British casualties, although several Germans were killed and one captured. As a result of his bravery Lt. Geary received the Military Cross (he was to die in an engagement two weeks before the Armistice). Unfortunately, the 6th Battalion's objective was not achieved and there was further

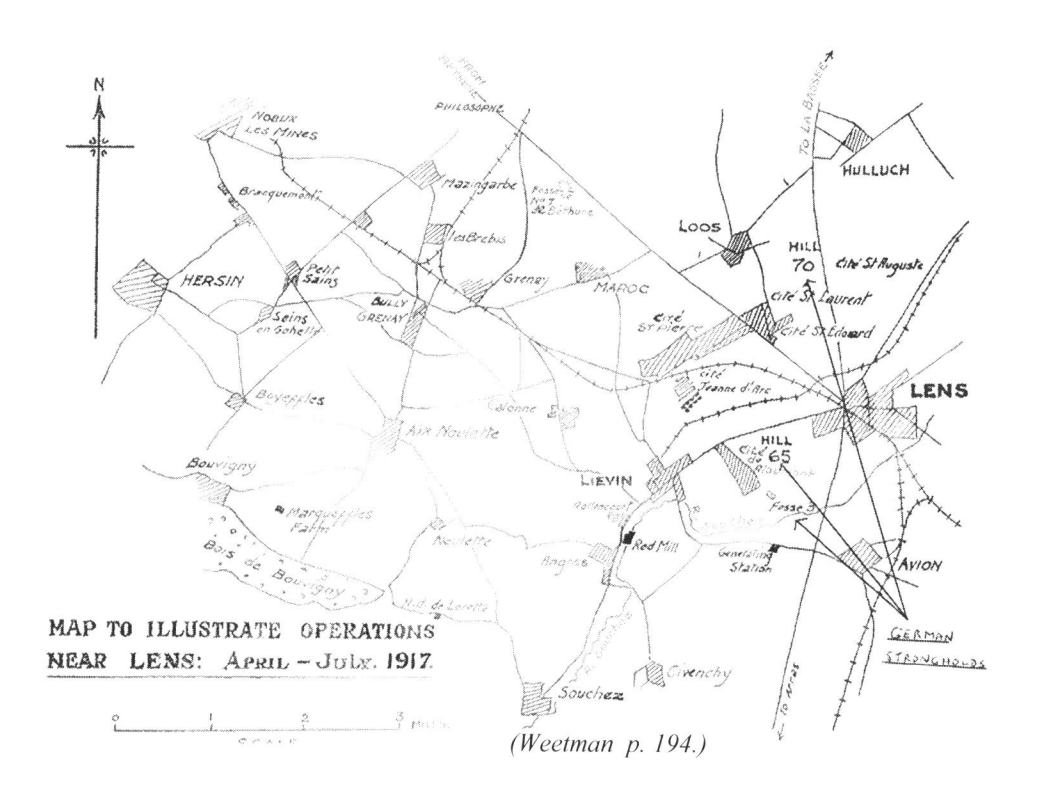

MAP TO ILLUSTRATE OPERATIONS NEAR LENS: APRIL – JULY 1917

(Weetman p. 194.)

fighting and a good deal of shelling during the night of 21/22nd April, resulting in a number of casualties, but no ground was given.

With only partial success, the officers were surprised to receive orders that members of the battalion were to attempt to capture Hill 65, with the 6th Battalion tasked with attacking Fosse 3 and clearing the enemy from the rest of the village. 'C' Company were chosen for this hazardous mission, but there was little time for proper reconnaissance prior to the attack. It seems that the Germans were aware that an attack was imminent as they opened up with their artillery on the forward trenches, and it was thought at one point that they were attacking. At 4.45 a.m. on 23rd April, before their promised tea and rum arrived, 'C' Company launched their attack under a barrage of artillery and trench mortars. There were some early casualties from 'friendly' fire as well as tremendous resistance from the enemy, and it soon became evident that the attack had been a mistake as the Germans held some adjacent positions. Casualties amongst 'C' Company were high, and with them being in imminent danger of being surrounded orders were given to withdraw. Sadly few made it back to their trenches and the immediate toll was 70 missing and 34 wounded. Amongst the dead was Corporal William Ward of Southwell, who had been moved into 'C' Company. The men were highly praised for their gallantry as were members of 'D' Company who had been involved in 'mopping up'. Unfortunately, the 6th Battalion had fared little better in their attempt to gain control of Fosse 3.

With the benefit of hindsight, the diarist noted that the intelligence report that the enemy was about to retreat was somewhat optimistic. He also made it clear that frontal attacks should not be made when there was danger of counter attack on a flank. In the event Hill 65 was only captured after two months of artillery preparation and the involvement, at intervals, of two brigades. In addition to these mistakes by the planners, it was to be another year before the Germans evacuated Lens, even after Hill 65 and later Hill 70 had been captured from them.

On 24th April the battalion went back into Brigade support and three days later the whole brigade was relieved by 137th Brigade and the 1/8th Battalion moved to Marqueffles Farm, which was described as a 'delightful spot'. The weather had improved and the men were extremely comfortable in the tranquil surroundings. 'C' Company were virtually wiped out at Hill 65 and with no replacements in the offing, transfers were made from other companies to equalise the numbers. From Marqueffles Farm on 6th May the battalion relieved the 5th Lincolns, taking over a section in front of Loos. Here the former German trenches were very shallow and, with the enemy having a good view of them, it was necessary to keep their heads down during daylight hours. The area was extremely desolate and made more unpleasant by bombardments of wing bombs, rifle grenades and gas bombs that caused 39 casualties with 8 deaths in the six days that they were there.

After this short tour the men were moved back to the Liévin sector where trench life was varied with some long distance patrols. On 29/30th May the Germans raided one of their trenches at a cost of 3 killed, 7 wounded and 2 men captured. During this period casualties were quite heavy and their depleted ranks were only partially replaced with reinforcements. At this time Cpl. John Thomas Templeman of Southwell was promoted to sergeant. To compensate for the shortage of men each company was reduced to three platoons from four. This situation illustrated the strain that was becoming evident in the British army with the high casualty rate.

Early June was spent in Brigade support at Liévin for six days and then the battalion returned to the line in front of Cité-St. Théodore, where they witnessed the pushing forward of several advance posts to protect the left flank of the 138th Brigade, together with some further long distance patrols. Following this brief spell they were again at Marqueffles Farm, where on 12th June they won first prize for the best turnout in the Brigade Horse Show. This was followed by a short tour as Brigade support in front of Loos. By now the battalion had experience of most of their immediate area and found little of it to their liking, as during their front line tours and in support there had been nothing but trenches to live in. In addition, as the Canadians and other British units had carried out raids on almost a daily basis, the enemy had retaliated with frequent shelling, which made life uncomfortable. One brighter aspect of their current location was that the local gardens were producing fresh vegetables and fruit with a good supply of early asparagus, gooseberries, and strawberries. An amusing diary entry refers to a greedy German who had wandered into the 6th Battalion's sector whilst filling his helmet with strawberries. He arrived at Battalion H.Q. minus his helmet full of fruit.

In spite of the earlier failures the High Command was still of the opinion that the Germans could be driven out of Lens and the 46th Division, together with the Canadians, were concentrating their efforts on bringing this about. However, it was a slow process as they nibbled away at the German front line. Two months earlier the 6th Battalion had failed to take Fosse 3 (at the same time as the Hill 65 disaster), but on 19th June the 138th Brigade finally achieved this objective. Three days later the 1/8th Battalion relieved the 5th Leicesters in 'Boot' and 'Brick' trenches near Calonne, having left the Loos area on 18th June. The two days they spent in these trenches were said to be the worst days in the history of the battalion. All four companies were in the line and there was hardly any shelter or accommodation. The shelling and trench-mortaring was very intense and they were in constant fear of attack. In this short period they suffered 10 killed and 31 wounded. The dead included Cpl. Arthur Humberstone of Southwell. They were relieved on

23/24th June, returning to Calonne. Even this was an unpleasant experience for 'A' Company who were targeted with gas shells and trench mortars, resulting in several casualties. A couple of days later 137th Brigade finally took Hill 65.

The battalion was moved back to Liévin, where they received orders to start digging assembly trenches at Cité-de-Riaumont. As the officers were receiving orders enemy shells knocked out a gun battery adjacent to them and also scored a direct hit on an ammunition dump, which resulted in explosions going on for several days. On the night of 27/28th June the battalion was moved to billets in Maroc. During this period further successes were chalked up and the Canadians got ever closer to Lens. These further gains convinced the High Command that the Germans were completely demoralized and that it wouldn't take much to capture Lens. They decided to put the whole division into this final effort on 1st July. The 1/8th Battalion were in support and 'A' and 'D' Companies were attached to the 6th Battalion, 'B' Company was attached to the 2nd Battalion, and 'C' to the 5th Battalion. Once again it seems there was an element of over confidence and initial gains were soon lost, with Lens remaining in enemy hands. The diarist notes 'July 1st is not a lucky day in the history of the 46th Division.'

The 1/8th Battalion was relieved on 3/4th July and taken to Chelers, which was described as a delightful village. They had been relatively lucky with only 6 wounded in the last debacle, but their experiences of the Lens operations amounted to 5 officers wounded; 3 missing; 42 other ranks killed; 180 wounded; and 72 missing. The diary records the first real hint of criticism of too much reliance being placed on poor intelligence and a warning for the future that more attention should be given to intelligence training.

St. Elie and Hill 70

July 4th 1917 – January 21st 1918

Following their three month period in the front line the battalion was moved to the relative quiet of Chelers. However, they were quite isolated with little opportunity for amusement; officers lucky enough to have a horse were able to visit St. Pol. Their billets were quite comfortable and Battalion Headquarters was housed in the local chateau, having a pleasant garden with a supply of fresh peaches. During this period the acting C.O. was Major John Kirkland Lane of Southwell.

Training continued, but with more emphasis on bayonet fighting. To hone their shooting skills there was a Divisional rifle competition; with the 1/8th Battalion winning a few prizes, and 'B' Company winning the Inter Company Snap-Shooting and Rapid Fire competition. The officers also had success at revolver shooting. To keep them on their toes there was the usual round of ceremonial inspections.

The calm of Chelers came to an end on 23rd July when the battalion, despite their low numbers, relieved the 1st Leicesters on the St. Elie front. The move heralded the longest period of continuous trench warfare that they had experienced, lasting for six months. Monotony was a big problem, apart from the occasional raid carried out by both sides. The Divisional Commander had ordered that raids should take place frequently, however, these were rarely a surprise to either side as cutting a gap in the wire and preliminary bombardments were a fair clue that a raid was in the offing.

St. Elie was reasonably familiar to the battalion as it was close to Hohenzollern and that particular section of the front had changed little since 1915. Mining was still a feature and the British had the upper hand in this particular offensive facet of warfare, as the 'Boche' were described as 'nervous miners'. The obvious evidence of mining was the large number of craters that had appeared following the detonation of mines. Another feature of this stretch of the line was the number of tunnels that had been dug to keep the troops out of view of the Germans who overlooked the area. Many of the dugouts had been fitted out with electric lights and underground barracks had been built within 100-400 yards of the Germans. The use of camouflage screens was also a new feature of the front.

A raid was planned by 'D' Company with the help of members of 'B' Company on 4th August. Despite careful planning it was not successful as 'D' Company were held up by heavy machine-gun fire, however, 'B' Company reached enemy trenches, but had to be recalled with both companies suffering casualties, with one death, as they returned. The following day, when the battalion was back in billets, they were heavily shelled, but escaped without casualties, although the Brigadier's dinner was delayed and he had to dine on cold 'bully beef', much to the amusement of the men.

On 15th August the Canadians captured Hill 70, which had been a long-standing objective and was to remain in Allied hands. The battalion now had ten days' rest at Verquin and the officers were fortunate enough to be invited to play tennis at the chateau, with partners for mixed doubles, followed by music in the drawing room after dinner. The other ranks enjoyed themselves in the village and were well looked after by the local miners, indeed they found the French to be very welcoming in this part of the front. The entertainment was enhanced by visits from the 'Whizz-bangs'. In addition Béthune, with its many attractions, was within walking distance of their billets.

The battalion continued with attack practice, and on 26th August they relieved the 23rd Battalion Royal Fusiliers in the Cambrin sector and remained there until 13th September. They were now north-west of the Hohenzollern Redoubt, which had an advantage over St. Elie in that it was not overlooked by the enemy. The first part of their tour in this sector was relatively quiet, however, on 30th August a small patrol reconnoitring a German post ran into difficulty, resulting in the death of an officer and Cpl. Harry Wright of Southwell. On 11th September a well-practised raid by 'C' Company and half of 'A' Company was caught in a bombardment and was forced to withdraw. There were high casualties with 3 deaths and 30 wounded and the following night 'C' Company were caught in a bombardment of trench mortars and suffered nine more casualties. The war diary roll of honour lists 11 deaths for 12/13th September, which was considerably worse than recorded in the text of the diary. Following these losses the 7th Battalion relieved them on 13th September and they moved to Fouquières for further training and refitting. A week later they moved to the front again and took over a section of Hill 70.

Hill 70 proved to be a useful spot for observation as they could see across the enemy lines for several miles. The only downside was that access to the sector was under German observation and they had to negotiate their way along a lengthy communication trench. There followed what was described as 'For seven weeks, probably the most monotonous in the history of the Battalion's trench warfare…' Tours in the trenches were on a six day rotation and whilst in reserve they had reasonably comfortable accommodation. With no real 'excitement' the battalion spent its time repairing and improving their trenches, which had been badly damaged during the battle for Hill 70. During the early part of October the weather had been hot and dry, but the rain returned and they were soon struggling in sticky mud.

The water supply to these trenches was, unusually, by pipes, which were occasionally ruptured by shells. Normal supplies were delivered by mules, which were a quiet and efficient method that was peculiar to this sector. In addition work had commenced on building tramlines up to Hill 70.

During this quieter period the men had little difficulty in carrying out General Carey's orders that they should shave every day and tea leaves were not to be disposed of in the trenches.

Although the diarist mentioned that the sector was quiet, this was all relative as he still recorded heavy shelling. On 4th October the battalion was shelled as the Germans attempted to raid the 7th Battalions trenches. 'B' Company were particularly badly hit and Sgt. William Drabble of Southwell was killed along with three others. The clearing of casualties and rescuing buried men was a difficult task for some of the men. There followed an uneventful period until 11th November when a raid on enemy trenches by a newly joined Subaltern, Lt. A. C. Fairbrother, and two men resulted in the shooting of one German. Fairbrother was awarded the M.C. for this daring raid. The battalion was withdrawn from Hill 70 on 15th November. Following this tour Major Lane was posted home for a tour of duty.

The battalion returned to the St. Elie sector until mid-January 1918, where they continued with a six-day rotation. As the weather had now turned very bad, the number of troops kept in the front line was reduced to the minimum. However, one bonus was that the battalion was out of the line over Christmas, which they spent at Verquin 'with much feasting and merriment'. Supplies of Christmas treats were very good and the local population appreciated the way that they enjoyed their festivities. On 28th December they returned to the line still full of Christmas cheer, and the diarist recorded that the four company commanders had a look about them that

Christmas Greetings from Southwell 1917 (Mike Kirton)

suggested 'another little drink wouldn't do us any harm'.

They were soon reminded of the war, when on 2nd January the Germans mounted a massive raid along the length of their line, but following careful preparation they were beaten off by a rain of Lewis gun fire. Luckily they only suffered 8 wounded and managed to capture two prisoners. The architect of their defence, Captain Simonet, received the M.C and a number of men had shown great gallantry.

Football, of course, played an important role in their recreation time, and a Divisional league was formed with each team being given a code name to avoid their identity being divulged to the Germans.

This period, whilst being described as monotonous at times, saw 35 men killed. As they prepared to move there were a number of personnel changes, including Captain Turner who had led 'B' Company for some time. Following this stint at the front the battalion was relieved and sent to Verquin, where they had a few days to clean themselves and their kit prior to a move on 21st January to Burbure in preparation for a long period of training.

Spring 1918

January 22nd 1918 – April 20th 1918

In January 1918, as the battalion was withdrawn from their six months in the forward area, there was an element of uncertainty as to what would be their next role. Following the Russian withdrawal from the war the Germans had many more troops available for the Western Front, and it was thought that the allies would have to take on a much more defensive role. With this fear of a German breakthrough much effort was being made in strengthening existing defensive lines. There was a particular fear that there would be a breakthrough in the area around Béthune. The 1/8th Battalion was ordered to send a party of 460 men, under the charge of Col. Blackwell, to Mazingarbe to help with the defensive work until 7th February.

With around half the battalion away the remainder undertook some training at Burbure. Their biggest gripe at this time was poor bathing and laundry facilities. The supply of clean clothes was rather scarce and the diarist complained that clothes sent to the laundry at Abbeville came back dirtier than when they went. However, supplies of other essentials were coming through quite well, but there was a shortage of motor lorries and it was becoming evident that money was quite tight at this stage in the war.

With economy being the order of the day there was a reorganization of the Brigade structure, which was reduced from four to three battalions. The 7th Battalion was the one to be broken up and the 2/8th also disappeared, as they merged into the 1/8th bringing them up to strength with a total of 53 officers and 987 other ranks – their highest number for some time. They were now to be known as the 8th Sherwood Foresters. Following these changes they marched off to Laires and by 13th February found themselves in the mining village of Enquin-les-Mines. Their Head Quarters were established at the Maire's House, which they found very comfortable, and all the officers were charmed by the Maire's attractive daughter, for some reason they had far more visitors than they would normally expect.

Recreation continued with the usual football competitions and 'B' Company reached the semi-final of the Brigade competition. Training was geared towards the expected German offensive as more divisions were brought in from the Russian front. This was quite a change from the offensive training they had recently been undertaking.

The training was cut short on 5th March and the battalion moved up to the front area at Béthune, where they were billeted at the orphanage for the third time. This move heralded a period of seven weeks of activity, although the first week it was quite peaceful with summer-like weather. On 12th March the battalion moved to the Cambrin sector, where they relieved the 5th Lincolns who were holding what was known as the Annequin Fosse at its colliery cottages. These had been made into a defensive position that was to be held in the event of a German breakthrough. There followed a few senior personnel changes, including Col. Blackwell the C.O. who had commanded the 8th since October 1915, he was replaced by Lt. Col. R. W. Currin. Other changes included Captain C. P. Elliott, who took over 'B' Company.

Within a few days the battalion took over the left sub-section of the Cambrin front, just as the tension was mounting as the Germans started an onslaught to the south of them, with their only problem being a heavy bombardment and gas, which was very unpleasant. However, on the night of 21/22nd March 'A' Company's long, sparsely manned sector was raided, preceded by the usual heavy bombardment that covered a wide area around them. The enemy managed to gain entry into their trenches and a fierce close-quarters fight ensued. Because of the ferocity of the bombardment, it had not been possible to get reinforcements up to them. The Germans' target was a tunnel that emerged into the front line trenches, which they were attempting to blow in. However, they did not achieve their objective and the outpost garrison did well to prevent this. After the raid 'the pools of blood and reeking bayonets of some of the rifles found' bore witness to the close-quarters fighting. The British eventually found the plans that the Germans had made for this daring raid and were impressed with the level of training that had taken place, including the troops being taught English words. In all 250 German troops had taken part and many were killed or wounded. On the British side there were 3 killed, 26 missing and 11 wounded.

Following this unwelcome visit from the enemy, the whole battalion was ordered to improve its defences by putting out more reels of barbed wire. By 24th March the battalion was relieved by the 6th Battalion. Half the 8th stayed in reserve and the remaining two companies moved to Beuvry. Tensions were still high as the Germans had made good progress in the south of the area and it was thought that they would attempt to move forward on a broader front. However, the threat did not materialise in their sector and the rumours were that an attempt would be made on Vimy. As a consequence the battalion was moved back to Lens to relieve the 72nd Canadian Battalion in the St. Emile sector on 27th March. The new sector was quiet and on 1st April they were relieved by the 6th Battalion and then moved to St. Pierre, where they were billeted in the cellars of damaged buildings. Unfortunately, the village was in full view of the Germans who still held Lens and they were subjected to frequent shelling and had to move around at night, which was not pleasant as gas shells were frequently fired on them. Bathing facilities were somewhat unusual in that they were in the crypt of a church, but quite safe.

After two days the battalion relieved the 5th Battalion, and then had six difficult days as they were subjected to heavy trench mortaring. On 9th April the 6th Battalion took over from them just as the Germans attacked the British line immediately north of the La Bassée Canal and the Portuguese in Neuve Chapelle. The canal was held by the British, but the Portuguese gave way and the Germans pushed west for quite a distance before being brought to a halt by the British and French. At this time the 8th Battalion was relieved and were put into reserve ready for a rapid move to wherever they were needed.

A further period of nervous waiting took place as they waited for the next German move, being caught in a prominent salient with the possibility of attack from the north and east. Several towns and mining villages were ordered to evacuate and the troops witnessed a sad stream of people trundling their meagre belongings and livestock to a safer area. Local miners had to cease work and were put to effective use in digging additional trenches in order to improve the sector's defences. The diarist noted that this was potentially the darkest period of the war and 'all indeed realised that we had our backs to the wall…' It was genuinely feared that the Germans could sweep through to the Channel and across to England.

In this period of tension a German prisoner informed them that they were planning a further attack on the La Bassée Canal. The battalion was moved to Sailly-Labourse in the early hours of 18th April, arriving as the enemy barrage began and suffering several casualties in the process. However, the attack took place at Givenchy where it was repelled. The 8th were kept in the line for two days until it was all quiet again and on 20th April they moved back to billets at Vaudricourt. This ended another three months' period of action during which eight were killed and many wounded.

Gorre and Essars

April 21st 1918 – September 6th 1918

Within two days of returning to Vaudricourt the division was called upon to relieve the 3rd Division to the north of the La Bassée Canal, which became known as the Gorre and Essars sector. The 8th Battalion left Vaudricourt and marched the short distance to Béthune where they were allocated French barracks. They were sorry to see that this once vibrant town was now wrecked by heavy German shelling.

Following a game of cricket on the Barrack Square on 24th April, the battalion marched to the front under cover of darkness to relieve the 2nd Royal Scots in the Essars right sub-sector. Fortunately some of the officers had been to check the area previously, otherwise they would have been in danger of losing their way as the promised guide failed to materialise. They found that they had to live in a collection of shell holes instead of the well dug trenches they had been used to. There were practically no defences and the area was very flat and in good view of the enemy. Consequently there were a limited number of hours in which they could work on improving their position. When they did start digging they found that the water table was very close to the surface, which meant that dugouts were out of the question. The first tour in the section lasted four days during which they were subjected to gas shelling. The 5th Leicesters relieved the battalion on 28th April and they moved back to Divisional Reserve at Fouquières, where they had to be ready for action at short notice as there were strong rumours of an imminent German attack. A few days later on 2nd May the 8th took over from the 6th Staffords, who had had almost half of their numbers affected by mustard gas during their stint. This relief interspersed their constant support of the Royal Engineers for whom they provided labour.

The next location saw the battalion witnessing the dreadful aftermath of a fierce battle to secure a strategic section known as 'Route A Keep'. The diarist described it as the unhealthiest part of the whole Divisional front. The area was a high piece of ground that partially overlooked German trenches. It had been fought over for some time and was finally taken some five days earlier on 29th April by the Stafford Brigade. Corpses of British and German soldiers lay on both sides, 'and made the place distinctly offensive'. Whilst the Germans had finally tired of attempting to retake the 'Keep', they continued to fire mortars and there was little in the way of defences. Upon arrival the 8th started digging an advanced trench to improve their security. Their rest periods were spent in bivouacs in Vaudricourt.

Throughout May there continued to be fears of a further attack being attempted on Béthune and other parts of the coalfield. In preparation the bridges over the La Bassée Canal were mined and guarded continuously, with instructions to blow the bridge in the event of a further withdrawal. Béthune was subjected to a daily bombardment and the church tower was mined as it commanded views for many miles over the front. However, a German shell hit the mines and destroyed the tower in a spectacular explosion. In view of the constant threat of an enemy attack the men in reserve spent a lot of time improving their defensive positions.

A further part of daily life was to salvage as much equipment and as many supplies as possible. Clearly the Army was becoming concerned at the mounting cost of the war. In between the defensive and salvage work the battalion was spending twelve days in the line and six days at rest. By the end of May the Germans had renewed their attacks near Rheims in the south, and Locre in the north, making some progress. Of the section of the line covered by the brigade, Essors was noted as the more preferable, if only on account of the excellent vegetables that grew there in large quantities, and, needless to say, found their way to the officers and men alike. The French had abandoned some of their livestock when the area had been evacuated and the fresh meat and vegetables were a welcome addition to army rations. Sadly, it was recorded that a cow being kept by the Battalion H.Q. came to an unfortunate end when it was gassed. Those in the front line had to have their food taken to them at night, although as the nights grew shorter the transport was under even more threat. They did, however, gain some cover from the growing crops in front of their trenches. During this period there were no raids by the enemy, but men were out on patrol, departing before dawn and laying up in a shell hole during the day where they could observe the German trenches, and returning again at night.

Selective training of officers and men took place to keep them up-to-date with changes in tactics and all the men were trained to use a Lewis gun. Alongside the training, ceremonial parades continued and on 28th May General Horne, Commander of the First Army, visited to inspect the division and to present medals. There was time for the occasional visit by the 'Whizz-bangs' and on 18th July the Battalion Sports Day took place. Two days later the Brigade Horse Show was held and the 8th Battalion won some prizes – all this to keep up moral.

During the summer period of moonlit nights, bombardments took place and there were air raids on the trenches. Whilst there were a few casualties in the line, the billets and transport suffered severely from these raids. Despite this the diarist described this period as 'somewhat humdrum', and the German offensive finally failed near Rheims on 15th July when the Germans suffered heavy casualties. On 18th July a force made up of French, American, British and Italian troops attacked the Germans, who finally started to withdraw in some sectors. In the area where the Portuguese had been overrun, the salient that had been created caused them problems as an effort was made to dislodge them.

August 1918 saw further German withdrawals and the battalion was able to move forward in short stages, although on 26th August they suffered a number of casualties as a result of a heavy bombardment. By September more and more positions were taken over by the 8th Battalion, and so much ground had been taken that those men who had been present in 1915 were now on familiar ground. Hurried instructions were given to launch an attack on their old front line near Neuve Chapelle, where the enemy front was around 2,000 yards west of the line. 'B' and 'C' companies were to lead with 'A' and 'D' in reserve. Fortunately the enemy offered little resistance and within a couple of hours the old British front line had been regained. Alongside, the 19th Division had a tougher time taking Neuve Chapelle.

Whilst the battalion had gained this ground and had a peaceful few hours, this was not maintained and on 5th September they suffered some serious shelling and Battalion Head Quarters suffered a direct hit from a 4.2 shell. All the officers except the Medical Officer, who was elsewhere, were wounded, ranging from a few scratches to broken limbs and the Intelligence Officer subsequently died. Even after the H.Q. was moved it was still targeted and the diarist noted that it had been a pretty grim day. That night the Division was relieved by the 19th and the men were sent back to Beuvry, some by light railway and others on foot. Their casualties during this period from late April amounted to 30 killed and many wounded.

Auchel to Pontruet

September 7th 1918 – September 26th 1918

The battalion left Beuvry on 7th September by light railway to Ferfay and marched the short distance to Auchel. This was another mining village, where the locals made them very welcome. Lt. Col. J.F. Dempster arrived from the 2nd Manchesters to take over as C. O. of the battalion. Further up the chain of command, Major-General Thwaites had been moved back to England, as Director of Military Intelligence, and was replaced by Major-General G.F. Boyd.

The new Divisional Commander had arrived with a wealth of experience from fighting in the south of the front. The officers were briefed on new techniques for attack. Attacking troops were now to advance in what the diarist described as 'Blobs'. This meant small formations of somewhat open groups to minimise the casualties from shelling and machine-gun fire. It seems that it had taken a long time to appreciate that advancing in long lines against machine-gun fire made the troops very vulnerable. They were also briefed on the introduction of tanks in moving warfare.

Within a few days the battalion was on the move southwards, travelling via Amiens to La Houssoye and were attached to General Rawlinson's 4th Army. Their new billets were in rolling countryside where those with horses were able to gallop across the chalk downs. The new camp was not far from Amiens, which was slowly coming back to life after being evacuated and had not suffered too much shell damage. The area around La Houssoye had been liberated by the Australians during August and gangs of Chinese labourers were clearing the battlefield. The British were somewhat amused by the Chinese carrying everything on poles, but were not amused by their industry. Meanwhile training continued with a good deal of Lewis gun work and learning how to follow up and occupy ground gained by tank advances. Some of the officers and NCOs had their first trip in an aeroplane courtesy of the officer commanding a bombing squadron that was stationed nearby.

In the midst of a training session on 18th September the battalion received urgent orders to move again. Their journey took them through a scene of

> … desolate ruin. For something like 40 miles, the Somme area, through which we were passing, was nothing but an immense wilderness – every village practically in ruins, and hardly sufficient remaining in many cases to identify their position …Not a scrap of ground was cultivated… Not a living soul was there except a few odd troops of our own, working mostly on roads and guarding dumps…

On 19th September they arrived at Poeuilly, where they were told to bivouac. The following day they relieved the 2nd Royal Sussex in Brigade Reserve at Pontru, seven miles north-west of St. Quentin.

Five days later the 8th Battalion relieved the 5th Battalion who were holding the western edge of Pontruet following a recent attack. The dugouts and cellars they occupied were swarming with flies and vermin and they were under frequent attack from enemy shelling. Fortunately, a couple of days later they were relieved by the 1st Black Watch and went to bivouacs off the Vendelles-Bihecourt Road.

During this short period there had been a few personnel changes and they had suffered 5 killed and 24 wounded. On the whole the battalion was said to be very fit and they awaited news of their next assignment, which was to come sooner than they expected.

Bellenglise

September 26th 1918 – September 29th 1918

The British Army planned a great effort to dislodge the enemy from the Hindenberg Line. With this in mind the St. Quentin Canal needed to be crossed and it was planned to do this between Bellenglise and Riquerval Bridge. The planning, as always, was very complex and several Brigades were involved, including French, Australian and American troops. Tanks were also to play their part in the planned attack. Preliminary attacks commenced on 27th September, with the main assault due two days later.

There were a number of obstacles to overcome, including the depth of water in the canal and the strongly protected German positions. Their defences were so strong it was realised that there would need to be a heavy bombardment to prepare the way for the ground assault. In preparation the diarist recorded '…the largest array of guns that ever was collected, at any rate in such a short space of time'. Supplies had to be maintained and railway lines were relaid by the engineers.

On the night of 27/28th September the 8th Battalion marched to their assembly point, which they navigated to without the help of markers and despite some gas shelling. The attack was to be carried out under a creeping barrage and their allotted part of the front was about 1,200 yards long. Careful planning was essential and the officers had very little time to make sure everything was in place. At 3.00 a.m. on the morning of 29th September the rum ration arrived and the battalion moved to their final assembly point on the eastern side of 'Ascension Valley'. It was not the healthiest point as the Germans had a habit of sending in high explosive shells and gas. It was difficult to see what they were doing because of the darkness and a thick fog which had descended, but they were in position in time, without incident, and ahead of zero hour set for 5.50 a.m. At the appointed hour the British bombardment commenced with '…the greatest concentration of artillery the World had ever seen…it was perfect pandemonium'. Speech was said to be impossible and whilst it was practically daylight, the fog was quite dense. They advanced by means of a compass and reached their first objective with little inconvenience despite a counter barrage by the Germans.

As they waited for their next advance they witnessed the wounded being brought back, together with many German prisoners – one group of prisoners was being led by a captured German officer using his compass. The battalion was holed up for around three hours before orders came through by runner - the telephone line had been broken – to cross the canal, which they did by plank footbridges.

At this point the battalion engaged the enemy in their defensive positions and isolated snipers and machine-gun posts had to be dealt with. 'A' Company took the brunt of the fighting as they worked their way along the canal. Most of the fighting was at close quarters and involved rushing machine-gun posts and subsequent bayonet fighting. 'C' Company came up to support their 'A' Company colleagues and eventually Bellenglise was cleared, but not without casualties. There were many acts of heroism recorded in the attack. 'B' Company lost direction and strayed into 138th Brigade positions, but eventually got back on track. By 11.30 a.m., just ten minutes behind schedule, the battalion had cleared the village and reached their next starting point.

The battalion was now on the so-called 'Brown Line' and were eventually joined by a company of five tanks. As they went forward again, the tanks were immobilised by enemy field guns firing at almost point blank range. However, the troops moved forward and met with little opposition, reaching their final objective at 12.15 p.m. They were exposed on their right flank and had to fight off two counter attacks. All in all the battalion was very pleased with itself and some degree of self-congratulation was in order.

The area had been devastated by the heavy bombardment and some 300 prisoners had been taken as the Germans surrendered when their dugouts were overrun. Casualties on the day were 14 killed and 80 wounded. In the aftermath of the battle the diarist recorded that it was '…a sight never to be forgotten'. Mopping up of the German trenches continued and equipment and guns were moved up. Prisoners were being taken back looking very bedraggled, and some had been put to work carrying back British casualties. Whilst the attack had been largely successful, the Germans still held parts of the Hindenberg Line and more was required. However, it was felt that '…the final defeat of the enemy was but a matter of days'.

Much of the success of the operation had been put down to the heavy fog that had prevented more casualties. It transpired that the High Command had not expected that they would achieve the crossing of the canal and Lt. General Sir John Monash, Commander of the Australian Corps, recorded:

> Quite early in the day news came in that the IX Corps on my right hand had achieved an astonishing success, that Bellenglise had been captured, and that the deep canal had been successfully crossed in several places. It was the 46th Imperial Division to which this great success was chiefly due. There can be no doubt that this success, conceived at first as a demonstration to detract attention from the Australian Corps' front, materially assisted me in the situation in which I was placed later on the same day.

The whole division had every right to be pleased with their achievements on that foggy September morning.

An article published by 46th Division in *Le Journal* on 5th October is transcribed below:

PRODIGIOUS EXPLOIT BY THE HEROES OF THE 46TH DIVISION

Whilst to the South and North of the La Bassée Canal, the army of Von Quast is retiring by forced marches, thus freeing for us the mining districts of Lens to Armentiers, a magnificent episode of the war has just occurred on the Hindenburg Line at Bellenglise:-

Here the trench system of the Field Marshall – 'He of nails' – consists of three lines, - one on the west covered by barbed wire, then the canal of St. Quentin, which is full of water, then again the other bank of the canal a further labyrinth of communication trenches and saps extending to a depth of one kilometre. A wonderful system you will agree, from which the enemy machine gunners naturally thought they could never be evicted. But the masterpiece of this gigantic mining work is a secret tunnel [several] feet high which passes under the canal joining the two trench systems, and which I have just come back from inspecting. This tunnel is two kilometres long, and is lit up like the passages of an underground railway by three powerful dynamos from the workshops of Leipsic [Leipzig]. A tramway runs along it in both directions and can be used in case of attack to bring up reinforcing troops in a few seconds under the cover of its concrete vaults. Never has anyone seen a better example of ingenuity combined with defensive art. It amounts to this - That there were two trenches, the canal and the tunnel, which had to be carried on the morning of the 29th before General Rawlinson's Army could break through on the North of St. Quentin and to enable General Debensy [semi-legible] to free the captive city.

The honour of overcoming all these difficulties fell to the 46th Division, composed of soldiers from the Midland Counties – The Sherwood Foresters Brigade of Territorials, North and South Staffordshire Brigade of Territorials, Lincolns and Leicesters Brigade of Territorials. The General commanding one of the Brigades is already known to you. Two years ago at the time of the first British Armies on the French Front, I told you about the almost epic adventure of the young General of the tiger-like red moustache who in former days was a Colonel in the Guards, and who like Roland at [illegible] led the charge on Lesboeufs, sounding on his silver horn the hunting calls of old Scotland, his name is [Brigadier] General Campbell, V.C., a brave man and a gallant hero. Two days before the attack, being in the line on the edge of the Somme Canal, he put his brigade through a general rehearsal for the crossing. The brave lads of the Midland Counties furnished with the same life-belts which they wear when crossing the canal on leave, threw themselves into the water - swimmers and non-swimmers alike, and all with the same courage. The rehearsal took place on a bitterly cold afternoon. Then came dawn of Sunday 29th, and on the whistle being sounded by the young leader, part of the Division under cover of the half light of daybreak, threw themselves into the canal under the direct fire of the Bosche's machine guns, touched bottom and hurling themselves into the bank, engaged and overcame the outposts in a bombing duel. Then having completed this mopping up, they threw out steel cable on to which clung the men who were coming to grief in the water. It is true there is a bridge at Bellenglise, but was it still standing (sic). *A corporal and four men slipping into the trenches on a further bank went off on a reconnaissance. On the approach to a bridge, still intact, they surprised three sentries, one was despatched to a better world, and another one to keep him company. The third kept quiet by the revolver of the corporal never budged. Willing or not he was obliged to point out the mine chambers hidden on the sides of the bridge. A soldier then cut the leads. A flare was the signal of the success of this mission and the whole division swarmed over. There remained the tunnel, a company man hauled a medium calibre gun and two mortars and then at the very entrance to the subterranean passage, opened a point blank fire, then came grenades as thick as hailstones followed by shrieks of horror and every sign of panic out of the smoke there emerged one by one two regiments of panic-stricken Huns…a thousand men livid with fear, were picked up here without further trouble than that of disarming them. Then the division, having overcome the fortifications pushed forward a strong patrol, surprising two batteries in the open, bayonetting the men serving the guns, and seized the guns and ammunition.*

By midday, the division had pushed forward to a depth of 6 kilometres and captured 70 guns and 6,500 prisoners. One prisoner went off struggling – a record for these days. The following day our cavalry burst through the gap. The Bosche retreated and the French entered St. Quentin.

46th Divisional Headquarters
5th October, 1918.[10]

---

[10] Transcribed from a carbon copy of the original article that formed part of the papers of Corporal C. R. Overton of Newark, a signaller in the 1/8th Battalion, Sherwood Foresters, who served for the duration.

Brigadier General J. Campbell V.C. addressing his troops after the battle at Requival.

Ramicourt and Montbrehain

September 30th 1918 – October 4th 1918

There was to be little rest for the members of the 8th Battalion following their successes of 29th September. They spent the following day in dugouts and trenches between Bellenglise and Lehaucourt. That day St. Quentin was taken by the French.

In the afternoon the 32nd Division moved forward to tackle the remainder of the Hindenberg Line and were supported by cavalry. The diarist reported that it was a most picturesque scene and the sight was one never to be forgotten. In the midst of this an endless stream of transport was observed ferrying supplies up to the new front line. The next phase of the advance was being planned carefully and the 8th were moved about a mile north to a trench system in 'Springbok Valley', just behind Magny-la-Fosse. The transport section was being put under great pressure to deliver all the stores that were required – many stores had been left behind earlier because of a shortage of transport. Their biggest problem was low flying German aeroplanes dropping bombs on the British lines. Horses seemed to be the main casualties from this action, although one German bomb landed in the middle of a concentration of troops who turned out to be German POWs and 40/50 of them were killed and as many wounded, together with 6 British soldiers. The diarist reported that the carnage caused by this was evident for a few days and was a dreadful sight.

In the period before the next action the battalion, now reduced to 46 officers and 752 other ranks, did its best to reorganise itself. At 4.30 p.m. on 2nd October orders were received for the next attack, which was to be in conjunction with the 2nd Australian Division and due to start early the next morning. The objective was to capture the villages of Ramicourt and Montbrehain, with the 8th acting with the 5th and 6th Battalions and a company of nine tanks. Zero hour was at dawn and they would be supported by a creeping barrage, although not as heavy as for the previous attack. The battalion's frontage in the attack was approximately 1,000 yards to be covered by 'A' and 'B' companies with 'C' and 'D' in support. The latter two were also to follow the 6th Battalion to mop up after them when they reached Montbrehain, their main objective. There had been no time to familiarise themselves with the countryside, other than from a few maps and brief observation.

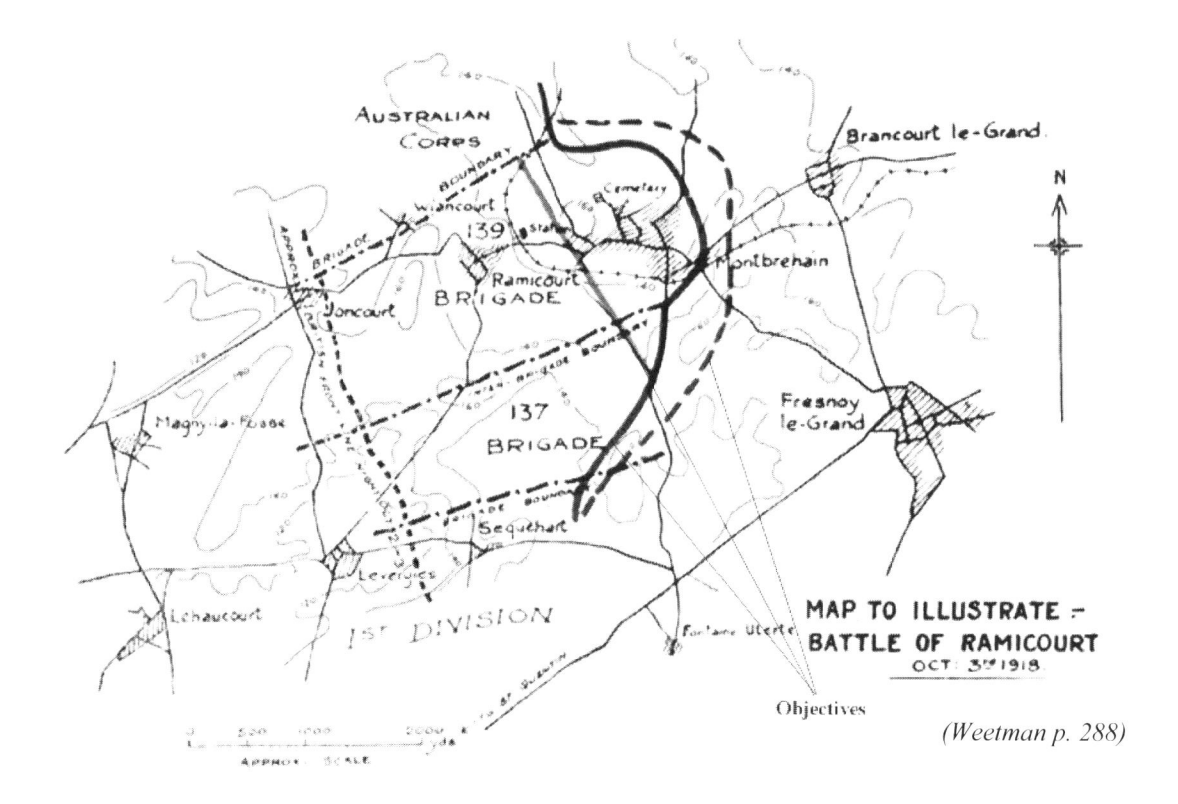

MAP TO ILLUSTRATE :-
BATTLE OF RAMICOURT
OCT 3RD 1918

(Weetman p. 288)

The troops set out just after midnight and after a most precarious time were assembled by 5.30a.m. on 3rd October. Once again there was some fog that made direction finding a little difficult. At 6.05 a.m. the barrage opened up, just as it was getting light. However, as the barrage was not as heavy as it had been at Bellenglise, the battalion were faced with much stiffer resistance than they had anticipated. The Germans had had time to call up reserves and were determined to hold on to their defensive positions. All of the machine-gun emplacements were operating, but the barrage had failed to cut any of the wire, which meant that the attacking troops had to manipulate it as best they could. The Australians had failed to make much progress and had not taken Wiancourt, which meant that the 8th Battalion's left flank was exposed. To avoid being attacked from this side they decided to take the village, which they achieved after some heroic fighting, including bayonet charges. The right was also making slow progress and 'C' Company, who were supporting the attacking troops, helped to secure the area. Again close-quarters fighting was involved and the Germans were overwhelmed and were either captured or killed. Intensive fighting was the nature of this attack as machine-gun posts were taken by a frontal attack or by being rushed from the rear. In the front, covered by the 139th Brigade, almost 200 Germans were killed and many taken prisoner.

The main Fonsomme Line had been won at a heavy cost and, as the troops had shifted too far left, they now concentrated on straightening their line and headed for Ramicourt, their ultimate objective. The next step was quite difficult as they were very exposed and were being shelled from behind Montbrehain. Fortunately supporting tanks that had been delayed now appeared and assisted them with the advance. 'B' Company, which had been involved with much of the fighting, joined forces with the other three companies and they were all then faced with firing from several machine guns and snipers hidden in some of the houses. The resistance was eventually overcome and the village was taken along with around 400 prisoners. All this had been achieved by 10.30 a.m. and they now awaited the 6th Battalion.

The 6th Battalion had suffered badly after crossing the Beaurevoir-Fonsomme Line when Col. Vann, who had been leading his men, was shot through the head. The 5th Battalion also lost Col. Hacking who was wounded in the arm. Both of these officers had served with the 8th Battalion earlier in the war. However, the 6th Battalion came through and went on to take Montbrehain, with the 8th now left considerably exposed, particularly from a machine-gun post to their left.

The gun position was taken with an element of subterfuge when a German prisoner was instructed to go over to his colleagues and suggest that they surrender. As he approached the position, the gun stopped firing and he disappeared into the ground, thus revealing the entrance to the position. Under cover of Lewis gun fire a couple of men rushed into the entrance and much to their surprise found 60/70 men and around 12 machine guns. After firing a few shots the Germans surrendered. This was certainly a story to go down in the history of the battalion.

In both Ramicourt and Montbrehain there were still around seventy French citizens who had refused to be evacuated by the Germans. They gave the liberators a very warm welcome and were quickly removed to a safe area. Having gained their objectives, the three battalions now found themselves somewhat exposed as the Australians had not caught up with their left flank and to the right the 137th Brigade had been forced to give ground, which meant that both flanks were exposed in an awkward salient. With the Germans launching a counter attack a strategic withdrawal was undertaken to just east of Ramicourt. The 8th took up positions at the railway and the sunken road, north-east of the village, and the Germans moved back into Montbrehain, but could get no further. Supplies were now very short, particularly ammunition, and arrangements had to be made to re-supply them. Fortunately they were left in peace for the rest of the day. The diarist recorded:

> …it had been a glorious day for the 8th Battalion. There was really no comparison between this battle and that of September 29th. The attack on September 29th was undoubtedly more spectacular, but in our humble judgement, having regard to the extremely short notice received, the strength of the enemy and the many difficulties encountered, the breaking of the Fonsomme Line on October 3rd may truly be counted as one of the most gallant exploits of the whole war.

None of this had been achieved without cost with a casualty count of 2 officers and 20 other ranks killed, and 2 officers and 86 other ranks wounded. The Medical Officer, Captain Homan, and Padre Sturt had worked for 24 hours non-stop, despite being gassed, tending to the casualties. Many prisoners had been taken and the 8th Battalion claimed a large share of the 30 officers and 1,500 other ranks that had been captured. In addition a large number of dead had been left on the ground for later attention.

Late in the night of 3rd October most of the battalion was relieved by the 4th Leicesters, although 'A' & 'D' companies had to remain in the line a little longer, despite being short of ammunition. Once again they had to bivouac.

The Last Fight

October 4th 1918 – November 11th 1918

Following the battle at Ramicourt the battalion spent what was left of 4th October cleaning up and reorganising the companies, which had been thinned out following the battle casualties, however, they were pleased to welcome 85 reinforcements. This was not without incident as the Germans continued to shell and bomb them causing further casualties. The following morning they were informed that there was still more work to be done and they were sent to relieve some of the 32nd Division, who had suffered heavy casualties. That night they relieved the 97th Brigade where casualties had been so heavy that each company relieved a battalion. These were Dorsets, Highland Light Infantry and Royal Scots.

Their new position was on a line through the village of Sequehart, on the extreme right of the British Front and next to the French. This new position was uncomfortable and the Headquarters of 'D' Company received five direct hits during the two days they were there. The commander of the company likened the situation to 'Bloody Ypres', as during their stay they suffered a constant barrage. This particular sector of the front had recently changed hands three times and they thought the Germans were about to launch another attack. The streets of Sequehart were littered with bodies from both sides making them all feel very uncomfortable.

The shelling was so bad that the C. O. and Second in Command were both wounded following a visit to the forward area, with Major V. O. Robinson from the 6th Battalion temporarily taking command. Following their two difficult days the battalion was relieved by the Monmouths and marched back to Lehaucourt. On 9th October they moved again, this time to Le Vergies and the following day to Méricourt. The neighbouring town of Fresnoy-le-Grand had been relieved by the 138th Brigade that morning. Fortunately it had not been badly damaged and was the first town of any size that they had been near for some time.

On 12th October the 8th was moved further forward to Jannecourt Farm, which had been captured a few days earlier by the Cavalry, and the battalion had the unpleasant task of burying the dead. However, they were able to refit and clean themselves up, taking advantage of the old

German baths in Fresnoy. A ceremony was held when the Divisional Commander presented 'Congratulatory Cards' to the N.C.O.s and men, followed by a march past to a military band.

The battalion was not left in peace for long as the Brigade prepared for another push to force the Germans back to the Sambre-Oise Canal, to take place on 17th October, which the 8th Battalion was to lead. Their objective was the consolidation of the line of the Andigny-les-Fermes – Bohain Road (the 'Blue Line'). They were to be assisted by tanks. As the attack was at right angles to the general line of the advance, it was impossible for them to rely on the usual barrage as troops would have been in the way. Along with the support of tanks they were to have assistance from the Life Guards Machine Gun Battalion.

With the planning in place and supplies ready to follow the battle, the men were fed on hot porridge, tea and rum and were ready to move to the front between 2.00 and 3.00 a.m. on 17th October. By 3.45 a.m. they were in position along a 1,200 yard front, but were thinly spread following their recent losses. The planned attack commenced at 5.20 a.m., but in the inevitable autumnal fog they soon strayed off course and the companies lost touch with each other very quickly. 'B' Company came up against stiff opposition and their commander, Captain Geary, was killed by machine-gun fire. In the confusion the battalion commander had difficulty in reaching his advanced headquarters. Once again they were faced with overcoming machine-gun positions. Incredibly, L/Cpl. Coombes of 'D' Company rushed a machine-gun post and killed six Germans with his revolver and a seventh with his Lewis Gun. Once the C. O. established his forward headquarters he managed to organise all the stragglers and sent out a party to clear the Germans who were between 'B' and 'C' Companies. They were led by Major Robinson who did a tremendous job as his impromptu team cleared a good number of machine-gun posts. Members of 'C' Company managed to clear one post with six machine guns and capture 40 prisoners. Shortly afterwards other members of the company surrounded a group of Germans and took the surrender of 140 men and 27 machine guns. Unfortunately, 'A' Company suffered quite badly, but were reinforced by two companies from the 5th Battalion, which enabled them to reach their objective. Major Robinson's group made good progress and moved into Regnicourt village, which was an important objective.

By late morning there was a fear that the Germans were regrouping for a counter attack, but headquarters managed to get the artillery to train their sites on them and they were dispersed. By noon the Germans had withdrawn from the Forêt d'Andigny. Following the reorganisation of the various companies, an outpost line had been formed and they managed to join up with the French on their right. During the attack the battalion had captured 220 prisoners and almost 100 machine guns, and there were many German casualties. This had been achieved at a heavy cost with the loss of 2 officers killed, 2 wounded, 25 other ranks killed and 54 wounded. There were many deeds of gallantry during this difficult battle.

The diarist noted that, in spite of their achievements, it had been an unsatisfactory day as they felt they '…hardly had our desserts for the gallant work done by all ranks against an enemy holding in much greater strength much more strongly fortified positions than had been anticipated'. He went on to say that the fighting had been harder than at Ramicourt: 'Regnicourt is apt to be looked on as a small matter, but for the 8th Battalion it was one of the most strenuously fought battles of the war.'

It was not until midnight that they were relieved by the 6th Battalion. During the following evening they marched to Fresnoy and were met by their drums, which cheered them up as they approached the village where they were greeted by General Harrington with a 'Well done, Sherwoods'.

A well-earned rest was the order of the day, together with a draft of 120 men of the Northumberland Hussars on their first tour abroad. The battalion now consisted of 34 officers and 745 other ranks. With the Germans in retreat the battalion had to keep moving forward and their next billets were in Bohain. As they arrived they were greeted by enthusiastic villagers and bands playing.

Whilst that fighting was moving on, the next hazard they faced was the damage undertaken by the retreating Germans and a large number of mines with delayed fuses of up to a month that were difficult to detect.

Following the benefit of a rest the battalion moved forward again and on 3rd November, having contended with heavy rain, they arrived at Escaufort, but were moved straight on to Catillon with orders to carry on the pursuit of the Germans. The following day they were in position by 8.30 a.m. and by the afternoon were moved to Meziers, staying the night in poor billets. By 6th November they were ordered to assist in the taking of Prisches[11] and Cartignies. 'A' Company had gained possession of Priches by 10.30 a.m. and were greeted to an unforgettable reception by the liberated villagers following four years of occupation and oppression. The whole village turned out and they were offered coffee, cider, cognac and fruit, and lots of appreciation. The battalion headquarters were eventually set up on the edge of the village. Their next objective was Cartignies and, with 'B' Company forming the advance guard, they arrived to find that half the village was still occupied and it was quite a lengthy process to clear the enemy out.

Prisches Church
(Mike Kirton)

It transpired that they had spent the night in 'No Man's Land' and the following morning they received another good reception from the villagers. The battalion's transport and supplies soon caught up with them. The diarist was pleased to note that the German withdrawal had speeded and on 10th November they moved on to Boulogne-sur-Helpe a few kilometres down the road. The diarist wrote: 'November 11th came in just the same as any other day, but quite early a wire from Brigade Headquarters stated that the Germans had agreed to our Armistice terms, and the Great War was over.'

Cartignies Church
A night in 'no man's land'
(Mike Kirton)

---

[11] The War Memorial inside the church shows evidence of civilian deaths on 5th and 7th November, suggesting they were caught in the cross-fire.

Boulogne-sur-Helpe
The battalion rested here on
11th November 1918

(Mike Kirton)

Home Again

November 12th 1918 – July 5th 1919

Following the armistice there was an element of uncertainty as to the immediate destination of the battalion. Several scenarios were considered: 'Would they set foot in Germany as part of a conquering army? Would they be sent home? Would they spend weary months scavenging in the fair land of France?' It soon became clear that they would not have the honour of moving into Germany, when at the end of the month General Sir H. S. Rawlinson sent the following letter:

> It is a matter of very deep regret to me that the 46th Division is not accompanying the Fourth Army to the Frontier. I desire, however, to place on record my appreciation of the splendid performances of the Division during the recent operations, and to congratulate all ranks on the conspicuous part they have played in the battles of the 100 days. The forcing of the main Hindenburg line on the Canal, and the capture of Bellenglise rank as one of the finest and most dashing exploits of the war. The attacks of October 3rd, and the subsequent operations about Bohain, together with the later advance towards the Sambre Canal, constitute a record of which all ranks of the Division may justly feel proud. I offer to all ranks my warmest thanks for their great gallantry, and to the leaders and staffs my admiration of their skilful direction and staff work throughout these battles. To every Officer, N.C.O., and man of the Division, I offer my warm thanks and hearty congratulations, and trust that at some future time they may again form part of the Fourth Army.

The next few months were a mixture of clearing battlefields, military training, sports, concerts, education and the occasional visiting dignitary. The battalion was based with the 139th Brigade and their visitors included the King, the Prince of Wales and various generals. Parades took place and medal ribbons were presented. On 8th December the Duke of Portland, Cols. Foljambe and Mellish, and the Bishop of Southwell visited them. The battalion's colours were collected from Newark and taken over to France.

Christmas 1918 nearly didn't happen as there was a breakdown in the supply chain, but fortunately the Christmas treats arrived by Boxing Day and they had a memorable time. By this time they had moved to Landrecies and organized a Christmas party for the local children. After a lengthy period of festivities they moved to Prisches and once again were involved in clearing the battlefields. Prior to Christmas all the men who had been miners before they joined were sent home as there was a pressing need to improve coal production. Further demobilization took place and their numbers were decreasing rapidly.

On 19th February, 1919 the remainder removed to Bethencourt where most of the horses and mules were sent for auction. By the end of April the battalion was reduced to 9 officers and 52 other ranks. Some had been sent home and others transferred to the 51st and 52nd Sherwood Foresters (Young Soldiers Battalion). By June the C. O. and other senior officers had returned to Newark and the colours returned on 21st June, following which on 23rd June there was an official welcome home ceremony at Newark Town Hall. This was almost five years since the battalion had left the market place for training prior to going to France. A memorial service took place at Southwell Minster on 5th July for the Nottinghamshire men who had died in the war. Following the service the attendees were given tea in the town.

From the time the battalion had left England to their return 193 officers and 2650 other ranks had served with them. The casualty list was dreadful, with 21 deaths from sickness and 4 from accidents. The battle casualties amounted to 26 officers and 507 other ranks killed or died of their wounds, 64 officers and 1500 other ranks wounded.[12]

Honours

D.S.O.	3
Bar	2
M.C.	28
Bar	1
2nd Bar	1
D.C.M.	20
Bar	1
M.M.	76
Bar	2
2nd Bar	1
M.S.M.	7
Mentioned in Despatches	32
Foreign Decorations	9

The casualty statistics were shocking and we will never know how many of those who returned were traumatized and suffered for years. However, we do know that most of them did not talk about their experiences and this has become more obvious having interviewed many of their surviving children and grandchildren.

---

[12] Casualty figures taken from the Regimental Annual, 8th Battalion Notes, 1920.

CHAPTER 4
'Because it was expected of them.'

John Keegan, in his book *The First World War,* when commenting on an incident involving Corporal William Holbrook of the Royal Fusiliers, said that his matter-of-factness 'epitomises the spirit of the old British Expeditionary Force, whose soldiers died in their thousands at Ypres not because of an ideal of self-sacrifice but because it was expected of them and, in any case, there was no alternative'. So many of them went off to do their duty and serve their country, and the following accounts of Southwell men are just a cross section of a generation's commitment. In the War Diary chapter there are many more accounts of service and sacrifice by the men of Southwell.

Edmund Henry Hynman Allenby

Edmund Allenby, the son of Hynman Allenby, a Norfolk landowner, and Catherine Anne Allenby (née Cane), was born on 23rd April 1861 at Brackenhurst Hall, Southwell, which was owned by his mother's parents. His early education was in Norfolk and in 1875 he was enrolled at a new public school, Haileybury and Imperial Service College, prior to attending Sandhurst. He left Sandhurst in 1882 and was commissioned as a Lieutenant into the 6th (Inniskilling) Dragoons.

Allenby's early military career was spent in South Africa, mainly in skirmishes against the Boers. In 1897 he was promoted to major and posted to the 3rd Cavalry Brigade, then serving in Ireland. When the Boer War broke out he returned to his regiment and the Inniskillings moved to Cape Town. He was involved in various actions throughout the war and in 1901 was promoted to lieutenant-colonel and brevet colonel in 1902. That year he became commanding officer of the 5th Royal Irish Lancers, by 1910 he was made major-general and appointed Inspector General of Cavalry. Upon the outbreak of war he was put in charge of the B.E.F. in Flanders.

The retreat from Mons at the end of August 1914 was Allenby's first major action, which was a chaotic affair, and he ended up joining a rear-guard action at Le Cateau. He was the leader of the Third Army at the 1st Battle of the Somme in July 1916 – the greatest one day loss of the British Army with around 60,000 casualties. The following year in April 1917 he did manage a four mile incursion at Arras, but when the advance came to a halt the Commander-in-Chief, Field Marshall Douglas Haigh, engineered his removal from the Third Army. All was not lost for Allenby and the Prime Minister, Lloyd George, saw him in a different light and he was transferred to take charge of the Egyptian Expeditionary Force. At this time the offensive against the Turks was at stalemate.

Upon arrival in Cairo Allenby set about a rapid reorganisation, moving the British H.Q. out of the comfort of a Cairo hotel to the military front and creating a cavalry unit of horses and camels, which was known as the Desert Mounted Corps. He left part of the army in Gaza and by the end of October attacked Beersheba. An Australian cavalry brigade charged the Turkish lines and the Turks retreated, with the British in pursuit. He then moved on Jerusalem, which fell on 9th December. The South Notts Hussars had been heavily involved in these successes in Palestine, prior to their transfer to France.

In the early part of 1918, with his army reinforcing the Western Front, he remained in Jerusalem until further reinforcements arrived. Meanwhile he had been supporting Colonel T. E. Lawrence in his guerrilla activities against the Hejaz Railway between Amman in Palestine and the southernmost Turkish garrison of Medina. Following the arrival of fresh troops he set about detailed planning for a further advance against the Turks.

The main operation took place between 19th and 21st October and the remaining Turkish forces were defeated at the Battle of Megiddo, which was looked upon as one of the best operations in British military history. Allenby moved on to take Nazareth, Damascus, Beirut, Homs and Aleppo. On 30th October 1918 Turkey capitulated and signed an armistice, which heralded the end of the Ottoman Empire that had existed since the 14th century.

Whilst Allenby had achieved considerable success in Palestine, it had been preceded by personal tragedy when his son was killed on the Western Front. On 29th July 1917 Horace Michael Hynman Allenby, M.C., Royal Horse Artillery and Royal Field Artillery, died of wounds at the Canadian Casualty Clearing Station and was buried in Coxyde Military Cemetery, West-Vlaandeven, Belgium.

Postwar, in 1919, Allenby was made Viscount, promoted to Field Marshall, and served as British High Commissioner in Egypt, continuing in public office until his retirement in 1925. Previously he had been made a KCB in 1915 (a GCMG would follow in 1917, a GCB in 1918, and a GCVO in 1934). He died in 1936 and was cremated, with his ashes being placed under a slab in Westminster Abbey.[1]

General Allenby approaching Jerusalem.

General Allenby showing respect as he dismounted and walked into the city of Jerusalem.

---

[1] Grateful thanks to Peter Baird of Southwell for allowing use of his article 'Brackenhurst to Beersheba', *The Southwell Folio* (Southwell: March/April, 2012) pp. 24-26. Additional material from the Oxford Dictionary of National Biography and other sources.

John Pickard Becher

For conspicuous gallantry and good service on several occasions:

On April 24, 1915 at Kemmel, when part of his trench was blown in, he organised the defence of the breach under heavy fire, and personally assisted in repairing the parapet and digging out buried men.

On June 1, at Kemmel, when part of his trench was blown in by mines, shelling, and trench mortars, he displayed great gallantry and coolness in reorganising the defence.

On July 30 and subsequent days, at Ypres, he displayed coolness, cheerfulness, and resource under trying circumstances when in temporary command of the battalion.

Derby Daily Telegraph, 16th September 1915 – Citation for his D.S.O.

John Pickard Becher (Loughton Collection)

The name Becher has been synonymous with Southwell for many years. John Pickard Becher, born in Southwell on 20th July 1880, was the son of John Henry Becher of Hill House, Southwell and Alice Mary Becher née Pickard, and great-grandson of Reverend John Thomas Becher, who was best known for his involvement in the Poor Law reforms of the early nineteenth century.

John Becher was educated at Malvern Links and abroad. Upon leaving school he entered the law, serving his articles in Louth with Mr H.F.V. Falkener and subsequently joined the firm of Larken & Co in Newark. He was appointed Magistrates' Clerk to the County Bench in 1909. In 1911 he married Gertrude Veronica Gale, the daughter of Henry Mark Gale and the Hon. Mary Emily née Strutt, third daughter of Edward, 1st Lord Belper. Gertrude's mother had been widowed and she subsequently married Dr Henry Handford[1]. Senior Consulting Physician to the Nottingham General Hospital and a retired Major in the R.A.M.C. (T.F.), living at Elmfield House, The Burgage, Southwell. The Bechers had three children: John Henry (1912); Mary Veronica (1913); and Margaret (1916 – born after John Becher's death). Gertrude Gale had two half-brothers: Henry Basil Strutt Handford (1894) and Everard Francis Sale Handford (1895), both of whom were to die in the war – see below.

John Becher's army career commenced on 1st November 1906, when he joined the Notts and Derby Territorials, and by the following June he was appointed Lieutenant; Captain on 9th May 1910; and Major whilst in the field in 1915. Captain Becher was the Commanding Officer of 'H' Company, 8th Battalion Sherwood Foresters, based in Southwell. He was well liked and respected by his men, as will become clear later. The photograph of him with the company football team, taken at Summer Camp held at Thoresby, is a good indicator. He led from the front and it is claimed that he would never ask a man to do anything that he would not undertake himself. Major Becher's exploits at the front are well documented in the battalion war diary in Chapter 3. However, more details of his last hours are worthy of inclusion at this point as they also cover the untimely deaths of his two brothers-in-law, Henry and Everard Francis Handford.

---

[1] Dr Handford was called up for military service on Cannock Chase in 1915.

(Loughton Collection)

Tragedy at the Hohenzollern Redoubt.
On the afternoon of October 12th, 1915, following a few days of recuperation at Fouquiers, the members of the 8th Battalion were ordered to collect fresh supplies and were marched via Vermelles, which was a seething mass of men and transport, to the front line in readiness to attack the German trenches. By lunchtime the following day the British artillery had opened up a barrage and by 1.00 p.m. greenish yellow smoke and chlorine gas was rolling towards the enemy on the breeze. By 3.00 p.m. they received orders to move forward and proceeded at a slow pace, as they were impeded by narrow trenches and a flood of wounded being carried back. The attack did not go to plan, as other units were held up by strong resistance, and finally came to a halt.

The following day, 14th October, orders were received for a further attack that would involve A and D Companies. As the light was fading Major Becher was instructed to go out with a flashlight to help guide the attack. The men went forward in the darkness with fixed bayonets and no covering artillery to try and surprise the Germans. As they progressed they came across a number of the dead from the earlier fighting, and wounded men still trying to return to their trenches. At times the men realised that they were going off course and had to change direction. Once the Germans spotted the advance they retaliated with heavy fire, causing many casualties. It was during this period that Everard Handford was killed instantly by a bullet in the head and several others died with him or were wounded. Shortly afterwards Henry Handford, and others, were killed in a hail of rifle and machine-gun fire as they attempted to re-supply the front-line trenches in daylight.

During the night it was realised that Major Becher was missing and Colonel Fowler, with Sergeant Stokes, had risked their lives by going out and trying to locate him. On the morning of 15th October a relief finally arrived for the battalion and, as they were preparing to move out, Colonel Fowler put his head above the parapet in a final bid to spot Major Becher, but tragically he was shot and killed by a sniper – a major loss for the battalion. Just as they were about to depart word came that John Becher had been found by an officer from another regiment. He had been wounded by a bomb, as had his batman Private Daniels who was with him. Company Sergeant-Major Haywood and Lance-Sergeant T. Martin went out to rescue him and carried him across 200 yards of open ground under, more or less, constant rifle fire. Sadly John Becher died of his wounds in hospital some ten weeks later on 1st January 1916. The battalion diarist noted:

> *In John Becher the Battalion lost one who was beloved by all, who had throughout ever had at heart the welfare of his men, whether in or out of the trenches, at work or at play. What he did at Kemmel, was known to few. Often he was out in 'No Man's Land', mainly for the sake of example, for it was part of his creed never to tell a man to do anything that he would not dare to do himself. He lies buried in the British cemetery at Abbeville. It was a hard fate that struck down John Becher and his two brothers-in-law, Basil and Everard Handford – two of the most promising young officers in the Battalion – within a few hours of each other.*[2]

John Becher's daughter, Mary Beaumont, in an interview later in life, recalled that she was on the beach at Bognor with her mother when she received a telegram advising her of his death.[3] Whilst John Becher is buried in a military grave at Abbeville, there is a memorial to him in the Southwell Minster Yard as illustrated on the title page to this book. In addition there is a magnificent stained glass window in the Pilgrim's Chapel dedicated to him. His two brothers-in-law also have a stained glass window in their memory, dedicated in 1918 by the Bishop of Newcastle, in the South Quire of the Minster.

Abbeville Military Cemetery
John Becher is buried here.

Loos Memorial The Handford Brothers are remembered here.

---

[2] Weetman, pp. 58-65.
[3] Doreen Stevenson, *Twentieth Century Lives of Southwell* (Southwell: J.L. & D.M. Stevenson, 2001), p. 55.

Charles Brown and his sons at war

Two generations of the Brown family of Victoria Terrace, Southwell committed themselves to the war effort. Charles Brown (b. 1871) and his two surviving sons, John Henry (b.1888) and Vincent Alphonso (b. 1889). A third son Francis had died in his eighteenth year in 1908.

Charles Brown

Charles Brown was born in Mansfield and following a period living in Nottingham and Thurgarton moved to Southwell, where his three sons were educated. He worked as a house painter, and for 21 years had been in the Volunteers and subsequently the Territorials, reaching the rank of Sergeant before his retirement at around age 40 in 1912, but remained on the reserve list.

In early 1915 the War Office sent out a notice to reservists asking if they were prepared to sign on for either active service or home defence. A report in the *Newark Advertiser* on 14th April 1915 stated that Dr Willoughby conducted a series of medical examinations at the New Drill Hall and 14 Southwell men, including Charles Brown, had been passed as fit. They were sworn in by Mr J.R. Starkey and were ready for deployment. Whilst Charles Brown's military records are not available, we know that he joined what eventually became the Royal Defence Corps[1]. A report in the *Newark Advertiser* on 19th September 1917 (reporting on his son Corporal J.H. Brown) mentions that he was guarding prisoners of war at a detention camp near Sutton Bridge, Lincolnshire. These duties were commensurate with him serving in the Royal Defence Corps and, of course, his age of 46. However, in April 1919 a further *Advertiser* report mentions that he was fighting at Archangel. A far cry from guarding P. O. W.s in Lincolnshire, and unusual for a man of his age – he must have volunteered, although there are no records. Charles Brown returned home and it is believed died in 1925.

---

[1] **The reserves of the Territorial Force**
The Territorial Force was created in 1908 as a form of part-time volunteer soldiering. Its original purpose was to provide a force for home defence and men were not obliged to serve overseas (until 1916). The troops undertook to serve full-time (to be "embodied") in the event of general mobilization.
1. Territorial Force Reserve
Most TF units struggled, until 1914, to attract sufficient men to fill their designed establishment and in consequence the reserves were well under strength. While theoretically the TF Reserve should have been one-third the size of the whole TF, by August 1914 it numbered only 2000 men.
2. National Reserve
The National Reserve was a register maintained by Territorial Force County Associations. Registration was voluntary but complex rules of eligibility applied. Its strength as at 1 October 1913 was 215,000 of all ranks. Detail of the National Reserve:
In October 1914 the National Reserve was formed into *Protection Companies*, which were attached to existing TF battalions, for the guarding of railways and other vulnerable points in Britain. That November, all Class I and II men were ordered to present themselves for enlistment. In March 1915 the *Protection Companies* were re-designated as *Supernumerary Companies TF*. In July 1915 there was a wide scale trawl of these companies to identify men capable of marching 10 miles with a rifle and 150 rounds of ammunition. Those who were classified as medical Category A went to Service battalions, while Category Cs were posted to Provisional battalions. Category B men were formed into the 18th-24th Battalions of the Rifle Brigade. These battalions were sent to Egypt and India at the end of 1915 to replace TF units committed to Gallipoli and Mesopotamia. The rump left in Britain eventually formed the 25th Battalion Rifle Brigade TF and served as a Garrison battalion at Falmouth. As for the Supernumerary Companies, they were eventually formed into the Royal Defence Corps.

John Harry Brown

Charles and Mary Brown's eldest son John was born at Thurgarton in 1888 and educated in Southwell. Upon leaving school, aged 13, he had been employed as an under gardener prior to joining the Royal Scots Fusiliers in 1907. The following year he went with his regiment to India and then on to Pretoria in South Africa (he was in South Africa at the 1911 Census). Following his army service John Brown returned to Southwell and was employed as a driver by J. H. Kirkby.

Shortly after the outbreak of war he enlisted with the 1st Battalion Sherwood Foresters and in May 1915 he was sent out to France where he fought at Ypres, the Somme and Cambrai. On 31st July 1917, Corporal Brown was wounded at Westhoek in Belgium (one report suggests it was at Arras), being shot in the right leg and fracturing it in two places. In the chaos of battle he lay there for two days before the stretcher bearers were able to rescue him. He was transported back to England and hospitalized for several months, undergoing a series operations to repair his leg. Upon leaving hospital he was discharged from the army on 10th July 1917.

Following his discharge John Brown returned to his job with J.H. Kirkby and delivered bread to Newark, where he became well known. Sadly, aged 31, he succumbed to pneumonia and died on 25th April 1919. Corporal John Brown was given a full military funeral and is buried in the Minster Church Yard. He left a wife, Ada, and two children.

The following inscription is on his tomb stone:

> HE ANSWERED HIS KING AND COUNTRY
> HE RALLIED TO THEIR CALL.
> HE ANSWERS NOW HIS MAKER,
> THE GRANDEST CALL OF ALL.

Vincent Alphonso Brown

Vincent Brown, born in Nottingham, was educated in Southwell and was the second son of Charles and Mary Brown. In 1907, aged 18, he enlisted with the 2nd Battalion, Sherwood Foresters and had been based in Wales, Plymouth and Sheffield prior to going to France in September 1914. His battalion took part in the Battle of Aisne, being in action at Chemin de Dames, where they suffered heavy casualties. Shortly afterwards they moved north and took part in fighting around Hooge in 1915. In December 1914 he wrote a long letter to his parents describing his harrowing experiences. Extracts from the letter were published in the *Newark Advertiser* on 23rd December (see the Southwell War Diary).

Little more was heard of Vincent Brown until 1916, when the 2nd Battalion were taking part in the continuing Battle of the Somme. On 13th September 'B' and 'C' Companies were moved to just south of the village of Ginchy, with 'A' and 'D' Companies in support in the reserve trenches. Around 4.00 a.m., after the attack had gone in, a patrol was sent out to find them. It appeared that 'C' Company had been held up and 'D' Company had managed to advance about 700 yards under heavy shelling and fire. 'B' and 'C' Companies were able to hang on to their gains. However, the battalion suffered heavy losses, including Vincent Brown on 16th September. He is buried at Guillemont Road Cemetery, Guillemont. Vincent Brown left a widow, Mary E. (Haywood), whom he had married in late 1913.

Vincent Brown
(Newark Advertiser)

A Family at War – The Hopewells of Southwell: Tragedy and Heroism

The Hopewells of Southwell were, even by the standards of the time, a large family with 9 surviving children – four having died in infancy. When the call came to defend their country the Hopewell sons did not shy away from their duty. Indeed four of them had been members of 'H' Company, 8th Battalion Sherwood Foresters for some time prior to the war. Five sons served during the course of the war, and typically two of them, Albert and John, died in the trenches of the Western Front within three months of each other in 1915. A third son, Arthur, was seriously wounded and the fourth son, William, was determined to avenge the deaths of his two elder brothers. When his chance came, he acquitted himself with exceptional bravery and was awarded the highest honour of any of the Southwell men. The youngest son, Gordon, enlisted much later and was taken Prisoner of War.

Whilst this family was not alone in suffering tragedy, their story is worth relating to help us to understand the horrors and the harsh reality of war, together with the emotional strain that must have affected those that were left behind on the 'Home Front'.

Tony Hopewell, of Upton, has kindly provided most of the family details that follow:

The family

The Hopewell family originate from Nottingham, where their father Henry (born 1861) worked for the lace manufacturer E. Carey & Sons of Bulwell. Carey's started to move their manufacturing to Southwell in 1900, and eventually the whole operation was transferred. Henry Hopewell moved his family to 8, Chatham Street, Southwell sometime between 1906 and 1911.

Henry and Alice Hopewell had a total of thirteen children:

William Henry   24/12/1882 – 2/1/83
Florence Annie 24/4/84
Robert Arthur   21/6/86
Albert Edward   8/9/88
John Henry   1/8/90
Millicent   11/10/81 – 28/1/83
William   11/2/94

Alice   6/4/96
Gordon   27/5/98
Evelyn   8/3/00
Ada   31/10/03 died before 1911
Elsie May   24/6/05
Ethel Ada   Born and died 1907

E. Carey & Sons were the largest employers in Southwell in the early part of the twentieth century and was not only the workplace of Henry, but also for (Robert) Arthur – he had worked in their Bulwell factory – Albert, John and William. As mentioned earlier in this book full military records are few and far between, but we are fortunate in having papers showing that John joined 'H' Company in December 1907 and Arthur in 1913 (he may have been a member earlier as they served on annual contracts). Albert is thought to have enlisted in 1908 and William sometime later.

In January 1913 William left home to join the Royal Marine Light Infantry as a professional soldier. When war was declared in August 1914 'H' Company were at their summer camp at Hunmanby and were sent home to prepare for mobilization, which order was given on 4th August. The Company were quickly entrained to Newark, prior to their march to Derby to join the other Nottinghamshire and Derbyshire Territorials, which brought the whole of the 8th Battalion together – a battalion of 'Pals'. Arthur was found to be unfit and was discharged on 6th August. However, it seems that he re-enlisted later in the war. John and Albert commenced intensive training with the 8th Battalion prior to being shipped to the Western Front in February/March 1915.

Albert Edward and John Henry Hopewell

On 3rd April 1915 the battalion had attended a Church Parade taken by the Bishop of London. It was a wet and windy day, and the men were miserable as they could not hear a word of the Bishop's address. On their mind was the start of the 'great adventure', as described by the battalion diarist, as they prepared themselves to take over a trench sector from the 1st Devons. For days they had been hearing the sound of battle and their moment for action was quickly approaching.

Albert Edward Hopewell (Newark Advertiser)

That night they set off in the dark from their billets in Kemmel Village and took their places in the trenches, with 'B' Company (Southwell and Newark men) in supporting points. The trench line varied between 25 and 300 yards' distance from the German front line.

The first few days were relatively quiet and the battalion suffered its first casualty on 6th April when Private J. Hyde was killed by a sniper. In those early days the men spent 4 days in the trenches and 4 days out, in which time they had to undertake support duties from their base at Locre. It was during this early period at the front that Albert was killed in action on 15th April. The battalion war diary does not record the specific event, but whilst at Kemmel, April – June, the battalion lost 49 men and 120 were wounded. It is difficult to imagine how this collection of 'Pals' from our area reconciled themselves to these violent deaths, and in particular John Hopewell who served in the same company. Albert Hopewell is buried in Grave E59 at Kemmel Chateau Military Cemetery at Hevvellard, West Vlaandeven, Belgium, about 8 miles from Ypres.

John Hopewell, who joined 'H' Company in 1908 at the same time as Albert, was about to enter an even more difficult period with the battalion. At the end of their stint at Kemmel on 20th June 1915, the 8th Battalion left Locre and took up positions in the 'Salient', recently christened by the Canadians as 'Bloody Ypres'. This part of the battalion's war is described in the previous chapter including their taking up position at Sanctuary Wood. The trenches were not comfortable and were badly affected by wet weather. On 29/30th July they relieved the 7th Battalion in trenches B3, 4, 7 and 8, and it was recorded that they didn't get out for a rest for 19 days. This period was described as the worst they had suffered. At this time Major Becher was in command of the Battalion.

July 30th was recorded as a perfect summer's morning and at 3.30 a.m. the battalion had been stood down. However, suddenly the wood was surrounded by a wall of fire and a heavy bombardment opened up. Under cover of the bombardment and behind 'flammenwerfer' (liquid fire) the Germans attacked. 'B' Company acquitted themselves very well in holding their trenches, but unfortunately John Hopewell was killed in the attack. His official date of death is recorded as 30th July, although the battalion record states 1st August – in the heat of battle it would have been difficult to be certain.

The 8th Battalion were finally relieved on 30th September. During this period they had suffered 61 fatalities, of which 22 had been between 30th July and 1st August, including Privates Charles Thorpe and Samuel Oliver, and Corporal Samuel Humberstone, all of Southwell. This was a shocking period for Southwell and illustrates the impact on a local area where 'Pals' battalions' had been recruited. Later in the war the policy was changed and men were spread out across different regiments.

The *Newark Advertiser* for 18th August 1915 contains a letter from a Southwell member of the 1/8th Battalion, which describes the skirmishes during this period. Also appearing in the *Advertiser* was the following report:

> *Mr. and Mrs. H. Hopewell, of 8 Chatham Street, lost their second son Pte. A.E. Hopewell, last April when he was killed in action and now they have received the sad intelligence that their third son, Pte. John Henry Hopewell has also made the supreme sacrifice. He was 25 years of age on the very day that he was shot. A native of Kimberley, he went to school at Bulwell, afterwards coming with his parents to Southwell, where he entered Messrs Carey and Sons' Lace Factory, and was also a member of the Boys' Brigade, being in the bugle band. Some seven years ago he joined the bugle band of the 8th Sherwood Foresters. A letter to his parents states that, "he always did his duty without grumbling and consequently was appreciated by his officers". Much sympathy is felt for the parents in their double loss.*

John Henry Hopewell (Newark Advertiser)

Robert Arthur Hopewell

Arthur's (as he was known) war history is somewhat vague. There are records to confirm that he joined 'H' Company in May 1913 with Service No. 1783. The record shows that he was medically discharged on 6th August 1914 just as the company was being sent for training. However, family sources state that he was injured in a shell burst later in the war and invalided out of the army. For several years he made frequent visits to the hospital to have shrapnel removed from his leg. Arthur had married in May 1910 and lived on the Burgage, whilst working for E. Carey and Sons. Post-war he lived in Old Basford, Nottingham, where he and his wife Ethel raised two daughters, Iris and Edna.

Gordon Hopewell

Gordon Hopewell was the youngest of the Hopewell boys and was called up later in the war. He served in the Machine Gun Corps in France, but was taken a Prisoner of War and released at the time of the Armistice.

William Hopewell

> *After the No. 1 and No. 2 of his Lewis gun section had become casualties in the ship in which Private Hopewell was serving, he took the Lewis gun ashore and brought it into action. He continued to fire the gun throughout the operation, and was almost the last man to retire, bringing his gun out of action with him until it was rendered useless by a direct hit by a shell.*
>
> London Gazette 30807
> 23rd July 1918
> To receive the Conspicuous Gallantry Medal

Along with his three elder brothers and his father, William Hopewell, after leaving school, worked for E. Carey & Sons as a threader. Family records suggest that he had been a member of the Church Lads' Brigade and was also a member of the Territorial Army, but in January 1913 he had a complete change of career and, aged 19, joined the Royal Marine Light Infantry. Although only 5' 4" he must have been a fit young man to be accepted into the RMLI prior to the outbreak of war. William served on several Royal Naval ships:

1914-17 H.M.S. Exmouth, which was originally part of the Northern Patrol, but in 1915 was sent to the Dardenelles to support the campaign. In late 1915 she was transferred to the Aegean and in 1917 sailed to the East Indies Section on escort duties. Whilst in the Mediterranean William Hopewell had been involved in the landing at Athens and in quelling the disturbances.

1918 H.M.S. Glory, which was the flagship of the British North Russia Squadron.

1918 H.M.S. Vindictive for the Zeebrugge Raid.

1919-1921 H.M.S. Ramillies

Late 1921 H.M.S. Hood, the new battle cruiser.

Following the death of his two brothers in 1915 William wrote to his aunt and vowed, 'I'll get my own back for what they did to Albert and John'. His opportunity came in 1918 when he volunteered to take part in the Zeebrugge Raid. It had been made clear that the possibility of not surviving was very high.

The Zeebrugge Raid

'...the finest feat of arms in the Great War'
Winston Churchill

German U-boats, based in the Bruges Canal, were responsible for sinking a third of Allied merchant shipping and during 1918 there was a fear that the ongoing threat to essential supplies could have starved Britain into submission. Britain started making plans to stop the submarines gaining access to the sea. The objective was to blow the lock gates and sink blocking ships in the channel. As Paul Kendall states in the introduction to his book about the raid, it was an audacious plan and its leader, Vice-Admiral Roger Keys, could only offer the prospect of death or capture to those who took part.[1] Selection for the volunteers was extremely rigorous and William Hopewell did well to be accepted. No doubt his experiences in the Dardanelles played a part. The volunteers were subjected to extensive and tough training and a number were rejected at this stage. Whilst the training was taking place around 2,000 workers were involved in fitting out the assault ships for the mission. Two submarines were filled with explosives with the intention of them destroying the viaduct that connected the Zeebrugge Mole to the shore. H.M.S. Vindictive was to land a raiding party of Royal Marines at the entrance to the Bruges Canal to create a diversionary attack and to destroy German defences and guns, whilst three old ships, packed with concrete, were manoeuvred into position to block the canal.

The raid was initially planned for 3rd April 1918, but due to an unfavourable wind direction it was postponed until 23rd April when the tides would be favourable. A large force came together for the raid, consisting of 168 vessels of various size and 1,780 officers and men, of which 690 were Royal Marine Light Infantry. All this as another raid was to take place on Ostend. Unfortunately, as the raiding party approached there was a change in wind direction and the smoke screen that had been laid was shifted, and the Germans spotted the approaching small

---

[1] Paul Kendall, *The Zeebrugge Raid 1918, The Finest Feat of Arms* (Brimscombe Port: Spellmount, 2008).

armada. The marines immediately came under heavy fire and a desperate fight ensued. Within less than an hour the order was given to withdraw and it was at this point that William Hopewell came into his own. As the Marines withdrew to H.M.S. Vindictive his Lewis Gun crew were providing covering fire. During the action two of his colleagues were wounded and William took the Lewis Gun on to the Mole and continued to fire at the enemy with no concern for his own safety. Eventually, as the citation mentions, he was almost the last man to retire to safety after his Lewis Gun had been hit by a shell and made inoperable. 227 men were killed and 356 wounded in the raid.

Despite such a supreme effort the raid was only partially successful, as the block ships failed to get into their correct positions and it was still possible for submarines to navigate in and out of the canal at high tide. However, the attack was deemed to be a success and provided a welcome boost to moral at a time when the Western Front was still at stalemate.

For their efforts 8 Victoria Crosses and 16 Conspicuous Gallantry Medals were awarded. William Hopewell narrowly missed a V.C., four members of the award committee voted for him, but insufficient to win the day. As well as his C.G.M. William was awarded the Croix de Guerre with a bronze palm – high honour indeed for this modest man.

William stayed in the marines until 1922 and when he returned home he went back to E. Carey & Sons. He later worked at the local gas works as a stoker, and at the Workhouse as a gardener. He had married Beatrice Hancock in 1919 and they had 3 sons and 3 daughters. His daughter Betty Thornton describes her father as very reserved and unassuming. When he returned home immediately after the raid the local band, press and dignitaries were waiting for him at the station. On spotting the reception committee he jumped off the train and ran home across the fields to Chatham Street. At the outbreak of the Second World War, aged 45, he volunteered again, but was rejected on age grounds and joined the Home Guard for the duration. William died on 9th May 1973.

William Hopewell (Tony Hopewell)

The Conspicuous Gallantry Medal

The Croix de Guerre

The Humberstone Brothers

The Humberstones were another family who were firmly wedded to the lace manufacturing trade. Originally from Nottingham they had moved to Southwell where three of their four sons are shown in the 1911 Census as working for E. Carey & Sons – Samuel, Arthur and William. Arthur was a noted footballer playing for Southwell City. Another son, Albert, had been a grocer's assistant prior to joining the 1st Battalion Royal Scots Fusiliers. Aged 22 in 1911 he is recorded as being based in South Africa as a signaller.[1]

Albert Humberstone

Albert Humberstone (born 1887) was a professional soldier who served in France during the war. Little is recorded about him, but we do know that he was gazetted in February 1915 on being awarded the D.C.M. whilst a Lance Corporal. It was recorded in the *Newark Advertiser* on 3rd March 1915 that he had been mentioned in dispatches for 'gallant and distinguished service in the field' – no further details were offered in the report. Later in the war he is reported as being a Sergeant-Instructor. In November 1915 the *Advertiser* reported his marriage to Mabel Sharpe of West Bridgford and formerly of Westgate, Southwell. Apart from a few further references in reports about his brothers there is little more on record, however, he is known to have survived the war.

Albert Humberstone
(Newark Advertiser)

The two middle brothers, Samuel (born 1889) and Arthur (born 1891), both volunteered for the Territorial Army in 1912 and were members of 'H' Company, Numbers 1424 and 1432 respectively. When 'H' Company was mobilized in August 1914 they both signed up for foreign service and following their intensive training went out to France in February/March 1915 with the 8th Battalion. Both men were promoted to corporal whilst in France.

Samuel Humberstone

As we know from the war diary the 8th Battalion were very quickly thrown into the heavy fighting around Ypres. Reports in the *Newark Advertiser* in June and July 1915 mention that a number of Southwell men had done excellent work following the Germans blowing three mines under the battalion's trenches, and one of these was Samuel Humberstone. Sadly Samuel was killed-in-action on 31st July during a heavy engagement in the 'Salient', in what was a very difficult time for the battalion. A scroll commemorating his death has been preserved in the private collection of local historian David Hutchinson. A memorial service was held in the Minster in August 1915 for Samuel and for Corporal Frank Wilcox, and Privates Frank Paling, Samuel Oliver and J Watson.

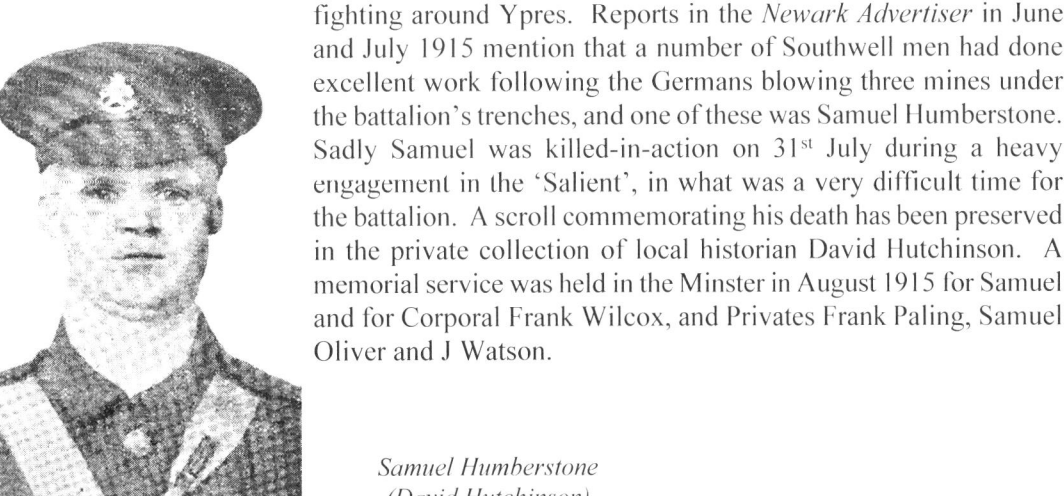

Samuel Humberstone
(David Hutchinson)

---

[1] On the same Census return in 1911 Lancelot Edward Becher, of Southwell, is shown as ADC to Lord Methuen, General, Royal Fusiliers, South Africa.

Similar scrolls to the one on the left were sent to all the families of men killed during the First World War.

(David Hutchinson - also applies to the letter on the following page.)

He whom this scroll commemorates was numbered among those who, at the call of King and Country, left all that was dear to them, endured hardness, faced danger, and finally passed out of the sight of men by the path of duty and self-sacrifice, giving up their own lives that others might live in freedom. Let those who come after see to it that his name be not forgotten.

Cpl. Samuel Humberstone
Notts. & Derby. Regt.

Arthur Humberstone

Arthur Humberstone had survived the onslaught in June and July, but it was reported in August 1915 that he had been wounded in the continuing fighting in the 'Salient'. Little more was recorded about Arthur until in early July 1917 when the *Newark Advertiser* reported that he had died of wounds on 23rd June 1917.[2] The family received a letter from the Chaplain:

---

[2] At this time the 8th Battalion had been sent back to Northern France and deployed near Lens between mid-March and early July. In this four month period the battalion had suffered 5 officers wounded, 3 missing, 42 other ranks killed, 180 wounded and 72 missing. It had been a black period for them.

Dear Mrs Humberstone, It is with deep regret that your son was brought into this hospital so badly wounded that he soon passed away, in spite of attempts to save his life. He was unconscious when he died, and it will comfort you to know that he suffered no pain. I saw him when he first came in, and he asked me to send you his love. Please accept my sincere sympathy in your great trouble. I shall bury him tomorrow at — , and will remember you in my prayers at the grave.

Arthur's brother William was close by at the time and had been allowed to visit him in hospital just prior to his death. He had a very difficult letter to write home:

I hardly know how to write this letter to tell you the news that poor Arthur has got severely wounded this morning with a trench mortar. I saw him when he was on the stretcher, but he hardly knew me. His wounds are in the neck and right side, and the doctor says they are very serious. In a later communication he states:– *I expect you have my letter telling you about Arthur being wounded. I am awfully sorry to tell you he died on Saturday, the 23rd, at 9 o'clock. I have got permission to leave the trenches to attend his funeral, and three chums are to go with me.*

A letter from the Reverend W. J. Conybeare followed to Arthur's widow:

*Arthur Humberstone
(Newark Advertiser)*

William Humberstone

The fourth brother, William, also served with the Sherwood Foresters and had gone to France in March 1915. It is assumed by his service number 2126 that he had also been a member of 'H' Company, but no records can be found. Neither was he on the original list of those who had left Southwell in August 1914, although he obviously went later.

William, fortunately, survived the war, but as with so many the death of his two brothers must have had a profound effect on him, particularly Arthur's as he had visited him at the hospital when he was wounded and subsequently died, and had had to relay the news to the family.

The Paling Brothers

The Paling family of Constance Villa, Station Road, Southwell (the house is now a part of Dornoch Avenue), suffered a double tragedy with two of their sons, Albert Edward and Frank, killed on the Western Front within a year of each other.

Albert, born 1896, worked as a miller at Caudwell's Flour Mill, and his brother Frank, born 1893, was a gardener and nurseryman with Henry Merryweather. The two volunteered shortly after the outbreak of war. Frank enlisted with the 1/8th Battalion Sherwood Foresters on 8th September 1914, and Albert followed on 28th October, initially with the 2/8th Battalion, but was quickly transferred to the 1/8th. Neither of them had been members of 'H' Company, but they would have been immediately amongst friends in the battalion. After intensive training the two brothers went out to the front, Frank in Early March 1915, and Albert followed in June.

As we know from the battalion war diary, the 1/8th Battalion were very quickly in action in the trenches and in the early days there were many casualties. On 12th June 1915, Frank was on sentry duty in a trench in the Kemmel area of Belgium when he was shot in the head by an enemy sniper and died within three quarters of an hour. Frank Paling was buried at the Kemmel Chateau Military Cemetery and his brother Albert was given leave to attend.

Albert stayed with the battalion and was very much in the thick of the fighting. In September 1915 he was in action at Sanctuary Wood, near Ypres, and on 10th September received a gunshot wound to his neck. It was not serious and he was sufficiently recovered to return to his unit by the end of the month. Within a few days, on 14th October, he suffered gas poisoning and was taken to the 18th Stationary Hospital, where he stayed until November 15th when he was transferred to the 48th Divisional Convalescence Depot at Rouen, from where he was discharged back to his unit. On 18th December Albert was promoted, in the field, to Lance Corporal, making full Corporal the following March.

Frank Paling
(Ann Warner)

Shortly after the commencement of the Somme offensive the 1/8th Battalion was moved to Bellacourt, south-west of Arras, where they were allocated a long frontage to defend. They were subjected to rifle and machine-gun fire as well as trench mortars, which caused a few casualties. Amongst them on 13th July 1916 Albert was wounded in his buttock and left thigh, which was fractured, and sadly he died of his wounds the following day at the 20th Casualty Clearing Station.

Albert's parents received a letter from one of the nurses:

Dear Mrs Paling,
I am afraid I have very sad news for you today. Your son Corporal A. Paling, 8th Sherwood Foresters, was admitted here on the 13th suffering from wounds in the thigh. His wounds were most severe and extensive and he was very exhausted on admission. By next morning the 14th he had rallied a little and it was necessary to give him an anaesthetic to examine his wounds, when it was also found necessary to amputate his leg and very little hope was given to his recovery.

This was about mid-day. During the afternoon he got much weaker and gradually sank and died at 4.50 p.m. He will be buried today in our little cemetery here. I expect our chaplain, Mr Swift, will be writing to you also. His effects will be sent to you in due course through the War Office. Please accept our sincere sympathy with you in your loss and believe me to be yours sincerely, sister-in-charge.[1]

There were various brief articles in the *Newark Advertiser,* including a report of a memorial service for Frank Paling in the Minster in August 1915. No doubt a similar service was held for Albert.

There was an elder third son, George, who was exempted from military service, following representation by his parents, as he worked on the land. His daughter, Mrs Ann Warner, has described that portraits and other memorials to her two uncles were on display in the house until very recently. The family never did fully recover from the deaths of their two young sons.

*Albert Paling
(Ann Warner)*

*The original cross marking the grave of Albert Paling at Walincourt Halte British Cemetery in the Somme area.
(Ann Warner.)*

---

[1] Foster, p. 38

Chris Rippin

The story of Chris Rippin is included in this section not because it is exceptional, but because it is excellent oral history being based on an interview granted to Doreen Stevenson for her book *Twentieth Century Lives of Southwell*, prior to his death in 1993. It is also included because years later he was still bitter about the way returning soldiers, particularly the wounded, had been treated and he questioned the existence of a 'land fit for heroes'. The text is taken from that interview.

Aged 13 Chris Rippin worked for J. J. Bates, the Southwell grocer. He was one of eleven surviving children (5 had died prior to the 1911 Census) – full details are included in the Roll Call of Servicemen section.

In 1916, Chris went to war; not the Royal Field Artillery where his brother was but to the South Staffs Regiment, where his ability with horses was needed. He was at Arras, Vimy Ridge and on the Marne and the Somme, taking food and ammunition up the line under cover of darkness. When moving from one offensive to another, 96lb (45kg) was carried on the back. It included a complete change of clothing, an overcoat, a blanket, a groundsheet and a haversack containing two dog biscuits, tea, a tin of bully beef and a tin of McConachy; meat, potatoes and vegetables that could be eaten hot or cold. 'Very tasty it was.'

The war was a horrible experience, the worst thing being the lice. The loosely-woven materials used for uniforms enable lice to reach even the seams. When the sun shone, lice could be seen everywhere; on hair, neck, clothes. Scrape a layer of soil and there would be lice. On one occasion, Chris and his group found a shed with a copper in it. They lit a fire underneath, added creosote to the water and proceeded to wash their clothing. The lice survived.....and the cleaned clothes burnt their skin. Southwell seemed a long way away.

November 11th, 1918 saw Chris in Calais where news of the cease-fire was received with jubilation. Bugles were blown continuously and guns fired out of windows. But the war was not over for Chris. He had to drive his wagon and two horses as part of an escort taking the enemy back to Dresden, travelling every day from 6 a.m. to 10 p.m. 'They were like us, not like the Germans of World War 2. They didn't want to fight.'

Chris Rippin in the South Staffs Regiment -
Private Collection Doreen Stevenson

In Germany, the farms and fields appeared immaculate. The farmers were forced to feed the English soldiers and also provide stabling for the horses. The Germans ate off the land. For the first time in two years, Chris slept in a white feather bed (although he was lousy) and had home-made bread and lard.

Back in England Chris was demobbed and given a gratuity of £27 which he spent on a holiday in London staying at a B & B that cost 12s:6d (62 ½ p) a night.

In Southwell, no one wanted to know about the war. The 'land fit for heroes' did not appear to exist and wounded soldiers thought they were unfairly treated by the government.

Pre-war jobs had not been kept while they were away fighting and many returning ex-soldiers could find nothing to do.

Chris obtained a job five miles away at Kelham. Amazingly he had to guard German prisoners-of-war who were camped at Kelham brickyard and worked on Kelham farm. The Royal Engineers were quitting Kelham Hall and selling off their horses so Chris bought one not yet broken into harness for £9 and on this he travelled to his job.

Chris had several jobs shortly after the war and later worked for J. H. Kirkby for twenty five years, before working for Dowse's the drapers and ironmongers. During the Second World War he was part of a contingent of the Red Cross and also helped run a volunteer ambulance service.[1]

---

[1] Doreen Stevenson, Chris Rippin, pp. 1-5.

Walter Frederick Saddington: The Old Warrior

Born in Oakham, Rutland, in 1866 Walter Saddington was a professional soldier who volunteered to serve as a Colour Sergeant Instructor to 'H' Company, 8th Sherwood Foresters, following 29 years' service with the former 2nd Battalion Derbyshire Regiment. At the age of 50 this old warrior served on the Western Front with his battalion. As an experienced soldier there is little doubt that his former service made him an excellent instructor for these part time soldiers and helped them earn the title of the 'Mad 8th' and for being part of the first territorial division to serve on the front line.

Colour Sergeant Saddington's army record matched his title as somewhat colourful. He joined the Derbyshire Regiment in October 1883 at just short of 18 years of age, having previously worked as a clerk. At that point in his life he was 5'6" tall and weighed a mere 9 stone. Today we would have described him as slight. By the time he matured he had grown a couple of inches and developed a 40 inch chest. Within a couple of years of joining he was severely reprimanded on several occasions, and also subjected to 19 days in detention. However, these offences were soon forgotten and did not hamper his career and by 1886 he was promoted to lance corporal and full corporal within a year. Promotion to sergeant came in 1890 and colour sergeant in 1896. Even as a sergeant he had brushes with discipline, mainly for drunkenness. In 1898 he had a set-back when he was arrested for fighting outside the sergeant's mess with another sergeant. To avoid a Court Martial he volunteered to take a reduction in rank back to sergeant. At this time correspondence in his military records shows that he made a well-written plea to his C.O. that his pension rights would still relate back to when he was first appointed a sergeant. His C.O. wrote a letter to the Brigadier in support of Walter Saddington and he confirmed that his pension rights would not be affected and reduction to sergeant was sufficient punishment. His C.O. clearly held Saddington in high regard.

Sergeant Saddington's army service was mainly spent overseas. In December 1885 he had been posted to the East Indies, returning for a brief period to the U.K. in 1893 and back East until 1899. From October that year he served in Malta before coming home for his last ten years of service and his first retirement in 1912. Whilst on foreign service he saw action and served in several campaigns, including the Sikkim Expedition in 1888.[1]

In September Walter Saddington married Helena Fitzgerald who was born in County Waterford and was his junior by nine years. They lived in married quarters. Helena bore them four children, but the first two died in infancy, the surviving children Frederick (1905) and Eveline (1907) were born in Southwell, where they lived in Westgate after he was appointed instructor to 'H' Company. The 1911 Census shows that he had regained his rank as colour sergeant. In 1912 he was discharged from the army, but it seems that he must have missed army life as in 1913 he reapplied at the age of 47 and special permission was given for him to return to his post with 'H' Company. Clearly it must have been recognised that he was an asset to the battalion.

---

[1] Sikkim was a small independent state of 3,600 square miles, wedged between Nepal and Bhutan. In 1888 the Tibetans occupied several border forts and a joint force of Indian and British troops were sent to remove them. Northern Sikkim then came under the rule of British India.

Whilst the photograph has been copied from the shot of 'H' Company going off to war, he did not go to France in 1915 as no doubt it was deemed that he was too old and was needed to train new recruits. However, in March 1916 in the rank of Quarter Master Sergeant he went out to the front for twelve months. His records show that life in the trenches took its toll and he suffered from cardiac debility and vertigo. Walter Saddington finally retired from the army in November 1919 after almost 36 years' service and aged 53.

This story is worth relating as it illustrates Q.M.S. Saddington's commitment to his men and to his country.

'H' Company Orders for 1912
(Roger Merryweather)

Thomas Scraton and William Henry Shepperson – Prisoners of War
On the 4th December 1918 the *Newark Advertiser* published an account of the above men's experience as Prisoners of War. Rather than include this article in the main text of the War Diary, it seemed appropriate to allow it separate coverage in order to illustrate the conditions suffered by some of the P.O.W.s.

'PRISONERS OF WAR HOME AGAIN
SLAVERY IN COAL MINES'

'Pte. W. Shepperson, Rose Cottage, Southwell, and Pte. Thomas Scraton, of Westhorpe, arrived home on Saturday last from Germany. Before the war Pte. Shepperson was a baker in the employ of Mr. J. H. Kirkby, and Pte. Scraton an employee of the local Co-operative Society. They joined up on Feb. 23rd, 1917, and went to France with the 6th Durhams on March 31st, 1918, saw much fighting at Armentiers and district, and were captured in the big push made by the Germans at Craonne on May 27th.

Taken behind the enemy lines, they were immediately put to work building bridges and laying railway lines right up to his front, and were often under shell fire from our own guns. The food was bad, consisting of coffee in the morning, made of burnt barley and water, and a small slice of brown bread. Dinner consisted of a small quantity of soup made from barley and mangolds [a beet cultivated as stock feed]. A German cook told them the black bread was made from sawdust, as they had nothing else. On the way to the billets the prisoners picked up nettle leaves, dandelion leaves, and ketlock stalks [?], boiled them with a few sticks and ate the lot. After six weeks they were taken in cattle trucks into Dulmin in Westphalia, and put to work in a coal mine. They had nothing to eat on the three days' journey but a few raw potatoes, which they picked up on the sidings. The mines were under Commandos No. 91 and 101, the men in charge being more like beasts than human beings. Our two prisoners went down the pit at 3 p.m. each day and came up at midnight. They had a long way to go to their billets. They were compelled to get 25 tons of coal daily from the seam, and load it on to the conveyor which carried it along and shot the coal into wagons. The seams were 15 feet from the conveyor and only five feet deep, so the work had to be done on knees and back. In some places they had to work in a space of three feet, carry a pick in one hand, a hacker in another, a saw tied to their foot for sawing props, and the lamp carried in their teeth. The conveyor was worked by hydraulic pressure. The food consisted of black bread made up of sawdust (each day's ration was eaten up as soon as it was handed out), and soup made of mangolds and black beans. The men were treated very badly. One man was struck on the head with a rifle and his head split open. It was the usual thing for prisoners' joints to be amputated without anaesthetics if they had an accident; and if the proper quantity of coal was not forthcoming they had to work a double shift. No food was allowed them in the mines. The foremen were brutes, and had no mercy for our half-famished men. The day the armistice was signed all was changed. The foremen came to them saying 'English now komerad. No more fights. English good', and later on the officers of the Revolutionary party in Germany came round and said, 'There will be no more fighting. We are comrades now.' The prisoners got no news, and did not have any idea how things were shaping. They were carried to the frontier, loaded up with parcels from home, in cattle trucks, and crossed the border into Holland on Nov. 20th. The Dutch treated them splendidly. Both prisoners speak in high praise of the work of the Red Cross Society, and the kind people at home who sent them the regular parcels of food, without which they could not have lived. In their district – Westphalia – butter is 22s. per pound, meat (when on sale) 22s. 6d. per pound; leather never seen, all people wear wooden clogs; cigars and cigarettes made of dried leaves, and few shops have anything to sell at all; but they have plenty of potatoes, and everybody is now living on them. The prisoners food on Sunday was cabbage soup and the bread left over from Saturday, if any, and many a man has been known to exchange his gold or silver wristlet watch for a bit of black bread. The two Southwell lads wish to thank all the friends who contributed in any way towards the parcels which had gone out so regularly.'

Other Prisoners of War

The *Newark Advertiser* and military records recorded a number of other Southwell P.O.W.s:

Dudley Dodson
George Hopkinson
Oscar Longmore
John (Jack) Partington
George W. Robinson
Frank Scraton
Alex Straw
Percy W. Toder (died of influenza on his journey home)[1]
Leslie F. Twidale

See the Roll Call of Servicemen for personal details.

There may have been others that were not recorded.

---

[1] A full report appears in the *Newark Advertiser* dated 18th December 1918.

John Sharman

John Sharman of The Holme, Westhorpe, Southwell lied about his age in 1911 when he joined 'H' Company, 8th Battalion Sherwood Foresters in Southwell. With a service number of 1245 he was certainly one of the earlier territorials. John was the son of Thomas Sharman, and one of 13 children – another large Southwell family. Born in Counthorpe, Lincolnshire in 1895 he had been educated at Woodborough, prior to the family moving to Southwell when he was moved to the National School in 1904. After leaving school he became a gentleman's servant for the Warrand family at Westhorpe Hall, and later he worked for Herbert Steel, the butcher, of Westgate Southwell. At some stage he became engaged to Mary Walters who was a domestic servant to a solicitor in Mapperley. Sadly he died before they could marry.

As war was declared in August 1914 he was with the rest of 'H' Company at summer camp and within a few days he was en route for intensive training and, along with most of his colleagues, had signed up for foreign service. He went to France in late February/early March 1915 with the rest of the battalion and they were very quickly deployed to trenches at Kemmel, near Ypres in Belgium.

John Sharman and Mary Walters (Robin Sharman)

Life near Kemmel was extremely difficult and the battalion soon started suffering heavy casualties. Mining was taking place by both sides and on 15th June the enemy exploded three mines under the 8th Battalion's trenches, accompanied by a heavy barrage for an hour, the likes of which they had not experienced before. Their telephone lines were severed and communications were lost with their headquarters. The isolated men were short of ammunition and were unable to make much response as the Germans tried to occupy the large crater that had been created by one of the mines. However, 'C' Company men were able to drive them off at bayonet point. John Sharman was the only man left in his trench and fought off an enemy attempt to take it over. In the fight he was hit on the leg by a dud bomb and injured, narrowly escaping more serious injury as a bullet passed through his haversack. In addition to the bravery of John Sharman, Corporal Humberstone had done excellent work, as had Lance Corporal Templeman and Private Tongue in repairing telephone wires. Casualties were high with 11 men killed and 29 wounded from the battalion. This had been one of the earliest raids by the Germans.

John Sharman managed to get home on leave in August and on 21st August it was reported in the *Newark Advertiser* that he had been awarded the Russian Medal of St. George, 4th Class for conspicuous bravery. He was also promoted to corporal in this period. Corporal Sharman was soon back in action, this time in what was known as the 'Salient' (Sanctuary Wood) and on 1st October the battalion was deployed to the Hohenzollern Redoubt. They were there for just over two weeks,

John Sharman, ready for departure (Robin Sharman)

which turned out to be their blackest period of the war – this is covered in the Battalion's War Diary.[1] John Sharman played a big part in the battle at this time and it is a testament to his bravery.

Towards the end of their deployment at Hohenzollern, on 13th October, 'B' Company were in a reserve trench waiting to attack. A shell exploded close by and stunned Private W. Gregory of Southwell, he was taken into a dugout by John Sharman and looked after until he was evacuated by stretcher bearers. By this time John Sharman had lost contact with 'B' Company, but at around 6.45 a.m. he found 'D' Company and one of their platoons was about to go 'over the top' lead by Sergeant Layhe. John Sharman decided to go over the parapet with them. As they reached the German wire he was hit in the head by a bullet and died instantly. He was originally posted as missing, but at a later inquest, based on evidence by Sergeant Layhe and Private Gregory, it was ruled that he had been killed in action. There is no known grave for John Sharman and he is commemorated on the Loos Memorial.[2]

On 10th November the *Newark Advertiser* reported that John Sharman's father had received a letter from an officer:

> *It is with the greatest regret that I have to write to tell you of the death of your son, Corpl. John Sharman. He was not with my Company at the time, but from what I can learn from the men with whom he was serving, there can be no doubt about it, I am afraid. He was an excellent fellow in every sense of the word and would have been a Sergeant in no time, if only he had been spared. He never knew what fear was, and I shall always remember him for the services he rendered, which earned for him the Russian Order of St. George. I cannot sufficiently express my sympathy with you in your great loss.*

The battalion's war diary records:

> *October 14th seemed a never-ending day for those in the Redoubt. Fortunately in a way, the lines were too close together for us to be shelled, but bombing went on almost uninterruptedly, and our casualties mounted rapidly.*

At the end of the chapter Captain Weetman, the battalion diarist, wrote:

> *Thus ended the more or less fruitless battle of Hohenzollern Redoubt. Though we held a portion of the Redoubt as a result of the fighting, it was of no tactical value, and indeed later on it was evacuated or blown up.*

---

[1] The Hohenzollern Redoubt was a raised area of ground, two miles from Loos and was a major German defensive position. On 2nd October the 16th Bavarian Reserve Regiment had been moved to the area, a member of which was the 26 year-old Adolph Hitler.
[2] Grateful thanks to the Sharman family historian, Robin Sharman, for much of the background information about John and his brothers. Olive Kitts also contributed with family details.

Samuel Spall – A Boy Soldier

It is well known that many young men who had been too young to enlist legally had joined the army and been killed or wounded. The rule in 1914 was that to fight abroad a soldier had to be 19 or over. Eighteen-year-olds could join up, but had to remain in the U.K. until they were eligible. It is thought that approximately 250,000 'boy soldiers' enlisted and fought in the war.[1] The fate of one of these Southwell boy soldiers, Arthur Leslie Arnold, is well documented. However, a further young volunteer has come to light.

Unbeknown to his living descendants, Samuel Spall, a butcher's errand boy born in 1897, volunteered for the army on 22nd October 1914. His military records show that he declared his age as 19. Samuel joined the 1/8th Battalion, Sherwood Foresters, having signed up as a territorial for the duration of the war. After his training he went out to France in June 1915, a month before his eighteenth birthday and joined many men from Southwell who may have known his true age, but it seems that this was not divulged otherwise he would have been sent home.

It is clear from the War Diary of the 8th Battalion that Samuel joined them in the midst of the fighting in the Salient. On 1st October they moved moved to the Hohenzollern Redoubt for that fateful period when several of the Southwell men were killed or wounded, including the Handford brothers and Major John Becher.[2] It is impossible to imagine the effect that all this death and destruction had on an impressionable eighteen-year-old.

Following the horrors of Hohenzollern, on the 18th October the battalion were sent down to Marseilles with the intention of them being shipped to Egypt. During their 'sojourn' in the South of France Samuel Spall was given three days 'Confined to Barracks' for 'Hesitating to obey an order.' The move to Egypt didn't happen and the battalion was transported back to Northern France on 6th March 1916 and were straight into the front line at Vimy Ridge. They joined the Somme offensive in late June 1916, leading up to the capture of Gommecourt in March 1917. The records suggest that Samuel had a period in England, as on 9th December he was charged at Saltfleet with overstaying his leave by three days and was disciplined. Just prior to the capture of Gommecourt Samuel Spall suffered a gunshot wound to his back and was sent to one of the Cheltenham Area V.A. Hospitals on 3rd March 1917, where he stayed until 24th December. This was the end of his service at the front and he was posted to the 5th Reserve

Samuel and Hannah Spall
(Carole Spall)

---

[1] www.historylearningsite.co.uk/boy_soldiers.htm (accessed 10th December, 2013).

[2] See the War Diary in Chapter 3.

Battalion, Sherwood Foresters at their depot. In March 1918, following his marriage in February, he was hospitalized for a further four months. The records state that he had a contused back and was suffering from shell shock, but had been admitted with German measles. After discharge he returned to the 5th Reserve Battalion. In mid-June he was granted leave, but was arrested by Military Police on Mansfield Station when he was 113 hours overdue to return. His punishment was the loss of 10 days' pay. The following month he was transferred to the 10th Battalion and was finally demobbed on 16th March 1919. Following his demob Samuel was awarded a 20% disability pension of 10s. 0d plus 3s. 0d for his wife, paid weekly. This was reduced two months later to 8s. 0d and 2s. 0d respectively. The pension award form stated that his disability was 'Hemashema' (sic), which may have been another term for anaemia or a similar blood condition.

Samuel Spall was typical of many who had fought in the First World War in that he did not wish to talk about it. His granddaughter, Carole Spall, who has supplied the photographs and some biographical information, was very close to him but had no idea that he was a 'boy soldier', nor that he had been wounded in the back. He blamed lung problems later in life on being gassed in the trenches, and whilst there is no record of this it may very well have been the case. Post war, working as a butcher, later as a chef at the Red Lion, Thurgarton and at the Saracen's Head he was well known and respected in Southwell and had a reputation for his excellent meat pies. He died in 1974.

Samuel, in later life, working at the Saracen's Head Southwell

(Carole Spall)

Philip Huskinson Warwick

The Warwicks were a family of brewers, part of the Warwick and Richardson brewery in Newark. The three sons of Richard H Warwick of Burgage Manor, Southwell, all served their country during the First World War. Richard Warwick's three sons were Hugh Branson Warwick (b. 1879), a professional soldier who served with the R.A.O.C. and Northumberland Fusiliers, rising to Lieutenant Colonel; Philip Huskinson Warwick (b.1880), a brewery director and territorial member of the South Nottinghamshire Hussars Yeomanry, who rose from Captain at the outbreak of war to Lieutenant-Colonel shortly after the war; Norman R.C. Warwick (b. 1892) who served in the

Jersey Brow, Aldershot, 1903.

2nd Lieutenant Warwick is pictured on the far left, front row.
(Photograph from Historical Records South Nottinghamshire Hussars)

East African Mounted Rifles. The elder son of John Warwick (brother of Richard Warwick, living at Upton Hall), John Cedric Geoffrey Warwick (b. 1895), also served in the South Notts Hussars and was drowned as a result of enemy action in 1918.

The war time career of Philip Warwick is well documented in the Regimental history, which has been used to write this chapter and serves to map out the progress of the South Notts Hussars throughout the First World War.[3]

The South Notts Hussars have a long and distinguished history and were first formed as a volunteer cavalry in 1794. In 1795 they had been used to scatter rioters in Nottingham's Market Place. Their first overseas deployment had been in the Boer War, and the First World War saw the regiment abroad once again, earning themselves a string of battle honours.

---

[3] George Fellowes, and Benson Freeman, *Historical Records of the South Nottinghamshire Hussars Yeomanry, 1794-1924* (Aldershot: Gale & Polden, 1928), pp. 212-337.

Philip Warwick had been a member of the Hussars from the turn of the century and is pictured on the previous page at a summer camp in 1903 at Jersey Brow, Aldershot as a Second Lieutenant.

Upon declaration of war in 1914 the South Notts Hussars were mobilized and the then Captain Warwick, with two others, set about making the necessary transport acquisitions. In common with the 8th Battalion Sherwood Foresters they had little transport available and acquired coal carts, brewery drays and horses from various sources. The field strength at the time was around 500 men, which included a small number from Southwell and district. By 8th August the men were on the move to Norfolk and several thousand people saw them off from Nottingham – it must have been an impressive site, despite the 'circus' like transport vehicles that followed them. The Hussars received a considerable amount of training in Norfolk prior to being deployed to Egypt in early April 1915. Upon arrival in Egypt they were quartered in Abbassia Main Barracks, Cairo, until July when they were moved to Kasr-el-Nil. By 11th August they were ordered to go dismounted to the Dardanelles.

Two squadrons, 'B' and 'D', were fitted out with infantry equipment, with squadron 'B' being commanded by Captain Warwick. The squadrons landed at Sulva Bay and quickly realised that they were to be engaged in an unpleasant war. They had to dig themselves in upon arrival whilst being shelled – this was the first experience of war for most of them. Conditions were very difficult and they were soon involved in the Battle of Scimitar Hill, where they suffered heavy casualties. This was an experience shared by many from various regiments. The *Newark Advertiser* printed letters from Lieutenant A.H. Chambers of the Sherwood Foresters on 29th September and 10th November 1915 that graphically illustrated the dreadful conditions. On 3rd November 1915 the South Notts Hussars left Gallipoli and went to Mudros for two weeks of rest prior to returning to Egypt. They received battle honours: 'Sulva', Scimitar Hill' and 'Gallipoli 1915'.

Once back in Egypt it was more training and the receipt of reinforcements prior to their despatch to Salonica in February 1916. Shortly after this deployment Captain Warwick took over command of 'C' Squadron. They were stationed near the Spanc River, where they were involved in several skirmishes whilst out on patrol. In July a high proportion of the regiment were hospitalised with malaria, this amounted to 50 officers and around 350 men. The regiment was moved to Guveyne in August to await the return of the men from hospital. Meanwhile they were involved in various actions against the Bulgarians. For a good proportion of their time in the Balkans outpost work was a feature, where they suffered frequent casualties. Not only had they to contend with Bulgarian Cavalry, but also German Dragoons and Uhlans, and later Turkish Cavalry.

In December 1916 Philip Warwick was promoted to Major, which was followed by a period of leave. He returned to the fray in early February 1917 and continued to command 'C' Squadron. By late June the South Notts Hussars left Macedonia, sailed for Egypt, arriving at Alexandria on 29th June 1917 and were rested for a while at Ismailia Ferry. Battle honours included 'Struma' and 'Macedonia 1916-17'. They were at Ismailia for six weeks and training commenced with machine-gun sections now being formed.

Little else happened until August, when on the 6th they were inspected by General Sir Edmund Allenby and six days later they marched with the brigade to Khan Yunus, near Gaza, on the Palestine frontier, followed by a most difficult journey for both men and horses over the Sinai Desert. At this point in the war the prestige of the British was at a low point following the evacuation of Gallipoli; the fall of Kut-el-Amara; and two unsuccessful attacks on Gaza in the spring of 1917. Turkish forces were on a wide front between Gaza and Beersheba – about 30 miles - and had the benefit of good roads and a railway. General Allenby undertook some reorganisation and formed the Desert Mounted Corps, of which the South Nottinghamshire Hussars Yeomanry were in the Corps Reserve. The total of British forces amounted to 76,000, of which 20,000 were mounted, with the enemy mustering 49,000. However, one of the problems was the heat at 110 degrees in the shade.

The South Notts Hussars undertook a good deal of reconnaissance duties towards Beersheba prior to the attack on there, which took place on 30th October 1917. The South Notts Hussars helped to overcome the Turks and Beersheba was secured, along with its important water resource. 'B' and 'C' Squadrons were involved in picking up Turkish stragglers after the battle. A letter from an officer illustrates the dreadful conditions they suffered:

Monday, November 5th, 1917
Whilst writing yesterday I got a message to move at once. Imagine our feelings, as we had just put up our bivouacs and I had had a lovely bath, and we hadn't slept under a bivy sheet since Monday. We moved about 4.30, and we had a terrible fourteen mile march in clouds of dust, as the traffic was awful. We lay down in the open at two o'clock this morning, and then they moved us at seven, and we arrived here (Shellal) at twelve, and have to be ready to move on at any time at half an hour's notice. We are supposed to have a rest now, as we have had a terrible week, and strong as I am, I really feel even I couldn't stand any more like it. Sleep is what we want, and a good square meal.

I must now continue my story of last Friday and Saturday – the latter we shall never forget. The twelve miles back to Beersheba was awful; our men suffered too horribly from thirst, and all our lips and tongues swelled up and cracked. A few more hours would have about finished some of them. Thirst is ghastly; I never saw men look like that. I think as regards thirst we suffered more than the Sherwood Rangers, though they had the more strenuous time fighting.

After we got in a lot of our horses died from exhaustion; they had had no water for two days, and had been climbing enormous hills both days. My letters are very disjointed, and everyone is on edge. We are a poor lot today.

A further letter tells the story of this rapid advance, and the restless activity it entailed:

To-night we shall be holding part of the line, which means no sleep, of course. When we got orders to move this morning we all felt at the end of our tether, for it has been the hardest week I ever remember, and even to sit down to one of our dirty meals and lie on a valise would seem the height of luxury!

A letter home from Major Warwick explains a little more of the situation:

Monday, November 12th
Just after writing on Saturday we got orders to move again. The squadrons had gone miles to water the horses, and didn't get back until 5.30, so the Colonel left me to bring on 'C' and 'B'. We left at 6.30 in pitch darkness, simply marching on a compass bearing, and we arrived without any difficulty about nine. It was a very rough march, as we had to cross dongas and wadis, and I had the regimental water-cart with me, *which was very precious.* It broke down and I had to leave it out all night with six mules and a subaltern, but it arrived yesterday.

We were here all day yesterday, but I never had a moment to write to you. We were on tenter-hooks all day and were actually turned out once, but had to return owing to lack of water. We expected all night to be turned out, but the order never came…

At 2.30 a.m. the limber arrived with rations and forage, and so I had to get up and see them issued – no easy matter in the dark. We had to do it at once because we can't carry the stuff in bulk if we get orders to move. At 4.30 we went back to bed, and then we had a thunderstorm, but I didn't get very wet, as I was sleeping under a tree and was fully dressed.

The last fortnight has played havoc with our clothes, but I believe there is a chance we may see our wagons with our valises to-morrow.

Following the success at Beersheba the next objective was El Mughar and another battle honour. At this point Lord Allenby summarised the successes in a despatch:

The enemy's army has now been broken up into separate parts, which retired north and east respectively, and were reported to consist of small scattered groups rather than formed bodies of any size.

In fifteen days our force had advanced sixty miles on its right and forty on its left. It had driven a Turkish Army of nine infantry divisions and one cavalry division out of a position in which it had been entrenched for six months, and had pursued it, giving battle whenever it attempted to stand, and inflicting on it losses amounting to nearly two-thirds on the enemy's original effectiveness. Over nine thousand prisoners, about eighty guns, more than a hundred machine guns, and very large quantities of ammunition and other stores had been captured.

The advance continued and they headed towards Jerusalem. The Turks attacked at Nebi Samwail in an effort to regain lost ground and there were ongoing battles with them.

Towards the end of November Major Warwick took over command of the South Notts Hussars. They continued to be involved in a good deal of close quarters fighting and at the end of 1917 Jerusalem was taken. In early January Major Warwick was awarded the D.S.O. By April 1918 further re-organisation took place and the South Notts Hussars paraded for the last time as Cavalry and became a machine gun regiment with the Warwickshire Yeomanry. Fighting continued and the South Notts earned four more honours: 'Gaza', 'El Mughir', 'Nebi Samwil' and 'Palestine 1917-18'.

The regiment was moved to Sidi Bishr Camp with Major Warwick as Senior Officer of the South Notts Hussars Machine Gun Companies from 10th April to 13th July 1918, prior to becoming Commanding Officer from 15th June. At this point the focus of training was on machine-gunning, bayonet fighting, gas drills and infantry drill, clearly a move to France was in mind.

On 22nd May 1918 the order came to embark for France and the regiment set off the following day in the Leasowe Castle within a small protected convoy. At 12.12 a.m. on 27th April the ship was struck by a torpedo[4]. An orderly evacuation commenced on a calm sea and all went well until one of the bulkheads gave way and the ship sank rapidly taking down 50 men with it (8 officers and 42 other ranks). The dead included Lieutenant John G. Warwick[5] of Upton. Had the sea not been so calm the death toll would have been much higher. Major Warwick was injured with a blow on the head from a spar as the ship was sinking. Within a few days he was back on duty and took command of the regiment again. They had returned to Alexandria and on 18th June set sail in the Caledonia and reached the Italian port of Taranto safely. They travelled on by train to Étaples in France from where a good number were sent off on leave, including Major Warwick.

---

[4] The Leasowe Castle, built by Cammell Laird & Co, was 9737 tons and was torpedoed by UB 51, the Captain was Kapitänleutnant Ernst Krafft (born 28/8/1885 in Berlin and died 27/7/54 in Vladimin Prison, a Soviet Camp, which suggests he served in both World Wars). The ship was part of a convoy of fast ships that included: the Canberra, the Caledonia, the Indarra, the Kasiar-i-Hind, the Malawa, and the Omrah.

[5] He was the cousin of Philip H. Warwick and had served with the South Nottinghamshire Hussars throughout.

From leave he and others went to Grantham for further training until September. On 13th July Lieutenant-Colonel Charles A Calvert took command of the regiment.

On 25th August they joined General Rawlinson's Fourth Army and were sent to Worley, near Amiens, and undertook intensive training, including improving their machine gun efficiency. During September the regiment moved to Trônes Wood in the area of Albert and by 9th September they were in action and once again suffering casualties. Within a week they were involved in the attempt to break through the Hindenburg Line. Later that month Major Warwick returned from training and took over as 2nd in Command. Their next objective was the St Quentin Canal and Bellinglise. At this point the war was fast moving and on 8th October the regiment was assisting in the attack on Le Cateau and its eventual recapture on 23rd October. The South Notts Hussars added another battle honour of 'Selle' and continued with the advance right up to the Armistice. Other battle honours were 'France and Flanders, 1918', 'Sambre', 'Beurevoir', 'St. Quentin Canal', 'Epehy', 'Hindenburg Line'.

By 6th December Major Warwick was left in command and promoted to acting Lieutenant-Colonel. In January demobilization had commenced and in mid-April Lt. Col. Warwick returned to England, and on Thursday 27th May 1919 a memorial service, led by the Bishop of Southwell, was held. Philip Warwick was gazetted as Commander of the South Nottinghamshire Hussars Yeomanry on 29th June 1920. By February 1922 the regiment was finally designated '107th (The South Nottinghamshire Hussars Yeomanry) Field Brigade, Royal Artillery (Army Troops)'. The South Notts were the only artillery unit to have a *Brigade* Cavalry sub-title.

Colonel Philip H. Warwick, D.S.O., T.D.,
Commanding 1918-1924
(Historical Records South Nottinghamshire Hussars)

The War Memorial to the South Notts Hussars at St Mary's Church, Nottingham is engraved with the following inscription:

IN MEMORY OF
THE OFFICERS, N.C.O.S,
AND MEN OF THE
SOUTH NOTTS HUSSARS
WHO FELL IN THE GREAT WAR
1914-1918
IN
EGYPT
GALLIPOLI
MACEDONIA
PALESTINE
FRANCE

It is worth noting that the battle honours, including 'South Africa, 1900-02', amount to eighteen distinctions – the third highest of the Yeomanry Regiments (they are exceeded only by the Queen's Own Oxfordshire Hussars with twenty, and the Warwickshire Yeomanry with nineteen).

Phillip Huskinson Warwick's family had lived at Burgage Manor for some years, but in 1911 the Census showed him as the occupant with three domestic staff. He later moved to Normanton Prebend and remained there until he died on 11th December 1954, leaving a widow Dulcie Joan Warwick née Turner.

Southwell Men in the South Nottinghamshire Hussars Yeomanry

There were at least 19 Southwell members of the South Notts Hussars as follows:

Walter W. Bates	Arthur Marshall
Joseph H. Bett	Rupert Mosedale
Charles H. Brown	John C. Peacock
C. Carding	Harold R. Peet
George A. Cottam	L. Wagstaff
W. Feathersone	William H. Wagstaff
Frank Foster K-in-A	Reginald Walker
S. Hallam	John G. Warwick (Upton)
B. Hibbert	Philip H. Warwick
	George W. Woodward

A regimental Christmas card (Artillery) from Alfred Merryweather
(Roger Merryweather)

CHAPTER 5
The Home Front

5.1 Women in the War and the Post-War Legacy

Much has been written about the legacy of the First World War and a great deal about the valuable role that women played on the home front, some, indeed, at the front. Whilst it is not the intention of this book to investigate the home front, it would be wrong not to highlight the important part women played and to mention a few changes that were the legacy of the war.

Women – Keeping the home fires burning.

Kate Adie in her recent book *Fighting on the Home Front* provides a valuable introduction to the role of women in the First World War:

> The war was immense, like no other in memory, and the country so tested, so stretched, that for once it needed the strengths and abilities of its women – otherwise there would be no victory. They rose to the challenge, proved themselves capable, and were partly granted the vote when peace returned. But they were then expected to give up their new jobs, return to their second-class status and forget their endeavours and achievements. However, they had achieved so much and demonstrated that they could weld, deliver the post, saw off a leg, drive a train, entertain troops to the sound of gunfire, read the lesson in church and play decent football in front of twenty thousand people – all previously thought utterly, completely beyond a woman – that they left indelible footprints of a great stride on the way to fairness and equality for their sex.[1]

Before the First World War the traditional female role had been confined to the domestic scene, although not necessarily in their own homes. In Great Britain out of a population of around 24 million adult women approximately 1.7 million worked in domestic service, 800,000 in the textile manufacturing industry and 600,000 in the clothing trades, with a further 500,000 in commerce and 260,000 working in local and national government, including teaching - jobs that were described as 'women's work'. As the war progressed, it soon became obvious that the gaps that were left as men went to the front had to be filled, as well as coping with increased production for the war effort. Women were put into roles that were outside the normal gender expectation. At the outset of the war the proportion of married women working was 14% and this increased over the war years to 40%.

Apart from volunteering as nurses, there was a demand for more women to go into teaching and commerce (not far removed from pre war work), and most of all into industry. There was an overriding need for munitions workers and, as was described in the introduction to this book, this was a dangerous, but necessary, occupation. Munitions factories employed the highest proportion of females in industry. Many women would have thought that they were 'doing their bit' in supporting husbands, fathers, and brothers who were fighting in the trenches. Additionally, there was an economic need for many of them to work in industry, which provided a better income than

---

[1] Kate Adie, *Fighting on the Home Front. The Legacy of Women in World War One,* (London: Hodder & Stoughton, 2013), p. 1.

domestic service, although at a lower rate than men were paid for equivalent work. The better off were more likely to have volunteered for the Red Cross or undertaking other duties in fund raising, sewing sand bags, knitting socks for the troops and providing other support. Nursing, particularly the Queen Alexandra's Army Nursing Corps, meant that some women were working close to the front. Others, such as those in the Red Cross and the Voluntary Aid Detachment, worked in the many hospitals that were set up across the country, such as Burgage Manor, Brackenhurst or the old fever hospital at Galley Hill in Southwell.

With many farmers' sons no longer able to escape conscription, there was a demand for women to work in agriculture. In 1915 the Board of Agriculture organised the Land Army and by 1917 over a quarter of a million women worked as farm labourers, of which 20,000 were in the Land Army.

Women working at the Chilwell Munitions Factory

Changes in society.

As the war progressed British society faced important changes at home. As Joanna Burke explains:

> Fear, grief, sorrow: these are the overriding emotions of war. For men, women, and children confined to the home front between 1914-1918 exhilarating surges of patriotic energies and the evaporation of many restraints were fleeting thrills when set against the loss of loved ones. Children woke to find their fathers had left for distant battlefields while they slept. Three hundred thousand never saw their fathers again: 160,000 wives received the dreaded telegram informing them that their husbands had been killed. Countless others discovered the meaning of suffering.[2]

Following the outbreak of war the government realised that they had to keep control and they passed the Defence of the Realm Act, which gave them many powers to control people's lives

---
[2] Joanna Burke, *The Guardian*, 'Another Battle Front', Tuesday 11th November, 2008.

and, if necessary, take over factories. Curfews and censorship were introduced, pub opening times were restricted, and as the war progressed rationing was introduced.

Women and the vote.

Pre war the suffragette movement had been very active, but as the war took hold many threw themselves into the war effort in an attempt to link their demands for citizenship with service during a national emergency.

By June 1917 there was a realization that women were valuable and perhaps should have a voice after all. In 1917 the Representation of the People's Bill was passed by 385 votes to 55. This act enabled an additional 5 million men to vote and 9 million women. However, the vote was only granted to women over 30 years old who were householders, wives of householders, occupiers of property of an annual value of £5, or university graduates. The millions of women outside these parameters who had worked in industry and the Land Army, etc., failed to qualify. It was to be 1928 before women gained the vote on the same basis as men.

A British Nurse Working near the front line. (Private Collection, Southwell Minster)

Improvements in the standard of living.

Whilst the vote was a long-time coming, women's efforts in the war had helped to improve working-class standards of living, with full employment, rent control, rising imports of bacon and increased consumption of eggs and milk, together with better social provision, working-class families were better off. In the period 1914-1920, and in the aftermath of the war and falling prices, the war-enhanced wage level was maintained. The great slump was yet to come.

The influenza epidemic.

As if the war had not inflicted enough death and misery upon the world, the 1918-1920 influenza epidemic caused even more misery and was one of the deadliest natural disasters in history. Across the world over 500 million people were affected, with a death toll of between 50 and 100 million people.[3] As the war came to an end there were many reports of the epidemic, and close to home the fate of Percy Toder of Southwell comes to mind. Percy Toder had been a prisoner of war and

---

[3] Estimates vary. Some suggest that between 3% and 5% of the world population died.

upon his release in a weakened state he had walked across Europe and reached Holland, where he died of pneumonia following catching influenza.

Improvements in healthcare.

Whilst the medical profession had not been able to find a cure for influenza, there were some positive advances in medical care as a consequence of the war, which had ongoing benefits. The war and health can best be described as a giant field trial, and a new feature was the medical administration and sanitation of vast armies. There had been a general lack of preparedness for war and medical services, but the UK drew on 11,000 civilian practitioners. Dr Handford of Southwell was one of those recalled to the army from civilian medicine and was posted to Cannock Chase. Dr Willoughby, a Southwell G.P., was responsible for some of the medical care at the military hospitals in Southwell and also for medical assessments for local recruits.

Whilst death rates were high – 10% of the armed strength (Britain and Empire) were killed and in some categories it was much higher - the mortality rate amongst the wounded was reduced to 10% from a figure of 39% recorded in the Crimean War. Sepsis almost inevitably followed a wounding on the battlefield. The treatment of wounds improved by better management of infection and more efficient means of killing bacteria. Many still died as a result of infection, and perhaps Major Becher might have survived if infection treatment had been better in 1915. During the course of the war it did improve.

Sanitation was an important area in the battle against infection, as was the prevention of disease by vaccination. Vaccination against typhoid helped a great deal. In the Crimea more men had died from typhus than from the war itself. Tetanus was prevented by prophylactic injections and the incidences fell by 90%. Inoculation in the British Army was voluntary and the death rate was 31 times higher among the unprotected. Eventually more men were persuaded, resulting in 98% of the army being inoculated, with positive results.

Further advances were made with orthopaedic innovation. For example, in the early months of the war a compound fracture of the femur had a mortality rate of 80% - mostly sepsis. It had become clear that specialist clinics needed to be set up and fracture clinics appeared in general hospitals, where orthopaedic specialists were able to control a patient's treatment. In addition ambulance crews were trained to fit splints at the front line, which proved to be a great help. This became a general first aid measure. The war speeded up the development of X-rays, which also improved diagnosis and treatment of wounds.

A further advance was the development of reconstructive surgery, again a technique that has developed over the years and was a great benefit for many of the facially wounded.

Blood transfusions were first used tentatively in the field at the First Battle of Cambrai in 1917, with blood being sent up to the front-line field ambulances prior to the battle. At that time blood could be safely kept for 12-18 hours.

There were several diseases associated with the appalling conditions in the trenches, e.g. trench fever, which had been identified as being transmitted by lice and, as a result, more care was taken with hygiene. Another well-known problem was trench foot, resulting from wet socks and boots in wet and muddy conditions. An adequate supply of clean dry boots was prescribed with facilities for drying footwear. The War Diary of the 8th Battalion, Sherwood Foresters mentions some of the preventative measures, including the use of anti-frostbite grease, which was later replaced with foot powder. The scourge of gassing was also tackled by the introduction of efficient stimulators.

This is a brief insight into the treatment of battlefield injuries and diseases, which were translated into general medical treatment after the war. There were also social advances in medical care.

Infant welfare advances meant that infant mortality dropped to 91 per 1,000 in England, the lowest on record, together with improvements in diet to fight diseases such as rickets. The profound changes in the treatment of injuries and disease, together with the social upheaval of the First World War, acted as a catalyst for changes in health care. In 1917 David Lloyd George set up committees to consider the future of healthcare; later health centres, based on an element of Royal Army Medical Corps organization, were introduced.[4]

It is clear that the war forced many improvements and changes to the treatment of the sick and the prevention of disease.

A land fit for heroes.

Once the euphoria of victory had passed, the poor response to the appeal for funds to help build a public hall and alms-houses for disabled ex-servicemen summed up the harsh economic reality of post-war Britain. The legacy of the war was all too obvious. One well known pacifist, Caroline Playne, admitted to being full of 'sickness and horror' at the 'sights of hundreds of men on crutches going about in groups'. More than 41,000 men had their limbs amputated during the war, with 272,000 suffering injuries to their legs and arms that did not require amputation. A further 60,500 were wounded in the head and eyes, with 89,000 suffering other damage to their bodies.[5] These awful statistics do not start to count those with psychological problems that we would now identify as 'post-traumatic stress disorder'. Most refused to discuss their experiences and this has been evident in researching this book, as descendants – children and grandchildren – have said 'he never talked about the war'. In the words of Joanna Bourke, 'The home front eventually welcomed back men and women whose war service abroad left scars, both visible and invisible, which were often difficult to speak about.' There are many stories of veterans struggling to survive with little or no support. Men wandered aimlessly, failing to scrape a living selling matches on street corners or openly begging. It is a sad reflection that the bold ideas of 1918-19 to build alms-houses in Southwell for disabled servicemen came to nought. Particularly as some of the traders in the town had profited from the war. Perhaps they thought that the government should have provided for them. Even the able-bodied struggled to find employment – the testimony of Chris Rippin (Chapter 4) illustrates the difficulties faced by many:

> In Southwell, no one wanted to know about the war. 'The land fit for heroes' did not appear to exist and wounded soldiers thought they were unfairly treated by the government. Pre-war jobs had not been kept while they were fighting and many returning ex-soldiers could find nothing to do.

In many ways Chris Rippin summarises the fate and feelings of numerous returning servicemen. However, he was fortunate to find employment close to home, albeit not with his previous employer. Whilst the men had been away fighting, women had taken over many traditionally male duties, but as seen above they were then expected to return to their subservient roles.

---

[4] J. D. C. Bennett FRCS, DHMSA, 'Medical Advances consequent to the Great War 1914-1918', *Journal of the Royal Society of Medicine,* Volume 83, (November 1990), pp. 738-742.

[5] Joanna Bourke

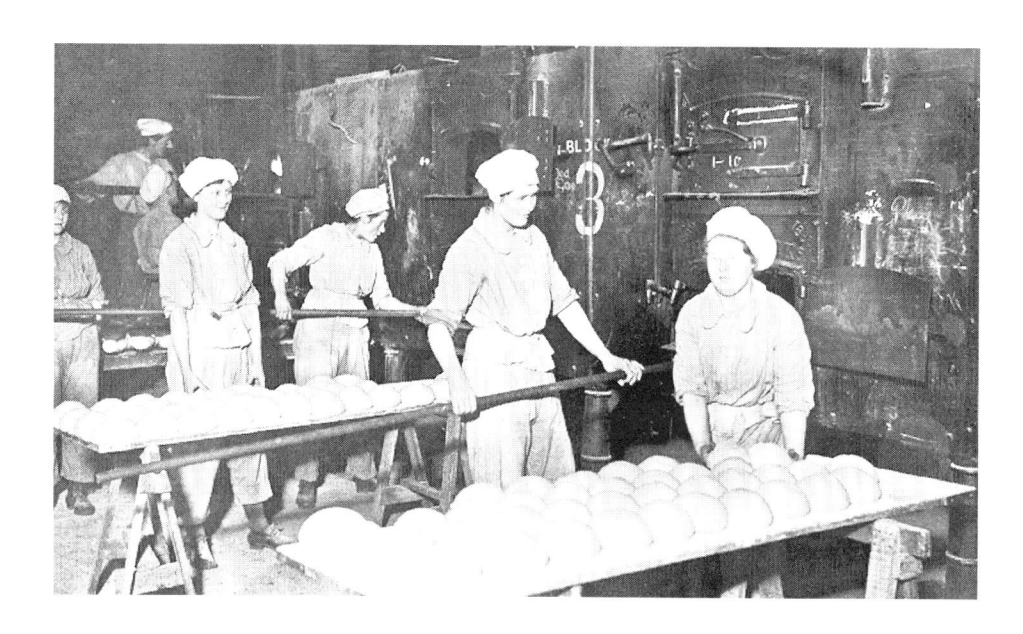

Women of the W.A.A.C baking bread in France
(Private Collection c/o Southwell Minster)

Wounded soldiers in Southwell
(Peter Cant)

5.2 Caring for the wounded - Burgage Manor and Brackenhurst Hall

The First World War produced an unprecedented number of casualties and it soon became clear that the existing hospitals, both military and general, would not be able to cope with the ever increasing volume of men needing care after being initially dealt with at the front. Many of those who did not require specialist treatment were allocated to Red Cross Hospitals that were established up and down the country and run by the Red Cross, with V.A.D. Support.[1] Large properties and country houses made ideal hospitals to treat and care for the recuperation of wounded men.

Shortly after the outbreak of war it was announced that Burgage Manor, Southwell, would become an auxiliary hospital.[2] The owner of the manor, Mr W.N. Hicking, took an ongoing interest in the running of the hospital and later in the war allowed his home, Brackenhust Hall, to be used as well.[3] It was to be April 1915 before the local branch of the Red Cross received notice to prepare the hospital, and the first fifteen wounded men arrived on Wednesday 21st April from Lincoln Hospital. Southwell's residents took a lively interest in the hospital and provided a great deal of support to the patients.

Within a month of the arrival of the first troops, the *Newark Advertiser* reported that the Reverend T.A. Lea and Mrs C.L. Maltby organised a concert at the hospital and took along the black and white minstrels. Shortly afterwards the more mobile patients were invited to the home of the Reverend H.K. and Mrs Warrand at Westhorpe Hall, where they were entertained to tea, played bowls and billiards, and were shown around the gardens.[4] Concerts for the patients at the hospital were regular throughout the war, with reports constantly appearing in the *Newark Advertiser* (see the War Diary).

The well-being of the men was uppermost and their general health was overseen by Dr Willoughby, J.P., a local general practitioner. Appeals were occasionally made for blankets, sheets, rugs, etc., together with personal comforts for the men such as face towels, dressing gowns and cigarettes. One of the ongoing voluntary efforts was the supply of eggs through the National Egg Collection Scheme, mainly undertaken by school children, and was another example of civilian support for the war effort. There were regular newspaper reports on the progress of the scheme, such as: '…the total eggs collected for the week amounted to 938, of which 280 were sent to Burgage Manor'.[5] [A copy of the National Egg Collection poster is on the rear cover of this book.]

Some of the patients offered their services in support of recruitment campaigns, and in August, 1915 it was reported that Sergeant Blundell, 'one of the wounded soldiers at the local Red Cross

---

[1] The Voluntary Aid Detachment (VAD) was a voluntary organisation providing field nursing services, mainly in hospitals, in the United Kingdom and various other countries in the British Empire. The organisation's most important periods of operation were during World War I and World War II. The organisation was founded in 1909 with the help of the Red Cross and the Order of St. John. By the summer of 1914 there were over 2,500 Voluntary Aid Detachments in Britain. Each individual volunteer was called a detachment, or simply a VAD. Of the 74,000 VADs in 1914, two-thirds were women and girls. At the outbreak of the First World War VADs eagerly offered their service to the war effort. The British Red Cross was reluctant to allow civilian women a role in overseas hospitals: most VADs were of the middle and upper classes and unaccustomed to hardship and traditional hospital discipline. Military authorities would not accept VADs at the front line.
[2] *Newark Advertiser*, 4th November 1914.
[3] Mr William Norton Hicking, with his father, founded G & W.N. Hicking lace bleachers and finishers of Nottingham. William Hicking was also the chairman of the Nottingham and Notts Banking Company. (He was knighted in 1917.)
[4] *Newark Advertiser*, 5th May 1915.
[5] *Newark Advertiser*, 19th May 1915.

Hospital' in Burgage Manor, went along to one such meeting to encourage men to volunteer for war service. He is reported as saying: 'Although Southwell had done magnificently in sending men to the war, yet he still saw strong, healthy young fellows walking about the streets who ought to be doing their bit in the trenches.'[6] This illustrates the pressure that was put upon young men to volunteer for the front.

Dr Willoughby, front row left, and Alfred Merryweather, back row second from right, with the first intake of wounded soldiers at Burgage Manor in 1915. (Peter Cant)

To support the morale of the hospitalized men there were frequent visits by notable people. In May 1916 the Duke and Duchess of Portland visited, and in July 1917 there was a large gathering of people, including thirty-six Southwell notables, to witness Corporal Allen Woodroffe, a patient, receive the D.C.M. for bravery at Potaguee Wood, Belgium, in 1915. (He was not a Southwell man.)

It was probably difficult to keep the men usefully occupied and different ways were introduced, including needlework, encouraging them to design regimental badges. This culminated in a competition with prizes presented by Miss Pavey of Westhorpe Lodge, who had taught the men the skill.[7]

All through the war the commandant of Burgage Manor had been Miss E.M. Small, who in 1919 was awarded the O.B.E., which had been introduced by George V in June 1917.

The present owner of Burgage Manor, Geoffrey Bond, O.B.E., still has the house visitors' book from the First World War period and this contains many appreciative comments about the care that patients received. One entry sums up the men's gratitude:

---

[6] *Newark Advertiser* 11th August, 1915.
[7] *Newark Advertiser* 7th November, 1917.

Private S. Hill, No. 8974, East Yorkshire Regiment

Wounded Feb. 14th 1915 at Hill 60 in hospital 5 weeks and returned to Regt. Again wounded May 5th St Julien, nr Ypres with shrapnel in left knee.
    My very best respects and thanks to the Hospital Staff at Burgage Manor, and also to the inhabitants of Southwell for the kind and generous assistance in making an all too short a stay so very happy.

S. Hill

One of the domestic staff, Edith Gibson[8], had been given a sizeable leather bound autograph book for Christmas 1914. When the soldiers started to arrive at Burgage Manor in 1915 she decided to take the book with her to work. As the men started to recover, many of them wrote messages or poems and some drew pictures in the book. This is a unique piece of history and, whilst there are too many to reproduce here, the following are an interesting sample:

Corporal Sydney Rathmell 955 A Company
B.E.F. West Yorks Regiment

There stands on Burgage little green
Where our wounded Tommies are often seen
At the Manor there all merry and bright
Who have done their best in this great fight
And I think you will say I am right
That the huns run away when our Baynotes they sight.

Private J. W. Horsley 1999 6th Northumberland Fusiliers

Wounded in the left hand
Lost a finger with rifle fire
Hill 60 Ypres

Many may have written
Many more may write
None can love you better
Than the one who writes tonight

Another Air Raid.

Extracts from Edith Gibson's Autograph Book. (Ann Hurt)

As the war progressed the need for more hospital beds increased and in May 1917 Mr W.N. Hicking allowed his home, Brackenhurst Hall, to be brought into service as a hospital and Mrs Hicking acted as commandant. Shortly afterwards she requested that seats be provided by the roadside en route to Southwell for those that wished to venture into town. As with Burgage Manor, efforts were made to raise funds for the men to enable them to be provided with additional comforts.

---

[8] Edith Gibson was born in 1899 and lived in a cottage on Westgate with her parents, and had two brothers serving in the war, George and Henry. She cared for her parents until they died and in 1947 married her long-term sweetheart Norman Powley. Norman died in 1972 and Edith survived until 2004, dying at the age of 105. (Grateful thanks to Ann Hurt for this information and sight of the Autograph book.)

In November 1917 the wounded at Brackenhurst were put through their paces with a needle and thread, and this time Mrs Warrand of Westhorpe Hall presented the prizes for the best regimental badge, following judging by Lady Savile of Rufford.[9] During August 1918 Sir William Hicking organized a large 'Patriotic Fête' at the hall, in aid of the Southwell Hospitals. This appears to have been a grand affair with a military band, various artists, games and dancing.

By February, 1919 the auxiliary hospitals were closed and the *Newark Advertiser* included an article praising the work of the two commandants, Lady Hicking and Miss E.M. Small, together with 'the highest praise' for the staff and nurses. Sir William Hicking was thanked for allowing both his houses to be used as hospitals.

In addition to these two hospitals, there was also a hospital at the old fever hospital on Galley Hill Road. Little is recorded about this facility, nor whether it was for isolation cases only.[10] The ballroom at the Admiral Rodney public house was also used for convalescing soldiers.[11]

Hospital Fête 1915 - Loughton Collection (By kind permission of the Dean and Chapter)

---

[9] *Newark Advertiser 21st November 1917.*

[10] Local Writers, *Southwell The Town and its People,* Peter O'Malley, Chapter 11, *Medical Facilities* (Southwell: Southwell and District Local History Society, 1992), p.178.

[11] Dobson, Roger, *Southwell Inns and Alehouses,* (Nottingham: Nottinghamshire County Council, 2008), p. 36.

5.3 Wartime School

The log books for the Church of England School (The National), Holy Trinity School, and St Mary's Infant School provide a fascinating insight into life in these schools in wartime Southwell. All walks of life were affected by the war, and not least of all education. Male teachers were being called up for service and their places were taken by women and young male trainees, until their time came to serve. In spite of this disruption the schools carried on working, making adjustments to their curriculum and changing school holidays to accommodate government needs to keep up production. The children were not protected from hearing about the war and, indeed, the boys had regular briefings and updates.

The First World War had broken out during the school holidays and upon reopening in early September the National School log reports that, 'the usual Geography lessons with classes 1 and 2 this week to take the war news'. The updates included reports of significant events:

30th November, 1914. Spoke to the school on the loss of the Bulwark.[1]

22nd October, 1915. Gave classes 1 and 2 a lesson on the Balkan Countries, in connection with Bulgaria joining the enemy.

23rd May, 1916. Continued lessons with classes 1 and 2 on the growth of the German Empire leading to the present war, Bismarck, defeat of Austria, France and Prussia, etc.

1st June, 1916. Spoke to school about the great Naval Battle in the North Sea.[2]

10th June, 1916. Spoke to the school about Lord Kitchener and his wonderfully full life for King and Country, and the loss of HMS Hampshire.[3]

18th September, 1916. Spoke to school about John T. Cornwell, the sailor hero of the battle of Jutland.[4]

17th November, 1916. Sergeant A. H. Chambers (ex-staff member) visited. He joined the forces in December, 1914 and is home on his first leave, having been through the Gallipoli Campaign, Egypt and is now in France.[5]

---

[1] HMS Bulwark entered service with the Royal Navy in 1902. Following the outbreak of war she was patrolling the Channel and on 26th November 1914 was anchored near Sheerness when she exploded due to an internal problem with the loss of 736 men.

[2] The Battle of Jutland.

[3] On 5th June 1916 Lord Kitchener was on board HMS Hampshire on a diplomatic mission to Russia. In a force 9 gale the ship struck a mine, that had been laid by a German U-boat, and sank. Lord Kitchener, his staff, and 643 crew of 655 drowned or died of exposure.

[4] Known as Jack Cornwell, at the age of 16 he was posthumously awarded the Victoria Cross. He had stayed at his post by one of the ship's guns when all his colleagues were either dead or wounded. When found he had shards of metal sticking from his chest, but was still awaiting orders. He died in Grimsby General Hospital on 2nd June, 1916.

[5] See *Newark Advertiser* 6/1/15, 29/9/15, 10/11/15 and 29/5/18. The September and November articles are particularly informative about life at the front.

9th January, 1917. Sergeant Major A. Deverill, R.F.C., an old boy, visited. He has seen much service in France and is now an instructor in the Flying School, Oxford.

1st October, 1917. Assembly concerning the U-boat menace and importance of food care.

Regular briefings on the U-boat menace and food shortages continued. Interspersed with the war briefings were the occasional records of patriotic lessons.

4th June, 1915. On the King's Birthday, the school sang the National Anthem. I spoke to the boys about the King and Patriotism…

Whilst the boys received these regular updates about the progress of the war, the girls seem to have been protected somewhat, although they did have some involvement with Empire Day celebrations.

4th May, 1918. Observed Empire Day. Patriotic teaching – Queen Victoria – King Edward VII and King George V, Empire and the war. The Union Jack, Patriotic songs, etc.

As food supplies became crucial the school was prompted into starting its own garden.

16th April, 1917. School Garden. A few weeks since a paragraph in Notts Education Committee Quarterly Circular advocated the formation of school gardens this year with a view to increasing production.

An arrangement was made to use a portion of the recreation field as a school garden at a nominal rent of 1/- per annum. Work started in earnest later in the month.

30th April, 1917. Class 1 continued work in the garden, taking the last lesson most mornings and afternoons. Plotted out different portions.

3rd September, 1917. Lifted some potatoes, each boy taking home a root or more of those he set.

In early September 1918 pupils started collecting blackberries for H.M. Forces.

11th October, 1918. The blackberry season closed – the school sent 1 ton 2 qts to the jam factory.[6]

The October half-term in 1918 was extended, 'to enable the children to help with potato picking'. The school had also been involved in the egg collection scheme that is mentioned in *Newark Advertiser* articles.

---

[6] Pickard's Jam Factory, Mansfield.

Agriculture played a big part in local life, and, with an increasing number of men being called up, farmers were becoming reliant upon women and young boys to fill the gaps. This started to have an impact upon education:

> 9th July, 1915. During the past five weeks 4 boys have left with Agricultural Certificates.

> 5th November, 1915. Six boys are now absent from school under 13 having been granted Agricultural Certificates by the Education Committee.

> 30th June, 1916. Closed school for a week's holiday with a view to the children helping with the hay and to enable teachers to have a needed rest in view of the Whitsun Holiday.[7]

> 14th December, 1917. The attendance is now approaching normal as far as Measles are concerned [see below], owing to the war causes it is much below the ordinary and many boys have left either with Agricultural Certificates or a year or two earlier than [they] would in Peace Time, the demand for labour being so great and wages high.

Not only had the farmers been requesting boys to fill the gaps in their workforce, other employers from the spring of 1915 had been contacting the school.

> 27th March, 1915. Received a number of applications from tradesmen for boys to take the places of men who had joined the forces.

> 25th February, 1916. Two boys left for work, one having a Proficiency Certificate and the other an Attendance Certificate, the former 12 and the latter 13 years old.

> 18th January, 1918. Three boys left this week for work having attained their 13th birthday and obtained Labour Certificates by attendance, the demand for labour has much thinned the upper classes.

The schools, in addition to disruption caused by staff being called up and other wartime disruption, had to try to make economies and encourage pupils to save towards the war effort:

> 6th March, 1916. A meeting of the managers of the different schools in Southwell was held at Trebeck Hall last week to consider educational questions with a view to economising during the war.

> 10th June, 1916. Read a circular on Thrift and the War Loan issued by the Postal Authorities.

> 22nd September, 1916. The School War Savings Association commenced on August 5th has now 59 depositors.

---

[7] The Whitsun Holiday had been postponed so as not to interfere with essential war production.

> 8th March, 1918. A number of new members joined the School War Savings Association and membership now totals 120, this includes some scholars, who have left but continue to deposit.

During the period of the school log books health issues were frequently mentioned. Measles was prevalent throughout the war and in an effort to contain the disease both the boys' and girls' sections of the school were closed:

> 18th April, 1916. The school was closed by order of Chief Medical Officer as a preventative to the spread of measles …

Again in June, 1917 schools were closed because of measles, this time it was from 18th June to 9th July. Another health problem was diphtheria:

> 14th November, 1916. Mabel Moore excluded on account of Diphtheria.

A number of other cases were mentioned, but epidemics of measles kept occurring with the school again closed for two weeks from 12th October 1917. Diphtheria, measles, whooping cough and scarlet fever were all prevalent at Holy Trinity School in July 1916, with 54 children listed as suffering from one of the four infections.

We know from several articles in the *Newark Advertiser* that there were a number of Belgian refugees in Southwell, and the following report appeared in the girls' log:

> 3rd August, 1916. A concert was held in the school playground in the evening in aid of the Belgian Relief Fund. The proceeds of the concert £2. 18. 00d was sent to the national committee.

Funds were also raised for Belgian children at Holy Trinity on 10th July 1916 amounting to 12/-. There is also evidence of Belgian children being enrolled at the schools. In addition the girls at the National School were involved in knitting socks for the troops, and needlework for the Red Cross.

> 20th November, 1917. The needlework report states that many garments have been made for the Red Cross, all of which were very well made.

Following the end of the war there is a note that the schools were heavily involved in a Peace Festival that took place on 19th July 1919. This followed the Easter welcome home service and the memorial service that took place in the Minster on 5th July, 1919. On 11th November the school log recorded the instructions for a remembrance ceremony with a, '2 minutes' silence throughout the Empire'.

Looking back over the 1914 – 1919 period the Church of England schools in Southwell took a practical approach to the war. The head teachers did not try to shelter their pupils from the war and, in particular, the boys received regular updates on various important events. However, there is no mention of the awful casualties that occurred in the Somme offensive and other battles. At this distance it is not clear if that was a result of censorship. However, the encouragement of patriotism seems to have been very important.

The education of young boys suffered as a number left school to take up employment on farms and elsewhere. This was a direct consequence of the war effort. However, it would seem that the biggest disruption to education was the recurring bouts of measles, and the occasional problem with diphtheria, with the schools closed for two weeks at a time in an effort to stop the spread of these infections.

There is no doubt that the schools 'did their bit' for the war effort and encouraged the children to take responsibility, the boys with their garden and the girls undertaking knitting for the forces and sewing for the Red Cross.

Church of England Infant School in 1915
(Loughton Collection - by kind permission of the Dean and Chapter)

5.4 The Minster Grammar School 1914-1919

In common with the National School and the infant and junior schools in the town, the Minster Grammar School had to adjust to operating in a country that was at war. Money was in short supply, able-bodied staff were called up for military service, and some of the older pupils had to abandon their studies to help out in family businesses when manpower was lost to the armed forces. Notwithstanding these ongoing difficulties, the school still managed to function with temporary staff covering the absences. The school records provide an interesting insight into its operation during the war period.

Buildings

When the war broke out the Minster Grammar School was situated at the top of Church Street in the red brick Georgian building now occupied by HSBC bank, with accommodation for both teaching and boarding of the boys. The school also owned the adjacent properties of the Crown Hotel and three shops along the frontage of the Market Place. In 1908-09 the school had undergone a significant renovation, with tenders existing from many Southwell, Newark and Nottingham builders to relay wooden floors, renew the drains, add new urinals, and put in new partitions, including bespoke glazed panelling across one of the large classrooms.

The school was also in possession of buildings, which were not directly used by the boys or Masters. The Crown Hotel was rented out to Eliza Taylor up to and during WWI to bring in rent (£38 p.a. reduced by the Governors in November 1916 to £25 for "the period of the war"). The Governors agreed to pay £25:15s for the fitting of a new kitchen range in 1916, as the old one had been "in daily use for cooking for over 20 years and is quite worn out", reported Mrs Taylor in a letter to the Governors.

In 1914 three other premises along the Market Place going west from the Crown were owned by the School. They were occupied by (going from the Crown); Mr Knowles, a painter; Pitchford's, a furniture dealer; and Mrs Lane in a domestic dwelling.

The science laboratory - pre war.
(Minster School)

In 1914 the school was in a heated debate with the Inland Revenue over the valuation of the non-school buildings. The Finance Act had brought in duties on land values and the Crown and three other properties had been assessed at over £2,000 for the purposes of the Act. The Governors not only disputed this figure, but had their own valuation of the properties to try to get the figure significantly reduced. Correspondence from 1915 seems to indicate that the Governors were successful in their appeals.

Finances

The war had a significant impact on the schools finances. In 1912-1913 the claim to the Board of Education for the annual grant was for £352, based on 80 pupils attending in the year 1912-1913. The impact of the war was dramatic as pupil numbers fell each year until 1915. Correspondence shows the difficulties families were having contributing towards their sons' education and boarding. The low point was in 1915-1916 when 54 pupils brought in a grant of £234. Finances did improve from 1917 onwards as the amount of grant per pupil was increased from £5 to £7. Not until the school year 1919-1920 did the pupil numbers climb back to the 1913 figure. The increased amount per pupil was outlined as a preliminary supplementary grant to all schools, as a means of establishing a national pension scheme for teachers in secondary education. The matter was being investigated by an Education Department Committee, which was expected to report in 1918 in favour of the 1914 recommendations on teachers' pay scales and pensions.

Fees from parents, which included boarding, also displayed a dramatic decline. In 1913 they stood at £584, but dropped to a low of £360 in 1916 and recovered slightly by the end of the war. Costs had to be trimmed accordingly. The Head's salary and bonus went down from £378 in 1914 to a low of £230 in 1916, partly because the bonus figure was arrived at by the number on roll, which was decreasing. Other staff expenses were similarly reduced from £439 in 1914, down to £399 by 1916. Part of the reduction can be accounted for through fewer staff, but also later in the war female staff were employed at a lower wage than their male counterparts. Further costs were added by the ongoing conflict, with the Governors taking out additional cover with the Ecclesiastical Insurance Office in March 1916 against the threat of damage by aircraft. The princely sum of £6:16s:6d was approved to cover the threat. Government regulations also created additional payments to cover the new Workmen's Compensation (War Addition) Act 1917.

In January 1917 the national financial situation had become so grave that the school received a letter requesting it deposit with the Treasury the £500 of Midland Railway Stock that it had held since 1904. The stock had been gifted to the school by Mr Lewis Starkey to create a self-perpetuating fund for a 'Starkey' scholarship and additional prizes. The Government request for the deposit of the stocks with the Treasury described the "urgent need for the immediate deposit" to stabilise the "American exchange". The Government's actions displayed their concern over the threat to the pound due to the massive deficit being run up in fighting the war. The school went further in its patriotic duty the following year with the Governors voting to buy £250 of War Bonds by taking money away from the school's Building Fund. Dividends on the War Stock were reported annually up to the 1941 accounts. Rents from the business properties owned by the school also went down, showing the depressed state of the town's commerce. On several occasions the Governors discussed the need to reduce rents for "the duration of the war". The Crown Hotel's rent was reduced from £38 to £25 in 1916. Overall rents reduced from £88:6:3 in March 1914 to £76:7:2 in March 1918. Even the students felt the cutbacks with no prizes or scholarships being awarded during the war but certificates only.

Staff

Through careful studying of the individual staff records during the period, there appears to have been 20 teachers and tutors employed at one time or another during the years 1914 – 1918. This included a number of peripatetic and visiting specialists, who only did a few hours per week and a number of very temporary appointments lasting for as little as one month. Including the Head (who taught), the main teaching staff seems to have been 5 – 6 teachers with another 3 or 4 part-timers to supplement them and bring specialisms such as Music and Drill. The Head, Reverend Wright, along with Harry Collins were the stalwarts and backbone of the teaching staff. Both served throughout the war.

Subtle changes can be observed as the conflict went on. On the very first day of the war Frederick Walker left the school's employment and was listed as "on war service" (aged 29). Not surprisingly he had been the "Sergeant Instructor" of "Drill". In December 1914 Mr Houseman took up a "Commission in ASC Northern Division". Mr Atkin, who left the school six days before the outbreak of war, was soon recorded as Lieutenant in the Gordon Highlanders. Mr Wilson (Drawing) joined the Royal Engineers (September 1916 listed as on "War Service"), and Mr Earp (Maths and Science) left in 1916 (aged 24) to join the Artists' Rifles. Another Drawing master left in July 1915 to take up a position in the Admiralty labs in Sheffield.

Interestingly the Governors' minutes reveal a hint at the change from voluntary enlistment and conscription, brought in by the Government in 1916. The Head asked the Governors to support Mr Earp if he had to appear "before any tribunal to obtain exemption from military service". As previously alluded Mr Earp left the school voluntarily and joined the forces.

In March 1916 the advent of another change was heralded by the arrival of Miss Dorothy Collier, aged 22, fresh from Manchester University. Female teachers had arrived. Her short stay (one month!) brought a replacement in Miss C. Butler in May, a 23-year-old Dublin girl. Shortly afterwards a third school Mistress, Miss Hilda Hedderley, arrived in September as a drawing teacher. Times were indeed changing!

The last year of the war was also noticeable because of the recruitment of two local vicars, the Reverend F. R. Dean (Vicar of Halam and Edingley) and the Reverend E. S. Longhurst (Rolleston, Morton and Fiskerton) to supplement the teaching staff, both were around 50 when appointed. Another interesting appointment was made in March 1917 when William Johnson-Coope, a 30-year-old, was employed to teach Drill. He was listed as a Sergeant in the Sherwood Foresters, and worked at the school for over 18 months - presumably he was a soldier discharged on medical grounds due to injury.

The conclusions seem clear, the older men "held the fort" whilst the young enlisted. Young women and older clerics filled the gaps of those going off to serve King and Country. In November 1918, in response to a circular from the Board of Education, the Governors replied that they "proposed to return to the employment of the normal staff…as soon as practicable".

Pupils.

Detailed numbers for the boys at the Minster School can be clearly ascertained as both the annual return documents survive in the archive and a range of correspondence exists between the school and the Board of Education between 1912-14. They wrangled over the number of free school places the Minster School should be making available annually, to receive a Government grant. The Board in 1912 discussed the "school being liable to the loss of a whole or part of the grant" unless "4 free places" were offered. The school managed to argue its case for a reduction in the number, but the board in September 1914 warned that [the free place students] were to be placed "as far as possible on the same footing as the fee paying pupils".

The figures clearly show a reduction in the numbers of boys attending with a significant drop between the 1914 and the mid-point of 1916, 82 down to 60. The Southwellian magazine (for old boys) reported at Easter 1915 that the year's football results "were disappointing" due "to the loss of players". The drop-off in older boys was particularly noticeable as many left to help their family businesses or gain employment because of the labour shortage. Only 4 pupils sat exams in 1917 and none in 1918. The Bishop of Newcastle, distributing certificates in 1917 (no prizes were given during the duration of the war), commented on the "diminution" of the school's numbers due to two causes: the uncertainty owing to the war, and the openings for earning money early in life.

Minster Grammar School pre the First World War.
(Minster School)

For these reasons the boys were leaving at a much earlier age than their parents had intended originally, but he urgently impressed upon all parents that "it was not wise to take short-term views of a boy's career". On closer examination of the record sheets for each pupil at the school, stories emerge, which illuminate further these difficult times. Individual tragedies cut short the school careers of some. The records show the departure of Albert Moore on March 22 1918 with the comment "Left without notice owing to death of father at the Front". His father, Thomas Henry Moore, ran a laundry business in West Bridgford and it can only be speculated that the 14 year old Albert was called home to help out in the business. Leonard Vickers Webster left school in April 1916 when the "firm by whom his stepfather [was] engaged ceased to pay his salary when he was called up for military service; hence unable to pay school fees". Arthur Lester left in July 1916 (aged 10) when his father Ernest, a leather merchant, was "called up for military service". Young John Frederick Milner left in February 1915 at 16 with the comment "Father could not get labour". Mr Milner senior was the Blacksmith at Kirklington. George Edward Harvey left in July 1916 (aged 14) "Father had to keep boy at home to help him". Mr Harvey senior was a Butcher in Easthorpe, Southwell. Happily George was able to return to his schooling in 1918 – 1920. Richard Jesson (16) left in December 1915 "because his father could not get labour on his farm". At least 8 other boys who left in the war had the comment "working on father's farm" in the remarks section of their records. These situations echo the experiences at the National School.

For the boys still at the school the diminished staff continued to deliver a full timetable, which included drill, a subject which had been taught before the war. The Governors requested in May 1918 that the school's uniformed cadet force be part of the Nottinghamshire Secondary Schools Battalion. The same subjects as listed in the pre and post war inspectors' report were taught as both annual awards were made for them, (certificates not prizes during the conflict) and staff were employed expressly to teach these topics, (see section on teachers) English, Maths, Religious Instruction, Chemistry, Physics, Biology, History, Geography, Music, Art, Woodwork, German, French, Latin, Greek, Games and, of course, Drill. All lessons, with the exception of games, were taught at the Grammar School buildings which had been the base for the school since 1819. Links with the Minster Church were strong with choristers singing daily, the school taking part in services and clergymen prominent as both governors and teachers. Every effort was expended to try to continue normality for the boys with cricket and football matches against Kirklington, Kelham, Nottingham and others throughout the war. Such a small school had a limited pool of talent and the results usually went against the Grammar school! A comprehensive list of all prize winners of the 1912 sessions shows the subjects taught then. The pupils were divided into four houses for competitive games and competitions; Aldred, Booth, Gray and Thomas. These were notable Archbishops of York (the Province of the church that Southwell came under).

The list of those pupils known to have been directly involved in the war is given in its most comprehensive form in an extract from the Southwellian magazine of 1919 listing 142 names of those who joined the colours during the conflict. The Minster School pupils who perished are listed below, a list of the other combatants appears at the end of this chapter.

Memorial to Old Southwellians
In the Minster Centre
(Minster School)

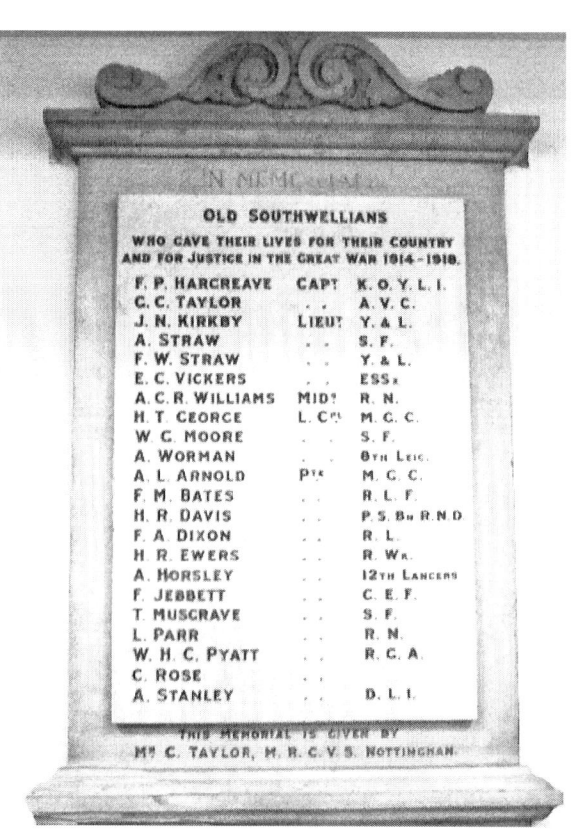

Killed in Action

A. L. Arnold*	Machine Gun Corps
F. M. Bates*	Royal Lancashire Fusiliers
H. R. Davis	Public Sch. Bn. R.N.D.
F. A. Dixon	King's Own Royal Lancasters
Lt. R. C. M. Douthwaite	Royal Field Artillery
H. R. Ewers*	Royal Warwicks
L. Cpl. H. T. George*	Machine Gun Corps
Capt. F. P. Hargreaves	King's Own Yorks Light Infantry
A. E. Horsley*	12th Lancers
F. A. Jebbett	Canadian Expeditionary Force
Lt. J. N. Kirkby*	Yorks and Lancashire Regt.
T. Musgrove*	Sherwood Foresters
Cpl. W. G. Moore	Sherwood Foresters
Leonard G. Parr	Royal Navy
W. H. C. Pyatt	Royal Garrison Artillery
C. P. Rose	Sherwood Foresters
A. G. Stanley*	Durham Light Infantry
Lt. A. Straw	Sherwood Foresters
Lt. F. W. Straw	Yorks and Lancashire Regt.
Capt. G. C. Taylor	Royal Army Veterinary Corps
Lt. E. C. Vickers*	Essex Regt
A. C. R. Williams	Royal Navy
L.Cpl. A. L. Worman	8th Leicesters

*Appear on the Memorial in Southwell Minster

There were a number of boys who left the area and it may well have been that they too fought for their country, but the records do not show that. At *least* 142 pupils and former pupils are reported to have taken part in the conflict and 23 are known to have lost their lives on active service. Snapshots of individual pupils' lives have been alluded to earlier with early leavers etc., but a couple of students have been selected here to try to give a brief insight into the individuals involved. It is right to give thanks respectfully to those who fell in the conflict, but also wrong to pass over those who returned, as if their experiences were of lesser merit. Two students have been chosen to illustrate these differences; Ernest Charles Vickers and George John Darcy Schumach.

Ernest Charles Vickers

Born 10th September 1894 in Southwell to Mr Wistow Vickers and Mrs Rachel V. of Westgate, Southwell. 1911 Census, aged 16, sisters Dorothy 14 and Elsie 6. Father – Coal merchant.

    Ernest attended Mrs MacDonald's private prep school in Southwell before entering the Minster School in January 1906. He was a day boy and attended until July 29th 1910. He was an excellent scholar with honours results in his Oxford Junior local exams in July 1908, 1909 and in the senior exams of 1910. In 1909 he was listed as the best candidate in Nottinghamshire. In recognition of his achievements he was confirmed in July 1909 in the Governors' minutes as being selected as the school's 'Starkey Scholar', an annual bursary set up in 1904 by Sir John Starkey. He won this again in the following year – a most unusual circumstance.

After leaving he took up a position as clerk in Union of London and Smith's Bank in Newark. He later moved on to the Nottingham and North Bank, where we believe he was at the outbreak of the war. In 1915 he enlisted and records show that he served with the 29th Royal Fusiliers, 7th Battalion of the Essex Regiment (Territorial Forces). On active service in France he is listed as Second Lieutenant Vickers. On the 26th January 1917 in action near Thiepval on the Somme he was killed, but his body was never recovered. With no grave he is listed along with commonwealth soldiers on the massive Thiepval Memorial Arch.

George John Darcy Schumach was born in December 1892 to Henry and Lucy (née Doncaster) Schumach. Henry was a taxidermist who ran a business in the town and had himself been a chorister and scholar at the Minster School in the 1860s. In 1901 the census records the family living at 19 Easthorpe with George (8) having an older sister Lucy (16) and brother Frederick (10). Frederick later joined the family business and took it over when his father died in 1913.

George initially attended the Church of England Elementary School, Southwell, but then transferred to being a pupil at the Minster School as a day boy between May 1900 and July 1911, a very considerable time – the Head specifically singled him out in his Speech Day address of 1911 saying; "never he thought, had they parted from one who had such a long record of attendance as Schumach; he entered as a chorister, a little boy, at the bottom of the school 11 years ago, and now, no longer a little boy, he had just passed the London University Matriculation Examination and was now reading for his Science degree at Nottingham University College, where they wished him every success." As the passage alludes, George was successful in his exams in 1908, 1909, 1910 and 1911 and trained as a teacher, being described in his file as an "Assistant Master under Notts Educational Authority". The Southwellian Magazine of 1912 tells us more about George; "Throughout the year the Cadet Corps were forced to drill without Schumach, the senior non-com, owing to his work for examinations." In the same publication the cricket season is reviewed with a roundup of team members; "Schumach. Reliable bat with good style and sound defence. Scores freely when set. Very good field and capable wicket keeper."

It seems that George was a real asset to the school in his time at the Minster! In 1915 he is noted in school records as having enlisted in the Sherwood Foresters as a Quartermaster Sergeant Major. According to military records he was in the 2/8 Sherwood Foresters. By that time his address is given as Church Street, Southwell. His older brother Frederick was then a Private in the Army Service Corps. George was promoted to Lieutenant in 1916. Service records show that he returned home from the war and was married in 1928 in Southwell to Miss Jessie Young. He lived a long life and died in Christchurch, Hampshire in June 1973, aged 80.

A final postscript on pupils must come from the Governors' minutes from 22nd November 1918 when, at the end of the meeting, it is recorded that an offer for "a memorial tablet of the pupils of this school who had fallen in the war was accepted" by those present. The benefactor was Mr Charles Taylor, a Nottingham Veterinary Surgeon, whose son, George Charles Taylor, serving with the Royal Army Veterinary Corps, died in an air raid on his camp. His death was one example of the tragedy of war, a war that took away far too many promising lives.

Bringing the story up to date

Throughout the latter part of the 20th Century the school's History Department taught generations of students about the horrors of the Great War. Students at 'O' Level, CSE and several versions of GCSE delved into the details of the key battles, methods of fighting, and generalship of the Western Front. In 1998, after much consideration, the History Department decided to instigate an annual school visit as part of the GCSE course to supplement and enhance the students' classroom learning. The visit, it was decided, should take place in February, giving the students a fuller experience of what it would have been like in Flanders and around the Somme in the winter months. The consequence, sleet, ice, snow, bitter winds and storm-tossed ferry crossings have brought home to the 1000 plus students, who have so far experienced the trip, the arduous nature of living outdoors at that time of year. The trip in 2012 being particularly notable for its daytime temperatures of -16°C!

The visit has evolved gradually over the 17 years it has taken place, but certain sites have always featured prominently. Around Ypres, the Menin Gate and Tyne Cot Cemetery amongst others. Further south, on the Somme, Lochganer Crater, Newfoundland Park, and Thiepval Memorial.

The spectacular memorial on the ridge at Vimy has been another permanent feature. At each site the students have been guided around the place, but then been allowed time to reflect on the significance of the sites and what they mean to us today. The visit to Langamar German Cemetery brings a different, and very poignant, opportunity to reflect on the wider issues of war and reconciliation.

In 2002 the Southwell Branch of the Royal British Legion were contacted to ask if a couple of the Southwell Burgage Remembrance Day wooden crosses might be taken with us to lay at the site of some of Southwell's war dead. Mr Andy Gregory was very keen to encourage this link with the town's young people and invited us to take annually two of the crosses on our visit to Belgium and France. In a very touching and sentimental request he asked that we did not wash the crosses, but take them with their "Southwell mud attached" to lay at the specific war grave locations visited. Each year since then the students have heard of the Southwell men who ventured forth in World War I, but never returned. Particular emphasis has been on those with no known grave and their names have been pointed out to the assembled groups before a student has laid our local cross at their memorial. In 2013 the sites were the Menin Gate and the Thiepval Memorial.

In more recent years this tradition has been extended and each student has been given a new wooden cross and asked to make their own personal choice where they would like to leave their own memorial token. A brief service and the laying of a wreath with readings has also become a feature of the visit in a private cloister at Tyne Cot Cemetery. The effect is quite dramatic and the response of the students from the town and surrounding communities has been a great credit to the young people with whom we are always deeply impressed.

Samuel Humberstone's Memorial Cross, taken from Southwell to the Western Front, 2013 (Minster School)

On our return to school the students have often shown a great ability to reflect in a mature way on the visit. Students

The Minster School group reflecting by the Menin Gate in February 2013, and below laying a wreath at the Tyne Cot Memorial. (Minster School). Next page a previous school year at Tyne Cot. (David Birkett)

have taken School Assemblies and one year they helped lead the Armistice Day Memorial Service in the Methodist Church, showing pictures of their visit and reflecting what it had meant to them. Below are examples of personal reflections from students who have been on the trip.

Our trip to Ypres – 2013

February 2013 was bitterly cold with biting winds freezing our hands and feet. As we trudged through the trenches at Ypres we realised that we were following in the footsteps of men who had stood in this very place merely 100 years ago. It is said that you cannot understand a person until you have walked in their shoes - well we tried to do just that and the experience was both moving and heartrendingly memorable. To imagine that hundreds and thousands of men - some as young as ourselves - would have stood in this very place for days, weeks and even months seemingly without an end in sight. Most poignant of all was the sight of the Danger Tree at The Beaumont-Hamel Newfoundland Memorial - which was the closest allied troops reached towards enemy lines. We could not comprehend that such an unremarkable landmark could signify so much. It is the memory of the soldiers who fought and died for us which will remain with me and should not be forgotten.

   By Charlotte Lock.

To me, visiting the battlefields of northern France and Belgium brought the First World War to life. It's one thing reading about the war with statistics and key points in study guides and books, but seeing the landscape and hearing the stories in the cold, damp weather amongst mud and rain, you can start to get an idea what life was like for those on the front line in the war. For any budding historian, it's a great catalyst for jumping into the study of a war that seems so far off yet is so relevant to our lives, societies and politics today. Two places on our visit stand out to me the most: first, when we went to a huge mine crater, it proved the savagery and strength of the war. Although it was an area once full of violence, today it is treated with reverence and respect – something that is so suitable this memorial year. Second was the Thiepval memorial to the missing of the Somme. This was so moving an area, as it highlights the extent of the numbers of men taken by the war. I found myself thinking of the impact on families at home when visiting these places, and over history's role in remembrance of the war. Visiting such important places allows us to recognise and understand what we can do today to prevent such a loss of life as the First World War again.

   By Owen Sparkes.

Former Minster Grammar School Boys who served in the First World War in addition to those who gave their lives.

Men who are already listed in the Southwell Roll Call are in italics.

Adams, Lt. J.F.:   Royal Engineers
Allcock, F.:   S/Foresters
Atkins, Capt. R.:   Royal Engineers
Bailey, F.L.:   Royal Garrison Artillery
Ball, C.:   *S/Foresters*
Ball, L.:   *S/Foresters*
Bates, W.W.:   *South Notts Hussars*
Beaumont, Capt. H.E.:   No record
Bennett, G.:   Canadian Engineers
Bently, L.:   S/Foresters
Bett, Joseph H.:   *South Notts Hussars*
Boyes, E.:   East Yorks
Bricknell, J.:   South Staffordshires
Burton, Lt. B.:   R.A.F.
Caldwell, A.:   R.N., H.M.S. Vernon
Carding, C.:   South Notts Hussars
Chambers, Lt. A.:   *S/Foresters*
Chambers, J.:   S/Foresters
Chambers, Sgt. H.W.:   *Royal Flying Corps*
Clarke, Lt. C.:   *S. Wales Borderers*
Clarke, W.J.:   *Royal Horse Artillery*
Coleman, Rev. N.D.:   Chaplain
Coleman, Lt. Col. T.E.: Royal Engineers
Cottam, G.A.:   *South Notts Hussars*
Dalgleish, O.:   No record
Dodd, J. J.:   *4th Hussars*
Dowling, A. E.: No record
Drury, W.S.:   11th Canadian
Earp, Lt. N.:   R.A.F.
Eaton, J.:   S/Foresters
Edmonds, Lt. H.S.:   Royal Warwicks
Ewers, Lt. L.F.:   *Border Regt.*
Featherstone, W.:   South Notts Hussars
Fleury, Sgt. A.: 50th Regt., France
Foster, H.:   *Army Service Corps*
Foster, W.:   *R.N., H.M.S. Queen*
Gant, Lt. L.:   No record
Gee, Rev. L.:   Chaplain
George, Lt. H.J.:   *Machine Gun Corps*
Gilbert, Major L.:   *Act. Lt. Col. S/Foresters*
Godber, Capt. J.: *Royal Army Vet Corps*
Gregory, G.:   *Midshipman R.N.*

Gregory, W.G.: *S/Foresters*
Hackett, L.:   No record
Hallam, L/Cpl. S.: South Notts Hussars
Handley, E.:   No record
Hardy, R.D.:   No record
Hassall, J.:   C.E.F.
Hibbert, Capt. W.:   Royal Army Medic Corps
Hibbert, Lt. B.:   South Notts Hussars
Hickling, Lt. H.:   West Yorks
Hill, G.:   Royal Sussex
Houseman, Lt. J.W.:   A.S.C. & S/Foresters
Huskinson, Lt. W.B.:   Welsh Fusiliers
Hyde, Capt. B.:   *S/Foresters*
Jackson, Lt. H.:   K.R.R.C.
Jackson, J. J.:   Royal Garrison Artillery
Jackson, R.:   No record
Jarvis, H.:   S/Foresters
Jebbett, A.:   Royal Army Medical Corps
Johnson, Capt. B.:   S/Foresters
Kirkby, Lt. J.H.:   *Yorks and Lancs*
Kirkby, Lt. S.:   No record
Larrington, L.:   *S/Foresters*
Leonard, H. T.:   *S/Foresters*
Lester, Lt. W.:   R.A.F.
Longmore, O.:   *S/Foresters*
Martin, J.E.: Royal Naval Air Service
Measures, Major H.:   R.A.F.
Mettham, M.C., E. D.: Leh. Frontiersman
Mills, A.:   S/Foresters
Mills, W.E.:   Sherwood Rangers
Moore, Sgt. G.:   S/Foresters
Musgrove, G.:   *S/Foresters*
Noble, A.D.:   Army Service Corps
Noble, F.W.:   Army Service Corps
North, R.E.:   Cheshires
Oldham, Lt. E.H.:   Royal Garrison Artillery
Paling, M.C., Capt. L.:   R.A.F.
Parker, Lt. S.A.:   S/Foresters
Parr, Lt. J.R.:   Royal Horse Artillery
Partington, J.L.:   *E. Lancashires*
Pitman, L.:   1st Middlesex
Pyatt, Lt. T.:   Army Service Corps

Redgate, C.H.: Royal Field Artillery
Redgate, G.: No record
Roberts, Sgt. C.: Hon. Artillery Co.
Rumford, Lt. E.C.: R.A.F.
Sail, J.: Royal Horse Artillery
Salt, Q.M.S., A.H.L.: North'land Fusiliers
Schumach, Lt. G.J.D.: S/Foresters
Smith, Capt. S.: West Yorks
Smith, S.V.: S/Foresters
Stanley, A.G.: Durham Light Infantry
Tatham, F.: Army Service Corps
Taylor, W.: Royal Navy
Tongue, E.: S/Foresters
Tongue, F.: S/Foresters
Truman, H.: R.N.D.
Truman, Lt. P.: South Lancashires

Vickers, Lt. S.: Canadian 5th Bn.
Wagstaff, W.H.: S/Foresters
Wagstaffe, Lt. L.: South Notts Hussars
Walker, J.: Royal Horse Artillery
Weldon, Lt. W.W.: D.A.C.
Westbury, F.S.: No record
Wilkinson, H.: Royal Garrison Artillery
Wilkinson, M.: Royal Empire Fusiliers
Wilkinson, R.: Lincolnshire Regt.
Wilson, W.: East Yorks
Winfield, Lt. A.G.: North'land Fusiliers
Witham, Lt. M.: R.A.F.
Woodward, C.G.: Royal Engineers
Wright, B.: South Staffordshire
Wright, Capt. G.: S/Foresters

Thirty-six of the above are listed in the Southwell Roll Call chapter of this book.

*Minster School pupils visiting the Lochnagar Crater
at La Boisselle, Somme.
(David Birkett)*

Aftermath

Have you forgotten yet?...
For the world's events have rumbled on since those gagged days.
Like traffic checked while at the crossing of city-ways:
And the haunted gap in your mind has filled with thoughts that flow
Like clouds in the lit heaven of life; and you're a man reprieved to go,
Taking your peaceful share of Time, with joy to spare.
But the past is just the same - and War's a bloody game . ..
Have you forgotten yet?...
Look down, and swear by the slain of the War that you'll never forget.

Do you remember the dark months you held the sector at Mametz –
The nights you watched and wired and dug and piled sandbags on parapets?
Do you remember the rats; and the stench
Of corpses rotting in front of the front-line trench -
And dawn coming, dirty-white, and chill with a hopeless rain?
Do you ever stop and ask, 'Is it all going to happen again?'

Do you remember that hour of din before the attack -
And the anger, the blind compassion that seized and shook you then
As you peered at the doomed and haggard faces of your men?
Do you remember the stretcher-cases lurching back
With dying eyes and lolling heads - those ashen-grey
Masks of the lads who once were keen and kind and gay?
Have you forgotten yet?...
Look up, and swear by the green of the spring that you'll never forget.

Siegfried Sassoon
March 1919

CHAPTER 6
Welcome Home – the band of heroes

'They'

*The Bishop tells us: 'When the boys come back
They will not be the same; for they'll have fought
In a just cause: they lead the last attack
On Anti-Christ; their comrades' blood has bought
New right to breed an honourable race,
They have challenged Death and dared him face to face.'*

*'We're none of us the same!' The boys reply.
'For George lost both his legs; and Bill's stone blind;
Poor Jim's shot through the lungs and like to die;
And Bert's gone syphilitic; you'll not find
A chap who's served that hasn't found some change.'
And the Bishop said: 'The ways of God are strange!'*

Siegfried Sassoon

As the four-year-old war was drawing to its conclusion, thoughts turned to welcoming back the men from the front, and considering an appropriate permanent memorial to the fallen.

In an article in the Diocesan Magazine of January 1919 the Bishop of Southwell addresses the immediate challenge facing the town of welcoming back the war-weary men and remembering the fallen. Clearly he had been moved when visiting a cemetery containing 17,000 graves, just as we are still moved today. It is interesting to note that the Bishop had recently visited the 46th Division in France and a full report of the action he refers to appears in the 8th Battalion's War Diary.

DEAR BRETHREN,
It has been my lot to catch a glimpse of the country over which our men have fought for four years. No language, no painting can describe the desolation or make clear the conditions under which the allied armies struggled to a glorious victory.

In that mighty contest for freedom and justice our Notts. and Derby men have won eternal honour.

It was our purpose to visit the Territorial Battalions and to take them in person a message, conveying our admiration for the prowess of the 46th Division in the late fighting across the Canal du Nord, and at Remicourt.

It is hard to describe our feelings when we arrived at Landrecies and found the 1/8th drawn up for inspection. I had not seen the Battalion since I had said farewell to them four years ago at Harpenden and Braintree. Now, there they stood, the hardened and tried soldiers of many a battle. Only a handful remained of that original band of heroes, but many of our country lads were there who had joined for over three years, and nearly all had been engaged in the late severe fighting.

I wish that I could convey to our people at home a sense of the smartness of the Band and the Battalion, or hand on the words of sincere admiration for the whole Division, uttered by General Boyd; or recount the deeds performed for which the Duke of Portland was asked to present medals.

But I cannot go into further particulars, for my purpose is now not to tell a story which will have to be told, but to remind those at home of the solemn duty left for us to perform.

As I wished them a happier Christmas, I also expressed the hope that we should soon see them back in our counties.

The Sherwood Foresters, and amongst them the Territorials, have done nobly, and now it will be for us at home to receive them worthily. At a later date this must be done in some public way, but at once we must put forth every effort to receive them as they return, singly or in driblets.

Here is a great task for our Clergy and members of the C.E.M.S. [Church of England Men's Society], and I hear with gladness of bands of welcomers who strive to welcome each returning comrade.

It is good and necessary work.

But beyond all this, I would beg you to remember the solemn duty we owe to those whose bodies are left in France or elsewhere. We stood in one cemetery of 17,000 men. Every grave beautifully kept, and every grave had its little cross with the name of the fallen soldier, symbolic not of death, but of victory and life.

It was such a sight as this which led me to suggest that here in the two great centres of Nottingham and Derby we should, amongst larger War Memorials, bear in memory of our heroic dead, and raise to their honour a Church, which should from generation to generation commemorate the spirit in which our men fought and died; and so stir us up in times of peace to labour for the advancement of the Kingdom of God.

This new year will be an eventful year, when large issues will come up for settlement.

Let us pray and strive for such a spirit of fellowship and zeal, that we may heal the wounds of a sorrowing world and establish a firm hope in the eternal justice and love of God.

Yours ever faithfully,

EDWYN SOUTHWELL[1]

An official welcome home service was held in the Minster and a report appeared in the May 1919 Southwell Diocesan Magazine. The service was held on Easter Sunday, 20th April, with the arrangements having been made by the Federation of Discharged Soldiers and Sailors. Approximately 200 men, headed by the Southwell Brass Band and the buglers of the Church Lads' Brigade,[2] marched to the Minster. Following a processional hymn the men were addressed by the Bishop, taking as his text:

> "Welcome Home" – Home to the families, Home to Southwell. Home to their Cathedral, where they had been so faithfully remembered and where their help and interest is so much needed if vitality is to be secured in the life of the Church.'[3]

Following a hymn and a special lesson, the Rector read the Roll of Honour containing 84 names[4] and the choir sang the anthem 'I know that my Redeemer liveth'. Prayers and further hymns followed.

At this time there were still a large number of troops waiting to return home, and the war was not over for those who had been sent to the Baltic States and Russia in connection with the Russian Revolution. The official county memorial service was delayed until Saturday, 5th July 1919.

---

[1] *The Southwell Diocesan Magazine,* January, 1919.

[2] Former members of the C.L.B. had distinguished themselves in the war.

[3] *The Southwell Diocesan Magazine,* May 1919.

[4] The eventual death toll for Southwell men was approximately 125 – there is some uncertainty as to the exact number as some names have been 'claimed' by other towns or villages. The passage of time has not helped to resolve the actual numbers.

Whilst the Church had put on a memorable service for the returning troops, the reality for many of the men was somewhat different. Many had no jobs to return to and women, who had filled their places so admirably, found themselves out of work. Some were probably happy to revert to their domestic role, but others would miss their responsible jobs.

Memorial Service and Celebrations

The day of the memorial service was one of mixed emotions in Southwell. Special trains had been laid on from Nottingham and Mansfield, which were full. Crowds of people lined the streets and the scene was captured by Alfred J Loughton, the Southwell photographer:

Victory Parade - A J Loughton Collection (by kind permission of the Dean and Minster Chapter)

The crowds were swelled by 'motorists, many in military uniform, who poured in from all parts of the country, and when the service commenced there was not a vacant seat in the vast edifice'.[5] A report in the Diocesan Magazine for August opened with:

> "This is not a funeral service at all. It is a most glorious period of victory." Offered the preacher at the county memorial service held in Southwell Cathedral on Saturday afternoon. Nevertheless, the many signs of grief – tear-stained faces and the general mourning worn – showed that the terrible losses which this war has inflicted are still uppermost in the thoughts of all classes, and dim, for the present, the glorious victory of right to which Mr Hales sought to direct the thoughts of the great congregation. The same mingling of sorrow and joy was evidenced in the muffled peals rung on the cathedral bells at the same time that the streets of the quaint little old-fashioned town were gay with bunting.

---
[5] *The Southwell Diocesan Magazine*, August 1919.

The official guests included the Duke of Portland (Lord-Lieutenant) along with local mayors, senior council officials, many dressed in their official robes and accompanied by mace-bearers.

The report continued:

The most striking spectacle, however, was the sight of the colour parties from three battalions of the Sherwood Foresters (the first, second, and the eighth). Every head was bared as they passed, carrying the emblems which mean so much to a soldier, and during the service the colours were handed to the sub-dean (Archdeacon Conybeare) by the Duke of Portland, reposed upon the nave altar in full sight of the congregation.

Colour Party
(A J Loughton Collection)

As the band of the 2nd Battalion, Sherwood Foresters approached the cathedral the men were met by the Bishop, Chapter, clergy and choir, and the civic representatives at the west door. A long list of senior military officers were recorded as representing the Sherwood Foresters and other regiments. There were special military contingents consisting of 100 men from the 1st Battalion, Sherwood Foresters, 40 from the Second, 8 from the Seventh, 80 from the Eighth, 9 Army Service Corps, 16 Field Ambulance, 6 South Notts Hussars, and 12 Horse Artillery.

The service contained an impressive list of hymns, and the sermon was preached by Rev. J.P. Hales, D.S.O., the Rector of Cotgrave, whose administrations to the men in the firing line had endeared him to thousands. This, indeed, seems to have been a most imposing and moving memorial service to the men of the diocese who gave their lives in the conflict. Meanwhile, in the town, many people had gathered to celebrate formally the end of the war, and this is illustrated in various photographs. Prior to the Cathedral services, discussions had commenced about a permanent memorial to the fallen and help to those who had returned home disabled. In early November 1918, the Rector, the Venerable

The Band arriving - A J Loughton Collection
(Both pictures by kind permission of the Dean and Chapter).

W. J. Conybeare, had written in the Diocesan Magazine that the town should be thinking about some form of permanent memorial. He made a suggestion that it could perhaps take the form of a building to be used for the good of the community, where lectures could be given, and where books could be read in quiet surroundings. His aim was to set the town thinking.[6] This he certainly did and two months later Southwell parish Council had considered various options. Their chairman, Arthur Salt, announced that they had taken the Rector's idea a little further, and mentioned that they had received several suggestions. These included a public hall, with offices for the council, a reading room and library, baths and washhouses, alms-houses for the disabled in the war, and a large public monument, along with various other schemes. It was decided that a committee be formed to consider the options.[7]

After these rather ambitious suggestions nothing more was heard until mid-June 1919, when it was reported in the *Advertiser* that the committee had decided, '…that a memorial hall, fully equipped, would cost £5,000, and it was agreed that the cost of either cottage homes or a memorial cross could be accommodated to the amount of subscriptions received.' It was decided that '… a scheme for a Public Hall be carried out'. There was some discussion as to how £5,000 could be raised. However, one firm resolution came out of the meeting: 'That a suitable cross be

Dedication of the War Memorial on the Burgage
A. J. Loughton Collection (by kind permission of the Dean and Chapter).

erected upon the Burgage Green as a war memorial.'[8] It would seem that the grand plan for a public hall failed miserably. A report appeared in the *Advertiser* on 19th September 1919 stating

---
[6] *Newark Advertiser*, 6th November 1918.
[7] *Newark Advertiser*, 8th January 1919.
[8] *Newark Advertiser*, 18th June 1919.

that the Southwell Memorial Fund had raised £466. 19s. 0d by that date. As we know, a memorial cross was erected on the Burgage Green and dedicated on Saturday 30th April 1921. The enthusiasm for a grander memorial seemed to have dimmed as post-war austerity had begun to bite.

The Bishop during the commemoration service
A. J. Loughton Collection (by kind permission of the Dean and Chapter).

They went with songs to the battle, they were young.
Straight of limb, true of eyes, steady and aglow.
They were staunch to the end against odds uncounted,
They fell with their faces to the foe.

They shall grow not old, as we that are left grow old:
Age shall not weary them, nor the years condemn.
At the going down of the sun and in the morning,
We will remember them.

They mingle not with their laughing comrades again;
They sit no more at familiar tables of home;
They have no lot in our labour of the day-time;
They sleep beyond England's foam.

Extract from *For the Fallen*, Laurence Binyon

BIBLIOGRAPHY

Primary Sources:

Absent Voters' List, Southwell and District, 1914, 1918

Births, Marriages and Deaths official records

Census Returns, 1881, 1891, 1901, 1911

Commonwealth War Graves Commission, www.cwgc.org

Military Service Records, www.ancestry.co.uk

Newark Advertiser, 1914-1919

Regimental Annual, *8th Battalion Notes* (Sherwood Foresters, 1920)

School Log Books:

    Holy Trinity School, Southwell

    National School, Southwell

    St. Mary's Infants' School, Southwell

School Admissions Records:

    Methodist School, Southwell

    Minster Grammar School, Southwell

    National School, Southwell

Soldiers Died in the Great War (The Naval and Military Press - Compact Disc)

Southwell Diocesan Magazine, July 1918, January 1919, May 1919, August, 1919

Southwell and District Roll of Honour, Trent to Trenches Project

Southwell Rural District Tribunal Records

Voters' List 1928 (included war veterans)

Secondary Sources:

Adie, Kate, *Fighting on the Home Front. The Legacy of Women in World War One* (London: Hodder & Stoughton, 2013)

Austin, Michael, *Almost Like a Dream, A Parish at War, 1914-1919* (Whitchurch: Merton Priory Press, 1999)

Ascoli, David, *The Mons Star: The British Expeditionary Force 1914* (London: Harper, 1981)

Blunden, Edmund, *Undertones of War* (London: Penguin, 2010)

Burke, Joanna, 'Another Battle Front', *The Guardian,* 11th November, 2008

Dobson, Roger, *Southwell Inns and Alehouses* (Nottingham: Nottinghamshire County Council, 2008)

Fellowes, George and Freeman, Benson, *Historical Records of the South Nottinghamshire Hussars Yeomanry, 1794 - 1924* (Aldershot: Gale & Polder, 1928)

Foster, Peter, *Memorials of the Great War, Nottinghamshire Cemeteries, Southwell* (Nottinghamshire: Foster, undated.)

Gardner, Brian, ed., *Up The Line To Death. The War Poets 1914-1918. An Anthology* (York: Methuen , 2007)

Keegan, John, *The First World War* (London: Pimlico, 1999)

Kendall, Paul, *The Zeebrugge Raid, The Finest Feat of Arms* (Brinscombe Port: Spellmount, 2008)

Local Writers, *Southwell, The Town and its People,* O'Malley, Peter, Chapter 11, 'Medical Facilities' (Southwell: Southwell & District Local History Society, 1992)

Pope, Stephen, Wheal, Elizabeth Anne, *The Macmillan Dictionary of the First World War* (London: Macmillan, 1995)

Stallworthy, Jon, ed., *The Oxford Book of War Poetry,* (London: BCA, 1995)

Stevenson, Doreen, *Twentieth Century Lives of Southwell* (Southwell: Stevenson, 2001)

Weetman, W.C.C., *The Sherwood Foresters in the Great War 1914-1919 - History of the 1/8th Battalion* (Nottingham: Thomas Forman, 1920 - reprint LCC/Qontro)

Loughton Collection of Photographs (Copyright The Dean and Chapter, Southwell Minster)

Internet Sources:

History Learning Site: www.historylearningsite.co.uk

Sherwood Foresters Museum: www.wfrmuseum.org.uk

INDEX - PEOPLE

The people index is in two parts. For the men from Southwell who served please see Chapter 1, where references to them in other chapters are indexed with their biographical details.

Adams, J.F. 306
Allcock, F. 306
Ashwell, Maj. 224
Atkins, R. 306

Bailey, F.L. 306
Barlow, Eustace 87
Bates, J.J. 89-90, 92-3, 110-11, 142, 162, 172-3, 175-6, 185-6, 190-1
Beaumont, H.E. 306
Becher, John Henry 89
Becher, J.T. 87
Becher, Joyce 100
Becher, Mrs 209
Bell, Joseph H. 279
Bennett, G. 306
Bently, L. 306
Bishop of London 208
Bishop of Southwell 246, 309
Blackwell, Col. 231-2
Blundell, Sgt. 287
Blunden, Edmund xiii
Boyd, Maj. Gen. G.F. 235, 309
Boyes, E. 306
Branston, Capt. H.P.G. 91
Bricknell, J. 306
Brown, Capt. 87
Browne, Harold 86, 154-5, 179-80
Burke, Joanna 282, 285
Burton, B. 306

Caldwell, A. 306
Carding, C. 306
Cauldwell, C.G. 86, 167, 173-4, 193-4
Chambers, J. 306
Clarke, Inspector 89-90
Clewes, Sgt. 218
Coleman, Revd. N.D. 306
Coleman, T.E. 306
Collier, Dorothy 298
Collins, Harry 298
Connybeare, Venerable W.J. 312-13
Coombes, L. Cpl. 243
Cornwell, John T. 291
Cottam, Wm. 85, 110-11, 197
Currin, Lt. Col. R.W. 232

Dalgleish, O. 306
Davis, H.R. 301
Dean, Rev. F.R. 298
Dixon, F.A. 301
Douthwaite, R.C.M. 301
Dowling, A.E. 306
Drury, W.S. 306

Earp, N. 298, 306
Eaton, J. 306
Edmonds, H.S. 306
Elliott, Capt. C.P. 232
Ellis, J.E. 86-7, 91, 148-9, 175-6
Fairbrother, A.C. 230
Featherstone, W. 306
Ferdinand, Archduke Franz xii
Fisher, Nellie 122-3
Fleury, A. 306
Foljambe, Lt-Col. G.S. 92-3, 246
Foster, Mr 85
Fowler, Lt. Col. G.H. 207, 211-2, 214

Gant, L. 306
Geary, Lt. 225, 243
Gee, Rev. L. 306
Gilstrap, Miss 209

Hackett, L. 306
Hacking, Archdeacon 86, 120-1, 132-3, 182, 193-4, 241
Hales, Revd. J.P. 215, 311-12
Hallam, S. 306
Handford, Dr H. 86, 115
Handley, E. 306
Hardy, R.D. 306
Hargreaves, F.P. 301, 306
Harrington, Gen. 243
Harvey, George 300
Hassall, J. 306
Hedderley, Hilda 298
Hibbert, B. 306
Hibbert, W. 306
Hicking, Lady N. 289-90
Hicking, Sir W. N., & Lady N. 84-5, 89-90, 105-6, 150-1, 153-5, 159, 170, 172, 177-8, 187-8, 193-4, 289-90

Hickling, H. 306
Hill, Capt. 221
Hill, G. 306
Hill, S. 289
Hindley, Canon 206
Homan, Capt. 242
Hopkinson, C. 208
Horne, Gen. 225, 234
Horsley, J.W. 289
Houseman, J.W. 306
Huskinson, W.B. 306
Hyde, Pte. 9
Jackson, H. 306
Jackson, H.T. 86, 190-1
Jackson, J.J. 306
Jackson, R. 306
Jarvis, H. 306
Jebbett, A. 306
Jebbett, F. 301
Jenks, Father David 102, 134
Jesson, Richard 300
Johnson, B. 306
Johnson-Coope, W. 298
King George V 215
Kirkby, J.H. 86, 89-92, 94-5, 99-100, 105-6, 110-14, 122-3, 125-6, 132, 138-9, 142, 147-9, 151, 155-6, 158-9, 160, 174-5, 182-3, 190-1, 193-4, 199
Kirkby, S. 306
Kitchener, Lord 94-6, 99, 120-1, 139, 161, 206, 291

Lea, Revd. T.A. 287
Lester, Arthur 300
Lester, W. 306
Lewin, Mr & Mrs H. 85, 148-9, 193-4
Lloyd George, David 285
Longhurst, Rev. E.S. 298

Maltby, C.L. 83, 86, 100, 105, 148-9, 157, 165-6, 190-1
Maltby, Mrs C.L. 287
Marshall. F.A. 86
Martin, J.E. 306
McMillan, Lt. 87
Measures, H. 306
Mellish, Col. 246
Merryweather, A.E. 87, 104, 135-7
Merryweather, E.A. 86, 191
Merryweather, H. 153-5, 186, 190-1
Merryweather, J.E. 86
Metcalf, A.T. 86, 148-9

Metcalf, N.A. 86, 114, 142, 146, 148-9
Mettham, E.D. 306
Millington, R.A. 86
Mills, A. 306
Mills, W.E. 306
Minding, Max Fredrik xii
Monash, Lt. Gen. Sir John 237
Moore, Albert 299
Moore, G. 306
Moore, Thomas H. 299
Moore, W.G. 301

Newcastle, Bishop of 299
Nicholls, Sir G. 87
Noble, A.D. 306
Noble, F.W. 306
North, R.E. 306

Oldham, E.H. 306

Paling, L. 306
Parker, S.A. 306
Parr, J.R. 306
Parr, L.G. 301
Partington, T.D. 90-1, 138, 142, 145, 154, 166-7, 186, 189, 196, 197-8
Pavey, Miss 288
Pigford, Capt. 221
Pitman, L. 306
Playne, Caroline 285
Pollock, C.T.A. 100
Polson, Dr 86, 107
Portland, Duke and Duchess of 92-3, 138, 246, 288, 309, 312
Prince of Wales 215
Pyatt, T. 306
Pyatt, W.H.C. 301

Rathmell, Sydney 289
Rawlinson, Gen. Sir H.S. 245
Redgate, C.R. 307
Redgate, G. 307
Ridgwell, Frank xi
Roberts, C. 307
Robinson, Maj. V.O. 242-3
Rose, C.P. 301

Sail, J. 307
Salt, A. 86, 142, 148, 155, 177-8, 186, 190-1
Salt, Arthur 313
Savile, Lady 290

Schumach, F. 302
Schwieger, Capt. Walter 119-123
Sharock, L.Cpl. 209
Shipley, Brig. C.T. 206, 219
Small, Miss E.M. 87, 133, 138, 149, 153-4, 164-5, 186-8, 288, 290
Smith, S. 307
Starkey, Hilda Margaret 100
Starkey M.P., J.R., 91, 100, 103, 141, 148-9, 153-4, 178-9
Starkey, Lewis 297
Starkey, Sir John 302
Stokes, Sgt. 214
Straw, A. 301
Straw, F. W. 301
Stuart-Wortley, Maj. Gen. 215
Sturst, Padre 242

Tatham, F. 307
Taylor, Charles 302
Taylor, G.C. 301
Taylor, George C. 302
Taylor, W. 307
Thwaites, Maj. Gen. 221-2, 235
Truman, H. 307
Truman, P. 307
Turner, Capt. 214, 221, 231

Vann, Capt. 209, 214, 221-2, 241

Vickers, S. 307

Wagstaffe, L. 307
Walker, Dr 86, 110-1
Walker, Frederick 298
Warrand, Mrs 287, 290
Webb, Mr 85
Weetman, Capt. W.C.C. xii
Weetman, W.C.C. 206
Weldon, W.W. 307
Westbury, F.S. 307
Whitting-Shaw, Hannah xi
Wild, The Ven. Archdeacon Herbert 87, 95, 97-8, 104-5
Wilkinson, H. 307
Wilkinson, M. 307
Wilkinson, R. 307
Williams, A.C.R. 301
Willoughby, Dr. J.F.D. 86, 99, 103, 105-6, 129-30, 149, 153-4, 284
Wilson, Mr 298
Wilson, W. 307
Winfield, A.G. 307
Witham, M. 307
Woodruffe, A. 86, 91, 110-2, 120-1, 125, 288
Worman, A.L. 301
Wright, B. 307
Wright, Revd. John 298
Wright, W. 90, 132-3

INDEX - GENERAL

Accrington Pals 202
Adinfer Wood 220
Admiral Rodney Hotel 86, 94-5, 96, 168-70, 194
Aerial Photography 94-5
Agricultural Certificates 293
Agricultural jobs 293
Alexandria 94, 125, 132, 156, 164-5
Amiens 225, 235
Andigny-les-Fermes 243
Annequin Fosse 231
Archangel 252
Archdeacon of Newark 89-90
Arras 247, 262
Ascension Valley 236
Assembly Rooms 86, 97-8, 103, 104, 177-8, 187-8
Auchel 235-6
Auxi-le-Chateau 222
Averdoignt 219

Bailleuval 222
Balkans 275
Baptist Chapel 85, 142, 156, 159
Bavincourt 221-2
Beersheba 247, 266-77
Belgian Refugees 83, 92-5, 99, 107, 114, 124
Belgian Relief Fund 294
Bellacourt 221, 262
Bellinglise 236-7, 239, 241, 245
Bethencourt 218, 246
Béthune 212, 213, 215, 229, 233
Beurevoir 278
Beuvry 235
Bienvillers 219, 221
Bishop of Newcastle 174-5
Bishop of Norwich 99
Bishop of Southampton 89
Bishop of Southwell 90, 99, 108-9, 116, 154-5, 174-5, 178-9, 180, 309-10
Bishop's Manor 89-90
Bishop's Stortford 207
Blood transfusions 284
Bocking 206
Boer War 247, 274
Bohain 243
Boulogne-sur-Helpe 244-5
Boy Soldiers 272
Brackenhurst Hall xiii, 84-5, 87, 89-90, 151-2, 158-9, 165-8, 170, 172, 179-80, 187-8, 247, 287-9
Braintree 206, 309
Bulgarian Cavalry 275

Bulwark, H.M.S., Loss of 291
Burbure 231
Burgage 287-10
Burgage Green Memorial 313
Burgage Manor xiii, 83-5
Burgage Manor Hospital 108-11, 113-4, 116-7, 125, 130, 136-8, 142-3, 145-9, 151, 154-6, 159-61, 164-6, 186-8, 190. 287-9

C of E Men's Society 310
Cairo 275
Caledonia, H.M.S. 208, 277
Calonne 227
Cambrin 231-2
Canal du Nord 309
Candas 215-6
Carency 217
Carey, E. & Sons 90, 104, 107, 112, 113-4, 116, 119-21, 130-2, 138, 142, 144-5, 150, 152-3, 156, 159, 165, 172-3, 177, 185, 187, 197, 199, 202, 252
Cartignies 244
Catillon 244
Caudwell's Mill 262
Chelers 228
Cheltenham Area V.A. Hospital 272
Church Lads' Brigade 87, 89, 101, 103, 122-3, 187
Cité-de-Riaumont 225, 228
Cité-St. Theodore 227
Clipstone Camp 100, 103, 105-6, 167, 178-9
Clothing trade 281
Commerce 281
Comrades' Association 84-5
Concert 85, 94-5, 118, 128-9, 135, 139, 142-6, 149, 155-6, 166-71, 179-80
Contay 224-5
County Magistrates 125, 128, 175-6
Crimea Veterans 84-5
Crimean War 284
Crown Hotel 296-7

Dardanelles 125, 129-31, 144, 275
Dartmouth, H.M.S. 194
Death rates 284
Defence of the Realm Act 83, 94, 133-5, 282
Desert Mounted Corps 247
Diphtheria 294
Domestic service 281-2
Drill Hall, Southwell 87-8, 91, 103, 163-4
Dummy Tree 218
Dunstable 207

Easthorpe Peace Celebrations 197
Écoivres 218
Egg Collection xiii, 84, 104, 106-8, 110, 114, 120, 135-6, 139, 143, 147, 149, 188, 190
Egypt 97-8, 125, 132, 134, 142, 145, 163-4, 216
Egyptian Expeditionary Force 272, 275
El Mughar 277
Empire Day 138
Enquin-les-Mines 231
Épehy 278
Escaufort 244
Essars 233-5

Federation of Discharged Soldiers & Sailors 136, 171, 174-5, 179-80, 187-9, 310
Fever Hospital 83-4
Flammenwerfer 211
Fonquevillers 219-20, 222, 224
Fonsomme Line 241
Food Controller 148, 150-1, 162-3, 168-9, 175-6
Food Rationing 147-8, 150-1, 179-80, 186
Food shortages 292
Forêt d'Andigny 243
Fouquières 212-14
Fresnoy-le-Grand 242-3
Fullerphone 218

Gallipoli 124-5, 128-32, 144-5, 155-6, 216, 275, 291
Gaza 247, 275, 277
German Dragoons 275
Girls' Friendly Society 143, 150, 157
Gommecourt 219, 222-4
Gorre 233-5
Grammar School 90, 92-3, 152, 170, 175, 178-9, 182-4, 197, 199
Guveyne 275

H Company 201-246
Harpenden 92, 95, 179-80, 206, 309
Healthcare 284
Hesperian, R.M.S. 119-20, 122
Hill 65 225-7
Hill 70 227-31
Hindenberg Line 237, 240, 245, 276
Hohenzollern Redoubt 212-15, 228-9, 250
Holy Trinity School 291
Honours - 8th Bn. 246
Hooge 211-2
Hooge, Battle of 122-3, 126-7

Horses 92-3
House of Correction 202
Humbercamp 219,
Hunmanby 88

Indian Mutiny Veterans 2
Infant welfare 285
Influenza 145, 184-5, 187, 189, 283
Irish Rebellion 102, 137, 152, 162
Ismailia Ferry 275
I-Tok 222

Jannecourt Farm 242
Jerusalem 247
Jutland, Battle of 291
Kasr-el-Nil 275
Kemmel 208-9
Khan Yunus 275
Killed-in-Action 83
King Edward Steamer 208
Kut-el-Amara 275

La Bassée Canal 216, 232-3
La Houssoye 235
La Souich 219
La Targette 217
Labour Certificate 293
Labourers' Union 189
Laires 231
Land Army 283
Land Workers' Rally 187-8
Landrecies 246, 309
Larken & Co 249
Le Cateau 247
Le Journal 237-8
Le Vergies 242
League of Nations' Union 199-200
Leasowe Castle, SS 277
Lehaucourt 239, 242
Lens 224-8
Liévin 225, 227
Local Government Board 87, 147-8, 150-1, 193, 195-6
Locre 208-9, 234
Loos 227
Lorette Ridge 217
Lusitania, R.M.S. 119-20, 122-3

Macedonia 275
Magny-la-Fosse 240
Maison Ponthieu 222

Malta 94, 125, 161
Mansfield Corps 201
Maroc 228
Marqueffles Farm 227
Marseilles 215-6
Mazingarbe 212, 231
Measles outbreak 293-4
Medina 247
Megiddo, Battle of 248
Memorial Services 104-5, 107, 117-8, 139, 156-7, 159, 175-6, 311-3
Mericourt 242
Merryweathers & Sons, H. 117, 121, 149, 190, 262
Meziers 244
Middlesex Wood 212
Mikado Café 85
Military Service Acts 83, 131-2, 134-7
Minster Grammar School 296-305
   Finances 297
     Pupils' reminiscences 305
   Staff 297-8
   Western Front 303-5
Minster Institute 110-11, 141, 167, 170-1
Minster Window Commemoration 174-5
Mons 247
Mont-Bernenchon 212
Mont St. Eloy 217
Montbrehain 239-42
Mr Ginnett's Circus 84, 87
Mudros 275
Mules 207
Munitions 281-2

National Deposit Friendly Society 102, 146
National Egg Collections 84, 104, 106, 107-11, 113-4, 120, 135-6, 139, 143, 147-9, 189-90, 287
National Patriotic Association 104
National Reserve 87, 91-3, 105-6, 120, 165-6, 182-3, 252
National School 291
National Service Campaign 149
Nebi Samwil 277
Neuve Chapelle 208, 232, 234
New Drill Hall 91, 103, 197
Newark Corps 201
Newark-on-Trent 246
Norfolk, H.M.S. 94
Norton Camp Altar 200
Norwood Park 84, 106, 114
Nottingham, Mayor of 85
Notts Rifle Volunteers 201

Nursing 281
Nursing Association 141

Ouderhom 209, 211-12
Oudezeele 208

P.O.W.s Food parcels 134
Palestine 248
Patriotic Sale 146
Peace Celebrations 196
Peace Festival 294
Pleasure Fair 84, 87
Poeuilly 235
Pommier 220
Pont Remy 216
Pontru 235
Pontruet 235-6
Poor Law 87, 191-2
Poperinghe 211
Prisches 243, 246

Quadrille Class 86
Queen Alexandra's Nursing Corps 282

Railway Reserve Trench 214
Ramicourt 239-43
Red Cross Society 84, 87, 89, 99, 103-4, 116-7, 125, 128-9, 130, 135-6, 138, 145-6, 150-2, 159, 175-6, 179-80, 185, 187-8, 281, 287, 295
Red Lion, Thurgarton 273
Regnicourt 243
Remicourt 309
Representation of the People Bill 283
Retford Corps 201
Revelles 225
Rheims 234
Ribeaucourt 216
Richebourg 215
Riqerval Bridge 236, 239
Robin Hoods 83, 92-3, 113-4, 119-20
Royal Defence Corps 252
Royal Proclamation 203
Russian Revolution 310

Salonica 275
Sambre 278
Sambre-Oise Canal 243, 245
Sanctuary Wood 210-11
Sandbags 110-11, 122-3
Sanitation 284
Saracen's Head 273

Scarbourough bombardment 207
School War Savings Association 293-4
Scimitar Hill 275
Sequehart 242
Sherwood Foresters 83
Sherwood Rangers Yeomanry 91
Sidi Bishr 277
Sikkin Revolt 266
Sinai Desert 275
Social class divisions 84
Society of the Sacred Mission 102, 134
Somme, Battle of 247
Somme, The 219
South Notts Hussars 87, 92-3, 102, 110-11, 122-3, 139, 247, 275-9
Southwell Aeroplane Week 177-8
Southwell Board of Guardians 83-7, 145, 147-9, 174-5, 189, 191-6, 197-9
Southwell Corps 201
Southwell Debating Society 86, 150
Southwell Evening Schools 198-9
Southwell Girls' Club 168
Southwell Lace Operatives' Society 197
Southwell Memorial Fund 313
Southwell Minster 90, 159, 171, 246
Southwell Parish Council 83, 99, 124, 140-1, 148-9, 151-2, 177-8, 186, 189-91
Southwell Rifle Club 84, 86, 103, 112
Southwell Rural District Council 83, 86, 92-3, 136-7, 158-9, 193-4, 199
Southwell Traders' Association 84-6, 142-3, 148-9, 157, 164-5, 173-5, 183-4, 186, 190-1
Southwell Tribunal 83, 134-8, 140-1, 179-80
Southwell Union 86
Spanc River 275
Sports Clubs 91-2
Springbok Valley 240
St Amand 224
St. Elie 228
St. Emile 232
St. Mary's Infants' School 291
St. Pierre 232
St. Quentin 235, 239
St. Quentin Canal 236, 278
St. Pol 228
Standard of living 283
Suez Canal 94
Suffragettes 283
Sulva Bay 132, 155-6, 275
Sunday Postal Delivery 142
Sussex Trench 213

Teaching 281
Territorial Reserve 252
Textile manufacturing 281
Thorneywood Corps 201
Thwanga, S.S. 94
Timeline xvi
Tincques 218-9
Tramps rationing 145, 150-1,
Transport 206
Trebeck Hall 90, 95, 101-2, 104-5, 108-11, 115, 118-9, 137, 143, 186-8, 197-8
Trench Foot 284
Turkish Cavalry 275

U-20 German Submarine 122-3
UB 51 277
U-Boats 257, 292
Uhlans 275

V.A.D. 282, 287
Vaudricourt 215, 233
Verdun 217
Vermelles 212-3, 250
Verquin 229-30
Victory Bond 193-6
Vieille Chapelle 215-6
Vimy Ridge 216-8, 225, 232, 272
Vote, The 84

War Declared 89
War Diary, 8th Bn. 206-46
War Loan 293
War Memorial 107, 182-3, 186, 191, 197-8, 313-4
War Savings Campaign 141, 195-6
Warwick Penny Bank 85
Welcome Home 310
Westrehem 225
Whooping Cough 294
Wiancourt 241
Wittes 216
Workers' Defence League 84, 168-70, 189-90
Workhouse 84-5, 133, 145, 147-8, 150-1, 198-8
Worksop Corps 201
Worley 278

Ypres 209
Ypres-Comines Canal 212

Zeebrugge Raid xiii, 173, 178-9, 257-8